Qualitative Methods for Reasoning under Uncertainty

Qualitative Methods for Reasoning under Uncertainty

Simon Parsons

The MIT Press
Cambridge, Massachusetts
London, England

This book was set in Times Roman by the author using the LATEX document preparation system and printed and bound in the United States of America.

Library of Congress Cataloging-in-Publication Data

Parsons, Simon.
  Qualitative approaches for reasoning under uncertainty / Simon Parsons.
  p.   cm.
Includes bibliographical references and index.
ISBN 0-262-16168-0 (hc. : alk. paper)
1. Qualitative reasoning. 2. Uncertainty (information theory). I. Title.

Q339.25 .P37   2001
006.3'3dc21   2001030492

...it comes, I tell you, immense with gasolined rags and bits of wire and old bent nails, a dark arriviste, from a dark river within.

Gregory Corso, *How Poetry Comes to Me*

Contents

	Preface	xi
	Acknowledgments	xvii
1	**Introduction**	1
2	**All about uncertainty**	7
2.1	Introduction	7
2.2	Taxonomies of uncertainty	9
2.3	Sources of imperfect information	15
2.4	Uncertainty and entropy	18
2.5	Human reasoning under uncertainty	20
2.6	Ground rules for formal systems	29
2.7	Summary	34
3	**Quantitative methods for reasoning with imperfect information**	37
3.1	Introduction	38
3.2	The main models	39
3.3	Other important models	65
3.4	Computational techniques	73
3.5	Quantified logics	97
3.6	Summary	105
4	**Qualitative methods for reasoning with imperfect information**	107
4.1	Introduction	108
4.2	Qualitative physics	109
4.3	Interval-based systems	117
4.4	Abstractions of quantitative systems	123
4.5	Defeasible reasoning	134
4.6	Combining and relating formalisms	155
4.7	Summary	166
5	**A framework for studying different methods**	169
5.1	Introduction	169

5.2	Eclecticism and the integration problem	172
5.3	A general framework	184
5.4	Examples of integration and incompleteness	191
5.5	Summary	199
6	**Using qualitative algebras**	201
6.1	Introduction	201
6.2	An algebra with qualitative values	202
6.3	An algebra of interval values	209
6.4	Other qualitative algebras	219
6.5	An example of handling integration	221
6.6	An example of handling incompleteness	228
6.7	Summary	233
7	**The theory of qualitative change**	237
7.1	Introduction	237
7.2	Basic concepts of qualitative change	239
7.3	Causal reasoning	247
7.4	Evidential reasoning	263
7.5	Handling incompleteness and integration	273
7.6	Summary	280
8	**Further results in the theory of qualitative change**	283
8.1	Synergy	283
8.2	Propagation in multiply-connected networks	296
8.3	Intercausal reasoning	311
8.4	Related work	322
8.5	Summary	327
9	**Implementing the qualitative approaches**	329
9.1	Introduction	330

9.2   Implementing qualitative algebras   330

9.3   Implementing the theory of qualitative change   336

9.4   Summary   351

10   Qualitative protein topology prediction   353

10.1   Introduction   354

10.2   Protein topology prediction   356

10.3   A first approach to modelling the uncertainty   358

10.4   A second approach to modeling the uncertainty   373

10.5   Discussion   387

10.6   Summary   389

11   Summary and conclusions   391

11.1   Summary   391

11.2   Conclusions   394

Appendix A: Proofs of theorems   401

Appendix B: Conditional belief calculations   445

Glossary   449
References   457
Index   499

Preface

He did swim in deep waters, on his belly, on his back, sideways with all his body, with his feet only, with one hand in the air.

Rabelais, *Gargantua*

The problem of reasoning with imperfect information is widely recognised as being of great importance within the field of artificial intelligence, and a wide range of formal methods has been proposed for dealing with the problem. Many of these methods rely on the use of numerical information to handle the imperfections. This, of course, is quite a natural way to address the problem since to handle information about random events, for instance, it is useful to have numerical information about the frequency with which the events occur. However, taking quantitative information as a base for models that solve the problem of handling imperfect information merely creates another problem—how to provide the quantitative information. In some situations this second problem can be easily solved, in others it proves more resistant to solution, and in recent years several authors have looked at a particularly ingenious way of tackling it. The methods that they suggest, while drawing inspiration from quantitative methods, in particular probability theory, do not require the kind of complete numerical information required by quantitative methods. Instead they provide information that, though less precise than that provided by quantitative techniques, is often sufficient.

This book proposes a number of new techniques with similar aims. In particular, it suggests means of handling imperfect information in accordance with the rules of well-founded methods such as probability theory, possibility theory, and the Dempster-Shafer theory of evidence, while not requiring the kind of numerical information normally assumed by those applying them. This is achieved through the use of qualitative methods, by which I mean methods that abstract away from numerical information, sometimes just retaining the most critical distinctions such as those between positive and negative information, and sometimes by allowing values to range across intervals. This book also provides support for another recent development—the recognition that rather than searching for the best method for handling all imperfect information, one should instead use whichever method best fits the problem at hand. Such an eclectic position leads naturally to the use of several techniques in the solution of a single problem, and hence to the problem of combining the results of applying these techniques. This then is the other focus of this book, to provide a solution to the problem of integrating different formalisms, and it turns out that qualitative methods provide such a solution.

The structure of the book is as follows. Chapter 1 discusses the handling of imperfect information in the context of artificial intelligence, and introduces the particular aspects of the problem that are addressed by this book. Chapter 2 then provides a survey of the literature of imperfect information, covering ground from economics via psychology to information theory. This is intended to give a flavour of the philosophical background to the problems of modelling imperfect information, and to provide support for some of the positions adopted later on. Chapter 3 builds upon this with a review of a selection of the formal techniques that have been developed for dealing with imperfect information, including the theories that form the basis of the qualitative methods developed in later chapters. The basic ideas behind each of these formalisms are discussed, and the essential axioms laid down. This is complemented by Chapter 4, which reviews previous work on qualitative approaches to reasoning with imperfect information, from naïve physics to models of argumentation, with particular emphasis on qualitative versions of quantitative formalisms. Chapter 5 then sets the scene for the more technical part of the book by describing the framework in which the work is carried out and providing examples that are used to illustrate the methods as they are developed. This framework borrows heavily from existing work on network representations in which models take the form of directed acyclic graphs. In such graphs nodes represent variables and arcs represent the dependencies between variables.

The technical work begins in Chapter 6, which introduces the idea of a qualitative algebra using an example from the literature, and then expands this and gives it a formal definition. Perceived limitations of this algebra lead to the definition of another that can handle interval values, and the use of both algebras to handle both integration and the problems caused by incomplete quantitative information about a situation is discussed. Chapter 7 presents a qualitative analysis of the use of probability, possibility, and evidence theories that provides a means of assessing the qualitative behaviour of networks from the conditional values controlling the interactions between nodes. The integration of formalisms and a solution to the problem of incomplete models using the results of the qualitative analysis is discussed. Chapter 8 extends the qualitative analysis to cover other classes of network and a number of different scenarios, including that of "explaining away." Chapter 9 describes the system Mummu (Multiple Uncertainty ManageMent techniqUes), which implements the ideas of Chapters 6, 7, and 8. Chapter 10 deals with the application of the techniques to the problem of protein topology prediction, and Chapter 11 concludes. There are also two appendices and a glossary. The first appendix contains the proofs of all new results stated in the book, which I wanted to keep separate in order to avoid interrupting what narrative thread there is. I trust that I have been successful in doing this in such a way that it is possible to read the book and understand it without having to refer to the proofs, though the reader is encouraged to examine the proofs in order to really understand what is going on. The second appendix contains some calculations that I felt rather disrupted the text but which needed to be included somewhere. The glossary was included to give a brief description of a number of commonly used terms which it did not seem appropriate to give in the main text, but which, if undefined, might prevent a full understanding. Most terms, including all those which are used at all extensively, are defined in the main text and will not be found in the glossary.

The focus on eclecticism in handling imperfect information and the need to integrate different approaches betrays the origin of the book. It started life as my PhD thesis, and the preparation of the thesis was funded by the European Commission as part of Esprit Basic Research Action 3085, Defeasible Reasoning and Uncertainty Management Systems (DRUMS). This project had as its aim the study of different formalisms for handling imperfect information and, in particular, their integration. However, the book is more than just a nicely bound edition of my thesis. In fact, the relation between my thesis and this book is rather similar to that between Boolos's *The Unprovability of Consistency* and *The Logic of Provability*, which he neatly summarised in the preface to the latter (Boolos, 1993):

"Is it a new book or [just] a second edition of your other book?" my colleagues have asked me. New book.
All right, there are borderline cases, aren't there? (Hmm, maybe books don't exist since we lack strict criteria of book identity.) And cases over the border, but near it, too. That's what I think the situation is with *The Logic of Provability*: there's enough new material in it for it to be a new book. Of course, when I thought I couldn't do better than I had done in *The Unprovability of Consistency*, I unashamedly copied sections from it. But I think I may call this work the "successor" to that.

In others words, this book is a substantially revised version of my thesis.

There are a number of reasons for this. The first is that I was unhappy with some of the limitations that time had imposed upon the results in my thesis, and wanted to rework them to put the proposed methods on a stronger footing. The second is that the anonymous reviewers of the original manuscript made a number of suggestions that I wanted to incorporate. The third, and possibly the most important, is that the field has moved on a good deal in the time that it has taken me to put this material together so that there are now so many other qualitative and eclectic approaches that the whole shape of this work has changed. Of course, as with any such work, there is more that could be done—more results that could be established and more approaches that could be compared and contrasted with mine.

To paraphrase Umberto Eco (1998), the process of writing academic books is the following. You spend many years thinking, getting your ideas straight in your own head, and writing them down. You then find out what other people think of your ideas. Sometimes you find you were wrong, and sometimes what other people think about your ideas leads you to change your mind. You then revisit what you wrote originally, making corrections and alterations, some of which contradict what you said earlier. This process then repeats. This book marks the second cycle of this process with respect to the work it contains. It has changed hugely since the first iteration, and doubtless it will change in the future, but for now it is the best I can do.

This seems an appropriate place to make a few remarks about what this book is and is not. In particular, I feel it is worth stressing that this is a research monograph rather than a textbook, so that the various methods considered within and the views expressed about them more reflect my personal opinions than the measured views of the field as a whole. The fact that this is a monograph does not mean that it turns its back upon all the other work on reasoning under uncertainty that already exists. Indeed, it contains a rather large amount of introductory and survey material (much of which was included at the suggestion of the reviewers) so that not only does it introduce many of the ideas that it uses by discussing them in the context of the work in which they were developed, but in doing so covers a large amount of material that is never used in the theoretical parts. The reason for doing this is to give a sound introduction to the state of the art in handling uncertainty at the time of writing. Actually, to be frank, it is really a snapshot of the field since, like snapshots of steppes, mountain ranges, and other landscapes with wide horizons, it only covers a part of the whole. As I sit here writing (in early 2001) the field seems sufficiently large that it can only be reasonably surveyed by a lengthy book and so, as it will no doubt continue to expand, I do not attempt to be comprehensive. Instead my aim is to focus on those developments that are most relevant to the work in the rest of the book. As a result the survey I give is rather uneven, covering some areas in a good deal of detail, but skimming over others. In particular, the detail is more often about older work since this is more foundational, and less often about more recent work, since the latter is frequently on particular topics (such as learning probabilistic networks) which are rather out of the scope of this book. With respect to this issue it should also be noted that throughout the book little space is given to discussion of decision making. While I acknowledge that making decisions is an important activity, I think of it, perhaps wrongly, as a topic that is distinct from reasoning under uncertainty and, certainly correctly, as a topic on which I currently have little to say.

As a research monograph this book has a two main aims. First, but not foremost, it is intended as a manifesto for the use of qualitative approaches to reasoning with imperfect information, which argues that they are useful and well-developed. It does this partly by highlighting the various qualitative systems that have already been developed, and partly by developing new ones and showing how they may be used. Second, this book is intended as a manifesto for the eclectic approach. As such it both argues that the eclectic approach is a natural way of modelling the various different forms of imperfection that may be present in models of the world when these may not be easily captured in a single model, and provides some practical assistance for those who wish to build eclectic systems by furnishing a theoretical means of combining information expressed in different formalisms. It should be noted that these two aims are, essentially, independent since qualitative methods are useful in building non-eclectic systems, and eclectic systems can be built (at least in principle) without resorting to qualitative methods.

Finally, a few words on the vexed question of personal pronouns. The use of the word "his" to denote an individual who may either be male or female will no doubt continue to be controversial for years to come. The use of "his/her" may well be correct, but, like Dawkins (1988) I find this too ugly to bear. However, unlike Dawkins I tend to use "her" in those cases where it is impossible to find a means of phrasing things to avoid those pesky pronouns. Like Hofstadter (1986) I feel that it is better to err on the side of the under-used alternative rather than the over-used one. Of course this choice is still going to make some people unhappy because they feel that it is silly, patronising, hypocritical, or just incorrect. Well, that's tough. Of course, if enough people object then maybe I'll change things next time I write a book. Which leads, naturally enough, to the usual statement that all comments on any aspect of this book, whether brickbats or accolades, are most welcome—comments via email especially so. The relevant address, for the foreseeable future, is `s.d.parsons@csc.liv.ac.uk`.

Acknowledgments

Angelheaded hipsters burning for the ancient heavenly connection to the starry dynamo in the machinery of the night,
who poverty and tatters and hollow-eyed and high sat up smoking in the supernatural darkness of cold-water flats floating across the tops of cities contemplating jazz.

Allen Ginsberg, *Howl*

This book would not have been realised without the help, encouragement and tolerance of many people, to all of whom I am extremely grateful. The somewhat convoluted history of the book means that these people fall into a number of quite separate groups.

The first group is comprised of those people who had a lot to do with my PhD. Of these, Abe Mamdani supervised me and, perhaps even more importantly, both employed me while I carried out much of the work that led to my thesis and got me involved in the DRUMS project without which the thesis would never have been written. John Bigham served as the internal examiner for my thesis, made many useful comments, and was encouragingly enthusiastic about my work throughout. Jim Baldwin was my external examiner, and was good enough to only insist on the most minor of corrections.

The second group are those people who have unstintingly filled in the many gaps in my knowledge of how to handle imperfect information. Within this group, invaluable technical advice on probability theory was provided by Gerhard Köstler, and David Speigelhalter; on possibility theory by Didier Dubois, Pascale Fonck, Jérôme Lang, and Henri Prade; on belief functions by Mike Clarke, Yen-Teh Hsia, Philippe Smets, and Nic Wilson; on qualitative reasoning by Mirko Dohnal; and on how to put it all together by Paul Krause. Serafin Moral, Alessandro Saffiotti, Prakash Shenoy, Elisabeth Umkehrer, and Hong Xu helped me to understand local computation, and Dominic Clark and Chris Rawlings were my main source of knowledge about protein topology. Marek Druzdzel, Linda van der Gaag, Max Henrion, Silja Renooij, and Mike Wellman helped to clarify my understanding of Qualitative Probabilistic Networks. In addition, Didier Dubois, Frank Klawonn, Rudolf Kruse, and Philippe Smets checked many of the technical results. In addition, I owe the initial inspiration for this work to John Fox, who has also proved an endless source of encouragement.

The third group are those people who helped me through two rather awful years of illness, and include Ann Radda, who got more than she bargained for but never looked like she couldn't cope with it; Brian and Tinker Parsons for endless trips to the hospital; all the doctors in the Leicester firm for perseverance in the face of adversity; and the nursing staff on Amyand Ward at St George's Hospital, Tooting, above all Sister Margaret Pryce, for care well beyond the call of duty. Also included are John Fox and John Bigham for believing that I could still do a good job while ill even though others doubted that this was possible.

The fourth group is made up of those people who have helped to make reasoning with imperfect information, and the DRUMS project in particular, such enjoyable and rewarding work. In addition to those mentioned already, these include Stephane Amarger, Salem Benferhat, Philippe Besnard, José Cano, Hélène Fargier, Jérôme Mengin, Victor Poznanski, Sandra Sandri, and Chris Whitney.

The fifth and final group are those who have had the misfortune to share an office with me over the years, and have yet continued to supply stimulating conversation and stimulating beverages in equal quantities. They include Tim Brown, Tim Chau, Andrew Coulson, David Glasspool, Lida Graupner, Saki Hajnal, Peter Hammond, Kate Hearne, Ana von Klopp, Anastasia Photiou, Jeff Pople, Claudia Roda, Paul Taylor, Richard Thomson, and Nick Theodoropoulos. Nick deserves special thanks for never objecting to my attempts to play squash in the office while he was working, as does Richard for withstanding my endless complaints about the Northern Line. I am grateful to Ana for introducing me to the wonders of Emacs, and Lida for both keeping my plants alive and for supplying the coffee grinder.

There are also some more specific thanks. Paul Krause, Peter McBurney, Brian Parsons, Alessandro Saffiotti, and Sandra Sandri proof-read drafts of this work, and their comments led to important improvements; the Imperial Cancer Research Fund was unstinting in providing funds for me to travel to present my ideas; Mike Wooldridge managed to walk the difficult line between encouraging me to finish this, and nagging me to get it done; and Ann Radda did more than anyone else simply by putting up with me while I was writing this.

The soundtrack heavily featured Dexter Gordon and The Jesus and Mary Chain, but sadly much more of the work was "The Hardest Walk" than "Fried Bananas."

Simon Parsons
London and Liverpool, 1995–2001

Qualitative Methods for Reasoning under Uncertainty

1 Introduction

Voices blurred soothingly in his ears. He cracked one puffy lid; everything indistinct, trimmed with foggy white; happy fungus growing everywhere. Ah, surfacing from anesthesia in Sick Bay ...

Seth Morgan, *Homeboy*

The discipline of artificial intelligence has as its aim the construction of computer-based systems that exhibit intelligence. However, the exact meaning of "intelligence" in this context is somewhat unclear. When work on artificial intelligence first began, the standard definition of "intelligence" in a computer program was that given by Alan Turing. Turing's proposal was that a computer program whose intelligence was to be gauged should be connected up to a terminal at which a person was sitting so that questions and answers could be exchanged between the two. If, after extensive questioning, the person was completely unsure whether or not the entity with which she was communicating was human or a computer program, then the program would be deemed to have intelligence. Sadly, despite the early optimism of workers in the field (McCorduck, 1979), it has become clear that no program is going to pass the so-called "Turing test" in the near future. Furthermore, the recent Leobner Prize Competitions, which offer cash rewards for programmers who are capable of building systems that can make a fair attempt at passing a restricted version of the Turing test (Russell and Norvig, 1995, page 5) seem to indicate, if anything, that systems which are good at fooling people into thinking that they are human are not those that show most intelligence. For instance, the winner of the first competition in 1991 (described in (Epstein, 1992)), engaged the judges in rather random whimsical conversation, while the winner of the 1994 competition (described in (Platt, 1995)) was a system that offered 380 stock pieces of advice about sex. Neither appear to be particularly smart, and neither comes close to being the kind of system popularly associated with the idea of computer intelligence, whether it is HAL from *2001: A Space Odyssey*, Wintermute (Gibson, 1993), or the *Arbitrary* (Banks, 1993). What characterises such systems is not the fact that they can hold conversations (though, of course, they do) but that they are capable of carrying out complex tasks like flying a spaceship, organising an armed robbery, or surveying a planet,[1] and it seems to me that it is this side of their cognitive ability—the ability to solve hard problems in a complex world—that marks them out as intelligent.

Now, by definition, solving such problems is a difficult matter, and the business of building a system to do so is far from trivial. There are difficulties, for instance, in

---

1 Though it could be argued that the *Arbitrary*'s fondness for collecting snowflakes or its ability to cheat amusingly when playing word games are even more telling signs of intelligence.

sensing the environment in which the task is to be carried out, and in planning how the task may be achieved. Even moving around is far from easy. However, one of the most fundamental problems is the handling of imperfect information. For those unfamiliar with the field, it is worth elaborating this point. A truely intelligent system needs to operate in the real world—it needs to be situated (Russell and Norvig, 1995, page 403). To interact successfully in the world the intelligent system needs some kind of representation of that world, a representation that may be explicit or implicit, and a means of reasoning with that representation. Now, when dealing with toy problems in a laboratory, all information about the world may be assumed to be present and correct, and providing a means of representing and reasoning with it is relatively simple. However, the real world is much more complicated. A moment's thought is sufficient to reveal the extent to which imperfect information is present in daily life and, as Morgan and Henrion (1990) point out,

we have evolved cognitive heuristics and developed strategies, technologies and institutions such as weather reports, pocket-sized raincoats, and insurance to accommodate or compensate for the effects of uncertainty.

It is exactly because information about the world is imperfect, that intelligent computer systems operating in the real world have to be able to represent and reason with imperfect information. Of course, there are strategies for "engineering out" (Cohen, 1985) the imperfections in a given situation to reduce the situation to one of perfect knowledge. This is the kind of approach adopted by Clark et al. (1994) to reduce the imperfections in genetic map data to manageable proportions, and advocated by Castro and Trillas (1993) for dealing with inconsistent information. However, while this approach may be suitable in some situations, in others ignoring or attempting to smooth out the imperfections can severely degrade the performance of the system (Uhrik, 1982). Thus there is often a need to deal with imperfect information when building intelligent systems. This need rules out the use of classical logic as the basis for these systems (Israel, 1987), and has stimulated the development of a number of so-called non-standard methods. Indeed, over the past twenty years a large number of formal methods have been proposed for the management of uncertainty in artificial intelligence systems including evidence theory (Shafer, 1976; Smets and Kennes, 1994), possibility theory (Dubois and Prade, 1988f; Zadeh, 1978), probabilistic networks (Jensen, 1996; Pearl, 1988b), and a host of other approaches (Smets et al., 1988).

These methods, by and large, involve attaching a numerical measure to items of information whose certainty is not known. The measure represents the degree to which it is certain, suspected, or believed that the item is true, and as different items are combined to reach a conclusion, the associated measures are combined to derive the degree to which the conclusion is certain, suspected, or believed, to be true. The methods are often specified in a precise mathematical way. As a result it is possible to precisely determine the meaning of the derived measure. It is also possible to precisely determine the conditions under which the measure is valid. These methods also require specific types of information to be known, and place specific conditions on how the measures are to be allocated—for instance the use of one method might require the attachment of a measure to each of a set of facts while another might only require a measure to be attached to at least one. Such conditions on the measures lead to quite stringent constraints on the situations in which models may be built using the methods. This, in turn, means that it is often the case that, when modelling a specific situation, no method exactly fits the data that is available. This raises a question that is largely avoided by people carrying out research into reasoning with imperfect information, which is:

How does one choose which method to adopt for handling imperfect information?

There are some exceptions to this avoidance of the question, including Heckerman (1990a), Heckerman and Shwe (1993), and Saffiotti et al. (1994), but the more usual position is to assume that the different methods are completely exclusive and that only the best method is worth bothering with. As a result the question that has been extensively explored is:

Which is the best method?

and much time and energy has been expended in assessing their relative worths.

Simplifying greatly, the argument has progressed along the following lines. Initially the mainstream view within the community of people doing research into artificial intelligence was that, despite its mathematical pedigree, probability theory was an inappropriate method because it both required infeasibly large amounts of information and did not handle imperfect information in the same way that people did. This led to the development of a number of models of reasoning under uncertainty that were supposed to be more easily applicable and more able to model the way that people deal with imperfect information. Three such models are certainty factors (Shortliffe, 1976), fuzzy sets (Zadeh, 1965), and the theory of evidence (Shafer, 1976). This provoked a number of people who were interested in the use of probability theory to argue that not only was it possible to apply probability theory when the right models were used (Cheeseman, 1985), but that it also provided the only properly rational means of handling uncertainty (Horvitz et al., 1986). This cause was greatly helped by the development of probabilistic causal networks (Pearl, 1986b) which provided a simple and efficient way to build probabilistic models, but this has not prevented an intense and, at times, rather acrimonious debate attempting to determine the best system. Notable contributions have been made by Pearl (1985), Cheeseman (1986; 1988b), Zadeh (1986), and Smets (1988b).

The debate now seems to have tailed off, and it seems to me that this is because the proponents of the different approaches no longer care if the supporters of other approaches agree with them or not. Each of the main methods has its own set of adherents who talk to each other, go to the same conferences, and tolerate (but are not necessarily convinced by) the point of view of other groups.

In recent years, however, an eclectic school of thought has emerged with authors such as Fox (1986), Saffiotti (1987), and Krause and Clark (1993) espousing the idea that the various methods are largely complementary. The argument runs along the lines that the different methods are often designed to model different aspects of imperfect information, require different preconditions, and provide different types of solution. This suggests not only that no one method can ever be shown to be better than every other under every condition, since each will be best under the conditions for which it was designed to operate. Such a position is reinforced by the work of Léa Sombé[2] (1990) who attempted to express some simple pieces of imperfect information in a number of different formal models and found that none was able to represent them all, and seems to be becoming well accepted in certain circles even if it is not directly stated as such. For instance, it is possible to read Darwiche's (1993b) position—that one should examine probability to see which features are desirable and adopt these as the basis of new methods—as being supportive of the eclectic viewpoint. Taking this viewpoint, of course, shifts the emphasis from answering the second question back to answering the first. Many clues as to the answer can be gleaned from existing work, including that of Léa Sombé, Kruse and colleagues (Kruse et al., 1991), Krause and Clark (1993), and Hunter (1996), but this remains an area in which much work still needs to be done.

Although this work is of major importance if the eclectic position is to be of practical use, there are other, equally important, issues. It is these other issues that are addressed in this book. The first of these stems from a more extreme version of the eclectic position, which is developed at length in Chapter 5. Briefly the argument is as follows. If the eclectic position is valid, and I strongly believe that it is, then no single model for handling imperfect information can handle every type of imperfect information that will be encountered. Therefore, there will be scenarios in which no single model will be able to handle the imperfect information that is present. Thus the best possible treatment of imperfect information in those cases will be achieved by using several formalisms in combination, and the pertinent question is:

How may the different models be combined together in a principled way?

Answering this question was one of the main aims of the research that led to this book, and results suggesting how this might be done are given in later chapters and constitute

---

2 The name is a pseudonym for a group of French researchers interested in the handling of imperfect information, and is an approximation to the expression "Les As sont Bs" ("The As are Bs"), one of the expressions that they attempted to capture in their work.

one of the key parts of the book. The other aims of the research described here are best summarised by considering another question about models of handling imperfect information. Since the models often require a good deal of numerical information to quantify the imperfections in the data, what must be done when the available data is not rich enough to satisfy the axioms of any model? In other words:

What must be done when data expressed in a particular formalism has missing values?

Well, one answer to this question is to make up the relevant data using some suitable assumption about the missing values. Another, and to my mind more reasonable, solution is to take whatever information is available and see what can be deduced from it, usually sacrificing some of the precision of the original methods. The development of such an approach constitutes the other main part of this book. Now this kind of approach, which has widely been termed "qualitative" is becoming quite widespread and, by happy coincidence, also provides a means of answering the previous question. This then summarises the remainder of the book—the development of a number of methods (well, two or three depending on what is counted as a method) that answer the questions of how to handle missing values in models for reasoning with imperfect information, and how to enable different models to be used in combination. There is a good way to go before such models can be defined, and the next chapter starts by considering the different types of imperfect information that these models have to handle.

2 All about uncertainty

The world is not knowable and there is not truth ... just as you can't learn the taste of salt with your nose, the smell of balsam with your ear, or the sound of a violin with your tongue, it's impossible for you to grasp the world with your reason.

Isaac Bashevis Singer, *Zeidlus the Pope*

This chapter, by way of introduction to the problems of handling uncertainty in intelligent systems, reviews a part of the treatment of the concept of uncertainty in the literature. In contrast to Chapters 3 and 4, which survey some of the theories introduced over the years for handling uncertainty, this chapter steers well clear of formal methods. Instead it leans towards the abstract and philosophical, making an attempt to establish a sense of the different nuances of uncertainty that intelligent systems must deal with. Some of the work that is reviewed is from outside the domain of artificial intelligence, and the intention is both to provide some justification for the main arguments that will be put forward in the following chapters, and to provide some background for the reader who is new to the field. Any impatient readers, even those who already know all about uncertainty, who think from this introduction that they should skip this chapter and jump ahead to where the real work begins, would be well advised to sit back and enjoy the show—after all some of this material is rarely considered by those working in artificial intelligence, and it does have a bearing on later chapters. However, like any good piece of hooptedoodle,[1] this chapter can be skipped by those determined enough, although such readers should definitely glance at the discussion (in Section 2.2.4) of the different terms used to describe types of uncertainty in order to avoid any later confusion.

2.1 Introduction

The investigation begins with the belief that perfect knowledge is never going to be available to man or machine when dealing with the real world. Of course in simple toy domains perfect knowledge is achievable with a few logical statements. However, in more complex environments knowledge is bound to be imperfect. For example, any intelligent system, human or otherwise, is constrained to have finite knowledge by virtue of its finite

---

1 "Sometimes I want a book to break loose with a bunch of hooptedoodle. The guy's writing it, give him a chance to do a little hooptedoodle. Spin up some pretty words maybe, or sing a little song with language. That's nice. But I wish it was set aside so that I don't have to read it. I don't want hooptedoodle to get mixed up in the story. So if the guy wants hooptedoodle, he ought to put it first. Then I can skip it if I want to, or maybe go back to it after I know how the story came out." John Steinbeck, *Sweet Thursday*.

storage capacity, so it will always be possible to find some fact that is unknown by a particular system. In addition there are facts that are inherently uncertain, such as the proposition "it will rain tomorrow in London," and any measurement that a system uses is bound to be imprecise since perfect precision of measurement is not achievable. This idea is not new. Chomsky (1992) credits Hume, among others, with the realisation that one has to depend upon an approximate model of the world. I quote Chomsky's summary of the situation at length since I cannot see how to better it:

In his study of the Scottish intellectual tradition, George Davie[2] identifies its central theme as a recognition of the fundamental role of "natural beliefs or principles of common sense, such as the belief in an independent external world, the belief in causality, the belief in ideal standards, and the belief in the self of conscience as separate from the rest of one." These principles are sometimes considered to have a regulative character; though never fully justified, they provide the foundations for thought and conception. Some held that they contain "an irreducible element of mystery," Davie points out, while others hoped to provide a rational foundation for them. On that issue the jury is still out.

We can trace such ideas to seventeenth century thinkers who reacted to the skeptical crisis of the times by recognizing that there are no absolutely certain grounds for knowledge, but that we do, nevertheless, have ways to gain a reliable understanding of the world, and to improve that understanding and apply it—essentially the standpoint of the working scientist today. Similarly, in normal life a reasonable person relies on the natural beliefs of common sense while recognizing that they may be parochial or misguided, and hoping to refine them as understanding progresses.

From the standpoint of this book, Chomsky's words could be considered as a statement that any intelligent system will require a means of representing an approximate model of the world that it can use to reason about the world in the absence of more correct information.

A similar viewpoint was expounded by Gallie (1957). He argues that while physical laws do express a certain amount of information, and can be interpreted to rule out certain consequences of certain situations, they are insufficiently informative to provide an

absolutely detailed forecast of any particular concrete example.

This, he suggests, means that whatever information is available, and however many rules for applying data are provided, there is always some degree of irreducible uncertainty in a situation. Gallie also uses the ubiquity of uncertainty to argue that from the time of Descartes' ideally rational man, who would never form expectations under uncertainty but would wait for detailed knowledge, scientists have been deluding themselves about the certainty of their knowledge. This, he argues, once again stresses the need for mechanisms for dealing with uncertain information. A similar point was made by Feynman who pointed out the

---

2 George Davie, *The Democratic Intellect*, Edinburgh University Press, 1961.

great value of a satisfactory philosophy of ignorance.[3]

Taking this view, it becomes evident that being uncertain is the natural state of things, and that it is rather foolish to consider reasoning about events under uncertainty as a fundamentally different process to reasoning about events in conformity with well-established laws. Any decision taken under uncertainty will be subject, to some degree, to some well-established law, and any decision made in conformity with some well-established law will be subject to some uncertainty.

Having argued that it is necessary to deal with uncertainty, this chapter begins by trying to identify what exactly is this "uncertainty" that must be dealt with. There are five main sections in this chapter. The first looks at different types of uncertainty, reviews some attempts to classify them, and creates a new classification from them. The terminology used in this book is drawn from this classification. The second section discusses sources of uncertainty, and how these relate to different varieties of uncertainty. Together these two sections help to identify what uncertainty is, and argue that it comes in many guises. The third major part of the chapter then looks at entropy and its relation to uncertainty, helping to clarify how information can be used to combat uncertainty. The fourth section surveys what has been learnt about human reasoning under uncertainty, and uses this to clarify what people can and cannot do, and why formal models are required. Finally, the fifth section looks at the properties required of formal models, and squares the circle by arguing that the variety of different requirements is really a call for a number of different models.

2.2   Taxonomies of uncertainty

If it is necessary to handle uncertainty, it is also necessary to know exactly what it is. An obvious way of finding out what the term "uncertainty" means is to look it up in the dictionary. The Collins English Dictionary that sits in my office yields

1. The state or condition of being uncertain. 2. An uncertain matter, contingency etc.

This definition suggests that looking up "uncertain" might be wise, and doing this gives a wealth of nuances:

1. Not able to be accurately given. 2. Not sure or confident. 3. Not precisely determined, established, or decided. 4. Not to be depended upon, unreliable. 5. Liable to variation, changeable.

To me, these meanings fall into three groups. Something can be uncertain because it hasn't been measured accurately enough (first and third meanings), because it might change (fourth and fifth meanings), or because the person who has the information is not confident

---

3 Attributed by Gleick (1992, page 372) to notes entitled *The Uncertainty of Science* that he found among Feynman's papers when writing his biography.

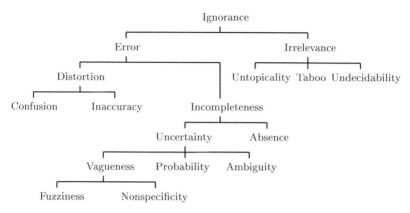

Figure 2.1
Smithson's taxonomy

about it (second meaning). Thus there are at least three ways in which uncertainty can arise. Indeed, the picture gets more complicated. According to Klir (1987) (Klir and Folger, 1988) Webster's New Twentieth Century Dictionary gives six groups of meanings for the term "uncertain":

1. Not certainly known; questionable; problematic. 2. Vague; not definite or determined. 3. Doubtful; not having certain knowledge; not sure. 4. Ambiguous. 5. Not steady or constant; varying. 6. Liable to change or vary; not dependable or reliable.

This definition adds the idea that something can be uncertain because one only has vague or ambiguous information about it, and one can go considerably further in identifying different types of uncertainty and their relations to one another. Several authors (Bonissone and Tong, 1985; Smithson, 1989; Bosc and Prade, 1997; Smets, 1997b) have carried out such an exercise, and while it is far from clear that the taxonomies that they provide are of fundamental importance, they do help to outline what uncertainty is.

2.2.1   Smithson's taxonomy

Smithson (1989) is interested in the problem of dealing with what he terms "ignorance," or "non-knowledge." He breaks this down into a number of areas, (summarised by Figure 2.1), which are defined using the following distinctions. It is possible to distinguish between "being ignorant" and "ignoring." When ignorant one is in some "erroneous state" compared to the state of perfect knowledge and is thus in error, whereas when a conscious decision to disregard something is made on grounds of irrelevance one is ignoring the information. Irrelevance can be split into "untopicality," "undecidability," and "taboo." Untopical matters are those that seem unconnected to the matter in hand, while undecid-

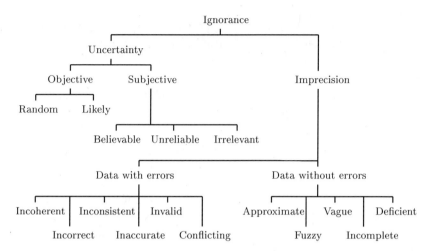

Figure 2.2
Smets' taxonomy

able things are those that stem from insoluble problems. Taboo matters, on the other hand, are those that people are not allowed to even ask about. As Smithson points out, taboo is often invoked within the scientific community to proscribe certain troublesome areas from analysis.

It is in the area of error that most work has been done in the scientific community. Errors are caused by incomplete and distorted data. Distortion is often caused by inaccuracy, but may also arise as a result of confusion. Incompleteness in Smithson's view may be due to the absence of information or uncertainty; that is incompleteness in the degree of certainty. This uncertainty can be broken down in a similar way to that adopted by the dictionary compilers whose work was quoted above. There is probability, the uncertainty that arises from events that are not completely predictable; ambiguity, which is the uncertainty that arises from not being able to distinguish between things; and vagueness, where problems arise from incorrectly drawn distinctions.

2.2.2 Smets' taxonomy

In a recent paper, Smets (1997b) has provided an alternative view, which can be summarised by Figure 2.2, and which is an extension of earlier thoughts on the subject (Smets, 1991c). He distinguishes between imprecision, where the difficulty is in the content of the information, and uncertainty, where the problem is related to the lack of information. Uncertainty can either be an objective property of the information or it can be a subjective property of the observer. If the uncertainty is objective then it can either be random infor-

mation that is subject to change, or likely information which is known frequentistically. If
the uncertainty is subjective, then it can relate to data that is believable but not completely
trustworthy, to data that is unreliable, or to data that is irrelevant, in which case the observer
does not care about it.

Imprecision is split into data without error and data with errors. Data without error
can be vague, in which case it is ambiguous and so has several possible meanings. Data
without error may also be approximate, in which case it is well-defined and known to be
close enough to the correct value to be considered correct. Alternatively error-free data can
be fuzzy, in which case it is not well defined. Error-free data can also suffer from missing
values that lead it to be incomplete. When the missing values are important, the data is said
to be deficient. Errors in data can be concerned with one or more pieces of information. A
single piece of data can be erroneous or incorrect, in which case it is completely wrong.
Data with errors can also be inaccurate, in which case it is well defined but too far from the
value it would have if correct to be considered correct. In addition, data with errors may
be invalid, in which case it would lead to incorrect conclusions. Several pieces of data that
contain errors can be conflicting, in which case they disagree. Such pieces of data may also
be incoherent, in which case the conclusions drawn from them are unclear or difficult to
understand. Finally, several pieces of data with errors may be inconsistent, in which case
the conclusions drawn from them may vary over time.

Although Smets and Smithson use the same terms to mean different things, it seems
that there is no great disagreement between them; they just have different viewpoints on the
same confused issue, and both can seem equally correct in different situations. Smithson
includes "uncertainty" as a sub-category of "error" because errors arise from uncertainty.
Smets has error-free uncertainty because uncertain data does not have to arise from errors
in measurement—in his classification uncertainty can also arise when information about
the value of data is missing.

2.2.3 Other suggestions

Though Smithson and Smets provide the most complete and detailed attempts to define
a taxonomy, there are other suggestions for classifying imperfect information. Bonissone
and Tong (1985) suggest that there are three fundamental types of ignorance of which uncertainty is one, and incompleteness and imprecision are the others. Incompleteness stems
from the absence of a value, imprecision from the existence of a value with insufficient
precision, and uncertainty arises when an agent must construct a subjective opinion about
a fact the truth of which it does not know for certain. Incompleteness can be existential
or universal. Existential incompleteness refers to situations in which a single piece of information is missing, as in the case of the statement "The author of *Naked Lunch* was
an important figure in twentieth century literature," which leaves the author's identity un-

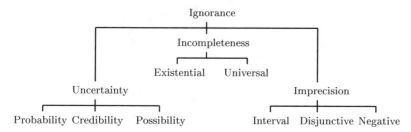

Figure 2.3
Bonissone and Tong's taxonomy

stated. Universal incompleteness refers to the situation in which a whole class of pieces of information are unknown, as in the statement "Allen Ginsberg wrote some very powerful poems," which fails to say what the names of any of the poems are. In this latter case it is the fact that none of Ginsberg's poems are named that makes the incompleteness universal.

Imprecision can be interval valued as in the statement "Simon is between 25 and 35," or fuzzy valued as in the statement that "Simon is thirtysomething." There is also disjunctive imprecision, which refers to such statements as "Simon is 33 or 34," and imprecision arising from negation as in the statement "Simon is not married to Ann." These classifications are not tied to any particular representation. Uncertainty, however, is tied down. It may be represented as probability, a degree of belief (credibility), or an epistemic possibility or necessity such as the possibility that Simon's height is 175 cm given that he is tall. This gives the taxonomy in Figure 2.3.

Bosc and Prade (1997) are in broad agreement with this. They suggest that uncertainty arises from a lack of information. Thus it arises because, for instance, it is not possible to decide if a given statement, such as "It will rain at 5pm," is true or false. As a result it is only possible to estimate the objective propensity or the subjective belief or credibility that the statement is true. Imprecision arises from the granularity of the language in which the data is represented. Thus the precise statement "Simon is 33 years and six months old" becomes the imprecise statement "Simon is between 33 and 34" years old when months are ignored. Bosc and Prade also consider disjunctive imprecision as discussed above and imprecision arising from negation. Vagueness, in their terminology, arises from the use of gradual quantifiers and statements that are neither true or false, while inconsistency stems from a clash of values, such as that between the statements "Simon is 33" and "Simon is 34," which make it impossible to determine one correct value. This time the taxonomy in Figure 2.4 results.

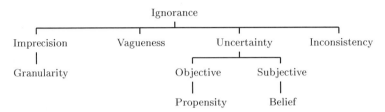

Figure 2.4
Bosc and Prade's taxonomy

2.2.4 Results of considering the taxonomies

There are a number of notable points that arise from this brief look at taxonomies of ignorance. The first is that the fact that four groups of authors can come up with four different taxonomies indicates that Elkan (1994a) is probably right in his assertion that

A complete and consistent analysis of all the many varieties of uncertainty involved in human thinking and revealed in human language is a philosophical goal that we should not expect to achieve soon.

However, the fact that these taxonomies do not agree on every point does not mean that they are useless. For a start, and this is the second notable point, they draw attention to the fact that there are a large number of different types of ignorance and uncertainty. This does not, in itself, mean that there is a need for a large number of methods of handling uncertainty. However, as will be discussed in later chapters, it does seem that the inventors of different formal methods only ever consider a few of these types when building any one model. In addition, and this is the third notable point, comparing all the different types of uncertainty suggested in the different classifications, it is possible to extract some common concepts, though they are somewhat obscured by the overloading of several of the terms.

For instance, all the authors have some idea of subjective *uncertainty*, where the lack of certainty about the truth of some event is in the mind of the beholder, either because of some error, or because of some ignorance or lack of accuracy of measurement. Likewise, they all have some notion of *vagueness* in the sense of something that is not well defined, though they differ in the way it is fitted into the hierarchy, and all but Smithson talk directly about *imprecision* as a failure to be adequately specific. Similarly, several deal with *incompleteness*, in the sense of lacking particular pieces of information, *inconsistency* in the sense of having two pieces of information that contradict each other, and Smithson talks of *ambiguity* as existing when there is no information that distinguishes between two alternatives. These, then, are the terms that will be used in the remainder of this book, and the senses in which they will be used. In addition, I will also talk of *imperfect information* as a catch-all for all the different terms mentioned here, although the word "uncertainty" will also be used in this sense where there is no chance of confusion. Finally, "ignorance" will be used to mean a lack of information about the certainty of information (a kind of second order term). In particular this term will be used in the context of the Dempster-Shafer theory to describe situations in which it is not possible to determine which of several alternatives is more certain—a sense in which it is closely related to "ambiguity."

Furthermore, and this is the last notable point, any of the terms defined here may be used in a second-order sense to refer to the information required by models of situations about which information is imperfect. Thus, considering the problem of diagnosing a disease given some observations, not only is the relation between observation and disease uncertain, but if a model of the relation is built using probability theory it is possible to encounter incompleteness in the model if necessary probabilities are missing.

2.3 Sources of imperfect information

One important matter when considering imperfect information concerns the origin of the imperfections. Obviously, if one holds that there is no such thing as perfect information, it is clear that some imperfections will always exist, but others can equally well be eradicated. The question then becomes, why aren't they? A partial answer is provided by Bonissone (1987a). He attributes the fuzziness of knowledge to the fact that observations are made concerning concepts that are ill-defined—it is easy to see that this can be either because they are not sufficiently thought through or because the concept in question is inherently fuzzy. In addition Bonissone attributes the randomness of knowledge to the fact that either measurements are taken inaccurately or the instruments used to take the measurements are not sufficiently reliable. Bonissone also suggests that uncertainty can arise in cases in which knowledge about the correlation between events is weak, so that rules relating these events are not completely correct in the form in which they are written. In a similar way, the imprecision of the language used to describe events and their inter-relationships gives rise to representations that are not correct models of what they represent. Other problems arise when trying to aggregate information from different sources, and such efforts typically lead to inconsistencies, or over-estimates of the likelihood of events due to assumed, but untrue, dependencies. Finally, Bonissone points out that knowledge about a domain is often incomplete, and this is a problem that can only grow with the scope of intelligent systems.

Similar considerations are provided by Motro (1997; 1990). Although Motro's main concern is with the types of imperfect information that may be found specifically in relational databases, the close relation between relational algebra and first-order logic means that his ideas can easily be adapted to the concerns of this book. He argues that within any relation between items, the value of individual items may be unknown, the applicability of a predicate to the objects contained in it may be vague, and relations themselves may be uncertain. Thus the salary of an employee may be unknown, the assignment of employees to projects may be undefined, though "employee" and "project" are themselves well defined, and the relationship between employee and department might be uncertain since some employees may belong to more than one. Queries on a set of logical facts may also introduce uncertainty, since the mapping of particular queries to facts might not be clear. For instance, a query on a set of facts about cars might request information about "sports cars." If the facts only record manufacturer and engine size, any answer to the query may be plausible (especially if it includes cars made by Ferrari and those with engines of 3.0 litres or more) but it will not be certain that it is correct. Thus in terms of the classification discussed above it is possible to have incomplete, vague, uncertain and imprecise data.

Motro then identifies the sources of these imperfections. They may result from unreliable sources, such as faulty sensors, input errors, or the inappropriate choice of representation (such as forcing an attribute with a disjunctive value to be single valued). He also discusses the problem of subjective errors introduced, for instance, by measuring time-varying quantities. In his view these are sufficient explanations for the unavailability of real, perfect information. However, this viewpoint is rather misleading since it assumes that real, perfect information exists, and could be attained if only the means of capturing it were good enough. If imperfection in data really is irreducible, as argued above, then perfect information will rarely be obtained.

Further discussion of the problems in compiling information comes from Kwan et al. (1997) who suggest a number of sources of uncertainty and incompleteness in information used in scientific applications, taking information about the human genome as an example. They suggest that some data is recorded statistically and so is inherently uncertain, while other data is deliberately made imperfect for reasons of security. Other data may not be measured accurately, due perhaps to some quantum mechanical effect, and so will include some irreducible uncertainty—a point of view that accords with mine in suggesting that perfect information is an unattainable ideal. In all of these cases there is a one-to-one mapping between real values and measured values. However, Kwan et al. also claim that it is very likely that some values will be missed because of imperfect measuring equipment. The different types of imperfection vary from application to application. Thus incomplete data, due to an inability to record every desired value, will characterise biomolecular databases, and these also have problems with measurement noise, while evasive and untruthful responses from people worried about higher taxes are apparently a big problem in introducing imperfections into economic data.

A similar analysis is provided by Riese (1993) who is concerned with observations of multi-agent systems. Reise points out that these observations may be incomplete because the system state may evolve too quickly for observations to be captured, because the internal state of the agents may be unobservable, or because there may be too much data generated for it all to be captured. The observations may also be uncertain because the observers make mistakes, may not be able to correlate what they see with what they think is happening, or because several observations from different agents may be confused.

Piatetsky-Shapiro (1997) has a slightly different focus, being interested in knowledge discovery from large quantities of information. In his view, imperfections stem from unreliable information, which, in the terms used here, is uncertain information and this, in turn, is the result of erroneous data, noisy data, or incomplete information. Furthermore, when dealing with several sources of information, different sources may conflict due to different terminologies and and scales of measurement, giving inconsistency, and it may be necessary to resolve the conflict before using the information.

The specific problems caused by imperfect information in information retrieval are the main concern of Turtle and Croft (1997), though their ideas clearly extend to other domains.[4] They identify three areas in which they claim uncertainty may be found. Firstly there is the problem of the representation of a document. Given the text of a document, people cannot agree on the set of concepts that should be used to represent it and automated procedures for creating descriptions will introduce considerable uncertainty. Further problems arise when attempting to represent the degree to which a document addresses the concepts in its description. The second problem is the representation of the kind of information that a user wishes to retrieve. Modelling this need is especially difficult since it typically changes during the search process. Thirdly, it is necessary to match needs to concepts, and the process of doing so would be approximate even if content and needs were precisely represented. In my terminology the problems do not seem to be so much of uncertainty as of vagueness and imprecision. The concepts by which a document is indexed, and the description of the document that the user wants to retrieve, are limited by the precision of the terms in which the descriptions are couched and the vagueness of the concepts. However, it is quite likely that some form of second order uncertainty will be introduced in that the imprecision and vagueness will be subject to some degree of subjective opinion.

Thus, the obvious conclusion seems to be that, as was the case for work on taxonomies, considering work on classifying the possible sources of imperfect information reinforces the idea that there are many types of imperfect information that must be handled by any intelligent system. However, despite the variety of sources discussed above, virtually all of them fall into the same broad category—sources of imperfect information that are due

---

4 As can be seen from the similarity between the protein structure prediction task discussed in Chapter 10 and the information retrieval task.

to some inability to measure the world precisely enough, either because of human frailty or because the necessary machinery is not accurate enough. The problem with this view is it suggests that given enough care it would be possible to engineer out the imperfection completely and have perfect information. This, I think, is misleading. As work in quantum mechanics has demonstrated, there are definite limits to the accuracy with which the world can be measured, so information about it will always be imperfect to some degree. Here there is a close connection between the work on sources discussed above and the "hidden variable" interpretation of quantum mechanics (Gribben, 1995), originally proposed by de Broglie to explain conundrums such as Schrödinger's cat. Much of the imperfection discussed above arises because information does not fit into the representation adopted. This suggests that were a suitable representation found, then the imperfection would disappear. In the "hidden variable" interpretation, there are aspects of the world that cannot be measured, the hidden variables, which would, were they measurable, allow completely precise predictions to be made. Both types of perfection, however, are equally illusory.

2.4   Uncertainty and entropy

Brillouin, one of the pioneers of information theory, offers an interesting discourse (Brillouin, 1964) on the properties of uncertainty by analogy with the concept of entropy from thermodynamics. Entropy is a property of all thermodynamic systems, and is captured by the following equation (van Wylen and Sonntag, 1985):

$$\Delta S \geq \frac{\delta Q}{T} \tag{2.1}$$

where ΔS is the change in entropy, δQ is the change in heat energy and T is temperature (temperature must be held constant for the equation to apply). From this equation it follows that whenever heat enters or leaves a system, there is a change in entropy. The interesting thing about this change in entropy is that it is positive for every interaction for every thermodynamic system. This is true whether the system being considered is the universe as a whole or is just the refrigerator in my kitchen. Entropy in part of the system can be reduced, but entropy for the system as a whole increases, and entropy can only be reduced at all by putting energy into a system. If no energy is input, entropy increases. It is this property of entropy that points to an analogy with uncertainty—just like entropy, uncertainty seems to increase of its own accord unless something is done to reduce it.

Brillouin was, to the best of my knowledge, the first to suggest that the principle of ever increasing entropy may be generalised to cover phenomena other than those of thermodynamics. As part of the ground work he introduces an idea of Schrödinger's, that of replacing entropy S with an expression of opposite sign which represents negative entropy $N = -S$. This negative entropy, known as negentropy for short, behaves more intuitively than entropy, steadily decreasing over time. In information theory, the idea of uncertainty is related to entropy, and the idea of information to that of negentropy. Brillouin gives the example of a container filled with a gas—a classic thermodynamic system. The gas is composed of many molecules all moving randomly and continuously. The only measurements that are known are the macroscopic measures of pressure and volume. These make it possible to determine the entropy of the system. The calculation takes into account all the possible internal structures that the system may have while satisfying the measurements. The greater the uncertainty, the larger the possible number of structures, and the larger the entropy. If there is some additional information about the system, some information relating to its original state, say, the structure may be more accurately determined, and both the uncertainty and entropy are decreased. Thus any additional piece of information increases the negentropy of the system. Brillouin then goes on to show that in a cycle:

Negentropy $\rightarrow$ Information $\rightarrow$ Negentropy   (2.2)

the quantity of negentropy lost in the first operation is greater than the negentropy gained in the second operation so that there is still an overall increase in entropy. In an information system, the increase in entropy is an increase in uncertainty.

It may be possible to extend Brillouin's analogy to the study of uncertainty in artificial intelligence. The results are not startling, but provide some support for ideas already in service. Brillouin's analogy suggests that not only are these ideas correct, but there is no point in trying to get around them. Firstly, and most obviously, there is the relation between information and uncertainty. Like entropy and negentropy each is the converse of the other. To decrease uncertainty in a system, more information must be applied to it. This, in turn, suggests that whenever uncertain data is available, additional information is always to be welcomed.[5]

Secondly, the loss of negentropy in any negentropy-information-negentropy cycle would seem to suggest that converting between different representations of uncertainty will in general cause the uncertainty of a system to rise. This, of course, may well be offset by the new information that the system can derive as a result of the conversion. The full extent to which the concepts suggested by Brillouin may be of use will only become known as the suggested interactions between information and uncertainty are investigated. For now their value is in suggesting that it is not at all surprising that uncertainty within a system is irreducible, or that uncertainty, where not limited by information, always increases.

---

5 There are, however, limits to the extent to which one can take this argument. Consider plotting a position by taking bearings from known locations. Two bearings will give a single location. Three invariably define an area.

Finally, and perhaps most importantly, the connection between entropy and uncertainty may be used to establish measures of uncertainty. If it is possible to establish the entropy of a given set of data, the uncertainty in it can be established. This idea has been used by Shannon (1948) and Klir (1987) to suggest measures of the amount of entropy in a given set of uncertain data, and, as will be discussed in Chapter 3, to provide the basis for techniques such as the principle of maximum entropy and principle of minimum specificity for establishing the best means of quantifying the uncertainty of data for which no numerical measure is known.

2.5   Human reasoning under uncertainty

Now, despite the fact that the discussion of uncertainty presented above makes it clear that the area is a rather complex and confusing one, it is nevertheless the case that people are extremely good at dealing with the problems posed by uncertainty—problems that surround them all the time. In general, people are quite happy with the incompleteness of their knowledge and the unpredictability of the world around them. They are eminently

capable of being in uncertainties, mysteries, doubts, without any irritable reaching after fact and reason[6]

and, more than this, are apparently capable of reaching decisions based only upon their limited knowledge of their environment. Given this fact, it seems worthwhile investigating exactly what they are capable of, and that is the focus of this section. It is not, of course, an exhaustive survey, but a summary of some of the more important results. More detailed studies are provided by Kahneman, Slovic and Tversky (1982), Arkes and Hammond (1986), and Wright and Ayton (1994).

2.5.1   Biases in human reasoning

Initial work by psychologists on human reasoning under uncertainty concentrated on comparing the way that people handled implicit or explicit probabilistic information with the way that the same information would be handled by a correct application of probability theory. This work appeared to uncover a number of systematic biases in human behaviour.

Experiments by Ward Edwards and colleagues on how subjects updated their beliefs in a variety of simple (Phillips and Edwards, 1966) and complex (Phillips et al., 1966) scenarios, showed that people are consistently conservative when compared with probability theory. That is they allow evidence about the rate of occurrence of events to change their belief in how probable the events are to occur less than is sanctioned by probability

---

6 John Keats, Letter to G. and T. Keats, 21st December 1817.

theory. This bias is referred to as "conservatism" and, though the precise reasons for it are controversial (Edwards, 1968), it appears to be consistent across a range of reasoning tasks (Peterson et al., 1965; Beach, 1966). The effects of conservatism have been shown to be reduced, though still present, in tasks involving normal distributions (DuCharme and Peterson, 1968), and when people accumulate experience with probability estimates (Schum et al., 1966). Furthermore, these effects appear to be more pronounced when more pieces of evidence are presented to the subjects (Phillips and Edwards, 1966). Thus, it seems that people under-estimate the force of the evidence that they are presented with, revising their beliefs less than they should do when compared with the amount of revision suggested by probability theory.

However, in other situations people have the opposite tendency. It seems (Kahneman and Tversky, 1973) that people often completely ignore prior values when they have evidence that strongly suggests a particular conclusion. Thus, despite knowing that a certain individual has a 70% chance of being an engineer, and only a 30% chance of being a lawyer, when given a description of a particular individual, people assess the likelihood that the individual is a lawyer purely by the degree to which the description fits their stereotypical view of a lawyer. When no specific evidence is presented people do use priors correctly, assessing the likelihood of an individual being an engineer as 0.7 when no personality sketch is given to them. This neglect of information about the base-rate of occurrence of an event is known as the "base-rate fallacy." Such behaviour is perhaps understandable since if evidence is strong enough it will tend to outweigh the effect of a base-rate, and all uncertainty handling formalisms will allow this kind of behaviour. However, it seems that people can over-estimate the importance of the evidence that they have, in direct contrast to their behaviour when exhibiting the conservatism bias .

This tendency can be so extreme that the base-rate is neglected even when there is no evidence suggesting a particular conclusion. For example, in another part of Kahneman and Tversky's study, subjects were asked to assess the probability of the following individual being an engineer:

Dick is a 30 year old man. He is married with no children. A man of high ability and high motivation, he promises to be quite successful in his field. He is well liked by his colleagues.

In a series of experiments the assessment of Dick being an engineer was given as 0.5 despite the knowledge that a randomly selected individual had a 70% chance of being an engineer, and the lack of useful information in the personality sketch.

The neglect of base-rates has also been observed in more serious situations. Eddy (1982) discusses an experiment with doctors who were experts in diagnosing breast cancer. The doctors were given the task of combining the results of an examination that indicated that a growth was benign, an X-ray that indicated that it was malignant, and knowledge about the accuracy of the test. The results showed that the doctors greatly overestimated the likelihood of cancer in those patients whom the X-ray indicated had malignant growths because they ignored the extremely low incidence of cancer in the population as a whole (though their failure to appreciate the fact that the X-ray could be wrong when indicating malignancy helped to distort the results).

Not only do people not reason in accord with probability theory, but they can also be bad at estimating probabilities to the extent that Keren (1994) claims that probability is not a good model of people's gambling behaviour. This is important since the assumption that human betting behaviour—the assessment and comparison of probabilistic odds—is good, is a major assumption in the justification of some systems based on probability. For instance, studies of how well calibrated[7] (Lichtenstein et al., 1982) people are, found that some groups of people, weather forecasters for example, are very well calibrated, while others such as doctors (worryingly) are rather bad. Indeed, doctors seem a favorite choice for the part of "bad intuitive probabilist." Meehl (1966) surveys 24 studies in which doctors' weighing up of evidence was found to be worse for making predictions than simple weighted-sum or statistical models,[8] and Kleinmuntz (1986) and Gustafon et al. (1986) each discuss another such study. Now, it might be thought that the reason that weather forecasters are good at estimating probabilities and doctors are bad is because the former have more practice of making numerical predictions than the latter. However, studies that involve telling people about the accuracy of their past predictions as a means of improving future predictions have proved inconclusive (Lichtenstein et al., 1982), and providing incentives has had similarly mixed success in improving performance.

This lack of calibration often takes the form of overconfidence, and this tendency has been called the "overconfidence bias." In a typical test, subjects would be given questions of the form:

Which is the world's longest canal? (a) Panama
(b) Suez

and then required to both indicate the answer that they believe to be correct, and to state how confident they are on a probability scale of 50% to 100% (since one of the answers is always correct, 50% is the probability of a guess being correct) (Ayton and Pascoe, 1995). Typically people give higher confidence values than is warranted by their performance, since their average confidence is greater than the percentage of answers they get correct.

In another blow to the idea that people are intuitive probabilists, it was found (Kahneman and Tversky, 1982a) that people are insensitive to the size of samples when assessing

---

7 If someone is well calibrated, their estimates of probability match up to the frequency of occurrence of the events whose probability of occurrence they are estimating.

8 Indeed, Kleinmuntz (1986) refers to a later work by Meehl in which he mentions 35 such studies.

probabilities. They seem to expect that the frequency of occurrence of events will not be greatly altered by increasing the number of measurements, whereas it can change a great deal because extreme estimates are quite likely to be made from small samples. A related result is one that demonstrates that even individuals with a sophisticated understanding of statistics have an inordinate belief in "the law of small numbers." Experiments on a group of leading psychologists (Tversky and Kahneman, 1971) showed that, despite a far greater familiarity with statistics than is common in the population at large, they still believed that events should occur with a randomness pleasing to the eye and that, because of this, a relatively small number of results should correlate well with a large number of results from the same experiment. The tendency to believe that events should behave this way is related to the "gambler's fallacy" after the observation (attributed to Dostoevsky (1966)) that roulette players tend to assume that after a particular number has come up it will not reappear for a while. The law of small numbers means that people believe that if an event happens two times out of three in a sample of five, then its frequency of occurrence is two thirds, and the gambler's fallacy means that people believe that if an event occurs, on average, one sample in ten then once it has occurred it cannot reoccur for another four or five samples.

In another set of experiments, Tversky and Kahneman (1983) tested people's adherence to the extension law of probability, which says that if the extension of A includes the extension of B, in other words $A \supseteq B$, then $\Pr(A) \geq \Pr(B)$. To see if people followed this rule in their intuitive reasoning, they were presented with some background information and a series of statements and were asked to rank the statements based on the information. For instance, one example involved information about a fictitious individual Linda:

Linda is 31 years old, single, outspoken and very bright. She majored in philosophy. As a student, she was deeply concerned with issues of discrimination and social justice, and also participated in anti-nuclear demonstrations.

Given this description, subjects then had to rank the following statements in order of likelihood of being true:

- Linda is a teacher in an elementary school.
- Linda works in a bookstore and takes Yoga classes.
- Linda is active in the feminist movement.
- Linda is a psychiatric social worker.
- Linda is a member of the League of Women Voters.
- Linda is a bank teller.
- Linda is an insurance salesperson.
- Linda is a bank teller and is active in the feminist movement.

If they followed the extension law, the subjects would judge statements of the form

"*A* and *B*," such as "Linda is a bank teller and active in the feminist movement" to be less likely than both the statements "*A*" and "*B*," such as "Linda is a bank teller" and "Linda is active in the feminist movement." However, while they correctly noted that "Linda is a bank teller and active in the feminist movement" was less likely than "Linda is active in the feminist movement," 85% of respondents thought that "Linda is a bank teller and active in the feminist movement" was more likely than "Linda is a bank teller," violating the laws of probability. People's tendency to indulge in this kind of reasoning has been called the "conjunction fallacy."

If probability is taken to be a normative theory, that is a theory that reflects the way in which people *should* reason under uncertainty, rather than describing how they actually *do* reason, then the conjunction and other fallacies are examples of non-normative behaviour.[9] Another example is people's response to what psychologists tend to call ambiguity, but in my terminology is ignorance. Ellsberg (1961) showed that people would rather place bets upon drawing a red ball from an urn with 50 red and 50 black balls than on drawing a red ball from an urn containing 100 red and black balls in unknown quantities. Since the two situations are, probabilistically speaking, equivalent, showing a preference for one in particular is non-normative, but this does not stop people systematically seeking to avoid this kind of lack of information (Curley and Benson, 1994; Baron and Frisch, 1994).[10] It is also worth noting that when faced with ambiguous information (in the sense that some of it is evidence for a particular conclusion, and some is evidence against), people's conservatism bias is more pronounced (Phillips and Edwards, 1966).

2.5.2   The use of heuristics

In their seminal paper (Tversky and Kahneman, 1974), and later in their collaboration with Slovic (Kahneman et al., 1982), Tversky and Kahneman suggested that the reason that people do not adhere to probability theory when reasoning under uncertainty is that, rather than use some intuitive version of the theory, they base their judgement on a limited number of heuristics that simplify the tasks of assessing numerical uncertainty values. These heuristics are often helpful but sometimes lead to severe systematic divergence from the results obtained using probability theory. The models Tversky and Kahneman describe are "representativeness," "availability," and "adjustment and anchoring." Representativeness is the heuristic by which the degree to which object *A* belongs to class *B* is determined by

---

9 Taking probability to be normative has led to behaviour which is non-normative being described as "irrational," in the sense that disagreeing with a theory that describes how one should behave is not a rational thing to do. However, this seems to me to be rather overstating the case.

10 Of course, one could also argue that this result is not surprising. To show the "probabilistic equivalence" of the two alternatives it is necessary to add information about the second, namely that in the absence of knowing how many black and red balls there are, it is reasonable to assume equal numbers. Thus maybe all the experiments show is that people are not comfortable with this assumption.

the degree to which *A* resembles *B*. Availability is used when the frequency of an event is assessed by the ease with which an occurrence may be brought to mind, and adjustment and anchoring are the related phenomenon of estimating by taking a guess and moving it as required.

For instance, Tversky and Kahneman suggest that when estimating the probability of the occurrence of events, people make use of the availability heuristic. This involves making estimates of the relative frequency of events on the basis of how easy or difficult they are to recall. This is doubtless a reasonable measure under some circumstances, but not under others. Kahneman and Tversky give the example of an experiment that asked people to compare the likelihood of a randomly chosen word beginning with a given letter and the likelihood of the word having the given letter as its third character. People tackle this problem by recalling words in both categories, and assess the relative likelihood by the relative ease of remembering. However, since it is easier to search for words by their first letter than by their third, the number of words with the given first letter is consistently judged more numerous. Thus the availability heuristic may account for people's lack of calibration when estimating probabilities.

The inability to correctly gauge probabilities can also be attributed to the use of the representativeness heuristic (Kahneman and Tversky, 1982a). If people judge the probability that something belongs to a class by the degree to which it is representative of the class, then an event might be very improbable even if it is highly representative. For instance, Tversky and Kahneman (1982b) give the example of judging the probability that somebody will complete a very hard task. If the person in question is highly representative of the kind of person expected to complete the task (because they are highly regarded by the judge) then a high probability may be given, even though the probability is really quite small because of the difficulty of the task. Representativeness clearly has some bearing on the conjunction fallacy as well. The reason that Linda is judged to be more likely to be both a feminist and a bank teller than just a bank teller is that the description seems to be so representative of someone who is "active in the feminist movement." Furthermore, the use of the representativeness heuristic may explain the base-rate and gambler's fallacy. In the case of the base-rate fallacy, if people base their judgment of the likelihood that Dick is an engineer on the degree to which they believe that he is representative of a stereotypical engineer, then it is understandable that they neglect base-rate information—it just does not seem to have any bearing on the situation. In the case of the gambler's fallacy, the representativeness heuristic suggests that people believe that the outcome of a random process should appear to be random even in the short term. In other words, a roulette wheel should appear to favour each number roughly the same number of times in a given set of roulette games. This argument leads people to believe that the same number cannot appear twice in quick succession because the resultant sequence of numbers would not appear to be random, and a similar application of the heuristic is what leads people to believe in the law of small numbers.

The remaining heuristic introduced by Tversky and Kahneman (1974), anchoring and adjustment, is used to explain the conjunction fallacy and the lack of calibration. In the former case, reasoning starts with an estimation of the probability of one of the conjuncts, and this value is then adjusted to reflect additional information about the other conjunct. Since adjustment is typically conservative, and the direction of adjustment is downwards, the final value that is generated is larger than that which is justified by the available information. In the case of calibration errors, the heuristic works as follows. Consider that the subjects are asked to give a value of the Financial Times 100 Share Index which has a probability of 0.8 of being above the actual value of the index on a particular day. Following the anchoring and adjustment heuristic, subjects make a best-guess estimate of the actual value of the index, and adjust upward. Since the adjustment is less than it should be, the values of the index given by the subjects are too low, leading to overconfidence in the subjects that the values they have given will be above the actual value.

These heuristics are not the only models that have been put forward to explain the observed biases—others include Tversky and Kahneman's (1982a) causal schema model, and the model put forward by Bar-Hillel (1980). However, those models already considered are sufficient to make the point that heuristic models exist and are reasonably compelling explanations of observed biases.

All in all results such as those presented above tend to suggest that human reasoning under uncertainty is non-normative when subjects are forced to use numerical values to quantify their uncertainty. Thus the heuristics provide a powerful argument for distinguishing between probability as a theoretical model and probability as a practical tool as Edwards (1954) does.[11] However, one should not lose sight of the proven ability of people to reason effectively under considerable uncertainty. Perhaps all that the results discussed in this section demonstrate is that human beings don't use numerical values to reason under uncertainty. In any case, the fact that people don't deal with numerical values in accordance with the laws of probability theory is not a good reason for abandoning numerical approaches to handling uncertainty.[12] Just as logic is used as a normative method of reason-

---

11 And, indeed, as most psychologists do, by distinguishing between "subjective probabilities," which are what people manipulate, and are created by some unknown process from the "objective probabilities" of the events with which they are concerned. With this nonclamenture, objective probabilities have all the mathematical properties of probability theory, while subjective probabilities have more or less of these properties depending on individual concerned, and may "describe the person who holds the opinion more than the event the opinion is about" (Edwards, 1968). This picture is complicated by the use, in artificial intelligence and statistics (Shafer, 1992), of the term "subjective probability" to distinguish those probabilities generated from individuals' beliefs, but which are constructed to obey the laws of probability, from those "objective probabilities" derived from statistical information (and which necessarily obey the laws of probability theory).

12 Though it is a good reason to try to model the way people do reason, if only to build systems that can predict

ing in artificial intelligence systems despite the fact that nobody uses logic in everyday life, so numerical methods can provide a normative approach to handling uncertainty despite being unintuitive to many people. However, before reaching any firm conclusions more recent evidence, which suggests that people are not so bad at numerical reasoning about uncertainty, should be examined.

2.5.3   Removing biases

As recorded in the previous sections, work by Tversky and Kahneman and those who followed their line of work, the so-called "heuristics and biases program," seemed to suggest that people were rather poor at using numerical values to reason under uncertainty, at least when compared with probability theory. However, there is considerable evidence to the contrary. For example, Beach, in (Beach and Braun, 1994), reports embarrassment at his

inability to find compelling evidence that subjects were rotten intuitive statisticians

when they were given experience with the events before being asked to assess probabilities. Perhaps, as Beach and Braun suggest, poor human performance is just cited more frequently than good performance, and to help set the record straight, they briefly survey a number of studies that report positive results.

The other alternative, of course, is that the biases being studied were more laboratory artifacts than real phenomena. Indeed, even while the original work on biases was taking place, there were results that suggested that they were due more to the way that experiments were carried out than to innate human deficiencies (Ayton and Pascoe, 1995). Such a conclusion certainly seems to follow from the work of Gigerenzer who, with various colleagues, has been steadily demolishing evidence of systematic biases. As an example, Gigerenzer et al. (1988a) have shown how base-rate neglect[13] can be reduced so that in some situations

subjects' judgements were indistinguishable from Bayesian performance.

This result leads them to conjecture that people are very sensitive to the presentation of problems and the information that they contain. The theory that two problems which have essentially the same structure can produce completely different results is supported by

---

their patterns of reasoning in order to interact with them more successfully as, for example, Vogel does (1996).

13 Base-rate neglect is a term they introduce and distinguish from base-rate fallacy—"base-rate neglect" is a term that describes a situation in which people do not use base rate information, while "base-rate fallacy" is a term that describes a situation in which base-rate information was neglected and should not have been. Gigerenzer et al. argue that, since in many cases it is not clear that ignoring the base-rate is necessarily incorrect (because in cases such as the "car and goats" problem (Deakin, 1992), it is not clear what answer probability theory should give), "base-rate neglect" is a more accurate term than "base-rate fallacy." The former also lacks the latter's pejorative overtones.

Gigerenzer et al.'s (1988b) investigation of the overconfidence bias. Based on a belief that the overconfidence bias is, in part, caused by the choice of questions, which tend to include a disproportionate number of elements such as the Panama/Suez question (which is deliberately chosen to be difficult), Gigerenzer et al. tested whether the bias was observed when the questions involved randomly selected elements. In particular they randomly selected pairs of German cities with more than 100,000 inhabitants and asked their subjects to indicate both which was larger, and what their confidence was. The results indicated no overconfidence. Furthermore, when dealing with the kind of "misleading" questions discussed above, Gigerenzer et al. found that the subjects were quite accurate when estimating their overall performance on the tests as opposed to their performance on individual questions.

Further evidence that the presentation of the problem is important is provided by (Gigerenzer, 1994). In this paper Gigerenzer advances the view that people might be bad at handling subjective probabilities, but that they are very good at handling objective probabilities, presented by stating problems in an explicitly frequentistic manner. As an example, he discusses the conjunction fallacy, suggesting the following restatement of the case of Linda:

Linda is 31 years old, single, outspoken and very bright. She majored in philosophy. As a student, she was deeply concerned with issues of discrimination and social justice, and also participated in anti-nuclear demonstrations.
There are 100 people who fit the description above. How many of them are

   (a) bank tellers

   (b) bank tellers and active in the feminist movement

With this version of the problem, the number of cases in which subjects demonstrated the conjunction fallacy fell dramatically when compared with the original formulation.

The conclusions of Gigerenzer's studies are backed up by two "real world" experiments. In the first (McNeil et al., 1986), data about the possible outcome of surgical and radiation therapy treatments for lung cancer was presented to a mixed group of patients, doctors and medical students. The subjects had to choose which treatment they preferred on the basis of the data they were shown. The results indicated that the subjects were influenced by the way that the data was presented, stating different preferences when presented with the same data in different ways. The second study (Gaeth and Shanteau, 1986) involved experts in hand soil analysis, and showed that including irrelevant factors in the information provided to the experts reduced the quality of their judgments, again suggesting that the presentation of the data is important.

2.5.4 Results of considering human reasoning

When taken as a whole, research on human reasoning under uncertainty presents a rather mixed message. Initial research suggested that people suffer from a series of consistent biases when their reasoning is compared with the gold standard of probability theory. This led to the proposal that people did not reason probabilistically, but instead used a series of "quick and dirty" heuristics to handle uncertainty. However, further research has called this idea into question by showing that many of the perceived biases can be made to disappear. Thus, it seems that people can either reason normatively or non-normatively when handling uncertainty—not a situation likely to inspire much confidence in anyone who is subject to a critical decision that takes place in uncertain conditions. This fact suggests that, at the least, it is wise to follow Meehl's (1966) suggestion that formal systems for handling uncertainty should be used as a means of backing up people who have to reason under uncertainty. This suggestion is supported by observations, such as those in (Sisson et al., 1986), that formal models may be necessary in order to ensure that the information available in uncertain situations is wisely used.

2.6 Ground rules for formal systems

In the years that the problem of reasoning under uncertainty has been studied, there have been a number of attempts to specify exactly what is required of a formal system for reasoning with imperfect information. Despite Dempster's (1988) disparaging remarks about such attempts, it seems that these are worth considering if only as a framework within which it is possible to discuss the differences between formalisms. The most notable of the specifications is the set of axioms laid down by Cox (1946), but the proposals made by Shackle (1961) and Bonissone (1987b) are also worth discussing.

2.6.1 Cox's fundamental properties

In a paper published in 1946, Cox (1946) laid down a set of axioms that he claimed any rational measure of uncertainty should adhere to. Forty years later Horvitz et al. (1986) reformulated the axioms for an artificial intelligence audience as a set of fundamental properties from which the axioms can be recovered. These are:

- Clarity: propositions should be well defined.
- Scalar Continuity: a single real number is both necessary and sufficient for representing a degree of belief.
- Completeness: a degree of belief can be assigned to any well-defined proposition.
- Context Dependency: the belief assigned to a proposition can depend on the belief in

other propositions.

• Hypothetical Conditioning: there exists some function that allows the belief in a conjunction of propositions to be calculated from the belief in one proposition and the belief in the other proposition given that the first is true.

• Complementarity: the belief in the negation of a proposition is a monotonically decreasing function of the belief in the proposition itself.

• Consistency: there will be equal belief in propositions that have the same truth value.

Despite the fact that they can be viewed as a post-hoc justification of probability theory, these properties are interesting because of the assumptions that they make, such as the degree of belief in a proposition being related to that in its negation, and the necessity of hypothetical conditioning. As Shafer (1988) points out, if these properties seem sensible it may well only be because probability theory is so widely known. Indeed, if one wants to criticise the properties, it is easy to attack several of the assumptions on the grounds that they are unintuitive. However, since most formal methods other than probability theory violate at least one of the properties, they are a useful framework within which to compare the methods (see Section 4.6).

2.6.2 Shackle's requirements

Shackle (1961), possibly the earliest proponent of possibility theory, also discusses what is required from a measure of uncertainty, using this discussion to motivate his departure from the tenets of probability theory. His starting point is that the base situation against which the uncertainty of all hypotheses should be compared is that of being "unquestionably wrong." He then claims that the essential choice in determining how a formal theory for reasoning with imperfect information should be developed is between values that sum to a fixed value ("distributional" values in his terminology, "additive" values in the usual terminology) and those that do not. Shackle requires that a useful system for handling imperfect information use non-additive values for a number of reasons. Firstly, he presents a number of familiar problems with additive measures. In particular, the problem that arises when the hypothesis set is incomplete. As he argues, the inclusion of a residual hypothesis to sweep up any unclassified outcomes makes any *a priori* distribution invalid since it is difficult to put a measure on "all other possible outcomes" that could possibly be valid. In addition to this, Shackle objects to the fact that when using an additive measure, the weight given to any hypothesis tends to be weakened when other possible new hypotheses are considered. This is a situation that he sees as patently ridiculous, and he likens it to allowing one's appreciation of a particular actor's performance to be lessened just because a number of other people happen to be on stage at the same time.

Shackle also has two other important requirements that he believes make probability inappropriate, and these are to model what he calls *non-divisible, non-seriable* experiments. Divisible experiments are those like predicting the number of times double six will be thrown when two dice are rolled 36,000 times, in which the experiment is divisible into a sufficiently large number of sub-experiments that statistical principles apply. Such experiments, he claims, should be distinguished from non-divisible experiments such as predicting the value of one roll of the dice. At first, therefore, his distinction seems to be between experiments that are performed once and so may not be modelled using statistical data, and those that are performed many times and so may be thus modelled. However, that is an over-simplistic view, since there are situations in which an experiment may only be performed once and yet statistical methods may be meaningfully applied. It is such experiments that Shackle calls "seriable," and they are characterised by the fact that, though single experiments, they may be investigated by pooling data about similar experiments. The obvious example here is the use of actuarial data where a decision about a particular life assurance policy (which is, in effect, a single experiment about longevity), is investigated using data about a large number of previous cases (other experiments in longevity).

Thus, in the case of a non-divisible, non-seriable experiment, there is only one experiment that cannot be broken down, and which is dissimilar to all others for which there is meaningful data. Of course, it is possible to analyse such experiments by pooling with dissimilar ones on the grounds that the possible loss in one is offset by the possible gain in another. However, Shackle argues that this approach is only meaningful and sensible when the acts themselves are of insignificant consequence, like buying a book or choosing a restaurant. For important decisions, like how to respond to the various crises in the Balkans that resulted from the break-up of what was Yugoslavia, Shackle claims that pooling is not a valid operation, and the decision can be regarded as non-seriable.

In summary, then, the result of Shackle's deliberations is the following set of requirements of a formal theory for handling imperfect information

1. A theory should explicitly model the idea of "unquestionably wrong."

2. The measure used by the theory should not be required to be additive.

3. The measure used by the theory should be applicable to non-divisible experiments.

4. The measure used by the theory should be applicable to non-seriable experiments.

While these are intended to argue against probability theory and for possibility theory, his argument for them has sufficient strength to warrant taking them as more general requirements of any system.

2.6.3   Bonissone's desiderata

As part of the motivation for his system of reasoning based on triangular norms, Bonissone (1987b) sets out a list of desirable properties, or desiderata, of formal systems for reasoning under uncertainty. Despite the suspicion that they are specially tailored to reinforce the argument for his possibilistic solution, these are worth looking at. The desiderata are structured into three sets, each corresponding to a layer of the architecture that Bonissone has defined for expert systems and which is used by the system RUM (Bonissone et al., 1987). These are the representation, inference, and control layers. The representation layer is concerned with how information about the world is represented by the formal system.

Representation layer

1. There should be an explicit representation of the amount of evidence that supports and refutes any given hypothesis.

2. There should be an explicit representation of the information about the evidence, such as the source of the evidence and the reason it supports or refutes a given hypothesis.

3. The representation should allow the user to describe the uncertainty of the information at the available level of detail.

4. There should be an explicit representation of consistency.

5. There should be an explicit representation of ignorance to allow the user to make non-committal statements.

6. The representation must at least appear to be natural to the user to allow her to describe input and interpret the output.

The inference layer is concerned with how the formal system uses the information that is available to infer new information, in particular how to combine measures of the uncertainty of pieces of information to discover the measure that should be associated with newly derived pieces of information.

Inference layer

7. The combination rules should not be based on global assumptions of independence of evidence.

8. The combination rules should not be based on global assumptions of the exclusivity and exhaustiveness of hypotheses.

9. The combination rules should maintain the closure of the syntax and the semantics of the representation.

10. Any function used to propagate uncertainty should have a clear semantics.

The control layer is concerned with the control of the inference process, and, in particular, the propagation of measures of uncertainty.

Control layer

11. There should be a clear distinction between a conflict in the information and ignorance about the information.

12. The aggregation and propagation of uncertainty through the reasoning process must be traceable so that conflicts may be resolved, support explained, and meta-reasoning performed.

13. It should be possible to perform pair-wise comparisons of uncertainty for decision making.

14. There should be a second-order measure of uncertainty so that it is possible to gauge the uncertainty of the information as well as the uncertainty of the measure.

15. It should be possible to select the most appropriate combination rule by some declarative form of control.

2.6.4   Results from considering the ground rules

Now, when reading the lists laid down by Cox, Shackle, and Bonissone there is no overwhelming reason to reject any of the requirements that they suggest. All the points they make seem, when viewed in isolation, to be very reasonable. Indeed some are supported by other results discussed in this chapter. For instance, the distinction that Shackle makes between divisible and non-divisible decisions is precisely the same distinction drawn by Gigerenzer (1994) in his argument for changing the representation for probability assessment exercises. Furthermore, they agree on some points, as illustrated by the fact that Shackle's argument against additivity makes essentially the same point as Bonissone's third desideratum. However, when placed side-by-side, the requirements conflict. For instance, Cox's insistence on the fact that a single number is both necessary and sufficient for representing a degree of belief (the "scalar continuity" property) conflicts with Bonissone's requirement for explicit representations of both consistency and information about the evidence (desiderata 2 and 4). In passing, it should also be noted that the scalar continuity property also conflicts with people's preferences—in many cases (Wallsten and Budescu, 1995) they would rather express uncertain information in the form of a "linguistic probability," of the form "quite likely," which covers a range of values. To me these relations between sets of requirements does not suggest that one set is right and the others are wrong. Instead it suggests that since the different requirements have been thought up with different scenarios in mind, they are applicable in different situations. Furthermore, since different formalisms conform to different sets of desiderata, it follows that different formalisms are applicable in different situations.

2.7   Summary

This chapter has looked at some of the background to formal systems for reasoning with imperfect information. The rationale for doing this was to put imperfect information in context by looking at what it is, where it comes from, and how it behaves before introducing formal models for reasoning under it. It turns out that there are a number of different varieties of imperfect information, each capturing a different aspect of the imperfections found in the knowledge that is available about the world. As a result, an attempt was made to define what these varieties are and how they relate to one another, providing an overarching framework for comparing the different formal models that will be discussed in later chapters.

This was followed by a discussion of entropy and uncertainty, which prompts the use of several mechanisms that will be discussed in later chapters. Next, having established to some degree what uncertainty is, the way in which human beings handle it was considered. This exposes both weaknesses and strengths in human reasoning under uncertainty, and provides some useful pointers for mathematical models for doing the same. Based on both these pointers, and a brief survey of the literature, some proposals for desirable features of formal systems were detailed and discussed.

From this survey it is possible to make a number of arguments concerning the handling of uncertainty. The first is that uncertainty is an unavoidable feature of the real world, and this means that any intelligent system which is going to deal with the real world will need to handle uncertainty. Allied to this is an argument about the nature of such intelligent systems. Since people, if not consistently then at least occasionally, do not handle uncertainty normatively, then it is arguably sensible to base methods used to handle uncertainty in an intelligent system on some kind of formally correct mathematical model rather than on a model of human reasoning. One might even extend Meehl's (1966) argument to claim that formal models, and possibly even intelligent systems based upon them, are necessary as a means of backing up human reasoning and guarding against faults in it.

Another line of reasoning that emerges strongly from the work surveyed in this chapter is that uncertainty comes in many guises and from many sources. This argument is further backed up by results from the psychology literature that have not been covered in this chapter, for instance (Kahneman and Tversky, 1982b; Teigen, 1994). The variety of types of uncertainty seems to have meant that different authors, whether compiling desiderata or deriving formalisms from those desiderata, have only dealt with a small part of the whole picture. This belief is supported by the survey of formal models covered in the following chapters that shows that, for instance, probability theory has no obvious mechanism for dealing with incomplete information, while default logic (Reiter, 1980) has no obvious mechanism for dealing with information in the form of subjective beliefs. This fact motivates the work in this book on extending numerical models to be applicable when the numerical information is incomplete. In addition, the fact that no one model covers all forms of uncertainty, along with the argument that additional information (when correctly handled) is useful in reducing uncertainty, suggests that when building intelligent systems it is sensible to use whatever different sources of information are available, even to the extent of employing a number of different formal models each of which captures different nuances of uncertainty.

The success of this approach, of course, is is dependent upon the existence of suitable methods for using the different models in conjunction—if they are used in an incoherent manner they will give incoherent results (on the garbage-in, garbage-out principle). As a result, a substantial portion of this book is concerned with developing methods which enable different formal models to be used together. Before doing this, however, it is necessary to look at some of those formal models.

3 Quantitative methods for reasoning with imperfect information

—Clever, Lenehan said. Very.
—Gave it to them on a hot plate, Myles Crawford said, the whole bloody history. Nightmare from which you will never awake.

James Joyce, *Ulysses*

In the previous chapter some attempts to categorise uncertainty were examined in an effort to understand exactly what must be dealt with when confronting the problem of reasoning under uncertainty. This chapter and the next build on this background by looking at a number of models for reasoning under uncertainty that have been proposed over the years. That these models are largely formal mathematical models may cause some alarm in some quarters, where perhaps it is felt that formality is pursued at the cost of clarity and deep insight (Birnbaum, 1991) or that building formal models before what is being modelled is exactly understood is a form of "premature mathematization" (Russell, 1997). However, I believe that there are good reasons for using formal models in this context. Indeed, the decision to concentrate upon formal models in this work was not because of any conviction that only formal mathematical models have anything to say about reasoning under uncertainty, but mainly because of two related reasons, both inherently practical. Firstly, as Bundy (1991) has pointed out, formally stating a model is the best way of conveying both accurately and precisely how it works. Given a good mathematical description of a model it is easy to understand it, and any error in understanding is the sole property of the interpreter. The creator of the model can make her creation no clearer. Secondly, one of the aims of this book is to compare and relate models. This is much easier to do if the models are described precisely, and so formal models are easier to compare than informal ones. The issue of clarity also ties up with the point made at the end of the previous chapter about formal methods being desirable as a way of ensuring that intelligent systems reason with imperfect information in a normative way. Describing a technique formally makes it possible to exactly determine its properties, and thus to check that it behaves as desired, sanctioning the right consequences. Of course, none of these arguments mitigate against the use of human insight in producing models for handling imperfect information, they just suggest that formalising such insights is advisable.

Now, as already mentioned, this book makes no pretence to include an exhaustive account of every model that has been proposed for dealing with imperfect information (and its coverage is also far from even). Instead it aims to cover a range of the most influential of the models that in some way take account of imperfections in data, including those which are drawn upon in the theoretical developments in Chapters 6 to 9. It deals especially with those that deal with uncertainty, though models covering incompleteness, vagueness, imprecision, and inconsistency are also covered. For those models used later in the book, the description is deep enough to make the book self-contained, while many of the other formalisms are sketched more briefly with pointers to sources of more detailed information where that is appropriate. Nevertheless, despite this focussing, there is sufficient material to make it prudent to split the survey into two parts. The first, which makes up this chapter, covers *quantitative* models in which the uncertainty about propositions is encoded by associating some number with the propositions. The second, which makes up Chapter 4, covers *qualitative* models in which the uncertainty about propositions is handled by the manipulation of symbols rather than numbers. Clearly there are many "semiqualitative" systems that fall in between the two camps, and these may be found in either chapter, depending on which they seemed to match most closely. The second chapter also contains a discussion of work that relates different formalisms together, and which attempts to integrate two or more such models.

3.1   Introduction

Just as the use of formal models might generate cries of alarm from some readers, so might the choice of models dealt with in this chapter. The chapter concentrates on the three most widely studied models, probability (Lindley, 1965), possibility (Dubois and Prade, 1988f; Zadeh, 1978), and evidence (Shafer, 1976; Smets and Kennes, 1994) theories. This choice is made on the grounds that since most people who are interested in uncertainty are interested in probability, possibility, or evidence theories (and if you doubt this, take a look at the contents page of the proceedings of any recent conference on uncertainty, bearing in mind that the use of fuzzy sets is implicitly the use of possibility theory) more people will be interested in work relating those models together than will be interested in work relating less popular models. This is not to say that only these three main models are worth thinking about, it is just that they get the most attention.

For theories that have traditionally been seen as rivals, one might expect that the big three would appear radically different, but this is not so. Indeed, they are remarkably similar, differing largely in subtleties of meaning or application. This is not entirely surprising since they are intended, essentially, to do the same thing, and, as Dubois and Prade have argued (Dubois and Prade, 1990c), possibility and evidence theories are variants of probability theory that extend it to be applicable in slightly different situations. The basic problem is how to weigh up the degree to which several uncertain events are considered to occur so that the most certain may be unambiguously identified. The basis on which the measure of uncertainty is assigned is a contentious issue, though the three main theories considered assume allocation by a *distribution function* that allocates some measure of uncertainty to at least some of the possible events under consideration. This measure may be distributed on the basis of statistical information, physical possibility, or purely subjective assessment by an expert or otherwise. The measure assigned is a number between 0 and 1, with 0 being the measure assigned to a fact that is known to be false, and 1 the measure assigned to a fact known to be true. The infinite number of degrees between the limits represent the various shades of uncertainty. Now, some formalisms restrict the measure—both probability theory and evidence theory do this by constraining the sum of all the measures assigned by a particular distribution function to be 1. This may be interpreted as meaning that one particular observer cannot believe in a set of uncertain events more than she would have believed in an event of total certainty. There is no such restriction on a possibility distribution, since one may conceive of several alternative events that are perfectly possible, and so have a possibility of 1. Probability theory, unlike the other theories, also introduces a strong restriction on the belief that may be applied to a hypothesis based on the belief assigned to its negation. Given the result of a distribution, the way in which the assigned measures may be manipulated is of interest. Given measures for two events, what is the measure appropriate for their disjunction or conjunction? More importantly perhaps, especially for artificial intelligence applications where it is often necessary to assess the measure applicable to a hypothesis given some evidence that has some effect on it, the propagation of the effects of pieces of evidence is of interest. The way in which this is done is based upon the interpretation that the theory gives to the measures it assigns, and thus it is not surprising that each theory should propagate values in a different way.

3.2   The main models

3.2.1   Probability theory

Probability theory has existed in one form or another for several hundred years. During this time various alternative formulations have been introduced and it is now difficult to say where the definitive account may be found. The introduction presented here is drawn from the discussion of probability theory in books by Lindley (1975) and Pearl (1988b).

BASIC CONCEPTS OF PROBABILITY THEORY

The fundamental notion behind probability theory is the *probability distribution*, which assigns a *probability measure* to events under consideration. The measure may be used as an estimate of the degree to which an uncertain event is likely to occur, and may be assessed by reference to a standard, such as the chance of drawing a black ball out of an urn containing five black balls and ten red balls. The probability distribution, $\Pr(\cdot)$, is a mapping from the set of events under consideration, U, to the unit interval $[0, 1]$, which is constrained by the conditions on the probability measures that it distributes. These conditions take the form of three axioms, or laws, that define the behaviour of the measure. The first law is the *convexity law*, which states that the probability measure assigned by a probability distribution to event A given information H is such that:

$$0 \leq \Pr(A|H) \leq 1 \tag{3.1}$$

There is also the *addition law*, which relates the probabilities of two events to the probability of their union. For two exclusive events A and B, that is two events that cannot both occur:

$$\Pr(A \cup B|H) = \Pr(A|H) + \Pr(B|H) \tag{3.2}$$

which is commonly written as:

$$\Pr(A \cup B) = \Pr(A) + \Pr(B) \tag{3.3}$$

without explicit reference to the information H, since the information is the same in all cases. Furthermore, the sum of the probabilities of a set of mutually exclusive and exhaustive events are constrained to sum to 1. The final law is the *multiplication law*, which gives the probability of two events occurring together; the probability of the intersection of A and B:

$$\Pr(A \cap B|H) = \Pr(A|H) \cdot \Pr(B|A \cap H) \tag{3.4}$$

Again this may be written as:

$$\Pr(A \cap B) = \Pr(A) \cdot \Pr(B|A) \tag{3.5}$$

without explicit reference to H. The probability measure $\Pr(B|A)$ is the *conditional probability* of B given A, the probability that B will occur, given that A is known to have occurred. If:

$$\Pr(B) = \Pr(B|A) \tag{3.6}$$

then the occurrence of A does not affect the occurrence of B and the two events are said to be *conditionally independent*. The multiplication law may be generalised:

$$\Pr(E_1, E_2, \ldots, E_n) = \Pr(E_n|E_1, E_2, \ldots, E_{n-1}) \ldots \Pr(E_2|E_1) \Pr(E_1) \tag{3.7}$$

This states that for n events, E_1, E_2, ..., E_n the probability of them all occurring, $\Pr(E_1, E_2, \ldots, E_n)$, may be written as the product of n conditional probabilities. Pearl (1988b) adds the basic tenet that a sure event, one that is known to occur, has probability of 1:

$$\Pr(\text{sure proposition}) = 1 \tag{3.8}$$

Now, it is obvious that any event A can be written as the union of the joint events $(A \text{ and } B)$ and $(A \text{ and } \neg B)$. The associated probabilities follow from 3.3:

$$\Pr(A) = \Pr(A, B) + \Pr(A, \neg B) \tag{3.9}$$

Note that the expressions $(A \cap B)$ and (A, B) are both widely used as representations of "both A and B." In accordance with this confusion as to the best representation, the two will be used interchangeably in this book. An important consequence of (3.8) and (3.9) is that a proposition and its negation must be assigned a total probability of 1 since one of the two events must occur. This results in the *total probability* formula:

$$\Pr(A) + \Pr(\neg A) = 1 \tag{3.10}$$

Clearly (3.10) can be derived from (3.3) and, in different places, both described as illustrating the *additivity* of probability measures. This property is important since it implies that the probabilities of two exclusive events are linked, so that one may be determined once the other is known, and serves to distinguish probability from other methods for reasoning under uncertainty.

As written above, (3.9) only applies to binary variables. However, it may be generalised so that B has a set of n possible exclusive and exhaustive outcomes. In this case, the probability of A is the sum across all the joint probabilities $\Pr(A, B_i)$, $i = 1, 2, \ldots, n$:

$$\Pr(A) = \sum_{i=1\ldots n} \Pr(A, B_i) \tag{3.11}$$

and this result may be used in conjunction with (3.4) to predict how the probability of any event A may be computed by conditioning it upon any set of mutually exclusive and exhaustive events B_i, $i = 1, 2, \ldots, n$:

$$\Pr(A) = \sum_{i=1\ldots n} \Pr(A|B_i) \Pr(B_i) \tag{3.12}$$

It should be noted that there is an important step rather hidden in these calculations. Whereas (3.4) deals with the case in which B is known to occur, (3.12) deals with the case in which the occurrence of B is uncertain (which is why the probability distribution across all values of B is taken into account). Jeffrey (1965) was the first to suggest this kind of extension of the use of conditional probabilities, and (3.12) is known as *Jeffrey's rule* as a result (Shafer, 1981b).

The results presented so far are sufficient to permit the kind of inferential reasoning that is widely used in artificial intelligence. Given a variable C, which can take values $\{c_1, c_2, \ldots, c_n\}$ and is known to be directly dependent only upon variable A, which can take values $\{a_1, a_2, \ldots, a_m\}$, and variable X, which can take values $\{x_1, x_2, \ldots, x_p\}$, then by (3.12) any value $\Pr(c)$ where $c \in \{c_1, c_2, \ldots, c_n\}$ may be determined by:

$$\Pr(c) = \sum_{\substack{A=a_1, \ldots, a_m \\ X=x_1, \ldots, x_p}} \Pr(c|A, X) \Pr(A, X) \tag{3.13}$$

Note that this expression is completely general. Any number of variables that affect C can be incorporated by replacing X. For instance, to establish the value of $\Pr(c)$ when C is affected by B, which takes values $\{b_1, b_2, \ldots, b_q\}$, and D, which takes values $\{d_1, d_2, \ldots, d_q\}$, in addition to A then:

$$\Pr(c) = \sum_{\substack{A=a_1, \ldots, a_m \\ B=b_1, \ldots, b_p \\ D=d_1, \ldots, d_q}} \Pr(c|A, B, D) \Pr(A, B, D) \tag{3.14}$$

A further rule concerning probability values that is important from the point of view of artificial intelligence is Bayes' theorem, also known as Bayes' rule—named after an English eighteenth century non-conformist clergyman who wrote on the subject of probability. This is not a fundamental law in the sense of those presented above, but may be derived from them. Bayes' theorem states that:

$$\Pr(a|c, x) = \frac{\Pr(c|a, x) \Pr(a, x)}{\Pr(c, x)} \tag{3.15}$$

for any three values a, c, and x of the variables A, C, and X. This is important since it allows the direction of reasoning to be reversed. That is, given the necessary conditional values to reason from A to C in (3.13), it is possible to apply Bayes' theorem to find out how to reason from C to A.

In addition, under the assumption that the events of interest are mutually exclusive, exhaustive, and conditionally independent, it is possible to obtain a version of Bayes' rule that is suitable for pooling evidence from a number of sources. This assesses the probability of a hypothesis h_i that is a member of the set $\{h_1, \ldots, h_n\}$ given a set of pieces of evidence $\{e_1, \ldots, e_m\}$, a set of probabilities of occurrence of the hypotheses, $\{\Pr(h_1), \ldots, \Pr(h_n)\}$, and a set of conditional probabilities for each piece of evidence given each hypothesis,

$\{\Pr(e_1|h_1), \Pr(e_1|h_2), \ldots, \Pr(e_m|h_n)\}$:

$$\Pr(h_i|e_1, e_2, \ldots, e_m) = \frac{\Pr(e_1|h_i)\Pr(e_2|h_i)\ldots\Pr(e_m|h_i)\Pr(h_i)}{\sum_{j=1,\ldots,n}\Pr(h_j)\Pr(e_1|h_j)\Pr(e_2|h_j)\ldots\Pr(e_m|h_j)} \quad (3.16)$$

This may be used, say, to reason about the likelihood of a particular disease (h_i), from a set of possible diseases $(\{h_1, \ldots, h_n\})$, given a set of recorded symptoms $(\{e_1, \ldots, e_m\})$. In recent years, however, this "naïve Bayesian" method of pooling evidence has fallen into disuse being replaced by the use of formulae such as (3.14) that do not make assumptions of conditional independence.

The reason for making the assumption that events are conditionally independent is that it greatly reduces the number of probabilities that must be provided to specify a probabilistic model. This number grows exponentially with the size of the problem being modelled (for a problem that includes N variables, there are 2^N joint probabilities in the full model). However, resorting to the assumption of conditional independence is not the only method of handling a lack of probabilistic information. It is also possible to fill in the gaps using some means of making assumptions about the unknown values. Possibly the most justifiable of these is to use the principle of *maximum entropy*.

One of the main proponents of maximum entropy was Jaynes (for instance (Jaynes, 1979)) while its use was first suggested in the context of artificial intelligence by Cheeseman (1983), and it is his presentation that is used here. Consider a system described by 3 variables, A, C and X, where A takes values $\{a_1, a_2, \ldots, a_m\}$, C takes values $\{c_1, c_2, \ldots, c_n\}$ and X takes values $\{x_1, x_2, \ldots, x_p\}$. The entropy H of the set of joint probabilities of all the possible combinations of values of A, C and X is:

$$H = -\sum_{\substack{A=a_1,\ldots,a_m \\ C=c_1,\ldots,c_n \\ X=x_1,\ldots,x_p}} \Pr(a, c, x) \log \Pr(a, c, x) \quad (3.17)$$

Because the various $\Pr(a, c, x)$ are probabilities, they must obey the constraint that:

$$\sum_{\substack{A=a_1,\ldots,a_m \\ C=c_1,\ldots,c_n \\ X=x_1,\ldots,x_p}} \Pr(a, c, x) = 1 \quad (3.18)$$

and in given situations, other constraints may apply. The principle of maximum entropy requires that a unique set of values be found for the $\Pr(a, c, x)$ that satisfies the constraints and at the same time maximises the value of H. The reasons for accepting these values as correct are discussed in (Jaynes, 1979), and centre around the fact that the principle of maximum entropy distributes probability across hypotheses as evenly as possible while taking the constraints into account. Thus it ensures that no hypothesis is favoured any more than is required by the available information.[1] Another argument for adopting the method is that made by Paris and Vencovska (1990) who advance seven principles that they believe any method for computing unknown probabilities should obey, and then prove that any method that does indeed obey them is equivalent to maximum entropy. Methods for calculating the values of $\Pr(a, c, x)$ that maximise H for a given set of constraints are provided by Cheeseman (1983) and Rhodes and Garside (1995). In the absence of constraints, other than the fact that the $\Pr(a, c, x)$ sum to 1, the commonly quoted solution is that H is maximised by making all the $\Pr(a, c, x)$ equal. Despite the nice properties that the principle of maximum entropy possesses, it is just one means of estimating missing probabilities and, as Wilson (1992b) points out, it may well make an estimation that is a long way from the actual value. This remark has echoes in the more recent work by Grove and Halpern (1997).

VARIETIES OF PROBABILITY

The previous section laid down some rules for the behaviour of probabilities. These rules were, historically at least, derived to describe probabilities that arise in games of chance (Shafer, 1991b). While there is no longer any argument over the validity of these rules, there are a variety of opinions as to the meaning of the numbers that obey them. Shafer (1988; 1991c) gives the following classification (which he attributes to Savage) and which can be contrasted with the different views of the meaning of the term "subjective probability" given in Chapter 2. There are three viewpoints, those of the "objectivists," "personalists," and "necessarians." The objectivists, who are sometimes referred to as "frequentists," believe that numerical probabilities may only be assigned in situations where a large number of repeated experiments can be carried out. The probabilities that they deal with are thus long-term ratios of numbers of outcomes of these experiments.

Personalists insist that rationality means that everybody expresses their belief about the validity of each and every proposition by assigning a numerical probability to it. If they do not, it should be possible to get them to bet in accordance with their beliefs and, since their beliefs do not accord to the probabilities of the events occurring, win an endless supply of money from them. Thus the probabilities that personalists deal with are not objective properties of the universe, but subjective estimates that may be interpreted as the rate at which the estimator would be prepared to bet on the proposition. The necessarians, on the other hand, believe that probabilities measure the degree to which propositions are supported by the evidence, and so measure the degree to which it is rational to believe

---

1 The idea that if there is no reason to give $\Pr(c|a)$ a higher value than $\Pr(c|\neg a)$ then it should be given the same value is known as the "principle of insufficient reason" or "principle of indifference" (Good, 1950, page 37). The first name is attributed to Bernoulli and the second to Keynes (Jaynes, 1979). Thus the principle of maximum entropy follows the principle of insufficient reason while ensuring that the constraints are obeyed.

that the propositions will be true. Both the personalists and the necessarians subscribe to the same "Bayesian" or "subjectivist" viewpoint of the way that probabilities are used to represent knowledge. Despite the apparent differences between the interpretations Shafer (1991c; 1992) stresses the underlying similarities and points out that different interpretations can prove useful in different situations.

Pearl (1988b) provides another perspective. He points out that the frequentist viewpoint is that all probabilistic knowledge is defined in terms of joint probabilities. That is to say that to define the system described by the binary variables A, B, C, and D it is necessary to specify the joint values $\Pr(A, B, C, D)$, ..., $\Pr(\neg A, \neg B, \neg C, \neg D)$, and to elicit the behaviour of the system it is necessary to measure these joint values. Under such an interpretation the idea of a conditional probability becomes an artifact relating joint values, and Bayes' theorem becomes a simple tautology. Bayesians on the other hand see conditional probabilities as absolutely fundamental. In their view the conditional probability is the basic means by which uncertain knowledge about the world is encoded, so that the conditional $\Pr(A|B)$ is related to the statement "I know A if I am given B." Thus the system involving A, B, C, and D would be described by the conditionals $\Pr(A|B, C, D)$, $\Pr(A|\neg B, C, D)$, ..., $\Pr(A|\neg B, \neg C, \neg D)$, ... , $\Pr(D|\neg A, \neg B, \neg C)$, implying that knowledge elicitation should concentrate on these values rather than the joint values. This concentration on conditionals means that Bayes' rule becomes a normative rule for updating probabilities in line with new information. Since, as discussed above, it follows from the basic ideas of probability theory, the use of Bayes' rule is not controversial. However, the interpretation of the rule is controversial.

OTHER PROBABILISTIC SYSTEMS

There have been several different uses of probability theory within the literature of artificial intelligence. These include the *odds-likelihood* formulation borrowed by Duda, Hart and Nilsson (1976) from statistics for their Prospector system. In this application of probability theory, prior and conditional probabilities are not used directly. For a hypothesis H and evidence E, Bayes' rule (3.15) may be used to write the probability of H given E:

$$\Pr(H|E) = \frac{\Pr(E|H)\,\Pr(H)}{\Pr(E)} \qquad (3.19)$$

while the probability of $\neg H$ given E can be written as:

$$\Pr(\neg H|E) = \frac{\Pr(E|\neg H)\,\Pr(\neg H)}{\Pr(E)} \qquad (3.20)$$

Now, dividing (3.19) by (3.20) gives:

$$\frac{\Pr(H|E)}{\Pr(\neg H|E)} = \frac{\Pr(E|H)}{\Pr(E|\neg H)} \cdot \frac{\Pr(H)}{\Pr(\neg H)} \tag{3.21}$$

eliminating $\Pr(E)$, which is the prior probability of the evidence—a quantity that can be rather difficult to assess. In (3.21) the first term is the posterior odds in favour of H over $\neg H$ (a measure of how much H is indicated by the evidence over $\neg H$), the third term is the prior odds of H to $\neg H$ (how much H was indicated before the evidence), and the second term is the likelihood ratio (a measure of the degree to which the evidence is more likely to occur given H rather than $\neg H$). Using this formulation of probability theory allows knowledge to be represented as rules of the form:

IF   evidence E
THEN hypothesis H

The uncertainty of the rule is quantified by attaching two likelihood ratios to it. λ is the likelihood ratio of (3.21) and represents the degree to which the rule supports the hypothesis, while $\neg\lambda$ is the likelihood ratio of (3.21) with $\neg E$ substituted for E, and represents the degree to which the rule is against the hypothesis. This approach seems attractive especially since it seems to promise a means of coupling probability theory, in a form that makes the acquisition of probability values easy, with rules. However, as discussed by Lam and Yeap (1992) the method has some problems, and, as with the naïve Bayes' model (3.16), has fallen out of favour in artificial intelligence. Of course, the idea of formulating probability in the odds/likelihood manner is still used by statisticians.

Another interesting adaptation of probability theory is the cautious approach adopted by INFERNO (Quinlan, 1983a,b). Instead of a point probability, INFERNO represents the validity of a proposition by means of probability bounds. The bounds chosen are the lower bound, $t(A)$, on the probability $\Pr(A)$ of A, and a lower bound $f(A)$ on the probability of $\Pr(\neg A)$. Quinlan claims two advantages of this approach over other probabilistic systems. Firstly, the uncertainty in knowledge about A is apparent as the difference between $t(A)$ and $1 - f(A)$, and secondly the values used to derive $t(A)$ and $f(A)$ are derived from separate pieces of evidence while the values themselves are maintained and propagated separately. The propagation mechanism is also interesting. INFERNO used non-directed propagation by constraint satisfaction in order to avoid problems when the underlying relations between propositions form a loop. For instance the piece of knowledge "A enables B with strength X" generates the two constraints of (3.22) and (3.23) using probability theory without the need for assumptions of conditional independence.

$$t(B) \quad \geq \quad t(A) \cdot X \tag{3.22}$$

$$f(A) \geq 1 - \frac{1 - f(B)}{X} \tag{3.23}$$

There are many other systems that deal with bounds on probabilities, and some will be considered in the next chapter along with other interval-based systems. However, there is one such system that deserves to be considered here. Given a set of hypotheses Θ, a "source triple" (Moral and Wilson, 1994) is defined to be a triple (Ω, P, Γ) where Ω is a finite set, P is a probability distribution over Ω, and Γ is a function from Ω to 2^Θ, the power set (set of all subsets) of Θ. The function Γ is a multivalued mapping, so that for any $\omega \in \Omega$, $\Gamma(\omega) \subseteq 2^\Theta$. This mapping can be thought of as a transformation whose outcome cannot be precisely pinned down. The result of this mapping is that for any set of hypotheses $X \subseteq \Theta$, there are two interesting measures that may be calculated from the distribution over Ω. One is the *lower bound* on the probability $\Pr_*(X)$ that must be assigned to X:

$$\Pr_*(X) = \sum_{\omega : \Gamma(\omega) \subseteq X} P(\omega) \tag{3.24}$$

and the other is the *upper bound* on probability $\Pr^*(X)$ that might be assigned to X:

$$\Pr^*(X) = \sum_{\omega : \Gamma(\omega) \cap X \neq \emptyset} P(\omega) \tag{3.25}$$

This idea was first considered by Dempster (1968), and forms the basis of the theory of evidence, which is discussed in Section 3.2.3.

3.2.2 Possibility theory

Possibility theory was introduced by Zadeh (1978) as a non-statistical means of quantifying uncertainty based on his fuzzy set theory (Zadeh, 1965) which is introduced in Section 3.3.2. This work has been extended by many authors, perhaps most notably by Dubois and Prade (1988f). The following description of possibility theory is largely drawn from (Dubois and Prade, 1991d).

BASIC CONCEPTS OF POSSIBILITY THEORY

Let U be a set that represents the range of possible values of a variable x. This variable, in general, stands for an unknown value taken by some attribute such as the age of a child or the temperature of a room. A *possibility distribution* π_x on U is a mapping from U to the unit interval $[0, 1]$ that is attached to x. The function π_x represents a flexible restriction of the values of x where:

$$\pi_x(u) = 0$$

means that $x = u$ is impossible, and:

$$\pi_x(u) = 1$$

means that $x = u$ is allowed. The flexibility in the restriction comes from allowing values of π_x between 0 and 1 for some u. $\pi_x(u)$ is the degree to which the assignment $x = u$ is possible, where some values u are more possible than others. If U is the complete range of values of x, at least one of the elements of U should be a completely possible value of x giving the *normalisation condition*:

$$\exists u, \pi_x(u) = 1 \tag{3.26}$$

This book will only deal with normalised possibility distributions. Such distributions make it possible to capture imprecise and incomplete information. Two important distributions model complete knowledge:

$$\exists u_0, \pi_x(u_0) \;=\; 1 \tag{3.27}$$
$$\forall u \neq u_0, \pi_x(u) \;=\; 0 \tag{3.28}$$

and complete ignorance:

$$\forall u, \pi_x(u) = 1 \tag{3.29}$$

Yager (1983) identified the importance of the concept of *specificity*, where for two distributions π_x and π'_x such that $\pi_x < \pi'_x$, π_x is said to be more specific than π'_x in the sense that it places a greater restriction on x taking value u than π'_x. In such a situation, π'_x is redundant and can be ignored. More generally it is possible to say that when there are several reliable sources of a particular piece of information, the possibility distribution that accounts for it is the least specific distribution that satisfies all the constraints induced by all the sources. This is known as the *principle of minimum specificity*. Given a binary variable x with no constraints on its possibility, the principle of minimum specificity suggests that both the possibility of x and that of $\neg x$ should be 1. Given two variables x and y with possibility distributions π_x and π_y respectively, then the principle of minimum specificity gives the joint possibility distribution $\pi_{x,y}$ as:

$$\pi_{x,y} = \min(\pi_x, \pi_y) \tag{3.30}$$

The principle of minimum specificity is the possibilistic analogue of the principle of maximum entropy. Both, in essence, call for the least informative distribution of values given particular constraints, and this is the one that makes least assumptions. In probability theory this is achieved by maximising H in (3.17). In possibility theory this is achieved by assigning the greatest degrees of possibility that are compatible with whatever constraints are known to hold since the smaller the degree of possibility assigned, the stronger the information it conveys. This might seem rather counter-intuitive at first, but may be clarified by considering that setting $\Pi(x)$ to 0 completely rules x out (since it is a statement that x is impossible), while setting $\Pi(x)$ to 1 merely means that x is not ruled out. The most obvious result of this difference is that while the principle of maximum entropy ensures that when there is no knowledge of the probability of x, $\Pr(x) = \Pr(\neg x) = 0.5$, when there is no knowledge of the possibility of x, the principle of minimum specificity ensures that $\Pi(x) = \Pi(\neg x) = 1$. Similarly, if x can take values $\{x_1, \ldots x_n\}$, then in the absence of any information about its probability or possibility, $\Pr(x_1) = \ldots = \Pr(x_n) = \frac{1}{n}$ while $\Pi(x_1) = \ldots = \Pi(x_n) = 1$.

By analogy with probability theory it is possible to introduce the idea of a *conditional possibility* distribution (Nguyen, 1978) over the set of possible values of x given information about the value of a variable y that has a set of possible values V. Given a possibility distribution π_x for the variable x and a conditional possibility distribution $\pi_{x|y}$, which is defined on the Cartesian product of U and V and which restricts the possible values of x when the value of y is given, then (Hisdal, 1978; Prade, 1983):

$$\forall u \in U, \forall v \in V, \pi_{x,y}(u, v) = \min(\pi_{x|y}(u, v), \pi_y(v)) \tag{3.31}$$

where $\pi_{x,y}(u, v)$ is the possibility distribution that expresses the possibility that x takes the value u and y takes the value v. From this it is possible to establish the possibility distribution relating to x:

$$\forall u \in U, \pi_x(u) = \sup_{v \in V} \left(\pi_{x|y}(u, v), \pi_y(v) \right) \tag{3.32}$$

From the idea of a possibility distribution it is possible to define the idea of the possibility of a particular proposition or set of propositions. A *possibility measure* is defined as $\Pi(u) = \pi(u)$, and this gives, for $A \subset U$:

$$\Pi(A) = \sup_{u_1, \ldots, u_n \in A} \pi_{x_1, \ldots, x_n}(u_1, \ldots, u_n) \tag{3.33}$$

It should be noted that possibility measures are not additive like probability measures. Instead, possibility measures are *subadditive* meaning that:

$$\Pi(A \cup B) \leq \Pi(A) + \Pi(B) \tag{3.34}$$

for exclusive events A and B. A possibility measure of an event A, $\Pi(A)$ evaluates the extent to which A is consistent with the possibility distributions $\pi_{x_1, \ldots, x_n}$. It is also possible to measure the extent to which A is entailed by the distributions, thus establishing a measure of certainty, known as necessity, that is dual to the possibility measure:

$$N(A) = \inf_{u_1,\dots,u_n \notin A} (1 - \pi_{x_1,\dots,x_n}(u_1,\dots,u_n)) \tag{3.35}$$

which means that:

$$N(A) = 1 - \Pi(\neg A) \tag{3.36}$$

Necessity measures are *superadditive*, meaning that:

$$N(A \cup B) \geq N(A) + N(B) \tag{3.37}$$

for exclusive events A and B. The idea is that for a given event A, the necessity and possibility measures together give a picture of the belief in its occurrence. The possibility of A measures the degree to which A happening is consistent with what is known, and the necessity of A measures the degree to which A happening is inevitable given what is known.

Now, (3.32), (3.33) and (3.35) may be used to write expressions for propagating possibility and necessity values (Dubois and Prade, 1991h) where the conditional possibility measures come from conditional possibility distributions:

$$\Pi(c) = \sup_{\substack{A=a_1,\dots,a_m \\ X=x_1,\dots,x_p}} \min\left(\Pi(c|A,X), \Pi(A,X)\right) \tag{3.38}$$

$$N(c) = \inf_{\substack{A=a_1,\dots,a_m \\ X=x_1,\dots,x_p}} \max\left(N(c|A,X), N(A,X)\right) \tag{3.39}$$

Of course, given a possibility distribution $\pi_{x_1,\dots,x_n}$ it is possible to establish both $\Pi(A)$ and $N(A)$ so it usually suffices to deal only with either possibility or necessity. This book follows the usual convention and deals mainly with possibility measures.

The expressions in (3.38) and (3.39) are analogous to those for probability theory given by the variations of Jeffrey's rule in (3.13) and (3.14). It is also possible (Dubois and Prade, 1993) to write a possibilistic version of Bayes' rule:

$$\min\left(\Pi(a|c,x), \Pi(c,x)\right) = \min\left(\Pi(c|a,x), \Pi(a,x)\right) \tag{3.40}$$

for any three values a, c, and x of the variables A, C, and X. This may be used to reverse the direction of reasoning so that it is possible to calculate the possibility of a when the possibility of c is known. Now, clearly the use of conditional possibility measures suggests the definition of conditional possibilistic independence, and the version that will be used in this book (there are several) will be that suggested by Fonck(1994). The possibility of variable A is conditionally independent of the possibility of variable B given the possibility

Table 3.1
Hans's breakfast

x	1	2	3	4	5	6	7	8
$\Pi(x)$	1	1	1	1	0.8	0.6	0.4	0.2
$\Pr(x)$	0.1	0.7	0.1	0.1	0	0	0	0

of C provided that:

$$\Pi(a|b, c) = \Pi(a|c) \tag{3.41}$$

and

$$\Pi(b|a, c) = \Pi(b|c) \tag{3.42}$$

for any three values a, b, and c of the variables A, B, and C. Note that in possibility theory the two conditions are not equivalent.

There is a connection between possibility and probability, since if something is impossible it is likely to be improbable, but a high degree of possibility does not imply a high degree of probability, nor does a low degree of probability reflect a low degree of possibility. This relationship can be illustrated with the example of Hans' breakfast (Zadeh, 1978). Consider the statement

Hans ate x eggs for breakfast.

It is possible to associate a possibility distribution with the set of possible values $\{1, 2, \ldots, 8\}$ of x based on the ease with which Hans can eat eggs, and a probability distribution over these values based on the likelihood that Hans will eat that number of eggs. Two suitable distributions are given in Table 3.1. This relationship can be refined. Indeed, Dubois and Prade (1988d) point out that a theoretical connection exists since:

$$\forall x, \Pr(x) \leq \Pi(x) \tag{3.43}$$

In addition, in his initial paper on possibility theory, Zadeh (1978) argued for a principle of consistency between probability and possibility values. The principle states that if a variable X can take values $x_1, \ldots, x_n$ with respective possibilities $\Pi(x_1), \ldots, \Pi(x_n)$ and probabilities $\Pr(x_1), \ldots, \Pr(x_n)$, there is a degree of consistency γ between $\Pr(x_i)$ and $\Pi(x_i)$:

$$\gamma = \Pi(x_1) \cdot \Pr(x_1) + \ldots + \Pi(x_n) \cdot \Pr(x_n) \tag{3.44}$$

that remains constant as the distributions are updated as a result of new information. The connection between probability and possibility is also discussed by Delgardo and Moral (1987) and Gupta (1993), the latter in the context of translating values between probability and possibility theories—work that will be considered further in Section 4.6.1.

OTHER POSSIBILISTIC APPROACHES

In possibility theory the basic mechanisms of the formalism are much less rigidly defined than in probability theory. For example, while the disjunctive combination of two possibility measures can only be achieved by the max operator, it is quite permissible to perform conjunctive combination by means of product rather than minimum (Dubois and Prade, 1991h). If the product operator were adopted, then propagation of possibility measures would be by:

$$\Pi(c) = \sup_{\substack{A=a_1,\ldots,a_m \\ X=x_1,\ldots,x_p}} \Pi(c|A, X)\Pi(A, X) \qquad (3.45)$$

rather than by (3.38). Dubois(1996) clarifies this matter by distinguishing between qualitative and quantitative approaches to possibility theory. The qualitative approach uses minimum to compute the possibility measure applicable to a conjunction and so only takes account of the order of the various measures. The use of numbers between 0 and 1 is thus just a convenience—they provide a suitable ordinal scale for possibility measures that has the attractive property that a third measure may be identified between any two existing measures (a property that is not true of the integers, for instance). The quantitative approach uses product to compute the measure applicable to a conjunction and is thus sensitive to the absolute magnitude of the measures. It is also possible to substitute other operations for minimum or product (Dubois and Prade, 1990b) giving other variants of the theory, but these have less satisfactory properties (Dubois, 1996). This choice of operators is not the only way in which possibility theory is flexible—there are also a number of different ways of combining possibility distributions, some of which are discussed in (Benferhat et al., 1997). Throughout this book only the qualitative approach to possibility theory will be considered in any detail, and the mechanisms for manipulating possibility values will be those mentioned above.

Further variety arises because there are different ways of defining conditional independence for possibility measures. Fonck (1994) also considers Zadeh's (1978) notion of *non-interactivity* as a form of conditional independence. The possibility measures of two variables are non-interactive given the possibility of a third variable if the possibility of their conjunction given the third factors into the conjunction of the possibility of either of them given the third. In other words, $\Pi(c)$ and $\Pi(a)$ are non-interactive given $\Pi(x)$ if:

$$\Pi(c, a|x) = \min\left(\Pi(c|x), \Pi(a|x)\right) \qquad (3.46)$$

provided that minimum is used to combine two conjuncts. Again this notion can be generalised to other combination operations, so that when product is used for conjunction, $\Pi(c)$ and $\Pi(a)$ are non-interactive given $\Pi(x)$ if:

$$\Pi(c, a|x) = \Pi(c|x).\Pi(a|x) \tag{3.47}$$

when product is used to combine two conjuncts. Other notions of possibilistic independence are studied by Fariñas del Cerro and Herzig (1994), Dubois et al. (1994b) and de Campos et al. (1995), and the effect of some of the different approaches has been studied by Benferhat et al. (1994a).

Finally, there has been some work on upper and lower possibilities—measures which stand in the same relation to probability as the upper and lower probability measures introduced by Dempster (1967) as mentioned above. The idea was introduced by Dubois and Prade (1983), and is direct analogous to Dempster's work. However, Dubois and Prade not only lay down the basis for a possibilistic version of evidence theory, but they also take account of generalising the multi-valued mapping Γ to a fuzzy relation. In essence this means that it is not only the case that it is not clear which one of a set of hypotheses is the result of the mapping, but also that it is not clear exactly what the set is either.

3.2.3   Evidence theory

Evidence theory is the term I will use to refer to the body of work initiated by Arthur Dempster (1968) and Glenn Shafer (1976) and often referred to as "Dempster-Shafer theory." Having covered Dempster's approach in sufficient detail for this book in Section 3.2.1, this section, in common with most current work on evidence theory, will broadly adopt Shafer's approach though some of the terminology and much of the perspective are taken from the work of Philippe Smets (Smets and Kennes, 1994).

BASIC CONCEPTS OF EVIDENCE THEORY

Evidence theory deals with the so-called *frame of discernment*, the set of interesting propositions $\Theta = \{\theta_1, \dots, \theta_n\}$, and its power set 2^Θ, which is the set of all subsets of the interesting elements. A *mass function* or *mass distribution function* $m(\cdot)$ establishes the measure of uncertainty or "basic belief mass" that is distributed to each member of the power set. This function has the following properties:

$$m : 2^\Theta \quad \rightarrow \quad [0, 1] \tag{3.48}$$

$$m(\emptyset) \quad = \quad 0 \tag{3.49}$$

$$\sum_{A \subseteq \Theta} m(A) \quad = \quad 1 \tag{3.50}$$

that is, it distributes a value in $[0, 1]$ to each element of 2^Θ; zero mass is assigned to the empty set, sometimes known as the *contradiction* to indicate that it is equivalent to the ever-false proposition; and the total mass distributed is 1. Since all possible subsets of the frame of discernment are considered, rather than members of the frame as in probability theory, it is possible to apportion the basic belief mass exactly as desired, ignoring assignments to those levels of detail about which nothing is known. This makes it possible to model ignorance about the correct mass to assign to particular members of the frame of discernment, $m(\Theta)$ being the belief mass that it is not possible, through lack of knowledge, to assign to any particular subset of Θ.

It is possible to define belief in a subset A of the set of all propositions as the sum of all the basic belief masses that support its constituents:

$$\text{Bel}(A) = \sum_{B \subseteq A} m(B) \tag{3.51}$$

A function $\text{Bel} : 2^\Theta \to [0, 1]$ is called a belief function if it is given by (3.51) for some mass assignment $m : 2^\Theta \to [0, 1]$. If there is no information about what to assign to which subset, knowledge is modelled by the *vacuous* belief function:

$$\text{Bel}(A) = \begin{cases} 0 \text{ if } A \neq \Theta \\ 1 \text{ if } A = \Theta \end{cases} \tag{3.52}$$

The basic belief mass assignment that generates the vacuous belief function is known as the vacuous mass assignment. This is unique in that there is only one basic probability assignment that produces a given belief function, and so the mass assignment may be recovered from the belief function:

$$m(A) = \sum_{B \subseteq A} (-1)^{|A-B|} \text{Bel}(B) \tag{3.53}$$

Now, it is possible to define a dual measure to the belief in A that gives the extent to which A might be true. This is called the plausibility of A and is defined as the probability mass not supporting $\neg A$:

$$\text{Pl}(A) = 1 - \text{Bel}(\neg A) \tag{3.54}$$

$$\text{Pl}(A) = \sum_{B \cap A \neq \emptyset} m(B) \tag{3.55}$$

This may be thought of as the total basic belief mass that may ever be assigned to A, and so forms an upper bound on the belief in A. As a result, in some interpretations of the theory the interval $[\text{Bel}(A), \text{Pl}(A)]$ is considered to be a measure of ignorance about A, and can vary from zero when all the mass concerning A is allocated to individual propositions, to 1 when A is supported by the vacuous belief function. There is a third measure that may be defined from the basic mass assignment—the commonality function:

$$Q(A) = \sum_{B \supseteq A} m(B) \tag{3.56}$$

This measures all the mass assigned to the supersets of the set in question, and although it has no obvious intuitive meaning, is useful in some of the developments of the theory. In particular, it has been used (Smets, 1983) to define a measure H_{Bel} of the information content of a mass distribution analogous the entropy of a probability distribution (3.17). The information content of a mass distribution is:

$$H_{Bel} = - \sum_{A \subseteq \Theta} \log Q(A) \tag{3.57}$$

Clearly this only makes sense when $Q(A)$ is greater than zero, but Smets suggests splitting the distribution into two parts to overcome this problem. It should be noted that since $Q(A)$ has a maximum value of 1, and that this is the value for the vacuous mass assignment, H_{Bel} is maximal for the vacuous mass assignment. Another suggestion is that of Dubois and Prade (1986) who give:

$$H_{Bel} = \sum_{A \subseteq \Theta} m(A)f(|A|) \tag{3.58}$$

where varying the function $f(\cdot)$ gives information measures with different properties. For instance, if $f(x)$ is $\log_2 x$ then $H_{Bel} = 0$ when $m(\cdot)$ allocates mass to each element in Θ, and is maximal for the vacuous mass distribution. Similarly, if $f(x)$ is $1/x$ then $H_{Bel} = 1$ when $m(\cdot)$ allocates mass to each element in Θ, and is minimal for the vacuous mass distribution. Either Smets' suggestion or Dubois and Prade's first suggestion could be used to specify a procedure for evidence theory that is analogous to the principle of maximum entropy. In addition, Dubois and Prade's second suggestion could be used as a basis of an evidence theory version of the principle of minimum specificity, and they in fact suggest a way of doing this (Dubois and Prade, 1986). Further suggestions, on what has become known as the *principle of minimum commitment* are provided by Hsia (1991b) and Moral and de Campos (1993).

Clearly the properties of a belief function are to some extent dependent upon which subsets of the frame of discernment the mass distribution function allocates belief mass to. Indeed, it is possible to distinguish between a number of different classes of belief function just by examining the *focal elements* as the subsets of the frame of discernment to which mass is allocated are called. If a mass distribution has just one focal element other than the whole frame of discernment, the resulting belief function is known as a *simple support function*. Because of their simplicity, simple support functions have been widely studied and widely used. If the focal elements $A_1, A_2, \ldots, A_n$ of a mass assignment are such that $A_1 \subset A_2 \subset \ldots \subset A_n$, then the resulting belief function is a *consonant belief function*. Consonant belief functions are particularly interesting because the measure of belief they allocate to a proposition is exactly the same as the necessity measure for that proposition, and the measure of plausibility they entail for any proposition is exactly the same as the possibility of that proposition (Dubois and Prade, 1988f). Since consonant belief functions are a special case of belief functions, it follows that belief functions are capable of representing more types of information than possibility and necessity measures, and so the theory of evidence can be thought of as a generalisation of possibility theory. Evidence theory can also be thought of as a generalisation of probability theory. In fact, just as every necessity and possibility distribution has a corresponding mass assignment that gives a consonant belief function, so every probability distribution has a corresponding mass assignment which gives a *Bayesian belief function*. A Bayesian belief function is again distinguished by the allocation of belief mass to its focal elements. A mass distribution that gives belief mass to focal elements which are singletons, that is individual elements of the frame of discernment rather than subsets of the frame of discernment, will generate a Bayesian belief function.

Thinking of belief as expressed by belief functions as being a generalisation of probability, is one way of looking at the relationship between the two formalisms. Another, is to think of belief functions as representing a more tentative view of the world. Whereas probability theory forces one to be very forthright and assign a measure to individual propositions, evidence theory allows one to dither a little and assign a measure to a set of propositions, pending further information. This further information can then re-assign any of the mass initially allocated to the set to any of its members. Thus one outcome of applying new information to a mass assignment might be to generate a Bayesian belief function, and this suggests that the belief actually allocated to a proposition will never exceed its probability. Indeed, as Dubois and Prade (1988d) have pointed out, the relationship between the belief in a proposition and its probability is such that:

$$\forall A, \mathrm{Bel}(A) \leq \mathrm{Pr}(A) \tag{3.59}$$

It should also be noted that beliefs are superadditive:

$$\mathrm{Bel}(A \cup B) \geq \mathrm{Bel}(A) + \mathrm{Bel}(B) \tag{3.60}$$

while plausibilities are subadditive:

$$\mathrm{Pl}(A \cup B) \leq \mathrm{Pl}(A) + \mathrm{Pl}(B) \tag{3.61}$$

Table 3.2
Applying Dempster's rule.

	{*Toyota, GM, Chrysler*} 0.8	Θ 0.2
{*Nissan, Toyota*} 0.4	{*Toyota*} 0.32	{*Nissan, Toyota*} 0.08
Θ 0.6	{*Toyota, GM, Chrysler*} 0.48	Θ 0.12

Mass assignments may be combined by *Dempster's rule of combination*. This computes the probability mass assigned to C, a subset of Θ, given A and B, also subsets of Θ, where A is supported by mass distributed by function m_1 and B is supported by mass distributed by m_2. The mass assigned to C is defined by:

$$m(C) = \frac{\sum_{A \cap B = C} m_1(A)m_2(B)}{1 - \sum_{A \cap B \neq \emptyset} m_1(A)m_2(B)} \tag{3.62}$$

This apparently complex rule becomes clearer when applied to an example. Consider a world (Cohen, 1985) with only four car manufacturers, Nissan, Toyota, GM and Chrysler, all trying to break into a new car market. The question at stake is which manufacturers will dominate the market; so there are four singleton hypotheses corresponding to the assertions that each of the four manufacturers alone will dominate. Consider the case in which there are two mass functions m_1 and m_2. Now, m_1 assigns 0.4 to {*Nissan, Toyota*}, the hypothesis that Japanese manufacturers dominate, and the remaining 0.6 to the set {*Nissan, Toyota, GM, Chrysler*}, modelling ignorance about the behaviour of American manufacturers. Similarly, m_2 assigns 0.8 to the set {*Toyota, GM, Chrysler*} and 0.2 to Θ, and Dempster's rule of combination assigns the product of the two belief masses to the intersection of the sets to which they are assigned. Table 3.2 explains the calculation. The masses after combination are as follows:

$$
\begin{align}
m_{12}(\{\textit{Toyota}\}) &= 0.32 \\
m_{12}(\{\textit{Nissan, Toyota}\}) &= 0.08 \\
m_{12}(\{\textit{Toyota, GM, Chrysler}\}) &= 0.48 \\
m_{12}(\Theta) &= 0.12
\end{align}
$$

The belief that Japanese manufacturers will dominate is computed from the sum of the belief masses of all the subsets of the hypothesis. Thus:

$$
\begin{align}
Bel_{12}(\{\textit{Nissan, Toyota}\}) =\ & m_{12}(\{\textit{Toyota}\}) \\
& + m_{12}(\{\textit{Nissan, Toyota}\}) + m_{12}(\{\textit{Nissan}\})
\end{align}
$$

$$= \quad 0.32 + 0.08 + 0$$

$$= \quad 0.4$$

For this simple example, no normalisation is required. Normalisation will be required when the initial computation assigns some mass to the empty set, and to normalise every mass is divided by 1 minus the mass assigned to the empty set.

As discussed below, normalisation is controversial, and it is possible to use Dempster's rule without it. The unnormalised version of (3.62) is:

$$m(C) = \sum_{A \cap B = C} m_1(A) m_2(B) \tag{3.63}$$

and it is this version of the rule that will be used in this book. When normalisation is not used, it is possible that $\text{Bel}(\emptyset) \neq 0$. If this is the case, Smets' (1988a) open-world assumption indicates that there is belief in a hypothesis that is outside the frame of discernment. This contrasts with the usual closed-world assumption, which assumes that all hypotheses are in the frame of discernment.

It is possible to cast the unnormalised version of Dempster's rule into a form comparable with that of (3.13) for propagation of belief values (Dubois and Prade, 1991h; Smets, 1991b):

$$\text{Bel}(c) = \sum_{\substack{A \subseteq \{a_1, \ldots, a_m\} \\ X \subseteq \{x_1, \ldots, x_p\}}} \text{Bel}(c|A, X) m(A, X) \tag{3.64}$$

This is, of course, just another variation on Jeffrey's rule, extended to cover belief functions. Now, the use of Dempster's rule in this way is only possible when conditional beliefs such as $\text{Bel}(c|a \cup \neg a, x)$ are available. Believing that such values may well be difficult to assess, Smets (1991a) has suggested an alternative combination rule. This generates the following expression (Smets, 1991b) for the propagation of belief values:

$$\text{Bel}(c) = \sum_{\substack{A \subseteq \{a_1, \ldots, a_m\} \\ X \subseteq \{x_1, \ldots, x_p\}}} m(A, X) \prod_{\substack{a \in A \\ x \in X}} \text{Bel}(c|a, x) \tag{3.65}$$

While Dempster's rule assumes that the relationship between the mass assigning functions is conjunctive, Smets' rule assumes a disjunctive relationship, and is known as the *disjunctive rule*. There are other rules for combining mass distributions, and they will be considered briefly a little later. To enable evidential reasoning across influences that are quantified with belief functions, Smets' has provided a generalisation of Bayes' theorem (Smets, 1991a) that makes it possible to calculate conditional beliefs such as $\text{Bel}(a|c, x)$

from conditional beliefs such as $\text{Bel}(c|a,x)$. For any $a \subseteq A, c \subseteq C, x \subseteq X$:

$$\text{Bel}(a|c,x) = \prod_{y \in \tilde{a}} \text{Bel}(\tilde{c}|y,x) - \prod_{z \in A} \text{Bel}(\tilde{c}|z,x) \tag{3.66}$$

where $\tilde{w}$ is the set-theoretic complement of w with respect to W, namely $W - w$. It is also possible (Smets, 1991a) to extend the notion of conditional independence to belief functions. The underlying idea is the same as for probability and possibility theories—the beliefs in two variables X and Y are independent if knowledge about the value taken by one of them does not affect belief in the value taken by the other. Formally this is expressed by:

$$\frac{\text{Bel}(x_1|y)}{\text{Bel}(x_2|y)} = \frac{\text{Bel}(x_1)}{\text{Bel}(x_2)} \tag{3.67}$$

for all $x_1, x_2 \subseteq X, y \subseteq X$. If two variables have this property, then they are said to be *conditionally cognitively independent*.

DIFFERENT VIEWS OF EVIDENCE THEORY

As is the case with probability theory, there is disagreement about what the measures manipulated by evidence theory actually mean. However, the disagreement is considerably greater, not least because, as Shafer (1990) himself admits, the

most comprehensive source of information on belief functions,

which is his monograph *A Mathematical Theory of Evidence* (Shafer, 1976),

says little about interpretation

thus leaving every adherent or opponent of the theory to dream up their own. This section attempts to clarify the situation a little by describing some of the main positions and providing pointers to more detailed discussion.

Shafer (1990) views evidence theory as a generalisation of Bayesian subjective probability. One might expect this to be the precursor to an argument that evidence theory is thus superior to probability theory and should therefore be used in place of probability theory. However, Shafer takes a more eclectic view, choosing to think of evidence theory and probability theory as two alternatives that are applicable in different situations, and which should only be used when applicable. In his view, when seeking to answer a particular question, probability theory is applicable when it is possible to provide probabilities for the possible answers to the question and evidence theory is applicable when it is only possible to provide probabilities for the possible answers to a related question. This point is clarified by the use of canonical examples (Shafer, 1986, 1990; Shafer and Tversky, 1985) of the kind of situations best modelled by the two theories. The two best known canonical examples of problems that Shafer claims are best tackled by belief functions are those of the randomly coded message (Shafer, 1981a) and the possibly unreliable witness. The latter is the simpler and is worth repeating here. This particular variation comes from (Shafer, 1990).

Suppose that Betty tells me a tree limb fell on my car. My subjective probability that Betty is reliable is 0.9; my subjective probability that she is unreliable is 0.1. Since they are probabilities, these numbers add to 1. But Betty's statement, which must be true if she is reliable, is not necessarily false if she is unreliable. So I say her testimony alone justifies a 0.9 degree of belief that a limb fell on my car, but only a zero degree of belief (not a 0.1 degree of belief) that no limb fell on my car. This zero does not mean that I am sure that no limb fell on my car, as a zero probability would; it merely means that Betty's testimony gives me no reason to believe that no limb fell on my car. The 0.9 and zero together constitute a belief function.

Thus Shafer sees belief functions as stemming from probabilistic information, but as computing a degree of belief that is quite distinct from probability. Indeed he stresses the fact that, in his view, interpreting a degree of belief as a lower bound on an unknown probability is quite wrong.

This, of course, has not prevented many people using this interpretation, and of course it does not mean that using such an interpretation is not possible—after all belief functions are, mathematically, just a subset of lower probability functions (as argued, for instance, by Kyburg (1987)) (such functions will be discussed in Section 4.3)—but if such an interpretation is to be used, care is required. This point is stressed by Halpern and Fagin (1992), who argue that the failure to distinguish between interpreting belief functions as modelling degrees of belief and as modelling lower probabilities is the reason why people have had problems in using evidence theory in practice. The nut of the problem, according to Halpern and Fagin, is that belief functions should be updated in different ways when interpreted in different ways. When the interpretation is as a degree of belief, Dempster's rule of combination is the appropriate method, and when the interpretation is as a lower probability measure, a suitable updating rule, along the lines of Jeffrey's rule, is the correct method. A particular method of updating, which is appropriate in the latter case, is detailed in another paper (Fagin and Halpern, 1991).

Another interpretation of belief functions that has a probabilistic flavour is Pearl's (1988b; 1990a) concept of the *probability of provability*. The idea here is as follows. Initially one has the usual set of focal elements, each of which has a basic belief mass, which for Pearl is just a probability, assigned to it. One then identifies the logical consequences of this set of elements, and computes the belief in a given consequence by summing the probabilities of all the focal elements that entail it. Under this interpretation, the belief in a proposition becomes the probability that the available information can prove that the proposition is true and that its negation is false. This interpretation has, as Pearl points out, the attractive property that it ties the idea of belief to that of a proof in classical logic, thus making belief a very concrete idea. Furthermore, since the idea of "logical proof" can be extended to other logics, it is possible to extend the use of belief functions to represent information expressed in a wide range of logics (Wilson, 1992c).

Despite the appeal of the probability of provability interpretation of belief functions, it is not the interpretation that will be used in this book—instead I will adopt Smets' (Smets, 1990; Smets and Kennes, 1994) *transferable belief model* interpretation, which completely rejects the notion that belief has anything to do with probability. Instead, the model has two parts, modelling reasoning that takes place at two levels. These are the *credal level* where beliefs are manipulated in order to reason about the world and the *pignistic level* where beliefs expressed as probabilities are used to make decisions. Reasoning at the credal level takes place using evidence theory as described above, using the open-world assumption, with the unnormalised version of Dempster's rule being the only justifiable means of combining two belief functions (Smets, 1990). In the various presentations of the model, Smets stresses the fact that the impact of a piece of evidence on a finite frame of discernment Θ is to allocate part of an initial unit of belief among the subsets of Θ. For any subset A of Θ, the basic belief mass $m(A)$ is the amount of belief supporting A, that, due to ignorance, does not support any strict subset of A. If new evidence is obtained that excludes some of the original hypotheses, and so points to the truth being in $\Theta' \subset \Theta$, then the basic belief mass $m(A)$ now supports $A \cap \Theta'$. Thus the evidence originally attributed to A is transferred to that part of A not eliminated by the new evidence, and it is this transfer that gives the model its name. Further relevant work (Smets, 1993) supports the use of evidence theory to model reasoning at the credal level by showing that a function that satisfies intuitively reasonable properties for reasoning at the credal level must be a belief function.

Part of the attraction of the transferable belief model is that this separation between credal and pignistic levels is a way of defending the use of belief functions from the argument that they are somehow unsound because they do not agree with probability theory. One forceful way of making the criticism is to point out that there are situations in which using belief functions can lead one to accept a series of bets in which one is sure to lose money. Smets and Kennes (1994) state that by making the pignistic transformation before deciding whether or not to accept a bet, it is possible to avoid such "Dutch book" situations, and this would seem a good defence. However, Snow (1998c) shown that even with the pignistic transformation, it is possible to construct a Dutch book against someone using belief functions, a result that suggests that there is still more work to be done in this area. However, from the perspective of this book, it is possible to sidestep this issue since it does not occur when dealing, as this book does, with credal level reasoning.

The interpretation of the theory of evidence is not the only area of controversy. Normalisation in the application of Dempster's rule has been criticised by Zadeh (1984a) who points out that it leads to counter-intuitive results when the mass assignments are contradictory. For instance, consider what would have happened if the mass assignments in the car market example had been $m_1(\{Nissan\}) = 0.01$, $m_1(\{Toyota\}) = 0.99$, $m_2(\{Nissan\}) = 0.01$, and $m_2(\{Chrysler\}) = 0.99$. This intuitively suggests that the most credible hypothesis is that either Toyota or Chrysler will dominate the market, and that one mass assignment is completely misleading. However, applying the normalised version of Dempster's rule will give $Bel_{12}(\{Nissan\}) = 1$. Smets (1988a) uses a similar counter-example to argue for the use of Dempster's rule without normalisation. It is worth noting, however, that Clarke (1988) and Dubois and Prade (1988g) have pointed out that the unnormalised rule is also counter-intuitive at times. When there is no normalisation, contradiction between sources of evidence will tend to reduce the total belief assigned, since that belief allocated to the contradiction by the combination will not be redistributed. In addition, Voorbraak (1991), for instance, challenges the use of the rule on the grounds that the requirements for its application are rather unclear in their original formulation, though Wilson (1993a) has since clarified this matter to some degree, in addition arguing that Dempster's rule may be justified when combining a finite number of simple support functions (Wilson, 1992c,a). Given Smets' result (Smets, 1995), which shows how any belief function may be decomposed into simple support functions, Wilson's argument could be considered to be the last word on the subject. Alternative rules for combination, in addition to those given above, have also been proposed. These include one provided by Dubois and Prade (1988g), based on disjunctive consensus, which gives an intuitively correct solution to the problem of contradictory mass functions, and Smets' generalization of the unnormalised version of Dempster's rule to a family of "α-junction" rules that model conjunction, disjunction, and exclusive-or relations between sources of evidence (Smets, 1997a).

There are numerous other papers on the subject of belief functions, many of which suggest alternative ways of interpreting them. For instance, Baldwin (1992) suggests an interpretation that is quite close to the upper and lower probability model. The major distinguishing factor of Baldwin's approach is his explicit rejection of Dempster's rule of combination, in favour of his own rule, which is in keeping with his voting model semantics. Another different interpretation is suggested by Dubois and Prade (1992a) who prefer to regard belief functions in terms of set-valued statistics. On the other hand, Neapolitan (1993) argues along the same line as Shafer, giving another canonical example of a class of problem that is best tackled using belief functions with Dempster's rule. Other authors have proposed variations on the basic form of evidence theory which was presented earlier in this section. In this vein van Dam (1996; 1998) considers a form of "tentative" belief while Guan and Bell (1993) show how evidence theory may be generalised to be applicable to arbitrary Boolean algebras, thus extending the number of situations that may be modelled using the theory. More recently Reece (1998) has suggested a "p-norm" version of the theory where the p-norm belief is defined by:

$$\mathrm{Bel}_p(A) = \left[\sum_{B \supseteq A} m(B)^p \right]^{\frac{1}{p}}$$

with other measures defined similarly. The ∞-norm version of this theory has many of the attractive computational features of possibility theory. Another proposal, this time for an interval valued system, is due to Driankov (1986). In Driankov's system there are degrees of belief and plausibility, related, as in the original theory of evidence, by $\mathrm{Bel}(A) = 1 - \mathrm{Pl}(\neg A)$. However, contradictory beliefs, where $\mathrm{Bel}(A) + \mathrm{Bel}(\neg A)) > 1$, are allowed. These ideas lead to the definition of a calculus of the belief intervals $[\mathrm{Bel}(A), \mathrm{Pl}(A)]$ in which explicit reasoning about the degree to which a proposition is believed and disbelieved is possible.

DECISION MAKING IN EVIDENCE THEORY

One major strand of work on evidence theory deserves special attention, and that is work concerning decision making. Although it is largely out of the scope of this book,[2] decision making is closely related to reasoning under uncertainty in that the need to make decisions in uncertain situations is a major motivation for studying reasoning under uncertainty. In other words in uncertain situations one reasons to find out how certain various outcomes are and then makes some decision based upon the results of the reasoning. The forcefulness of this observation is apparent as soon as one reflects upon all the decisions that must be made under uncertainty, and the crucial nature of those decisions—decisions such as whether or not a particular investment should be made, whether or not a certain patient should be treated with a particular drug, and whether or not a particular deployment of troops represents a threat or not. As a result, any theory for reasoning under uncertainty that ties in with some way of deciding which of a set of options is to be preferred is highly attractive. This goes some way towards explaining the popularity of probability theory, since probability theory is a part of classical decision theory (Raiffa, 1970), and also helps to explain why there has been considerable interest in supplying a decision theory for evidence theory (it also makes it remarkable that until recently there has been no great

---

2 That is, decision making in the sense of decision theory (Raiffa, 1970) where the focus is on combining the value of the outcomes of various actions along with a measure of their chance of occurrence given a particular choice of action.

attempt to couple most other uncertainty theories with a decision making mechanism).

The attempts to provide a means of making decisions based upon calculations of beliefs fall into two main categories. The first are those based around the interval interpretation of beliefs—that $\mathrm{Bel}(A)$ is a lower bound on the probability of a and $\mathrm{Pl}(A)$ is an upper bound on the probability of A. An early attempt at providing this kind of mechanism in the area of artificial intelligence (the problem had already been considered by decision theorists) is that of Loui (1986) who discusses problems in generalising classical decision theory to interval probabilities. The classical mechanism is to determine the probability of occurrence of each outcome under consideration (the probability of occurrence under the action about which the decision is being taken) and the utility (usefulness to the decision maker) of those outcomes. Combining respective probabilities and utilities and summing over the possible outcomes gives the expected utility of the decision. Loui points out that combining interval probabilities with utilities gives expected utility intervals and that the best means of comparing such intervals is not, in general, obvious. As a result he makes a number of suggestions for making the comparison, of which the most interesting is the idea that the discovery that there is no clearly best solution should be an indication that the initial probability intervals should be revised. Starting from a similar position, Jaffray (1988) suggests a particular solution—the use of Neumann-Morgenstern linear utility theory—to make it clear which decision should be taken given the decision maker's attitude towards risk and ambiguity. A particularly influential piece of work on a similar vein is that of Strat (1989b; 1989a) who makes the suggestion that it is possible to choose between intervals by constructing probability distributions over the expected utility intervals and using these distributions to calculate particular points within the intervals that may be used as the basis of a comparison. The most appealing part of the suggestion is the way in which there is a clear separation of the calculation of expected utility, which reflects the underlying lack of knowledge about the probabilities of the outcomes (by using intervals), and the assumptions about how the intervals should be interpreted, which are clearly modelled by the additional probability distributions. This approach is further developed by Mellouli (1994), who suggests a means of analysing the belief functions that support given hypotheses to determine information about them, in particular information about their precision, with the aim of using this to determine how confident one should be in a decision based upon them.

The second category of methods for decision making in evidence theory are inspired by Smets' transferable belief model. As discussed above, in this model rather than beliefs being interpreted as lower bounds of imprecisely known probabilities, they are interpreted as something completely different—they are taken to be the natural means of representing beliefs at the credal level whereas decisions are made at the pignistic level. It is possible to move from the credal level to the pignistic level by means of the *pignistic transformation*

(Smets, 1988a) This transformation takes a mass distribution and converts it to a probability distribution. It is as follows:

$$\Pr(B) = \sum_{A \cap B \neq \emptyset} m(A) \frac{|A \cap B|}{|A|} \qquad (3.68)$$

where $|A|$ is the number of elements in A. The justification for this transformation is the *principle of generalised insufficient reason*, which specifies that the principle of insufficient reason be applied to each focal element of the belief function. Having established this probability, it is then possible to use decision theory in the normal way. The pignistic transformation is not without its critics, for instance (Clarke, 1988), and in the light of this Wilson (1993b) has provided an interesting analysis of its properties. The main result of this analysis is that while the probability distribution generated by the pignistic transformation depends upon the choice of frame of discernment, the effects of this choice do not result in different decisions from those that would be generated by taking beliefs to be upper and lower probabilities. This result can be taken two possible ways—either as a defence of the pignistic transformation against the charge that it generates arbitrary decisions (because the choice of frame of discernment is often rather arbitrary) or as an indication that the pignistic transformation has little use. Perhaps, as Wilson points out, it merely suggests that the pignistic transformation should be adopted in situations in which there is an obvious choice of frame of discernment, and not used when the frame is not so evident. This is a conclusion that I am happy to agree with since it suggests that even in decision making the eclectic position has some validity.

3.3 Other important models

As mentioned in the introduction to this chapter, there are many different models for dealing with uncertainty that have been proposed at one time or another. This section looks at a few of them—the ones I consider to be the most important, either because they are widely used, have been widely used, or, I suspect will be widely used.

3.3.1 Certainty factors

Certainty factors (Shortliffe and Buchanan, 1975; Shortliffe, 1976; Buchanan and Shortliffe, 1984), perhaps because of their simplicity and intuitive appeal, have been widely used to handle uncertainty. The certainty factor approach is tied to the use of rules of the form:

IF   evidence E
THEN hypothesis H

and thus to the context of rule-based systems. Every fact dealt with by the system is characterised by two measures of uncertainty, *MB* which is the degree to which all the known evidence supports the fact, and *MD* which measures the degree to which the evidence suggests that the fact should be disbelieved. When a rule is fired, the degrees of belief and disbelief in all the antecedents of the rule are combined, and the result modified using the weight attached to the rule, to establish an *MB* and *MD* for the consequent. These values may then be combined with the output of other rules, and the resulting values propagated. When the overall measure of strength of a conclusion is required, the certainty factor is computed from *MB* and *MD*:

$$CF = \frac{MB - MD}{1 - \min(MB, MD)} \tag{3.69}$$

When introduced, the idea of a certainty factor was given a probabilistic interpretation, but it can also be expressed in terms of possibility measures (Dubois and Prade, 1991h).

Since its introduction, several people have challenged the validity of the certainty factor model. Adams (1976) showed that implicit assumptions made by the model, such as the independence between hypotheses, may not always be valid, while Heckerman (1986) showed that the original definition of the model is flawed since the belief in a hypothesis given two pieces of evidence will depend upon the order in which the effect of the pieces of evidence is computed. In addition, Heckerman and Horvitz (1987; 1988) have argued that the model does not comply with one of its basic tenets since, under some conditions, it is not possible to add new knowledge in a modular fashion. However, as van der Gaag (1990) points out, these flaws have not prevented certainty factors from being widely used.

3.3.2   Fuzzy sets

The theory of fuzzy sets (Zadeh, 1965) is undoubtedly one of the most influential models for dealing with imperfect information, having been widely applied, especially in the area of control. However, it is not of major importance from the point of view of the work in this book, except in so far as it forms the basis for possibility theory, since fuzzy sets are used to model vague information, rather than uncertain information—a point discussed at some length by Dubois, Prade and Smets (Dubois and Prade, 1988c; Dubois et al., 1994c; Dubois and Prade, 1994)—and representing uncertain information is the main focus of this work. The following brief description is included for completeness, and to make the connection with possibility theory. Comprehensive introductions to fuzzy set theory have also been given by Dubois and Prade (1980), Klir and Folger (1988), and Kruse, Gebhardt and Klawonn (1994), and descriptions of both applications of fuzzy sets and further developments of the theory may be found in any issue of the journal *Fuzzy Sets and Systems*.

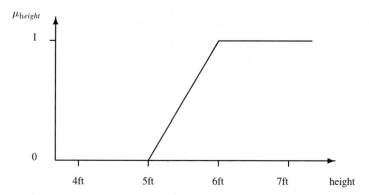

Figure 3.1
The fuzzy set of tall people

In simple terms, the notion of a fuzzy set is a generalisation of the ordinary mathematical notion of a set that aims to allow the representation of sets whose boundaries are not clear. For example, the set of all triangles is a classical, or "crisp" in the language of fuzzy sets, set because given any object it is possible to say whether or not it is a member of the set of triangles. Indeed, it is possible to conceive of a membership function $\mu_{triangle}(\cdot)$ that indicates whether or not any object in the universe U is in the set of triangles. Any object is either in, in which case the function returns 1, or out, in which case the function returns zero:

$$\mu_{triangle} : U \mapsto \{0, 1\} \qquad\qquad (3.70)$$

It is not so easy to determine the members of other sets. Consider, as Zadeh (1965) did, the set of animals. It is clear that the set of all animals includes all dogs and cats, and does not include rocks and quasars, but it is less clear if it should include bacteria or viruses. To incorporate this "fuzziness" Zadeh essentially suggested that the membership function $\mu_{animal}(\cdot)$ should not just say whether or not an object was in the set, but should say to what degree it was a member of the set. Thus:

$$\mu_{animal} : U \mapsto [0, 1] \qquad\qquad (3.71)$$

The result of applying $\mu_{animal}(\cdot)$ to an object gives the *degree of membership* of that object with respect to the set of animals.

Fuzzy sets can also be defined over continuous domains. For example, Figure 3.1 gives a typical fuzzy set—the fuzzy set of tall people. For a given person whose height is known it is possible to read off the degree of membership of that person in the set of tall people.

Thus a person who is 4 feet tall is not in the set of tall people to any degree, someone who is five foot eight inches tall has a degree of membership of around 0.7, and anyone over six feet tall has a degree of membership of 1. In his initial work, Zadeh (1965) not only defined the notion of a fuzzy set, but also suggested how fuzzy sets could be manipulated. In particular, he suggested that the membership function $\mu_{S'}$ of the complement S' of a fuzzy set S with membership function μ_S is defined by:

$$\mu_{S'}(x) = 1 - \mu_S(x) \tag{3.72}$$

for all x, while the union of two fuzzy sets S_1 and S_2 is a fuzzy set S_3 with the membership function:

$$\mu_{S_3}(x) = \max\left(\mu_{S_1}(x), \mu_{S_2}(x)\right) \tag{3.73}$$

and the intersection of S_1 and S_2 is a fuzzy set S_4 with the membership function:

$$\mu_{S_4}(x) = \min\left(\mu_{S_1}(x), \mu_{S_2}(x)\right) \tag{3.74}$$

Fuzzy versions of other mathematical notions can also be proposed. As an example, Dubois and Prade (1979) propose fuzzy maximum and minimum operations that are best described by the example that is given in Figure 3.2. Consider superimposing the membership functions of S_1 and S_2, then the maximum of the two sets is a combination of the rightmost sections of the two membership functions, and minimum a combination of the leftmost sections.

Subsequent authors have suggested other ways of combining fuzzy sets. In particular, some, including (Weber, 1983), have advocated the use of the class of complementary functions known as triangular norms and triangular conorms, introduced originally in the mathematics literature as abstract operations on semi-groups (for instance they are discussed by Schweitzer and Sklar (1963)) that are binary, monotonic, commutative, and associative and operate on values from the unit interval. The results of applying the functions at the extreme values of the $[0, 1]$ range obey the requirements of the logical conjunction and disjunction, permitting the claim to be made that the t-norms and t-conorms, as they are commonly known, are (Bonissone and Wood, 1989):

the most general families of binary functions that satisfy the requirements of the conjunction and disjunction operators.

Zadeh's minimum and maximum operations are respectively a specific t-norm and a specific t-conorm.

Clearly the membership function that defines the set in Figure 3.1 is highly subjective, in this case it represents my personal notion of the term "tall," and it is this aspect of the membership function that ties the notion of fuzzy sets to possibility theory. Since the fuzzy

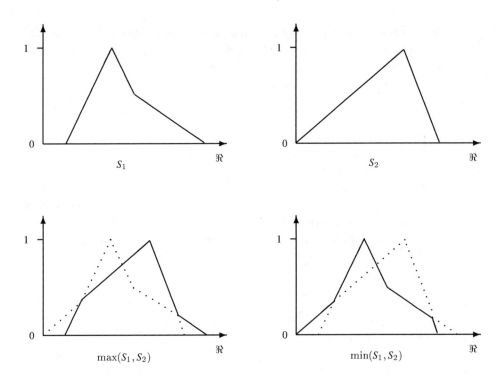

Figure 3.2
Fuzzy maximum and minimum operations

set represents my idea of how to interpret the term "tall," it can be used to quantify the uncertainty inherent in any prediction with which I will view a particular person as being tall. Clearly it is certain that I will regard anyone who is five feet or less in height as not being tall, and anyone over six feet tall as definitely being tall. For people between five and six feet tall it is possible to some degree that I will regard them as being tall, the degree being defined by the membership function. Thus Figure 3.1 can also be regarded as a possibility distribution over the set of possible heights (Zadeh, 1978).

Possibility theory is not the only way in which fuzzy sets can be used to handle uncertain (as distinct from vague) information. An alternative is the use of "fuzzy probabilities," that is probabilities that, rather than being numerical, are (Zadeh, 1984b):

exemplified by the perceptions of likelihood which are commonly labelled as *very likely, unlikely, not very likely,*

and so on. The idea is simple—each *linguistic quantifier* equates to a fuzzy set of probability values that are combined using the usual methods for combining fuzzy sets. The idea of combining probability and fuzzy sets into fuzzy probabilities has been taken on board by Bonissone and his co-workers in their "Reasoning Under Uncertainty" (RUM) system which is described in a sequence of papers. The first, (Bonissone, 1987b), introduces a family of calculi, of varying properties, based on a number of sets of linguistic probabilities such as "very low chance." These are represented as fuzzy sets of probabilities and combined using sets of different triangular norms and triangular conorms. A single set of fuzzy probabilities, a t-norm, and a t-conorm define one member of the family.[3] The properties of the members of the family are examined and compared in (Bonissone and Decker, 1986) providing data about their behaviour that, while it cannot really be usefully summarised here, is necessary for anyone intending to make use of them. The final papers, (Bonissone et al., 1987; Bonissone and Wood, 1989) describe aspects of the RUM system which has been successfully used to handle the uncertainty in "battle management."

3.3.3   Rough sets

Fuzzy sets provide a natural means of handling vague and imprecise information, a fact that explains their success in the field of automatic control where they are used to handle imprecise control information, blending different control strategies together. Rough sets, like fuzzy sets a generalisation of classical set theory, may be considered as a tool for modelling non-fuzzy vagueness (in Smithson's terms), or possibly even for modelling ambiguity. In other words, what rough sets model is information that, like naturally fuzzy information, cannot be spilt into "clean" classes such that any object is either in the class or out of the class. Instead some objects appear to be both the kind of object that should be in the class and the kind of object that should be out of the class. However, unlike the kinds of classes modelled by fuzzy sets, those modelled by rough sets are such that the "neither-in-nor-out" objects cannot be distinguished from one another by different degrees of membership. As a result all these objects must be treated all together and this makes a reference to them as a group completely ambiguous (since it will never be clear which member is being referred to).

Rough sets were first introduced by Pawlak (1982) and have since proved a popular topic of research, which has been documented both in a monograph by Pawlak (1991) and collections of papers, for example (Słowinski, 1992; Ziarko, 1993). This description of rough sets is drawn from (Pawlak, 1992). The concept of a rough set is relative to some knowledge base $K = (U, \mathbf{R})$ where U is a set of objects, and $\mathbf{R}$ is a set of equivalence

---

3 In fact the original papers also include "averaging operators" that "are located between conjunctions and disjunctions" (Bonissone and Decker, 1986), and "detachment operators" which allow the generalisation of classical modus ponens (Bonissone, 1987b), but these do not appear in the descriptions of the final system.

Table 3.3
Some rough knowledge

U	a	b	c	d	e
1	1	0	2	1	0
2	0	0	1	2	1
3	2	0	2	1	0
4	0	0	2	2	2
5	1	2	2	1	0

relations over U such that

$$\mathbf{R} = \{R_1, \ldots, R_n\}$$
$$R_i \subseteq U \times U$$

The set of equivalence classes of a member of $\mathbf{R}$ given U, that is the set of sets of members of U that may be distinguished using a given R_i, is denoted by U/R. Now, for any $\mathbf{P} \subseteq \mathbf{R}$, it is the case that the intersection, $\bigcap_i P_i$, of all the equivalence relations P_i in $\mathbf{P}$ is also an equivalence relation. This relation is known as an *indiscernibility relation* over $\mathbf{P}$ and is written as $IND(\mathbf{P})$. Every knowledge base $K = (U, \mathbf{R})$ has an associated pair $S_K = (U, \mathbf{A})$ where $\mathbf{A}$ is a set of attributes of the objects in U. That is every member a_i of $\mathbf{A}$ is an attribute of the objects in A, and so can be considered a mapping from a given object $u_i \in U$ to a value:

$$a_i : u_i \mapsto V_{a_i}$$

where V_{a_i} is the set of possible values of attribute a_i. Now, every subset of attributes $\mathbf{B} \subseteq \mathbf{A}$ has an associated indiscernibility relation $IND(\mathbf{B})$ that classifies two members of U as equivalent if, for every attribute in $\mathbf{B}$, the values of the attributes are the same.

As an example of the kind of information that may be represented in this way, consider Table 3.3. Here the universe consists of five objects denoted 1, 2, 3, 4, and 5 and the set of attributes is $\mathbf{A} = \{a, b, c, d, e\}$. The set of possible values of a and e is $\{0, 1, 2\}$, the set of possible values of b is $\{0, 2\}$, and the set of possible values of d and e is $\{1, 2\}$. Some of the equivalence classes due to the attributes are as follows:

$$U/IND(\{a\}) = \{\{1, 5\}, \{2, 4\}, \{3\}\}$$
$$U/IND(\{b, c\}) = \{\{1, 3, 4\}, \{2\}, \{5\}\}$$
$$U/IND(\{a\}) = \{\{1\}, \{2\}, \{3\}, \{4\}, \{5\}\}$$

For every $X \subseteq U$ and $\mathbf{B} \subseteq \mathbf{A}$ it is possible to define two sets

$$\underline{\mathbf{B}}X = \bigcup \{Y \in U/IND(\mathbf{B}) : Y \subseteq X\}$$

$$\overline{\mathbf{B}}X = \bigcup\{Y \in U/IND(\mathbf{B}) : X \subseteq Y\}$$

These are known as the *B-lower approximation* and *B-upper approximation* respectively, and together form the *rough set* approximation of X with respect to **B**. The attraction of rough sets is that they may be used to establish approximate classifications (Pawlak, 1984; Pawlak et al., 1986)—that is sets of objects can be classified into rough sets with respect to certain attributes—and these can then be used to establish decision rules of the form

IF   attributes $a_1, \ldots, a_n$ have values $v_1, \ldots v_n$
THEN object is in class C

permitting a form of approximate learning as discussed by Kubat (1991) and a number of authors in (Słowinski, 1992).

3.3.4 Spohn's epistemic beliefs

As already discussed, it is possible to argue that probability theory is a good means of representing beliefs, but it is also possible to argue that there are reasons why probability is not a good means of representing beliefs. One such argument against probability is that put forward by Spohn (1990) who starts from the position that there is an intuitive notion of *plain belief* that is not captured by probability theory. If some proposition is believed, Spohn argues, it is not the same thing as that proposition having a probability of one, because beliefs can be revised while probabilities of one cannot change. Furthermore, representing the fact that a proposition is believed by giving it a probability close to 1 will not work either because if A and B are both believed then, in most cases, so is $A \wedge B$ but even if both A and B have a probability above whatever threshold has been chosen it is unlikely that their conjunction will also. Spohn therefore proposes a new formalism that may be used to represent plain belief, a formalism that is based around the notion of a natural conditional function (also known as an ordinal conditional function).

    However, despite the fact that the theory was proposed because of the shortcomings of probability theory, it turns out (Spohn, 1990), that it can be interpreted in terms of probabilities that are infinitesimally close to 1, and that is the way in which it is presented here. The basis of the presentation is taken from Pearl (1989), and an equally good, but less terse, presentation is given by Shenoy (1991b). The starting point is a probability distribution over a set of possible worlds w_i,[4] that assigns to every possible world a probability which is a polynomial function of some small positive number ϵ. Thus possible probabilities are α, $\beta\epsilon$, $\gamma\epsilon^2$. From these probabilities, it is possible to determine the probabilities of a set of possible worlds A and conditional probabilities such as $\Pr(A|B)$.

---

4 In other words, a probability distribution over a set of conjunctions of propositions—in a world described by two propositions a and c, there are four possible worlds, $a \wedge c$, $a \wedge \neg c$, $\neg a \wedge c$, and $\neg a \wedge \neg c$.

The ordinal conditional function $\kappa(\cdot)$ (which Shenoy calls a "disbelief function") is then defined in terms of these probabilities.

$$\kappa(A|B) = n \tag{3.75}$$

where n is the smallest integer such that

$$\frac{\Pr(A|B)}{\epsilon^n}$$

is finite but not infinitesimal for infinitesimal ϵ. This means that $\kappa(A|B)$ takes the value n if and only if $\Pr(A|B)$ is of the same order as ϵ^n. This is quite a coarse mapping, and less coarse mappings have been explored (Giang and Shenoy, 1999).

The reason for calling $\kappa(\cdot)$ a disbelief function is that as $\kappa(A)$ gets bigger, the $\Pr(A)$ gets smaller. Thus $\kappa(A)$ increases as the (probabilistic) degree of belief in A gets smaller. The properties of the disbelief functions are as follows:

$$\kappa(A) = \min_{w_i \in A} \kappa(w) \tag{3.76}$$

$$\kappa(A \cup B) = \min(\kappa(A), \kappa(B)) \tag{3.77}$$

$$\kappa(A \cap B) = \kappa(A|B) + \kappa(B) \tag{3.78}$$

and at least one of $\kappa(A)$ and $\kappa(\neg A)$ is zero. These properties are clearly those of probability theory where addition has become minimum and product has become addition. However, they also look a good deal like those for possibility theory, and it turns out that $\kappa(A)$ can also be interpreted as $-\ln(\Pi(A))$ (Dubois and Prade, 1991h). A further interpretation of epistemic beliefs, in terms of a slightly different type of probability, is given by Wilson (1995).

Now, even though disbelief functions give no representational advantage over probability and possibility theories, they do have their uses. In particular they give a computationally efficient method for computing probabilities. However, disbelief functions only approximate probabilities since all $\Pr(x_i)$ that are of the same order as ϵ^n map to n. As approximations to probabilities, ordinal conditional functions are discussed further in Chapter 4.

3.4   Computational techniques

The major reason that probabilistic methods were initially shunned by the artificial intelligence community was because they were thought to be impractical. Given a system that involves n variables it is necessary to obtain 2^n probabilities to fully specify the probabilistic relationships between those variables. For expert systems in which n is reasonably large this suggests that vast numbers of probabilities both need to be obtained and then updated during inference. Similar objections have been made about Dempster-Shafer theory of evidence. Because the naïve application of Dempster's rule to combine a mass distribution that has m focal elements with another that has n involves mn multiplications, it is clear that the naïve application of the rule will lead to a combinatorial explosion. However, rather than prompting researchers to give up using the theories, these difficulties instead prompted them to search for computationally efficient techniques.

3.4.1 Causal networks

Causal networks were proposed as an attempt to overcome some of the computational problems posed by probability theory, and have subsequently been adopted as a useful tool by proponents of some of the other major theories as well.

PROBABILISTIC CAUSAL NETWORKS

Considering the computational and representational demands made by probability theory, Pearl (1988b)[5] realised that although in general a large number of probabilities are required to specify a probabilistic system, in practice one often needs many fewer probabilities. This is because the kind of knowledge that is represented in artificial intelligence systems does not usually involve inter-relationships between many variables. The relationships that do exist, and thus the probabilities that are required, may be exposed by the construction of a network in which variables are represented by nodes and the explicit dependencies between them by arcs.[6] As an example, consider the network in Figure 3.3, which represents medical knowledge about a set of related conditions. From the network it is clear that both the occurrence of increased calcium and the occurrence of brain tumours are dependent upon the occurrence of metastatic cancer, while the occurrence of severe headaches is dependent upon the occurrence of a brain tumour and the occurrence of coma is dependent jointly upon the occurrence of increased calcium and a brain tumour. Thus when eliciting the probabilities that concern coma it is not necessary to bother with metastatic cancer or severe headaches, reducing the necessary number of probabilities from 2^5 to 2^3. Of course, in order to get the network in the first place, it is necessary to elicit all the dependencies between variables, but in general it seems that this is reasonably straightforward since the dependencies that exist tend to be reflected in notions of which factors "cause" which others. While there is some dispute as to whether or not it is fair to say that these networks

---

5 Pearl's original proposal was made in a series of papers in journals and conferences, including (Pearl, 1982; Kim and Pearl, 1983; Pearl, 1986a,b). The book (Pearl, 1988b) covers all this material and has become the benchmark reference for belief networks.

6 This suggestion was apparently first made by Wright (1921).

Metastatic cancer

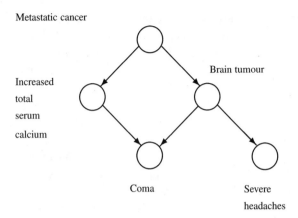

Increased

total

serum

calcium

Brain tumour

Coma   Severe

                              headaches

Figure 3.3
Some medical knowledge

really encode causality (for contributions to the debate see (Heckerman and Shachter, 1994a,b; Pearl, 2000)), it is often taken to be the case that they do, and this is reflected in the fact that they are often called causal networks[7]. This is the name by which they will be known in this book.

In addition to this representational advantage, Pearl (1988b) showed that the use of networks had a significant computational advantage. Because a node in the graph is only connected directly to those nodes whose values directly affect it, it is possible to calculate the probability of the variable represented by a node just from the probabilities of the variables represented by the nodes to which it is connected, and the conditional probabilities that relate to them. This, in turn, means that when the probabilities of variables represented by particular nodes change, it is possible to calculate the effects of these changes locally—by looking at which nodes are directly affected, calculating the relevant changes, then looking to see which nodes are affected by these new changes. This propensity for local computation makes it possible to propagate values through the network in a way that is reasonably efficient when the network is sparse, and such a scheme is proposed by Pearl (1988b). Pearl's method for updating values works for all singly-connected networks—

---

7 These structures go by many names. They are known as "probabilistic networks," "Bayesian networks" (in honour of Thomas Bayes, and because they are mostly used with subjective probabilities), belief networks (since the subjective probabilities are taken to be measures of subjective belief), and "Bayesian belief networks," and of course any of these names can be used with the word "network" abbreviated to "net." However, as Neapolitan (1990) has pointed out, most of the names are misleading, and the networks should really be known as "independence networks" since what they encode is explicit conditional independencies between variables. It should also be noted that these networks are closely related to "path diagrams" as used in sociometrics, paths diagrams having grown out of Wright's (1921) work.

those networks in which there is at most one route (disregarding the direction of the arrows) between any pair of nodes. If a network is multiply-connected, in other words if it is not singly-connected, then conventional wisdom was that it was only possible to use Pearl's method if it were extended (Pearl, 1988b) with additional mechanisms such as "conditioning" and "stochastic simulation" (Pearl, 1987, 1988b). Efficient methods for implementing these extensions have been suggested by a number of authors, for instance (Henrion, 1988; Peot and Shachter, 1991; Suermondt and Cooper, 1991), all of which required that the network be acyclic, meaning that it is not possible to follow directed links from one node around a in a cycle back to the same node. Recently, though, it has been shown (Murphy et al., 1999; Weiss and Freeman, 1999) that Pearl's original algorithm can perform accurate approximate calculations of probabilities even in acyclic networks[8].

Another method of propagating probability in acyclic singly or multiply-connected causal networks, which has the nice property of only requiring local computations, is the approach of clique-tree propagation developed by Lauritzen and Spiegelhalter (Spiegelhalter, 1986; Lauritzen and Spiegelhalter, 1988). As the name suggests, the actual propagation does not take place using the causal network, but uses another structure—the causal network is turned into an undirected graph, which is then triangulated to ensure that any loop contains at most three nodes.[9] Finally from this the "join-tree," "Markov tree," or "clique-tree" (all three terms denoting the same structure) is built. This latter has nodes that represent sets of variables, a set of variables being a clique, and it is through this kind of tree that the variables are propagated. Further research has made the original method more efficient, for example (Olesen and Andersen, 1988; Jensen et al., 1990; Madsen and D'Ambrosio, 1999; Madsen, 1999), and has generalised it so that formalisms other than probability may be propagated using it (Lauritzen and Jensen, 1996).

It should be noted that, despite the fact that most applications of causal networks have no significant computational problems, this is largely due to the sparseness of the networks that are necessary. Cooper (1990) has investigated the computational complexity of the approach and has shown that propagating probabilistic information in an arbitrarily complex belief network is NP-hard, a result that suggests that there will never be an algorithm which efficiently calculates the exact probabilities for every node of every possible network. As a result, there has been a good deal of research on methods for calculating probabilities approximately, for example (Pearl, 1987; Henrion, 1988; Hrycej, 1990; Jensen and Andersen, 1990; Jaakkola and Jordan, 1996, 1999; Cheng and Druzdzel, 2000; Salmerón et al., 2000). However, even this work seems doomed to failure in the general case by Dagum and Luby's (1993) result, which shows that it is not possible to find polynomial-time al-

---

8 This work goes by the name of "loopy belief propagation."
9 In doing so, the graph is made "moral" by "marrying" (connecting) those "parents" (predecessors) of a node that are unconnected.

gorithms which can calculate a required probability with greater accuracy than to say that it falls in the interval $[0, 1]$ when the relevant conditional probabilities can be arbitrarily close to zero.[10] Thus it seems that the best kind of algorithm that one can hope to establish is an anytime algorithm (Dean and Boddy, 1988) that can always give some kind of approximation to the required probability (even if it is just $[0, 1]$), and will gradually give better approximations if given more time. Such algorithms are described by a number of authors including Horvitz, Suermondt and Cooper (1989), Poole (1993a), Draper and Hanks (1994), and Jitnah and Nicholson (1997).

Another approach that aims to avoid the predicted combinatorial explosion is one which aims to reduce the amount of irrelevant information considered when calculating particular probability values. In many cases only a small proportion of the given evidence will bear upon values of interest, so that a large part of the network may be ignored when answering particular queries, and providing a mechanism for doing this is the aim of Xiang et al. (1993). One way of looking at the work of Xiang et al. is as an approach that makes use of the fact that a given query on a probabilistic network—a request to compute a particular probability given a particular set of observations—may have features that can be exploited to make the computation more efficient. This has also been explored with the idea of context specific independence (Boutilier et al., 1996) where conditional independencies which only occur for particular instantiations of of a set of variables. It seems that context specific independence can be exploited to speed up the various exact propagation algorithms discussed above (Boutilier et al., 1996; Zhang and Poole, 1999).

The idea of exploiting features of specific queries was taken to its extreme in the notion of a Query DAG (Q-DAG) (Darwiche and Provan, 1997). Given a probabilistic network, it is possible to construct a corresponding Q-DAG that essentially compiles all the results of all the queries which would be asked of the network. The construction of the Q-DAG is thus a computationally complex process, but the resulting structure can be evaluated efficiently. Q-DAGs are therefore useful for delivering the functionality of probabilistic networks for use on limited hardware platforms, or where real-time performance is required.

Since they were originally proposed, the use of probabilistic causal networks has become quite widespread, and there are numerous applications that make use of them. Some of the more notable are the MUNIN system for the interpretation of electromyographic findings (Andreassen et al., 1987; Olesen et al., 1989), the ARCO system for financial forecasting (Abramson, 1991), and the Pathfinder system for diagnosing lymph-node diseases (Heckerman et al., 1992; Heckerman and Nathwani, 1992). There are many others, including the CONVINCE system for situation assessment (Kim and Pearl, 1987), the VPROP

---

10 More recent work has suggested that in some cases an approximation to the required probability can be efficiently computed, but the pessimistic result holds in the worst case, when the number of observations that need to be taken into account is large (Dagum and Luby, 1997).

system for reducing the complexity of information presented to human operators in complex domains (such as space shuttle mission control) (Horvitz et al., 1992), and a system for analysing adverse drug reaction (Cowell et al., 1991; Spiegelhalter et al., 1990). Probabilistic causal networks have even been proposed as a means of establishing the best document to retrieve from a document database (Fung and Del Favero, 1995; Turtle and Croft, 1990, 1997), as a method to support visual recognition (Agosta, 1990) and ship classification (Musman and Chang, 1993), as a technique to generate advice on insulin therapy (Horvorka et al., 1992), and as the basis for troubleshooting systems (Heckerman et al., 1995). A variation on the latter application is doubtless familiar to many users of Microsoft's Windows operating system, since a probabilistic causal network lies at the heart of a number of the system utilities. It is also worth noting that, despite the fact that some of their many names suggest that these networks are limited to using subjective probabilities, there is nothing to prevent them being used with experimentally determined objective probabilities as is done in the QUALQUANT (Sucar et al., 1993) system.

In addition to this growing list of applications of probabilistic causal networks, there are a growing number of implementations of the various schemes for propagating probabilities—shells that can be instantiated to build new applications. One of the best known of these is the commercial system HUGIN (Andersen et al., 1989), which is essentially the inference engine from MUNIN. Another system that is widely used is IDEAL (Srinivas and Breese, 1990, 1989), a set of LISP macros which implement many of the propagation algorithms described in this section, as well as several that have not been considered here. Also worthy of note is Darwiche's CNETS system (Darwiche, 1994b,a), Cozman's JavaBayes, Microsoft Bayesian Networks, and Knowledge Industries' DXpress.

This, then, completes a brief look at some of the more important results concerning probabilistic causal networks. There is a great deal of other such material in what is an expanding field, though much of the more recent research seems to concentrate on the fine detail of propagation mechanisms (as for example (Becker and Geiger, 1996) does) and so is rather arcane. A large proportion of this ongoing work can be found in the proceedings of the annual Conference on Uncertainty in Artificial Intelligence. There are also several good introductory works on various aspects of probabilistic causal networks, for instance (Horvitz et al., 1988; Henrion, 1990; Neapolitan, 1990; Henrion et al., 1991; Charniak, 1991; Jensen, 1996), and a growing number of detailed descriptions of the underlying theory (Castillo et al., 1997; Cowell et al., 1999).

NON-PROBABILISTIC CAUSAL NETWORKS

Now, there is nothing inherent in the idea of causal networks that means that they may only be used in conjunction with probability theory. As mentioned above, all the networks really do is to provide a means of structuring knowledge about a domain to expose the dependencies between the key concepts in the domain. These dependencies are then represented in such a way that the representation may be used to determine what calculations need to be carried out to propagate new information about the domain. The key property of the network representation is, roughly speaking as follows. If there is a single path through a network between nodes X and Y, and that path passes through node Z, then X and Y are *d-separated* by Z. A much fuller definition, may be found in Section 5.3.2 and the best discussion of d-separation that I know of may be found in Jensen's book (1996, pages 12–14). If X and Y are d-separated by Z then the probabilities of the nodes represented by X and Y are conditionally independent of one another given the probability of the variable represented by Z (Verma and Pearl, 1990). Thus, it is possible to determine something about the conditional independence relations between the probabilities of the variables represented by nodes in the network from the structure of the network. So, if it is possible to show that conditional independencies between the possibilities of, and beliefs in, the variables may also be inferred from the structure of the network, then such networks may be used to guide the propagation of possibility and belief values.

Such results have been provided by Fonck and Smets respectively.[11] Fonck (1994) showed that the notion of conditional possibilistic independence introduced in (3.41) is such that the possibilities of two d-separated nodes are conditionally independent, in the "non-interactive" sense, of one another.[12] Thus it is possible to propagate possibility values in causal networks. Indeed, Fonck and Straszecka (1991) have looked at this kind of propagation of possibility values in a singly-connected network and have provided the kind of mathematical machinery necessary to propagate possibility values by local computation in the same way that Pearl propagates probability values. Smets (1991a) shows that it is possible to combine belief functions using Dempster's rule (3.64), the disjunctive rule of combination (3.65) and his generalisation of Bayes' theorem (3.66) provided that the belief functions are conditionally cognitively independent as defined in (3.67). As a result, provided that any two nodes in a network are taken to be conditionally cognitively independent given that they are d-separated, values can be propagated through the network using local computation, as discussed in (Xu and Smets, 1991). It should be stressed, however, that this local computation can only be carried out in singly-connected networks. If multiply-connected networks need to be handled, they must be transformed into singly-connected networks by having single nodes represent several variables.

---

11 The idea of using a graphical representation to represent dependencies in evidence theory was also investigated by Lowrance, Garvey and Strat (1986) and used in their system Gister.

12 Actually Fonck showed that the possibilistic conditional independence relation implied by her notion of conditional possibilistic independence was a "graphoid" (Pearl, 1988b) for the kind of combination used in (3.38), but the two ideas are equivalent.

Several other authors have looked at the construction of possibilistic causal networks. Of particular interest is the work of Gebhardt and Kruse and that of Benferhat and co-workers. Benferhat et al. (Benferhat et al., 1995b, 1996) have looked at some of the forms of reasoning that may be captured by possibilistic networks in which conditional independence is equivalent to non-interactivity. Gebhardt and Kruse (1994; 1995) build up their own notion of conditional independence, basing it on the same graph-theoretic properties as conditional independence for probabilities, finding that it more-or-less coincides with the notion of non-interactivity. Gebhardt and Kruse's approach has been implemented in the system POSSINFER (Kruse et al., 1994), and allows networks to be learnt from data (Gebhardt and Kruse, 1995; Borgelt and Kruse, 1997).

3.4.2   Valuation networks

This section, despite its title, covers not just valuation networks (although these are a major focus since they are used later in the book) but also the wider issues of the methods of local computation initially introduced by Shenoy and Shafer. These methods can be seen as standing in the same relation to evidence theory as probabilistic causal networks stand in relation to probability theory[13]—as a way of breaking down the problem of computing a global distribution over many variables into the problem of computing many local distributions over a few variables. However, the local computation methods discussed here can also be seen as a generalisation of probabilistic causal networks since they can be used to propagate probability values as well as belief values, and indeed can propagate many different types of value from many different methods for handling uncertainty.

The work on local computation begins[14] with (Shenoy and Shafer, 1986), which generalises the idea of conditional probability to the more general notion of qualitative conditional independence. Briefly, for a frame of discernment Θ with sets of Φ_i (for which the constituent sets are non-empty and disjoint), then $\Phi_1 \ldots \Phi_n$ are qualitatively conditionally independent given Φ if:

$$P \cap P_1 \cap \ldots \cap P_n \neq \emptyset \tag{3.79}$$

where $P \in \Phi$, $P_i \in \Phi_i$ and $P \cap P_i$ for all i. Using this form of conditional independence makes it possible to build qualitative Markov trees in the same way that probabilistic conditional independence makes it possible to build up probabilistic causal networks. Having obtained such a tree, it is possible to propagate probabilities and beliefs through it only using local computations. A more technical exposition of the ideas expressed in

---

13 This is certainly how they were devised.

14 A more comprehensive, and amusing, summary of the work on local computation is provided by Saffiotti (1989b) who also gives a clear introduction to the detail of the local computation mechanism (Saffiotti, 1989a).

(Shenoy and Shafer, 1986) may be found in (Mellouli et al., 1986; Shenoy et al., 1988) and (Shafer et al., 1987), and more general work on independence in this framework may be found in (Shenoy, 1992a). Smets (1991a) has adapted the idea of qualitative Markov trees, providing the mathematical framework necessary to propagate belief functions in directed graphs similar to those discussed by Pearl (1988b). This work includes the full derivation of the generalisation of Bayes' rule, begun in (Smets, 1986), which was given in (3.66).

Since the method for propagating values in Markov trees could capture both the propagation of belief functions and probability, it was clear that the work on local computation was extremely general. This generality was made even clearer in (Shenoy and Shafer, 1990). This paper uses a hypergraph representation, a hypergraph being a generalisation of a graph in which a node represents a set of variables and an edge represents a relationship between sets of variables, and in particular a kind of hypergraph that is known as a hypertree. Now, every hypertree has an associated Markov tree, so if it is possible to represent a set of probability or belief information as a hypertree, then it is possible to use the local computation mechanism to propagate it through the associated Markov tree, and so find the value of any variable in the tree. The generality arises because Shenoy and Shafer show that it is possible to describe the operations, known as *combination* and *marginalisation*, which are used to propagate values in very general terms, and give a set of three axioms concerning these operations. These operations and axioms are given in detail in Chapter 9 when they are used to implement the qualitative systems developed in Chapter 6. Now, given any formalism it is only necessary to define combination and marginalisation functions and show that they obey the axioms in order to be able to propagate values in that formalism by local computation. The key stage in the process is moving from a hypergraph representation to a hypertree representation since every scenario can be expressed as a hypergraph but not every hypergraph is a hypertree. As a result, not every hypergraph has an associated Markov tree. It turns out that any hypergraph can be converted into a hypergraph that is a hypertree, but at the cost of making some of its edges larger, and this may have a negative impact on the efficiency of the technique since the complexity is dependent on the size of the largest edge.

The generality of this framework has been exploited by Dubois and Prade (1991f) who show that the local computation mechanism can be used to propagate possibility values in hypergraphs, and by Shenoy (1991b) to show that the local computation scheme can be used to propagate values from Spohn's theory of epistemic beliefs. It has also been used to handle logical deduction (Kohlas et al., 1999; Wilson and Mengin, 1999).

In introducing the axioms for local computation, Shenoy and Shafer introduced the idea of a valuation—an assignment of values to a set of variables. Taking the idea of a valuation as primitive, Shenoy (1989) developed the idea of a valuation-based system in which all information is represented as valuations, and inference is carried out by means

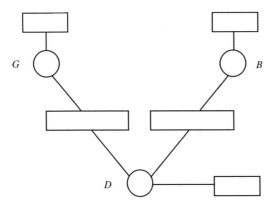

Figure 3.4
An example valuation network

of operations on valuations (just as in a rule-based system information is represented as rules, and inference is by operations on rules). This initial paper discusses valuation-based systems to represent categorical knowledge, and the use of belief function valuations for reasoning with uncertain and defeasible information. A later paper (Shenoy, 1992c) additionally discusses the use of probability and Spohn's epistemic belief, providing the example valuation network[15] of Figure 3.4. This figure represents the interaction between variable D, which represents the occurrence of diabetes, variable B, which represents the occurrence of the symptom "blue toe," and G, which represents the occurrence of glucose in urine. The rectangles represent valuations, and there is a valuation for each variable and a valuation for each relationship between variables.

Following the introduction of valuation-based systems, Shenoy has argued that they may be used as a convenient method of building expert systems that incorporate uncertainty handling methods. In particular he has advocated their use in building systems that use evidence theory (Shenoy, 1994a) and possibility theory (Shenoy, 1992b). The latter paper is noteworthy since it points out that within valuation based systems the best combination operation for possibilistic valuations is product rather than minimum in contrast to the suggestion made by Dubois and Prade (1991f) (this is to avoid problems when using normalised possibility values). Of course, as discussed above, there is no conflict between these two views since possibility theory can use either product or minimum as a combination operation. Shenoy has also shown that valuation systems can be used to solve both discrete optimisation problems (Shenoy, 1990b) and decision problems (Shenoy, 1990a) (even those that are asymmetric and thus defeat some other methods of decision analysis

---

15 A valuation network is a graphical representation of a valuation-based system.

(Shenoy, 1994b)), and has provided a detailed comparison of valuation networks and other methods of decision analysis (Shenoy, 1990c). This work has been complemented by the derivation of an algorithm, a hybrid of local computation methods for propagating values and local computation methods for discrete optimisation, for solving decision problems that are modelled as a valuation-based system (Shenoy, 1991a), and Xu's work on decision making with belief functions in valuation-based systems (Xu, 1992a), which uses Strat's (1989a) method for interpreting what a belief means to a decision maker.

There have also been further developments in the underlying computational theory. Shafer (1991a) has shown that the propagation of values through hypertrees can be generalised so that the values that may be propagated are members of any commutative semigroup, and that the members of the edges of the hypertree, through which the propagation takes place, may be the elements of any lattice. Generalisation is also the theme of (Lauritzen and Shenoy, 1995), which shows how the propagation of values in the valuation network setting relates to methods that use join trees. Another development is that of Xu (1995) who shows how it is possible to change the structure of a Markov tree without changing the information in its vertices. This makes it possible to obtain values for arbitrary subsets of the variables in the tree, rather than just subsets of those represented by a single node, without the need to recompute the values for the whole tree. In a slightly different vein, there have been improvements to the propagation algorithm (Shenoy, 1997; Schmidt and Shenoy, 1998), reducing the number of calculations required, and thus speeding up the propagation.

There are a number of implementations based upon the work on local computation, including Zarley's Delief (Design of Beliefs), Hsia's MacEvidence, Xu's TresBel (Tool for reasoning with belief functions) and VBSD (Valuation Based System for Decision Analysis), and Saffiotti and Umkehrer's Pulcinella (Propagating uncertainty through local computation).

The first of these systems was Delief (Zarley, 1988; Zarley et al., 1988), which allows a user to enter a series of nodes representing variables, and a series of relations between them that may be quantified using probability or evidence values. This evidential network is then converted into a Markov tree and propagation is carried out by using the method described by Shafer et al. (Shafer et al., 1987). The system is written in Symbolics Lisp, and so its portability is rather limited. This limited portability makes Delief rather less useful than its successor MacEvidence (Hsia and Shenoy, 1989a,b) which, as its name suggests, is a stand-alone Macintosh application. One of the problems with both Delief and MacEvidence is that they perform a number of redundant computations—the result of the same marginalisation or combination operation is needed several times by one node for instance. Xu (1991a) shows that by storing more information at each node, such redundant computations can be significantly reduced. Furthermore, the same stored information can be used to ensure that if some of the prior beliefs are altered so that there is a need to re-propagate values, and the underlying Markov tree has not been changed, recomputations involving values that have not been changed can be avoided. The algorithms presented in (Xu, 1991a) form the basis of TresBel (1991b; 1992b) along with the use of bit arrays to store the frame of discernment of the belief functions it handles and bit level operations to manipulate these frames. A full description of the these methods for speeding up computation is provided in (Xu and Kennes, 1994).

   Pulcinella (Saffiotti and Umkehrer, 1991a,b), implements much of Shenoy's work on local computation and valuation systems and some of Xu's work on efficient computation of belief functions. Pulcinella thus provides both a means of representing probabilistic, possibilistic, evidential, and logical information, and an inference mechanism suitable for propagating probability, possibility, evidence, and Boolean values through any valuation system. Pulcinella is also easily extensible to cope with other formalisms[16] that obey the local propagation axioms, and for which a valuation representation may be devised. The initial version of Pulcinella was written in Allegro Common Lisp using Flavors and ran both on Macintosh and Sun machines. There was also a version of Pulcinella that ran as a stand-alone application on the Macintosh. Sadly this stand-alone version was killed off by the advent of the System 7 release of the Macintosh operating system, which introduced some problems in file-handling (there was no subsequent version of Allegro Common Lisp), but this problem is somewhat overcome by the fact that Pulcinella has subsequently been rewritten to run under any Common Lisp, including freely available versions such as Kyoto.[17] Pulcinella has subsequently been extended (Xu et al., 1993) to include Shenoy's mechanism for solving decision problems in the valuation-based system framework, forming the tool VSBD. This may then be used along with TresBel as a decision support system that implements the transferable belief model and Smets' method for making decisions based upon it. Thus, beliefs are used to model the problem, the effect of evidence is established using TresBel, the resulting beliefs are then converted to probabilities using the pignistic transformation, and the resulting decision problem is solved using VSBD. More recently work on implementing these ideas has been carried out by Kohlas and his co-workers (Anrig et al., 1997; Haenni, 1998; Lehmann and Haenni, 1999).

   Inspired by Shenoy and Shafer's work on local computation, Cano et al. (1993) have considered how a similar scheme could be devised to cover propagation in directed acyclic

16 The system is so easy to use that I was able to extend it to propagate a new formalism (one of the qualitative systems discussed in Chapter 6) in one afternoon without any prior knowledge of the internal operation of the system.

17 For more details of the system, including information on how to obtain a copy, see the Pulcinella Web page at http://iridia.ulb.ac.be/pulcinella/Welcome.html.

graphs. It turns out that such a scheme is derivable, generalising Pearl's propagation scheme to be applicable to formalisms other than probability theory. The scheme works for any formalism that obeys the three axioms required by Shenoy and Shafer's method plus three additional axioms,[18] but it should be noted that possibility theory is not among these. This work has been extended by Ben Yaghlane and Melloulli (1999) to deal with the case in which the directed graph is quantified with belief functions. Fonck (1992) has published some interesting work related to this. She takes the axioms identified by Cano et al., and from them determines the restrictions on the combination and marginalisation operators allowing the easy selection of operations that conform to them. In doing so she manipulates "certainty values" in an anonymous formalism that is defined only by the operations over it, and which could be considered an abstraction of all the formalisms that may be propagated by the scheme.

3.4.3   Dynamic construction of network models

Initially systems that made use of probabilistic causal networks were constructed by eliciting the knowledge required by the system from someone knowledgeable about the domain in which the system was intended to operate. For example, in the case of the Pathfinder system (Heckerman et al., 1992) the procedure was roughly as follows. An expert was selected and, through a series of consultations, helped Heckerman et al. to structure their knowledge of the domain in terms of a set of important concepts, the influences between them, and the strengths of those influences. The concepts then became the nodes in the network, the influences became the arcs, and the strengths of the influences became the conditional probability tables. The problem with this procedure is that it is very time-consuming, and so is not very helpful in dynamic domains. In addition, it relies very much on the existence of the domain expert, and so is not applicable in areas in which such experts cannot be found. It is not too surprising, therefore, that there has been a considerable amount of work over the past few years on methods for the automatic construction of networks (Wellman et al., 1992), and in this section a number of proposals are discussed.

One of the earliest attempts to provide for automated construction was that of Srinivas et al. (1989) who take a number of different types of qualitative information, such as "A is a cause of B" or that "A is independent of B given C," obtained from an expert, and use these, together with a black box that tests for independence, to create networks. Clearly this approach finesses one of the harder problems in ignoring the test for independence, but it is nevertheless obvious that the algorithm that they provide could be usefully linked with

---

18 In fact, Cano et al. argue that the fourth of their axioms was in fact considered by Shenoy and Shafer, but not included as an axiom.

an automated reasoning system to build networks from logical statements. In addition the system is implemented as part of the IDEAL package. In contrast with this "expert centered" approach, Cooper and Herskovits (1991a) developed an algorithm that can deduce the most likely structure of a causal network linking a set of variables given a database of cases of the form "in Case 1, A is present, B is absent, and C is present." The derivation of the network is based upon the assumptions that the database explicitly mentions all the relevant variables, that the cases mentioned in the database are independent, and that all the cases are complete. This algorithm has been tested on a moderately sized database of $10,000$ cases generated by an existing causal network. The algorithm took around 15 minutes on a Macintosh II to generate a network that was nearly identical to the original. This compares favourably with their initial experiments with a method based on finding the maximum entropy distribution (Herskovits and Cooper, 1990) for a network based on a set of cases that took nearly 24 hours to handle the $10,000$ case database. The same authors (Cooper and Herskovits, 1991b) have also considered the problem of assessing the conditional probability values necessary to perform probabilistic inference in the causal network. Wen (1991) takes a slightly different approach. Starting from a database that records statistical data of the form "D and E occur with A, B, and C on 2048 occasions," Wen discusses how to reduce sets of relations into fourth normal form, which correspond to the cliques of the equivalent causal network, and from which the necessary conditional probabilities may be learnt. He also discusses methods based on the principle of maximum entropy for completing sets of conditional probabilities.

The other major disadvantage with network based formalisms is the fact that they are inherently propositional. Consider Pearl's (1988b) seminal example about Mr Holmes and his burglar alarm. Either an earthquake or a burglary would cause the alarm to sound, an earthquake would most likely result in a radio announcement, and the sounding of the alarm would cause Holmes' neighbour Mrs Gibbon to telephone him at work. This may be represented by a causal network (see Figure 3.5) and the result used to predict the most likely cause of the alarm sounding given that Mrs Gibbon calls. The problem with this model is how to extend it to cover the case, for instance, in which Dr. Watson, another neighbour who is more reliable than Mrs Gibbon, also telephones, and the case when Inspector Lestrade, who happens to be passing, telephones to report a suspicious person hanging around the Holmes residence, or even the case when Watson rather than Gibbon is the only one to call. The model as it stands does not allow universally quantified statements such as "a ringing alarm would cause a neighbour to telephone," restricting expressiveness to statements to such as "the alarm would cause Mrs Gibbon to telephone."

Breese (1992) addresses the removal of this restriction for probabilistic causal networks, showing how to build such networks from a database of facts and rules in first order horn clause logic, statements of probabilistic influence, and additional information (such

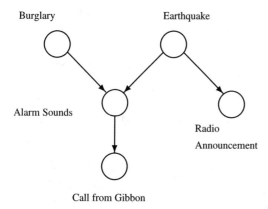

Figure 3.5
The events surrounding Mr Holmes

as the mutual exclusivity of some values of some variables). He not only proves that the method produces networks that do not ignore any probabilistic dependencies, but also argues forcefully that dynamic construction allows only relevant information to be taken into account, so improving efficiency. Xiang et al. (1993) argue from a similar position. Another similar approach is adopted by Poole (1991; 1993b) who uses first order horn clause logic to represent the variables in a belief network and the relationships between them, attaching an associated probability to each. The logical clauses are then used to deduce various facts such that the probability associated with the facts is the probability that would be established for them using the equivalent network. Thus the network is never built, but is implicit in the computation, and this differentiates the approach from the earlier work presented by Horsch and Poole (1990). In this latter, horn clauses are used to provide general statements that are then instantiated at run-time and used to explicitly construct Bayesian networks. More recently, Poole's approach has been extended to include negation as failure and to allow for the modelling of multiple agents (Poole, 1995).

Saffiotti and Umkehrer (1994) present a related method for dynamically constructing valuation networks suitable for their system Pulcinella. Facts and relations are represented in first order logic, and resolution used to build a proof path from which a network can be constructed. The network may then be fed to Pulcinella for evaluation. The implementation described is proven sound and complete when evidence theory is used as a means of quantifying the uncertainty in the facts and relations, though it is possible to extend the approach to other uncertainty handling formalisms and representation languages. Another method in the same vein is that of Goldman and Charniak (1990), who are also interested in explicitly building Bayesian networks in dynamic environments. Their approach differs in that it uses a specialised network construction language rather than first order logic and, being motivated by understanding natural language, is not goal directed in the same way as the methods listed above.

It should be noted that all of the network construction techniques mentioned so far build networks that are correct at a particular instant in time, but do not allow for changes in the network. Provan (1991) deals with the latter problem using a sensitivity analysis to determine when better decisions would have been taken using a different model, and gives an algorithm for performing the updating. The need to update networks is often due to the fact that the problem being solved changes over time, and so the history of the problem becomes important. This time dependency is handled in Provan's system Dynasty, which also allows different levels of granularity of problem description to be considered. Similar issues are addressed by Dagum et al. (1992) who synthesize belief networks with time-series analysis to create dynamic network models for use in forecasting, as do Glesner and Koller (1995). Another factor that has been disregarded in all the systems considered so far is the problem of separating the construction of a model from using that model. In a resource bound environment this could lead to the query-driven construction of a network that could not be evaluated in reasonable time. Goldman and Breese (1992) consider how to alleviate this difficulty by integrating the two stages to give an anytime algorithm for query evaluation that will always give a solution and gives successively better solutions the longer it is allowed to run. In addition to always providing a solution, the method allows solutions that are of no use to be identified at an early stage, and its deductive style brings the use of numerical methods almost full circle and back to the logical methods discussed above.

Finally, it should also be noted that there are some striking similarities between the representation of data in probabilistic networks and in relational databases. Pittarelli (1994) pointed out that his probabilistic databases allow the computation of the same probability distributions as belief networks given information about the dependencies between different data. In other words, if the graphical structure is known, then the probabilistic information that is stored in his system is sufficient to establish a unique joint probability distribution for all the pieces of data in the database. Similar findings were reported by Studený (1990) in his attempt to characterise the nature of conditionally independent pieces of information. Despite starting from a completely different position, Studený spotted a close analogy between his definition of conditional independence and the idea of embedded multi-valued dependencies, which are a means of describing relational databases. However, he also showed that there were some differences between the ideas. Finally, Wong and his co-workers (Wong et al., 1994) have shown that probabilistic causal networks networks can be represented as relational databases, and have explored some of the properties of this representation (Wong and Wang, 1994; Wong et al., 1995). Rather as one might expect given the work discussed above by Poole (1993b; 1991), and the close correspondence between predicates and the tuples in a relational table, it seems that if a probability distribution is given over a set of relational tables, it is possible to perform correct probabilistic inference using just the project and join operations that one would expect of a relational database. Thus when new evidence is obtained its effects may be propagated through the database in a manner consistent with the underlying dependencies. Since new information can easily be added to the database at any time, this appears to give a means of dynamic network construction without explicitly creating the network. However, the method does rely upon the prior structuring of the relations in order to represent the conditional independencies.

Once again it should be stressed that this section just scratches the surface of the work on the construction of networks. Now that the basic computational problems of probabilistic methods have been sorted out, and the techniques have been applied to a number of illustrative examples, building the networks automatically seems to be one of the main areas of research being carried out by people interested in this kind of model. Some recent contributions are by Lam and Bacchus (1994), Heckerman and co-workers (Heckerman et al., 1994; Heckerman, 1995), Acid and de Campos (1996), Kleiter and Jiroušek (1996), and Jensen (1999), while a good survey of the area is provided by Krause (1998).

3.4.4   Other network models

There are three other important types of model that have a network representation. These are influence diagrams, similarity networks, and Bayesian multinets. The former can be thought of as an extension of probabilistic causal networks (though influence diagrams actually predate them) to include explicit information about decisions, while the latter two are extensions of probabilistic causal networks that allow the representation of independence information that cannot be captured by probabilistic causal networks.

INFLUENCE DIAGRAMS

Influence diagrams were originally developed as a modelling tool to help in decision analysis (Miller et al., 1976; Howard and Matheson, 1984). The latter is the usual reference for information on influence diagrams while a very readable introduction to the topic may be found in (Howard, 1990). Like probabilistic causal networks, influence diagrams represent a particular situation by means of a graph that shows the interactions between a set of variables, the variables being denoted by nodes in the graph. Like causal probabilistic networks, influence diagrams represent random variables and the probabilistic influences between them, but they also explicitly represent decisions and the quantity whose value

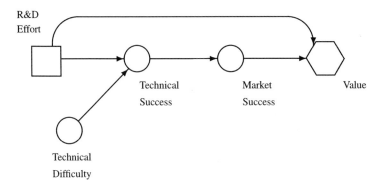

Figure 3.6
An influence diagram for a research and development decision

is to be optimised by the decision being analysed. As an example, consider the influence diagram in Figure 3.6 (which is taken from (Howard, 1990)). The round nodes represent random variables, and are called *chance* nodes, the square node represents the decision to be taken and is known as a *decision* node, and the hexagonal node represents the value to be optimised and is known as a *value* node. Here the decision is the amount of money to be spent on research and development.

As introduced, influence diagrams were intended as a tool to help decision analysts in their task of assisting a decision maker to make the decision pictured in the diagram. In such a scenario the emphasis was on structuring the problem and ensuring that it was properly represented. Once the representation of the problem was settled, the idea was that the influence diagram would be converted into an alternative representation, such as a decision tree, so that it could be evaluated. However, it was always intended that, eventually, some procedure would be devised to permit the automated evaluation of the models, and such procedures were provided by Shachter (1986b; 1986a) and Rege and Agogino (1988). These procedures are rather different to those discussed above for the evaluation of probabilistic causal networks and valuation networks since they involve the transformation of the diagram—nodes are removed until all the chance nodes have disappeared, the decision nodes indicate the optimal decisions, and the value node gives the maximum value of the quantity being optimised. Shachter's procedure is automated in DAVID (Shachter, 1988), and both Shachter's and Rege and Agogino's procedures are automated in the IDEAL package mentioned above.[19] Commercial implementations include Demos from Lumina Decision Systems (an early version of which is described in the

---

19 IDEAL actually stands for Influence Diagram Evaluation and Analysis in Lisp.

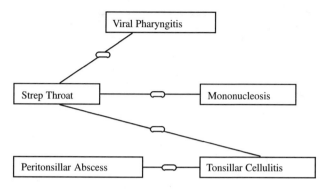

Figure 3.7
A similarity graph

context of risk analysis by Henrion and Morgan (1985; 1990)), and DXpress. More recent work (Shachter and Peot, 1992) has produced a method for evaluating influence diagrams using the kind of local computation algorithms developed for probabilistic causal networks.

Other notable contributions on the subject of influence diagrams include Henrion and Cooley's (1987) comparison of influence diagram and rule-based representations for the diagnosis of root disorders in apple trees, and Shachter and Ndilikilikesha's (1994) generalisation of the influence diagram to a structure known as a "potential influence diagram" in which the arcs between nodes are not constrained to be quantified by conditional probabilities.

SIMILARITY NETWORKS

Similarity networks (Geiger and Heckerman, 1996) were invented by Heckerman (1991a; 1990b) during the construction of the Pathfinder system (Heckerman et al., 1992; Heckerman and Nathwani, 1992). In the initial stages of the development of the system it was assumed that the various lymph-node diseases that the system was being built to diagnose were mutually exclusive and exhaustive, while the symptoms produced by the diseases were conditionally independent of one another. However, while the mutual exclusivity and exhaustiveness of the diseases was a reasonable assumption, the first because of the nature of the domain and the second because the system had such a wide scope, the conditional independence of the features was not. Now, the domain expert, despite agreeing that this was the case, was not happy with having to assess the conditional dependencies between certain features, and it was this problem that similarity networks were intended to address. They also have the feature of reducing the number of probabilities that need to be established.

A similarity network is a similarity graph and a set of local belief networks. In the

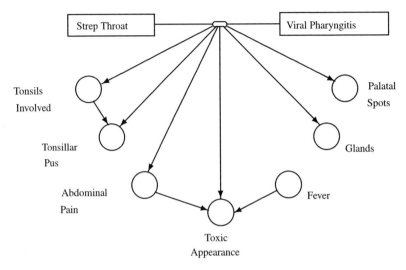

Figure 3.8
A local belief network

context of Pathfinder, a similarity graph is a set of nodes representing diseases that have related symptoms, and edges which connect similar diseases. A similarity graph from Pathfinder is given in Figure 3.7. For each edge in the similarity graph, there is a local belief network that relates particular symptoms that bear on making a distinction between the diseases related by that edge. One of the local belief networks for the similarity graph in Figure 3.7 is given in Figure 3.8. It is easy to see that the representation makes it clear exactly which symptoms are used to distinguish which diseases—distinctions that are lost in a global probabilistic causal network—and this is the representational advantage that similarity networks have over probabilistic causal networks.

The original intention behind similarity networks was that they were a tool for building probabilistic causal networks. The idea was that once all the local belief networks were specified they would be composed to get the global network, and Heckerman provides an algorithm for doing this (Heckerman, 1991b). However, it is also possible to perform inference using the similarity network alone (Geiger and Heckerman, 1996). The extension of similarity networks to the case in which there is no assumption that only one disease occurs at a time is described in (Heckerman, 1991b), and there is a tool called SimNet (Heckerman, 1991a) that helps in the construction of similarity networks.

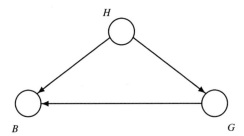

Figure 3.9
A probabilistic causal network for the secure building example

BAYESIAN MULTINETS

Bayesian multinets (Geiger and Heckerman, 1991, 1996) provide a means of encoding asymmetric independence, a situation that is best described by Geiger and Heckerman's example of the secured building:

A guard outside a secure building expects three types of person to approach the entrance of the building: workers in the building, approved visitors, and spies. As a person approaches the building, the guard can note their gender and whether or not they are wearing a badge. Spies are mainly men. Spies always wear badges in an attempt to fool the guard. Visitors don't wear badges because they don't have one. Female workers tend to wear badges more than male workers. The task of the guard is to identify the type of person entering the building.

This situation can be represented by the network in Figure 3.9 where *H* represents the correct identification and has values *worker*, *visitor*, and *spy*, while *G* and *B* are binary variables representing the person's gender and whether or not they wear a badge. The arcs between *H* and *B* and *G* represent the influence between the type of person and their gender and badge-wearing tendency, while that between *G* and *B* reflects the relationship between gender and badge-wearing tendency. However, this representation obscures the fact that spies always wear badges and visitors never wear badges, so that *B* and *G* are conditionally independent given that someone is known to be a spy or a visitor. Thus the link between *B* and *G* is only included to cover the case in which the person is a worker.

   This fact suggests that the situation would be better represented by the two networks of Figure 3.10. Here the first network represents the case in which the person is a spy or a visitor and makes it clear that in this case whether or not someone wears a badge only depends upon what type of person they are, while the second represents the case in which the person is a worker, and makes it clear that in this case gender and badge wearing are related. Geiger and Heckerman call the kind of representation illustrated in Figure 3.10 a "Bayesian multinet," and both show that it holds sufficient information to compute the

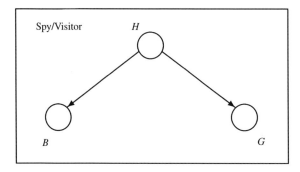

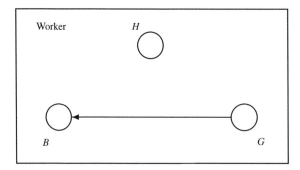

Figure 3.10
A Bayesian multinet for the secure building example

joint probability distribution over all the variables it contains and provide an algorithm to achieve this. They also give an algorithm for converting similarity networks into multinets.

3.4.5   Other computational techniques

The major problem with building systems using evidence theory is the computational complexity of Dempster's rule of combination. If the rule is applied naïvely, that is as it is applied in Section 3.2.3 by taking the intersection of all the focal elements of the various belief functions and combining the mass assignments over them, then the application of the rule is computationally hard [20](Orponen, 1990; Provan, 1990). Thus computing the application of Dempster's rule is not possible in reasonable time for large numbers of mass distributions and focal elements.

Even before Orponen's result it was clear that Dempster's rule was a source of computational problems, and several authors had looked at ways of applying the rule in compu-

---

20 Orponen shows that the application of Dempster's rule is #P-complete while Provan shows it is NP-complete.

tational efficient ways. Barnett (1981) showed that the apparent exponential time requirement of the theory could be reduced to simple polynomial time if the theory was applied
to singleton hypotheses, rather than sets of hypotheses, and the evidence combined in an
orderly fashion. Gordon and Shortliffe (1985) extended Barnett's approach to compute approximate beliefs in a space of hierarchically organised sets of hypotheses in linear time.[21]
This approach was then subsumed by that of Shafer and Logan (1987), who provided an
exact algorithm for hierarchically organised sets of hypotheses that is also linear in time
while being slightly more general than that of Gordon and Shortliffe.

More general algorithms have also been sought by a number of authors. For example,
Wilson (1992c) has proposed a method in which the explicit use of Dempster's rule of
combination is avoided, permitting an exact calculation of belief to be performed in worse
than polynomial but better than exponential time. Sandri (1991) has shown that careful
structuring of the focal elements of mass distributions can lead to improvements in complexity over the naive application of Dempster's rule. Another improvement is suggested
by Smets and Kennes (Smets and Kennes, 1991; Kennes, 1992; Xu and Kennes, 1994)
who suggest the use of the Möbius transform. In particular they develop algorithms that
are provably among the fastest for computing Möbius transforms, and show that these may
be used to establish commonality functions from mass distributions, and then plausibility
functions from commonality functions. This rather roundabout route for computing plausibility functions might seem rather baroque but, due to the efficiency of the transform
algorithms, it considerably reduces the number of arithmetic operations required when
compared to the naive approach (for a frame of discernment of 20 elements the transform
method uses up to 35,000 times fewer additions and 10^6 fewer multiplications). However,
despite the various successes of these approaches, Orponen and Provan's results suggest
that, in general, none of these will be particularly efficient.

Luckily this is not a great problem in practice. The intractability result only applies to
exact computations, so that it seems that it is quite possible to find efficient approximate
methods. Indeed, Dempster's formulation (see Section 3.2.1) suggests such an approximate
method based on Monte-Carlo algorithms (Kämpke, 1988; Pearl, 1988b; Wilson, 1991,
1992a,c). Such an approach, as Wilson shows, gives results that are arbitrarily close to the
exact solution, and that may be performed in linear time even when the hypotheses are not
hierarchically structured. This method is always efficient under the open-world assumption
since there is no need to normalise belief after the use of Dempster's rule. However, if
normalisation is required, the method becomes inefficient when there is a large degree of
conflict between pieces of evidence. In such cases Moral and Wilson (1994) show that

---

21 The fact that Gordon and Shortliffe heaped extravagant praise upon the ability of the evidence theory to
handle hierarchies of hypotheses led Pearl (1986c) to show that the same kind of reasoning could be performed
in probability theory.

the application of Markov Chain Monte-Carlo algorithms provides an efficient solution. This approach has recently been even further refined (Wilson and Moral, 1996), and the same authors have also considered the use of Monte-Carlo methods based on importance sampling (Moral and Wilson, 1996). This remains an active area of research (Moral and Salmerón, 1999).

Other approximate techniques, based on the isomorphism between computing belief and network reliability, are discussed by Provan (1990), while Dubois and Prade (Dubois and Prade, 1990a) describe the approximation of belief functions by possibility measures. In addition, Voorbraak (1989) discusses the use of what he terms Bayesian approximations of belief functions. The Bayesian approximation $\underline{\mathrm{Bel}}(\cdot)$ of a belief function $\mathrm{Bel}(\cdot)$ is that established from the mass distribution $\underline{m}(\cdot)$ in the same way in which $\mathrm{Bel}(\cdot)$ is obtained from a mass distribution $m(\cdot)$, and $\underline{m}(\cdot)$ for a particular proposition is obtained from a given $m(\cdot)$ by:

$$\underline{m}(A) = \frac{\sum_{A \supseteq B} m(B)}{\sum_{c \supseteq \Theta} m(C).|C|} \tag{3.80}$$

if A is a singleton, otherwise $\underline{m}(A) = 0$. Finally, Tessem (1993) presents a method of approximation that reduces the number of computations required to combine mass functions by ignoring those focal elements with the lowest mass, showing that the approach performs well when compared with the consonant and Bayesian approximations.

It should be noted that, as mentioned by Wilson (1991), the methods discussed in this section are complementary to the use of valuation systems. Valuation systems provide an efficient means of computing marginal beliefs because they avoid computing the global distribution, computing only the belief on valuations over a subset of all the variables in the system. However, if the largest valuation in a valuation system is relatively big, computing the belief on that valuation will still be computationally expensive and this will increase the time taken to compute any given marginal. In such a situation, using one of the approximate methods to perform the combination has considerable attractions. It should also be pointed out that local computation methods flirt with intractability in another area. As Provan (1990) points out, the efficiency of local computation methods hinges upon finding a good representation of the evidential or valuation network as a hypertree (which can then be reduced to the Markov network in which propagation takes place). This is because using any old hypertree can increase complexity exponentially, and finding a good hypertree representation is an NP-hard problem. As a result, local computation is not guaranteed to give efficient calculation, it just often manages to.

3.5 Quantified logics

While approaches that reason directly with numerical distributions (either with or without the use of networks of some kind) are the most interesting methods for applying quantitative models of uncertainty from the point of view of this book, it is also worth considering some of the attempts to combine these models with logic since, as Bacchus (1990b) points out, logical systems are more expressive than systems such as causal networks,[22] and can have quite a transparent semantics.

3.5.1 Probabilistic logics

The classic paper on reasoning combining logic and probability is that of Nilsson (1986), though, unbeknown to him, he was restating for an artificial intelligence audience work that was originally carried out by Smith (1961) and de Finetti (1975). The paper considers the consequence of combining the probabilities assigned to P and $P \supset Q$, "$\supset$" standing for material implication, when the two are combined using modus ponens. In general the probabilities on a set of sentences do not completely determine the underlying joint distribution so that it is only possible to determine the bounds on derived sentences. Thus when deriving Q from P and $P \supset Q$ only the bounds on $\Pr(Q)$ may be obtained:

$$\Pr(P) + \Pr(P \supset Q) - 1 \leq \Pr(Q) \leq \Pr(P \supset Q) \tag{3.81}$$

However, this disadvantage is offset to some extent by the fact that because imprecise probabilities are derived, the formalism can handle incompletely specified probabilistic models. There are some difficulties, however, in reconciling Nilsson's work with standard probability theory. Chief among these is the fact that it uses probabilities of material implications rather than conditional probabilities. Since the probability of a material implication is rather different to a conditional probability, the logic is open to criticism (Dubois and Prade, 1990b, 1987c) on the grounds that the probability of Q is not correctly updated when information is learnt about P. In a more recent paper Nilsson (1993) suggests that associating the conditional value $\Pr(Q|P)$ with the implication $P \supset Q$ gives more natural results that include:

$$\Pr(Q|P)\Pr(P) \leq \Pr(Q) \leq 1 \tag{3.82}$$

However, this does not really solve the problem. The updating of $\Pr(Q)$ might now be more natural, but because the probability associated with $P \supset Q$ is no longer its probability $\Pr(P \supset Q)$, there is now a gap between the underlying logical mechanism and the proba-

---

22 In the sense that logical systems can be first order while causal networks, as mentioned above, are propositional.

bilistic propagation. Despite this problem, Nilsson's work has been extended by McLeish (1989; 1988) in a number of ways. The first extension is to use Cheeseman's (1985) maximum entropy method to improve the bounds on the probability of the propositions derived using the logic. The second extension is to cover cases in which:

$$\Pr(P) + \Pr(P \supset Q) < 1 \tag{3.83}$$

since these give invalid results for reasonable probability values in Nilsson's scheme. McLeish's last extension replaces the probabilities of P, $P \supset Q$ and Q with the relevant belief functions allowing her to explore notions of belief function entailment while still using the maximum entropy method. It is worth noting that in doing so she uses both the open and closed world assumptions discussed in Section 3.2.3. More recently Frisch and Haddaway (1994) have considered another extension of Nilsson's approach that has the useful property of possessing a deductive procedure that is an anytime algorithm thus finessing the computational problems of Nilsson's approach.[23]

Bundy (1985) has proved that any logic in which any uncertainty values, including probability, are directly associated with formulae cannot be truth-functional. In other words the truth of a compound formula cannot be computed directly from the truth of its parts. However, he argues that truth functionality is desirable since it would enable the tightest possible bounds on the uncertainty value of a formula to be calculated. As a result, Bundy has developed the incidence calculus (Bundy, 1985, 1990), a logic that enables truth functional probabilistic reasoning. In incidence calculus, probabilities are not associated with propositions, instead incidences are associated with formulae, and probabilities calculated from these incidences. An incidence is a set of possible worlds, each of which has an associated probability, and the incidence of a formula is the set of possible worlds in which the formula is true. Thus incidence has much in common with Carnap's (1962) view of probability, as well as being related to ideas of modality (Hughes and Cresswell, 1968) and rough truth (Parsons et al., 1992, 1995).

Further considerations are provided by Bacchus (1990b) who examines the semantics of probabilistic logic in considerable detail. He argues that a reasonably expressive language will need to be first order, and that a first order probabilistic language should distinguish between propositional probabilities, which involve degrees of belief such as "I believe that there is a 50% chance that tomorrow will be sunny," and statistical probabilities such as "25% of all April days in London are sunny." To handle these he devises two logics (the second is also described in (Bacchus, 1990a)) each with a different semantics, and then shows how the two types of probability can be combined. Similar results are pro-

---

23 Nilsson's approach is NP-complete for the propositional case—the case considered by Frisch and Haddaway—and undecidable for the first order case.

vided by Halpern (1989; 1990)[24] who takes the solution to the problem of dealing with statistical probabilities provided in (Bacchus, 1990a) and, arguing that it is often useful to combine reasoning using statistical information and information about beliefs, shows that it is possible to find a common framework for both kinds of knowledge. The resulting logic has also been proposed as the basis for another method of building probabilistic causal networks (Bacchus, 1993). The link between statistical probabilities and degrees of belief is also explored in (Bacchus et al., 1996).

Another interesting advance in combining probabilistic methods with deductive techniques is made by Güntzer et al. (1991). They deal with rule-based reasoning where every rule in the knowledge base has an associated conditional probability, and provide a set of inference rules for deducing connections between various events that are implicit in the knowledge base. These inference rules enable the bounds on the conditional probabilities of these new connections to be deduced, and the soundness of these bounds is proved. Clearly the new connections and their associated probabilities allow new facts to be deduced along with a probabilistic quantifier. It seems at first as if this formalism is a new probabilistic logic. However, the kind of links over which the probabilities are propagated are not logical implications, but a form of "causal" relation. Thus the formalism provides an alternative notation for probabilistic causal networks, providing a means of performing correct probabilistic calculations without explicitly building the causal network. Like causal networks, the representation is inherently propositional, and the proof procedure for any one query may not be used to answer another query. In a later paper (Thöne et al., 1992) the same authors demonstrate that their approach can handle multiply-connected networks to give the same results as Lauritzen and Spiegelhalter (1988), while arguing that it is really just a more accurate version of Quinlan's INFERNO (Quinlan, 1983b).

This work bears many similarities to that of Amarger et al. (1991). Although they tie their work in with the use of default rules, what Amarger et al. are essentially doing is to take a series of propositions, whose relationships are stated using imprecisely known probabilities, and inferring new probabilistic relations between them. Thus given the information that between 70% and 90% of students do sport, and between 85% and 90% of students are young, they show how to conclude what proportion of young people do sport. The most interesting point about the method that they propose, which is based upon local rules for calculating the tightest possible bounds just like Güntzer et al.'s, is that they require no prior probabilities, and that the existence of loops[25] in the graph of dependencies

---

24 The somewhat convoluted history seems to be that Bacchus' thesis dealt with statistical probabilities which were then refined by Halpern and combined with probabilities for dealing with belief. Bacchus then revised his thesis turning it into a book, covering probabilities for dealing with belief along the way, and devising a combined framework that, unlike Halpern's system, is complete.

25 Loops and cycles only occur in multiply-connected networks, and are distinguished as follows. In a loop two arcs meet head to head at one node and two arcs meet tail to tail at another node while in a cycle all the directed

between propositions serves to improve the bounds.

Other relevant work has been carried out by Ng and Subrahmanian who have considered the use of probabilities in deductive databases and logic programs (Ng and Subrahmanian, 1992b, 1991b). To do this they allow logical clauses to be annotated with probability intervals and provide rules for establishing the bounds on combinations of clauses that do not make the kind of restrictive assumptions about the independence of clauses required by previous efforts in logic programming (van Emden, 1986). The propagation rules are backed up by a full proof procedure, fixpoint theory, and a formal model theory that is shown to be probabilistic. This work is extended in (Ng and Subrahmanian, 1991a) to cover the use of nonmonotonic negation, which makes it possible to capture some kind of default reasoning, and in (Ng and Subrahmanian, 1992a) to cover objective probabilities. Now, it might not seem that objective probabilities raise any problems not covered by a scheme that can handle subjective probabilities, but this is not the case because of a technical hitch with Herbrand universes. Despite this problem Ng and Subrahmanian provide a means of answering queries and ensuring the consistency of the database when objective probabilities are used.

3.5.2   Possibilistic logic

Possibility theory has been extended by Dubois and Prade (1987b) to create a numerically quantified logic called possibilistic logic. In this formalism either a possibility or a necessity measure is attached to every formula of classical first order logic with non-vague predicates, and classical inference patterns, such as modus ponens and the resolution principle, are extended for such weighted clauses. As a result possibilistic logic provides a basis for theorem proving under uncertainty (Dubois et al., 1987) that, thanks to the combination rules for possibility measures, does not suffer from some of the problems of probabilistic logic. In particular, possibility theory allows the possibility of the conditional $\neg p \lor q$ to be interpreted as a conditional possibility. In addition it has been proved that inference using a linear resolution strategy generates a solution with the greatest possible lower bound on necessity, giving a simple means of determining the most certain conclusion that may be inferred from a set of uncertain clauses. Further work (Dubois et al., 1989, 1994a; Dubois and Prade, 1990d) has extended the system in a number of ways. Perhaps the most important extension is that of the resolution principle so that a clause weighted with a possibility measure can be combined with one weighted with a necessity value. In addition, a scheme for including vague predicates has been introduced, and possibilistic logic has been shown to be complete in the sense that any logical inconsistency in a set of clauses will be detected by repeated applications of the resolution principle. This compares well with probabilistic

---

arcs point in the same direction (clockwise or anticlockwise) (Pearl, 1988b, page 195).

logic, which can be shown to be incomplete. Other soundness and completeness results for possibilistic logic may be found in (Dubois et al., 1991a).

Some additional developments in possibilistic logic are worth mentioning. Just as in classical logic one can discover whether a clause is satisfiable either by syntactic or semantic means, so one can consider semantic ways of performing inference in possibilistic logic to go with the resolution method mentioned above. This is demonstrated by Lang (1990) who gives a method for finding the best interpretation, in the sense that it has the largest necessity measure, of a set of clauses of possibilistic logic. Around the same time Dubois and Prade (1991c) were considering the relationship between possibilistic logic and Gardenförs' (1988) idea of epistemic entrenchment[26] showing that, at a qualitative level, the relation between necessity measures is almost identical to the relation that defines epistemic entrenchment. This leads to the suggestion that possibilistic logic is a suitable method for handling inconsistent information since the inconsistencies can be eliminated using Gardenförs' method (Dubois and Prade, 1991e).

Possibilistic logic has been implemented in a number of interesting ways; as the POSLOG system, a possibilistic logic programming language, and as a possibilistic ATMS. POSLOG (Dubois et al., 1990a) is an automated theorem prover based on resolution refutation for first order clauses weighted with lower bounds on their possibility or necessity degree. The system is complete in that it has been proved that it finds optimal refutations— those refutations with maximal possibility or necessity degrees. In an extension of this work, the same authors (Dubois et al., 1991b) lay the groundwork for a logic programming environment based on Prolog in which clauses may be quantified with possibility measures. Such a logic programming language looks to be useful for solving min-max computations as well as reasoning with uncertain knowledge. The possibilistic ATMS (Dubois et al., 1990b) is an ATMS (de Kleer, 1986) in which both assumptions and justifications may be associated with a possibility weight and, since the propagation of the weights is carried out for every clause in the ATMS, there is no separation of the management of uncertainty from the usual functionality of an ATMS. Furthermore, the possibilistic ATMS allows inconsistent knowledge bases to be revised using the principles of epistemic entrenchment (Gärdenfors, 1988). Finally, it should be noted that Lang has provided a comprehensive discussion of computational aspects of possibilistic logic (Lang, 2000).

3.5.3 Belief function logics

There have also been a number of efforts to build a logical deductive system that employs evidence theory to deal with uncertain propositions. McLeish's (1989) combination of

---

26 Epistemic entrenchment can be thought of as a means of assigning priorities to propositions that enables a decision to be taken on how to revise a set of such propositions when some inconsistency is discovered.

logic and belief functions has already been mentioned. Hsia (1990) reformulates the theory of evidence in a way that is explicitly non set-theoretic with the aim of making the theory more applicable in domains which are not themselves set-theoretic. As a result he creates an alternative notation that leads naturally to systems of natural deduction. This work is extended in (Hsia, 1991a,c). In (Hsia, 1991a) the non-monotonic System P of Kraus et al. (Kraus et al., 1990) (see Section 4.5.1) is recreated using a logic quantified with belief functions where updating beliefs is carried out by Dempster's rule of conditioning. In the companion paper (Hsia, 1991c), the same quantified logic is justified from a philosophical standpoint. Hsia differentiates between "uncertainty of belief," which is quantified by subjective probabilities, from "uncertainty about belief." This new type of belief, it turns out, is nicely quantified by belief functions. Updating is, as noted above, carried out using Dempster's rule of conditioning, which allows Hsia to justify the use of Dempster's rule of combination on the basis of his rule of conditioning. Another attempt to combine logic and belief functions is Saffiotti's belief function logic (Saffiotti, 1992, 1991). In this system every sentence of a first order logic language is quantified with a pair of numbers $[a, b]$ that represent respectively the degree to which the sentence is known to be true, and the degree to which the sentence may be true. The quantification makes the logic a generalisation of standard first order logic that boasts a well defined semantics and notion of deduction in which the sentences that may be derived are determined by the rules of the underlying logic and the degrees to which they are believed are determined using the rules of belief functions. The logic also handles reasoning by cases and by, using the open-world assumption, provides a means of coping with partial inconsistency in a similar way to that proposed for possibilistic logic.

3.5.4   Other logical systems

The ideas of fuzzy sets can be combined with classical logic to form a "fuzzy logic" in which propositions can be true to some degree, and which can be used to reason with "linguistic quantifiers" such as "large" and "tall" by manipulating the relevant fuzzy sets. The pioneering work in combining fuzzy sets and logic to allow the representation of, and inference with, vague information was performed by Zadeh (for instance in (Zadeh, 1977, 1979, 1983a,b)). He described a system that generalised both two-valued and multi-valued logic by allowing all predicates, quantifiers, and the relations between predicates, to be described by fuzzy sets. Thus within fuzzy logic it is possible to provide a mathematical description of the statement:

If Hans has a new red Porsche then it is likely that his wife is young,

which Zadeh claims is able to take account of the natural fuzziness of the terms "new," "likely" and "young." Representation is handled by defining fuzzy sets for these fuzzy terms, and inference by applying methods for inferring the fuzzy term that is implied by what is known. A number of methods are proposed, including one that involves solving a non-linear program, but the most widely used is a generalisation of the classical inference pattern of modus ponens to fuzzy syllogisms of the form (Zadeh, 1985; Dubois and Prade, 1988e):

$$Q_1 As \ are \ Bs$$
$$\frac{Q_2(A \ and \ B)s \ are \ Cs}{QAs \ are \ (B \ and \ C)s}$$

where A, B and C are fuzzy sets and Q_1, Q_2 and Q are fuzzy quantifiers. A typical syllogism is:

$$most \ students \ are \ young$$
$$\frac{most \ young \ students \ are \ single}{most^2 \ students \ are \ young \ and \ single}$$

where $most^2$ indicates the product of *most* with itself. Such syllogisms, which are clearly generalisations of the kind of reasoning considered by Amarger et al. (1991), allow the inference of one fuzzy predicate from another and are intended to form the basis for the implementation of intelligent systems that use fuzzy logic.

The idea behind Zadeh's proposal is extremely appealing, and many people have been moved to build upon his work. There are many applications of fuzzy logic—see for example those collected by Mamdani and Gaines (1981) and those mentioned by Zadeh (1994), bearing in mind that the term "fuzzy logic," which originally only referred to the kind of system discussed in the last few paragraphs, has now been broadened (Zadeh, 1994) to cover any kind of work involving the notion of fuzzy sets—especially in the domain of control where a vast number of successes have been reported. There has also been a lot of theoretical work done on fuzzy sets, ranging from philosophical assaults on the basis of the theory (Haack, 1979; Elkan, 1993, 1994b) and their rebuttals (Fox, 1981; Dubois and Prade, 1994; Dubois et al., 1994c; Watkins, 1995),[27] to detailed elaborations of the nature of the connectives it uses, for example (Smets and Magrez, 1987).

Building on the theoretical work on fuzzy logic, there have been several approaches to providing some form of fuzzy logic programming environment. One could consider FRIL (Baldwin and Zhou, 1984) to be such an environment, though it is based upon the mathematics of relations rather than the predicate calculus, with a fuzzy degree of membership being associated with each tuple of a relation. As Dubois and Prade (1991a) point out, such a degree may be interpreted in a number of ways—as a degree of association

---

27 Indeed, there is a whole journal issue (IEEE Expert, 1994) devoted to one skirmish between the supporters and opponents of fuzzy logic.

between the elements of a tuple (that is the degree to which they all belong together in the tuple) as a measure of confidence about the information that is stored in the tuple (that is as a measure of the certainty of the information) and as an estimate of the degree to which the tuple is a typical example of the relation to which it belongs. Baldwin and Zhou opt to take the degree of membership attached to a tuple to be the degree to which it satisfies the relation it belongs to, and, in order to answer a query on a set of fuzzy relations, FRIL combines relations and the fuzzy degrees of membership of the members of the relations to compute which facts fit the query and to what degree. Thus FRIL is inherently fuzzy, but can also deal with point, interval and fuzzy probabilities (Baldwin, 1986; Baldwin and Martin, 1996).

A subsequent development (Baldwin, 1987), which has now been combined with the fuzzy relational inference mechanism described above, is support logic programming. In this system each clause is quantified with a *support pair*, that is a pair of numbers that represent the possible and necessary degree to which the statement is supported. Roughly speaking, the possible support is the largest degree of support that might be provided for a clause and the necessary support is the smallest degree of support that is known to be provided. These degrees of support are related to possibility measures (and their dual necessity measures) and the measures introduced in Shafer's (1976) theory of evidence as discussed below (Section 4.6). Another approach to providing fuzzy logic programming is FProlog (Martin et al., 1987), which is a fuzzy Prolog interpreter. This builds the association of a degree of membership to clauses into the proof mechanism, so that each time a fuzzy fact is used to define a subgoal the degree of membership of the goal within the set of true facts is adjusted according to the rules of fuzzy logic. This means that the degree of membership is in fact a degree of truth. In the FProlog system, backtracking may be triggered by partial failure when a truth value falls below a certain threshold, and the *not* operator is extended so that when the query X succeeds with truth value v, $not(X)$ succeeds with degree $1 - v$. A number of other fuzzy logic programming environments are surveyed in (Dubois et al., 1991a).

It is also possible to build systems that combine rough sets and logic, both for reasoning about data (Fariñas del Cerro and Orłowska, 1985; Pawlak, 1991) and for handling uncertainty (Parsons et al., 1992, 1995), as well as systems that combine logic with other ideas on how to handle uncertainty. It is even possible to abstract away from a specific model of uncertainty, providing general frameworks for combining logic with any of a number of different models (Parsons and Fox, 1994; Lakshmanan and Shiri, 1996).

3.6 Summary

This chapter has surveyed a number of formal systems that handle different types of imperfect information. All the methods discussed may be considered "quantitative" since they use numbers to specify the degree of imperfection which should be attached to particular pieces of information, and may be contrasted with the "qualitative" approaches that will be covered in the next chapter (though in places the distinction is so fine as to be invisible).

The main models considered were probability, possibility, and evidence theories—three models that are similar in many ways. In particular, all three are intended to offer ways of handling uncertainty, that is in the sense of handling the kind of imperfection that arises due to imperfect observations. Such observations lead to the problem of not knowing whether a particular fact is true or not, so that all that can be said about the fact is that there is some probability, possibility, or belief that it is true (or is false). The exact way in which this information is represented differs from model to model, as does the way in which pieces of information expressed using the model are interpreted (indeed, different variants of the models have different interpretations), but it is essentially the same kind of information that is being represented.[28] This means that the bulk of this chapter, whether discussing models based on logic or models based on networks, has concentrated on uncertainty to the exclusion of other types of imperfection. Even when not covering probability, possibility, and evidence theories, this chapter has looked mainly at methods for handling uncertainty, since this is also the domain of Spohn's ordinal conditional functions and certainty factors. This seems entirely appropriate given the fact that handling uncertainty is the main focus of this book.

---

28 Though evidence theory does, of course, provide a neat way of handling a lack of information about what belief should be attached to a piece of information and so could be considered to provide a model for representing incomplete information, "ignorance" in the terms used in Chapter 2.

4 Qualitative methods for reasoning with imperfect information

Men make their own history, but not of their own free will; not under the circumstances they themselves have chosen but under the given and inherited circumstances with which they are directly confronted.

Karl Marx, *The Eighteenth Brumaire of Louis Bonaparte*

The previous chapter surveyed systems that deal with uncertain and imprecise information by attaching numbers to the propositions with which they deal. In these systems the numbers are then interpreted as measures of the certainty or precision of the information. In using numbers in this way, such systems employ perhaps the most obvious method of dealing with imperfect information, though using the term "obvious" is not intended to be disparaging. Indeed, in many ways the fact that the methods are obvious is one of their strengths—it is quite clear how to interpret one degree of certainty relative to another, and the interval $[0, 1]$ clearly has more than enough alternative values to make all the necessary distinctions. However, there are problems with purely numerical approaches. These include the well-known objection that is often levelled at probabilistic systems:

where are all the numbers coming from?

Before dismissing this kind of objection as a partisan attack, it is worth remembering that even as ardent a probabilist as Peter Cheeseman has made exactly this point (indeed these are his words (Cheeseman, 1988a)). When building an expert system, the obvious reply is to get the numbers from some domain expert, but, as Cheeseman points out, even this expert may well not have sufficient information to establish valid probabilities. A better solution is to build a second system that can learn the necessary values[1] and, as discussed in Chapter 3, research in this area is becoming quite widespread. However, not having complete numerical information about a situation can still be a problem and a growing number of authors have considered different models for reasoning that can handle such situations.[2] Their work is the subject of this chapter, along with a survey of some of the work on relating and integrating different models.

---

1 Provided, of course, that enough data exists for the values to be inferred with sufficient accuracy.
2 Obviously there are other solutions, one being the use of methods such as the principle of maximum entropy, and some discussion on the relative merits of such solutions is given in Chapter 5.

4.1 Introduction

The systems discussed in this chapter may be classified as being able to cope with either partial numerical information, or a complete lack of numerical information, and it is in these senses of "not completely quantitative" that they are referred to as "qualitative." Some of these models are closely connected with those discussed in Chapter 3. For instance interval probability systems (Section 4.3), which allow for the representation of, and reasoning with, imprecisely known probabilities, are close to both probability theory and evidence theory, though not under the transferable belief interpretation used in this book. Many of the models discussed here fit the description given by Wellman (1994) for "qualitative probabilistic methods." He defines such models as being concerned with imprecise statements about belief where:

an imprecise statement involving degrees of belief (is) a statement that the degrees of belief satisfy some constraint. Thus, whereas a fully precise description of an uncertain belief state will assign a unique number to the probability of each proposition, an imprecise description will merely constrain the probability to belong to some set.

Other models considered here are rather different. These include the methods of qualitative physics (Section 4.2), which are included partly because they are used in later chapters, and partly because they are used to model particular aspects of the world when there is little or no numerical information available—the fact that the aspects concerned are rather different from the usual ones considered in research into handling imperfect information do not make them irrelevant. However, most of the systems covered in this chapter lie somewhere between the two extremes with enough non-numerical aspects to warrant calling them "qualitative" rather than "quantitative" (though "symbolic" would be equally good as a description).

These qualitative systems do not fall into easy and obvious classifications, so a few words about their organisation are relevant. The first part of this chapter considers systems for qualitative reasoning about physical systems under the heading "Qualitative Physics." Since this ends with a look at systems that use interval values it seemed natural to have the next section consider interval probability and associated ideas, and so it does. This then leads to a section on abstractions of quantitative systems, in which all the systems that are essentially numerical, but which abstract away from actually using numbers, are grouped. Such systems were once neatly described by David Poole, and I paraphrase, as being those in which the calculations are numerical, but which one squints at from a distance without using one's glasses. The result is that rather than seeing the exact numerical results, all that can be discerned is that one number is bigger than another, or that one number increases and another decreases. Since there is a good deal of commonality between such systems and systems for carrying out defeasible reasoning, that is reasoning where new information can invalidate old conclusions, the following section is on defeasible reasoning. Finally, in preparation for later work on combining and relating different methods, existing work in this area is considered.

4.2   Qualitative physics

The paper that is always cited as being the foundational work in qualitative reasoning is Hayes' Naïve Physics Manifesto (Hayes, 1978) in which he urged practitioners of artificial intelligence to (Hayes, 1985b):

put away childish things by building large scale formalizations.

His suggestion was that real progress in the field would come about by attempting to model a large part of human commonsense knowledge about the real world, and his first attempt created an initial theory of the behaviour of liquids (Hayes, 1985a). This work was built upon first order logic, the traditional tool of symbolic artificial intelligence. At the same time, and to some extent as a result of Hayes' proposal, work that modelled complex systems in a way that mirrored the kind of approach adopted by engineers was emerging.

4.2.1   Qualitative reasoning

There are, broadly speaking, three such approaches to building such engineering models. These approaches have in common the fact that they deal with abstractions of real numbers into positive, negative, and zero valued quantities rather than dealing with numbers them-selves. The first approach is that of Kuipers (1984) who takes a set of differential equations, abstracts them to just consider their qualitative impact, and then uses them as a set of con-straints on the possible values of the state variables. This approach has been implemented as the QSIM software system (Kuipers, 1986). The second approach, taken by de Kleer and Brown (1984) and Williams, (1984) is to build libraries of components, each of which has a well defined qualitative behaviour described by sets of qualitative differential equations, and connect these components together to build a qualitative model. Some of this work is implemented as the ENVISION software system, which takes its name from the process of "envisionment" by which behaviour is inferred from the structure of the system. The final approach not only models components, but also the processes that they may undergo. Work on this approach is primarily due to Forbus (1984), and is closest in spirit to the work on naïve physics. In addition, Forbus's approach goes further than the others in allowing sets of objects to have group behaviours over and above their individual ones, thus providing a far richer modelling language. This is, of course, just an introductory sketch of the field that has, at the time of writing, eluded a definitive study. Papers by Cohn (1989) and Coiera

Table 4.1
Qualitative addition

⊕	[+]	[0]	[−]	[?]
[+]	[+]	[+]	[?]	[?]
[0]	[+]	[0]	[−]	[?]
[−]	[?]	[−]	[−]	[?]
[?]	[?]	[?]	[?]	[?]

(1992) come closest to providing such a survey, while Kuipers' book (Kuipers, 1994) gives a detailed treatment of the work of his group.

The core of the first two approaches described above is the idea of qualitative differential equations. Rather than attempting to deal with a mass of numerical data, values are only distinguished as positive ([+]), zero ([0]), negative ([−]), or unknown ([?]),[3] the so-called *quantity space*. These values are sufficient to identify many of the interesting features of the behaviour of the important variables in a given system. Briefly, this works as follows. Consider a very simple system that may be described by the equations:

$$\frac{dx}{dt} + x = k_1$$

$$\frac{d^2x}{dt^2} + k_2 = 0$$

where k_1 and k_2 are positive constants and x is a state variable. The qualitative abstraction of these equations, in which all numerical values are replaced by [+], [0] or [−] is:

$$\frac{dx}{dt} \oplus x = [+]$$

$$\frac{d^2x}{dt^2} \oplus [+] = [0]$$

where $\oplus$ is qualitative addition, as described by Table 4.1. To solve the pair of equations, sets of qualitative values that satisfy them are sought. For instance:

$$x = [+]$$

$$\frac{dx}{dt} = [+]$$

$$\frac{d^2x}{dt^2} = [−]$$

In other words, x is positive, its first time derivative is positive, but its second time derivative is negative. This set of values indicates that the value of x over time will rise over time to some limiting value as in Figure 4.1. The limit may be unknown, but it is clear

---

3 These symbolic values are often also written as +, 0, −, and ?.

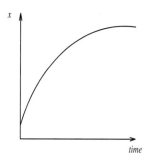

Figure 4.1
The qualitative behaviour of x

that the value of x will eventually stop rising, and this less precise information may be sufficient for the task in hand. Clearly if it is necessary to establish that x has a maximum value then the information that may be deduced is quite adequate, and in many cases the fact that it is possible to learn something from qualitative reasoning far outweighs the fact that what may be learnt is not very detailed.

Qualitative methods have been widely used, a fact that is not surprising when one considers that much of the original work was driven by the desire to model real systems. Two of the early papers on qualitative reasoning (de Kleer, 1984; Williams, 1984) were concerned with the analysis of digital circuits, and similar attempts with a distinct flavour of naïve physics are provided by Davis (1984), Genesereth (1984) and Barrow (1984), while Mohammed and Simmons (1986) have considered the use of qualitative simulation in modelling the fabrication of semiconductor devices. More recently, Ormsby et al. (1991) have applied qualitative techniques to the diagnosis of faults in the electrical systems of automobiles. However, electronics is far from being the only domain to which qualitative methods are applicable. Falkenheiner and Forbus (1988) have tackled the simulation of a more complex system, namely the steam plant of a naval vessel, albeit with a number of simplifying assumptions, and Kuipers (1987) has used QSIM to model processes in the human body, the human body being a system that is considerably more complex than any man-made artifact, and certainly less well understood. Ardizzone et al. (1988) have modelled cell growth with a qualitative system, Hunt and Cooke (1994) have modelled photosynthesis, and Rickel and Porter (1994) have modelled plant physiology. Farley and Lin (1991) and Brajnik and Lines (1998) have modelled economic systems,[4] while Hangos et al. (1992) discuss the control of a distillation column by using a qualitative model both to determine what actions will give the correct response and to predict the result of a given

---

4 Qualitative reasoning has a long and distinguished tradition in economics, having first been used to model economic systems many years before the inception of artificial intelligence.

M, V   *m, v*

Figure 4.2
Two colliding masses

action, and Hurme et al. (1991) make a similar analysis of a chemical recycling process but with the aim of using the qualitative simulation to identify the conditions under which profit can be maximised. Finally Koivisto et al. (1989) and Catino (1993) discuss applications in chemical engineering.

4.2.2   Order of magnitude systems

Despite the success of qualitative methods, there are some problems with qualitative reasoning that make it unsuitable for modelling certain systems. These problems stem from the limited number of values that any constant or variable can adopt. Raiman (1986) illustrates this with a simple example from mechanics. Consider two masses that collide while travelling towards one another along the same line (Figure 4.2). One has a large mass M and velocity V, the other has a small mass and velocity m and v. The net momentum from left to right above is given by the law of the conservation of momentum as:

$$MV_{net} = MV - mv$$

Since M, V, m, and v are all positive values, they all have qualitative value $[+]$, and the net rightwards momentum is established by the calculation:

$$MV_{net} = [+] \otimes [+] \ominus [+] \otimes [+]$$

where $\ominus$ is the operator representing the difference of two qualitative values and $\otimes$ is the operator representing the product of two such values (see Table 4.2). It is clear that the product of two positive values will itself be positive so that the calculation reduces to:

$$MV_{net} = [+] \ominus [+]$$

Now, applying $\ominus$ to determine the difference of two values that are only known to be positive will give a result which may be either positive, negative or zero, depending on the relative sizes of the values. Thus qualitative reasoning can only deduce that the overall rightwards momentum will be $[?]$, while intuitively it is possible to see that it will be $[+]$

Table 4.2
Qualitative subtraction and multiplication

⊖	[+]	[0]	[−]	[?]
[+]	[?]	[+]	[+]	[?]
[0]	[−]	[0]	[+]	[?]
[−]	[−]	[−]	[?]	[?]
[?]	[?]	[?]	[?]	[?]

⊗	[+]	[0]	[−]	[?]
[+]	[+]	[0]	[−]	[?]
[0]	[0]	[0]	[0]	[0]
[−]	[−]	[0]	[+]	[?]
[?]	[?]	[0]	[?]	[?]

because MV is much larger than mv.[5]

The problem of coping with situations like this, which cause difficulties for qualitative reasoning techniques but that are readily handled by people in everyday life, has been investigated by a number of authors. The first solution was proposed by Raiman (1986). He introduced a system called FOG that allowed the representation of "order of magnitude" concepts. Thus it allows the statement that, for instance, A is negligible with respect to B, A Ne B, or that A has the same sign and order of magnitude as B, A Co B. These relations are then used to define a set of inference rules such as:

$$\frac{A \quad Ne \quad B}{A \quad Ne \quad C}$$
$$B \quad Co \quad C$$

So that if A is much smaller than B, which is about the same size as C, then A is much smaller than C. In all Raiman provides 30 such rules of inference, giving a semantics for the approach that is based on non-standard analysis, and FOG has been used to model analog circuits (Dague et al., 1987). The FOG approach has also been discussed by Dubois and Prade (1989b; 1991g) who have considered the problem that is caused by the use of non-standard analysis as a basis for a semantics—namely that the results are only valid in the limit. In order to cope with situations in which A Co B does not mean that A and B are infinitely close together, they propose a new interpretation in terms of an interval on the ratio of A to B. This allows them to validate the inference rules, and allows a sensible limit on the chaining of inferences such as:

---

5 To some extent this problem is a straw man. Certainly systems such as QSIM provide a way around it. Faced with such a situation, QSIM would identify that the result of the subtraction would depend upon the relative magnitudes of MV and mv. Rather than return the overall momentum as ?, the system would introduce the quantity $MV - mv$ as a landmark value and give three possible behaviours, one for each qualitative value of the landmark. Thus it would predict that if $MV - mv$ is positive, the net momentum would be leftwards, if $MV - mv$ is negative, the momentum would be rightwards, and if $MV - mv$ is zero, the net momentum would be zero. However, Raiman's main point is still correct—resolving this problem, even with the branching behaviours, involves stepping outside the qualitative reasoning and selecting one output from many (and a typical qualitative model will throw out many such branch points).

$$
\begin{array}{ccc}
30 & Co & 31 \\
31 & Co & 32 \\
\hline
30 & Co & 32
\end{array}
$$

to be established that prevents the derivation of 30 Co 1000 without the need for an arbitrary cut-off. In the later paper Dubois and Prade also consider the application of the system to probabilistic reasoning. Work on a system that is rather similar to FOG has also been carried out by Dormoy and Raiman (1988), and more recently both Raiman (1991) and Yip (1993; 1996) have worked on other systems that attempt to capture the form of reasoning hinted at by FOG in which certain factors are disregarded because they are so much smaller than others. Further work on similar ideas has been carried out by Dague who gives a means of obtaining smooth changes between the orders of magnitude that are recognised (Dague, 1993b), and of incorporating numerical information (Dague, 1993a). These ideas are implemented in systems known as ROM[K] and ROM[ℜ] respectively.

Another scheme for order of magnitude reasoning is due to Mavrovouniotis and Stephanopoulos (1987; 1989) who have formalised the representation of relations such as $A > B$ to give a system called O[M] that they claim is expressive enough for all engineering problems, and that compares well with FOG. The semantics of the relations is provided in terms of the bounds on the ratio between A and B, and two possible interpretations are given. The first is mathematically correct, but conservative, and the second is heuristic, but more aggressive in the inferences it sanctions and so provides results that are closer to those produced by people. O[M] has been applied to problems in process engineering (Mavrouniotis and Stephanopoulos, 1988).

4.2.3 Qualitative algebras

Order of magnitude methods provide one means of making qualitative reasoning slightly less abstract and therefore less prone to making the vacuous prediction that a quantity could be positive, negative or zero. Another approach to reducing abstraction is to use more quantitative information alongside the qualitative information. This was the approach taken by Berleant and Kuipers (Kuipers and Berleant, 1988; Berleant and Kuipers, 1992) who developed a system in which both qualitative and quantitative information is maintained and used simultaneously during a simulation, allowing qualitative values to be checked against their quantitative counterparts to remove over-abstract values. A very similar idea is that suggested by Williams (1988). He extends the idea of having a set of qualitative equations that describe a system to the idea of having a set of equations some of which are qualitative and some of which are quantitative. These equations are written in terms of an algebra known as Q1, which has operands that include both the real numbers and the standard quantity space and has operations over both. By using the purely quantitative

Figure 4.3
A set of semiqualitative intervals

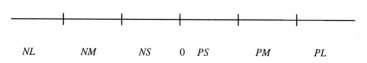

Figure 4.4
A set of interval values

information to establish the quantitative value of interesting variables, and then mapping
these into qualitative values where appropriate, Williams shows that it is possible to
establish conclusions that would be unobtainable in a system in which all quantitative
information was mapped into qualitative values before any reasoning took place. Q1 was
later reformulated as an algebra SR1 (Williams, 1991) that has a combined domain of
qualitative values and reals so that it is possible to, for instance, add $[+]$ to 25, while
something very similar to SR1 was suggested in the context of probability theory by Fox
and Krause (1990) (this will be discussed in more detail in Chapter 6). Other work in the
same vein is that of Goyal and Shoham (1993).

A slightly different approach to using qualitative and quantitative information is to effectively combine the reals and the standard qualitative values by using a set of interval
values rather than keeping them separate and reasoning over both sets of values. In its simplest form this provides a system of semiqualitative reasoning (Parsons and Dohnal, 1992,
1995) (the name contrasting nicely with Kuipers' (1994) "semiquantitative reasoning"), in
which the values of variables and constants are restricted to a set of $2k + 1$ intervals, for
instance those in Figure 4.3. This set of intervals covers all numbers from ∞ to $-\infty$, and
the intervals are continuous and non-overlapping, so that any real number falls into one,
and only one, interval. The intervals are symmetric about zero, which is a distinguished
value, and there are k positive and k negative intervals. The boundaries of the intervals
may be set by an arithmetic or geometric progression, or may be chosen to reflect what
are considered to be interesting values. Despite intense discussions of the validity of this
approach (Struss, 1988a; Kuipers, 1988; Struss, 1988b), it has proved rather popular—it
is, for instance, possible to capture the O[M] system using exactly this method (Parsons,
1993).

The idea of a set of interval values is also the basis for Travé-Massuyès and Piera's

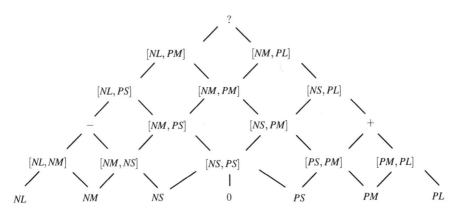

Figure 4.5
A set of sets of interval values

attempt (Piera and Travé-Massuyès, 1989) to provide a:

unifying mathematical framework for qualitative models using in qualitative reasoning

In a series of papers (Piera and Travé-Massuyès, 1989; Travé-Massuyès and Piera, 1989; Travé-Massuyès et al., 1989), the limits of interval-based or semiqualitative methods were explored. The nut of their suggestion is that from an arbitrary partition of the real numbers it is possible to build up a nested family of sets of interval values. Thus from the set of values in Figure 4.4, in which *NL* denotes "negative large," *NM* denotes "negative medium," and *NS* denotes "negative small," it is possible to build up the family of values in Figure 4.5. Then, provided that the operations defined over the intervals obey certain conditions, the different sets of intervals form a family of qualitative algebras that are capable of describing situations at differing levels of precision. Furthermore, Travé-Massuyès and Piera show that it is possible to use the algebras together in combination, making use of the trade-off between being precise and saving computational expense, and switching between them to maintain the optimal degree of abstraction. This idea is rather similar to that suggested by Murthy (1988).

Of course when taking the interval-handling route, there is no reason to restrict oneself to crisp intervals. It is perfectly possible to use fuzzy intervals, and a number of authors have chosen this direction. One of the earliest suggestions is that of Nordvik et al. (1988), though they do little more than point out that fuzzy sets could be usefully employed to reduce some of the overabstraction typical of qualitative approaches. A more complete proposal is that of Dubois and Prade (1989a) in which interval values such as "negative large"[6] are interpreted as overlapping fuzzy sets as in Figure 4.6, and the combinator tables for the usual quantity space expanded to cover these new operands. Other systems that

---

6 Indeed these values were originally suggested by Dubois and Prade in this paper and borrowed by Travé-Massuyès and Piera.

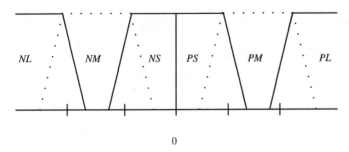

0

Figure 4.6
A set of fuzzy interval values

combine fuzzy sets and qualitative reasoning are described by Shen and Leitch (1993) and Bousson and Travé-Massuyès (1993).

Finally, it should be noted that there have been numerous other attempts to extend qualitative reasoning using limited amounts of numerical information, including (Féray Beaumont, 1991; Steyer et al., 1992; Sticklen et al., 1991; Gao and Durrant-Whyte, 1994).

4.3   Interval-based systems

As mentioned above, one of the main motivations for qualitative approaches to reasoning with imperfect information is the difficulty of obtaining the mass of detailed numerical information required by quantitative models. One obvious response to a lack of such information is to relax the requirement for point values, allowing interval values to be specified. This has been discussed by a number of authors. Indeed, several such approaches have already been covered. Evidence theory, when interpreted as talking about upper and lower probabilities, is a theory of interval probabilities, and so much of the work of Fagin and Halpern (Fagin and Halpern, 1991; Halpern and Fagin, 1992) discussed in Section 3.2.3 falls into this class. Similarly, since most of the work that has been done on probabilistic logics involves interval values, all the work surveyed in Section 3.5.1 may be considered as work on interval-based systems. This section discusses a number of other suggestions.

Before beginning, however, it is worth noting that there is something of a conundrum at the heart of work on interval probabilities. When talking about intervals of some measure of uncertainty one is clearly specifying a second-order distribution of this measure irrespective of whether this is done implicitly or explicitly. As several authors have pointed out, for instance Kyburg (1989) and Neapolitan (1996), higher-order probability distributions achieve nothing that lower order distributions cannot do equally well, and probability intervals can always be reduced to point values. So why are interval probabilities so popular? I am not sure that I can provide an answer, but I think that the reason is likely to be bound up with the fact that interval representations, whether of probability or not, are intuitively attractive because they make the imprecision clear. That this imprecision can be reduced to give a point value matters not a jot—it is still nice to be able to see that it exists (a fact that might be related to the results reported by Ellsberg and discussed in Section 2.5.1).

If probabilities are allowed to take on interval values, two consequences immediately follow. The first is that a distribution of interval values will not be additive since, typically, the upper probability values of a distribution will sum to more than one and the lower values will sum to less than one. The second is that a single distribution of interval values will be consistent with a whole set of distributions of point values, and it is therefore no surprise that many people have studied interval probabilities by means of studying sets of probabilities. From this set-based point of view (1990), the upper probability of a proposition A may be determined from the set S of probability distributions across A:

$$\Pr^*(A) = \sup_{\Pr \in S} \Pr(A) \tag{4.1}$$

as may the lower probability:

$$\Pr_*(A) = \inf_{\Pr \in S} \Pr(A) \tag{4.2}$$

and these two values are duals of one another:

$$\Pr^*(A) = 1 - \Pr_*(\neg A) \tag{4.3}$$

Provided that A and B are disjoint events:

$$\Pr^*(A \cup B) \ \leq \ \Pr^*(A) + \Pr^*(B) \tag{4.4}$$
$$\Pr_*(A \cup B) \ \geq \ \Pr_*(A) + \Pr_*(B) \tag{4.5}$$

while:

$$A \subset B \ \implies \ \Pr^*(A) \leq \Pr^*(B) \tag{4.6}$$
$$A \subset B \ \implies \ \Pr_*(A) \leq \Pr_*(B) \tag{4.7}$$

Set functions that have these properties are the *capacities* studied by Choquet (1953). If in addition $\Pr^*(A)$ obeys the condition:

$$\Pr^*(A \cup B) + \Pr^*(A \cap B) \leq \Pr^*(A) + \Pr^*(B) \tag{4.8}$$

then in Choquet's terminology it is a 2-alternating capacity. If $\Pr^*(A)$ is a 2-alternating capacity then $\mathrm{Pr}_*(A)$ obeys the condition:

$$\mathrm{Pr}_*(A \cup B) + \mathrm{Pr}_*(A \cap B) \geq \mathrm{Pr}_*(A) + \mathrm{Pr}_*(B) \tag{4.9}$$

and is a 2-monotone capacity. The theory of capacities provides a means of comparing different interval methods. Thus Weichselberger and Pöhlmann's (1990) interval probabilities are Choquet capacities of order two, while belief and plausibility measures are Choquet capacities of infinite order—capacities for which the inequalities of (4.8) and (4.9) hold for any number of disjoint events.

A particularly neat approach to the manipulation of these sets of probability distributions is permitted if the sets are constrained to be convex. Indeed, if, as is usually the case, the set of probabilities is not just convex but also a polytope then (Snow, 1986) it is easy to define the set, and computationally cheap and simple to revise when new probabilistic information becomes available. In particular, there are methods for updating values that are based on linear programming (Snow, 1991). Other important work on the subject of convex sets of probabilities is that of Moral and colleagues, which can be thought of as taking place within their axiomatic approach to propagating uncertainty measures by local computation (Cano et al., 1993) (though they began working on convex sets before considering local computation). The first part of the work that will be considered here (Moral and de Campos, 1991; Cano et al., 1991) discussed previous results concerning the different ways convex sets of probabilities could be updated given new evidence, and proposed suitable combination rules. Since the sets of measures generated by these rules are not necessarily probabilities, further work was required (Moral, 1992) to produce a method for transforming them. Once this was achieved, it was possible to use the combination method along with the local computation scheme to propagate the values through directed acyclic graphs (Cano et al., 1992). Further work has investigated the relationship between convex sets of probabilities and other interval methods (de Campos et al., 1994), the use of approximate methods for the propagation of such convex sets (Cano et al., 1994), and a number of different concepts of independence that may be proposed in such a framework (de Campos and Moral, 1995). More recently Cozman has also been studying notions of independence in the context of convex sets and their use in Bayesian networks (Cozman, 1997, 1999, 2000).

However, despite all the attractive properties of convex sets of probabilities, there are some problems with using them. As Kyburg and Pittarelli (1992) point out, convex sets are actually too weak a representation in that it is possible to construct a convex set from two convex sets of probabilities that contains probability distributions which are not compatible with the information that the set was constructed to reflect. Furthermore, there are situations that cannot be represented by any convex set of probabilities but which can be easily represented by other sets of probability distributions. Together these seem to be a good argument for the adoption of the same authors' set-based Bayesian approach (1996). In this formalism imprecise beliefs are quantified by sets of probability distributions that are subsets of convex sets, thus providing a more precise representation and one that will not generate incompatible distributions. Another solution applicable in situations in which convex sets are not appropriate is that of Snow's (1994b) ensemble of sets of distributions. In particular, ensembles of sets permit the representation of situations in which probabilities of propositions are initially unordered, but become partially ordered as evidence is gathered. A further alternative is provided by Kleiter (2000).

A system that has many of the same properties as convex sets of probabilities but is semantically rather different, is that of Walley's lower previsions (Walley, 1996). The idea is that the lower prevision of A, $\underline{\Pr}(A)$, represents the highest price that one is prepared to pay for the gamble A while the upper prevision of A, $\overline{\Pr}(A)$, represents the minimum price for which one would be prepared to sell A. In a similar way, the lower conditional prevision $\underline{\Pr}(A|B)$ represents the maximum price one would pay for the gamble A were B known to be true. Walley argues that this is a better semantic foundation than that of imprecise probabilities, which is used by most interval probability methods, and shows that there are situations that lower previsions can model better than other interval methods. Another formulation of this approach, in the form of a logic, is provided by Wilson and Moral (1994).

Another approach to dealing with interval probabilities that differs slightly from those discussed so far is to use a fixed set of intervals onto which imprecisely known values are mapped rather than specifying bounds on the values. Thus, given an event X, rather than specifying that $\Pr(X)$ is known to be in the interval $[0.3, 0.5]$, it is possible to break up the unit interval of probabilities into values "unlikely," "quite likely," and "very likely" that correspond to the intervals $[0, 0.3]$, $[0.3, 0.6]$, $[0.6, 1]$ and associate the "linguistic" value "quite likely" with X. One of the most theoretically satisfying analyses of this kind of reasoning is that provided by Dubois et al. (1992), who also make the connection with the qualitative algebras of Travé-Massuyès and Piera (1989). Another nice analysis is that of Lamata and Moral (1994) who describe the propagation of linguistic terms represented by fuzzy and interval probabilities using the local computation framework defined by Cano et al. (1993). There are also numerous more pragmatic applications of the idea although these frequently do not appear in the mainstream artificial intelligence literature. For instance, Fox et al. (1980) developed a system for the diagnosis of dyspepsia in which the conditional probabilities of disease given symptoms were mapped onto a simple qualitative indication for or against the disease. When compared with a full probabilistic analysis (carried out using the, then standard, assumption of conditionally independent evidence, and combining evidence using (3.16)) it was found that the diagnoses produced by the qualitative approach were virtually identical to those produced by the probabilistic approach. A second diagnostic system (Fox et al., 1985), this time for lukaemia diagnosis, also provided similar results. In this case the full numerical analysis used certainty factors, and the linguistic values (though this terminology was not used in the paper) distinguished between "certain" influences which took value 1, and "non-certain" influences which took value 0.5. In this case, the diagnostic accuracy of the non-numerical system was actually higher than its numerical counterpart, agreeing with the domain expert in 69% rather than 64% of cases. More recently, Chard (1991) considered the use of different sets of linguistic values in the diagnosis of gynecological complaints finding that:

a Bayesian system does not seem to be grossly affected by the use of subjective (linguistic)[7] probability estimates, provided that the system is focussed on conditions with relatively high prior probability.

Tu et al. (1993) also make use of linguistic values in assessing the eligibility of patients for clinical trials, though the way that they manipulate the values suggests that they are closer to possibilities than probabilities, and they stress the fact that this kind of analysis produces complementary information to that provided by the use of numerical probabilities. Linguistic values have also been considered in the context of Aleliunas' (1990) probabilistic logic and it is also possible to use such values in combination with evidence theory. Finally I (Parsons, 1994) have made a very straightforward attempt at using linguistic values in evidence theory, an attempt that is heavily influenced by the work of Dubois et al. (1992). The resulting method identifies which member of the frame of discernment is most supported by a number of pieces of evidence whose values are, at best, specified as intervals.

Of more direct use to those interested in applying network models in the absence of precise probabilistic information than many of the methods covered so far is the work of Fertig and Breese (1990). These two authors consider how interval probability values, defined in terms of the lower bounds of probabilities on propositions, may be propagated through influence diagrams using the transformations suggested by Shachter (1986a). Initially the approach only considered networks built using chance nodes, but in a later paper (Breese and Fertig, 1991) it was extended to networks including decision and value nodes. A similar approach is that proposed by van der Gaag (1991), in which an incomplete set of probabilities is taken as a set of constraints upon the joint probability distribution and the probability intervals are computed by solving a linear program. The approach differs, though, in that it is applied within the context of join trees rather than influence diagrams.

As mentioned above, all of these interval approaches make the implicit or explicit

---

7 In the original, the term "qualitative" is used here. Chard uses this term in exactly the same sense as I use "linguistic," and the substitution is therefore made to avoid confusion with the use made of "qualitative" in the rest of this book.

assumption that a given probability interval for a proposition spans all the possible values of the probability of the proposition, and there is no way of telling which of these values is more likely. In other words they all assume that little can be said about the second-order probability distribution (the distribution of the distributions) other than its extreme values. A more general approach is that of Paaß (1991) who explicitly models the second-order distribution, though he restricts himself to binomial and normal distributions. His work permits the use of intervals in which, for instance, a probability is 90% certain to lie, and he demonstrates the use of his system on a cyclic inference network. However, the main reason for the development of this technique seems to be less the need to represent imprecise information than the need to reconcile inconsistent pieces of information (where the inconsistency arises from the departure, by those assessing the probabilities, from the laws of probability) by taking into account their reliabilities.

Of course, once the idea of explicitly modelling the second order uncertainty present in interval estimates is taken on board, there is no reason that such modelling should be restricted to the use of probability distributions over probability distributions. Indeed, in the discussion of fuzzy sets (Section 3.3.2) another such approach has already been considered—fuzzy probabilities are, of course, interval probabilities in which there is a possibility distribution over the possible values that the probabilities may take. A slightly different approach is that suggested by Jain and Agogino (1988) who deal with what they call "Bayesian fuzzy probabilities." These are distinguished from ordinary fuzzy numbers by the fact that they are constrained to obey the laws of probability. Jain and Agogino then develop suitable versions of the the arithmetic operations required for a probabilistic analysis—addition, multiplication, division, and the calculation of expectation—that obey the laws of probability and are consistent with Bayes' rule. These can then be used to perform probabilistic analyses in which the mean of the resulting fuzzy probability is the result that would be obtained from the standard probabilistic calculation if that were performed with the means of the initial fuzzy probabilities, and the bounds on the resulting fuzzy number represent the outcome of some kind of sensitivity analysis. This approach is then extended (Jain and Agogino, 1990) to the use of Bayesian fuzzy probabilities within influence diagrams, a move that enables decisions to be analysed in terms of fuzzy expected values (the use of non-monetary utilities are not considered), with a number of mechanisms for making this choice being available. It is equally possible to conceive of systems in which second-order information about possibilities is summarised using probabilities. In the sense of interpreting a fuzzy interval as having some kind of probability distribution associated with it, this idea seems to have first been suggested by Dubois and Prade (1987a) and it has also been proposed (though in a different context) by Boutilier (1993).

One view of this work is that it is a way of coping with imprecise information about probabilities. Another view is that it provides a way of talking about probabilities that abstracts away from precise numerical information in the same way that qualitative physics abstracts away from precise numerical models of physical systems. Taking such a viewpoint, it is clear that the systems discussed in this section are much closer to the semi-qualitative systems of Section 4.2.3 than the purely qualitative systems of Section 4.2.1. This leads naturally to the question of whether there are any probabilistic systems that are closer to purely qualitative systems than those discussed in this section. The short answer is "yes," and the long answer may be found in the next section.

4.4 Abstractions of quantitative systems

There are, to my mind, three classes of system that use practically no quantitative information yet are clearly qualitative versions of systems that are normally largely numerical. These are *strict* abstractions, in which the only distinctions are those from Section 4.2.1 between positive, negative, and zero values, *infinitesimal* abstractions, in which the distinctions are between sets of values arbitrarily close to one, and *symbolic* abstractions, in which the formalism manipulates symbols that have no obvious numerical equivalent.

4.4.1 Strict abstractions

The most influential work among the systems of strict abstraction is that of Wellman on qualitative probabilistic networks (QPNs). This work also has many similarities with the method developed in Chapters 7 and 8, and so is worth considering in some detail. Wellman was concerned with planning under uncertainty, and wanted to deal with the problem of choosing the best plan under such conditions in a probabilistic way without having to commit to the use of precise probabilities, arguing that this means that, in situations in which the precise numbers were not available, the results are more reliable since they are not dependent upon the assumed values. Since he was interested in decision making, the decision being which plan to choose, Wellman's work was set in the context of influence diagrams,[8] and, roughly speaking, proceeded by replacing the conditional probability table linking two nodes with a *qualitative influence* of one node upon the other. The idea of a qualitative influence was initially (Wellman, 1988) defined for binary variables and a variable A, with possible values a and $\neg a$, was said to have a positive influence on variable C, with possible values c and $\neg c$, if and only if:

$$\Pr(c|a, X) \geq \Pr(c|\neg a, X) \tag{4.10}$$

---

8 Making the name "qualitative probabilistic network" a little confusing.

where X is every value of every other variable that bears upon C.[9] In other words, the inequality holds whatever the state of all the other variables that affect C. Zero and negative influences are similarly defined. The effect of such an influence is to induce a partial order over the conditional values that would make up the conditional probability table which is replaced by the influence, and it is thus clear that an influence represents much weaker information than is held in such a table.

If A positively influences C, then this fact is denoted by $S^+(A, C)$ while the negative influence of C on D is represented by $S^-(C, D)$. From these two pieces of information it is possible to ascertain that the influence of A on D is:

$$S^{+\otimes-}(A, D)$$

where $\otimes$ is exactly the same operation as the $\otimes$ of Table 4.2 (as discussed by Wellman (1988)), so that A has a negative influence on D, $S^-(A, D)$. If there is a second influence on D, $S^-(B, D)$, then the overall influence on D is computed using the operation $\oplus$ from Table 4.1 to be:

$$S^{-\oplus-}(A \wedge B, D) = S^-(A \wedge B, D)$$

Wellman also shows that it is possible to reverse influences, in other words finding the influence of C on A from the influence of A on C, and proves that a simple application of Bayes' rule implies that reversed links have the same qualitative value as the original ones.

When variables with more than two values are considered, things get a little more complex. In such cases, rather than thinking of qualitative influences being between the probabilities of values of the variables, it is useful to think of them as being between the probabilities of sets of values of the variables. In particular, Wellman (1990a; 1990b) suggests thinking of the positive influence of a many-valued variable A on a many-valued variable C as implying that the occurrence of higher values of A make higher values of C more likely, where the concept of "higher" is taken to be in the sense of some defined order over the values. To capture this idea of ordering, Wellman adopts the idea of *first order stochastic dominance* (Whitmore and Findlay, 1978), making use of a result by Milgrom (1981) to show that a necessary and sufficient condition for the stochastic dominance interpretation of the positive qualitative influence of A on C is that for all values $a_1 > a_2$, c_0, and X:

$$\Pr(c \geq c_0|a_1, X) \geq \Pr(c \geq c_0|a_2, X) \tag{4.11}$$

---

9 Where there is more than one such variable, X may be thought of as any truth assignment to the conjunction of all those variables.

As before negative and zero influences are similarly defined. This definition reduces to the binary one if "true" is taken to be greater than "false," and the same influence combination and reversal properties hold. This allows Wellman to define qualitative analogues of Shachter's (1986a) procedures for the transformation of influence diagrams that permit the reduction of any diagram so that the effect of the decision node upon the value node may be determined.

When modelling real situations, such as the effect of a dose of digitalis on a patient's well-being, it turns out that qualitative influences are not sufficient to capture all the interactions between variables. Instead it is necessary to introduce some means of identifying the effect that a pair of variables might have in unison on a third. This is done in terms of what is known as *qualitative synergy*, and A and B are said to exhibit positive *additive* synergy with respect to C[10] if, for all $a_1 > a_2$, $b_1 > b_2$, c_0, and X:

$$\Pr(c \geq c_0 | a_1, b_1, X) + \Pr(c \geq c_0 | a_2, b_2, X) \geq \qquad\qquad (4.12)$$
$$\Pr(c \geq c_0 | a_1, b_2, X) + \Pr(c \geq c_0 | a_2, b_1, X)$$

and is written $Y^+(\{A, B\}, C)$. Zero and negative additive synergy are similarly defined. The term "additive" reflects the addition in the synergy condition, and provides a contrast with "product synergy," a concept introduced by Wellman and Henrion (1991) in their investigation of the phenomenon of "explaining away." The latter was first identified by Pearl (1988a) as the kind of reasoning in which on observing an event, knowledge that makes one of its causes more likely makes another cause less likely. Wellman and Henrion showed that if a particular value c_0 of C is known to be the case, then explaining away of A by B (or vice versa) will occur if there is negative *product* synergy between A and B. This is the case if, for all $a_1 > a_2$, $b_1 > b_2$, and X:

$$\Pr(c_0 | a_1, b_1, X) \Pr(c_0 | a_2, b_2, X) \leq \Pr(c_0 | a_1, b_2, X) \Pr(c_0 | a_2, b_1, X) \qquad\qquad (4.13)$$

and is denoted $X^-(\{A, B\}, c_0)$. Again it is also possible to define positive and zero versions of the condition. Wellman and Henrion also investigated the relationship between product and additive synergy showing that they are rather different concepts but are related under some circumstances.

This work was then extended by Druzdzel, both in his thesis (Druzdzel, 1993), and in a number of papers with Henrion (Henrion and Druzdzel, 1991; Druzdzel and Henrion, 1993b,c,a). This contribution can be split into three main parts. The first part was an extension of the analysis of explaining away, initially generalising it to encompass all forms of interaction between two causes of the same event—a form of reasoning that was termed

---

10 The idea of synergy was introduced in (Wellman, 1990b), but the terminology used here is adopted from (Wellman and Henrion, 1991).

"intercausal" (Henrion and Druzdzel, 1991)—and showing why this kind of reasoning might be important.[11] This line of work was then further extended (Druzdzel and Henrion, 1993c) to take account of the effects of causes other than the two whose interaction was studied by Wellman and Henrion, and to investigate the kinds of intercausal reasoning that might occur when it is not the event with the common causes which is observed, but some effect of that event. This work is not only an advance on that of Wellman and Henrion, but also on that of other authors who have investigated intercausal reasoning (Agosta, 1991; Tzeng, 1992).

The second part of Druzdzel and Henrion's contribution was to provide an efficient means of evaluating qualitative probabilistic networks. The suggestion for doing this by propagating qualitative values through networks rather than transforming the network as Wellman had originally suggested, first appeared in (Henrion and Druzdzel, 1991). It was then further developed, with particular emphasis on intercausal reasoning, by Wellman and Henrion (1991). The main work on the propagation mechanism appeared in (Druzdzel and Henrion, 1993c) where a complete algorithm was presented,[12] and the complexity of the algorithm was determined to be quadratic in the number of nodes in the network to which it is applied. Additional wrinkles in the propagation mechanism were explored in (Druzdzel, 1993) and (Druzdzel and Henrion, 1993a).

The third part of the work by Druzdzel and Henrion was the use to which they put qualitative probabilistic networks. Whereas Wellman had been interested in finding out the influence of a particular decision on a particular utility and was thus very much in the decision-making domain, the main motivation behind Druzdzel and Henrion's work was to be able to explain to people what was going on in a probabilistic system in order to get them to accept the recommendations that it might make (Druzdzel, 1993). This motivation places their work firmly in the same context as most work on reasoning under uncertainty in artificial intelligence—their main concern is assessing the impact of new evidence—and explains their interest in developing a belief propagation rather than a graph reduction method. Indeed, the networks through which they consider propagating qualitative values are qualitative versions of the kind of probabilistic network popularised by Pearl (1988b) rather than being qualitative versions of influence diagrams like those considered by Wellman.

More recently, work on QPNs has been further developed by Renooij and van der Gaag in a number of interesting ways.[13] The first of these (Renooij and van der Gaag, 1998) is to extend the algorithm developed by Druzdzel for use in QPNs that include value nodes.

---

11 Intercausal reasoning is discussed in detail in Sections 5.3.2 and 8.3.
12 The algorithm is discussed in detail in Section 9.3.2.
13 All of these approaches are covered in Renooij's thesis (Renooij, 2000).

This, then, makes the algorithm applicable to the kind of networks originally considered by Wellman and a qualitative analogue of the message-passing algorithms for evaluating influence diagrams mentioned in Section 3.4.4. Another line of work that Renooij and van der Gaag have followed is that of resolving trade-offs, a problem that is closely related to Raiman's qualitative reasoning example of the colliding masses discussed in Section 4.2.2. Consider a variable A that positively influences another variable C while a third variable B has a negative influence on C. If the probabilities of A and B both increase, then the combined qualitative influence on C is $S^?(A \wedge B, C)$ indicating that the influence is unknown. Of course, this situation arises because the actual strengths of the influences are unknown, and one way to resolve the situation is to use some information about strengths. Renooij and van der Gaag do this in a particularly elegant way (Renooij and van der Gaag, 1999a) by distinguishing between strong and weak influences, where the strengths themselves have arbitrary absolute values but the weakest strong influence is stronger than the strongest weak influence. This makes it possible to generalise the message passing algorithm by adapting the $\otimes$ and $\oplus$ operators thus making the approach much closer to the spirit of QPNs than other attempts to solve the problem (Parsons, 1995; Liu and Wellman, 1998). More recent work on the problem (Renooij et al., 2000a) has concentrated on identifying nodes at which trade-offs occur, making it possible to establish automatically, in the context of the example above, that if the influence on A on C is greater than that of B on C then the combined influence of A and B on C is $S^+(A \wedge B, C)$.

Tradeoffs are an important issue in QPNs because they lead to ambiguous results— knowing that the combined influence of A and B on C is $S^?(A \wedge B, C)$ means that it is not possible to determine the way that the probability distribution over C will change as those over A and B do. A similar difficulty arises if the influence between A and C, say, is non-monotonic, in other words if it is $S^?(A, C)$. Such a situation will mean that, in the original formulation of QPNs, the effect in changes in the probability distribution over C (and those variables that C itself influences) cannot be predicted from changes in the probability distribution over A. However, Renooij and van der Gaag (1999b) have shown that if there is another variable B that influences C, then the additive synergy between A and B on C can sometimes[14] be used to determine whether the influence of A on C is positive or negative when the value of B is observed.

The final aspect of QPNs studied by Renooij and van der Gaag (Renooij et al., 2000b) is that of propagating the effect of multiple observations. In a standard probabilistic causal network, it is possible to accommodate any number of observations by setting the

---

14 In the example, the non-monotonicity can be resolved if the variables are binary-valued and B is both the only other node directly influencing C and the source of the non-monotoniicty. If there are other nodes influencing C, then it is necessary to know which one is causing the non-monotonicity. If the nodes are not binary-valued, then the non-monotonicity might stem from the order over the values of the nodes.

appropriate probabilities to 1 or 0 (if A is observed to take the value a_i, then $\Pr(a_i) = 1$ and $\Pr(a_j) = 0$ for all values a_j of A such that $i \neq j$). Using any propagation algorithm on the resulting network will give the correct posterior probabilities for all variables represented by the network. Multiple observations in a QPN can be naïvely handled by simply identifying all the relevant changes in probability, those induced by the multiple observations, and running Druzdzel's algorithm. However, this will then compute the effect of the observations in what is essentially a serial manner, with the effect of each observation being established given all the observations handled before it. As shown in (Renooij et al., 2000b), the outcome of the computation can then be sensitive to the order in which the observations are processed, and this effect can be eliminated by an appropriate modification of the algorithm.

It is worth noting that Druzdzel was interested in using linguistic probabilities in conjunction with qualitative influences in constructing his explanations, and that in more recent work with van der Gaag (Druzdzel and van der Gaag, 1995) this idea has been extended to use a mixture of qualitative and quantitative information about probabilities to determine second-order probability distributions over probabilities of interest. This points to an application of QPNs as a step in the knowledge acquisition process for probabilistic networks—they are an intermediate step between learning the arcs in a network and learning the full set of conditional probabilities. Qualitative influences can also be used in the process of learning such conditional values (Wittig and Jameson, 2000).

A formalism that is rather similar to qualitative probabilistic networks is that of monotonic influence diagrams (Michelena, 1991; Michelena and Agogino, 1993a,b). Deterministic monotonic influence diagrams (Michelena and Agogino, 1993b) look much like qualitative probabilistic networks, but the signs on the arcs correspond to the qualitative values of the partial derivatives linking the quantities joined by the arcs rather than the kind of probabilistic influence between them. They may be manipulated in ways that are very similar to those proposed for influence diagrams (Shachter, 1986a), and thus, when used to represent the effect of design factors on some aspect of a design, they may be reduced so that it is possible to see which factors must be adjusted to optimise the design. The concept of deterministic influence diagrams may be generalised to cover probabilistic relationships between variables (Michelena and Agogino, 1993a), and this increase in expressiveness allows the techniques to be applied to a wider range of problems, including decision making in the presence of random variables (Agogino and Michelena, 1993) while leaving the graph reduction method largely unaltered. The idea of combining qualitative probabilistic influences and deterministic dependencies has also been explored by Wellman (1991) who stresses the ability of such hybrids to represent information that cannot be captured by either qualitative probabilistic networks or deterministic influence diagrams.

Considering the fact that qualitative probabilistic networks and monotonic influence diagrams are specified in terms of relative values (in the case of monotonic influence diagrams these are the values of partial derivatives relative to zero) makes it clear that these techniques are related to methods based upon orderings of probabilities. Now, the use of such "qualitative"[15] probability methods has a lengthy history (Suppes, 1994) that is not relevant from the point of view of this discussion because they have not been widely applied in artificial intelligence. There is, however, one interesting development that is similar.

This development is Snow's work on what has come to be called "ignorant induction." This line of work began in (Snow, 1992) with an attempt to mark out the bounds of what may be represented by probability theory by investigating what kind of assumptions are required to move from an order over a set of propositions to a probability distribution over them. To put it another way, the work identified what information was necessary, over and above information about which propositions were thought to be more probable than others, in order to build a full probabilistic model of a situation. This position was then extended (Snow, 1994a) to allow the representation of information by a partial order over the probabilities of a set of propositions while enabling an upper bound on the probabilities of the propositions to be calculated if desired, and to demonstrate (Snow, 1994b) that such a partial order captures the "ensemble of sets" representation introduced in the author's earlier work. Most recently (Snow, 1996a), the method has been developed to enable prior information, which expresses no ordering over propositions, to be resolved into a posterior ordering using only conditional information about whatever evidence is available. The approach makes it possible to decide what order holds between any pair of propositions. In a similar vein, the use of a preference relation to specify belief functions has been studied by Wong and Lingras (1994), and the compatibility between beliefs represented using preferences and those represented using belief functions has also been considered (Wong et al., 1991).

4.4.2 Infinitesimal abstractions

Another qualitative approach, albeit one that has some semiqualitative features, is the work on infinitesimal probabilities. This approach is based upon Spohn's epistemic beliefs which, as discussed in Section 3.3.4, may be interpreted as order of magnitude approximations to probabilities. Thus if a proposition A has an epistemic belief $\kappa(A) = n$ then the

---

15 The scare quotes are there to distinguish this notion of qualitative probability from that denoted by the term elsewhere in this book.

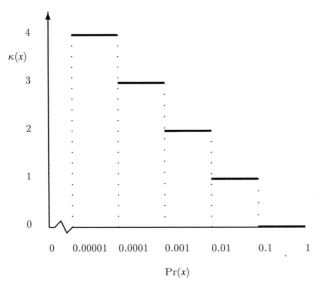

Figure 4.7
Mapping from probabilities to epistemic beliefs using $\epsilon = 0.1$

probability of A is constrained by:

$$\epsilon < \frac{\Pr(A)}{\epsilon^n} \leq 1 \tag{4.14}$$

where ϵ is a small positive number. Thus any probability between ϵ^n and ϵ^{n+1} will map to the same value n. This is illustrated, for $\epsilon = 0.1$ by Figure 4.7. This interpretation means that it is possible to use epistemic beliefs as a way of applying probability theory when a full set of probabilities is available but the precise values are not known. Instead of specifying the probabilities one specifies a set of "kappa values" so that $\kappa(x)$ is known for every x in the domain. This task may well be easier than specifying probabilities because it only involves identifying the interval into which the probability falls. These values can then be used in conjunction with (3.76)–(3.78) to propagate the effects of new information generating a new set of kappa values that may either be used as they stand or translated back into probabilistic intervals.

When considered in this light, there are a number of pieces of work on epistemic beliefs that are of interest. Foremost among these is Shenoy's (1991b) work on using epistemic beliefs in the framework of his local computation scheme. Obviously this is important because it provides a computationally efficient means of propagating the effects of evidence expressed in terms of epistemic beliefs, but Shenoy's work has some other useful features as well. In particular, Shenoy devises a new means of updating epistemic beliefs that has some attractive properties, including the fact that it can be used to construct the epistemic belief in a large set of variables from the beliefs in smaller sets. Giang and Shenoy (1999) have recently investigated alternatives to (4.14) as a means of building kappa distributions from probability distributions, and have identified the mapping that preserves the maximal amount of information.

Another interesting piece of work is that of Goldszmidt and Pearl (1992) where a similar means of updating epistemic beliefs is proposed, and it is shown that Spohn's original rule is equivalent to Jeffrey's rule for kappa values. This then leads naturally to the idea (Goldszmidt and Pearl, 1996; Geffner, 1996) of using kappa values instead of probability values in conjunction with causal networks, and Darwiche's CNETS system (Darwiche, 1994b,a) makes it possible to propagate these values. However, the widest application of infinitesimal probabilities is in the area of defeasible reasoning, and this will be discussed later in Section 4.5.2.

It should also be stressed (Goldszmidt and Pearl, 1996) that kappa values may be considered as another form of linguistic probability where linguistic terms relate to probability values as follows:

$$
\begin{array}{lll}
\Pr(A) = \epsilon^0 & A \text{ and } \neg A \text{ are possible} & \kappa(A) = 0 \\
\Pr(A) = \epsilon^1 & \neg A \text{ is believed} & \kappa(A) = 1 \\
\Pr(A) = \epsilon^2 & \neg A \text{ is strongly believed} & \kappa(A) = 2 \\
\Pr(A) = \epsilon^3 & \neg A \text{ is very strongly believed} & \kappa(A) = 3 \\
\vdots & \vdots & \vdots
\end{array}
$$

In addition to these theoretical results, there have been a couple of attempts to compare the results obtained by the use of epistemic beliefs and the results obtained from a full probabilistic analysis. Henrion and colleagues (Henrion et al., 1994) performed a number of experiments on a diagnosis example[16] that aimed to assess the effect on the relative performance of kappa values and probabilities of the choice of value of ϵ, the range of prior fault probabilities, and the amount of evidence provided. The results indicated that, as expected, there is a trade-off between using small values of ϵ (which gives accuracy) against a large value of ϵ (which gives a large number of intervals and hence good resolution), and that for this example the optimal value of ϵ is around 0.1. In particular, the results also showed that the infinitesimal scheme performed well, provided that the prior probability of faults was below 0.03, in that for lower priors the diagnoses agree well with those provided by ordinary probabilities. Similar results are provided by Darwiche

---

16 The particular example diagnosed problems related to the electrical system of a car.

and Goldszmidt (1994) who supplement their work with an analysis of the ways in which kappa and probability values differ. They found that whereas the effect of probabilistic evidence decreases along a chain of influences, the effect of kappa evidence is constant, and that the kappa value of the common cause of a number of effects changes in a very different way to the probability value as the effects are incrementally observed.

Given the close relationship between probability theory and decision theory, it is no surprise to find that there has been some work on qualitative decision theory using kappa values, and it is worth considering this briefly. The initial work on this subject was carried out by Pearl (1993) who devised a decision model that combined a κ-ranking over events with a similar utility ranking and could distinguish clearly dominating choices. This approach was then extended by Tan and Pearl, firstly (Tan and Pearl, 1994b) to allow utilities to be described as a set of conditional preferences of the form "if β then α is preferred to $\neg\alpha$," and then (Tan and Pearl, 1994a) to allow the fact that some choices might take precedence over others in some situations and not in more specific situations.

A more general approach to handling infinitesimal probabilities has been provided by Wilson (1996). He takes standard probability theory and extends it to be applicable both to real numbers and to infinitesimals, creating a theory that can combine ordinary probabilities with the kind of probabilities represented by kappa values in the same distribution. Wilson has also considered a theory of decision making that uses extended probabilities (Wilson, 1995), which turns out to be similar to, but fixes some problems with, Pearl's (1993) original suggestion.

4.4.3 Symbolic abstractions

The use of abstractions can be seen as being motivated by the wish to get all the advantages of quantitative approaches to reasoning under uncertainty, such as a powerful and well-founded theory, without having to commit to the use of numbers. Indeed, this is the specific aim of Darwiche's thesis (Darwiche, 1993b), and his work has resulted in a number of symbolic approaches. Essentially, Darwiche's approach is to abstract away from probability theory to provide a general framework (Darwiche and Ginsberg, 1992) for defining the degree to which a proposition is supported, and the operations by which this degree is computed. Instantiating this framework with particular degrees of support and combination operations gives probability and possibility theories, along with Spohn's ordinal conditional functions. The framework also supports objections (Darwiche, 1992) where the degree of support attached to a proposition is a condition under which it would not be true. Thus the sentence "Today is a good day for a picnic" might have the objection "It is raining today." Whatever type of degree of support is chosen, Darwiche shows that it is possible to structure information as a causal network, and to propagate values through it using generalisations of standard probabilistic algorithms.

It is also possible to approach the situation from a different angle and, rather than seeing what kind of probability theory can be built by throwing the numbers away and replacing them with something else (which is my colloquial reading of the work in Darwiche's thesis), trying to find out what kind of logical theory can be built using those bits of probability theory that are attractive. In more recent years this is one of the things that Darwiche has worked on. In particular, he has investigated how probabilistic notions of independence might be incorporated into propositional logic. This he achieves (Darwiche, 1993a) by recording the *arguments* for propositions, and since arguments record which propositions were used in derivations, it is possible to identify which propositions have no effect on one another and so are, in some sense, "independent" of each other. This line of inquiry has been extended (Darwiche and Pearl, 1994) to build probabilistic notions of causality into propositional logic databases, by associating a causal network with every logical database, in order to prevent non-intuitive conclusions from being derived. In a slightly different context (once again that of defeasible reasoning), this kind of approach has been proposed by Pearl and Geffner. Initially (Pearl, 1988a), this was done by distinguishing between casual and evidential rules and only sanctioning particular kinds of deduction with each. Later (Geffner, 1990), the mechanism was the use of a "causes" modality, and most recently (Geffner, 1994), the idea has evolved into one in which rules are causally directed and a distinction is made between forward and backward reasoning. This idea can be extended (Parsons, 1998) to build a logic that captures the kind of reasoning possible in QPNs.

There has also been some work on abstractions of evidence theory that are rather far removed from the abstractions that have been considered so far. The way in which these abstractions work is by identifying sets of propositions that support particular propositions and which are implied by certain pieces of evidence (and thus give results similar to those generated by logical approaches) rather than determining the qualitative and semiqualitative values that should be associated with the propositions according to the evidence. The first work to attempt to do this explicitly is that of Kohlas and his co-workers though, as they acknowledge, the idea was already implicit in the idea of interpreting belief as the probability of provability.

The first papers on the subject (Kohlas, 1993; Kohlas and Monney, 1993) argued that uncertain information may be modelled as logical formulae that include explicit assumptions to which a measure of uncertainty is attached. When such formulae are used to prove some conclusion, it is possible to identify the set of true and assumed propositions that are used in this proof and which form the symbolic *support* for that proposition. This set is analogous to the belief in the proposition, and if probabilities are attached to the assumptions, the belief may be calculated from it. In addition, the support may be determined by using Shenoy and Shafer's local computation scheme (Shenoy and Shafer,

1990). In fact, as stressed in (Kohlas and Brachinger, 1994), evidence theory can be seen as a hybrid logical and numerical method in which an initial symbolic stage is followed by a numerical calculation. Thus the belief in, or support for, a proposition is taken to be the probability of provability of a proposition, and this is calculated by looking at those sets of propositions from which the proposition in question could be proved. These form the "support set" for that proposition. This idea is extended in (Besnard and Kohlas, 1995) to allow the logical stage to be based on any logical system and the idea of the support for a proposition may be defined in terms of what is provable in that system. One of the main results of this work is a combination rule that is a generalisation of Dempster's rule, and which does not make assumptions about the independence of evidence. This symbolic approach to evidence theory has been applied in model-based diagnosis (Kohlas et al., 1995) and has been implemented in the interactive tool Evidenzia (Haenni, 1996, 1998) which runs on Macintosh computers under the CLOS system.

4.5 Defeasible reasoning

Defeasible reasoning is usually taken, by the artificial intelligence community at least, to be reasoning in which initial conclusions may need to be retracted in the light of new information. It is important as a means of handling incomplete information about the world—if information about the world is complete and perfect, then initial conclusions can always be correct since they can be based on what is known to be true (though of course if information changes over time, conclusions may need to be withdrawn). However, if it is necessary to reason using information that is not available, then the best way to proceed is to make some assumption from which some conclusion may be drawn while noting that the conclusion may need to be retracted if the assumption is invalid. For example, to estimate one's time of arrival when the train timetable is not known, one might assume that trains run every half an hour allowing the conclusion that one will arrive at 3pm, at the latest, to be reached. However, when it turns out that the trains run less frequently at the weekend, then this estimated arrival time may have to be revised.

From the point of view of the artificial intelligence community, the problem of reasoning defeasibly is bound up with the problem of representing information about typicality and prototypical objects. For instance, to take the usual example, it is clear that, generally speaking, birds fly. Thus, when confronted by a particular bird Tweety, one naturally assumes that Tweety can fly, although this is not known for sure, and despite the fact that there are many types of bird (penguins, dead birds, and birds whose feet have been set in concrete are the most commonly quoted ones) that cannot fly. This assumption may be used to draw new conclusions, about the wisdom of letting Tweety out of her cage when the window is open for example, and as the basis for making decisions based on those conclusions. However, it is also possible that the assumption is invalid, as in the case that Tweety's wings have been clipped precisely because of her predeliction for open windows, and so conclusions and decisions must be revised in the light of this new information. The connection between defeasible reasoning and reasoning about typicality is recognised in the use of the term "default reasoning" to refer to much of this work. It should be noted that making assumptions that are later contradicted adds the problem of resolving inconsistency to the problem of handling incomplete information, a problem that has partly been addressed by the use of truth maintenance systems (Doyle, 1979; McAllester, 1980; de Kleer, 1986; McDermott, 1991; Forbus and de Kleer, 1993).

4.5.1 Defeasible reasoning with logic

The first context in which defeasible reasoning was investigated was that of logic. In classical logic it is not possible to carry out defeasible reasoning because the monotonicity of classical logic prevents conclusions being withdrawn. As a result, the artificial intelligence community has invested a lot of time and effort in producing nonmonotonic logics and there is now a vast number of such systems. This section deals with three of the original nonmonotonic formalisms and some of their descendents. Some of the other formalisms are covered in the collection edited by Ginsberg (1987), others may be found in the books by Brewka (1991) and Besnard (1989), a special issue of the *Journal of Applied Non-Classical Logics* (JANCL, 1991), and the proceedings of any conference on artificial intelligence.

One of the first nonmonotonic systems to be proposed was Reiter's default logic (1980). This augments standard first order logic with a set of default rules that explicitly state what assumptions may be made. A default rule is a statement of the form:

$$\frac{a(x) : b(x)}{c(x)} \qquad\qquad\qquad (4.15)$$

which has the meaning that if $a(t)$ is true of some individual t and there is no reason to conclude that $b(t)$ is not the case, then $c(t)$ may be concluded. Thus, to make it possible to infer that a given bird can fly, unless there is information to the contrary, the following default rule may be written:

$$\frac{bird(x) : fly(x)}{fly(x)}$$

The statement of rules outside the logic that say how assumptions can be made is very appealing, and default logic has, perhaps as a result, proved very enduring. It has, however, had some technical problems. The first main problem is that in the original formulation there was no constructive procedure for building the *extension* of a set of defaults, that is the set of all their consequences, and this frustrated attempts to build an efficient implementation. The second main problem is the interpretation of the notion of consistency that is implicit in the idea of a default. Given that first order logic is only semi-decidable, it is not necessarily possible to decide, for instance, that Tweety cannot fly, and so it is not necessarily clear whether it is possible to apply a default about Tweety's ability to fly. The third main problem is that a set of defaults is not guaranteed to have an extension unless the defaults are all *normal*, that is of the form:

$$\frac{a(x) : b(x)}{b(x)} \tag{4.16}$$

which rather restricts their expressiveness. However, it turns out that normal defaults have an additional nice property—they are *semi-monotonic* that is they are monotonic with respect to default rules. Thus, once an extension is determined from a set of normal defaults, adding more defaults will not cause any conclusions to be retracted. A number of other authors have worked on default logic. Łukaszewicz (1985) proposes translations between different types of default. Thus he suggests replacing the general default of (4.15) by the *semi-normal* default (a semi-normal default is any default of this type):

$$\frac{a(x) : b(x) \wedge c(x)}{c(x)} \tag{4.17}$$

and the semi-normal default:

$$\frac{a(x) : b(x) \wedge c(x)}{c(x)} \tag{4.18}$$

by the normal default:

$$\frac{a(x) : b(x) \wedge c(x)}{b(x) \wedge c(x)} \tag{4.19}$$

The first of these translations is non-controversial, but the second, despite being applicable for a large range of practically occurring defaults, has some rather alarming exceptions (Etherington, 1988). By using both translations sequentially, it is possible to replace the eminently sensible:

$$\frac{has\_motive(x) : guilty(x)}{suspect(x)}$$

by the rather unreasonable:

$$\frac{has\_motive(x) : suspect(x) \wedge guilty(x)}{suspect(x) \wedge guilty(x)}$$

In a further paper, Łukaszewicz (1988) generalises default logic, providing an alternative formalisation of an extension, and proving that semi-normal default theories are guaranteed such extensions. He also shows that semi-normal default theories are semi-monotonic with respect to such extensions. More recently, Wilson (1993b) has proposed yet another formalisation of an extension that has the advantage that every default theory has such an extension and that default theories are semi-monotonic with respect to such extensions. In fact these different formulations are just some of the many variants of default logic that have been proposed. Many more are catalogued by Antoniou (1996; 1997; 1998).

Another early scheme for nonmonotonic reasoning is circumscription (McCarthy, 1980, 1986). Unlike other techniques, circumscription applies a set of rules of conjecture that are based on syntactic manipulation rather than appeals to undecidable provability or consistency. Broadly it attempts to formalise the idea that, unless otherwise specified, things that are not known to hold may be assumed to not hold (in much the same way as would be possible when a normal default was applied). This kind of reasoning is known as *closed world reasoning* and attempts had already been made to place it on a formal footing using methods such as the closed world assumption (Reiter, 1978) and negation as failure (Clark, 1978) (which is one of the mechanisms used by logic programming languages to infer negative information). However, both the closed world assumption and negation as failure were originally proposed in the context of database systems (logic programs being essentially databases in which some deduction is possible), and a number of problems became apparent when they were applied to more general situations. Circumscription addresses these.

Predicate circumscription (McCarthy, 1980) was the first variant to be introduced, and consequently it is the most studied of the differing varieties of circumscription. Predicate circumscription allows explicit assumptions of completeness to be made as required, providing a way of applying a closed world assumption to a particular predicate at a given moment. A schema for a set of first order sentences is generated, and then instantiated by replacing predicate variables with particular predicates, the choice determining the composition of the extension of the circumscribed predicate. This has the effect of asserting that the only positive instances of that predicate that exist are those known to exist at that time within the circumscribed domain. Any instances that are not known to be positive are assumed to be negative. Predicate circumscription has been amended and refined to handle various technical difficulties that have been discovered in the years since the formalism was introduced. These refinements include formula circumscription (McCarthy, 1986), which permits arbitrary predicate expressions to be circumscribed, and which forms the basis of a simple means of implementing commonsense reasoning commonly known as *abnormality theory*. This allows the "birds fly" example to be encoded as:

$$bird(x) \land \neg abnormal(x) \rightarrow flies(x)$$

and if penguins are distinguished as abnormal birds, formula circumscription does not sanction the inference that penguins can fly. There is also pointwise circumscription (Lifschitz, 1986) in which the circumscription, instead of being carried out everywhere simultaneously, is performed by minimising one point at a time, and domain circumscription (Etherington, 1988), which provides a formalisation of the so called domain closure assumption; the assumption that the only individuals that a system must deal with are those explicitly named. Work on new variants of circumscription continues including, for example, work on a new approach to domain circumscription (Doherty et al., 1996).

While default logic attempts to formalise particular assumptions, and circumscription and other closed world methods attempt to formalise the basis for assuming that something is not true, a third approach to nonmonotonic reasoning was proposed. This line of work suggested using notions of what is known as a basis for deciding what could be assumed to be true, where the concept of "known" is drawn from modal logic (Hughes and Cresswell, 1968). The first of these modal approaches to be introduced was McDermott and Doyle's non-monotonic[17] logic I (McDermott and Doyle, 1980), which was based on the use of a consistency operator M where Mp is assumed to be true of any p for which $\neg p$ is not provable. The conclusions that may be derived from a set of facts then includes everything that may be derived from the original facts using classical logic and the intersection of all the maximal sets of assertions of the form Mp that are consistent with them. Unfortunately, as McDermott and Doyle point out, the logic does not ensure that Mp and $\neg Mp$ are necessarily inconsistent, and this leads to a number of anomalies. This weakness in the notion of consistency, among other things, led McDermott (1982) to define nonmonotonic versions of the modal logics T, S4 and S5 (Hughes and Cresswell, 1968). Unfortunately nonmonotonic S5, whose axioms intuitively suggest it captures the ideas about consistency of beliefs that McDermott wanted for his logic, collapses to monotonicity, leaving only the less desirable nonmonotonic T and S4.

Moore (1983; 1985; 1988) identifies the problem with McDermott's systems as being the acceptance of the characteristic axiom of the T system:

$$Lp \supset p \tag{4.20}$$

which may be read as "whatever is believed is true," and, after rejecting it as only being appropriate for dealing with infallible agents, goes on to define autoepistemic logic. Moore claims that autoepistemic reasoning is the kind of reasoning intuitively employed in many situations, giving the example of how he determines whether or not he has an elder brother. He argues that it is not that case that he knows that he has no elder brother because he has

---

17 Such systems were iniitally called "non-monotonic" logics, but as they became more familiar they became "nonmonotonic" logics.

been explicitly told that no such person exists, nor because he has carefully sifted all the available evidence, but simply because if he had an elder brother he would know about him. Moore formalises this style of reasoning by introducing autoepistemic logic, defining the conclusions of a consistent set of premises A that may be maintained by an ideally rational agent as being those sets of beliefs T such that:

$$T = Th(A \cup \{Lp : p \in T\} \cup \{\neg Lp : p \notin T\}) \tag{4.21}$$

where Lp means that p is believed, and $Th(X)$ indicates all the conclusions of the set of facts X that may be determined using the rules of inference of the logic. Thus the conclusions include everything that may be derived from the set composed of the original facts plus assumptions about what should and should not be believed. In its original form autoepistemic logic was a purely propositional logic, with no means of incorporating quantifiers or individual variables. Konolige (1988; 1989) extended Moore's approach to a first order system initially (Konolige, 1988) to a system that does not allow "quantifying in" to the scope of a modality, and later (Konolige, 1989) to a full first order system.

Following autoepistemic logic, a whole host of nonmonotonic modal logics have been proposed. A particularly elegant example is Besnard and Siegel's (1988) supposition-based logic in which expressions are written in terms of the modality "suppose," while Levesque (1990) has used the modal approach to allow the formalisation of a system's knowledge of the limits of its knowledge. Other suggestions include (Bochman, 1995; Lifschitz, 1994; Wainer, 1992) and an attempt (Weber, 1996) to produce a system whose notion of what is known lies somewhere between that assumed by Moore in autoepistemic logic and that assumed by McDermott in his nonmonotonic version of S5.

One way of looking at subimplication (Bossu and Siegel, 1985) is as another attempt to extend the idea of closed world reasoning, providing a specific system that is intended to make applying the closed world assumption consistent and closed under deduction. However, from another point of view, subimplication introduces a very important way of looking at nonmonotonic logics in general. From this second viewpoint, subimplication is important because it orders models (the ordering being based on the number of base facts that are true in the model), and uses the order to decide what may be concluded. A very similar idea was later suggested by Shoham (1987; 1988) who went on to show that the idea of a preference order over models could be used to capture a number of existing models by varying the preference order. This then leads to a broad classification of nonmonotonic logics into the class of logics, such as circumscription, which construct a set of minimal models, and the set of logics, such as default logic, which iteratively apply rules for making assumptions until a fixed-point[18] is reached. A system that makes use of

---

18 A fixed-point is a set of facts and assumptions that is both consistent and maximal in that no more assumptions

the preference-based semantics is Lin and Shoham's (1992) GK. This has two modalities, one for representing the beliefs a system starts with, and one for representing those beliefs that a system derives from its base set. Lin and Shoham prove that GK subsumes default and autoepistemic logic and, in doing so, give a clear model-theoretic semantics for default logic (which until then had been an open problem), and claim that, since GK is based on the idea of logical minimization, it provides a bridge between circumscription and fixed-point nonmonotonic logics. A similar result is provided by Voorbraak (1993) who shows that it is possible to give a preference-based semantics for default logic when the idea of a preference order over models is generalised to become an order over sets of models.

A slightly different approach to nonmonotonic reasoning is suggested by Kraus et al. (1990) who start from the point of view of defining a nonmonotonic consequence relation $\mid\!\sim$ [19] and dealing with its properties in conjunction with the set of minimal models it relates to. For example, they consider the use of the rule named "Cautious Monotonicity:"

$$\frac{a \mid\!\sim b, \quad a \mid\!\sim c}{a \wedge b \mid\!\sim c} \tag{4.22}$$

which says that if it is possible to nonmonotonically infer both b and c from a, then it is possible to nonmonotonically infer c from the conjunction of a and b. Taking a set of such rules, Kraus, Lehmann and Magidor define a number of systems, arguing that they are intuitively more correct than default logic and circumscription in some situations. The most interesting of these systems, System P, turns out to be equivalent to that studied much earlier by Adams (1975), and seems to include all the properties that are definitely required from a nonmonotonic reasoning system. However, there are useful properties that System P does not satisfy, foremost among which is the property that Kraus et al. call *rational monotonicity*. This requires that:

$$\frac{a \mid\!\sim c, \quad a \not\mid\!\sim \neg b}{a \wedge b \mid\!\sim c} \tag{4.23}$$

In other words, if it is possible to infer c from a and it is not possible to infer $\neg b$ from a then it is possible to infer c from a and b together. Since this form of rationality seems so attractive, not least because it permits a "lazy" approach to the updating of consequences, it was then further studied by Lehmann and Magidor (Lehmann, 1989; Lehmann and Magidor, 1992) who showed that it was a property of systems in which the preference order over the minimal models is ranked.

This approach to nonmonotonic reasoning has been adopted by a number of authors,

---

may be consistently added.

19 An idea that was first developed by Gabbay (1985) and can be detected in his work even earlier (Gabbay, 1982).

including Dubois and Prade (1991b) and Benferhat et al. (1999) who have compared it with approaches based on conditional probabilities and possibilities. One of the more interesting pieces of work in this vein is by Pinkas and Loui (1992) who survey a number of different approaches and study the relationships between them. In particular, Pinkas and Loui suggest that the idea of *cautiousness*, which had been bandied about the literature at least since McDermott's (1982) paper on non-monotonic logic II, should be used to distinguish between different consequence relations. Informally, a reasoning system is *credulous* or *brave* if it accepts conclusions that may well be wrong (relying on realising that they are wrong and being able to recover) and a system is *skeptical* or *cautious* if it only accepts conclusions which, so far as it knows, must be true. Pinkas and Loui formally define cautiousness as a partial order on consequence relations allowing them to come up with a taxonomy of consequence relations, clarifying their relative cautiousness.

All of the nonmonotonic reasoning systems discussed here were originally presented in such a way that there is no mechanism for enumerating the extensions of a given theory. Several researchers have presented theorem provers for deciding if particular formulae are true in restricted versions of particular nonmonotonic logics. For example, Ginsberg (1989) and Doherty et al. (1995) have dealt with circumscription, Brewka (1986) with non-monotonic logic I, and Niemelä (1988) with autoepistemic logic, while Bossu and Siegel (1985) suggested a theorem proving procedure known as saturation, which may be used to decide whether one set of formulae entail another set by subimplication. Besnard et al. (1983) used a modified version of saturation to tackle theorem proving in a subset of Reiter's default logic, Mengin (1995) extended the approach for the whole of Reiter's default logic, and Nicolas and Duval (1995) have provided a theorem prover for a subset of Łukaszewicz's default logic. With this support for establishing which defaults hold, and with additional support such as that provided by (Nicolas and Schaub, 1998; Cholewiński et al., 1999; Linke and Schaub, 1999, 2000), authors are beginning to look at the use of default logic in applications such as information retrieval (Hunter, 1995).

A further problem is that of dealing with multiple extensions. The failure of default logic to provide a means of choosing between several extensions is often stated as a fatal flaw in the formalism. However, as Reiter and Criscuolo (1981; 1983) point out with reference to the "Nixon diamond"[20] there are many situations in which it is inappropriate for the formalism to choose between extensions. This may be justified on the grounds that such choices, when they may be made intuitively, depend on information implicit in the premises that is not accessible to the syntactic mechanism of the logic (a point reiterated by Bourne (1999)). If it is not necessary to make choices between extensions then a reasoner

---

20 The Nixon diamond is one of the classic problems in nonmonotonic reasoning. It deals with an individual Dick who is both a Republican and a Quaker. If Quakers are generally pacifists and Republicans are generally not pacifists, is Dick pacifist or not?

may use default logic alone. If choices are necessary, some suitable mechanism must be appended to the basic default logic, or a different formalism that can cope with making decisions must be used instead. Selman and Kautz (1990) discuss just such a formalism that makes choices using the specificity of information as a basis. Preferences can also be used in conjunction with default logic as a way of making this choice. This has been studied by, for instance, Delgrande and Schaub (2000).

Alternatively, it is possible to pick an extension and use it until one of the deduced facts is found to be contrary to the state of the world, at which point an alternative extension that excludes the relevant fact is adopted as a basis for reasoning. This is an approach closely related to the behaviour of justification based truth maintenance systems (Doyle, 1979), and the difference between the approaches relates back to McDermott's distinction between brave and cautious systems. A brave system, using a model based on default logic, will believe anything that may be true in one extension, while a cautious system that uses circumscription will only believe facts that may be deduced in every possible world view. Clearly, one type of system will be applicable to particular types of tasks, and the other to different tasks. The fact that the selection criteria for brave systems is likely to be task specific is an argument for the correctness of standard default logic in providing no mechanism for choosing between extensions. Such a mechanism is a feature that the designer of a reasoning system based upon default logic can introduce if and when it is required.

The final limitation of nonmonotonic reasoning systems is their inability to distinguish between different degrees of belief. Once facts have been derived, either from true axioms or plausible assumptions, they are regarded as true in their own right. It is thus impossible to formalise statements such as "I almost believe that A is true, but not as much as I believe B is true" in any way that approximates the meaning of the original. There have been attempts to classify nonmonotonic reasoning within the framework of multivalued logics (Ginsberg, 1988), and to relate inference to the ease with which the fact may be removed from a knowledge base (Gärdenfors, 1988), which may help to remedy this problem. There is, however, a more obvious way to remedy this problem, namely incorporating some uncertainty handling mechanism, and this is the subject of the next section.

While there are still many people working in the area of nonmonotonic reasoning, recent years have seen a move away from the idea that nonmonotonic logics are the best way of providing such reasoning. Moses and Shoham (1993) capture what seems to be the prevailing view when they suggest that McCarthy's slogan[21]:

modality—*si*, modal logic—*no!*

---

21 Which seems to have originally made its way into the literature via (Lifschitz, 1989).

should be augmented by:

nonmonotonicity—*si*, nonmonotonic logic—*no!*

and the belief system that they propose is entirely in this vein, permitting defeasible reasoning without being a nonmonotonic logic by explicitly stating the assumptions under which beliefs are held. An overview of some of the many systems in this style, which I have classified as being systems of argumentation since many of them explicitly deal with arguments for and against propositions, is given in Section 4.5.3.

4.5.2   Defeasible reasoning with numbers

Classical logic might find it difficult to handle the retraction of conclusions, but classical probability theory has no such problems. This is because the conditionalisation mechanism of probability allows the probability of a proposition to be revised when new information is obtained. The prior probability of a, $\Pr(a)$ can be much greater or much smaller than $\Pr(a|b)$, so finding out that b is the case can indicate either than a has become very likely or very unlikely.[22] Realising this, many people have suggested using probability and other numerical methods as a means of performing defeasible reasoning.

DEFEASIBLE REASONING USING PROBABILITY

An early suggestion in this line was that of Rich (1983) who makes the point that it is possible to consider the fact that birds usually fly as a statement about the likelihood that a given bird does fly. Quantifying defaults with certainty factors to acknowledge this, Rich shows that it is possible to handle some of the problems discussed with reference to nonmonotonic logics, such as the Nixon diamond, and the propagation of properties in inheritance hierarchies. Ginsberg (1984; 1985) investigates the extension of this idea to the situation in which default rules are quantified using evidence theory with an explicit upper and lower probability pair. In particular he is concerned with the problem of conflicting rules such as:

$$tweety \xrightarrow{(1\ 0)} bird$$
$$bird \xrightarrow{(0.9\ 0.02)} flies$$
$$tweety \xrightarrow{(1\ 0)} ostrich$$
$$tweety \xrightarrow{(0\ 1)} flies$$

---

22 Of course, strictly speaking, probability does have a problem. If a proposition is proved or disproved (and so has a probability of 1 or 0), which is exactly what classical logic deals with, then no amount of evidence will change that value. However, it is simple enough to consider something "true" or "untrue" when it has an arbitrarily high or low value, in which case its status can be changed.

The numbers Ginsberg attaches to a rule are $\mathrm{Pr}_*(\textit{rule holds})$, the lower bound on the probability that the rule holds, and $\mathrm{Pr}_*(\textit{rule does not hold})$, the lower bound on the probability that the rule does not hold. This latter is, of course, one minus the upper bound on the probability of the rule holding, $1 - \mathrm{Pr}^*(\textit{rule holds})$. Thus the second rule given above is interpreted as meaning that the probability of something flying given that it is a bird, $\mathrm{Pr}(\textit{flies}|\textit{bird})$, is constrained to lie in the interval $[0.9, 0.98]$. With this interpretation, a vacuous rule is quantified with $(0, 0)$, and the outcome of two conflicting rules is obtained by the use of Dempster's rule, which ensures that vacuous rules have no effect on conclusions while certain rules are never outweighed by default rules.

Nilsson's probabilistic logic has also been applied to the problem. Grosof (1988) considers how to extend probabilistic logic in a way analogous to the way in which nonmonotonic logic extends classical logic. In other words, Grosof's extension allows the inference of probabilistic information that is not justified by what is known, but which would commonly be inferred by people in the absence of information to the contrary. Thus the system would permit the inference that $\mathrm{Pr}(c|a, x) = \mathrm{Pr}(c|a)$ when there is no information about how x bears upon c, an inference that would not be sanctioned by probability theory and probabilistic logic. Formalising default reasoning is also one of the things that McLeish considers doing with the extensions of probabilistic logic that were discussed in Section 3.5.1. She first describes how Nilsson's scheme can be used to permit nonmonotonic reasoning (McLeish, 1988) by allowing for logical inconsistencies, and then extends the scheme to use belief functions rather than probabilities to quantify the defaults. This latter framework is then further extended in (Deutsch-McLeish, 1991).

Perhaps a more interesting scheme for default reasoning is that suggested by Bacchus (1990b; 1991). As mentioned in Section 3.5.1, Bacchus distinguishes between propositional and statistical probabilities, and proposes a framework in which they can both be used. He also proposes that they can be used in combination with one another so that statistical information about the proportion of birds that can fly may be used to inform the belief that a given bird does fly. Because it makes the initial distinction between the two types of probabilistic information, Bacchus's system is more convincing than others that assume that the two things are the same (or do not acknowledge that there are two different things to distinguish), and it also offers the option of expressing beliefs about statistical assertions, making it far more advanced than any similar system. This scheme is further developed in (Bacchus et al., 1992, 1993). The first of these papers develops a number of schemes for deciding how to use statistical knowledge about various classes of individuals that have various characteristics to determine beliefs about the likelihood of a particular individual having particular characteristics given that she is a member of particular classes. The second paper then incorporates these schemes into Bacchus' original reasoning mechanism. The final word on the subject may be found in (Bacchus et al.,

1996), which combines and expands the previous two.

Another interesting system in this class is that of Neufeld (1989; 1990). Neufeld is interested in creating a system that is capable of default reasoning, but which uses probability to justify the inferences made. Thus each rule has a probabilistic meaning. If c can be inferred by default if a is known, then:

$$\Pr(c|a) > \Pr(c) \tag{4.24}$$

while if c is known to be true if a is true, then:

$$1 = \Pr(c|a) > \Pr(c) \tag{4.25}$$

Neufeld's system also distinguishes monotonic and nonmonotonic rules by which knowledge about a affects knowledge about c. These are represented, respectively, by:

$$1 = \Pr(\neg c|a) > \Pr(\neg c) \tag{4.26}$$

and

$$\Pr(\neg c|a) > \Pr(\neg c) \tag{4.27}$$

The fact that knowledge in this system is represented by an "inference graph" (in which each type of rule is represented by a different type of arc) makes the connection with probabilistic causal networks quite clear—inference graphs encode exactly the same information as such networks. However, despite the graphical notation, the system is basically logical, inferring the change in belief in propositions by means of rules of inference rather than graphical propagation. Furthermore, Neufeld concentrates on classic nonmonotonic reasoning conundra, such as determining whether or not a particular bird flies, rather than classic reasoning under uncertainty conundra like determining whether or not a patient has tuberculosis (though he does discuss simple diagnosis problems).

The discussion of the system was later extended (Neufeld, 1990) to cover its application to a whole range of problems in default reasoning and inheritance hierarchies. In addition this later paper contains a brief comparison of Neufeld's work and Wellman's QPNs that is of particular interest given the connection between QPNs and the work in later chapters of this book. Casting the definition of a positive influence (4.11) into its form for binary variables gives:

$$\Pr(c|a, X) \geq \Pr(c|\neg a, X) \tag{4.28}$$

from which it follows that:

$$\Pr(c|a, X) \geq \Pr(c) \tag{4.29}$$

can be deduced. Thus a positive qualitative influence corresponds to a default rule that c can be inferred by default if a is true. However, the additional conjunct in the qualitative influence means that $\Pr(c)$ always increases when $\Pr(a)$ does, so that if c is influenced by b as well as a, then it is influenced by $a \wedge b$. This property does not hold for Neufeld's system which, instead, can handle problems of exceptional subclasses that defeat QPNs. The other obvious difference between QPNs and Neufeld's system is that QPNs do not distinguish the case in which knowing that a is true makes c true. However QPNs can easily be extended to make this distinction (Parsons, 1995).

It should also be noted that Garbolino (1996) has suggested a system that is very similar to that suggested by Neufeld (and thus also very similar to that suggested by Wellman) and which he uses to reason about relations between probabilities in a probabilistic causal network.

DEFEASIBLE REASONING USING INFINITESIMAL VALUES

It is also possible to use the work on infinitesimal probabilities discussed in Section 4.4.2 to provide a form of non-monotonic reasoning using probability theory. If conditional kappa values are associated with logical implications, then it is possible to use Spohn's (1990) epistemic beliefs as a means of quantifying statements of the form "Birds are likely to fly" and then making the right kind of defeasible deductions. However, to use the model requires a full specification of all the kappa values of all the possible worlds and, as Pearl (1989)[23] points out, this may be impossible even when the assessment is simplified by using techniques from causal probabilistic networks—for instance default information is rarely specified in sufficient detail to identify all the propositions that might affect a given default. This might appear to rule out the use of infinitesimal probabilities in any practical case, but Adams (1975) provides a mechanism that can be used for drawing conclusions from partially specified epistemic belief models for which the kappa values are 0 or 1. This works by using those values that are known as constraints on the kappa distribution, and drawing conclusions which, given those constraints, are guaranteed high probability. This system provides a probabilistic semantics for System P but, like System P, it also has some less desirable properties. In particular, it suffers from the problem of "irrelevance." Thus if it is known that birds fly, and that Tweety is a red bird, the system cannot detect the irrelevance of the information about Tweety's colour when considering her ability to fly and so cannot conclude that she flies. This, of course, is exactly the same problem that plagues Neufeld's (1990) system.

This problem may be resolved by allowing kappa values other than 1 and 0 and then

---

23 This paper provides a useful summary of the developments in probabilistic semantics for nonmonotonic reasoning up to 1989, and (Pearl, 1991) gives a slightly more recent one.

selecting higher probability worlds in preference to lower probability ones. However, doing this generates another problem—how to assign values to defaults in such a way that the correct worlds have the highest probability, and the solution is somewhat roundabout. If all sentences have kappa values of 1 or 0, a set of defaults is consistent if there is a probability assignment over them that satisfies the constraints imposed by their kappa values. This consistency can be detected just by looking at the models of the defaults, and proceeds by iteratively removing groups of defaults from the complete set. The order in which the defaults are removed gives a kappa ranking to the defaults that is known as the Z-ranking (Pearl, 1990b). This ranking can then be used to give a ranking to the models of a set of defaults and this, in turn, can be used to define the consequences of the set. The system that uses the Z-ranking to define the consequences of a set of defaults is known as System-Z. System-Z has the property of rational monotonicity (4.23) in addition to those properties possessed by Adams' system and also solves the problem of irrelevant information. However, System-Z cannot handle the associated problem of "inheritance blocking." That is, given the information "most birds fly," "penguins are birds," "penguins do not fly," and "birds have legs" it cannot conclude that penguins have legs—the inheritance of this property from birds to penguins is blocked. This problem can, however, be handled by the maximum entropy approach of Goldszmidt et al. (1990) at the cost of introducing some rather odd additional properties and by Geffner and Pearl's (1992) conditional entailment, which combines the infinitesimal approach to defeasible reasoning with the logical one at the cost of drawing rather weak conclusions.

Despite its limitations, System-Z has been widely studied and there are a number of results concerning it that are worth considering. For instance, Goldszmidt and Pearl (1991a) have extended the test for consistency of a set of defaults to be applicable to mixed sets of defaults and strict rules. In the same paper they also showed that testing for consistency is identical to determining entailment—a set of rules and facts is inconsistent if the facts are not entailed by the rules. System-Z has also been extended so that the ranking it produces takes account of pre-defined priorities between defaults, producing a system known as System-Z^+ (Goldszmidt and Pearl, 1991b, 1996), which assigns a value $\kappa^+(w)$ to every possible world. System-Z^+, while still suffering from the problem of inheritance blocking, is appealing because (Goldszmidt and Pearl, 1992) it is both computationally tractable and can handle "soft evidence," that is evidence of the form "the probability of A being true is n," as well as "hard evidence," that is evidence of the form "A is true." Recently the appeal of System-Z^+ has been increased by an extension (Tan, 1994) that allows it to solve the problem of inheritance blocking, and System-Z has been extended (Tan and Pearl, 1995) to correctly handle reasoning about the inheritance of properties from class to subclass. This area has also been studied by Weydert (1995; 1996), and has recently been extensively revisited by Bourne (Bourne, 1999; Bourne and Parsons, 1999b), who has given a new algorithm for applying maximum entropy to the problem. Bourne's approach allows defaults to have variable strengths and solves the problems with Goldszmidt et al.'s work (Goldszmidt et al., 1990) as well as capturing other extensions to System-Z (Bourne and Parsons, 1999a). The complexity of inference in these systems is discussed in (Eiter and Lukasiewicz, 2000).

It should also be noted that recent work by Snow (1999) seems to achieve much of what System-Z does without the need to use infinitesimal probabilities. What Snow demonstrates is that given a set of sentences, it is possible to construct a probability distribution over them that has the same conclusions as Lehmann and Magidor's (1992) default entailment (with rational monotonicity (4.23)) under the interpretation that

$$A \mid\sim B \text{ implies } \Pr(A, B) > \Pr(A, \neg B) \tag{4.30}$$

This suggests that Lehmann and Magidor's scheme is rational in a probabilistic sense, and offers a way of carrying out default reasoning in the sense suggested by Lehmann and Magidor using standard probabilistic methods. Snow's method for constructing the distribution has much in common with Giang and Shenoy's (1999), although it predated the latter by several years.[24]

Just as work on default reasoning with probabilistic logic can be extended to give default reasoning with belief functions, so can work on infinitesimal probabilities be extended to give default reasoning with infinitesimal beliefs. Exactly this has been done by Benferhat et al. They start (Benferhat et al., 1995a) from a mass assignment that allocates masses of zero, ϵ or $1 - \epsilon$, where ϵ is the usual small positive number, and from these build beliefs which are clearly polynomials in ϵ. These infinitesimal beliefs, in turn, allow the definition of a nonmonotonic consequence relation that is better behaved than other suggestions. In particular, the consequence relation satisfies the postulates proposed by Kraus et al. (1990) for System P, as well as correctly handling the problems of irrelevance, inheritance blocking, ambiguity and redundancy, though it does not have the property of rational monotonicity (4.23). The extended version of the paper (Benferhat et al., 2000) also includes a detailed comparison with other similar systems.

DEFEASIBLE REASONING USING POSSIBILITY VALUES

Of course, there is no particular reason why if default information is going to be quantified it has to be quantified with probability or evidence values—it can equally well be quantified with possibility values. One of the first attempts to use possibility values in a way that directly attempts to perform the kind of defeasible reasoning that is possible using

24 I first came across this work of Snow's at a conference in 1996, but the work did not appear in the conference proceedings.

nonmonotonic logics is that of Yager (1987). Yager considers how information such as that about birds generally flying can be handled using Zadeh's theory of approximate reasoning (Zadeh, 1979) (which was briefly discussed in Section 3.5.4). To do this he takes the defeasible rule:

If x is a bird then in most cases x will fly

to mean that:

If x is a bird, and it is possible that x is a flying bird, then x flies

This second rule then has a number of degrees of possibility associated with it; that x is a bird given what kind of animal it is, that x is a flying bird given that it is a bird, and that a flying bird actually flies. All of these degrees of possibility are derived from the fact that all the classes of objects being talked about (birds, flying birds, and flying things) are fuzzy sets. Then, given fuzzy information about x, the degree of possibility that x flies can be computed. This style of defeasible reasoning is then extended by Dubois and Prade (1988b) to remedy the flaws that it does not capture the fact that the conclusions of default rules are in some sense uncertain (since they are less certain than the conclusions of rules that always hold), and that it does not handle interacting defaults in a suitable manner.

Another approach to using possibility theory to provide a method of defeasible reasoning is that discussed by Farreny and Prade (1985). Their approach associates a conditional possibility distribution $\Pi(q|p)$ and $\Pi(\neg q|p)$ with a rule "if p then q," where varying the possibility degrees gives rules of different strengths. Thus a certain rule will have $\Pi(q|p) = 1$ and $\Pi(\neg q|p) = 0$, and an uncertain rule will have $\Pi(q|p) = 1$ and $\Pi(\neg q|p) = \lambda$. The smaller the value of λ the more certain the rule, so Farreny and Prade propose that default rules are simply uncertain rules in which λ is small. They also discuss extensions of classical rules of inference that fit in with their scheme.

While it is clear that Yager and Dubois and Prade succeed in providing a possibilistic way of performing the same kind of reasoning about likelihood suggested by Rich and Ginsberg, it is not clear how directly their approach relates to nonmonotonic logics. In contrast, it is clear how reasoning about likelihood using possibilistic logic is related to nonmonotonic logics. Firstly, as discussed in Section 3.5.2, Dubois and Prade (1991c) showed that qualitative necessity measures are a special case of Gardenförs' epistemic entrenchment (Gärdenfors, 1988). This relation between possibilistic logic and epistemic entrenchment suggests that there is some kind of connection between possibilistic logic and nonmonotonic logics since both Gardenförs and people working in nonmonotonic logic are concerned with revising inconsistent sets of information. Secondly, Dubois and Prade (1991e) proved that possibilistic logic is a member of the family of nonmonotonic logics based on preference models that were first discussed by Shoham (1987) and discussed above.

An extension to this line of work (Benferhat et al., 1992) established the relationship between possibilistic logic and Pearl's System-Z (1990b). In doing so, Benferhat et al. showed that System-Z is completely captured by possibilistic logic in that it is possible to build a possibilistic knowledge base that can encode a set of default rules which have been ordered by System-Z, and from which exactly the same conclusions can be drawn as when using System-Z. Furthermore, they show that the ranking used by System-Z is equivalent to a possibility distribution generated by the principle of minimum specificity, and that possibilistic logic can go further than System-Z in handling problems of inheritance. A further extension (1994) showed how to capture normal defaults and how to find a possibility distribution that can capture both defeasible and certain information.

4.5.3 Argumentation

In recent years, a third branch of research into defeasible reasoning has developed—that of argumentation. In argumentation, reasoning is essentially logical, but the idea is that there is not one line of logical reasoning that proves or disproves a conclusion, but that there are several which concern it and are taken into account when deciding whether to accept it. The first use of argumentation in artificial intelligence is due to Birnbaum and colleagues (Birnbaum et al., 1980) who were not concerned with defeasible reasoning, but with getting computers to engage them in arguments. Interested in natural language processing, they constructed a system that could take either side in the following kind of argument:

Arab: Who started the 1967 war?

Israeli: The Arabs did, by blockading the Straits of Tiran.

Arab: But Israel attacked first.

Israeli: According to international law, blockades are acts of war.

From the point of view of reasoning with imperfect information, their system is significant because it required the ability to handle the inconsistent information expressed by the two sides and to decide upon a response that backed up its case. The ideas of "support" and "attack" between statements were further developed by McGuire et al. (1981) and were extended to take account of prototypical argumentation structures by Birnbaum (1982) and Flowers et al. (1982). Other work on argumentation structures is that of Robin Cohen (1987), and argumentation as a whole has been widely used in work on natural language (see, for instance, (Reed, 1998; Zukerman et al., 1999)).

While this work is interesting from the point of view of handling inconsistent information, it says little about how such mechanisms can be used to handle other types of imperfect information. To make the connection, it is necessary to turn to Paul Cohen's theory of endorsements (Cohen, 1985; Cohen and Grinberg, 1983a,b), which was concerned with handling uncertainty. Cohen's aim was to replace the handling of uncertainty by attaching numerical values to uncertain facts by heuristic reasoning about the nature of the uncertainty. Facts and rules in SOLOMON, the implementation of the Cohen's model, have labels, known as endorsements, attached to them specifying the degree to which uncertainty is inherent in them. Thus, for instance, rules may be labelled "maybe too general," and data is tagged with its source to allow its reliability to be assessed. The knowledge about the different forms of uncertainty associated with each continuing inference, and the reason that the particular inference is being propagated, are then used to control the spread of uncertainty in pursuit of a particular deduction. Cohen argues that dealing with the reasons for the existence of the uncertainty that pervades real life problems, gives a far deeper, and more accurate, means of handling uncertainty than using a flat numerical measure. Thinking of these reasons as arguments for and against the certainty of the information makes the connection with argumentation clear.

The theory of endorsements has been tested in FOLIO (Cohen and Lieberman, 1983), a system that manages financial portfolios, and it seems to have been successful in this domain. However, there are some problems with the model. Chief among these is the fact that a conclusion inherits all the endorsements of all of its premises, as well as any that are inherent in the rule that generates the conclusion. This can rapidly lead to every interesting fact being dogged with large numbers of endorsements after only a few rules have been fired. Since the model contains no scheme for combining the endorsements, indeed this is explicitly forbidden (Cohen, 1985),[25] it is difficult to see how such large bodies of structural information can be assessed either by the system or the operator when a decision is required.

Now, at no point did Cohen claim to be talking about arguments, and he was clearly not interested in incomplete information or defeasible reasoning. For the first work that actually claims to be about argumentation as a means of dealing with incomplete information, it is necessary to look at (Lin and Shoham, 1989; Lin, 1993). Lin and Shoham were concerned with various formalisations of nonmonotonic reasoning, and proposed their system of argumentation as a general model. Their idea was that this general model could be instantiated, by judicious choice of base language and the addition of suitable predicates and modalities, to provide systems equivalent to default logic, autoepistemic logic, negation as failure and circumscription. In Lin and Shoham's terms, an argument is a tree whose root is the proposition of interest, and whose branches are sequences of rules that are chained

---

25 This position appears to be contradicted by the claim in a later paper (Sullivan and Cohen, 1985) that combinations of endorsements should be partially ordered. Sadly, however, there is too little information in the later paper to resolve the apparent inconsistency.

together to prove the proposition. This is a powerful and interesting approach, but it should be noted that it does have considerable similarities to nonmonotonic logics, especially in the way in which it differentiates between monotonic and nonmonotonic rules and uses this distinction, rather than any notion of attack and defeat of arguments, in order to determine which of two conflicting conclusions to favour.

In contrast, Loui (1987) describes a system that uses just such notions of attack and defeat in order to perform defeasible reasoning. He incorporates rules that are explicitly denoted as being defeatable, and discusses ways of constructing arguments from such rules, along with criteria for resolving conflicts between arguments based on preferences between premises and the amount of evidence used by the arguments. These meta-level reasons for preferring one argument over another are interesting because they combine rules of thumb, such as the shortest path heuristic, equally with better founded notions of arguments attacking each other's premises. Loui later extended this work in conjunction with Simari (Simari and Loui, 1992) to provide a formal framework in which the notion of defeat is explicitly bound up with the notion of specificity—one argument defeats another if their conclusions disagree and the one is more specific than the other.

Another important system of argumentation is that which is discussed in detail by Fox and co-workers (Fox et al., 1992; Krause et al., 1995). It is particularly interesting because it was explicitly designed to perform both defeasible reasoning, and reasoning under uncertainty. The basic idea behind this system is that it should be possible to say more about the certainty of a particular fact than may be expressed by quantifying it with a number between 0 and 1. In particular, it should be possible to assess the reason why a fact is thought to hold, and use this *argument* for the fact as its quantification. An argument in this system is thus a tentative proof. A proof is tentative because argumentation allows the proof of a fact being true to co-exist with the proof of a fact being false. The advantage of constructing arguments for facts, and using these arguments as quantifiers of the certainty of the facts is that it is possible to reason about the arguments themselves. This reasoning about arguments can be used to determine which facts are most acceptable.

Reasoning about arguments in the system proposed by Fox and colleagues takes a number of different forms. Firstly, it is possible to use this system of argumentation to combine different arguments. Thus it is possible to combine an argument for a proposition A with one for B to get an argument for A *and* B, or to establish an argument for B from one for A and one for A *implies* B. Secondly it is possible to aggregate arguments, so that a number of arguments for A can be combined to get a single argument with a suitable strength, for instance by applying an improper linear model (Dawes, 1979) or by counting the number of steps in the argument. The result of the combination can then be used to rate A against competing hypotheses. Finally, and most interestingly, the structure of arguments can be analysed (Elvang-Gøransson et al., 1993). In this process, an argument is classified into one of six classes based upon its "acceptability," which is determined by examining the arguments for and against a given proposition to see whether any of the steps in the arguments themselves have any arguments against them. The advantage of this approach is that the degree of confidence of the proposition is determined by the structure of the reasoning rather than being imposed by the assignment of a numerical measure. Of course, it is perfectly possible to use numerical measures to quantify the uncertainty present in arguments. Krause et al. (1995) discuss the attachment of numerical measures to both facts and rules, and show that they can be interpreted both as probabilities and possibilities. Using such a measure means that this system of argumentation can be used to combine both uncertain and default reasoning (Krause and Fox, 1994; Parsons and Fox, 1994). Furthermore, it is possible to quantify arguments with qualitative probabilities (Parsons, 1996a,b) in a way that captures much of the functionality of qualitative probabilistic networks and Neufeld's probabilistic commonsense reasoning.

It is worth noting that this particular form of argumentation has been quite widely applied—much more so than any similar system. Most of the applications have been in decision support in the medical domain, and include systems for diagnosing disease, prescribing drugs, interpreting mammograms, and ensuring that medical protocols are adhered to. Some of these applications are discussed by Fox (1996).

A method that is more closely related to classical first order logic is that of Poole (1989) who builds his system on top of earlier work on the Theorist system (Poole et al., 1988), which carries out default reasoning and diagnosis by identifying hypotheses that are consistent with what is known. This method of proceeding has been shown (Poole, 1988) to be equivalent to default logic. Poole considers what should be predicted when classically inconsistent information, such as the fact that both A and $\neg A$ are true, is deduced, and considers a number of different ways of interpreting the contradiction. Thus it is possible to say that the contradiction indicates that either A or $\neg A$ may be true, or that neither is definitely true. It is also possible to argue that even though there is a contradiction, some things may be still be predictable, for instance because B follows from A and C follows from $\neg A$ while D is true if B or C is true. These considerations produce a number of criteria for selecting particular predictions based on how much one is prepared to deduce from the contradictions, and these criteria are clearly close to the acceptability classes mentioned above.

Pollock, a philosopher who is interested in defeasible reasoning, has been working for a number of years on the problem of building an agent, called OSCAR (Pollock, 1996a), which uses argumentation as a means of dealing with defeasible reasoning. Some of the more important material is presented in four main papers (Pollock, 1987, 1991, 1992, 1994) and a book (Pollock, 1995). The system, an initial version of which is described in (Pollock, 1987), distinguishes between certain and defeasible rules (known as "reasons" and "*prima facie* reasons"), and decides what should be believed by taking into account the interactions between different lines of reasoning, in particular which propositions are "rebutted" and "undercut." Propositions are rebutted if there is a reason to believe their negation, and undercut if there is a reason to disbelieve the line of reasoning that supports it, and the ideas of rebuttal and undercutting are used to provide a general theory of warrant, which determines whether or not a proposition should be believed. A proposition is warranted if there are no arguments that rebut or undercut it, or, if there are, such arguments are themselves undercut or rebutted. This basic system has been extended in a number of ways. Firstly (Pollock, 1991), it has been extended with considerations of how an intelligent system should attempt to establish what it believes, and how arguments of differing strengths should be incorporated. Secondly (Pollock, 1992), it has been extended to introduce a means of suppositional reasoning, that is hypothesising something and then seeing if it can be justified from what is known. Thirdly (Pollock, 1994), it has been extended to handle some particularly difficult instances of defeasible reasoning. The most recent work on OSCAR (Pollock, 1996b) has been to extend it to reason about the persistence of facts over time.

Another important system of argumentation is that of Dung (1993; 1995). Dung bases his system upon the idea of the "acceptability of arguments," claiming that an argument is acceptable if it can attack every attack (an attack being a rebuttal in the terminology used by Pollock) that is made on it. From this simple notion he builds up a theory that is a generalisation of several schemes of nonmonotonic reasoning, including Reiter's default logic (Reiter, 1980), some parts of Pollock's system of argumentation, and the general paradigm of logic programming. This latter aspect has also been explored in conjunction with Kakas and Mancarella (Kakas et al., 1994) and further extended by Jakobovits and Vermeir (1996), while the use of argumentation to capture different forms of non-monotonic reasoning is exhaustively explored with Bondarenko et al. (1997). This work suggests that Dung's form of argumentation is a powerful tool for building systems capable of handling imperfect information. The system is even more powerful when equipped with a mechanism, like that introduced by Amgoud (1999), for incorporating information about how strongly particular pieces of information are believed to be true.

In this context it is also worth mentioning the work by Benferhat and colleagues, which first appeared as (Benferhat et al., 1993) and was then revised and expanded as (Benferhat et al., 1994b) and (Benferhat et al., 1994c). In the first of these revisions, Benferhat et al. (1994b) look at a number of different ways in which inconsistent knowledge can be used to draw conclusions, including the approach advanced by Simari and Loui (1992) and different ways of revising the knowledge to remove inconsistencies, building up a taxonomy of different approaches whose properties are then compared and contrasted. The results are reminiscent of those provided by Pinkas and Loui (1992), though somewhat more detailed. This work is then further developed in (Benferhat et al., 1994c) where the authors consider the situation in which the various formulae that make up the inconsistent knowledge are given priorities (expressed as possibility measures) which reflect the degree of confidence in the formulae.

There is a great deal of other work on argumentation and topics related to it. For instance, Vreeswijk (1989) presents a number of conclusions about which arguments should be defeated and when, Prakken and Sartor (1996) discuss a form of argumentation whose basis is in legal reasoning, and Cayrol (1995) compares different systems of argumentation with work on non-monotonic consequence relations. There are also two extensive surveys of argumentation systems (Carbogim et al., 2000; Prakken and Vreeswijk, 2000). It should also be noted that, in addition to the work in artificial intelligence, there is a well developed branch of philosophy whose concerns include the modes of non-logical reasoning, "informal logic," and rules for the conduct of arguments and discourses (van Eemeren et al., 1996).

4.6 Combining and relating formalisms

Many different formalisms have been proposed for reasoning under uncertainty; those presented here are a small but influential fraction. It is not surprising therefore that there have been a number of attempts to establish the formal relationships between formalisms or even combine them in some way. Some of these attempts will be considered in the following sections.

4.6.1 Combining and relating quantitative formalisms

The combination of several formalisms within one framework is not straightforward, and even the elucidation of the relationships between them is not straightforward. As discussed in (Dubois and Prade, 1987c), the various numerical techniques have been independently developed, rely on different modelling assumptions, and use different inference techniques. Some formalisms handle vague knowledge where the boundaries of the situations dealt with by a statement are not clear. Other formalisms are concerned with precisely stated situations about which possibly incorrect facts are known. A third group of formalisms deal with both incorrectness and vagueness, using approaches that differ from those employed by the dedicated calculi. Despite this there has been some interesting work on comparing and relating some of the many quantitative formalisms. An early attempt to do this in an experimental fashion was made by Tong and Shapiro (1985). Their work, set in the context of a rule-based information retrieval system, investigated different ways of using fuzzy probabilities, comparing the approaches by their ability to retrieve information relevant to particular queries. Though the results are not terribly interesting from the point of view of this book, the fact that they made some kind of experimental study is. Another experimental comparison was carried out by Wise and Henrion (1986) who looked at the performance of fuzzy probability, certainty factors and an early form of Bayesian networks on a diagnosis problem relating to nuclear reactor accidents, finding that the Bayesian network approach performed best. Another comparison (Heckerman, 1990a), this time concerning a simple probabilistic model, certainty factors and a simple method based on evidence theory, put the strictly probabilistic model ahead of the others.

While these results are useful, they do not provide information about how the formalisms differ theoretically—a topic that is of more interest from the point of view of this book. However, there are results which do, and some of the most interesting of these have involved looking at the axioms that underpin the theories. In particular, Cox's "fundamental properties of belief" (Cox, 1946), introduced in Section 2.6.1, have been widely discussed. The reason for the popularity of Cox's properties is that from them it is possible to prove the axioms of probability theory. That is, if the properties are assumed, there exists a continuous monotonic function ϕ such that:

$$
\begin{aligned}
\phi(Q|e) &\geq 0 \\
\phi(Q|e) &\leq 1 \\
\phi(TRUE|e) &= 1 \\
\phi(Q|e) + \phi(\neg Q|e) &= 1 \\
\phi(Q|e) \cdot \phi(R|Q \wedge e) &= \phi(Q \wedge R|e)
\end{aligned}
$$

This means that $\phi(Q|e)$ satisfies the axioms of probability theory. Thus Cox's properties have been used as a justification for the use of probability theory as the only measure suitable for expressing belief (Horvitz et al., 1986; Cheeseman, 1988b), and in particular for the justification for the use of probability with no reference to frequency information and thus the Bayesian interpretation of probability. This is a very strong claim, and there has been much discussion of it.

To me, and here I am grateful to Paul Snow for his elucidation of some of the discussion (Snow, 1998b), which helped me through these particularly deep waters, it seems that the discussion has two main threads. The first is concerned with the correctness of Cox's results, and the second is concerned with the degree to which Cox's result, if true, rules out formalisms other than probability theory. In the first thread, a number of authors, including (Paris, 1994; Snow, 1998a; Halpern, 1999a,b), have examined Cox's work in detail and identified some gaps in his argument. These gaps, they argue, can be filled by making additional assumptions which are in the spirit of what Cox intended. The result of this thread, then, indicates that Cox's properties, when suitably amended, are sufficient to justify the use of probability. The second thread deals with the extent to which the properties necessarily imply the use of probability theory. In this line, Snow (1995) shows that a qualitative probability model is in accordance with Cox's properties, and (Snow, 1998b) points out that a close reading of later work by Cox indicates his acceptance of set-based probabilistic methods. Thus Cox does not appear to interpret his properties as only supporting standard probability theory. In addition, Reece's (1998) "p-norm" version of evidence theory appears to obey the properties. This thread, then, seems to suggest that adhering to Cox's properties does not rule out the use of formalisms other than probability.

Now, there is another use for Cox's properties besides arguing for the necessity or otherwise of probability. As Dempster (1988) remarks, the distillation of assumptions represented by the properties is interesting as it provides a means of comparing the assumptions made by different formalisms. Thus evidence theory relaxes the completeness property (see Section 2.6.1) (Dempster, 1988) so that it is not necessary to assign a measure of a belief to those propositions about which there is no information, and it also does not enforce complementarity (meaning that $\text{Bel}(a)$ cannot be determined from $\text{Bel}(\neg a)$).

In a similar vein it is possible to relate possibility theory to probability theory by identifying which properties are violated by possibility measures. As Dubois and Prade (1988a) point out, possibility theory clashes with the complementarity property and with a property related to hypothetical conditioning (see Section 2.6.1) that is not explicitly stated by Horvitz et al. This is that, in order to ensure that the axioms of probability theory emerge from the "fundamental properties," the function that combines the "belief in one proposition and the belief in the other given that the first proposition is true" must have a continuous second order derivative. However, as Dubois and Prade argue, this seems an unnecessarily strong assumption to be made on merely technical grounds (and left unstated). The equivalent operation in possibility theory is usually taken to be the minimum operation, which violates the assumption, but, as Dubois and Prade go on to argue, if the assumption is relaxed, then possibility theory does obey Cox's axioms. Furthermore possibility theory also permits the use of product (Dubois and Prade, 1988a), which does obey the assumption.

Dubois and Prade have extended their analysis of Cox's axioms in two ways. The first (Dubois and Prade, 1990b) is by considering "measure-free" conditioning. Thus they examine what it means for A to depend on B irrespective of the formalism in which this dependence is discussed, and the properties that conditioning should have whatever formalism is being considered. From this consideration a number of axiomatic properties are identified, properties that it could be argued that any formalism should obey. Dubois and Prade then show that Cox's axioms correspond to some of these axioms, and that subsets of the other axioms lead to versions of possibility theory in which product or minimum is used for combination. This seems to me to place Cox's axioms in their proper perspective—

they are a minimalist statement of the behaviour of probability measures, identifying the assumptions about uncertainty that probability measures make. There are other possible sets of assumptions leading to other systems, and anyone choosing a system would be well advised to look at the assumptions to see whether they accept them. However, in general, no set of assumptions is necessarily better than any other set. All this work on Cox's axioms proceeds from the abstract to the specific, postulating general principles and then drawing out specific examples. Dubois and Prade's second extension (Dubois and Prade, 1991h) works the other way around. In this latter paper they pick out a number of different conditioning rules proposed in various places for probability, possibility and evidence theories, and relate them to one another, showing which generalise which, and which have similar ways of behaving.

Other authors have taken a similar approach, attempting to draw out similarities between quantitative formalisms by considering the different ways in which they achieve similar things. A good example of such work is Studený's paper on conditional independence (Studený, 1993). In this paper Studený gives a precise mathematical definition of different forms of conditional independence for different uncertainty formalisms (including probability, possibility and evidence theories) and compares them. This comparison shows, for instance, that the notion of conditional independence suggested for evidence theory does not generalise that for possibility theory—a result that Studený finds objectionable. A more informal comparison is provided by Walley (1996). Here a number of formalisms, including point probabilities, belief functions, possibility measures and lower previsions are compared against a number of criteria including factors such as their ability to model partial ignorance and the availability of computationally feasible mechanisms for computing the valid conclusions from a set of initial information. While Walley's paper is very readable, his criteria seem rather carefully chosen to illuminate the advantages of lower previsions—his preferred model—and this in turn suggests that he has a rather partisan agenda (though one that is considerably less partisan than others such as Cheeseman (1986), for instance). However, despite this reservation, Walley's work does give some kind of a basis for identifying which formalism will be best to adopt in particular situations suggesting that it is useful from the eclectic viewpoint being considered here.

Evidence theory, being a very general formalism, has been related to a number of other formalisms (some of these relations have already been mentioned). Dubois and Prade (1988g) discuss the relationship between belief functions and possibility theory. The paper presents an interpretation of the theory of evidence that aligns it with a general view of reasoning under uncertainty. Dubois and Prade are able to relate possibility theory to evidence theory by interpreting possibility measures as special cases of plausibility measures in which the underlying belief functions are consonant. Similarly, necessity measures are special cases of belief measures for which the belief functions are consonant.

Further comparisons lead to the conclusion that the conjunctive scheme embodied in Dempster's rule is not the only, nor, in the general case, the best way to combine belief functions. In addition, they show that the blind use of combination rules can lead to incorrect results where important information about the sources of the evidence is not taken into account, and it is suggested that some scheme, such as Cohen's endorsements (Cohen, 1985), may be necessary to record the reasons for the numerical uncertainties that are being combined. This analysis is generalised to consider the commonalities between a number of non-additive systems (including possibility and evidence theories) in (Dubois and Prade, 1988d). This latter paper also proposes that possibility and necessity measures can be viewed as special cases of upper and lower probability measures, and this relationship is further explored in (Dubois and Prade, 1992b).

In addition, evidence theory has been related to the incidence calculus by da Silva and Bundy (1990). As the authors mention, the formalisms are very similar, both having been established as interval based extensions of probability theory, and both having had semantics based upon possible worlds proposed for them. Bundy and da Silva suggest that under the interpretation of belief functions suggested by Halpern and Fagin (1992), it is possible to define a common probability space over which both incidences and belief functions may be constructed. Given this common structure, it may be proved that the distribution of incidence and the distribution of belief are equivalent in the sense that any incidence distribution is a belief distribution and any belief distribution is an incidence distribution.

The generality of evidence theory suggests that it might be possible to use it to integrate different formalisms, and this approach has been adopted by Baldwin (1992) who has provided one possible framework for combining probability, possibility and belief measures. The central mechanism for combining the formalisms is the generalised mass assignment (Baldwin, 1990), which distributes uncertainty values across a set of propositions. Since the propositions are common to all formalisms it is possible to combine the different assignments. However, the interpretation of the models that is necessary to perform the combination requires the adoption of Baldwin's voting model semantics, which while it seems sensible is not universally accepted, and the rejection of Dempster's rule of combination for combining belief mass assignments. The combination of generalised mass assignments is possible within the framework provided by support logic programming (Baldwin, 1987), discussed in Section 3.5.4.

A number of authors have also suggested connections between probability theory and possibility theory. One of the earliest suggestions is due to Dubois and Prade who, in (Dubois and Prade, 1991h), show that the measure manipulated by Spohn's ordinal conditional functions is related to the natural logarithm of a possibility measure. Thus, for some proposition A, the possibility of A, $\Pi(A)$ and the kappa value of A, $\kappa(A)$ are related by:

$$\Pi(A) = 1 - e^{-\kappa(A)}$$

Since, as discussed above, ordinal conditional measures can also be interpreted as a probabilities, these measures can be regarded as a bridge between probability and possibility theories. In a similar vein, Snow (1996b) has shown that possibility measures, in some circumstances, can be used to represent the same information as probability measures so that under these circumstances the two theories may be considered to be equivalent.

The most comprehensive body of work on relating quantitative formalisms to one another is that of Gebhardt and Kruse (1993a; 1993b). Their approach, termed the context model, provides an general framework in which different formalisms may be captured. In particular, the framework can encompass probability theory, evidence theory (Gebhardt and Kruse, 1993a) and possibility theory (Gebhardt and Kruse, 1993b). What the context model provides is a way of identifying differences between the different formalisms, giving an objective basis for comparing their different features, and thus giving some basis on which to select the best model for given data. However, the downside is that in order to place the various models into the framework, they need to be re-interpreted in the terms of the context model and this seems to suggest that the versions of the formalisms being compared in the context model differ, at least semantically, from the versions espoused by other researchers. So, while the context model gives a fine basis for comparison if one is happy with the context model interpretation, it is not the only means of comparing the formalisms in question.

Of equal interest are two rather similar pieces of work that relate to the use of different formalisms in conjunction. These are Saffiotti's (1990) hybrid belief system and González and Fernández' system ENAMORA (González and Fernández, 1990a). The hybrid belief system arises from the idea that in the pursuit of suitable methods for handling uncertainty, the use of knowledge representation techniques have been abandoned unjustly. To rectify this situation, Saffiotti proposes a unifying formal framework for representing uncertain knowledge composed of categorical knowledge to which data about its uncertainty is attached, thus treating uncertainty as meta-knowledge. The system handles the categorical knowledge, the knowledge component, as separate from the uncertainty component, treating the uncertainty component as information about the validity of the knowledge. This is a rather limited view of uncertainty, and whether it is possible to generalise this view is open to question. The system provides an abstract knowledge base built around operations, "Empty," which initialises the knowledge base, "Tell," which updates it, and "Ask," which queries it. Any knowledge representation scheme and uncertainty handling formalism may be built into the system by supplying the appropriate functions. In general, "Ask" is a function that returns the degree to which an item of knowledge is believed, and "Tell" is a function which adds a piece of information to the knowledge base. To separate the knowledge and uncertainty components of a particular piece of data, Saffiotti distinguishes between the intension of a sentence, which is its meaning and thus the knowledge component, and the extension, which is the object it denotes, here the truth value corresponds to the uncertainty component. This structure allows the abstract knowledge base to be decomposed into two modules, one to handle knowledge, and one to handle uncertainty, each dealing with a different part of the sentences that make up the uncertain information passed to the system. The whole system turns on the use of the sentences, and the fact that both the knowledge representation and uncertainty handling systems deal with complementary parts of them. In this light Pulcinella (Saffiotti and Umkehrer, 1991a) may be seen as the uncertainty handling component for a hybrid belief system that is capable of using different formalisms to solve different problems in different situations.

ENAMORA (González and Fernández, 1990a) is an environment in which different approaches to handling uncertainty may be studied, as a basis for developing a deeper theoretical understanding of their capabilities by means of comparative testing. Identifying the need to vary control knowledge between methodologies, González and Fernández (González and Fernández, 1990b; González, 1989) propose that this problem is handled by holding the necessary information, including the interpretation of operators and inference rules, as meta-knowledge. This allows ENAMORA to be constructed from a general database of knowledge that does not change between uncertainty handling formalism and representation and domain. Considering domain independent information, it is clear that the general information corresponds to Saffiotti's (1990) set of sentences that link uncertainty representation to knowledge representation. This, in turn, suggests that the hybrid belief system and ENAMORA are essentially two different ways of looking at the same functional system, and that the most important features in both are the set of facts that relate the uncertainty and knowledge components and the mappings between them.

Although it is somewhat off the main track of this book, it is also worth briefly pointing out that there has been some work that looks at the relationship between rough sets and other systems. In particular, while rough and fuzzy sets might initially look rather similar (a rough set looking a lot like a fuzzy set for which the degree of membership is merely 0, 1, or some unknown number between 0 and 1), Pawlak (1985) argues that the two concepts are in fact rather different. Dubois and Prade (1990e) take a more eclectic line, arguing that the two approaches are complementary, with rough sets attempting to model the idea of objects being indiscernible while fuzzy sets try to model the fact that certain boundaries are are ill-defined. As a result of this argument they suggest that there are two ways to combine the two approaches, by producing rough approximations of fuzzy sets, and also by fuzzifying rough sets. This latter method, which involves giving membership functions to the upper and lower approximations that make up the rough set, has also, apparently independently, been proposed by Nanda and Majumdar (1992). Perhaps of more interest from the perspective of this work are the remarks that Dubois and Prade (1990e) make about the relationship between rough sets and the structure of the frame of discernment over which belief functions are defined. This idea has also been pointed out by Grzymala-Busse (1987), who also showed that the lower and upper approximations of rough sets are belief and plausibility measures respectively, and Wong and co-workers (Wong et al., 1992) who discuss in detail the mathematical structure common to belief functions and rough sets.

4.6.2   Combining and relating qualitative formalisms

There has also been a fair amount of work published on combining and relating qualitative formalisms, although this work has only been concerned with nonmonotonic logics, and, in particular, with default logic, circumscription, and autoepistemic logic. One of the earliest attempts in this vein is that of Imielinski (1985) who considered the relationship between default logic and circumscription, being particularly concerned with ways in which translations could be effected between different classes of defaults and circumscription. In the final version of the paper, Imielinski (1987) proves that it is possible to translate normal and semi-normal defaults without prerequisites into abnormality theories in a *modular* way, where modularity is taken to mean that, given a default theory and a set of additional pieces of information, the translation of the default theory and the new information together is the new information plus the translation of the default theory. However, it is not generally possible to translate normal defaults into circumscription in a modular way. The same two formalisms were considered by Etherington (1987), whose results are primarily of interest where they complement Imielinski's by showing that there are cases in which information expressed using circumscription can be translated into default theories.

At around the same time as these results were appearing, work was going on to establish the relationship between default logic and autoepistemic logic. Konolige (1988) showed that it was possible to translate default theories into autoepistemic logic so that the consequences of the resulting autoepistemic theories were the same as the consequences of the initial default theories. He also showed that it was possible to translate autoepistemic theories into default logic so that the consequences of the resulting default theories were the same as the consequences of the initial autoepistemic theories. Now, in order to get this kind of equivalence, Konolige had to modify autoepistemic logic slightly, altering the consequences that may be derived from a particular autoepistemic theory. As Marek and Truszczyński (1989) point out, the same kind of result could have been achieved by altering default logic, and this is the route that they followed, comparing their results with those of Konolige. More recently, Gottlob (1993) has shown that altering either autoepistemic logic or default logic is not necessary by providing a translation from default logic into standard autoepistemic logic (though he also showed that a modular translation between the two is impossible), and Schwarz (1996) has improved upon this translation. Konolige has also (Konolige, 1989) presented results on the relation between autoepistemic logic and circumscription, while Lifschitz (1989) has carried out work on a modification of circumscription that has no modal operators but has many similarities with autoepistemic logic.

Also worth mentioning here are two attempts to classify and relate the many variations on the theme of default logic. Moinard (1993) makes his comparison on the basis of the various ways in which the valid consequences are defined by the variants, finding some surprising similarities. Froidevaux and Mengin (1994), on the other hand, devised an alternative formulation of a whole range of different versions of default logic in terms of a new set of concepts, allowing them to classify the relationships between the different systems in terms of these concepts. It is also worth noting that Konolige and Myers (1989) have studied the use of Konolige's modified version of autoepistemic logic as a knowledge representation system in its own right, concluding that it has some advantages in representing default information. Finally, the work by Bondarenko et al. on how Dung's system of argumentation can capture various nonmonotonic logics (Bondarenko et al., 1997) can be seen as a way of relating those logics to one another.

4.6.3   Combining and relating qualitative and quantitative formalisms

The most difficult part of the task of combining and relating formalisms is the part that considers mixtures of symbolic and numerical techniques. The difficulty is partly due to the fact that the two types of formalism are intended to deal with different types of imperfect information—many of the qualitative formalisms deal with incomplete information, whereas most quantitative ones do not. Furthermore, the two different types of formalism have a different concept of what it means to perform inference. As Dubois and Prade (1987c) point out, many qualitative formalisms use deductive approaches in which inference techniques from classical logic (such as modus ponens and modus tollens) are extended in some way. In this case the material implication $p \rightarrow q$, which is the usual basis of deductive reasoning about p and q, sanctions inferences about belief in q based on knowledge about belief in p and the strength of the implication. This may be contrasted with the reasoning used by numerical methods, which is often essentially abductive. Here the inference is based around conditional measures such as $\Pr(B|A)$ and has a different direction to that of deductive reasoning. [26] This difference is particularly clear when the reasoning schemes are written as follows, for deductive reasoning in qualitative approaches:

---

26 Though the direction can be reversed using Bayes' rule, it is more usually abductive than deductive.

A is believed to be true
(*A* implies *B*) is believed to be true
_____
B is believed to be true

and for abductive reasoning:

A is a cause of *B*
B is observed
_____
A becomes more credible

Perhaps the most obvious attempts to combine qualitative and quantitative approaches to dealing with imperfect information have already been mentioned in the discussion of systems that provide a combination of logical rules and measures of certainty. However, since such systems add numerical measures to classical logic, and classical logic is not really a tool for handling imperfect information, these systems do not really count as combining numerical and non-numerical approaches. However, one system that does count as a combination is graded default logic (Froidevaux and Grossetête, 1990), which combines default logic and possibility theory. Attaching a numerical weight to the logical sentences changes none of their basic properties, so normal techniques can be used to propagate inference alongside some piece of computational machinery that propagates the possibility measures. Thus when two clauses are combined, or a default rule fired, the antecedents are logically combined to give a consequent that has a possibility measure that is the result of the correct combination of the measures associated with the antecedent. The fact that the two processes, although simultaneous, are independent means that a theorem prover for graded default logic may be obtained by augmenting a standard theorem prover for the underlying logic with a means of propagating the numerical measure. Froidevaux and Mengin (Froidevaux and Mengin, 1990; Mengin, 1991) take this course, adapting saturation (Bossu and Siegel, 1985) in the style of Besnard et al. (1983) and adding the correct style of measure propagation. Something rather similar is provided by Neufeld and Poole (1989) in their system, which suggests computing the probabilities of extensions of default logic as a means of choosing between them.

A development that ties default logic even more closely to numerical methods is the discovery of relationships between default logic and evidence theory. Wilson (1990) considers the similarities between belief functions and default logic and shows that, despite their initial dissimilarities they are, in fact, closely related. Indeed, when using Łukaszewicz's (1988) modification of default logic, the extensions of general closed default theories correspond to the sets of formulae whose beliefs, calculated by the theory of evidence, tend to 1 when the reliability of the sources of evidence tend to 1. This work is extended in (Wilson, 1993b) where, by modifying the Dempster-Shafer framework, Wilson is able to capture the full expressiveness of default logic. The existence of a strong relationship between default logic and the theory of evidence is borne out by Smets and

Hsia (1990; 1991) who demonstrate how to represent normal defaults (both with and without prerequisites) using the transferable belief model. As part of this analysis they build valuation networks that capture these defaults, and propagate values through the networks using MacEvidence. This representation will be revisited in Chapter 10.

Both these approaches to combining default logic and evidence theory proceed by embedding defaults into evidence theory. A different approach to combining different inference techniques, which overcomes the problem of having to integrate them fully, is to apply them to a given problem sequentially. This has particular advantages if one of the formalisms is computationally expensive since it allows the more time-consuming method to be applied to a group of hypotheses that has already been restricted to a most plausible set. Systems in which the first inference is by symbolic methods dominate the attempts to combine reasoning techniques. These apply logical techniques to establish a set of possible hypotheses from a larger initial set of exhaustive hypotheses, and then use numerical techniques to rank the plausible set. Typical of such systems are those of Provan (1988), Bigham (1990) and Laskey and Lehner (1990). In all three of these systems, the semantic equivalence of the assumption based truth maintenance (ATMS) (de Kleer, 1986) and evidence theory, proved by Provan, is exploited ensuring that no information is lost in the initial round of inference. Bigham's system is particularly interesting in that it includes an extension of the clause based approach of McAllester's LTMS (McAllester, 1980) as a symbolic inference engine, and also permits possibility values to be propagated.

There are a number of other similar proposals. Three other hybrids of logic and evidence theory set within the context of assumption-based truth maintenance systems are those proposed by D'Ambrosio (1989), Provan (1990) and Kohlas and Monney (1993) while Poznanski (1990) and van Dam (1996; 1998) depart from the norm by combining evidence theory with justification-based truth maintenance systems (Doyle, 1979). Given the close relation between evidence theory and the ATMS, this might seem a strange decision, but it is one that makes sense in the context with which both Poznanski and van Dam were working. In both cases they were interested in establishing a single best solution and so the multiple solution approach of the ATMS was unnecessarily expensive to obtain. Furthermore, both authors were interested in using belief measures to identify which pieces of information were most contradicted, and so use the beliefs to control the truth maintenance system in contrast to most other authors who use the truth maintenance system to compute the beliefs. Also worth mentioning is de Kleer and Williams' (1987) GDE system for fault diagnosis. In this system all inference directed at discovering the fault is carried out by symbolic methods, with probabilities of component failure invoked, not to determine the most likely of several solutions in a static analysis, but to suggest the next measurement. Thus the numerical computation sparks off another round of symbolic inference, and the cycle continues until the fault is found.

4.7 Summary

As before, it is instructive to match the various systems that have been reviewed in this chapter against the various types of imperfect information discussed in Chapter 2. Firstly, consider those systems that might be found under the umbrella of qualitative physics, that is all formalisms for qualitative and order of magnitude reasoning about physical systems. These may deal with a mathematical tool (differential equations) that lies outside the traditional domain of artificial intelligence, but they deal with incomplete information as surely as any logical formalism does. This is also true, to some degree of the interval systems discussed in Section 4.3. While these systems clearly deal with uncertainty in the same sense that probability and possibility theories deal with uncertainty, they also deal with incomplete probabilistic knowledge—which is why they give interval rather than point results—a point that is often acknowledged by saying that the systems can deal with *partial ignorance*. By this it is meant that the systems can cope with situations in which whoever is specifying the necessary probabilities is partially ignorant of the true probability distribution and so cannot give all the values. Regardless of how it is named, the result is the same—the knowledge is incomplete. However, this incompleteness is rather different to the incompleteness modelled by qualitative algebras, for instance. The difference is that while qualitative algebras and order of magnitude systems model knowledge that is incomplete, interval probability systems model information that is uncertain and incomplete. In fact, interval probability systems model information for which there is incomplete knowledge of how uncertain the information is. Thus the incompleteness is "second order." It is an imperfection in knowledge of the imperfection of knowledge. Indeed, it is this kind of information that is modelled by all abstractions of quantitative systems whether they are qualitative probabilistic networks or systems built on kappa values. In contrast, all the defeasible systems really just aim to handle first order incomplete information. These are therefore largely concerned with how to make assumptions about pieces of information which are not explicitly given, though those that make use of numbers are capable of handling uncertainty as well—they are, of course, all based on methods for handling uncertainty[27]—as are some of those that are based on argumentation. Indeed, one of the attractive features of some systems of argumentation is that fact that they promise to be able to handle both uncertainty and incompleteness with similar ease.

One notable exception in types of incomplete information covered in this chapter is inconsistent information. That does not, however, mean that systems that can handle in-consistency have not been considered in the literature. Indeed, one could consider any

---

[27] Provoking the tangential thought that perhaps there is not much difference between handling incomplete information and handling uncertain information. But that is another story.

nonmonotonic logic to be a system for handling inconsistency since the reason for retracting assumptions is precisely to prevent inconsistencies occurring. In addition systems of argumentation can be used as a means of handling inconsistency (Elvang-Gøransson and Hunter, 1995), though it should be noted that there are many formal systems not mentioned here whose main purpose is ensuring that sensible conclusions can be reached from a set of inconsistent formulae. Examples of such systems are discussed by Rescher and Manor (1970), Roos (1992), and Hunter (2000).

This marks the end of the review part of this book. What the review was intended to provide is a context in which to set the theoretical developments of the later part of this book. From the material that has been covered it is clear that there are many types of imperfect information and that only some of these are actually handled by the different formalisms that have been proposed. It is also clear that many different methods have been proposed, all of which have quite a narrow field of application, some handling only uncertain information and others only handling incomplete information. There have been some attempts to combine systems with different areas of application in order to create more widely applicable systems but such efforts have not succeeded in combining many different formalisms. This is a point that will be reconsidered in the next chapter. Having established this overview of the handling of imperfect information, this book now focuses on the specific area of handling uncertain information, and, in particular, on qualitative versions of the models for handling uncertainty provided by probability, possibility, and evidence theories. As the next chapter will argue, there are three problems with using the theories as they stand, and it is solutions to these problems that are the main topic of the remainder of the book.

5 A framework for studying different methods

The world is an interminable chain of causes and effects and each cause is also an effect.

Jorge Luis Borges, *Avatars of the Tortoise*

The previous two chapters introduced a number of systems for handling imperfect information. In particular, Chapter 3 discussed probability, possibility, and evidence theories, three formalisms for handling uncertain information (evidence theory also being well adapted for handling ambiguous information) in some detail. The next chapter sees the start of the main theoretical results that this book presents, results that centre on the use of these three theories. There is a considerable gap between the knowledge imparted in Chapter 3 concerning the three theories and that required to understand the material in Chapter 6 and beyond—a gap that is more one of focus and intent than of technical information. It is intended that the contents of this chapter should fill that gap. This is done in a number of ways. The first way in which the gap is filled is by expanding on points made in Chapter 1 concerning problems in applying formal methods for handling uncertainty—problems that are not currently handled by any of the available methods. In particular, the problems of not having all the information required by a model, of not having information about the specific problem to which the model is being applied, and the problem of not being able to fit the available data into the model are discussed. A particular solution to these problems that has many similarities to some of the qualitative systems described in Chapter 4 is then introduced, concluding the first thread of the chapter. The second way in which the reader is prepared for Chapter 6 is by stating quite precisely the focus of the later technical developments. This focussing provides some early insights into how the work will progress, defines some key terms, and describes exactly how the formalisms will be employed. The third and final way in which the gap between Chapters 4 and 6 is filled is by providing a pair of examples that will be used in the remaining chapters to demonstrate the approaches being developed.

5.1 Introduction

As mentioned in Chapter 1, there are a number of problems that are common to many of the commonly used techniques for handling uncertainty.[1] The most important of these from the point of view of this book are those that will be referred to here as the *incompleteness*

---

1 From here on the term "uncertainty" is used in the specific sense introduced in Chapter 2 of a form of subjective imperfection introduced due to some observer's lack of perfect knowledge.

problem, the *robustness problem*, and the *integration problem*.

The incompleteness problem arises from the fact that many of the methods for reasoning under uncertainty are numerical and therefore anyone who wishes to use them must acquire a large amount of detailed numerical information about the domain to which they intend to apply the model. As argued in the introduction to Chapter 4 this is a problem that has been widely acknowledged, and the wealth of work in that chapter is a testimony to the seriousness with which it is viewed. However, despite the advances chronicled in Chapter 4, there are no completely satisfactory methods that are capable of handling incomplete information about probabilistic, possibilistic and belief models. It could be argued that such methods are not necessary, since each of these three main theories have methods such as the principle of maximum entropy and the principle of minimum specificity that may be used to "fill in" the missing values, and such arguments have considerable virtue. However, all such methods make some assumptions about how the values should be filled in, and these assumptions, like all assumptions, may be wrong at times. Thus the existence of methods such as the principle of maximum entropy does not make the study of other methods of handling incomplete information worthless. Of course, it should be noted that the methods investigated here as means of handling the incompleteness problem make their own assumptions that the reader may accept or reject as desired—the point is that they provide a different solution to the problem than existing methods. The main kind of solution that they provide is a qualitative one, where the word "qualitative" is interpreted in the same broad way as it was in Chapter 4[2] and broadly takes the form of replacing missing precise values with qualitative ones.

The robustness problem is closely allied to the incompleteness problem, and in some ways may be considered as a particularly extreme version of it. The problem arises from the fact that when precise numerical information is used as the basis of a system that handles uncertainty, the system can be extremely sensitive to the particular values that are built into it, and hence particularly sensitive to the sample data that is used to establish the numbers. Although it is possible, through diligence and hard work, to reduce this effect, it remains the case that a numerical model is less effective when used on examples that are not drawn from the same pool as those used to build the model. Thus a medical diagnosis system might be built using patient data from a particular clinic. This system might show very high diagnostic accuracy when used on patients attending that clinic, but it is likely to exhibit considerably less impressive performance when used in a similar clinic in a distant city because the characteristics of the population on which it is used will have changed. The problem was stated in a particularly pithy form by Wellman (1990a) when he used

---

2 That is to indicate any method that uses coarser grained information than precise numbers thus covering the whole terrain from narrow intervals to symbolic increments.

the robustness problem to motivate his work on QPNs and qualitative decision making. He argued that:

knowledge bases (of the kind that are commonly developed) constrain the problem solver to a narrow decision context applicable only to a restricted set of selected cases.

The robustness problem, then, is the problem of making models for handling uncertainty sufficiently robust that it is possible to transfer models built using them from one narrow context to another without seriously degrading their performance. It can be viewed as a more extreme version of the incompleteness problem since, strictly speaking, after shifting a model from one set of subjects to another none of the numerical information actually applies. Thus the robustness problem is the incompleteness problem applied to the whole model. In practice, however, the information often does not differ enough to have a huge effect on the performance of the model, and improving robustness is a matter of ensuring that the initial model does not break down too badly, either by choosing values that are valid over several sets of subjects, or by tweaking the values after the move. Whichever view is taken, it is clear that methods such as the application of the principle of maximum entropy have little to say about the robustness problem, not least because they are sensitive to the part of the model that is complete when they are applied. The solutions that are proposed for the robustness problem here draw both on the use of qualitative values such as are used in the solution of the incompleteness problem, and on a method that is very similar to that proposed by Wellman (1990a). Both the robustness problem and the incompleteness problem are problems of second-order imperfect information in that they are problems to do with specifying the various models used to handle imperfect information. Providing solutions to them may be seen as reducing the burden on the user of such models (Wellman, 1994).

The integration problem is the problem of integrating two or more uncertainty handling techniques so that they may be applied in combination to the same problem. Briefly, the reason that this arises can be explained as follows. From the discussions in Chapters 3 and 4 of how techniques map to types of imperfect information, it seems that a suitable way of handling any incompleteness in a probabilistic model would be to use a set of default rules that specify which probabilities should be adopted and when. However, this solution immediately poses its own problem—how should these defaults and the rest of the probabilistic model be used in conjunction. There is more to the integration problem than this, as hopefully will become clear in the next section, but this suffices to show that there is a problem, and one to which this book proposes a partial solution. The form of the solution will give the alert reader no cause for surprise. Indeed, even before investigating the problem in more detail, it is not giving much away to reveal that the solution once again is the use of qualitative methods, in fact exactly the same methods that are proposed as possible solutions to the incompleteness and robustness problems. Thus it is clear that the remainder of this book also serves the additional purpose mentioned in the introduction, namely to broadcast my strong opinion that qualitative methods have an important place in the armoury of anyone who has to combat the problems of representing and reasoning with uncertainty.

5.2   Eclecticism and the integration problem

Methods for handling uncertainty have traditionally been regarded as exclusive alternatives, and for many years, researchers have indulged in ideological tracts in which the formalism that they championed was compared with its "competitors" and found to exhibit superior performance. Examples of this behaviour abound, and it is only recently that a more moderate view has emerged (Fox, 1986; Saffiotti, 1987; Clark, 1990; Krause and Clark, 1993; Shafer, 1994; Hunter, 1996) that acknowledges that different formalisms are useful for the solution of different problems. A general realisation of the strength of this eclectic position has motivated research both into ways in which different formalisms may be used in combination to solve interesting practical problems, and into establishing the formal differences and similarities between different systems. Because of the relation between this approach and the work that is presented in the following chapters, it seems appropriate to discuss the eclectic approach in some detail.

5.2.1   The eclectic position

The best summary of the eclectic position that I have found is that provided by Shafer (1994) who asserts that:

managing uncertainty in artificial intelligence means choosing, on a case-by-case basis, between different formalisms and different ways of using these formalisms.

The argument for adopting this position runs along the following lines. Each and every formalism was invented with particular goals in mind. Those that motivated the development of probability theory are somewhat obscure but seem to have been based upon the desire to profit in games of chance (Shafer, 1991b). Possibility theory was intended to represent vague and incomplete knowledge (Dubois and Prade, 1991d). Evidence theory was intended (Dempster, 1988) to extend probability theory by dropping the completeness axiom (as discussed by Cox (1946) and in Sections 2.6.1 and 4.6.1), though it can equally well be seen as being intended to be an axiomatically justified model of subjective belief (Smets, 1993). All of the formalisms can achieve their aims given a suitable application, and perform admirably on their home ground as demonstrated by many of the papers that champion them, for instance (Zadeh, 1986; Lauritzen and Spiegelhalter, 1988;

Smets, 1988b). Probability theory is perfectly adapted for handling objective frequentistic information and also provides a normative model of subjective belief when it is possible to assign a belief to every one of a set of mutually exclusive and exhaustive hypotheses. Possibility theory provides a neat way of combining data defined in terms of fuzzy variables, and evidence theory is a beautifully intuitive way of redistributing belief as ignorance is resolved.

However, as discussed in Chapter 2, there are many different types and sources of imperfect information, and any one formalism is only designed to work on some of them. If an attempt is made to apply a formalism to model a form of imperfection it was not designed to handle, problems may emerge. For example, if it is desired to use probability theory where the prior probability of some variable is unknown then it is necessary to use some assumption, such as maximum entropy, in order to get the values that are required. This might be a less intuitive means of encoding the information than would be adopted by evidence theory. Another problem emerges when the data that is available is not of the right kind for a given model, as, for instance, is the case when the data is largely statistical, and the model is possibilistic. In some cases it may be possible to squeeze the data into the model (Garriba et al., 1988), but in some other cases this "shoehorning" of data may cause a distortion of the problem. A good example of this latter phenomenon is provided by the Pathfinder system (Heckerman et al., 1992) in which the performance of the system (as judged by the domain expert) improved substantially when changing from using evidence theory to using probability theory. In another case, it has been demonstrated that engineering uncertainty out (in Cohen's (1985) phrase) of a diagnosis system altogether, which is an extreme form of shoehorning, impairs the diagnostic ability of the system (Saffiotti and Umkehrer, 1991c; Saffiotti et al., 1994). A desire to avoid shoehorning was also the concern of Gupta (1993), motivating his work on translating possibilistic information into probabilistic information, and prompted Bogler (1987) to use evidence theory rather than probability theory in target identification.

A further problem that can arise is that applying a particular approach may involve constructing a hugely complex model. For instance, in the case discussed by Cheeseman (1986), it seems clear to me that it would be much simpler to use a possibilistic approach rather than the probabilistic approach he is advocating. He, of course, is not really arguing that probability is the best way of tackling the problem, only that it may be used to tackle the problem—it is the baroque nature of his model that suggests that there are better ways to do the modelling. All of these problems point to the adoption of the eclectic position. This resolves all the problems by suggesting that each approach should just be used in exactly those conditions in which it is best, either because it is simpler or because it makes fewer assumptions, and thus provides a means of dealing with situations in which the available data does not fit into a given model.

Now, adopting the eclectic position is a relatively simple matter when problems are small and there is one formalism that is clearly the best. In such situations one can follow the course suggested by Saffiotti and colleagues (Saffiotti and Umkehrer, 1991c; Saffiotti et al., 1994). This procedure, which has been applied to the problem of diagnosing faults in an electricity distribution network, is to encode the uncertain information in probability, possibility, and evidence theories and to make a decision as to which is best on the basis of their comparative performances. This is a good method for choosing a single representation, but it does not deal with the underlying issue. If it is accepted that particular pieces of information are represented best in a particular formalism, then eventually a situation will arise in which a single problem has elements that are best encoded in different formalisms. One approach would be to extend Saffiotti's method and find the formalism that encodes all elements with the least distortion. However, the best approach seems to be to use the best formalism in each case and integrate the information where necessary.

The idea of combining approaches to provide a better solution than is possible using any single approach is not new.[3] It has been widely adopted in the knowledge representation community where the superiority of the use of several formalisms over one has long been realised, for example (Brachman et al., 1983; Reichgelt, 1991). Combined knowledge representations have many advantages. They may be computationally more efficient because the result of "shoehorning" is often a clumsy expression that takes a long time to evaluate, and they often give a more natural means of expression since they extend the expressive capabilities of any one system. Both of these advantages also apply to combined uncertainty handling formalisms, and the success of eclecticism in knowledge representation is a powerful argument for its adoption in uncertainty handling. Additional motivation for studying the problems of integrating formalisms comes from the field of multi-agent systems where much interest is concentrated on the problem of getting several intelligent systems to co-operate with one another. Since these systems may well have been developed before it was decided to make them work together, as was the case in the ARCHON system (Jennings, 1994), they may well use different uncertainty handling formalisms. As Zhang (1992) points out, if the systems use different uncertainty handling formalisms it is necessary to provide them with a means of integrating the formalisms that they use so that they may pass useful information to one another.

5.2.2 Integration and incompleteness

There are many forms of integration. Some of the work discussed in the previous chapter where one formalism has been theoretically related to another, for instance (Wilson, 1990), may be claimed to be integration. Similarly it could be claimed that when one formalism

---

3 Indeed, it could be taken as a model for scientific advances in general.

can be partially fitted into another, as Smets and Hsia (1991) fit default logic into evidence theory, the two formalisms have been integrated. This is not the kind of integration that will be considered in this book. For the eclectic position to be useful it must be possible to integrate values expressed in different formalisms in the sense that they may be combined together. Thus, for instance, given two pieces of evidence about an event, one expressed in possibility theory and one in probability theory, it must be possible to combine them together to get a single measure that indicates either how probable or how possible the event is.

There are a number of ways in which this kind of integration can be achieved. The first is the formation of a *super-formalism*, which combines the features of several formalisms, and can thus handle information expressed in more than one. In such a system one would first encode the information in the best fitting formalism and when wanting to combine this with information in a different formalism use the super-formalism as the format into which both could be translated. This is an attractive idea but as it requires a large amount of theoretical work and, since each new development will require that the super-formalism be painstakingly crafted to handle it, the superformalism is always liable to lag behind the cutting edge of developments in reasoning under uncertainty. However, having said this, a restricted form of this super-formalism is already in existence in the form of the context model (Gebhardt and Kruse, 1993a). However, it does not appear, as yet, to provide a means of translating values between probability, possibility, and evidence theories. Instead it provides a means of comparing the semantic foundations of the theories, pointing out common features and those operations that are compatible across formalisms, and highlighting their common basis in random sets.

A second form of integration is integration by the translation of values between formalisms, a step that replaces the integration problem with a *translation problem*—to provide a means of translating values from one formalism to another. This can be done in a number of ways. When given information in n formalisms it is possible to integrate by translating all the information expressed in $n - 1$ of the formalisms into the nth, perhaps that in which the most relevant information is expressed. This approach has the disadvantage of appearing to be "shoehorning" by another name. Perhaps a better option is to begin reasoning in any formalism, and then translate into, or out of, that formalism when information that is not expressed in that formalism is required. Either way, the translation of values from one formalism to another is an important means of achieving the integration of uncertainty handling formalisms, and one that it is difficult to achieve at the moment. As discussed already, Smets (1988a; 1989), among others, has given a means of translating from belief measures to probability and it is possible to convert probability values to belief functions. However, less can be said about other formalisms. Possibility values do not easily translate to either probability or belief values, though under some circumstances plausibility may equate to possibility and necessity to belief (Dubois and Prade, 1988d) and a possibility can be taken as an upper bound on the probability of a variable (as discussed in Section 3.2.2), and a translation has been proposed by Gupta (1993). Zhang (1992; 1994) has suggested a general approach to translation between different formalisms and has applied it to translations between the Prospector model (Duda et al., 1976) and the two types of certainty factor used by MYCIN (Buchanan and Shortliffe, 1984) and EMYCIN (van Melle, 1980). However, the keystone of this approach is that the extreme values of the measures between which the translation is made must be equivalent. This makes it inappropriate for translations between many theories. In particular, it makes the approach inappropriate for translations between probability, possibility and evidence theories since $\Pi(x) = 1$ expresses something rather different from $\Pr(x) = 1$ and $\text{Bel}(x) = 0$ expresses something rather different from $\Pr(x) = 0$. In addition, Agustí-Cullell et al. (1991) have proposed a method for translation between the different multi-valued logics used by the MILORD system. However, this method seems to rely on the fact that the different logics have the same semantics—they are just different-grained views of the same set of values. This means that their approach does not provide a solution to the translation. There has been little other work done on translation, and it should be noted that those translations that have been proposed often disagree with one another, as is the case with those given by Smets' pignistic transformation (Smets, 1989) and Dubois and Prade (1988d), and are not always accepted even by those who do not offer an alternative, as is the case with Clarke (1988) who disagrees with Smets (1988a).

A third form of integration is achieved through the assessment of the impact of evidence expressed in one formalism upon values expressed in another. For instance, consider a hypothesis H whose probability is known and suppose that some new evidence is obtained about a related fact G whose possibility changes as a result. If it were possible to determine how this change in possibility affects the probability of H then the initial possibilistic information about G, the information relating G and H, and the probabilistic information about H would have been integrated. Although at first sight this form of integration may seem to be less important than the others, it can be argued that this is not so. Assessing the impact of evidence is, as is clear from Chapter 3, the biggest concern of all the major uncertainty theories. Indeed the way that values change often seems to be of far greater concern to authors than the values that they change to and dealing with exactly these kinds of changes in value is the focus of much of the work on abstractions of numerical systems discussed in Chapter 4. This mention of qualitative methods brings the argument full circle and it is time to turn to the question of why qualitative methods are useful as a means of integration between formalisms, in particular as a means of achieving the kinds of integration discussed above, as the basis for constructing intelligent systems based upon the eclectic approach to reasoning under uncertainty. The next section discusses how this might be done when some intuitively reasonable assumptions are made.

5.2.3   Integration and degrading

Section 5.2.1 presented a statement that purported to summarise the eclectic position that has emerged from the literature, and it was argued that this naturally led to the need to integrate formalisms, in particular by translating values from one formalism to another. This statement has an important corollary. If it is possible to translate values from one formalism to another then the values must encode the same basic information. That is not to say that $\mathrm{Bel}(A)$ and $\Pi(A)$ are equivalent since they are clearly not. The belief value is a subjective statement of some agent's internal view of the world, while the possibility value is determined by fuzzy restrictions that describe the state of the world. However both encode the same basic piece of information, namely that there is some reason to think that A will occur. This reason can be based on subjective belief or physical possibility. It may be the result of a simple observation or a complex argument. However, when it is degraded to the extent that only its basic semantic content remains, it is the same whatever the formalism in which it was initially expressed. At this basic level, all the semantic subtleties are lost and every last measure, expressed in whichever formalism is chosen, is reduced to the same thing; a reason to think that an event may occur. This leads to the idea of "degrading" measures of uncertainty, a process that is summed up by the following *principle of degrading*:

Assumption 5.1 *For any event X any measure of uncertainty about X, such as the probability of X, $\mathrm{Pr}(X)$, encodes the same basic information about X as any other measure of uncertainty such as the possibility of X, $\Pi(X)$, or the belief in X, $\mathrm{Bel}(X)$. This basic information is that there is a reason to think that X may occur.*

This idea of degrading makes the second kind of integration discussed above, value integration, possible. If it is known that $\mathrm{Pr}(A) = 0.2$ then there is a reason to believe that A will occur, and so there is a non-zero value for $\Pi(A)$. This value of $\Pi(A)$ may then be combined with other possibility values to learn things about $\Pi(C)$, for instance, that were previously unknown. Unfortunately, the value of $\Pi(A)$ is unknown, all that is known is that it is greater than 0 and less than or equal to 1 when $n > 0$, and 0 when n is zero. In other words the translation is:

$$\mathrm{Pr}(A) = n \mapsto \Pi(A) \in (0, 1]$$

when $n > 0$ and:[4]

$$\Pr(A) = 0 \mapsto \Pi(A) = 0$$

This does not appear to be very useful at first sight. However, as discussed in Chapter 4, qualitative reasoning provides a means of dealing with "somethings," and in Chapter 6 the way in which qualitative reasoning may help to extract the maximum information possible from the translation of values by degrading is examined. It is worth noting that what the principle of degrading says is very weak. Any measure of the uncertainty of X is reduced to a statement that "X may occur," even when the measure implies that to some degree X must occur, as $N(X)$ does for instance. The reason for choosing this weak principle is that it is universally applicable to all formalisms, whereas a stronger statement, that degraded measures to "X is known to occur" would only be applicable to measures of certainty such as $N(X)$ and $\mathrm{Bel}(X)$.

However, the principle of degrading does not apply equally across all formalisms. For instance, while knowing that $\Pr(A) = 0$ implies that $\Pi(A) = 0$, knowing that $\mathrm{Bel}(A) = 0$ does not mean that $\Pi(A) = 0$. So, for the three formalisms considered here, the implications of the principle of degrading are, for $n > 0$:

$$\Pr(A) = n \quad \mapsto \quad \Pi(A) = (0, 1] \tag{5.1}$$
$$\Pr(A) = n \quad \mapsto \quad \mathrm{Bel}(A) = [0, 1] \tag{5.2}$$
$$\Pi(A) = n \quad \mapsto \quad \Pr(A) = (0, 1] \tag{5.3}$$
$$\Pi(A) = n \quad \mapsto \quad \mathrm{Bel}(A) = [0, 1] \tag{5.4}$$
$$\mathrm{Bel}(A) = n \quad \mapsto \quad \Pr(A) = (0, 1] \tag{5.5}$$
$$\mathrm{Bel}(A) = n \quad \mapsto \quad \Pi(A) = (0, 1] \tag{5.6}$$

while:

$$\Pr(A) = 0 \quad \mapsto \quad \Pi(A) = 0 \tag{5.7}$$
$$\Pr(A) = 0 \quad \mapsto \quad \mathrm{Bel}(A) = 0 \tag{5.8}$$
$$\Pi(A) = 0 \quad \mapsto \quad \Pr(A) = 0 \tag{5.9}$$
$$\Pi(A) = 0 \quad \mapsto \quad \mathrm{Bel}(A) = 0 \tag{5.10}$$
$$\mathrm{Bel}(A) = 0 \quad \mapsto \quad \Pr(A) = [0, 1] \tag{5.11}$$
$$\mathrm{Bel}(A) = 0 \quad \mapsto \quad \Pi(A) = [0, 1] \tag{5.12}$$

---

4 Note that this latter mapping assumes, as we do throughout this book, that the measures are defined on a finite set. Thus the variables whose probabilities and possibilities are under discussion have a finite set of possible values.

The principle of degrading also enables the third kind of integration discussed above—integration by change in value, which from this point on is known as "integration by change." Of course, dealing with changes involves dealing with the value of the change, but the given names will be used to distinguish the methods. To see how integration by change works, consider the following. As discussed above, if $\Pr(a) = 0.1$ then $\Pi(A) = x$, where x is unknown but greater than 0 and less than or equal to 1. If some evidence about B is obtained, which bears upon A such that, as a result of this evidence, $\Pr(A)$ increases to 0.5, what can be said about $\Pi(A)$? It seems reasonable to assume that since $\Pr(A)$ and $\Pi(A)$ are both fundamentally measuring the same thing that if it is known that $\Pr(A)$ goes up, then something can be said about changes in $\Pi(A)$. Because it is assumed that a change in $\Pr(A)$ is somehow carried over into a change in $\Pi(A)$, this assumption is referred to as a *monotonicity assumption*. In fact, there are a whole range of monotonicity assumptions that may be made. The first is perhaps the most desirable since it is the strongest and so allows precise predictions to be made:

Assumption 5.2 *If one measure of uncertainty concerning a variable X, say the probability of X, $\Pr(X)$, increases, then any other measure such as the possibility of X, $\Pi(X)$ also increases. Similarly if one measure decreases then so does the other.*

Unfortunately this version of the assumption is rather too strong since, recalling the example of Hans' eggs from Chapter 3, if the probability of Hans eating n eggs for breakfast is reduced (perhaps because he was advised to cut his cholesterol intake) it would mean that the possibility of him eating n eggs, which is a function of his ability to eat eggs, would also be reduced. Thus the assumption does not make sense for this pair of formalisms, though it may be valid for others. Instead a weaker second monotonicity assumption can be proposed:

Assumption 5.3 *If one measure concerning a variable X, say the probability of X, $\Pr(X)$, increases, then any other measure such as the possibility of X, $\Pi(X)$, cannot decrease. Similarly if one measure decreases no other may increase.*

This avoids the problems of the first assumption by allowing the possibility of Hans eating a given number of eggs not to change when the probability falls. However, Prade (1993) has pointed out that as it stands this assumption is flawed in certain cases. In particular, when reasoning with evidence theory it is possible for a hypothesis to initially have a low belief and a high plausibility, and for these to converge as evidence is obtained. Thus as $\mathrm{Bel}(X)$ increases, $\mathrm{Pl}(X)$ decreases. Thus, while the use of the second monotonicity assumption need not be problematic, as argued in Chapter 7, there are situations in which it breaks down.

To overcome this flaw, the assumption needs to be restated in terms that capture the difference between upper and lower certainty values (Saffiotti, 1993) such as plausibility and belief. In particular it is necessary to relate the change in an upper certainty value of a hypothesis to the lower certainty value of the complement of that hypothesis and vice-versa. That is $Bel(X)$ must be related to $Pl(\neg X)$ and $Pl(X)$ must be related to $Bel(\neg x)$. Taking this need into account, a third version of the monotonicity assumption may be obtained:

Assumption 5.4 *If a lower measure of the certainty of a hypothesis in one formalism increases, the lower measure of the same hypothesis in any other formalism does not decrease, and the upper measure of the complement of the hypothesis in any formalism does not increase.*

Similarly, if the upper measure of the certainty of a hypothesis in one formalism increases, the upper measure of the same hypothesis in any other formalism does not decrease, and the lower measure of the complement of the hypothesis in any formalism does not increase.

A similar assumption may be made for decreases in value. What this version of the assumption means for the probability, possibility and belief measures that are considered here is that given some hypothesis H, if $Pr(H)$ is known to increase then $Bel(H)$ will not decrease, and $\Pi(\neg H)$ will not increase. Similarly, if $\Pi(H)$ increases, then $Pr(\neg H)$ will not increase and neither will $Bel(\neg H)$. Again, this assumption may fail to hold in some cases—it is, after all, a heuristic. However, like the others it does make it possible to make useful deductions in those situations in which it is thought reasonable to employ it. The use of any of these assumptions clearly raises questions of semantic coherence and necessitates the adoption of a suitable semantic model such as that of "degrading." There is one final version of the monotonicity assumption that may be employed:

Assumption 5.5 *If one measure concerning a variable X, say the probability of X, $Pr(X)$, increases, then any other measure such as the possibility of X, $\Pi(X)$, either increases, decreases, or does not change. Similarly if one measure decreases any other either increases, or decreases, or does not change.*

While this might at first sight seem to be too weak to make any useful deductions, it is not necessarily the case when translating into possibility theory. This matter will be discussed further in Chapter 7.

In addition to the fact that these assumptions seems intuitively acceptable, it is possible to argue slightly more formally for their adoption. As mentioned in Section 3.2.2 Zadeh has suggested formalising the relationship between probability and possibility via the possibility/probability consistency principle expressed in (3.44). Given a belief distribution across $x_1, \ldots, x_n$, $\mathrm{Bel}(x_1), \ldots, \mathrm{Bel}(x_n)$, two further principles may be suggested to formalise similar connections between belief and probability, and between belief and possibility. These will be known as the *probability/belief consistency principle* and the *possibility/belief consistency principle*. The first says that the probability distribution and the belief distribution have a degree of consistency ϱ:

$$\varrho = \mathrm{Pr}(x_1) \cdot \mathrm{Bel}(x_1) + \ldots + \mathrm{Pr}(x_n) \cdot \mathrm{Bel}(x_n) \qquad (5.13)$$

which remains constant as the probability and belief distributions are updated. The second says that the possibility distribution and the belief distribution have a degree of consistency ζ:

$$\zeta = \Pi(x_1) \cdot \mathrm{Bel}(x_1) + \ldots + \Pi(x_n) \cdot \mathrm{Bel}(x_n) \qquad (5.14)$$

which remains constant as the possibility and belief distributions are updated. Similar principles could be laid down for other pairs of types of certainty value, particularly necessity and belief, necessity and probability, necessity and plausibility, and probability and plausibility. Given the above principles, it is possible to show that no assumption forces the degree of consistency between two sets of values to change as the values change, making it possible to state:[5]

THEOREM 5.6:   All monotonicity assumptions are consistent with the principles of consistency between probability, possibility, and belief values expressed in (3.44), (5.13), and (5.14).

What this means, essentially, is that the monotonicity assumptions enforce less constraints on the relation between the theories than the consistency principles. This, of course, does not completely prove the validity of the monotonicity assumptions, not least because as Zadeh points out, with reference to the probability/possibility consistency principle, the principles are just approximate statements of the connections between the formalisms. Instead the theorem merely shows that the probability/possibility consistency principle, and its obvious extension to other formalisms, do not rule the monotonicity assumptions out.

---

5 The proofs of all theorems may be found in Appendix A.

Now, given the monotonicity assumption it is possible to reason, for instance, that knowing how $\Pr(A)$ changes provides information on how $\Pi(A)$ changes. In other words there is a translation:

$$\Delta \Pr(A) = n \mapsto \Delta\Pi(A) = m$$

where n and m are both qualitative values. Once again this may seem of little use, since the only methods for dealing with arbitrary increases and decreases in measures of certainty are Wellman's qualitative probabilistic networks (Wellman, 1990a) and Neufeld's (1990) probabilistic defaults. As a result it would seem that it is only possible to make meaningful translations into probability theory since there are no analogous methods for other formalisms. However, Chapters 7 and 8 describe a uniform method for reasoning with changes in probability, possibility, and evidence theories and this may be used to make meaningful translations into those formalisms.

5.2.4   Incompleteness and degrading

Taking an eclectic approach to reasoning under uncertainty, the choice of formalism is guided by the available data. This makes it possible to overcome, to some extent, problems in which the data under consideration does not fit into a particular formalism. If the data does not fit, the formalism is simply replaced with another. However, it is possible that certain data will not fit into any formalism because particular crucial values are not available. From the point of view of the closest fitting formalism, there will be certain values that are missing and so the model will be in a state of incompleteness. The question addressed here is how the qualitative approaches outlined above as solutions to the translation problem may be used to resolve this kind of incompleteness problem.

Well, it is reasonably clear how qualitative values may be used to resolve this problem. The principle of degrading is applied in much the same way that it is applied when translating between formalisms. If a probabilistic model is being considered, and the incompleteness that plagues the model is the lack of a probability $\Pr(A)$ for the event A, and if a non-zero possibility value $\Pi(A)$ for A is available, then it is possible to say that there is a non-zero probability for A. Furthermore, qualitative values may be used to represent this non-zero probability allowing it to be combined with other probabilistic information. This idea may be employed even when there is no possibilistic information about A, or indeed any knowledge about A expressed in any formalism. It is possible to say something about the missing value, namely that $\Pr(A)$ is some value not less than 0 and not greater than 1. This is almost exactly what is known about $\Pr(A)$ if the value of $\Pi(A)$ is known, the difference being that 0 is now a plausible value for $\Pr(A)$. This approach may be summarised by:

$$\Pr(A) = ? \mapsto \Pi(A) \in [0, 1]$$

where ? should be read as "unknown" and be distinguished from [?]. Just as in the case of translation, this imprecise knowledge about the value of $\Pr(A)$ can be represented using a qualitative value and combined with the other data in the model.

The way in which qualitative changes may be used to handle incompleteness is less obvious. The idea here is that by considering qualitative changes of the kind described by Wellman, it is not necessary to have precise numerical values in order to build models. Instead, it is sufficient to establish the qualitative influences between variables. This may be done in two ways. The first is through knowledge of the domain. Rather than assess the precise values of the conditional probabilities relating variables in the domain, it is sufficient to assess the influence of one variable on another. So to model the interaction between A and C, it is only necessary to decide whether or not it is appropriate that the probabilities of values of C increase when the probabilities of values of A do, and not necessary to establish the precise conditional probabilities that relate the two. Of course in specifying that a probabilistic influence holds between two variables, assumptions are being made about the conditional values, assumptions that ensure that the reasoning being performed using the influences is in accordance with probability theory. If A is said to positively influence C, then by (4.11):

$$\Pr(c|a, X) \geq \Pr(c|\neg a, X)$$

for all other variables X that also have an influence on the probabilities of values of C. Of course, if the conditional probability values are known, there is no reason why they should not be used in order to determine the qualitative influences—it is just that there seems to be little reason to degrade precise numerical information into qualitative information. However, even if some of the conditional values are not available, but it is still clear what their relative magnitude is in relation to values that are known, then the use of qualitative influences seems appropriate. Thus, when relating two binary variables A and C (where the latter is only influenced by the binary variable B in addition to A), then if one value, say $\Pr(c|a, \neg b)$, is unknown, conventional probabilistic techniques may not be applied. However, if it is clear that the following conditions hold:

$$\Pr(c|a, b) \geq \Pr(c|\neg a, b)$$
$$\Pr(c|a, \neg b) \geq \Pr(c|\neg a, \neg b)$$

the first from the values that are known and the second from knowing that A taking the value a has a positive effect on the probability of C taking the value c, then A positively influences C. Thus the values that are known help to focus attention on what information is required about those that are not known, in this case whether the missing value was greater than or equal to $\Pr(c|\neg a, \neg b)$.

This second method of establishing what qualitative influences hold between variables immediately suggests a solution to the incompleteness problem. If values are missing from a model, the entire model can be converted into one that uses qualitative changes. Existing values can be used to establish many of the influences, and further can be used to determine what exactly needs to be known about those values that are missing in order to establish the remaining influences. Having established the influences they may then be used to carry out reasoning that would not have been possible previously. Thus in the case of A and C, initially nothing could be said about how the probabilities of the value of C changed when new information became available about A. However, once the influence of A on C is established, it may then be used to determine how the probabilities of the values of C are affected when the probabilities of values of A change.

The first method of establishing what qualitative influences hold may also be used to solve the incompleteness problem. Indeed, it can be used to build models that are totally incomplete in that there is no precise information at all about probability values. All that is required is sufficient knowledge of the domain so that the influences between variables may be established. Again, once the influences are established, it is possible to use them to draw conclusions that could not have been reached without using the method. Since this use of qualitative changes is capable of dealing with this extreme kind of incompleteness, it is obviously capable of providing a solution to the robustness problem, a point originally made by Wellman (1990b). He argues that transferring a system from the data which was used to build it to the data on which it will be used, will not change the underlying influences because, even though the particular conditional values relating to variables will alter, they will not alter enough to reverse the conditions on their relative magnitudes. Given that Wellman has thus already proposed a solution to the incompleteness and robustness problems for probability theory, the main contribution of this book as regards those problems is to suggest how they might be solved when using possibility and evidence theories and to provide a general approach for solving the problems that could be extended to other formalisms.

5.3   A general framework

The following ideas frame the development of methods for reasoning under uncertainty that is carried out in later chapters. It should be noted that the framework, while wide-reaching, is not completely general. This kind of focusing is a necessary prerequisite for any comparative discussion of uncertainty formalisms since it is impossible to deal with every possible scenario and paradigm that has been introduced. In brief, it seems sensible to focus only on the three main uncertainty handling formalisms, though it should be stressed that it is straightforward to extend the methods introduced to deal with most formalisms. It is also sensible to only consider the use of the methods within the context of network representations, partly because they are so widely used, and partly because they conveniently limit the problems being considered.

5.3.1   An abstract description of uncertainty

Many of the intuitive terms for representing quantitative uncertainty have become associated with particular formalisms. This is especially true of terms like "belief" and "possibility," which are used both as a reference to a precise mathematical concept, and more loosely to represent different types of uncertainty. This is unfortunate because it creates a particular problem. As a result of the fact that the integration of different formalisms is being considered, a lot of space in the next few chapters will be devoted to talking of probability, possibility, and belief values all at the same time. Consequently it is useful to have a single term for referring to them all that is not tainted by associations with particular formalisms. As a result the term "certainty value" will be used to refer to quantitative uncertainty values since it is distinct from "certainty factor" and has a similar intuitive meaning of a value that encodes how certain or uncertain an event is. The expression "certainty value of x," which is abbreviated to both $\text{Val}(x)$ and "certainty of x," will be used in two separate ways. The first is as an abbreviation for "probability, possibility, or belief," as in the statement:

in probability, possibility, and evidence theories, $\text{Val}(x)$ takes values between 0 and 1.

This is its most common usage. In this sense, the formal definition of the term "certainty value" is as follows:

DEFINITION 5.1:   The *certainty value* of a variable X taking value x, $\text{Val}(x)$, is either the probability of x, $\text{Pr}(x)$, the possibility of x, $\Pi(x)$, or the belief in x, $\text{Bel}(x)$.

The terms "certainty value" and "$\text{Val}(x)$" will also be used in the sense of "an anonymous numerical measure of uncertainty," as in the statement:

when it is necessary that $\text{Val}(x)$ always decreases as $\text{Val}(\neg x)$ increases, probability theory must be used.

In this way the use of "certainty value" and "$\text{Val}(x)$" helps to stress the fact that the methods outlined in this book may be extended to cover every existing formalism, as well as any formalisms that may emerge in the future. When used in this way $\text{Val}(x)$ is similar to the abstract measure of uncertainty introduced by Fonck (1992), and the use made of the symbol "$\mathrm{Val}(\varphi, \mathcal{H})$" by Dubois, Lang and Prade (1991a) to represent either a possibility measure or a necessity measure.

In some places, as in the third monotonicity assumption, it will be necessary to distinguish between *upper certainty values*, written $\mathrm{Val}^*(\cdot)$, which, like possibility, measure the upper bound on the degree to which a hypothesis might occur, and *lower certainty values*, written $\mathrm{Val}_*(\cdot)$, which, like belief, measure the lower bound on the degree to which a hypothesis must occur. For both possibility and evidence theory, the upper certainty value of a hypothesis may be established from the lower certainty value of the complementary hypothesis (Dubois and Prade, 1988d), and vice versa:

$$\mathrm{Val}^*(x) = 1 - \mathrm{Val}_*(\neg x) \tag{5.15}$$

Thus a belief value may be related to a plausibility value (Shafer, 1976), and a possibility value may be related to a necessity value (Dubois and Prade, 1988f). In the case of probability theory, of course, the upper certainty value and the lower certainty value coincide.

The work described in later chapters is set in the framework of directed graphs in which the nodes represent variables, and the edges represent explicit dependencies between the variables. These are called *certainty networks*. Sometimes attention will be restricted to singly-connected graphs. However, many of the techniques described in this book can be extended to multiply-connected networks with loops, and the precise limitations of the systems are described when they become apparent. When the edges of such graphs are quantified with probability values they are those studied by Pearl (1988b), when possibility values are used the graphs are those of Fonck and Straszecka (1991) and when belief values are used the graphs are those studied by Shafer et al. (1987) and Smets (1991a).

Each node in a graph represents a variable with two or more values. All such variables are taken to have a finite set of values. The convention that will be used is that the name of the node is a capital letter, often related to the name of the variable it represents, and that the possible values taken by the variable are indicated by lower case letters, usually the lower case letters appropriate to the name of the node. Thus a node X represents some variable, say "The average price of a Xylophone in dollars," which has set of possible values such as "The average price of a Xylophone is two dollars" and "The average price of a Xylophone is twenty dollars" and which are denoted by $x_1, \ldots, x_n$. These values will also often be referred to anonymously as x_i. Where X represents a binary variable the usual notation is adopted with the two values taken to be x, which stands for the value "The variable represented by X is true," and $\neg x$, which stands for the value "The variable represented by X is false." The set of values $\{x_1, \ldots, x_n\}$ is sometimes written as $\mathbf{X}$. The probability values associated with X are written as $\mathrm{Pr}(x_1), \ldots, \mathrm{Pr}(x_n)$, and the possibility values associated with X as $\Pi(x_1), \ldots, \Pi(x_n)$. Belief values may be assigned to any subset of the values of X, so it is possible to have up to 2^n beliefs associated with X—$\text{Bel}(\{x_1\}), \ldots, \text{Bel}(\{x_n\}), \ldots, \text{Bel}(\{x_1, \ldots, x_n\})$. For simplicity these will be written as $\text{Bel}(x_1)$, $\text{Bel}(x_n)$ and $\text{Bel}(x_1 \cup \ldots \cup x_n)$ respectively. Even this rather lapse notation will be abused later on by using expressions such as $X \in \{x_1, x_3 \cup x_4\}$ to mean that X either takes value $\{x_1\}$ or takes value $\{x_3, x_4\}$, and expressions like $x_i \in X$ to mean that x_i can take any of the values $x_1, \ldots, x_n$. Note that throughout this book we will assume that there are no conditional belief measures of the form $\text{Bel}(\emptyset | \mathbf{X}')$, $\mathbf{X}' \subseteq \mathbf{X}$, although such values are permitted under Smets' open world assumption.

To build a certainty network, a procedure based on that of Fonck and Straszecka (1991) is adopted. Consider a set of variables $\mathbf{V} = \{V_1, V_2, \ldots, V_n\}$ such that V_i takes values from $\{v_{i_1}, \ldots, v_{i_m}\}$. A network is then constructed based upon the influences between the variables. The variables are represented by the nodes of the network, and the influences between the variables are represented by the links between the nodes. The strength of the influences is represented by the numerical certainty value assigned to the link, and any node X, representing a given variable V_i, is only connected to those nodes that represent variables that influence V_i or are influenced by V_i. Links between nodes are added so that the correct conditional independence relations for the different formalisms may be inferred from the links (as discussed in Section 3.4.1). Thus if the network is quantified with probabilities, links are added so that if two nodes are d-separated by a third, then the probabilities of the two are conditionally independent given the probability of the third. Similarly, if the network is quantified with possibilities, links are added so that if two nodes are d-separated by a third, then the possibilities of the two are conditionally independent given the possibility of the third in the sense of (3.41), and if the network is quantified with belief functions, links are added so that if two nodes are d-separated by a third, then the beliefs of the two are conditionally cognitively independent given the belief of the third. Thus the network encodes all the available information about the dependencies between the variables in $\mathbf{V}$, and the strength of those dependencies.

5.3.2 On the use of graphs

Since the work described by this book is set within the context of directed acyclic graphs, it is inevitable that some use will need to be made of graph-theoretic notions. Some of these have been met already, and most of the remainder will be introduced in this section.[6] The introduction given here will be heavily influenced by the needs of the rest of the book. For more general introductions to the relevant parts of graph theory see Chapter 3 of (Neapolitan, 1990) and for an introduction to graph theory as a whole see (Even, 1979)

---

6 Some additional concepts, necessary for developing the algorithms in Chapter 9, are given in that chapter.

Rain last night   Sprinkler was on

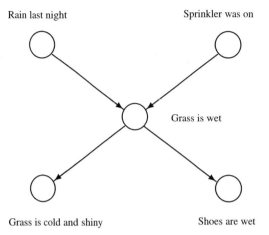

Grass is wet

Grass is cold and shiny   Shoes are wet

Figure 5.1
The graphical representation of the sprinkler example

or (Berge, 1973).

    The reason for using graphs as a means of representation is, as already discussed, to enable the dependencies between variables to be identified. Two nodes are connected by an arc if the certainty values of the variables they represent have an influence on one another. The reason for using directed graphs is to distinguish between different types of influence. In particular, directed arcs are used to distinguish between causal and evidential influences. Consider the graph in Figure 5.1 (appropriated from (Pearl, 1988a) via (Wellman and Henrion, 1991)). The direction of the arcs indicates causal influence so that both "it rained last night" and "the sprinkler was on" are causes of "the grass is wet," while "the grass is wet" is a cause of both "the grass is cold and shiny" and "my shoes are wet." Observation of any cause leads to a prediction that its effect will be the case, thus learning that it rained last night leads one to believe that the grass will be wet, and observing that the grass is wet leads one to believe that it will be cold and shiny. Such reasoning is referred to as *causal* or *predictive* reasoning.

    As Pearl (1988a) points out, there is a fundamental difference between causal reasoning and reasoning in the opposite direction to the arcs. Such reasoning is, of course, possible since observing cold and shiny grass is evidence for the grass being wet, and this in turn is evidence for either rain or the sprinkler having been on. Indeed, such reasoning is extremely common, not least in diagnosis where reasoning proceeds from the observation of a patient's symptoms to the disease most likely to cause them, and this is reflected in the fact that this style of proceeding is known as *diagnostic* as well as *evidential* reasoning.

The asymmetry between causal and evidential reasoning is illustrated by the following. Observing a cause, such as "rain last night," allows a prediction of "grass wet" along with both "cold and shiny grass" and "wet shoes" but provides no evidence about the possibility of "sprinkler on." Observing an effect, such as "wet shoes" allows a diagnosis of "wet grass" and this, in turn, allows a prediction of "cold and shiny grass" to be made along with a suggestion that both "rain last night" and "sprinkler on" are possible.

There is also a third kind of reasoning that is possible in the sprinkler example, the *intercausal* reasoning discussed in the context of qualitative probabilistic networks (Section 4.4.1). Here if it is known that the grass is wet and there is evidence for it having rained last night, then this may change the certainty value of the hypothesis "the sprinkler was on." Often this relationship will be negative, so that observing one cause tends to make it less believable that the other occurred. This is the phenomenon of *explaining away* mentioned in Section 4.4.1, and arises because knowing one cause generates an explanation that does not require the other. This is a natural interpretation of the intercausal interaction in the sprinkler example when it is assumed that the conjunction of the two causes is relatively unlikely and so (as Wellman and Henrion (1991) point out) it is reasonable to make the Occam's razor type assumption that only one cause should be present. However, it is perfectly possible that the relationship between the causes can be positive (as in Wellman and Henrion's drink-driving example), which enables a form of reasoning that has been termed *explaining in* (Benferhat et al., 1996). The causes may also have no effect on one another.

Given these distinctions, the following definitions may be made. These are based on definitions in (Pearl, 1988b), (Geiger et al., 1990), and (Druzdzel and Henrion, 1993c). Note that while the context limits many definitions to directed acyclic graphs, many of these also hold for any directed graph. The most widely used definitions are those that relate a node to those connected to it—the definitions of parent and child nodes:

DEFINITION 5.2: Given a node C in an acyclic directed graph, any node from which there is an arc to C is said to be a *parent* of C.

DEFINITION 5.3: Given a node C in an acyclic directed graph, any node to which there is an arc from C is said to be a *child* of C.

This familial analogy extends to cover the *siblings* of a node (all the nodes with at least one parent in common with the node), the *predecessors* or *ancestors* of a node (all the parents of the node and the parents of the parents and so on), and the *descendants* of a node. Having settled these ideas, it is possible to mix metaphors and identify the extreme nodes of a graph:

DEFINITION 5.4:   A *root node* of a directed graph is one with no parents.

DEFINITION 5.5:   A *leaf node* of a directed graph is one with no children.

In general a graph will have many roots and many leaves, and since in the graphs considered here all nodes are connected to at least one other node, no node will be both a root node and a leaf node. Next, the idea of different routes through a graph must be considered. In an undirected graph there is only one kind of route, and this will be called a track:

DEFINITION 5.6:   A *track* through an undirected graph is an alternating sequence of nodes and arcs so that each arc joins the nodes immediately preceding and following it.

In a directed graph things are more complicated. It is possible to have routes through the graph that only follow links in the directions of those links. Such a route will be called a path:

DEFINITION 5.7:   A *path* in a directed acyclic graph is an alternating sequence of nodes and arcs such that each node in the sequence is the parent of the subsequent node.

It is also possible to have routes through the graph that do not respect the orientation of the links. Such routes are are called trails:

DEFINITION 5.8:   A *trail* in a directed acyclic graph is an alternating sequence of nodes and arcs that form a track through the underlying undirected graph.

DEFINITION 5.9:   A trail connecting A and B is said to be a *minimal trail* between them if no node appears more than once.

The concept of a trails makes it possible to formally capture the idea of *d*-separation, but first it is necessary to define a couple of associated concepts:

DEFINITION 5.10:   A node C is called a *head-to-head* node with respect to a trail T if there are two consecutive arcs, one directed from a node A to C and the other directed from a node B to C, on T.

DEFINITION 5.11:   A trail T connecting A and B is said to be *active* given a set of nodes **L** if (1) every head-to-head node in T is either in **L** or has a descendant in **L** and (2) every other node in T is outside **L**.

Finally it is possible to provide a formal definition of *d*-separation:

DEFINITION 5.12: If **J**, **K** and **L** are three disjoint sets of nodes in some directed acyclic graph *D*, then **K** is said to d-*separate* **J** from **L** if no trail from a node in **J** to a node in **L** is active given **K**.

Thus two sets of nodes are *d*-separated by a third set if that third set manages to inactivate all the trails between them. In other words two sets of nodes are *d*-separated if there is no way of propagating changes in certainty value between them. This is why the idea of *d*-separation is so important—it exactly characterises which nodes are "connected" to which others in the sense of being able to influence their certainty value. It is thus a key property when considering how certainty values are propagated through networks and as such will loom large in Chapter 9 when such matters are discussed.

5.4 Examples of integration and incompleteness

The previous two sections have discussed the way in which the work presented here will address three of the fundamental problems in handling uncertainty, and detailed the framework in which this work will take place. This section presents the remaining part of the triptych promised in the introduction—examples of the incompleteness and integration problems that will be used to demonstrate the solutions as they are provided.

5.4.1 An example of integration

The following scenario illustrates the integration problem. Consider the network of Figure 5.2 to have been generated from medical knowledge stored by the Oxford System of Medicine (Glowinski et al., 1989) by some intelligent system using one of the forms of dynamic network construction discussed in Section 3.4.3. Based on the information provided by the Oxford System of Medicine on the relationships between various medical conditions, this network encodes the fact that joint trauma (*T*) leads to loose knee bodies (*K*), and that these and arthritis (*A*) cause joint pain (*P*). The incidence of arthritis is influenced by dislocation (*D*) of the joint in question and by the patient suffering from Sjorgen's syndrome (*S*). Sjorgen's syndrome affects the incidence of vasculitis (*V*), and vasculitis leads to vasculitic lesions (*L*). However, the strengths of the influences between the variables is not available since such information is not recorded in the Oxford System of Medicine.

Consider further that the intelligent system that built the network is part of a community of intelligent agents who operate in this medical domain. Other agents in the domain can supply information about the strength of the influences between the variables. How-

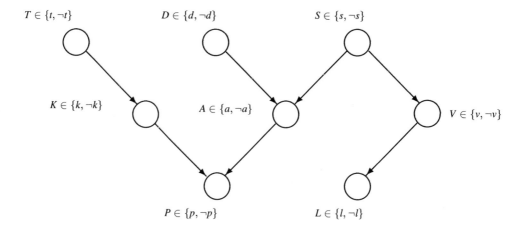

Figure 5.2
The network for the trauma example.

Table 5.1
The probabilities for the trauma example

$\Pr(k\|t)$	=	0.6	$\Pr(a\|d,s)$	=	0.9
$\Pr(k\|\neg t)$	=	0.2	$\Pr(a\|\neg d,s)$	=	0.6
			$\Pr(a\|d,\neg s)$	=	0.6
$\Pr(v\|s)$	=	0.1	$\Pr(a\|\neg d,\neg s)$	=	0.4
$\Pr(v\|\neg s)$	=	0.3			

ever, like the modular expert systems discussed by Agustí-Cullell et al. (1991; 1992), each system can only supply values for a part of the network, and each uses a different formalism. Thus, some of the influences are given as probabilities, reflecting the fact that there is good statistical data relating the various complaints. For instance, it is known that loose knee bodies are uncommon in people who have not suffered trauma, but quite common following joint trauma of the knee, while vasculitis is generally uncommon, and even less so in sufferers from Sjorgen's syndrome. In addition, data on arthritis sufferers shows that arthritis is a common complaint, but is more common in those suffering from Sjorgen's syndrome or with dislocations. This data gives the probability values of Table 5.1. It is also known that vasculitic lesions are entirely possible in patients with vasculitis, and that it is less possible for patients without vasculitis to form the lesions. It is also on record that it is perfectly possible for a patient to not have lesions whether or not she is suffering from vasculitis. However there is no statistical data, so that only the possibilistic data of

Table 5.2
The possibilities for the trauma example

$\Pi(l\|v)$	=	1	$\Pi(\neg l\|v)$	=	1
$\Pi(l\|\neg v)$	=	0.8	$\Pi(\neg l\|\neg v)$	=	1

Table 5.3
The beliefs for the trauma example

$\mathrm{Bel}(p\|k,a)$	=	0.9	$\mathrm{Bel}(p\|k,a\cup\neg a)$	=	0.7
$\mathrm{Bel}(p\cup\neg p\|k,a)$	=	0.1	$\mathrm{Bel}(p\cup\neg p\|k,a\cup\neg a)$	=	0.3
$\mathrm{Bel}(p\|k,\neg a)$	=	0.7	$\mathrm{Bel}(\neg p\|\neg k,\neg a)$	=	0.5
$\mathrm{Bel}(p\cup\neg p\|k,\neg a)$	=	0.3	$\mathrm{Bel}(p\cup\neg p\|\neg k,\neg a)$	=	0.5
$\mathrm{Bel}(p\|\neg k,a)$	=	0.7	$\mathrm{Bel}(\neg p\|\neg k,a\cup\neg a)$	=	0.4
$\mathrm{Bel}(p\cup\neg p\|\neg k,a)$	=	0.3	$\mathrm{Bel}(p\cup\neg p\|\neg k,a\cup\neg a)$	=	0.6
$\mathrm{Bel}(p\|k\cup\neg k,a)$	=	0.6	$\mathrm{Bel}(\neg p\|k\cup\neg k,\neg a)$	=	0.4
$\mathrm{Bel}(p\cup\neg p\|k\cup\neg k,a)$	=	0.4	$\mathrm{Bel}(p\cup\neg p\|k\cup\neg k,\neg a)$	=	0.6

Table 5.2 is available. Finally some subjective beliefs are available about the relationship between joint pain, arthritis and loose knee bodies. These are given in Table 5.3. The information available is rather incomplete and so is represented using belief functions rather than probability theory since this better allows the representation of ignorance. Broadly it is known that pain is likely to occur if either arthritis or loose bodies occur in the joint. Belief in the absence of pain is not directly related to belief in the occurrence of pain, and it is believed that pain is unlikely to occur if the patient has neither arthritis or loose knee bodies. All conditional values other than those given are zero.

There is also some information about the general state of the world as regards factors bearing in aching knees and vasculitic lesions. Within the population that is of interest, that is the patients in the School for the Study of Joint Aches and Vasculitis, the prior probability of a patient suffering from joint trauma is known to be $\Pr(t) = 0.4$, while records show that the prior probabilities of a patient suffering from dislocation $\Pr(d)$ and Sjorgen's syndrome $\Pr(s)$ are 0.3 and 0.1 respectively. In the absence of any other information about vasculitis one may, if one accepts that it is reasonable to do so, apply the principle of minimum specificity. This reflects the total ignorance about whether a patient will suffer from vasculitis or not by predicting that it is entirely possible for a patient to have vasculitis, so that $\Pi(v) = 1$, and that it is entirely possible for a patient not to have vasculitis, so that $\Pi(\neg v) = 1$.

With the above information it is possible, at the moment, to carry out a limited amount of reasoning. The existing prior probabilities can be used with (3.13) to establish the prior probabilities of a patient suffering from loose knee bodies and suffering from arthritis:

$$\Pr(k) = \Pr(k|t)\Pr(t) + \Pr(k|\neg t)\Pr(\neg t)$$

$$
\begin{aligned}
&= (0.6 \times 0.4) + (0.2 \times 0.6) \\
&= 0.36
\end{aligned}
$$

$$
\begin{aligned}
\Pr(a) &= \Pr(a|d,s)\Pr(d)\Pr(s) + \Pr(a|\neg d,s)\Pr(\neg d)\Pr(s) \\
&\quad + \Pr(a|d,\neg s)\Pr(d)\Pr(\neg s) + \Pr(a|\neg d \neg s)\Pr(\neg d)\Pr(\neg s) \\
&= (0.9 \times 0.3 \times 0.1) + (0.6 \times 0.7 \times 0.1) \\
&\quad + (0.6 \times 0.3 \times 0.9) + (0.4 \times 0.7 \times 0.9) \\
&= 0.483
\end{aligned}
$$

It is also possible (3.13) to calculate that the prior probability of vasculitis:

$$
\begin{aligned}
\Pr(v) &= \Pr(v|s)\Pr(s) + \Pr(v|\neg s)\Pr(\neg s) \\
&= (0.1 \times 0.1) + (0.3 \times 0.9) \\
&= 0.28
\end{aligned}
$$

and to compute the prior possibilities relating vasculitic lesions to vasculitis using (3.38):

$$
\begin{aligned}
\Pi(l) &= \sup\left(\min\left(\Pi(l|v),\Pi(v)\right),\min\left(\Pi(l|\neg v),\Pi(\neg v)\right)\right) \\
&= \sup\left(\min(1,1),\min(0.8,1)\right) \\
&= 1
\end{aligned}
$$

$$
\begin{aligned}
\Pi(\neg l) &= \sup\left(\min\left(\Pi(\neg l|v),\Pi(v)\right),\min\left(\Pi(\neg l|\neg v),\Pi(\neg v)\right)\right) \\
&= \sup\left(\min(1,1),\min(1,1)\right) \\
&= 1
\end{aligned}
$$

Nothing, however, can be said about the prior value of any belief in the patient being in pain because nothing is known about the belief in loose knee bodies or arthritis.

It is also not possible to carry out much reasoning with new evidence. For instance, if the patient is observed to be in pain, it is clear that $\mathrm{Bel}(p) = 1$, and it is desirable to establish, for instance, how this bears upon the probability of a dislocation. Now it is possible to use (3.66) to establish conditional beliefs relating pain to the incidence of arthritis, so that, for instance[7]:

$$
\mathrm{Bel}(a|p) = 0.4
$$

and this may then be used to determine that when the patient is observed to be in pain:

$$
\mathrm{Bel}(a)^* = 0.4
$$

---

7 The interested reader may find the rather lengthy calculation of the conditional beliefs in Appendix B.

This posterior belief indicates that it possible to say with some certainty that the patient has arthritis but that it is not completely certain (which is reasonable since the pain could be caused by loose knee bodies—if loose knee bodies could be ruled out, belief in arthritis would increase). However, this information about belief in arthritis cannot be used to give any indication of what the posterior probability of dislocation is.

Furthermore, it is also not possible to do much with new information about vasculitic lesions. It is possible to use (3.40) to establish the relevant conditional possibilities, provided that the use of the principle of minimum specificity to establish $\Pi(v)$ and $\Pi(\neg v)$ is accepted. This gives:

$$
\begin{aligned}
\min(\Pi(v|l), \Pi(l)) &= \min(\Pi(l|v), \Pi(v)) \\
\min(\Pi(v|l), 1) &= \min(1, 1) \\
\min(\Pi(v|\neg l), \Pi(\neg l)) &= \min(\Pi(\neg l|v), \Pi(v)) \\
\min(\Pi(v|\neg l), 1) &= \min(1, 1) \\
\min(\Pi(\neg v|l), \Pi(l)) &= \min(\Pi(l|\neg v), \Pi(\neg v)) \\
\min(\Pi(\neg v|l), 1) &= \min(0.8, 1) \\
\min(\Pi(\neg v|\neg l), \Pi(\neg l)) &= \min(\Pi(\neg l|\neg v), \Pi(\neg v)) \\
\min(\Pi(\neg v|\neg l), 1) &= \min(1, 1)
\end{aligned}
$$

from which it is clear that $\Pi(v|l) = 1$, $\Pi(v|\neg l) = 1$, $\Pi(\neg v|l) = 0.8$, and $\Pi(\neg v|\neg l) = 1$. These values may then be used along with the observation that vasculitic lesions occur, so that $\Pi(\neg l) = 0$, to calculate the posterior possibilities relating to vasculitis:

$$
\begin{aligned}
\Pi(v)^* &= \sup(\min(\Pi(v|l), \Pi(l)^*), \min(\Pi(v|\neg l), \Pi(\neg l)^*)) \\
&= \sup(\min(1, 1), \min(1, 0)) \\
&= 1 \\
\Pi(\neg v)^* &= \sup(\min(\Pi(\neg v|l), \Pi(l)^*), \min(\Pi(\neg v|\neg l), \Pi(\neg l)^*)) \\
&= \sup(\min(0.8, 1), \min(1, 0)) \\
&= 0.8
\end{aligned}
$$

but again this information again cannot be used to obtain any further information.

In contrast, if translation between values is possible, more specific deductions can be made from the data. The use of qualitative methods to implement integration by value allows a prior value for the belief in the patient suffering from painful knees to be established. It also allows new information to be inferred from evidence about pain and vasculitic lesions, allowing a posterior value for the probability of Sjorgen's syndrome to be calculated. In addition, integration by change allows the changes in the probability induced by the various pieces of evidence to be established. This information is only in terms of "the probability of dislocation increases," but this kind of information can be useful. Indeed, as described in Chapter 4, it is sufficient for such tasks as explaining the effect of evidence (Henrion and Druzdzel, 1990; Druzdzel, 1993), solving design problems (Michelena, 1991) and choosing between classes of plans (Wellman, 1990a). This example will be used to illustrate exactly how integration improves matters when the integration methods themselves have been examined.

Note that when integration by change takes place in a network, it takes place at a node. The conditional values that control the propagation of values between nodes are always in a single formalism. When a change is propagated from D to A and then on to P, the change in $\Pr(b)$ is calculated from the change in $\Pr(d)$, this is converted into a change in $\mathrm{Bel}(d)$, and this latter change is propagated to establish the change in $\mathrm{Bel}(p)$. In contrast, integration by value may take place at any point in a network so that it is possible to translate $\Pr(d)$ in $\Pi(d)$ and $\Pr(v|s)$ into $\Pi(v|s)$. Note also that a large part of the reasoning that is possible in the absence of a solution to the translation problem is only possible if the principle of minimum specificity is accepted. Without it or another solution to the incompleteness problem, very little could be inferred. This serves to illustrate the connection between the translation and incompleteness problems.

5.4.2   An example of incompleteness

As discussed above, the methods developed in this book may also be used to handle incompleteness. That is they may be used is to deal with the situation in which no model of uncertainty can be applied because none fits the relevant data. In order to illustrate the effectiveness of the various solutions suggested, the following example will be used. The problem of incompleteness, like that of integration, can be illustrated using information from the Oxford System of Medicine. Consider that the same system as before builds the network of Figure 5.3, which represents the following medical information. Both alcoholism (S) and hypertension (H) influence the occurrence of gout (G), while alcoholism and hepatitis (E) influence the occurrence of cirrhosis (C). Cirrhosis causes liver failure (L), and gout causes arthritis (A), while alcoholism is caused by a high intake of alcohol (I).

Once again no values for the strength of these influences are given by the Oxford System of medicine, so that if the system that built the network wants to reason about the certainty of the different conditions, it must ask other systems in its community to give it suitable values. In this case one of the other systems can supply most of the necessary values as probabilities (see Table 5.4). The only missing values in Table 5.4 are the conditional probability relating the probability of cirrhosis to the probabilities of alcoholism and hepatitis $\Pr(c|s, e)$ and the conditional probability relating the probability

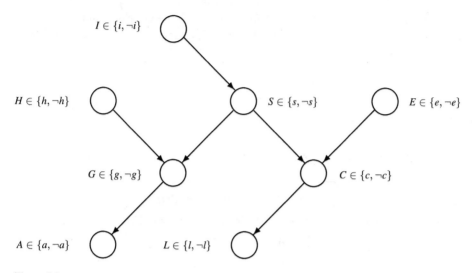

Figure 5.3
The network for the gout example.

Table 5.4
The probabilities for the gout example

$\Pr(g\|h, s)$	=	0.8			
$\Pr(g\|\neg h, s)$	=	0.6	$\Pr(c\|s, \neg e)$	=	0.7
$\Pr(g\|h, \neg s)$	=	0.6	$\Pr(c\|\neg s, e)$	=	0.3
$\Pr(g\|\neg h, \neg s)$	=	0.2	$\Pr(c\|\neg s, \neg e)$	=	0.3
$\Pr(s\|i)$	=	0.8	$\Pr(l\|c)$	=	0.8
$\Pr(s\|\neg i)$	=	0.1	$\Pr(l\|\neg c)$	=	0.2
$\Pr(a\|g)$	=	0.7			

of arthritis to the probability of not having gout $\Pr(a|\neg g)$. $\Pr(c|s, e)$ cannot be measured accurately since there are few alcoholic patients who have had hepatitis, although it is known to be greater than $\Pr(c|s, \neg e)$, and there are insufficient records of the right kind to establish $\Pr(a|\neg g)$, though it is suspected that it is less than $\Pr(a|g)$. Unfortunately, no other systems in the community can supply the missing conditional (in any formalism), so the system that built the network must live with the incompleteness. Some prior probability values, based on a survey of patients entering the Centre for the Treatment of Gout and Hepatitis, are also available. These are the prior probability of a patient having a high intake of alcohol $\Pr(i) = 0.4$, of suffering from hypertension $\Pr(h) = 0.6$, and of having suffered from hepatitis, $\Pr(e) = 0.1$.

With the missing values, it is not possible to establish the prior probabilities of all of the medical conditions. It is obviously possible to establish the prior probability of a patient suffering from alcoholism:

$$
\begin{aligned}
\Pr(s) &= \Pr(s|i)\Pr(i) + \Pr(s|\neg i)\Pr(\neg i) \\
&= (0.8 \times 0.4) + (0.1 \times 0.6) \\
&= 0.38
\end{aligned}
$$

and this can be used along with the given prior probability of a patient being hypertensive, $\Pr(h)$, to establish the probability of gout:

$$
\begin{aligned}
\Pr(g) &= \Pr(g|h, s)\Pr(h)\Pr(s) + \Pr(g|\neg h, s)\Pr(\neg h)\Pr(s) \\
&\quad + \Pr(g|h, \neg s)\Pr(h)\Pr(\neg s) + \Pr(g|\neg h \neg s)\Pr(\neg h)\Pr(\neg s) \\
&= (0.8 \times 0.6 \times 0.38) + (0.6 \times 0.4 \times 0.38) \\
&\quad + (0.6 \times 0.6 \times 0.62) + (0.2 \times 0.4 \times 0.62) \\
&= 0.546
\end{aligned}
$$

However, nothing may be established about the probability of the patient having gout or cirrhosis, and thus nothing can be said about how likely the patient is to experience liver failure or to suffer from arthritis. Furthermore, as in the integration example, it is not possible to tell much from any evidence that may be gathered. If it is observed that the patient has liver failure, the posterior probability of cirrhosis cannot be established, because applying Bayes' rule (3.15) to get:

$$
\Pr(c|l) = \frac{\Pr(l|c)\Pr(c)}{\Pr(l)} \tag{5.16}
$$

requires the prior probabilities of cirrhosis and liver failure $\Pr(c)$ and $\Pr(l)$. Unless one is happy to apply the principle of maximum entropy and assume that $\Pr(c) = \Pr(\neg c) = 0.5$ and $\Pr(l) = \Pr(\neg l) = 0.5$ nothing further can be inferred.[8] Furthermore, it is not possible to carry out any kind of updating when there is evidence about arthritis. To apply Bayes' rule to establish the conditional values $\Pr(g|a)$ and $\Pr(g|\neg a)$ it is necessary to have prior values for $\Pr(a)$ and $\Pr(\neg a)$, and these are not available.

Using qualitative values to handle incompleteness makes it possible to hypothesise values for the missing conditionals, and these may then be combined with the existing values to establish $\Pr(c)$, the prior probability of cirrhosis and $\Pr(a)$, the prior value of

---

8 Of course, if the principle of maximum entropy is applied, then from (5.16) $\Pr(c|l) = \Pr(l|c) = 0.8$, so the posterior probability of cirrhosis when liver failure is known to have occurred is 0.8, and similar updating is possible in the other incomplete parts of the model.

arthritis. The former value may then be used to establish $\Pr(l)$, the probability of liver failure. Although the probabilities that are calculated when using qualitative values to defeat incompleteness in this way may well not be very precise, they may still be valuable, and the lack of precision may not be a problem if, for example, the established value is going to be translated into another formalism. Knowing these values also makes it possible to propagate the effects of evidence, so that, for example, the posterior probability of gout may be calculated when there is evidence about arthritis, and the posterior probability of hepatitis may be calculated when there is evidence about liver failure. Qualitative changes can also be used to resolve the incompleteness. Even in its incomplete state, there is enough information about the problem to establish the qualitative influences between the variables, and these may be used to establish the impact of evidence. The use of this approach also illustrates how the robustness problem may be solved. If the system is required to make predictions about gout patients in another clinic, the results of the qualitative change analysis are likely to be transferable.

5.5 Summary

This chapter has set the scene for the theoretical work of this book by specifying the kind of work that will be done and the exact framework in which it will be carried out. The chapter began with a statement of three problems in reasoning under uncertainty, the incompleteness problem, the integration problem and the robustness problem. Justifying consideration of the integration problem led to a discussion of the eclectic position as an alternative to the exclusive use of one of the formalisms introduced in the previous chapters. This in turn led naturally to the idea of integration by translation between formalisms, and when the idea of degrading values to their central message of "a reason to think that X will occur" was added, the result was to focus on two possible types of integration, integration by value and integration by change. It was also argued that the mechanism at the heart of these integrations provides a means of solving the incompleteness and robustness problems. Having established that qualitative methods were worthy of further study, a suitable framework for carrying out the study was introduced. The current interest in the uncertainty community on reasoning in networks when handling uncertainty suggested that propagation in networks should be considered, and to be able to study integration it is necessary to deal with networks in which uncertainty is represented in more than one formalism. These networks were christened certainty networks since their arcs are quantified in terms of certainty values—values that are either probabilities, possibilities or beliefs—and some of the basic concepts of such networks were introduced. Finally this chapter introduced a pair of examples that will be used throughout the remainder of the book in order to illustrate the benefits of the different schemes for integration and handling incompleteness. These are set within the context of a community of intelligent agents that have a body of medical knowledge concerning joint pain, arthritis, vasculitis and related diseases. The strength of the relations between the different diseases are encoded in a number of formalisms, since different parts of the relevant knowledge belong to different systems, and there are missing values. The examples were discussed with reference to the extent of the knowledge that may be inferred without integration or dealing with missing values, and the expected benefits from integrating and handling incompleteness. Now that the scene has been set for work on qualitative methods, the next chapter begins the work to establish qualitative methods for handling incompleteness and robustness, and for integrating values between formalisms. These methods are based upon both qualitative values and qualitative changes in value, and the first to be considered are those based upon the use of qualitative values.

6 Using qualitative algebras

What's your road, man? Holyboy road, madman road, rainbow road, guppy road, any road. It's an anywhere road for anybody, anyhow ...

Jack Kerouac, *On The Road*

The previous chapter discussed possible solutions to the problems of integration, incompleteness, and robustness. In particular it discussed methods based on the principle of degrading, that is the idea that the underlying meaning beneath any certainty value for a proposition X is "a reason to think that X is the case," showing that this principle opens the way for solutions in which missing or translated values are treated as bounded yet unknown values. The idea is that having established that there is something that specifies the certainty value of X, however imprecise it is, it may then be combined with more precisely known values, to reach conclusions that would otherwise be unattainable. However, in order for this approach to work it is necessary to provide a way of expressing "a reason to think that X is the case" in the various formalisms, preferably in a way that makes as few assumptions as possible and permits what is expressed to be combined with numerical values. The suggestion is that this should be done using qualitative algebras similar to those discussed in Section 4.2.3. This chapter concentrates on the definition of two such algebras, both of which make it possible to perform arithmetic operations of the kind needed by uncertainty handling formalisms on mixtures of qualitative and numerical values. The first, known as $Q2$, deals with values of the kind used in work on qualitative physics. Thus it produces quite coarse-grained information, only being able to distinguish between positive and zero values. However, it is argued that this may be useful in some situations. The second algebra, which is known as $Q3$, uses a more precise interval representation and so is able to generate more fine-grained results. For both algebras, the way in which values expressed in probability, possibility, and evidence theories may be propagated is described in detail. The ways in which both algebras may be used to solve the incompleteness and integration problems is also discussed (though no solution is offered to the robustness problem using the algebras). In addition, the use of both algebras is illustrated on the pair of examples introduced in the last chapter.

6.1 Introduction

Now, as discussed in Chapter 4, qualitative reasoning (Bobrow, 1984; Kuipers, 1994) gets around the problem of dealing with incomplete complex models by using the symbolic values $[+]$, $[0]$, and $[-]$, instead of numerical values. When turning a quantitative value into a qualitative one, every strictly positive value becomes $[+]$, and every strictly negative value becomes $[-]$. Thus when confronted with a $[+]$, it is not possible to tell what value it represents, it is only possible to say that it is "something strictly positive." This is exactly the kind of value that is required as the result of a translation since the principle of degrading says that, for instance, a belief is equal to "some non-zero probability" but refrains from saying what that probability is. To use $[+]$ as the result of a translation it is necessary to combine it with other values that are not qualitative. To do this requires the use of an algebra that mixes both qualitative and quantitative values rather like Williams' (1991) SR1, which was mentioned in Chapter 4. The algebras discussed here are a little different from SR1 mainly because they are focussed on handling uncertainty. This means that they are concerned with providing extensions to the operations used by the various uncertainty handling formalisms to make those operations function over sets of operands that cover qualitative values as well as numerical ones. Thus in order to propagate probabilities that include $[+]$, extensions of addition and multiplication that manipulate $[+]$ are provided. The algebras are not fully described since it is anticipated that the operations over them will be extended in order to encompass additional formalisms. This is also the reason that the set of operands extends beyond the $[0, 1]$ interval used by probability, possibility, and evidence theories. For instance, negative numbers make no sense in probability theory, but are natural when dealing with certainty factors or Spohn's ordinal conditional functions. It is also important to stress that the algebras say nothing about what formalism to use and how the formalism should be interpreted; this is left to the user of the formalism. The algebras make no attempt to enforce axioms such as $\Pr(x) + \Pr(\neg x) = 1$. Such constraints are the concern of the formalisms that are applied, they are not the concern of the algebras. All the algebras do is to provide a language in which it is possible to handle "something positive" and combine it with numerical values.

6.2   An algebra with qualitative values

Inspired by work such as Williams' (1988) Q1, Fox and Krause (1990) suggested strengthening ordinary arithmetic with operations over qualitative values, and applying this to reasoning under uncertainty. In particular they suggested using the system as a means of combining "somethings" generated by non-numerical methods with quantitative information. Their system, though rather incomplete, appeared to me to be a good basis for a qualitative algebra that could solve the incompleteness and translation problems and so I extended it to make this possible. The extended system, known as $Q2$ in acknowledgement of Q1, first appeared in (Parsons and Fox, 1991), having been developed in ignorance of Williams' presumably contemporaneous work on SR1 (which first appeared for a general audience in (Williams, 1991)). What follows is a definition of $Q2$ that differs slightly from the version that was first published.

6.2.1   A formal definition

The qualitative operations of $Q2$ are valid over a single set of operands $\mathcal{S}' = \{[-], [0], [+],$ $[?]\} \cup \Re$ so that $\mathcal{S}' = \mathcal{S} \cup \Re$ where $\mathcal{S} = \{[-], [0], [+]\} \cup \{[?]\}$, the union of the standard quantity space (Bobrow, 1984; Kuipers, 1994), with the qualitatively indeterminate value $[?] \equiv [-\infty, \infty]$. Note that the set of real numbers $\Re$ is now part of the set of qualitative operands. The members of the set of operands $\mathcal{S} = \{[-], [0], [+], [?]\}$ are related to $\Re$ by the mapping $[\cdot] : \Re \mapsto \mathcal{S}$ (Williams, 1988), which is used to assess the qualitative value of a variable. For any $x \in \Re$:

$$[x] = \begin{cases} [+] & \text{if } x > 0 \\ [0] & \text{if } x = 0 \\ [-] & \text{if } x < 0 \end{cases} \tag{6.1}$$

Many of the properties of this kind of algebra are explored by Kuipers (1994). The members of $\mathcal{S}$ are also the result of applying one of the binary combining functions that are defined over $\mathcal{S}'$ to a member of $\Re$ and a member of $\mathcal{S}$. This may be summarised by stating that there is at least one operator $\odot \in \mathcal{OP}_{Q2} : \Re \times \mathcal{S} \mapsto \mathcal{S}$, where $\mathcal{OP}_{Q2}$ is the set of all operators over $\mathcal{S}'$.

An important consequence of including $\Re$ in the operand set is that there is no need to have two sets of operators, one for the reals and one for the qualitative operands as is necessary in Q1. Instead there is a set of extended arithmetic operators that can operate on all members of $\mathcal{S}'$. The extended operators, which are analogous to the usual set of arithmetic operators on $\Re$, $\{+, -, \times, \div\}$, are written as $\{\oplus, \ominus, \otimes, \oslash\}$, and along with the operator $[\cdot]$ they form an algebra that combines arithmetic on real values with the robustness of pure qualitative algebras. Thus, for instance, the operator $\oplus : \mathcal{S}' \mapsto \mathcal{S}'$ is equivalent to the addition operator for reals, the qualitative addition operator, and a combined addition and mapping operator converting reals into qualitative values:

$$\oplus : \Re \times \Re \mapsto \Re$$
$$\oplus : \mathcal{S} \times \mathcal{S} \mapsto \mathcal{S}$$
$$\oplus : \Re \times \mathcal{S} \mapsto \mathcal{S}$$

The effect of the remaining extended operators $\{\ominus, \otimes, \oslash\}$ are similarly dependent on the type of their operands, and the properties of their counterparts over $\Re$. To specify the results of the operators, the combinator table given for the extended addition operator $\oplus$

Table 6.1
Combinator tables for $Q2$

⊕	ℜ+	[+]	[0]	[−]	ℜ−	[?]
ℜ+	ℜ+	[+]	ℜ+	[?]	ℜ?	[?]
[+]	[+]	[+]	[+]	[?]	[?]	[?]
[0]	ℜ+	[+]	[0]	[−]	ℜ−	[?]
[−]	[?]	[?]	[−]	[−]	[−]	[?]
ℜ−	ℜ?	[?]	ℜ−	[−]	ℜ−	[?]
[?]	[?]	[?]	[?]	[?]	[?]	[?]

Addition

⊗	ℜ+	[+]	[0]	[−]	ℜ−	[?]
ℜ+	ℜ+	[+]	[0]	[−]	ℜ−	[?]
[+]	[+]	[+]	[0]	[−]	[−]	[?]
[0]	[0]	[0]	[0]	[0]	[0]	[0]
[−]	[−]	[−]	[0]	[+]	[+]	[?]
ℜ−	ℜ−	[−]	[0]	[+]	ℜ+	[?]
[?]	[?]	[?]	[0]	[?]	[?]	[?]

Multiplication

⊘	ℜ+	[+]	[0]	[−]	ℜ−	[?]
ℜ+	ℜ+	[+]	U	[−]	ℜ−	U
[+]	[+]	[+]	U	[−]	[−]	U
[0]	[0]	[0]	U	[0]	[0]	U
[−]	[−]	[−]	U	[+]	[+]	U
ℜ−	ℜ−	[−]	U	[+]	ℜ+	U
[?]	[?]	[?]	U	[?]	[?]	U

Division

⊖	ℜ+	[+]	[0]	[−]	ℜ−	[?]
ℜ+	ℜ?	[?]	ℜ+	[+]	ℜ+	[?]
[+]	[?]	[?]	[+]	[+]	[+]	[?]
[0]	ℜ−	[−]	[0]	[+]	ℜ+	[?]
[−]	[−]	[−]	[−]	[?]	[?]	[?]
ℜ−	ℜ−	[−]	ℜ−	[?]	ℜ?	[?]
[?]	[?]	[?]	[?]	[?]	[?]	[?]

Subtraction

by Fox and Krause (1990) is repeated, and additional ones for multiplication, division, and subtraction are provided in Table 6.1. The occurrence of $ℜ+$ designates a particular positive number, and the occurrence of $ℜ−$ designates a particular negative number. The $ℜ+$, $ℜ−$ or $ℜ?$ that is the result of applying the qualitative operator to two $ℜ$s is simply the result of applying the relevant real operator to the two operands so that, for instance, $x \otimes y \equiv x \times y$ when x and y are both real numbers. $ℜ?$ differs from $[?]$ in the same way that $ℜ+$ differs from $[+]$ and $ℜ−$ differs from $[−]$. That is to say, while $[?]$ represents an unknown quantity somewhere in the range $[-\infty, \infty]$, $ℜ?$ represents a real number somewhere in the same range that may be uniquely determined from the operator and operands. U represents an undefined value, in particular the result of dividing by 0 or a value that includes 0.

Since these combinator tables are correct for all the possible combinations of qualitative and real operands in the range $[-\infty, \infty]$, they are complete for all operands that may be encountered in any formalism. However, in considering integration between, and incompleteness and robustness in, probability, possibility, and evidence theories, it will only be necessary to deal with values in the range $[0, 1]$. As a result, attention will usually be limited to the non-negative operands of $Q2$ whose values are less than or equal to 1.

6.2.2 Propagating values in $Q2$

The propagation of values through networks using $Q2$ is based on the use of combinator tables such as those in Table 6.1. For instance, to propagate probabilistic information from A to C in Figure 6.1 (page 206), the following version of (3.13), in which standard addition

Table 6.2
More combinator tables for *Q2*

$\max_{Q2}$	$\Re+$	$[+]$	$[0]$	$[?]$
$\Re+$	$\Re+$	$[+]$	$\Re+$	$[+]$
$[+]$	$[+]$	$[+]$	$[+]$	$[+]$
$[0]$	$\Re+$	$[+]$	$[0]$	$[?]$
$[?]$	$[+]$	$[?]$	$[+]$	$[?]$

Maximum

$\min_{Q2}$	$\Re+$	$[+]$	$[0]$	$[?]$
$\Re+$	$\Re+$	$[+]$	$[0]$	$[?]$
$[+]$	$[+]$	$[+]$	$[0]$	$[?]$
$[0]$	$[0]$	$[0]$	$[0]$	$[?]$
$[?]$	$[?]$	$[?]$	$[?]$	$[?]$

Minimum

and multiplication are replaced by $\oplus$ and $\otimes$, is applied:

$$\Pr(c) = \bigoplus_{\substack{A=a_1,\dots,a_m \\ X=x_1,\dots,x_p}} \Pr(c|A,X) \otimes \Pr(A,X) \tag{6.2}$$

In a similar way, for information expressed as beliefs, it is possible to propagate using the following versions of equations (3.64) and (3.65)

$$\mathrm{Bel}(c) = \bigoplus_{\substack{A\subseteq\{a_1,\dots,a_m\} \\ X\subseteq\{x_1,\dots,x_p\}}} m(A,X) \otimes \mathrm{Bel}(c|A,X) \tag{6.3}$$

$$\mathrm{Bel}(c) = \bigoplus_{\substack{A\subseteq\{a_1,\dots,a_m\} \\ X\subseteq\{x_1,\dots,x_p\}}} m(A,X) \otimes \bigotimes_{\substack{a\in A \\ x\in X}} \mathrm{Bel}(c|A,X) \tag{6.4}$$

To do the same with possibilistic values it is necessary to define new tables for *Q2* equivalents of the max and min operations, known as $\max_{Q2}$ and $\min_{Q2}$. These are defined in Table 6.2 and are based upon the generalisation of the maximum and minimum operations suggested by Dubois and Prade (1979) and discussed in Section 3.3.2. Using these operations, the maximum of $[+]$ and some positive value $\Re+$ is the interval $[\Re+, \infty)$, which cannot be expressed more precisely than $[+]$ in the language of *Q2*. Similarly, the minimum of $[+]$ and $\Re+$ is the interval $(0, \Re+]$, which again is represented by $[+]$. The similarity between the tables stems from the fact that when using this ordering the maximum and minimum of pairs of values are often "equal." The generalised max and min operators make it possible to write down the following expression to determine $\Pi(c)$ from $\Pi(a)$ in the network of Figure 6.1:

$$\Pi(c) = \sup_{Q2} {}_{\substack{A=a_1,\dots,a_m \\ X=x_1,\dots,x_p}} \min_{Q2}(\Pi(c|A,X), \Pi(A,X)) \tag{6.5}$$

where $\sup_{Q2}$ is to supremum as $\min_{Q2}$ is to ordinary minimum. Note that the combinator tables may be replaced with others that implement a different means of establishing the maximum and minimum of two operands in *Q2*. There is nothing in this algebra that specifies what orderings and combinator tables are correct any more than there is anything

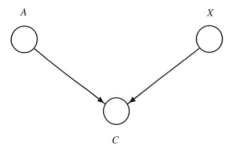

Figure 6.1
A simple directed graph.

that specifies which uncertainty handling formalism to use. The algebra simply provides a framework for combining qualitative and numerical values using whatever methods one wishes to use. Of course, the other equations in Chapter 3 may also be converted for use in $Q2$. Thus Bayes' rule (3.15) may be modified to establish the conditionals necessary to propagate values from C to A in Figure 6.1:

$$\Pr(a|c,x) = (\Pr(c|a,x) \otimes \Pr(a,x)) \oslash \Pr(c,x) \tag{6.6}$$

and the possibilistic (3.40) and belief function (3.66) versions of Bayes' rule may be similarly modified:

$$\min_{Q2}\left(\Pi(a|c,x), \Pi(c,x)\right) = \min_{Q2}\left(\Pi(c|a,x), \Pi(a,x)\right) \tag{6.7}$$

$$\mathrm{Bel}(a|c,x) = \bigotimes_{y\in\tilde{a}}\mathrm{Bel}(\tilde{c}|y,x) \ominus \bigotimes_{y\in A}\mathrm{Bel}(\tilde{c}|y,x) \tag{6.8}$$

In the same vein, there are many other models for propagating values that are present in the literature, some of which are mentioned in Chapters 3 and 4, and any of these may be adopted and the arithmetic operators they use replaced by the analogous operators in $Q2$. Of course, it is possible to propagate values without using any such models, at least not directly. Instead it is possible to modify any of the computational models discussed in Section 3.4, and this is exactly the course adopted in Chapter 9 where a modification of Shenoy and Shafer's local computation approach is adapted for $Q2$.

Note that here, as elsewhere in this book, no account is given of the propagation of plausibility and necessity values. The reason for this is twofold. Firstly the rules for the propagation are easy to establish as duals of those for belief and possibility, and secondly the plausibility and necessity values themselves may be established from the corresponding belief and possibility values since $\mathrm{Pl}(a) = 1 - \mathrm{Bel}(\neg a)$, and $\mathrm{N}(a) = 1 - \Pi(\neg a)$.

6.2.3   Handling translation and incompleteness in $Q2$

The problem of translation is solved by the use of the qualitative values introduced in $Q2$. Consider a translation function $F(\cdot) : F_1 \mapsto F_2$ that, when applied to a value v_1 expressed in a formalism F_1, provides a precise value v_2 expressed in a different formalism F_2:

$$F(v_1) \mapsto v_2 \tag{6.9}$$

Assuming the existence of such a translation function, which seems reasonable, implies that there is some value v_2 for every v_1. This suggests that there is another translation function $H_{Q2}(\cdot) : F_1 \mapsto F_2$ between the two formalisms, one that is less informative, which only gives:

$$H_{Q2}(v_1) \mapsto x \tag{6.10}$$

where x is a "something." Recalling the principle of degrading, as summarised by (5.1)–(5.12), this translation may be restated for probability, possibility, and evidence theories when $Q2$ is used. Remembering that for these theories $0 \equiv [0]$, $(0, 1] \equiv [+]$, and $[0, 1] \equiv [0]$ or $[+]$, which is written as $[0, +]$,[1] for $n > 0$:

$$H_{Q2}(\Pr(A) = n) \mapsto \Pi(A) = [+] \tag{6.11}$$
$$H_{Q2}(\Pr(A) = n) \mapsto \mathrm{Bel}(A) = [0, +] \tag{6.12}$$
$$H_{Q2}(\Pi(A) = n) \mapsto \Pr(A) = [+] \tag{6.13}$$
$$H_{Q2}(\Pi(A) = n) \mapsto \mathrm{Bel}(A) = [0, +] \tag{6.14}$$
$$H_{Q2}(\mathrm{Bel}(A) = n) \mapsto \Pr(A) = [+] \tag{6.15}$$
$$H_{Q2}(\mathrm{Bel}(A) = n) \mapsto \Pi(A) = [+] \tag{6.16}$$

while:

$$H_{Q2}(\Pr(A) = 0) \mapsto \Pi(A) = [0] \tag{6.17}$$
$$H_{Q2}(\Pr(A) = 0) \mapsto \mathrm{Bel}(A) = [0] \tag{6.18}$$
$$H_{Q2}(\Pi(A) = 0) \mapsto \Pr(A) = [0] \tag{6.19}$$
$$H_{Q2}(\Pi(A) = 0) \mapsto \mathrm{Bel}(A) = [0] \tag{6.20}$$
$$H_{Q2}(\mathrm{Bel}(A) = 0) \mapsto \Pr(A) = [0, +] \tag{6.21}$$
$$H_{Q2}(\mathrm{Bel}(A) = 0) \mapsto \Pi(A) = [0, +] \tag{6.22}$$

---

1 This notation is just a convenient shorthand, so that no new value is being introduced. To calculate the result of combining $[0, +]$ with another qualitative value one simply calculates the result of the requisite combination with $[+]$ and $[0]$ and composes the two. $[0, +]$ and its dual $[0, -]$ crop up again in Chapter 7.

These translations would obviously be modified if the formalism that was the result of a translation had values outside the range $[0, 1]$ as would be the case if it were Spohn's theory of ordinal conditionals. There are two notable points about the translations. The first is that they are "assumption free" in the sense that they generate a value that makes no assumptions about the value that they translate to. The second is that they agree with the ideas of Brillouin, discussed in Section 2.4, in that in the absence of any specific information, they lead to a decrease in precise knowledge.

Using the translation, if it is necessary to determine $\Pr(c)$ from $\Pr(a)$, and $\Pi(c|a)$ is known rather than $\Pr(c|a)$, it is possible to translate the latter to obtain $\Pr(c|a) = [+]$, and use this to get:

$$\Pr(c) = (\Pr(a) \otimes [+]) \oplus (\Pr(\neg a) \otimes \Pr(c|\neg a)) \tag{6.23}$$

The qualitative values manipulated by $Q2$ also provide a mechanism for handling the problem of incomplete information. If a necessary probability, possibility or belief value is missing, it is possible to substitute $[+]$ or $[0, +]$ for it in exactly the same way as is done when translating into the formalism, and with exactly the same justification. The value is known to exist, but it is not known what it is. Therefore it will be taken to be $[0, +]$ or $[+]$ (depending on whether or not it may be zero), which makes no assumptions about the value and yet provides a value that may be used alongside those that are known. This same mechanism may be used to solve the incompleteness and translation problem in all formalisms that have values in the range $[0, 1]$ by suitable extension of the principle of degrading and the substitution of suitable values. Other formalisms may be accommodated by use of other qualitative values. For instance, when using certainty factors, it is possible to represent missing or translated values with $[?]$, and in Spohn's ordinal conditional functions missing or translated values could be represented by $[-]$ or $[0, -]$.

Irrespective of the way in which qualitative values are introduced, they always tend to proliferate. Combining a qualitative value with a real value often gives a qualitative value. Thus, at the end of some reasoning process it is possible to end up with a number of hypotheses whose uncertainty is quantified as being $[+]$. In some cases simply knowing that the certainty of a hypothesis is non-zero is sufficient. However, there are cases in which it is desirable to rank hypotheses. Since it is impossible to tell which of two $[+]$ values is the greater, in $Q2$ it is not possible to distinguish between a qualitative value that has been combined with many low certainty values, and thus may be assumed to be a low, though unknown, value, and one that has been combined with many high values, and may thus be assumed to be high but unknown.[2] Ideally it would be desirable to preserve some of

2 The fact that it is not possible to distinguish between two $[+]$ values follows directly from qualitative reasoning—when viewed through the lens of qualitative reasoning the values are equal since that lens distinguishes no more than the sign of a quantity. From a perspective that distinguishes values more precisely, doing

the information that is abandoned when it is assumed that the missing or translated value is "something positive." Since certainty values are being considered, and these have well defined bounds, the limits on the value of the unknown quantity are known. If these upper and lower values are manipulated, it is possible to get more precise answers, and that is the idea elaborated in the next section.

6.3   An algebra of interval values

A new algebra, $Q3$, which operates over real numbers and intervals can be defined. $Q3$ combines the robustness of $Q2$ with a sound computational mechanism that generates results of a greater precision than those produced by its predecessor. The operand set of $Q3$ includes the set of exact values, which are individually written as $m, \ldots, n$ rather than $\Re+$ making it clear that they are distinct values. The operand set of $Q3$ also contains 0 and $(0, 1]$, which is equivalent to $[+]$ except that it specifically refers to the interval $0 < x \leq 1$. The algebra also deals with operands of the form $[p, q]$, $(r, s]$, $[t, u)$ and (v, w), which specify the intervals $p \leq x \leq q, r < x \leq s, t \leq x < u$ and $v < x < w$ respectively. $Q3$ provides a means of handling uncertainty that is similar to that of Jain and Agogino (1990) but which uses crisp rather than fuzzy intervals, and general arithmetic operations rather than those specific to probability theory. Since fuzzy intervals are a generalisation of crisp intervals, the results presented here can be generalised to fuzzy intervals, and probability specific operations can be introduced (Parsons, 1990).

6.3.1   A formal definition

More formally, $Q3$ deals with a set of values $\mathcal{S}'_* = \mathcal{S}_* \cup \Re_{[0,1]} \cup \{[0, 1], (0, 1]\}$ where the set $\mathcal{S}_* = \{[y, z] : 0 \leq y \leq z \leq 1\} \cup \{(y, z] : 0 < y \leq z \leq 1\} \cup \{[y, z) : 0 \leq y \leq z < 1\} \cup \{(y, z) : 0 < y \leq z < 1\}$ and $\Re_{[0,1]} = \{x : x \in \Re, 0 \leq x \leq 1\}$. There is a mapping $[\![\cdot]\!]$ that relates $\Re_{[0,1]}$ to $\mathcal{S}_*$, such that if $x \in \Re_{[0,1]}$ then $[\![x]\!] = [x, x]$. Thus every real number in the zero-one interval is equivalent to a point, or degenerate (Moore, 1966), interval. The members of $\mathcal{S}_*$, the set of intervals whose bounds are between 0 and 1 inclusive, other than those point intervals of the form $[x, x]$, may not be obtained by applying a mapping function to $\Re_{[0,1]}$, and are established either through operations applied to members of $\mathcal{S}'_*$, or by way of quantifying vague information. As in the case of $Q2$, it is possible to say that there is at least one $\odot \in \mathcal{OP}_{Q3} : \Re \times \mathcal{S}_* \mapsto \mathcal{S}_*$, where $\mathcal{OP}_{Q3}$ is the set of all operators over $\mathcal{S}'_*$.

Members of $\mathcal{S}_*$ may also be created by the quantification of vague information. This

---

this is applying a heuristic. However the heuristic is a cautious one and so seems justifiable. Note the contrast with the approach in (Renooij and van der Gaag, 1999a).

is one of the main strengths of the algebra, allowing the incorporation of values that are not known precisely. There is a mapping $\{\!\![\cdot]\!\!\}$ that maps from imprecise data to $\mathcal{S}_*$, so that $\{\!\![\{x : y \leq x \leq z, 0 \leq y \leq 1, 0 \leq z \leq 1\}]\!\!\} \mapsto [y, z] \in \mathcal{S}_*$, $\{\!\![\{x : y < x \leq z, 0 \leq y \leq 1, 0 \leq z \leq 1\}]\!\!\} \mapsto (y, z] \in \mathcal{S}_*$, $\{\!\![\{x : y \leq x < z, 0 \leq y \leq 1, 0 \leq z \leq 1\}]\!\!\} \mapsto [y, z) \in \mathcal{S}_*$ and $\{\!\![\{x : y < x < z, 0 \leq y \leq 1, 0 \leq z \leq 1\}]\!\!\} \mapsto (y, z) \in \mathcal{S}_*$. Two special cases are distinguished. These are the value $[0, 1]$, which expresses complete ignorance about the value of x when x is a value in an uncertainty handling formalism whose range of values is between 0 and 1, and the value $(0, 1]$ where x is only known to be strictly positive. Arithmetic operations over closed intervals are defined by Moore's (1966) interval analysis, such that for any arithmetic combinator $\odot \in \mathcal{OP}_{Q3}$:

$$[a, b] \odot [c, d] = \Big[\min(a \odot c, a \odot d, b \odot c, b \odot d), \max(a \odot c, a \odot d, b \odot c, b \odot d) \Big] \quad (6.24)$$

where $\max$ and $\min$ have their usual meanings. This system of arithmetic generalises easily to cover open intervals:

$$(a, b) \odot (c, d) = \Big(\min(a \odot c, a \odot d, b \odot c, b \odot d), \max(a \odot c, a \odot d, b \odot c, b \odot d) \Big) \quad (6.25)$$

as well as intervals with one end open and one end closed. When dealing with such "mixed" intervals, any interval whose end value is established using a value from the open end of an interval is itself open. Thus:

$$(1, 2] + [3, 4] = (4, 6]$$

The only price to be paid for using this simple system stems from the ultra-cautious nature of interval arithmetic; it always selects the widest possible bounds, and this can be a problem when dealing with a large amount of imprecise data. However, this is partially compensated for by the following result (Moore, 1966):

THEOREM 6.1:   Let $f(x_1, \ldots, x_n)$ be a rational function of n variables. Consider any sequence of arithmetic steps which serve to evaluate f with given arguments $x_1, \ldots, x_n$. If the arguments x_i are replaced by the corresponding intervals X_i, where $i = 1, \ldots, n$, and the arithmetic steps in the sequence used to evaluate f are replaced by the corresponding interval arithmetic steps, then the result will be an interval $f(X_1, \ldots, X_n)$ which contains the value of $f(x_1, \ldots, x_n)$ for all $x_i \in X_i$, $i = 1, \ldots, n$.

This result guarantees that the interval generated by the application of the rules of interval arithmetic never excludes any value that it should include.

It should be noted that the use of $Q3$ to handle interval uncertainty values is a reflection of the imprecision of the values, nothing more. Thus an interval probability is an imprecise probability, not a pair of upper and lower probabilities (Dubois and Prade, 1988d) and is unrelated to upper and lower previsions (Walley, 1996) though they can be given meaning in terms of acceptable limits on gambles. This means that there is no duality between the upper bound of $\Pr(A)$ and the lower bound of $\Pr(\neg A)$ that is enforced by the algebra. In a similar vein a possibility interval represents an imprecise possibility, and an interval belief an imprecise belief, where the belief is known to be in a particular range.

6.3.2   Propagating values in $Q3$

The propagation of values through a network using $Q3$ is very straightforward. Interval arithmetic is defined over all the usual arithmetic operators, so all the operations required to propagate inference in all commonly used uncertainty handling formalisms are covered. Every normal arithmetic operation is replaced by its interval arithmetic counterpart, as defined by (6.24). For instance, to propagate from A to C in Figure 6.1 using probability values, the following formula is used:

$$\Pr(c) \;=\; \left[\sum_{\substack{A=a_1,\ldots,a_m \\ X=x_1,\ldots,x_p}} \Pr(c|A,X)_L \Pr(A,X)_L \,, \right.$$

$$\left. \sum_{\substack{A=a_1,\ldots,a_m \\ X=x_1,\ldots,x_p}} \Pr(c|A,X)_U \Pr(A,X)_U \right] \tag{6.26}$$

where all the probabilities are of the form $\Pr(a) = [\Pr(a)_L, \Pr(a)_U]$, and $\Pr(a)_L \leq \Pr(a)_U$. Now, while this equation and the others in this section only apply to closed intervals it is simple to write down versions that apply to open intervals and intervals which are open at one end and closed at the other. To propagate possibility values from A to C in Figure 6.1, the following is used:

$$\Pi(c) \;=\; \left[\sup_{\substack{A=a_1,\ldots,a_m \\ X=x_1,\ldots,x_p}} \min(\Pi(c|A,X)_L, \Pi(A,X)_L) \,, \right.$$

$$\left. \sup_{\substack{A=a_1,\ldots,a_m \\ X=x_1,\ldots,x_p}} \min(\Pi(c|A,X)_U, \Pi(A,X)_U) \right] \tag{6.27}$$

Clearly the effect of applying maximum and minimum operations in interval arithmetic is the same as applying Dubois and Prade's fuzzy maximum and minimum with crisp intervals and so is consistent with $\min_{Q2}$. It is also simple to determine the formulae for propagation in evidence theory by Dempster's rule and the disjunctive rule respectively:

$$
\text{Bel}(c) \;=\; \left[\sum_{\substack{A \subseteq \{a_1,\ldots,a_m\} \\ X \subseteq \{x_1,\ldots,x_p\}}} m(A,X)_L \text{Bel}(c|A,X)_L \,, \right. \tag{6.28}
$$

$$
\left. \sum_{\substack{A \subseteq \{a_1,\ldots,a_m\} \\ X \subseteq \{x_1,\ldots,x_p\}}} m(A,X)_U \text{Bel}(c|A,X)_U \right]
$$

$$
\text{Bel}(c) \;=\; \left[\sum_{\substack{A \subseteq \{a_1,\ldots,a_m\} \\ X \subseteq \{x_1,\ldots,x_p\}}} m(A,X)_L \prod_{\substack{a \in A \\ x \in X}} \text{Bel}(c|A,X)_L \,, \right. \tag{6.29}
$$

$$
\left. \sum_{\substack{A \subseteq \{a_1,\ldots,a_m\} \\ X \subseteq \{x_1,\ldots,x_p\}}} m(A,X)_U \prod_{\substack{a \in A \\ x \in X}} \text{Bel}(c|A,X)_U \right]
$$

Once again Bayes' rule (3.15) may be modified to establish the conditionals necessary to propagate values from C to A in Figure 6.1:

$$
\Pr(a|c,x) = \left[\frac{\Pr(c|a,x)_L \Pr(a,x)_L}{\Pr(c,x)_U}, \frac{\Pr(c|a,x)_U \Pr(a,x)_U}{\Pr(c,x)_L} \right] \tag{6.30}
$$

and the possibilistic (3.40) and belief function (3.66) versions of Bayes' rule may be similarly modified. The possibilistic rule is:

$$
\min\left(\Pi(a|c,x), \Pi(c,x)\right) = \min\left(\Pi(c|a,x), \Pi(a,x)\right) \tag{6.31}
$$

which, for interval valued possibilities, may be written as:

$$
[\min(\Pi(a|c,x)_L, \Pi(c,x)_L), \min(\Pi(a|c,x)_U, \Pi(c,x)_U)] \tag{6.32}
$$
$$
= \;[\min(\Pi(c|a,x)_L, \Pi(a,x)_L), \min(\Pi(c|a,x)_U, \Pi(a,x)_U)]
$$

The version of the rule for belief functions is a suitably adapted version of (3.66):

$$
\text{Bel}(a|c,x) \;=\; \left[\prod_{y \in \tilde{a}} \text{Bel}(\tilde{c}|y,x)_L - \prod_{y \in A} \text{Bel}(\tilde{c}|y,x)_U \,, \right.
$$

$$
\left. \prod_{y \in \tilde{a}} \text{Bel}(\tilde{c}|y,x)_U - \prod_{y \in A} \text{Bel}(\tilde{c}|y,x)_L \right]
$$

As with $Q2$ these are not the only models that may be used—any model proposed in the literature may be adopted and used in $Q3$ by changing every arithmetical operator for its interval equivalent, and again it is easy to adapt existing computational schemes to use interval values.

Now, a problem with the use of interval arithmetic arises when trying to rank hypotheses based upon the interval values of their associated certainty measures. Interval arithmetic only supports the ordering of non-overlapping intervals:

$$[a, b] < [m, n] \text{ iff } a < b < m < n \tag{6.33}$$

In general this is no use for choosing between interval certainty values since these often overlap. To get around this problem it is necessary to decide what is meant by an interval value in some formalism and use this assumption to determine how to compare two of them. The obvious ordering to use is that implied by the the maximum and minimum operations suggested by Dubois and Prade (1979). This ordering, which will be termed $\leq_{Q3}$, follows almost immediately from Dubois and Prade's definition:

THEOREM 6.2:   An interval $[a, b]$ is considered less than or equal to a similar interval $[m, n]$, $[a, b] \leq_{Q3} [m, n]$, iff $a \leq m$ and $b \leq n$.

This is the ordering used in the implementation of $Q3$ discussed in Chapter 9. Clearly this is a generalisation of the ordering of (6.33). In addition, the notion of equality engendered by $\leq_{Q3}$:

$$[a, b] =_{Q3} [m, n], \text{ iff } [a, b] \leq_{Q3} [m, n] \text{ and } [m, n] \leq_{Q3} [a, b] \tag{6.34}$$

is equality as defined by interval arithmetic (Moore, 1966):

$$[a, b] = [m, n] \text{ iff } a = m \text{ and } b = n \tag{6.35}$$

It is, of course, equally possible to make a completely different assumption about the meaning of an interval, coming up with a different ordering, for instance the "average" ordering of interval values suggested by Voorbraak (1989) may be adopted, justifying this choice as follows.

An interval $[m, n]$ represents a value that is known to lie between m and n but whose precise value is not known. Since there is no information to suggest otherwise, the real value is equally likely to be any point value in this interval. In other words, by the principle of maximum entropy there is uniform second order probability distribution across the set of possible values, and an equal finite probability that the value will be in the interval $[m, x]$, $m < x < n$, or in the interval $[n + m - x, n]$. Such an interpretation makes it possible to

Table 6.3
The probabilities for Jack's model

$\Pr(s\|c)$	$=$	$[0.7, 1]$	$\Pr(c\|w, d)$	$=$	$[0.2, 0.6]$
$\Pr(s\|\neg c)$	$=$	$(0, 0.4]$	$\Pr(c\|\neg w, d)$	$=$	$[0.8, 1]$
			$\Pr(c\|w, \neg d)$	$=$	$(0, 0.2]$
$\Pr(g\|d)$	$=$	$[0.8, 1]$	$\Pr(c\|\neg w, \neg d)$	$=$	$[0.4, 0.6]$
$\Pr(g\|\neg d)$	$=$	$(0, 0.1]$			

calculate the probability that the value whose bounds are known will exceed a particular value and this provides the basis for comparing intervals. An order $\leq'_{Q3}$ is defined by:

$$[a, b] \leq'_{Q3} [m, n] \text{ iff } \Pr(x \leq y) \leq \Pr(y \leq x) \text{ where } a \leq x \leq b \text{ and } m \leq y \leq n. \qquad (6.36)$$

This is, of course, expected mean dominance for identical distributions (Whitmore and Findlay, 1978). This gives:

THEOREM 6.3:   An interval $[a, b]$ is considered less than or equal to a similar interval $[m, n]$, $[a, b] \leq'_{Q3} [m, n]$, iff $(a + b) \leq (m + n)$.

If this ordering is adopted, it is important to remember that it is imposing a particular interpretation upon the interval and so, following the advice that Strat (1989b) gives for his similar interpretation of belief functions, the ordering should only be used to rank alternatives at the end of a calculation so that the calculation itself is not distorted.

6.3.3   An example using $Q3$

The year before last, Jack Dulouz, spontaneous bop-prosodist and ardent student of qualitative approaches to reasoning under uncertainty, was climbing a mountain with his friend Japhy Ryder. As they neared the summit it became clear that if they continued climbing they might not be able to complete the subsequent descent before nightfall. This would be disastrous since they had no camping gear. Being keen to reach the top, Japhy suggested that they leave their packs by the side of the trail, arguing that they could climb quicker that way and so both reach the summit and safely descend before dark. Jack was less convinced, worrying that the wind, which he feared would begin to blow quite strongly, would prevent them from reaching the summit anyway. He was also worried that without the packs, which contained all their food, they would become very hungry. To help him analyse the problem, he sketched the graph of Figure 6.2 in the dirt by the side of the trail to help him decide what he thought of their chances of reaching the top of the mountain. The proposition "wind blows" is represented by the node W, "climb fast" by the node C, "discard packs" by the node D, "get hungry" by the node G, and "reach summit (and descend by nightfall)" by the node S.

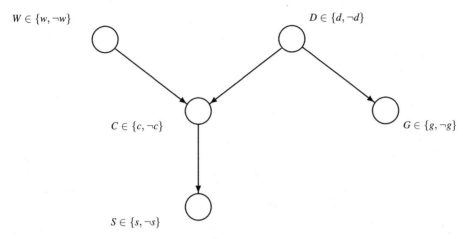

Figure 6.2
Jack's model of mountain climbing

Jack had no accurate numerical information with which to quantify the model, but after some thought decided that $\Pr(s|c)$ must be greater than 0.7, by which he meant that if he had a bet with Japhy such that Japhy would pay him \$1 were they able to reach the summit and descend before nightfall given that they are able to climb quickly, then the minimum price that he would be happy to exchange that bet for was 70c. Similar reasoning led him to set the maximum value of $\Pr(g|d)$ as 0.8, the minimum value of $\Pr(c|\neg w, d)$ as 0.8, and the maximum value of $\Pr(c|w, \neg d)$ as 0.2. In all cases he was sure that the probabilities were non-zero. Chuckling to himself at the thought of the problems that such imprecise information would cause people who did not know about qualitative methods, he drew up the conditional probability table replicated in Table 6.3, filling in the missing values with intervals that fitted with his imprecise estimates of the other values. Then he used $Q3$, in particular (6.26), to determine that, if they discarded the packs and took the probability of the wind picking up to be 0.6, it followed that:

$$
\begin{aligned}
\Pr(g) &= [0.8, 1] \\
\Pr(c) &= [0.2, 0.6][0.6, 0.6][1, 1] + [0.8, 1][0.4, 0.4][1, 1] \\
&= [0.12, 0.36] + [0.48, 0.6] \\
&= [0.6, 0.96] \\
\Pr(s) &= [0.7, 1][0.6, 0.96] + (0, 0.4](0, 0.3] \\
&= [0.42, 0.96] + (0, 0.12]
\end{aligned}
$$

Table 6.4
The possibilities for Japhy's model

$\Pi(s|c)$	=	$[0.7, 1]$	$\Pi(c|w, d)$	=	$[0.2, 0.6]$
$\Pi(s|\neg c)$	=	$(0, 1]$	$\Pi(c|\neg w, d)$	=	$[0.8, 1]$
			$\Pi(c|w, \neg d)$	=	$(0, 1]$
$\Pi(g|d)$	=	$[0.8, 1]$	$\Pi(c|\neg w, \neg d)$	=	$[0.4, 1]$
$\Pi(g|\neg d)$	=	$(0, 1]$			

$$= \quad (0.42, 1]$$

where the final figure is arrived at by capping the interval generated by interval arithmetic at 1 (since it cannot be greater). Jack pointed the results of his calculation out to Japhy, arguing that it meant that they were nearly certain to be hungry, but did not have that much chance of getting to the summit and returning safely.

Being a keen student of possibility theory, and a believer in an eclectic outlook on life, Japhy insisted that they consider the results of a possibilistic analysis. To do this he took Jack's probabilities and applied Dubois and Prade's version of the possibility/probability consistency principle (3.43) to obtain the possibilities of Table 6.4 along with $\Pi(w) = [0.6, 1]$, and then estimated $\Pi(\neg w)$ and all conditionals of the form $\Pi(\neg c|W, D)$ to be 1. Concluding that leaving their packs should be modelled by setting $\Pi(d) = 1$ and $\Pi(\neg d) = 0$, Japhy calculated that:

$$\Pi(g) = \text{sup}(\text{min}([0.8, 1], [1, 1]), \text{min}((0, 1], [0, 0]))$$
$$= [0.8, 1]$$
$$\Pi(c) = \text{sup}(\text{min}([0.2, 0.6], [0.6, 1], [1, 1]), \text{min}([0.8, 1], [1, 1], [1, 1])$$
$$\text{min}((0, 1], [0.6, 1], [0, 0]), \text{min}([0.4, 1], [1, 1], [0, 0]))$$
$$= \text{sup}([0.2, 1], [0.8, 1], [0, 0], [0, 0])$$
$$= [0.8, 1]$$

Similarly,

$$\Pi(\neg c) = [1, 1]$$

Thus:

$$\Pi(s) = \text{sup}(\text{min}([0.7, 1][0.8, 1]), \text{min}((0, 1], [1, 1]))$$
$$= \text{sup}([0.7, 1] + (0, 1])$$
$$= [0.7, 1]$$

showing that while it was perfectly possible that they would get hungry, it was also possible to make the summit and still descend safely.

Seeing that Jack was still wavering, Japhy then pointed out that it was possible to use $\leq'_{Q3}$ to compare the interval probability results with point values and that doing so makes $\Pr(s)$ equivalent to 0.71. Even though the same calculation made $\Pr(g)$ equivalent to a point value of 0.9, this was enough to convince Jack, and the two of them left their packs and set off for the summit. As it happened, only Japhy reached the summit in the end, but both Japhy and Jack made a safe descent before nightfall.

6.3.4 Handling translation and incompleteness in $Q3$

The problem of translation is handled using $Q3$ in the same way as it is in $Q2$, by importing "something" values. For example, consider that it is necessary to carry out the probabilistic propagation described by (6.26). However, assume that this is frustrated by the fact that there is no available value for $\Pr(c|a)$, instead there is a non-zero value available for $\Pi(c|a)$. It is possible to obtain $\Pr(c|a)$ from $\Pi(c|a)$ by using an assumption free translation:

$$H_{Q3} : \Pi(x) \mapsto \Pr(x)$$

which is defined by[3]:

$$\forall x, \Pi(x) \in (0,1], H_{Q3}(\Pi(x)) = [0,1] \tag{6.37}$$

Giving:

$$\begin{aligned} \Pr(c) &= \Pr(c|a)\Pr(a) + \Pr(c|\neg a)\Pr(\neg a) \\ &= (0, \Pr(a)] + \Pr(c|\neg a)\Pr(\neg a) \\ &= \left(\Pr(c|\neg a)\Pr(\neg a), \Pr(c|\neg a)\Pr(\neg a) + \Pr(a) \right] \end{aligned}$$

which is a tighter interval, and thus a more informative value, than that which would be generated by $Q2$ if it were applied to the same situation. In general the translation function is:

$$H_{Q3}(v_1) = x \tag{6.38}$$

where x is a a "something." Again recalling the principle of degrading, as summarised by (5.1)–(5.12), this translation may be restated for probability, possibility, and evidence theories for $n > 0$ as:

$$H_{Q3}(\Pr(A) = n) \quad \mapsto \quad \Pi(A) = (0,1] \tag{6.39}$$

$$H_{Q3}(\Pr(A) = n) \quad \mapsto \quad \mathrm{Bel}(A) = [0,1] \tag{6.40}$$

---

3 In fact $H_{Q3}(\Pi(x)) \subseteq [0,1]$, but since it is not known which subinterval it lies in, I trust that this slight abuse of notation will be excused by the reader.

$$H_{Q3}(\Pi(A) = n) \quad \mapsto \quad \Pr(A) = (0,1] \tag{6.41}$$

$$H_{Q3}(\Pi(A) = n) \quad \mapsto \quad \mathrm{Bel}(A) = [0,1] \tag{6.42}$$

$$H_{Q3}(\mathrm{Bel}(A) = n) \quad \mapsto \quad \Pr(A) = (0,1] \tag{6.43}$$

$$H_{Q3}(\mathrm{Bel}(A) = n) \quad \mapsto \quad \Pi(A) = (0,1] \tag{6.44}$$

while:

$$H_{Q3}(\Pr(A) = 0) \quad \mapsto \quad \Pi(A) = [0,0] \tag{6.45}$$

$$H_{Q3}(\Pr(A) = 0) \quad \mapsto \quad \mathrm{Bel}(A) = [0,0] \tag{6.46}$$

$$H_{Q3}(\Pi(A) = 0) \quad \mapsto \quad \Pr(A) = [0,0] \tag{6.47}$$

$$H_{Q3}(\Pi(A) = 0) \quad \mapsto \quad \mathrm{Bel}(A) = [0,0] \tag{6.48}$$

$$H_{Q3}(\mathrm{Bel}(A) = 0) \quad \mapsto \quad \Pr(A) = [0,1] \tag{6.49}$$

$$H_{Q3}(\mathrm{Bel}(A) = 0) \quad \mapsto \quad \Pi(A) = [0,1] \tag{6.50}$$

Again this translation would have to be modified if the formalism that was the result of the translation had values outside the range $[0,1]$. As before, the translation follows Brillouin's dictum (Section 2.4) that unless there is any additional information, uncertainty increases when translating from one formalism to another. Of course, this does not mean that the translation is not useful if even the less precise information is more information than was otherwise available. A more precise translation is possible if additional information is present in the form of the suggestions for relating formalisms that have been put forward in the literature, and the assumptions required by those suggestions are accepted. For instance, it is possible to use the relations between its probability, possibility, and belief values suggested by Dubois and Prade (1988d) (see (3.43) and (3.59)) to put limits on the values generated by these translations. Doing so gives the following results:

$$H'_{Q3} : (\mathrm{Bel}(x) = (\!(n,m)\!)) \quad \mapsto \quad (\Pr(x) = (\!(n,1])) \tag{6.51}$$

$$H'_{Q3} : (\mathrm{Bel}(x) = (\!(n,m)\!)) \quad \mapsto \quad (\Pi(x) = (\!(n,1])) \tag{6.52}$$

$$H'_{Q3} : (\Pr(x) = (\!(n,m)\!)) \quad \mapsto \quad (\mathrm{Bel}(x) = [0,m)\!)) \tag{6.53}$$

$$H'_{Q3} : (\Pr(x) = (\!(n,m)\!)) \quad \mapsto \quad (\Pi(x) = (\!(n,1])) \tag{6.54}$$

$$H'_{Q3} : (\Pi(x) = (\!(n,m)\!)) \quad \mapsto \quad (\mathrm{Bel}(x) = [0,n)\!)) \tag{6.55}$$

$$H'_{Q3} : (\Pi(x) = (\!(n,m)\!)) \quad \mapsto \quad (\Pr(x) = (0,n)\!)) \tag{6.56}$$

where the last mapping holds provided $n > 0$ (otherwise the lower end of the interval is closed), and $(\!(n,m)\!)$ is shorthand for an interval that is either open or closed so that if $\Pr(x) = (0.2,0.3]$ then $\Pi(x) = (0.2,1]$ but if $\Pr(x) = [0.2,0.3]$ then $\Pi(x) = [0.2,1]$. The translations are stated in terms of interval values for generality, however, they are equally applicable to degenerate intervals. As ever with qualitative algebras, every possible way of doing things has not been stated. There are other translations possible if different assumptions are made; in fact any desired assumption can be made and any one of a vast number of possible translations may be carried out. $Q3$ does not force the choice of a particular translation, it merely provides the mechanism to enable translations into interval values since these seem to be an appropriate way to represent the results of inexact translations.

As in $Q2$, it is possible to handle incompleteness in a similar way to that by which translation is performed. If there is a missing value in a database of probability, possibility or belief values, it may safely be assumed that it is $(0, 1]$, and as a result interval arithmetic may be used to combine this with other values in the database. Thus if it is known that $\Pr(fever|measles) = 0.5$, but there is no information about $\Pr(fever|\neg measles)$, it is possible to assume that $\Pr(fever|\neg measles) = (0, 1]$ and use this in (6.26) along with $\Pr(measles) = 0.2$ to learn that $\Pr(fever) = (0.1, 0.9]$. However, this is not the only way that it is possible deal with incompleteness. $Q3$ also allows the use of more detailed values to handle missing information. Consider the measles example again. Since it is known that measles tends to cause a fever, it is possible to deduce that $\Pr(fever|measles) \geq \Pr(fever|\neg measles)$. Thus it is known that $\Pr(fever|\neg measles)$ lies in the interval $(0, 0.5]$. This value may then be manipulated using $Q3$ to give the more precise result that $\Pr(fever) = (0.1, 0.5]$.

6.4   Other qualitative algebras

The qualitative values of $Q2$ and the interval values of $Q3$ represent two extreme ways of splitting the real numbers into sets. The first splits the real numbers into three sets, the positive numbers, the negative numbers, and zero. The second divides the real numbers into an infinite number of overlapping intervals which vary in breadth from the infinitesimal to the infinite, although in practice the upper positive bound is 1, and the lower bound is 0. Of course, as discussed in Chapter 4, there are many other ways of splitting up the real numbers. For instance, one may wish to use the set of intervals introduced by Dubois and Prade (1989a) and discussed in Section 4.2.3. It is quite possible to use such partitionings of the set of real numbers as the basis of a qualitative algebra that is then used to handle values expressed in some uncertainty handling formalism. Exactly this has been done (Parsons and Dohnal, 1993). Indeed, it is even possible to show (Parsons and Dohnal, 1992) that the intervals of $Q3$ and the various semiqualitative algebras obtained by arbitrary divisions of the real numbers form a family of semiqualitative algebras in the sense of Travé-Massuyès and Piera (1989). This result means that for every algebra other than $Q2$, there is a sub-algebra that represents a coarser partitioning of the set of real numbers, and so it would be possible to use the whole family of algebras in conjunction, switching from coarse partitions to fine partitions when greater precision was required. However, since arithmetic operations tend to cause semiqualitative intervals to agglomerate (Dubois and Prade, 1989a), and thus become less precise, the greatest precision is maintained by the use of *Q3*. As a result the use of semiqualitative algebras for handling uncertainty is considered no further here. Another obvious extension of the algebras is to fuzzify them, and a fuzzy *Q3* would be a general version of the formalism introduced by Jain and Agogino (1990). Again, having suggested the idea it will not be pursued any further.

It is also possible to imagine another form of qualitative algebra—one that manipulates qualitative influences of the kind discussed by Wellman and subsequent authors rather than dealing with qualitative values that are abstractions of real values. Such an algebra would deal with changes in value rather than with the values themselves in the way that *Q2* and *Q3* do. It is simple enough to provide most of this algebra (Parsons, 1991), but there is a real problem when it comes to providing mappings between quantitative and qualitative values. When dealing with probability theory it is, of course, possible to take Wellman's (1990a) condition and have (for binary variables) *a* "positively influencing" *c* if:

$$\Pr(c|a, X) \geq \Pr(c|\neg a, X)$$

However, there are other equally plausible suggestions for the condition. For instance one might sum over the instantiations of X to make the relevant condition:

$$\Pr(c|a) \geq \Pr(c|\neg a)$$

or compare the probability of c given a is known with the unconditional probability of c as proposed by Neufeld (1990) in which case the condition for "positive influence" becomes:

$$\Pr(c|a) > \Pr(c)$$

Alternatively the condition could be taken to be:

$$\Pr(c|a) > \Pr(\neg c|a)$$

or even

$$\Pr(c|a) > 0.5$$

as discussed by Dubois and Prade (1991b). It is not at all clear which is the best mapping to choose. Unlike the mapping into qualitative values proposed in *Q2* and *Q3*, here the choice of mapping will have a fundamental effect on the kind of reasoning that can be performed using the algebra. Furthermore, there are no obvious mappings for other formalisms, and

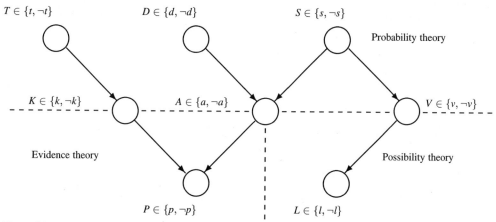

Figure 6.3
The network for the trauma example.

further to that, even if other mappings were proposed, it is not obvious how it would be possible to capture the same idea of a "positive influence" in those other formalisms.

Together these difficulties suggest that constructing an algebra of qualitative influences is rather pointless since it will never be possible to create anything as simple and easy to apply as $Q2$ and $Q3$. Once one has done the work of establishing a set of mappings in different formalisms that have captured the same idea of "positive influence" (which is effectively what is done in Chapters 7 and 8) then nothing is gained by dressing it up as an algebra.

6.5   An example of handling integration

In this section, the integration example of Section 5.4.1 is discussed, using the qualitative algebras $Q2$ and $Q3$ to translate between values. The reader will recall that the network in question was that of Figure 6.3 (annotated to identify how uncertainty is handled in different parts of the model), which encodes the following medical information. Joint trauma (T) leads to loose knee bodies (K), and that these and arthritis (A) cause pain (P). The incidence of arthritis is influenced by dislocation (D) of the joint in question and by the patient suffering from Sjorgen's syndrome (S). Sjorgen's syndrome affects the incidence of vasculitis (V), and vasculitis leads to vasculitic lesions (L). The strengths of the influences are given by the probabilities of Table 6.5, the possibilities of Table 6.6, and the beliefs of Table 6.7. The prior probabilities of joint trauma, $\Pr(t) = 0.4$, Sjorgen's syndrome $\Pr(s) = 0.1$, and dislocation, $\Pr(d) = 0.3$, are also known. Ignorance about the

Table 6.5
The probabilities for the trauma example

$\Pr(k\vert t)$	=	0.6	$\Pr(a\vert d,s)$	=	0.9
$\Pr(k\vert\neg t)$	=	0.2	$\Pr(a\vert\neg d,s)$	=	0.6
			$\Pr(a\vert d,\neg s)$	=	0.6
$\Pr(v\vert s)$	=	0.1	$\Pr(a\vert\neg d,\neg s)$	=	0.4
$\Pr(v\vert\neg s)$	=	0.3			

Table 6.6
The possibilities for the trauma example

$\Pi(l\vert v)$	=	1	$\Pi(\neg l\vert v)$	=	1
$\Pi(l\vert\neg v)$	=	0.8	$\Pi(\neg l\vert\neg v)$	=	1

Table 6.7
The beliefs for the trauma example

$\mathrm{Bel}(p\vert k,a)$	=	0.9	$\mathrm{Bel}(p\vert k,a\cup\neg a)$	=	0.7
$\mathrm{Bel}(p\cup\neg p\vert k,a)$	=	0.1	$\mathrm{Bel}(p\cup\neg p\vert k,a\cup\neg a)$	=	0.3
$\mathrm{Bel}(p\vert k,\neg a)$	=	0.7	$\mathrm{Bel}(\neg p\vert\neg k,\neg a)$	=	0.5
$\mathrm{Bel}(p\cup\neg p\vert k,\neg a)$	=	0.3	$\mathrm{Bel}(p\cup\neg p\vert\neg k,\neg a)$	=	0.5
$\mathrm{Bel}(p\vert\neg k,a)$	=	0.7	$\mathrm{Bel}(\neg p\vert\neg k,a\cup\neg a)$	=	0.4
$\mathrm{Bel}(p\cup\neg p\vert\neg k,a)$	=	0.3	$\mathrm{Bel}(p\cup\neg p\vert\neg k,a\cup\neg a)$	=	0.6
$\mathrm{Bel}(p\vert k\cup\neg k,a)$	=	0.6	$\mathrm{Bel}(\neg p\vert k\cup\neg k,\neg a)$	=	0.4
$\mathrm{Bel}(p\cup\neg p\vert k\cup\neg k,a)$	=	0.4	$\mathrm{Bel}(p\cup\neg p\vert k\cup\neg k,\neg a)$	=	0.6

possibility distribution over the values of V permits the minimum specificity assumption that $\Pi(v) = 1$ and $\Pi(\neg v) = 1$.

6.5.1 Handling integration in $\mathcal{Q}2$

Consider propagating values in the network of Figure 6.3 by means of operations over the algebra $\mathcal{Q}2$. Using (6.2) it is possible to combine the probability values given above to establish that the probability of the patient suffering from loose knee bodies $\Pr(k)$, the probability of the patient suffering from vasculitis $\Pr(v)$, and the probability of the patient suffering from arthritis $\Pr(a)$ are:

$$\Pr(k) = \Pr(k\vert t)\otimes\Pr(t)\oplus\Pr(k\vert\neg t)\otimes\Pr(\neg t)$$
$$= (0.6\otimes 0.4)\oplus(0.2\otimes 0.6)$$
$$= 0.36$$
$$\Pr(a) = \Pr(a\vert d,s)\otimes\Pr(d)\otimes\Pr(s)\oplus\Pr(a\vert\neg d,s)\otimes\Pr(\neg d)\otimes\Pr(s)$$
$$\oplus\Pr(a\vert d,\neg s)\otimes\Pr(d)\otimes\Pr(\neg s)\oplus\Pr(a\vert\neg d\neg s)\otimes\Pr(\neg d)\otimes\Pr(\neg s)$$
$$= (0.9\otimes 0.3\otimes 0.1)\oplus(0.6\otimes 0.7\otimes 0.1)$$

$$\oplus \; (0.6 \otimes 0.3 \otimes 0.9) \oplus (0.4 \otimes 0.7 \otimes 0.9)$$
$$= \; 0.483$$

It is also possible to calculate the prior probability of vasculitis:

$$
\begin{aligned}
\Pr(v) \; &= \; \Pr(v|s) \otimes \Pr(s) \oplus \Pr(v|\neg s) \otimes \Pr(\neg s) \\
&= \; (0.1 \otimes 0.1) \oplus (0.3 \otimes 0.9) \\
&= \; 0.28
\end{aligned}
$$

In addition, the prior possibility of vasculitic lesions may be calculated using (6.5) provided, as discussed in Chapter 5, the principle of minimum specificity is adopted to provide values of $\Pi(v)$ and $\Pi(\neg v)$. Doing this makes the following calculation possible:

$$
\begin{aligned}
\Pi(l) \; &= \; \sup_{Q2} \left(\min_{Q2} \left(\Pi(l|v), \Pi(v) \right), \min_{Q2} \left(\Pi(l|\neg v) \right), \Pi(\neg v) \right) \\
&= \; \sup_{Q2} \left(\min_{Q2}(1,1), \min_{Q2}(0.8,1) \right) \\
&= \; 1
\end{aligned}
$$

Since no qualitative values have been used at this point, the values obtained are exactly those that would result from calculations using operations over just the set of real numbers.

Now, by the principle of degrading, it is possible to say that because there are non-zero probability values for a, $\neg a$, k, $\neg k$, v, and $\neg v$, there are non-zero possibilities for v and $\neg v$ and that the belief values of a, $\neg a$, k, and $\neg k$ are $[0, +]$. Thus $\Pi(v) = \Pi(\neg v) = [+]$ while $\mathrm{Bel}(a)$, $\mathrm{Bel}(\neg a)$, $\mathrm{Bel}(k)$, and $\mathrm{Bel}(\neg k)$ are non-negative. These values may then be used with (6.4) and (6.5) to compute $\mathrm{Bel}(p)$, $\mathrm{Bel}(\neg p)$, $\Pi(l)$ and $\Pi(\neg l)$ (the latter without needing to make use of the principle of minimum specificity):

$$
\begin{aligned}
\mathrm{Bel}(p) \; &= \; \bigoplus_{\substack{A \subseteq \{a, \neg a\} \\ K \subseteq \{k, \neg k\}}} m(A,K) \otimes \mathrm{Bel}(p|A,K) \\
&= \; \bigoplus_{\substack{A \subseteq \{a, \neg a\} \\ K \subseteq \{k, \neg k\}}} m(A)m(K) \otimes \mathrm{Bel}(p|A,K) \\
&= \; [0,+] \bigoplus_{\substack{A \subseteq \{a, \neg a\} \\ K \subseteq \{k, \neg k\}}} \mathrm{Bel}(p|A,K) \\
&= \; [0,+] \\
\mathrm{Bel}(\neg p) \; &= \; \bigoplus_{\substack{A \subseteq \{a, \neg a\} \\ K \subseteq \{k, \neg k\}}} m(A,K) \otimes \mathrm{Bel}(\neg p|A,K)
\end{aligned}
$$

$$= [0, +]$$

$$\Pi(l) = \sup_{Q2} \left(\min_{Q2} \left(\Pi(l|v), \Pi(v) \right), \min_{Q2} \left(\Pi(l|\neg v) \right), \Pi(\neg v) \right)$$

$$= \sup_{Q2} \left(\min_{Q2} \left(\Pi(l|v), [+] \right), \min_{Q2} \left(\Pi(l|\neg v) \right), [+] \right)$$

$$= [+]$$

$$\Pi(\neg l) = \sup_{Q2} \left(\min_{Q2} \left(\Pi(\neg l|v), \Pi(v) \right), \min_{Q2} \left(\Pi(\neg l|\neg v) \right), \Pi(\neg v) \right)$$

$$= [+]$$

Thus strengthening the set of real numbers by adding qualitative values makes it possible to perform some kind of integration of values between different formalisms. As a result, it is possible to say that from some probabilistic data about arthritis, trauma, dislocation and Sjorgen's syndrome one can derive that fact that vasculitic lesions are perfectly possible, and that the patient being in pain cannot be ruled out. It is also possible to establish something about the way in which these values change when the patient is known to be in pain. Applying the relevant version of Bayes' rule (6.8) to establish the conditional beliefs relating P to A gives:

$$\text{Bel}(a|p) = 0.4$$

as established in Chapter 5 and Appendix B. As Appendix B explains, it is also possible to establish that:

$$\text{Bel}(\neg a|p) = 0$$

Using these two results it is possible to propagate back the effect of knowing that $\text{Bel}(p) = 1$ and $\text{Bel}(\neg p) = 0$ (for instance because a patient is observed to be in pain). This gives the following:

$$\text{Bel}(a)^* = \text{Bel}(a|p)$$
$$= 0.6$$
$$\text{Bel}(\neg a)^* = \text{Bel}(\neg a|p)$$
$$= 0$$

These values can then be translated into probability theory to give $\Pr(a)^* = [+]$ and $\Pr(\neg a)^* = [0, +]$, which can be further propagated to say something about $\Pr(d)$ and $\Pr(\neg d)$. However useful this information is, there will be situations in which more detailed information will be required, and in these cases $Q3$ offers some improvements.

6.5.2 Handling integration in $Q3$

Using $Q3$ permits essentially the same calculations as $Q2$, but with results that are, in general, more accurate. Equation (6.26) makes it possible to combine the probability values relating joint trauma to loose knee bodies, Sjorgen's syndrome to vasculitis, and dislocation and Sjorgen's syndrome to arthritis.

$$
\begin{aligned}
\Pr(k) &= \Pr(k|t)\Pr(t) + \Pr(k|\neg t)\Pr(\neg t) \\
&= ([0.6, 0.6] \times [0.4, 0.4]) + ([0.2, 0.2] \times [0.6, 0.6]) \\
&= [0.36, 0.36] \\
\Pr(a) &= \Pr(a|d, s)\Pr(d)\Pr(s) + \Pr(a|\neg d, s)\Pr(\neg d)\Pr(s) \\
&\quad + \Pr(a|d, \neg s)\Pr(d)\Pr(\neg s) + \Pr(a|\neg d \neg s)\Pr(\neg d)\Pr(\neg s) \\
&= ([0.9, 0.9] \times [0.3, 0.3] \times [0.1, 0.1]) + ([0.6, 0.6] \times [0.7, 0.7] \times [0.1, 0.1]) \\
&\quad + ([0.6, 0.6] \times [0.3, 0.3] \times [0.9, 0.9]) + ([0.4, 0.4] \times [0.7, 0.7] \times [0.9, 0.9]) \\
&= [0.483, 0.483]
\end{aligned}
$$

It is also possible to calculate the prior probability of vasculitis:

$$
\begin{aligned}
\Pr(v) &= \Pr(v|s)\Pr(s) + \Pr(v|\neg s)\Pr(\neg s) \\
&= ([0.1, 0.1] \times [0.1, 0.1]) + ([0.3, 0.3] \times [0.9, 0.9]) \\
&= [0.28, 0.28]
\end{aligned}
$$

and the prior possibility of vasculitic lesions (using (6.27)):

$$
\begin{aligned}
\Pi(l) &= \sup\left(\min\left(\Pi(l|v), \Pi(v)\right), \min\left(\Pi(l|\neg v), \Pi(\neg v)\right)\right) \\
&= \sup\left(\min([1, 1], [1, 1]), \min([0.8, 0.8], [1, 1])\right) \\
&= 1
\end{aligned}
$$

The results are that the probability of the patient suffering from loose knee bodies $\Pr(k) = [0.36, 0.36] = 0.36$, the probability of the patient suffering from vasculitis $\Pr(v) = [0.28, 0.28] = 0.28$, and the probability of the patient suffering from arthritis $\Pr(a) = [0.48, 0.48] = 0.48$. As is the case with $Q2$, the values obtained are exactly those that would result from calculations using operations over just the set of real numbers.

Now, by the principle of degrading, it is possible to say that because there are non-zero probability values for a, $\neg a$, k, $\neg k$, v, and $\neg v$, there are non-zero possibilities for v and $\neg v$ and the belief values for a, $\neg a$, k, and $\neg k$ are non-negative. Thus $\mathrm{Bel}(a) = \mathrm{Bel}(\neg a) = \mathrm{Bel}(k) = \mathrm{Bel}(\neg k) = [0, 1]$ and $\Pi(v) = \Pi(\neg v) = (0, 1]$. These values could then be used with (6.28) and (6.27) to compute $\mathrm{Bel}(p)$, $\mathrm{Bel}(\neg p)$, $\Pi(l)$, and $\Pi(\neg l)$, obtaining values similar to those produced by $Q2$. However, $Q3$ makes it possible to improve upon this. It is possible to use (6.53) to obtain:

$$
\begin{aligned}
\Pr(a) &= [0.48, 0.48] &\mapsto& \quad \mathrm{Bel}(a) = [0, 0.48] \\
\Pr(\neg a) &= [0.52, 0.52] &\mapsto& \quad \mathrm{Bel}(\neg a) = [0, 0.52] \\
\Pr(k) &= [0.36, 0.36] &\mapsto& \quad \mathrm{Bel}(k) = [0, 0.36] \\
\Pr(\neg k) &= [0.64, 0.64] &\mapsto& \quad \mathrm{Bel}(\neg k) = [0, 0.64]
\end{aligned}
$$

from which the relevant mass distributions can be established:

$$
\begin{aligned}
m(a) &= [0, 0.48] \\
m(\neg a) &= [0, 0.52] \\
m(a \cup \neg a) &= [0, 1] \\
m(k) &= [0, 0.36] \\
m(\neg k) &= [0, 0.64] \\
m(k \cup \neg k) &= [0, 1]
\end{aligned}
$$

From these it is possible to use (6.28) to obtain the following[4]:

$$
\begin{aligned}
\mathrm{Bel}(p) &= \left[\sum_{\substack{A \subseteq \{a, \neg a\} \\ K \subseteq \{k, \neg k\}}} m(A, K)_L \mathrm{Bel}(p|A, K)_L \, , \sum_{\substack{A \subseteq \{a, \neg a\} \\ K \subseteq \{k, \neg k\}}} m(A, K)_U \mathrm{Bel}(p|A, K)_U \right] \\
&= \left[\sum_{\substack{A \subseteq \{a, \neg a\} \\ K \subseteq \{k, \neg k\}}} m(A)_L m(K)_L \mathrm{Bel}(p|A, K)_L \, , \right.
\end{aligned}
$$

$$
\left. \sum_{\substack{A \subseteq \{a, \neg a\} \\ K \subseteq \{k, \neg k\}}} m(A)_U m(K)_U \mathrm{Bel}(p|A, K)_U \right]
$$

$$
\begin{aligned}
&= [0, 0.48 \times 0.36 \times 0.9 + 0.52 \times 0.36 \times 0.7 + 1 \times 0.36 \times 0.7 \\
&\quad + 0.48 \times 0.64 \times 0.7 + 0.52 \times 0.64 \times 0 + 1 \times 0.64 \times 0 \\
&\quad + 0.48 \times 1 \times 0.6 + 0.7 \times 1 \times 0 + 1 \times 1 \times 0] \\
&= [0, 1]
\end{aligned}
$$

This indicates that on the basis of the available information, nothing can be said about how

---

4 The final value $[0, 1]$ being that adopted when the upper bound of the interval overflows its maximum possible value.

certain pain is. However, it is also possible to calculate belief in the patient not being in pain:

$$\text{Bel}(\neg p) = \left[\sum_{\substack{A \subseteq \{a, \neg a\} \\ K \subseteq \{k, \neg k\}}} m(A)_L m(K)_L \text{Bel}(\neg p | A, K)_L , \right.$$

$$\left. \sum_{\substack{A \subseteq \{a, \neg a\} \\ K \subseteq \{k, \neg k\}}} m(A)_U m(K)_U \text{Bel}(\neg p | A, K)_U \right]$$

$$= [0, 0.63]$$

This information, like that which may be inferred using $Q2$, could not be established if a qualitative algebra was not used to perform the translation. The result is also more informative than that possible using $Q2$.

The algebra may also be used to establish something about the possibility of lesions. Since it is known that $\text{Pr}(v) = [0.28, 0.28]$ and $\text{Pr}(\neg v) = [0.72, 0.72]$, it is possible to use (6.54) to perform the following translation:

$$\text{Pr}(v) = [0.28, 0.28] \quad \mapsto \quad \Pi(v) = (0.28, 1]$$
$$\text{Pr}(\neg v) = [0.72, 0.72] \quad \mapsto \quad \Pi(\neg v) = (0.72, 1]$$

This can then be used along with (6.27) to determine $\Pi(l)$ and $\Pi(\neg l)$:

$$\Pi(l) = \left[\sup_{V = \{v, \neg v\}} \min(\Pi(l|V)_L, \Pi(V)_L), \sup_{V \in \{v, \neg v\}} \min(\Pi(l|V)_U, \Pi(V)_U) \right]$$

$$= [0.8, 1]$$

$$\Pi(\neg l) = \left[\sup_{V = \{v, \neg v\}} \min(\Pi(\neg l|V)_L, \Pi(V)_L), \sup_{V \in \{v, \neg v\}} \min(\Pi(\neg l|V)_U, \Pi(V)_U) \right]$$

$$= (0.72, 1]$$

Again this information could not have been attained without the use of some means of translation, and is more precise than the information attained using $Q2$. Of course, just as in $Q2$, it is possible to establish new results when new evidence is obtained. For instance, if the patient is observed to be in pain it is clear that $\text{Bel}(p) = 1$ and it is possible to propagate the effect of this new information backwards through the model. As before,

$$\text{Bel}(a|p) = 0.4$$

and this may then be used to give the posterior belief in the patient having arthritis when pain is observed:

$$\mathrm{Bel}(a)^* \ = \ 0.4$$

This value may then be translated into a probability using (6.51):

$$\mathrm{Bel}(a)^* = 0.4 \ \mapsto \ \mathrm{Pr}(a)^* = [0, 0.4]$$

Clearly this value could be propagated further to find out the posterior probability of dislocation $\mathrm{Pr}(d)^*$. It is also possible to take an observation about vasculitic lesions, use this to establish the posterior possibility of vasculitis, and then use this latter value to establish the probability of vasculitis. This probability could then be used to find the posterior probability of Sjorgen's syndrome. Both these calculations are rather lengthy to complete by hand and so are left as an exercise for the interested reader, but it is clear that they can easily be carried out. Thus using $Q3$ makes it possible to integrate probability, possibility and belief values to get interval-valued possibilities and beliefs. These results are more precise than those attained using $Q2$, making it possible to establish bounds on the probability of the patient having a dislocation when belief in the patient being in pain is known, and to establish bounds on the probability of Sjorgen's syndrome given knowledge about the possibility of vasculitic lesions.

6.6   An example of handling incompleteness

Having looked at how $Q2$ and $Q3$ may be used to give translations between formalisms, the use of the algebras to deal with incomplete information will be considered in the the example introduced in Chapter 5 and pictured in Figure 6.4. This figure depicts the following medical information. Both alcoholism (S) and hypertension (H) influence the occurrence of gout (G), while alcoholism and hepatitis (E) influence the occurrence of cirrhosis (C). Cirrhosis causes liver failure (L), and gout causes arthritis (A), while alcoholism is caused by a high intake of alcohol (I).

A full set of probability values that indicate the strengths of the influences between the conditions are available for most of the arcs in the network, and these are given in Table 6.8. In fact, the only missing values are the conditional probability relating cirrhosis to alcoholism and hepatitis $\mathrm{Pr}(c|s, e)$, and the conditional probability relating arthritis to not having gout $\mathrm{Pr}(a|\neg g)$. The first is known to be greater than $\mathrm{Pr}(c|s, \neg e)$, and the second is thought to be less than $\mathrm{Pr}(a|g)$. The prior probabilities of a patient having a high intake of alcohol, $\mathrm{Pr}(i) = 0.4$, of suffering from hypertension, $\mathrm{Pr}(h) = 0.6$, and of having suffered from hepatitis, $\mathrm{Pr}(e) = 0.1$, are also known.

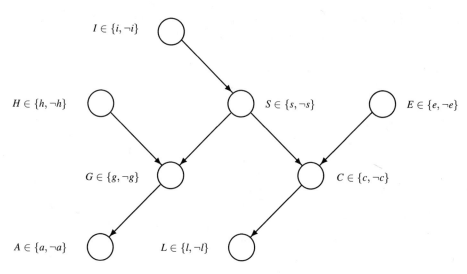

$I \in \{i, \neg i\}$

$H \in \{h, \neg h\}$ $S \in \{s, \neg s\}$ $E \in \{e, \neg e\}$

$G \in \{g, \neg g\}$ $C \in \{c, \neg c\}$

$A \in \{a, \neg a\}$ $L \in \{l, \neg l\}$

Figure 6.4
The network for the gout example.

Table 6.8
The probabilities for the gout example

$\Pr(g\|h, s)$	=	0.8			
$\Pr(g\|\neg h, s)$	=	0.6	$\Pr(c\|s, \neg e)$	=	0.7
$\Pr(g\|h, \neg s)$	=	0.6	$\Pr(c\|\neg s, e)$	=	0.3
$\Pr(g\|\neg h, \neg s)$	=	0.2	$\Pr(c\|\neg s, \neg e)$	=	0.3
$\Pr(s\|i)$	=	0.8	$\Pr(l\|c)$	=	0.8
$\Pr(s\|\neg i)$	=	0.1	$\Pr(l\|\neg c)$	=	0.2
$\Pr(a\|g)$	=	0.7			

6.6.1   Handling incompleteness in $Q2$

As discussed in Chapter 5, it is possible to establish several of the probabilities of the various conditions without having to deal with incompleteness. For instance, it is possible to establish the probability of alcoholism, $\Pr(s) = 0.38$, and the probability of gout, $\Pr(g) = 0.55$, among the patients whose medical records made up the survey from which the conditional probability values were established. These values may also be obtained using $Q2$. The difference between propagating values in $Q2$ and the usual set of real numbers is that $Q2$ allows the replacement of the missing values with the qualitative value $[+]$. This may be done in the first case since it known that the missing value is greater than the non-zero $\Pr(c|s, \neg e)$, while $\Pr(a|\neg g)$ is non-zero since there are some who have arthritis but not gout. Using these values with equation (6.2) gives:

$$
\begin{aligned}
\Pr(a) &= (\Pr(a|g) \otimes \Pr(g)) \oplus (\Pr(a|\neg g) \otimes \Pr(\neg g)) \\
&= 0.7 \otimes 0.55 \oplus [+] \otimes 0.45 \\
&= [+] \\
\Pr(c) &= \bigoplus_{\substack{S \in \{s, \neg s\} \\ E \in \{e, \neg e\}}} \Pr(c|S, E) \otimes \Pr(S) \Pr(E) \\
&= [+] \otimes 0.38 \otimes 0.1 \oplus 0.7 \otimes 0.38 \otimes 0.9 \\
&\quad \oplus 0.3 \otimes 0.62 \otimes 0.1 \oplus 0.3 \otimes 0.62 \otimes 0.9 \\
&= [+] \\
\Pr(l) &= (\Pr(l|c) \otimes \Pr(c)) \oplus (\Pr(l|\neg c) \otimes \Pr(\neg c)) \\
&= 0.8 \otimes [+] \oplus 0.2 \otimes [+] \\
&= [+]
\end{aligned}
$$

so that it is known that the prior probability of a patient having cirrhosis and liver failure is non-zero, which is not much, but is more than could have been deduced when not using $Q2$. In addition, when it is learnt that the patient does not suffer from arthritis, so that $\Pr(a) = 0$, $\Pr(\neg a) = 1$, then it is possible to use $Q2$ to determine something about the posterior probability of gout. First (6.6) is applied to establish the relevant conditional values:

$$
\begin{aligned}
\Pr(g|\neg a) &= (\Pr(\neg a|g) \otimes \Pr(g)) \oslash \Pr(\neg a) \\
&= [+] \otimes 0.55 \oslash 1 \\
&= [+]
\end{aligned}
$$

and then (6.2) is used to establish the probability of gout:

$$
\begin{aligned}
\Pr(g)^* &= \Pr(g|\neg a) \otimes \Pr(\neg a) \\
&= [+] \otimes 1 \\
&= [+]
\end{aligned}
$$

which shows that gout is not ruled out by the absence of arthritis. Thus $Q2$ makes it possible to handle missing values by replacing them with a qualitative value of $[+]$. This in turn makes it possible to determine whether certain nodes, whose values would otherwise have been unknown, are zero or not. However, for the more detailed information that is often required, it is again necessary to turn to $Q3$.

6.6.2   Handling incompleteness in $Q3$

When using $Q3$, it is once again possible to establish the probabilities of alcoholism, gout and arthritis with the same precision as if real numbers rather than intervals were being used as operands. Thus $\Pr(s) = [0.38, 0.38] = 0.38$ and $\Pr(g) = [0.55, 0.55] = 0.55$. However, things are rather different when the incompleteness caused by the missing value of $\Pr(c|s, e)$ is considered. This may be tackled in a very similar way to that adopted by $Q2$, taking $\Pr(c|s, e) = (0, 1]$ on the grounds that $\Pr(c|s, e)$ is clearly not equal to zero. If this is done it is possible to use (6.26) and establish that:

$$\Pr(c) = \left[\sum_{\substack{S \in \{s, \neg s\} \\ E \in \{e, \neg e\}}} \Pr(c|S, E)_L \Pr(S)_L \Pr(E)_L, \sum_{\substack{S \in \{s, \neg s\} \\ E \in \{e, \neg e\}}} \Pr(c|S, E)_U \Pr(S)_U \Pr(E)_U \right]$$

$$= (0.43, 0.46]$$

$$\Pr(l) = \left[\sum_{C \in \{c, \neg c\}} \Pr(l|C)_L \Pr(c)_L, \sum_{C \in \{c, \neg c\}} \Pr(l|C)_U \Pr(C)_U \right]$$

$$= (0.45, 0.49)$$

However, this is not making the best use of all the available knowledge. As remarked above, it is clear that the probability of a patient having cirrhosis given that they suffer from alcoholism and hepatitis is going to be greater than the probability that they have cirrhosis given that they suffer from alcoholism but not hepatitis. Thus $\Pr(c|s, e) = [0.7, 1]$. Using this value it is possible to obtain the more precise results that:

$$\Pr(c) = (0.45, 0.46]$$
$$\Pr(l) = (0.47, 0.48)$$

$Q3$ will also give precise results when faced with more missing values, allowing reasonable probability values to be obtained when little could be deduced if intervals were not employed. For instance, consider what would happen if reliable estimates were not available for $\Pr(g|\neg h, \neg s)$ (because, for example, there are very few cases of gout in which the patient does not suffer from alcoholism or hypertension), and $\Pr(s|\neg i)$ (since it is not easy to identify alcoholics who do not have a large alcohol intake). With these values missing, it is not possible to establish the probability of gout or arthritis unless a qualitative algebra is used. When $Q3$ is employed it seems reasonable to assume that $\Pr(g|\neg h, \neg s) = (0, 0.6]$

and $\Pr(s|\neg i) = (0, 0.8]$. These values may then be used in (6.26) to determine that:

$$\Pr(s) = \left[\sum_{I \in \{i, \neg i\}} \Pr(s|I)_L \Pr(S)_L, \sum_{I \in \{i, \neg i\}} \Pr(s|I)_U \Pr(S)_U \right]$$

$$= (0.32, 0.8]$$

$$\Pr(g) = \left[\sum_{\substack{H \in \{h, \neg h\} \\ S \in \{s, \neg s\}}} \Pr(g|H, S)_L \Pr(H)_L, \Pr(S))_L \, , \right.$$

$$\left. \sum_{\substack{H \in \{h, \neg h\} \\ S \in \{s, \neg s\}}} \Pr(g|H, S)_U \Pr(H)_U, \Pr(S))_U \right]$$

$$= (0.32, 1)$$

and thus, assuming that $\Pr(a|\neg g) = (0, 0.7]$ because gout tends to make arthritis more likely, it is possible to obtain:

$$\Pr(a) = \left[\sum_{G \in \{g, \neg g\}} \Pr(a|G)_L \Pr(G)_L, \sum_{G \in \{g, \neg g\}} \Pr(a|G)_U \Pr(G)_U \right]$$

$$= (0.22, 1)$$

It is also possible to use the value of $\Pr(s)$ to establish bounds on the probabilities of cirrhosis and liver failure, finding these to be:

$$\Pr(c) = (0.28, 0.79)$$
$$\Pr(l) = (0.27, 0.77)$$

Furthermore, as with $Q2$, it is possible to establish the effects of new evidence. For instance, if it is learnt that the patient has arthritis, then it is possible to compute that the posterior probability of gout is:

$$\Pr(g)^* = \Pr(g|a)$$
$$= \left[\frac{\Pr(a|g)_L \Pr(g)_L}{\Pr(a)_U}, \frac{\Pr(a|g)_U \Pr(g)_U}{\Pr(a)_L} \right]$$
$$= (0.22, 1)$$

and this value could, of course, be used to establish the posterior probabilities of hepatitis and alcoholism.

Thus $Q3$ makes it possible to replace missing values with intervals reflecting their bounds as determined by common sense. This absorbs incomplete information while still giving reasonably precise results. Despite the fact that this example only deals with an incomplete probabilistic model, it is quite possible to use exactly the same method to handle the problem of having models with missing possibility and belief values. Indeed, it is possible to use this kind of approach to solve the incompleteness problem in any uncertainty handling formalism.

6.7 Summary

This chapter has proposed the use of qualitative algebras to enable integration between disparate formalisms and to handle incompleteness. Such algebras support integration by providing translations between formalisms that either make no assumptions about the translated value or enable the theoretical bounds on the precision of such translations to be explicitly maintained. The algebras use extended arithmetic operations over real numbers and the qualitative and interval values that result from the translations. This means that values may be manipulated in the algebras in different formalisms using any combination model from the literature. All that is required is that the usual arithmetic operators over the real numbers are replaced with the extended operators. Incompleteness is handled in a similar fashion. Missing values are replaced by "assumption-free" values[5] and these are then combined in the same fashion as translated ones. Two algebras that combine qualitative real and interval values are proposed. One, known as $Q2$, combines standard qualitative values with reals to provide robust reasoning in situations where it is sufficient to determine whether or not a value is non-zero. The other, $Q3$, mixes reals and intervals to compute the bounds on ill-known values, and is thus suitable for situations where it is desirable to get the most accurate answer possible.

The second algebra, $Q3$, has similarities with a number of systems discussed in earlier chapters. Firstly, there are obvious connections with the work on interval methods for handling uncertainty, discussed in Section 4.3, which has mainly been concerned with interval probabilities. The main difference between the use of $Q3$ to propagate interval probability values and the work reported in Section 4.3 is that $Q3$ does not attempt to compute good probability bounds. Instead $Q3$ is merely concerned with establishing bounds quickly, providing a quick and dirty solution that is easily extensible to other formalisms such as possibility and evidence theories. Of course, there is nothing in the formalism that prevents the use of more sophisticated methods. However, in the context of translation and handling incompleteness most of the values are point values, and under

---

5 Though, of course, they could equally be replaced by values which were determined by some set of assumptions if so desired.

such conditions the simple approach offered by $Q3$ seems to be adequate. The connection between $Q3$ and interval methods is emphasised by the fact that $Q3$ provides a means of handling uncertainty that is similar to that of Jain and Agogino (1990) but which uses crisp rather than fuzzy intervals, and general arithmetic operations rather than those specific to probability theory. Since fuzzy sets are a generalisation of crisp intervals, the results presented here can be generalised to fuzzy intervals, and probability specific operations can be introduced over our crisp intervals (Parsons, 1990). Secondly, there are similarities between the work reported here and that of Zhang (1992; 1994) in the provision of a method for translation between different uncertainty handling formalisms. Like the approach described here, Zhang's method does not place much emphasis on the meaning of the numbers he is transforming, but it has a rather serious limitation. This limitation is that when translating between two formalisms, it is necessary to take the maximum and minimum values that may be expressed in the two formalisms to be equivalent. Thus when translating from probability to possibility theory (which as yet is not possible using Zhang's method) it would be necessary to have $\Pr(x) = 0$ translate to $\Pi(x) = 0$ and $\Pr(x) = 1$ translate to $\Pi(x) = 1$. Finally, the use of the $[0, 1]$ interval to represent an unknown probability that is then combined with known values to obtain an interval estimate finds echoes in (Thöne et al., 1992) and (Draper and Hanks, 1994).

This chapter has not discussed ways in which the $Q2$ and $Q3$ can be used to solve the robustness problem. This is because they do not provide a very convincing solution. It is possible to handle the robustness problem by treating every value in a model as if it were a missing value—the algebras make this possible and so provide some kind of a solution. However, the results that may be obtained by doing this will not usually be very helpful. Without some precise values to combine with the imprecise "assumption-free" values, the only values that will be generated by such models will be $[+]$ or $[0, 1]$.

It is also important to bear two things in mind. Firstly the algebras do not in any way restrict the choice of formalism that may be used to model a problem. Examples using probability, possibility and evidence theories were given, but the algebras could equally well be employed for manipulating values expressed using certainty factors (Shortliffe, 1976), Spohn's ordinal belief measures (Spohn, 1990), or any other formalism. Secondly the algebras in no way restrict the way the formalisms are employed. Whichever formalism is used, the algebras place no restriction on the mechanisms for propagation and no restriction on the way in which the values are interpreted. The algebras simply provide a syntactic framework that stipulates how mathematical operations may be carried out, and in so doing provide new structures that permit the handling of values translated from other formalisms. All semantic dogma is avoided. Any algebra may be used with any semantics one is happy with since the algebras do not enforce a particular semantics. Even the ordering over the intervals $\leq_{Q3}$ introduced in Section 6.3.2 is only one way of ordering intervals—if another ordering based upon another interpretation of what an interval represents is required, then it may be introduced. However, as Henrion (1993) and Klawonn (1991), among others, have pointed out, this does not mean that one may be agnostic with respect to semantics. Some semantics must be adopted, but whatever semantics are desired, qualitative algebras may be used.

7 The theory of qualitative change

An endless swallow and flow; flood alternating with ebb and ebb with flood; waves pouring in, some big, some small; brooks and rivulets flowing in from all sides.

Alexander Solzhenitsyn, *The Gulag Archipelago*

The last chapter developed a theory, based upon the use of qualitative algebras, which could support the kinds of extensions to existing systems for dealing with uncertainty discussed in Chapter 5. This was successful in providing methods of solving the problems of incompleteness and integration when dealing with certainty values. These methods were formalism independent and very simple to implement. However, as discussed in Section 6.4, when dealing with changes in certainty values, the qualitative algebra approach breaks down, since it is not obvious how to provide formalism-independent methods for dealing with changes. It seems that in order to deal with changes in value it is necessary to work in a formalism-dependent way, and that is exactly what this chapter does. It develops a general framework, called *qualitative certainty networks* (QCNs), for talking about changes in certainty values in terms of influences between variables, and then investigates how the different formalisms fit into it. In doing so it becomes clear that it is possible to deal with changes in a way that can be regarded as formalism-independent, but it is a different kind of formalism-independence than is possible when dealing with values themselves. When dealing with values, the mapping from value in an ordinary formalism (probability, possibility or belief) to value in a qualitative formalism is the same for all formalisms. However, the way in which the values are propagated is formalism-dependent. When dealing with changes, the reverse is true. All changes in value are propagated in the same way, but the way in which the numerical description of influences between variables are mapped into qualitative influences is formalism-dependent and as robust as that which forms the basis of QPNs. Thus it is necessary to do more work to establish the mappings than is necessary when using qualitative algebras, but the payoff is a solution to the robustness problem.

7.1 Introduction

As discussed in previous chapters, one way of tackling the problems of incompleteness, robustness, and integration when dealing with values is to abstract away from the precise numerical values used by most methods for reasoning under uncertainty and deal instead with the idea of "some value" that is not exactly known. This idea may be extended, when dealing with changes in value rather than values themselves, so that precise changes in value are abstracted into "some change" that is not exactly known. Such unknown changes are clearly very similar to the qualitative values handled by $Q2$ and may be manipulated in much the same way. The crucial difference, of course, is that while the qualitative values handled by $Q2$ are propagated by combining them with other qualitative values that are determined by the same mapping $[\cdot]$, qualitative changes are propagated by combining them with qualitative influences, and qualitative influences are definitely not established that easily. Indeed, since the qualitative influence between two variables is determined by the way in which values are combined when propagated, the mapping is obviously dependent upon the formalism in question. Furthermore, it is not immediately clear, even when the formalism is fixed, exactly how the value of a given qualitative influence may be determined—this, of course, is exactly why the attempt to find an algebra of influences that was as formalism-independent in the same way as $Q2$ and $Q3$ failed (see Section 6.4).

It is, however, not that difficult to determine the mapping between the quantitative probabilistic, possibilistic, and evidential influences between variables, and the qualitative influences that link them. Indeed the machinery for doing so has already been encountered in Chapter 4 in the discussion of qualitative physics. In qualitative physics, systems are described in terms of the qualitative value of key variables, and these are related to one another by sets of qualitative differential equations that state how changes in one variable affect changes in other variables. These sets of equations allow the propagation of changes in value to take place, so that the effects of a set of changes in value of certain variables can be established given the changes in other variables. This is, of course, exactly what a system of qualitative changes in certainty value requires.

There are two possible ways to construct the necessary set of equations. The first is to analyse a given numerical model to establish its qualitative behaviour. This might well be done if the numerical model was to be integrated with another since the resulting qualitative model could be combined with another qualitative model using "integration by change." This might also be done in order to make the model more robust—having built it using a set of data that is specific to one situation, the general shape of the interactions between variables could then be extracted for use in a similar situation giving it the advantages that Wellman claims for qualitative probabilistic networks. Alternatively the model could be specified qualitatively from an understanding of the interaction between variables. In this second mode the model can be built in the face of considerable incompleteness since it is not necessary to know what the probabilities, possibilities or beliefs are, just (as will become clear) their relative sizes. Whichever way the model is built, its construction will depend upon exactly what it means to say that, for instance, the derivative relating $\Pr(a)$ to $\Pr(b)$ is positive, and the body of information that explains this is the "theory of qualitative change" referred to in the title of this chapter, and developed both here and Chapter 8.

This chapter introduces the ideas that form the basis of the theory of qualitative change, identifies the different types of influence that can hold between the probabilities and possibilities of, or beliefs in, variables and how these may be used to propagate changes through networks, and derives the conditions under which these different kinds of influence hold in singly-connected networks quantified by the different formalisms. It then extends the notion of influences to cover those between effect and cause as well as cause and effect, and shows how the theory of qualitative change may be used to overcome the problems of incompleteness, robustness and integration by solving the problems posed in Section 5.4. Chapter 8 then extends the theory to cover influences in multiply-connected networks as well as considering the phenomena of synergy and intercausal reasoning, and examining how they may be captured using qualitative changes.

7.2   Basic concepts of qualitative change

Given two nodes in a network, A and C, where A is the parent of C, the theory of qualitative change is concerned with the way in which a change in the certainty value of some value of A, $\mathrm{Val}(a)$, influences the certainty value of some value of C, $\mathrm{Val}(c)$. Thus the theory is concerned with the way in which $\mathrm{Val}(c)$ changes when $\mathrm{Val}(a)$ changes. This information about changes may then be used to model the effect of evidence upon a model. It is possible to model the impact of evidence that affects the value of A in terms of the changes in certainty value of all its possible values relative to their value before the evidence was known. Having established this information, it is then possible to use knowledge about the way that a change in the certainty values of the possible values of A affects the certainty values of the possible values of C to propagate the effect of the evidence. Thus information about the changes in certainty value of observable variables may be propagated through a network to discover the changes that are implied in the certainty value of variables of interest.

The following relationships are defined in order to describe the different ways in which the value of a variable X changes when the value of a variable Y is altered by new evidence. Any such relationship is said to be a *qualitative influence* and there are three obvious kinds of influence that Y may have on X—a change in certainty of a given value of Y may lead to a similar change in a given value of X, a change in the opposite direction, or it may have no effect at all:

DEFINITION 7.1:   The certainty value of a variable X taking value x is said to *follow* the certainty value of variable Y taking value y if $\mathrm{Val}(x)$ increases when $\mathrm{Val}(y)$ increases, and $\mathrm{Val}(x)$ decreases when $\mathrm{Val}(y)$ decreases.

If $\text{Val}(x)$ follows $\text{Val}(y)$, y is said to have a *positive influence* on x.

DEFINITION 7.2:   The certainty value of a variable X taking value x is said to *vary inversely* with the certainty value of variable Y taking value y if $\text{Val}(x)$ decreases when $\text{Val}(y)$ increases, and $\text{Val}(x)$ increases when $\text{Val}(y)$ decreases.

If $\text{Val}(x)$ varies inversely with $\text{Val}(y)$, y is said to have a *negative influence* on x.

DEFINITION 7.3:   The certainty value of a variable X taking value x is said to be *qualitatively independent* of the certainty value of variable Y taking value y if $\text{Val}(x)$ does not change as $\text{Val}(y)$ increases and decreases.

When it is clear that the type of independence being considered is qualitative, the term "qualitative" will sometimes be dropped. If $\text{Val}(x)$ is qualitatively independent of $\text{Val}(y)$, y is said to have *zero influence* on x.
    Note that the influences are defined between particular possible values of the variables. As a result the relationship between X and Y will be described by a number of qualitative influences. Unfortunately, it turns out that when dealing with possibility theory the terms defined in Definitions 7.1–7.3 are not sufficient to describe every relationship that can exist between values of variables. It is also necessary to have the following concepts that describe situations in which the relationship between X an Y only holds for particular types of change:

DEFINITION 7.4:   The certainty value of a variable X taking value x is said to *follow* the certainty value of variable Y taking value y *up* if $\text{Val}(x)$ increases when $\text{Val}(y)$ increases, and $\text{Val}(x)$ does not change when $\text{Val}(y)$ decreases.

DEFINITION 7.5:   The certainty value of a variable X taking value x is said to *follow* the certainty value of variable Y taking value y *down* if $\text{Val}(x)$ does not change when $\text{Val}(y)$ increases, and $\text{Val}(x)$ decreases when $\text{Val}(y)$ decreases.

Clearly the relationships between $\text{Val}(x)$ and $\text{Val}(y)$ described by these two terms are related to those introduced previously since $\text{Val}(x)$ follows $\text{Val}(y)$ if and only if it both follows $\text{Val}(y)$ up and down. It is also possible to introduce the idea that the relationship between $\text{Val}(x)$ and $\text{Val}(y)$ is not known exactly, so that it may be the case that $\text{Val}(x)$ changes when $\text{Val}(y)$ does but it may also be the case that $\text{Val}(x)$ does not change when $\text{Val}(y)$ does. To cope with these situations, four additional definitions are required, the first two are adjuncts to the definitions of "follows" and "varies inversely with:"

DEFINITION 7.6:   The certainty value of a variable X taking value x is said to be related to the certainty value of variable Y taking value y such that $\text{Val}(x)$ *may follow* $\text{Val}(y)$ if $\text{Val}(x)$ either follows $\text{Val}(y)$ or is qualitatively independent of it.

DEFINITION 7.7:   The certainty value of a variable X taking value x is said to be related to the certainty value of variable Y taking value y such that $\text{Val}(x)$ *may vary inversely with* $\text{Val}(y)$ if $\text{Val}(x)$ either varies inversely with $\text{Val}(y)$ or is qualitatively independent of it.

The next two definitions are adjuncts to the definitions of "follow up" and "follow down."

DEFINITION 7.8:   The certainty value of a variable X taking value x is said to be related to the certainty value of variable Y taking value y such that $\text{Val}(x)$ *may follow* $\text{Val}(y)$ *up* if $\text{Val}(x)$ either follows $\text{Val}(y)$ up or is qualitatively independent of it.

DEFINITION 7.9:   The certainty value of a variable X taking value x is said to be related to the certainty value of variable Y taking value y such that $\text{Val}(x)$ *may follow* $\text{Val}(y)$ *down* if $\text{Val}(x)$ either follows $\text{Val}(y)$ down or is qualitatively independent of it.

Note that this terminology is sometimes extended to create terms such as "may always follow" and "may always follow ... up." These new terms are used to describe relationships that, unlike the majority of relationships in the theory of qualitative change, hold between variables irrespective of the conditional values which relate them. Thus they are abbreviations for "it is always the case that ... may follow" and "it is always the case that ... may follow ... up."

It is also possible introduce further relationships relating to the sub-parts of the "varies inversely" relation and their tentative counterparts, but these have not been found necessary to date. It is, however, useful to be able to capture the idea of an indeterminate relationship between variables:

DEFINITION 7.10:   The relationship between the certainty value of a variable X taking value x and the certainty value of variable Y taking value y is said to be *indeterminate*, if $\text{Val}(x)$ either follows $\text{Val}(y)$ or varies inversely with $\text{Val}(y)$ or is qualitatively independent of it.

When a qualitative influence has a value other than zero, it is referred to as a *non-zero influence*. Thus all relationships between X taking the value x and Y taking the value y other than independence are captured by non-zero influences.

Having defined the different types of influence between variables, the next stage is to define how these relationships are handled within the theory of qualitative change. This is done by borrowing from the differential calculus—the use of the differential calculus is the other big idea that the theory takes from qualitative physics—a suitable introduction to which may be found in (Stewart, 1991). The relationship between the certainty values of particular values of variables X and Y, $\mathrm{Val}(x)$ and $\mathrm{Val}(y)$, is characterised by the partial derivative $\partial\mathrm{Val}(x)/\partial\mathrm{Val}(y)$. Partial derivatives are used because it is often the case that $\mathrm{Val}(x)$ is a function of values other than $\mathrm{Val}(y)$ yet the relation that it is necessary to capture is that which holds irrespective of changes in these other values, and it is exactly this relation that is given by the partial derivative. When the value of the derivative is known, the change in $\mathrm{Val}(x)$ can be established from the value of the change in $\mathrm{Val}(y)$[1]:

$$\Delta\mathrm{Val}(x) = \frac{\partial\mathrm{Val}(x)}{\partial\mathrm{Val}(y)}\Delta\mathrm{Val}(y) \tag{7.1}$$

Now, it is only necessary to know the direction of the change, so it is only necessary to consider the qualitative values of the above terms:

$$[\Delta\mathrm{Val}(x)] = \left[\frac{\partial\mathrm{Val}(x)}{\partial\mathrm{Val}(y)}\right] \otimes [\Delta\mathrm{Val}(y)] \tag{7.2}$$

where the mapping $[\cdot]$ is exactly that considered in Section 4.2. Thus, $[\Delta\mathrm{Val}(x)]$ is $[+]$ if $\Delta\mathrm{Val}(x)$ is positive, $[-]$ if $\Delta\mathrm{Val}(x)$ is negative, $[0]$ if $\Delta\mathrm{Val}(x)$ is zero, and $[?]$ if it is not possible to determine whether $\Delta\mathrm{Val}(x)$ is any of the above. The symbol "$\otimes$" denotes qualitative multiplication as defined in Table 4.2, and terms such as $[\partial\mathrm{Val}(x)/\partial\mathrm{Val}(y)]$ are known as *qualitative derivatives*. Just as it is helpful to distinguish between zero and non-zero influences between variables, it is helpful to distinguish between zero and non-zero changes in certainty value. A change in certainty value $\mathrm{Val}(x)$ is known as a *zero change in value* iff $[\Delta\mathrm{Val}(x)] = [0]$ and is known as a *non-zero change in value* otherwise.

In order to use qualitative derivatives in any useful way, it is necessary to provide a mapping between such derivatives and the properties of influences introduced above. In particular, it is easy to show that the following equivalences hold:

THEOREM 7.1:   Qualitative influences are related to qualitative derivatives such that:

$$\mathrm{Val}(x)\ follows\ \mathrm{Val}(y) \quad \Leftrightarrow \quad \left[\frac{\partial\mathrm{Val}(x)}{\partial\mathrm{Val}(y)}\right] = [+]$$

$$\mathrm{Val}(x)\ varies\ inversely\ with\ \mathrm{Val}(y) \quad \Leftrightarrow \quad \left[\frac{\partial\mathrm{Val}(x)}{\partial\mathrm{Val}(y)}\right] = [-]$$

1 Of course, this is only generally true for infinitesimal changes in $\mathrm{Val}(y)$ and this point is discussed in detail in Section 7.3.4.

Table 7.1
Multiplication for qualitative changes

$\otimes$	$[+]$	$[\uparrow]$	$[0]$	$[\downarrow]$	$[-]$	$[?]$
$[+]$	$[+]$	$[+]$	$[0]$	$[0]$	$[-]$	$[?]$
$[0]$	$[0]$	$[0]$	$[0]$	$[0]$	$[0]$	$[0]$
$[-]$	$[-]$	$[0]$	$[0]$	$[-]$	$[+]$	$[?]$
$[?]$	$[?]$	$[0,+]$	$[0]$	$[0,-]$	$[?]$	$[?]$

$$\text{Val}(x) \text{ is independent of } \text{Val}(y) \quad \Leftrightarrow \quad \left[\frac{\partial \text{Val}(x)}{\partial \text{Val}(y)}\right] = [0]$$

This neat equivalence can be extended to the full range of relationships between $\text{Val}(x)$ and $\text{Val}(y)$ but only at the cost of introducing two new qualitative values:

DEFINITION 7.11:   The fact that $\text{Val}(x)$ follows $\text{Val}(y)$ up is denoted by:

$$\left[\frac{\partial \text{Val}(x)}{\partial \text{Val}(y)}\right] = [\uparrow]$$

and the fact that $\text{Val}(x)$ follows $\text{Val}(y)$ down is denoted by:

$$\left[\frac{\partial \text{Val}(x)}{\partial \text{Val}(y)}\right] = [\downarrow]$$

To handle the new values $[\uparrow]$ and $[\downarrow]$ it is necessary to extend the qualitative multiplication operator of Table 4.2 to get the operator $\otimes$ defined in Table 7.1. In this table the columns hold the values of qualitative derivatives such as:

$$\left[\frac{\partial \text{Val}(x)}{\partial \text{Val}(y)}\right],$$

the rows the values of $[\Delta \text{Val}(y)]$, and the cells give the corresponding values of $[\Delta \text{Val}(x)]$. The results are trivial to establish, just as they were for the original qualitative multiplication operator. However, this does not mean that they are ill-defined. They are precisely the only sensible ways to combine changes in value. Thus, the product of an increase in value (top row), and a positive derivative (left column) is an increase in value, while the product of an increase in value and a derivative that indicates the relationship in question is "follows down" (fourth column) is no change. These new derivatives naturally lead to changes that are represented by combinations of $[+]$ and $[-]$ with $[0]$ since they are possible increases and decreases. An example is the combination of $[\uparrow]$ with $[?]$, which produces a result that is either $[+]$ or $[0]$ since $[?]$ represents a value that is $[+]$, $[0]$ or $[-]$. For simplicity, a value that is either zero or positive is denoted $[0, +]$ or $[+, 0]$ (no distinction is made between

Table 7.2
Addition for qualitative changes

⊕	[+]	[0]	[−]	[?]
[+]	[+]	[+]	[?]	[?]
[0]	[+]	[0]	[−]	[?]
[−]	[?]	[−]	[−]	[?]
[?]	[?]	[?]	[?]	[?]

the two) and it is also possible to write down values such as $[0, \uparrow]$. With respect to this, it should be noted that the symbol $[+]$ has exactly the same meaning here in the theory of qualitative change, as it has in qualitative physics and in $Q2$. That is it represents a strictly positive quantity. In this it differs from the $+$ used by Wellman (1990a) or the $'+$ used by Druzdzel (1993) since these latter symbols denote a non-negative quantity. However, the value $[0, +]$ is exactly the same as Wellman's $+$ and Druzdzel's $'+$. Similar remarks apply to $[-]$, $-$ as used by Wellman and $'-$ as used by Druzdzel.

Given these new values, it is then possible to characterise the remaining possible relationships between $\mathrm{Val}(x)$ and $\mathrm{Val}(y)$ uniquely in terms of qualitative derivatives:

THEOREM 7.2:   Qualitative influences are related to qualitative derivatives such that:

$$\mathrm{Val}(x) \; may\, follow \; \mathrm{Val}(y) \quad \Leftrightarrow \quad \left[\frac{\partial \mathrm{Val}(x)}{\partial \mathrm{Val}(y)}\right] = [0, +]$$

$$\mathrm{Val}(x) \; may\, vary\, inversely\, with \; \mathrm{Val}(y) \quad \Leftrightarrow \quad \left[\frac{\partial \mathrm{Val}(x)}{\partial \mathrm{Val}(y)}\right] = [0, -]$$

$$\mathrm{Val}(x) \; may\, follow \; \mathrm{Val}(y) \; up \quad \Leftrightarrow \quad \left[\frac{\partial \mathrm{Val}(x)}{\partial \mathrm{Val}(y)}\right] = [0, \uparrow]$$

$$\mathrm{Val}(x) \; may\, follow \; \mathrm{Val}(y) \; down \quad \Leftrightarrow \quad \left[\frac{\partial \mathrm{Val}(x)}{\partial \mathrm{Val}(y)}\right] = [0, \downarrow]$$

and the relationship between $\mathrm{Val}(x)$ and $\mathrm{Val}(y)$ is indeterminate if and only if:

$$\left[\frac{\partial \mathrm{Val}(x)}{\partial \mathrm{Val}(y)}\right] = [?]$$

The effect of "may follow" and similar derivatives may be established by considering the two effects that they represent. Thus the effect of combining $[0, \uparrow]$ with $[+]$ is $[0] \otimes [+]$ or $[\uparrow] \otimes [+]$. This comes to $[0]$ or $[+]$, which of course is $[0, +]$. Note that because qualitative addition only ever combines two changes in value, and because changes never have the value $[\uparrow]$ or $[\downarrow]$, the original operator, as defined by Table 4.1 and repeated here in Table 7.2, suffices.

As will become clear a little later, when establishing $[\partial \mathrm{Val}(x)/\partial \mathrm{Val}(y)]$, it is necessary to take into account the fact that the certainties of values of Y other than y change when $\mathrm{Val}(y)$ changes. In other words, the certainty values $\mathrm{Val}(y_i)$ of the possible values of Y are dependent variables. However, it is also possible to treat them as independent variables provided that the changes in each and every one of them are taken into account. That is, rather than computing the change in $\mathrm{Val}(x)$ using a single partial derivative that implicitly takes account of changes in all the values of Y, it is possible to use a form of derivative which only takes account of the change in a single value of Y provided that every value of Y is explicitly taken into account. This latter form of derivative will be termed *separable* and denoted by $\partial_s \mathrm{Val}(x)/\partial_s \mathrm{Val}(y_i)$, and a change in $\mathrm{Val}(x)$ may be computed using such derivatives as follows:

$$[\Delta \mathrm{Val}(x)] = \bigoplus_i \left[\frac{\partial_s \mathrm{Val}(x)}{\partial_s \mathrm{Val}(y_i)}\right] \otimes [\Delta \mathrm{Val}(y_i)] \tag{7.3}$$

where "$\oplus$" is qualitative addition (as defined in Table 7.2), and y_i ranges over all the possible values of Y. Any of the possible relationships between variables may hold for changes determined using partial or separable derivatives. When it is important to distinguish that separable derivatives are being referred to, the fact is indicated by appending the adverb "separably" to the relationship. Thus to say $\mathrm{Val}(x)$ separably follows $\mathrm{Val}(y)$ means that $[\partial_s \mathrm{Val}(x)/\partial_s \mathrm{Val}(y)] = [+]$.

Given this background, it is not hard to see that to determine the change at a node C, with possible values $c_1, \ldots, c_n$, given the change at node A, with possible values $a_1, \ldots, a_m$, it is possible to use either partial or separable derivatives, and, using the matrix notation from Farreny and Prade (1985) the calculations may be written as:

$$\begin{bmatrix} [\Delta \mathrm{Val}(c_1)] \\ \vdots \\ [\Delta \mathrm{Val}(c_n)] \end{bmatrix} = \begin{bmatrix} \left[\frac{\partial \mathrm{Val}(c_1)}{\partial \mathrm{Val}(a_i)}\right] \\ \vdots \\ \left[\frac{\partial \mathrm{Val}(c_n)}{\partial \mathrm{Val}(a_i)}\right] \end{bmatrix} \otimes [\Delta \mathrm{Val}(a_i)] \tag{7.4}$$

or:

$$\begin{bmatrix} [\Delta \mathrm{Val}(c_1)] \\ \vdots \\ [\Delta \mathrm{Val}(c_n)] \end{bmatrix} = \begin{bmatrix} \left[\frac{\partial_s \mathrm{Val}(c_1)}{\partial_s \mathrm{Val}(a_1)}\right] & \cdots & \left[\frac{\partial_s \mathrm{Val}(c_1)}{\partial_s \mathrm{Val}(a_m)}\right] \\ \vdots & \ddots & \vdots \\ \left[\frac{\partial_s \mathrm{Val}(c_n)}{\partial_s \mathrm{Val}(a_1)}\right] & \cdots & \left[\frac{\partial_s \mathrm{Val}(c_n)}{\partial_s \mathrm{Val}(a_m)}\right] \end{bmatrix} \otimes \begin{bmatrix} [\Delta \mathrm{Val}(a_1)] \\ \vdots \\ [\Delta \mathrm{Val}(a_m)] \end{bmatrix} \tag{7.5}$$

where a_i denotes any of the possible values of X.

Now, the difference between (7.2) and (7.4) and between (7.3) and (7.5), is that the former consider changes in the certainty values of individual values of variables represented by a node in a graph, whereas the latter consider changes in the certainty values of all the values of variables represented by a node. This distinction, between changes associated with individual variable values and those associated with the values of a variable as a whole, is an important one and one that is acknowledged by some new terminology. Whereas changes in certainty value of individual values of variables are referred to as "changes in value", changes in certainty of all the values of a variable as a whole are referred to "changes at a node." In particular a distinction is drawn between *zero change at a node*, when the change in every value of the relevant variable is itself zero, and *non-zero change at a node*, when at least one value of the variable experiences a non-zero change.

When the certainty value of a node is influenced by changes at several other nodes the overall change is obtained by using the principle of superposition (Stewart, 1991), which gives the compound change to be the sum of the changes that would be induced by each influencing node on its own. Thus if node C is influenced by changes at X, which has possible values $x_1, \ldots, x_p$, as well as those at A, the overall change in the certainty of a particular value c of C is given by the sum of the change at C due to the change at A plus the change at C due to the change at X. This sum may be established by the use of either partial or separable derivatives:

$$
\begin{bmatrix} [\Delta \mathrm{Val}(c_1)] \\ \vdots \\ [\Delta \mathrm{Val}(c_n)] \end{bmatrix}
=
\begin{bmatrix} \left[\frac{\partial \mathrm{Val}(c_1)}{\partial \mathrm{Val}(a_i)}\right] \\ \vdots \\ \left[\frac{\partial \mathrm{Val}(c_n)}{\partial \mathrm{Val}(a_i)}\right] \end{bmatrix} \otimes [\Delta \mathrm{Val}(a_i)]
$$

$$
\oplus \begin{bmatrix} \left[\frac{\partial \mathrm{Val}(c_1)}{\partial \mathrm{Val}(x_j)}\right] \\ \vdots \\ \left[\frac{\partial \mathrm{Val}(c_n)}{\partial \mathrm{Val}(x_j)}\right] \end{bmatrix} \otimes [\Delta \mathrm{Val}(x_i)] \tag{7.6}
$$

$$
\begin{bmatrix} [\Delta \mathrm{Val}(c_1)] \\ \vdots \\ [\Delta \mathrm{Val}(c_n)] \end{bmatrix}
=
\begin{bmatrix} \left[\frac{\partial_s \mathrm{Val}(c_1)}{\partial_s \mathrm{Val}(a_1)}\right] & \cdots & \left[\frac{\partial_s \mathrm{Val}(c_1)}{\partial_s \mathrm{Val}(a_m)}\right] \\ \vdots & \ddots & \vdots \\ \left[\frac{\partial_s \mathrm{Val}(c_n)}{\partial_s \mathrm{Val}(a_1)}\right] & \cdots & \left[\frac{\partial_s \mathrm{Val}(c_n)}{\partial_s \mathrm{Val}(a_m)}\right] \end{bmatrix} \otimes \begin{bmatrix} [\Delta \mathrm{Val}(a_1)] \\ \vdots \\ [\Delta \mathrm{Val}(a_m)] \end{bmatrix}
$$

$$
\oplus \begin{bmatrix} \left[\frac{\partial_s \mathrm{Val}(c_1)}{\partial_s \mathrm{Val}(x_1)}\right] & \cdots & \left[\frac{\partial_s \mathrm{Val}(c_1)}{\partial_s \mathrm{Val}(x_p)}\right] \\ \vdots & \ddots & \vdots \\ \left[\frac{\partial_s \mathrm{Val}(c_n)}{\partial_s \mathrm{Val}(x_1)}\right] & \cdots & \left[\frac{\partial_s \mathrm{Val}(c_n)}{\partial_s \mathrm{Val}(x_p)}\right] \end{bmatrix} \otimes \begin{bmatrix} [\Delta \mathrm{Val}(x_1)] \\ \vdots \\ [\Delta \mathrm{Val}(x_p)] \end{bmatrix} \tag{7.7}
$$

where x_j denotes any of the possible values of X. In this book partial derivatives are used to manipulate probability and belief values and, because of the difficulty of determining how $\Pi(x_j)$ affects $\Pi(x_k)$ where $j \neq k$, separable derivatives are used to manipulate possibility values. Strictly speaking, it is not possible to establish any kind of derivative in possibility theory since the maximum and minimum operations used by the theory may not be differentiated.[2] However, it is possible to establish the sign of $\delta\mathrm{Val}(x)/\delta\mathrm{Val}(y)$ (the way in which a small change in value rather than an infinitesimal change in value is propagated) and this is what will be manipulated in the case of possibility theory. I trust that the reader will excuse the slight abuse of notation that allows $\partial_s\mathrm{Val}(x)/\partial_s\mathrm{Val}(y)$ to stand for $\delta\Pi(x)/\delta\Pi(y)$ since it limits the proliferation of notation. It should also be noted that separable derivatives are used when the theory of qualitative change is extended to take account of order of magnitude information (Parsons, 1997b, 1999; Parsons and Saffiotti, 1996) though the latter mistakenly calls partial derivatives "total" and separable derivatives "partial."

7.3 Causal reasoning

Having established this basic framework for talking about changes in certainty values, it is clear how to establish the way in which changes are propagated between a particular pair of nodes X and Y. If the change in a particular value of Y, $\mathrm{Val}(y_1)$ say, is known, and the change in a particular value of X, $\mathrm{Val}(x_1)$, is required, then the way in which the one affects the other is established by determining the qualitative value of either $\partial\mathrm{Val}(x_1)/\partial\mathrm{Val}(y_1)$ or $\partial_s\mathrm{Val}(x_1)/\partial_s\mathrm{Val}(y_1)$. Thus this section is concerned with how to establish such derivatives.

7.3.1 Establishing qualitative relationships

At one level it is quite clear how to establish the qualitative derivatives— it is achieved by taking an expression that relates $\mathrm{Val}(x_1)$ and $\mathrm{Val}(y_1)$, such as (3.13), and taking the partial or separable derivative of it with respect to $\mathrm{Val}(y_1)$. This is simple to do for all separable derivatives as will become clear below, and simple to do for partial derivatives in the binary case (as shown elsewhere (Parsons and Mamdani, 1993)), but slightly more complex for the multi-valued variables considered here. The problem is that given an expression:

$$\mathrm{Val}(x_1) = f(\mathrm{Val}(y_1), \ldots, \mathrm{Val}(y_n)) \tag{7.8}$$

in which:

$$\mathrm{Val}(y_1) = g(\mathrm{Val}(y_2), \ldots, \mathrm{Val}(y_n)) \tag{7.9}$$

the partial derivative of x with respect to y_1 is not defined. Since all the equations that might be used to relate certainty values of x and y_i in both probability and evidence theories are of exactly this form, this is a significant difficulty. However, it is a difficulty that can be

---

2 The use of maximum clearly also prevents differentiation when the variant of the theory that uses product rather than minimum is adopted, though that version of the theory is not considered in any detail here.

overcome to some degree. The actual form of the equations that relate $\mathrm{Val}(x_1)$ to $\mathrm{Val}(y_i)$ for both probability and evidence theories is:[3]

$$\mathrm{Val}(x_1) = k_1\mathrm{Val}(y_1) + \ldots + k_n\mathrm{Val}(y_n) \tag{7.10}$$

$$\mathrm{Val}(y_1) = 1 - (\mathrm{Val}(y_2) + \ldots + \mathrm{Val}(y_n)) \tag{7.11}$$

and under such conditions it is possible to determine the qualitative value of the partial derivative of $\mathrm{Val}(x_1)$ with respect to $\mathrm{Val}(y_1)$. Indeed, the following result holds.

LEMMA 7.1: If (1) $u_1 = k_1 v_1 + \ldots + k_n v_n$, (2) $v_1 = 1 - (v_2 + \ldots + v_n)$ and (3) $\Delta v_1 \geq \max_{2 \leq i \leq n} \Delta v_i$, where $k_1 \ldots k_n$ are constant values with respect to v_1, then:

$$\left[\frac{\partial u_1}{\partial v_1}\right] = \left[k_1 - \frac{\max}{\min}_{i=2\ldots n} k_i\right]$$

where $[k_1 - \frac{\max}{\min}_{i=2\ldots n}k_i]$ is shorthand for the qualitative value of the interval obtained by subtracting the maximum and minimum of the k_i from k_1. In other words it is the qualitative value of the interval:

$$\left[k_1 - \max_{i=2\ldots n} k_i, k_1 - \min_{i=2\ldots n} k_i\right]$$

The same qualitative value is obtained from the expression:

$$\left[k_1 - \min_{i=2\ldots n} k_i\right] \oplus \left[k_1 - \max_{i=2\ldots n} k_i\right]$$

or indeed

$$\bigoplus_{i=2,\ldots,n} [k_1 - k_i]$$

Either way the qualitative value is $[+]$ if k_1 is bigger than at least one of the k_i and no smaller than the others, zero if k_1 is equal to all the k_i, and $[-]$ if k_1 is smaller than at least one the k_i and no bigger than the others. In all other cases, the value is $[?]$.

Having established Lemma 7.1, it is possible to determine the values of the qualitative derivatives that relate probability, possibility and belief values in singly-connected networks so that the way in which qualitative changes are propagated through such networks may be predicted. The general situation in which this propagation will take place is that depicted by Figure 7.1 where the aim is to determine how the certainty values of the pos-

---

3 Though it should be noted that in evidence theory the summation is over all the subsets of the frame of discernment rather than over its members. There is a fine distinction to be made between $m(\cdot)$ and $\mathrm{Bel}(\cdot)$ and this is given due attention below.

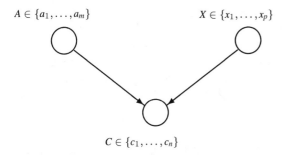

$A \in \{a_1, \ldots, a_m\}$ $X \in \{x_1, \ldots, x_p\}$

$C \in \{c_1, \ldots, c_n\}$

Figure 7.1
A simple directed graph.

sible values of C alter when changes in the certainty values of the possible values of A are known—X summarises the effect of all variables that have an influence on C other than A and its predecessors. That is, the direction of propagation is the same as the direction of the directed arcs joining the nodes between which propagation takes place. Underlying all this work is the assumption that that the conditional value table that controls propagation over the link is written in terms of values such as $\mathrm{Val}(c_i|a_j)$ and that, because such tables are usually elicited most easily in terms of causal influences, A causes C. Thus this form of propagation is causal in the sense discussed in Section 5.3.2.

Now, because the graph is singly-connected, A and X are known to be conditionally independent of one another when the value of C is not known. Thus, if the network in this scenario is quantified with probability theory, it is possible to determine that:

THEOREM 7.3:   Consider a variable C, with possible values $c_1, \ldots, c_n$, which is part of a singly connected network. If C has parents A, with possible values $a_1, \ldots, a_m$, and X, with possible values $x_1, \ldots, x_p$, the probability of C taking value c_1 follows the probability of A taking value a_1, if, for all other values a_i of A and all values x of X:

$$\Pr(c_1|a_1, x) > \Pr(c_1|a_i, x)$$

The situations in which the probability of C taking value c_1 varies inversely with, and is qualitatively independent of, the probability of A taking value a_1 are determined analogously, replacing $>$ with $<$ and $=$ respectively, and the situations in which the probability of C taking value c_1 may follow, or may vary inversely with, the probability of A taking value a_1 are also determined in a similar way, replacing $>$ with $\geq$ and $\leq$ respectively.

Note that here, as throughout the work on qualitative change discussed in this book, results are stated in terms of the certainty values of C taking value c_1 and A taking value

a_1 rather than in terms of C taking value c_i and A taking value a_j. This is purely to avoid a profusion of anonymous subscripts, and of course c_1 and a_1 could be any of the possible values of C and A. Also note that throughout the main results are stated in terms of the strict inequality—for reasons that will become apparent when looking at evidential reasoning, using strict inequalities has a payoff in terms of providing the strongest predictions.

Since many of the examples given here involve binary variables, it is worth bearing in mind the following corollary of Theorem 7.3:

COROLLARY 7.1:   Consider a variable C, with possible values $\{c_1, c_2\}$, which is part of a singly connected network. If C has parents A, with possible values $\{a_1, a_2\}$, and X, with possible values $x_1, \ldots, x_p$, then:

$$\left[\frac{\partial \Pr(c_2)}{\partial \Pr(a_2)}\right] = \left[\frac{\partial \Pr(c_1)}{\partial \Pr(a_1)}\right]$$

$$\left[\frac{\partial \Pr(c_1)}{\partial \Pr(a_2)}\right] = [-] \otimes \left[\frac{\partial \Pr(c_1)}{\partial \Pr(a_1)}\right]$$

$$\left[\frac{\partial \Pr(c_2)}{\partial \Pr(a_1)}\right] = [-] \otimes \left[\frac{\partial \Pr(c_1)}{\partial \Pr(a_1)}\right]$$

Thus when variables are binary, once one of the qualitative derivatives relating C and A is established, all the others are immediately defined.

If the network is quantified with possibility values, it is not, as discussed above, possible to obtain derivatives by differentiation. However, it is possible to perform a kind of perturbation analysis, considering what happens when $\Pi(a_1)$ changes value. Thus, for example, it is possible to argue that for a node C with parent A, since:

$$\Pi(c_1) = \sup_{a_i} \min(\Pi(c_1|a_i), \Pi(a_i))$$

the only way in which $\Pi(c_1)$ will follow $\Pi(a_1)$ up and down will be if

$$\Pi(a_1) < \Pi(c_1|a_1)$$

and:

$$\min(\Pi(c_1|a_i), \Pi(a_i)) > \sup_{a_i, i \neq 1} \min(\Pi(c_1|a_i), \Pi(a_i))$$

Thus the value of $\Pi(c_1)$ is equal to that of $\Pi(a_1)$ alone so that if $\Pi(a_1)$ changes $\Pi(c_1)$ must also change. Carrying out such an analysis gives the following result:

THEOREM 7.4:   Consider a variable C, with possible values $c_1, \ldots, c_n$, which is part of a singly connected network. If C has parents A, with possible values $a_1, \ldots, a_m$, and X, with possible values $x_1, \ldots, x_p$.

1. The possibility of C taking value c_1 follows the possibility of A taking value a_1 if, for some value x_j of X and all other values a_i of A and x_k of X:

$$\Pi(a_1) < \Pi(c_1|a_1, x_j), \Pi(x_j)$$
$$\Pi(c_1, a_1, x_j) > \Pi(c_1, a_i, x_k)$$

2. The possibility of C taking value c_1 may follow the possibility of A taking value a_1 up if, for some value x_j of X and all other values a_i of A and x_k of X:

$$\Pi(a_1) < \Pi(c_1|a_1, x_j), \Pi(x_j)$$
$$\Pi(c_1, a_1, x_j) \leq \Pi(c_1, a_i, x_k)$$

3. The possibility of C taking value c_1 may follow the possibility of A taking value a_1 down if, for some value x_j of X and all other values a_i of A and x_k of X:

$$\Pi(a_1) \geq \Pi(c_1|a_1, x_j)$$
$$\Pi(c_1, a_1, x_j) > \Pi(c_1, a_i, x_k)$$

or

$$\Pi(a_1) \geq \Pi(x_j)$$
$$\Pi(c_1, a_1, x_j) > \Pi(c_1, a_i, x_k)$$

In all other cases the possibility of C taking value c_1 is qualitatively independent of the possibility of A taking value a_1.

It should be noted that the exclusive nature of the conditions in this theorem means that it is only possible for the possibility of c_1 to follow one parent. Even if, initially, $\Pi(a_1)$ and $\Pi(x_j)$ are equal so that according to Theorem 7.4 $\Pi(c_1)$ may follow either of them down, as soon as one does fall, $\Pi(c_1)$ is qualitatively independent of the value of the other. Thus, even though there are a number of different trails through a graph that end at C, the possibility of a given value of C can only be affected by one of them, a phenomenon which will be called "blocking." This is in contrast to probability theory where the probability of a given value of a node can be influenced by changes at a number of other nodes. Note that blocking can also occur at a node on just one trail.

An important special case of Theorem 7.4 is obtained when there is initially no information about which values of A and X are more favoured. In such a situation one might reasonably take $\Pi(a_i)$ and $\Pi(x_j)$ to be 1 initially for all values of i and j, since that is the value that they will have by the principle of minimum specificity. In this case Theorem 7.4 gives:

COROLLARY 7.2:   Consider a variable C, with possible values $c_1, \ldots, c_n$, which is part of a singly connected network. If C has parents A, with possible values $a_1, \ldots, a_m$, and X, with possible values $x_1, \ldots, x_p$, if nothing is known about the prior distributions over A and X, then applying the principle of minimum specificity means that the possibility of C taking value c_1 may follow the possibility of A taking value a_1 down if, for some value x_j of X and all other values a_i of A and x_k of X:

$$\Pi(c_1|a_1, x_j) > \Pi(c_1|a_i, x_k)$$

Otherwise the possibility of C taking value c_1 is qualitatively independent of the possibility of A taking value a_1.

Applying the principle of minimum specificity is not the only way of overcoming the problem of not knowing the prior possibility distributions over A and X. It is also possible to ask what the derivatives would be if the priors are allowed to take any value between 1 and 0. This question can be answered by looking at what the derivatives would be according to Theorem 7.4 with priors of both 1 and 0 and taking the union of these values. Doing this gives:

COROLLARY 7.3:   Consider a variable C, with possible values $c_1, \ldots, c_n$, which is part of a singly connected network. If C has parents A, with possible values $a_1, \ldots, a_m$, and X, with possible values $x_1, \ldots, x_p$, if nothing is known about the prior distributions over A and X, then the possibility of C taking value c_1 may always follow the possibility of A taking value a_1 up, and may follow the possibility of A taking value a_1 down if, for some value x_j of X and all other values a_i of A and x_k of X:

$$\Pi(c_1|a_1, x_j) > \Pi(c_1|a_i, x_k)$$

Clearly this latter result may well give:

$$\left[\frac{\partial \Pi(c_1)}{\partial \Pi(a_1)} \right] = [\uparrow, \downarrow]$$

The reason that Corollaries 7.2 and 7.3 are important is that they provide a means of determining the qualitative influence between A and C even when the prior possibility distribution over A is unknown. As a result it is possible to argue that the corollaries will sufficient to determine the qualitative behaviour of many possibilistic networks—prior possibility values will be unknown and so the Theorem 7.4 will provide no additional information. It should be noted, of course, that the reason Corollary 7.2 gives more precise answers than Corollary 7.3 is that it only applies in conjunction with the principle of minimum specificity and that it is to be expected that reasoning with more precise information will give more precise results. It should also be noted that even if Corollary 7.3 produces a derivative with value $[\uparrow, \downarrow]$, which might appear vacuous, it is still useful—as will be illustrated in Section 7.5.2—thanks to the blocking of changes in one direction.

Taking Theorem 7.4 and Corollary 7.2 together it becomes clear that the derivatives

$$\left[\frac{\partial_s\Pi(c_1)}{\partial_s\Pi(a_1)}\right] \cdots \left[\frac{\partial_s\Pi(c_n)}{\partial_s\Pi(a_m)}\right]$$

which may be established by these results are not, despite the fact that they are separable, completely unaffected by each other's value. This is because the the value of each member of the set of derivatives

$$\left[\frac{\partial_s\Pi(c_1)}{\partial_s\Pi(a_1)}\right] \cdots \left[\frac{\partial_s\Pi(c_1)}{\partial_s\Pi(a_m)}\right]$$

depends upon the relative value of the joint possibility value $\Pi(c_1, a_i, x)$, $i = 1 \ldots m$ compared with all the other $\Pi(c_1, a_j, x), j \neq i$. If a particular $\Pi(c_1, a_i, x)$ is greater than all the $\Pi(c_1, a_j, x)$ then the relevant derivative

$$\left[\frac{\partial_s\Pi(c_1)}{\partial_s\Pi(a_i)}\right]$$

will have value $[+]$ and all the other derivatives will have value $[\uparrow, 0]$ or $[0]$. This means that if $\Pi(a_i)$ does not decrease in value, applying (7.7) means that $\Pi(c_1)$ cannot be $[?]$.

Considering the scenario of Figure 7.1 again, but with the network quantified with belief functions, there are two possible results. The first is for the case in which conditional beliefs of the form $\mathrm{Bel}(c_1|a_1 \cup a_2 \cup \ldots \cup a_n, X)$ are known, in which case Dempster's rule of combination may be used to combine values. In this case the qualitative derivative may be determined as follows:

THEOREM 7.5: Consider a variable C, with possible values $c_1, \ldots, c_n$, which is part of a singly connected network. If C has parents A, which has possible values $a_1, \ldots, a_m$, and X, with possible values $x_1, \ldots, x_p$, belief in C taking value c_1 follows belief in A taking value a_1 if, for all other values $\mathbf{y} \subseteq A$, $a_1 \in \mathbf{y}$, and all values x of X:

$$\mathrm{Bel}(c_1|a_1, x) > \mathrm{Bel}(c_1|\mathbf{y}, x)$$

when the relevant beliefs are combined using Dempster's rule of combination.

The situations in which belief in C taking value c_1 varies inversely with and is independent of belief in A taking value a_1 are determined analogously, replacing $>$ with $<$ and $=$ respectively, and the situations in which belief in C taking value c_1 may follow and may vary inversely with belief in A taking value a_1 are also similarly determined by replacing $>$ with $\geq$ and $\leq$ respectively. If none of these relations hold, then the belief in C taking value c_1 is indeterminate with respect to belief in A taking value a_1.

The other possible result is for the case in which conditional beliefs of the form $\mathrm{Bel}(c_1 | a_1 \cup a_2 \cup \ldots \cup a_n, X)$ are not known, and the only conditionals available are of the form $\mathrm{Bel}(c_1 | a_1, X)$. In such a case, if the use of the disjunctive rule of combination is sanctioned, the following result may be obtained:

THEOREM 7.6:   Consider a variable C, with possible values $c_1, \ldots, c_n$, which is part of a singly connected network. If C has parents A, with possible values $a_1, \ldots, a_m$, and X, with has possible values $x_1, \ldots, x_p$, belief in C taking value c_1 may always follow belief in A taking value a_1 if the relevant beliefs are combined using the disjunctive rule of combination.

In other words, when the disjunctive rule is used, it is always the case that:

$$\left[\frac{\partial \mathrm{Bel}(c_1)}{\partial \mathrm{Bel}(a_1)} \right] = [0, +]$$

whatever the value of the conditionals.

With these last two results, it is important to note that the results only hold for singletons, making them directly analogous to the results obtained for possibility and probability theories. Thus while it is possible to use Theorems 7.5 and 7.6 to determine the qualitative derivative relating any singleton value of C to any singleton value of A, it is not, for instance, possible to determine $\left[\partial \mathrm{Bel}(c_1 \cup c_2) / \partial \mathrm{Bel}(a_1 \cup a_2) \right]$ from them. This is due to the fact that the proof relies upon the equivalence of $m(z)$ and $\mathrm{Bel}(z)$ for singleton hypotheses z. This restriction is relaxed in Section 8.2.2.

For completeness, it is also worth determining how probabilities and beliefs change when only separable derivatives are used. These are given by the following two theorems:

THEOREM 7.7:   Consider a variable C, with possible values $c_1, \ldots, c_n$, which is part of a singly connected network. If C has parents A, with possible values $a_1, \ldots, a_m$, and X, with possible values $x_1, \ldots, x_p$, the probability of C taking value c_1 may always separably follow the probability of A taking value a_1.

THEOREM 7.8:   Consider a variable C, with possible values $c_1, \ldots, c_n$, which is part of a

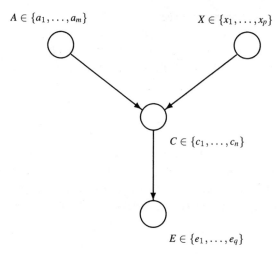

$A \in \{a_1, \ldots, a_m\}$

$X \in \{x_1, \ldots, x_p\}$

$C \in \{c_1, \ldots, c_n\}$

$E \in \{e_1, \ldots, e_q\}$

Figure 7.2
A larger network

singly connected network. If C has parents A, with possible values $a_1, \ldots, a_m$, and X, with possible values $x_1, \ldots, x_p$, belief in C taking value c_1 may always separably follow belief in A taking value a_1.

In other words, it is always the case that:

$$\left[\frac{\partial_s \Pr(c_1)}{\partial_s \Pr(a_1)}\right] = [0, +]$$

$$\left[\frac{\partial_s \mathrm{Bel}(c_1)}{\partial_s \mathrm{Bel}(a_1)}\right] = [0, +]$$

So in the separable case there is no difference between the using Dempster's rule and the using the disjunctive rule.

7.3.2   The modularity of propagation

All the results given so far, and all those that will be given in the remainder of this chapter and the next, are obtained by considering how values are propagated across single arcs in a network. Focussing in this way makes it easier to obtain the results, but it begs the question of how the results that have been obtained may be used to propagate values through the wider network. For example, given the situation in Figure 7.2, how is it possible to take a change in $\mathrm{Val}(a_1)$ and use this to determine what the change is in $\mathrm{Val}(e_1)$?

The intuitive answer is to use the relationship between A and C to determine the changes in the certainty values of the possible values of C, and then use the relationship between C and E to determine the changes in certainty of the possible values of E. It turns out that this intuition is exactly what is sanctioned by the differential calculus (in particular the chain rule), which gives:

$$[\Delta \mathrm{Val}(e_1)] = \left[\frac{\partial \mathrm{Val}(e_1)}{\partial \mathrm{Val}(c_i)}\right] \otimes \left[\frac{\partial \mathrm{Val}(c_i)}{\partial \mathrm{Val}(a_1)}\right] \otimes [\Delta \mathrm{Val}(a_1)]$$

for any value c_i. Thus the change in $\mathrm{Val}(e_1)$ is just the qualitative product of the change in $\mathrm{Val}(a_1)$ with the intervening derivatives. In a more general case in which there are more intervening nodes, the product of derivatives part just grows. In the general case in which a node A and a node C are separated by a number of intervening nodes $N_1, \ldots N_p$, the change in $\mathrm{Val}(c_1)$ is

$$[\Delta \mathrm{Val}(c_1)] = \left[\frac{\partial \mathrm{Val}(c_1)}{\partial \mathrm{Val}(n_{p_i})}\right] \otimes \cdots \otimes \left[\frac{\partial \mathrm{Val}(n_{1_i})}{\partial \mathrm{Val}(a_1)}\right] \otimes [\Delta \mathrm{Val}(a_1)] \qquad (7.12)$$

where n_{p_i} denotes any of the possible values of the variable associated with the node N_p. This product of derivatives turns out to be a useful concept, and so it is worth relating it to the concept of qualitative influence. Recalling the graph-theoretic notions introduced in Chapter 5 gives:

DEFINITION 7.12:   Given a trail through a graph from node A, with possible values $\{a_1, \ldots, a_m\}$, through nodes $N_1, \ldots N_p$ to C, with possible values $\{c_1, \ldots, c_n\}$, the *qualitative influence* of $\mathrm{Val}(a_1)$ on $\mathrm{Val}(c_1)$ *along the trail* is given by:

$$\left[\frac{\partial \mathrm{Val}(c_1)}{\partial \mathrm{Val}(a_1)}\right] = \left[\frac{\partial \mathrm{Val}(c_1)}{\partial \mathrm{Val}(n_{p_i})}\right] \otimes \cdots \otimes \left[\frac{\partial \mathrm{Val}(n_{1_i})}{\partial \mathrm{Val}(a_1)}\right]$$

Just as with a qualitative influence between variable values, it is helpful to distinguish between a *zero influence along a trail* in which case the influence along the trail has value $[0]$, and a *non-zero influence along a trail*, in which case the influence has a value other than $[0]$.

Although the discussion so far has only developed the theory supporting propagation in the direction of the causal arcs, and so only applies to paths through a graph, the result applies to the more general concept of trails (which ignore the direction of the arcs) and so applies to evidential reasoning, as discussion in Section 7.4 as well as causal reasoning. As ever, when it is clear that the influence being discussed is a qualitative influence, the term "qualitative" will be dropped.

The fact that the influence of one value on another is just the product of the intervening influences, which is another way of stating Definition 7.12, is important because it makes propagation modular. To find the effect of a change at one node in a network on other nodes it is possible to progress by calculating the effect arc by arc. The change at any one node can be calculated by looking at the changes in nodes to which it is directly connected. This locality of calculation is exploited in Chapter 9 when devising an algorithm to propagate the effects of a given set of changes in certainty value through a network.

In addition to establishing the qualitative influence between values along a trail, it is possible to establish the qualitative influence of one node on another node along a trail. Adapting the matrix notation of (7.4), gives the following definition.

DEFINITION 7.13:   Given a trail through a graph from node A, with possible values $\{a_1, \ldots, a_m\}$, through nodes $N_1, \ldots N_p$ to C, with possible values $\{c_1, \ldots, c_n\}$, the *qualitative influence of a node A on a node C along a trail $N_1, \ldots N_p$* is given by

$$
\left[\begin{bmatrix} \frac{\partial \mathrm{Val}(c_1)}{\partial \mathrm{Val}(a_1)} \end{bmatrix} \\ \vdots \\ \begin{bmatrix} \frac{\partial \mathrm{Val}(c_n)}{\partial \mathrm{Val}(a_1)} \end{bmatrix} \right]
=
\left[\begin{bmatrix} \frac{\partial \mathrm{Val}(c_1)}{\partial \mathrm{Val}(n_{p_i})} \end{bmatrix} \\ \vdots \\ \begin{bmatrix} \frac{\partial \mathrm{Val}(c_n)}{\partial \mathrm{Val}(n_{p_i})} \end{bmatrix} \right]
\otimes \cdots \otimes
\left[\begin{bmatrix} \frac{\partial \mathrm{Val}(n_{1_i})}{\partial \mathrm{Val}(a_1)} \end{bmatrix} \\ \vdots \\ \begin{bmatrix} \frac{\partial \mathrm{Val}(n_{1_i})}{\partial \mathrm{Val}(a_1)} \end{bmatrix} \right]
$$

Once again it is useful to distinguish zero influences, and in this case a *zero influence between nodes along a trail* is one for which all the values in the resulting vector are zero. A *non-zero influence between nodes along a trail* is any influence that is not a zero influence. Note that summarising a trail into a single vector of qualitative derivatives is essentially doing the same as Wellman's graph reduction (Wellman, 1990a) for that trail.

To get the feel of the kind of reasoning that may be carried out using these results, the next section gives a small example that will be used, in various forms, throughout this and the next chapter.

7.3.3   An example of propagation

Late last year, Jack Dulouz received a long letter from his friend Cody Pomeroy in which Cody mentioned that he had just taken a job fixing tyres at the local tyre shack in order to have enough money to support his wife and children. In the letter he complained about the manager of the tyre shack, a most unscrupulous sort, who immediately sacks any employee if they become ill or if he suspects that they drink alcohol. This made Jack worry about Cody's prospects, since he was well aware of Cody's fragile health and the fact that Cody often drank heavily, especially when writing poetry. Jack was so worried that he went to

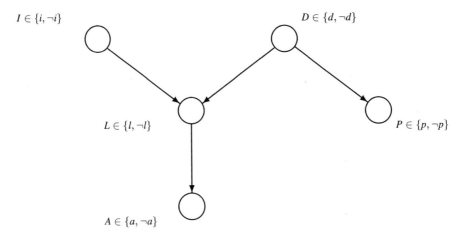

$I \in \{i, \neg i\}$ $D \in \{d, \neg d\}$

$L \in \{l, \neg l\}$ $P \in \{p, \neg p\}$

$A \in \{a, \neg a\}$

Figure 7.3
A network describing Jack's beliefs about Cody

the lengths of drawing up the directed graph in Figure 7.3 in order to analyse the problem. In the graph node I represents the variable "ill," L represents the variable "lose job," D represents the variable "drink alcohol," P represents the variable "write poetry", and A represents the variable "adequate income." Note the causal direction of the link between D and P. This arises because in addition to knowing that there is a correlation between Cody's drinking and poetry writing, Jack believed that it is Cody's drinking that prompts his attempts to write.

In contrast to the situation on the mountain with Japhy, when considering Cody's employment prospects Jack had no numerical information. However, this did not prevent him from applying the theory of qualitative change. When considering the use of probability theory to express his beliefs he could reason in the following way.

1. Cody's description of the tyre-shack manager seemed to indicate that the probability of the proposition "lose job" may follow the probability of "ill" and "drinks alcohol."

2. For this to be true, Theorem 7.3 showed it is necessary that:

$$\Pr(l|i, d) \ge \Pr(l|\neg i, d)$$
$$\Pr(l|i, \neg d) \ge \Pr(l|\neg i, \neg d)$$

This, Jack decided, was a reasonable interpretation of Cody's description of the tyre-shack manager. The same process of reasoning told him that assuming that the probability of "adequate income" varied inversely with the probability of "lose job" meant accepting:

$$\Pr(a|l) < \Pr(a|\neg l)$$

and assuming that the probability of "write poetry" follows the probability of "drink alcohol" meant accepting:

$$\Pr(p|d) > \Pr(p|\neg d)$$

Since both of these latter conditions also appeared to Jack to be reasonable, based upon his knowledge of Cody's ability to get another job and his poetry-writing habits, he was happy with the model as described.[4] Jack then used his model to speculate about Cody's prospects, using (7.4) in conjunction with Table 7.1 to reason as follows. If Cody either drank or got ill then either:

$$[\Delta \Pr(i)] = [+]$$

or

$$[\Delta \Pr(d)] = [+]$$

The first would mean that:

$$
\begin{aligned}
[\Delta \Pr(a)] &= \left[\frac{\partial \Pr(a)}{\partial \Pr(l)}\right] \otimes \left[\frac{\partial \Pr(l)}{\partial \Pr(i)}\right] \otimes [\Pr(i)] \\
&= [-] \otimes [0,+] \otimes [+] \\
&= [0,-]
\end{aligned}
$$

and the second would mean that:

$$
\begin{aligned}
[\Delta \Pr(a)] &= \left[\frac{\partial \Pr(a)}{\partial \Pr(l)}\right] \otimes \left[\frac{\partial \Pr(l)}{\partial \Pr(d)}\right] \otimes [\Pr(d)] \\
&= [-] \otimes [0,+] \otimes [-] \\
&= [0,-]
\end{aligned}
$$

This makes it clear that either way Cody's prospects did not look good. Furthermore, if $\Delta \Pr(d) = [+]$, then:

$$[\Delta \Pr(p)] = \left[\frac{\partial \Pr(p)}{\partial \Pr(d)}\right] \otimes [\Pr(d)]$$

4 Note that the model only takes into account what happens *if* the manager notices Cody's illness or suspects him of drinking—it makes no attempt to model the manager's propensity to make such observations given that Cody is ill or drinking (though such a model could be built by adding in additional nodes between D and L and between I and L respectively).

$$= [+] \otimes [+]$$
$$= [+]$$

This means that if Cody drank it was more likely that he would write poetry. Influenced by Japhy's eclecticism during their conversation on the mountain, Jack also considered the use of possibility and evidence theories to quantify his model, discovering, for instance that to entertain the thought that belief in "adequate income" varies inversely with belief in "lose job" meant accepting:

$$\text{Bel}(a|l) \quad < \quad \text{Bel}(a|l \cup \neg l)$$

while considering that the possibility of the proposition "write poetry" might follow the possibility of "drink alcohol" up meant accepting:

$$\Pi(p) \quad < \quad \Pi(p|d)$$
$$\Pi(p,d) \quad \leq \quad \Pi(p,\neg d), \Pi(\neg p, d), \Pi(\neg p, \neg d)$$

Although, once again, these conditions seemed reasonable, Jack preferred to muse on the Diamond Sutra than to use the models that they entailed to predict Cody's future.

7.3.4 The validity of propagation

Now, since the form of the propagation of values is determined by the qualitative value of a derivative, it is only guaranteed to be correct when changes in value of $\text{Val}(a_1)$ are infinitesimal. Since the theory of qualitative change needs to handle changes that are significantly larger than infinitesimal, it is necessary to check that using the value of qualitative derivatives for these substantial changes will give results that agree with those which would have been obtained by a calculation that took into account the fact that the changes are not infinitesimal—results that will be termed "correct." What this means, is that the qualitative changes predicted using the qualitative derivatives derived above, should be *compatible* with the values that would be attained were the changes in $\text{Val}(a_1)$ taken into account. To show this, it is necessary to introduce the notions of inclusion and compatibility between two qualitative values:

DEFINITION 7.14: The qualitative value *x includes* the qualitative value *y* if and only if one of the following three conditions hold:

1. $x = [+, 0]$ *and* $y = [+]$ *or* $y = [0]$
2. $x = [-, 0]$ *and* $y = [-]$ *or* $y = [0]$
3. $x = [?]$

DEFINITION 7.15: Two qualitative values x and y are *compatible* if they are the same, or either includes the other.

Thus [?] is compatible with anything, and $[0, +]$ is compatible with $[+]$ and $[0]$, but is not compatible with $[-]$. Compatibility is the strongest condition that may be considered when determining the agreement between two qualitative values. If z is calculated by one method to be $[+]$ and by another to be [?], the two values are compatible—there is nothing in the second calculation that rules out the possibility of z being $[+]$. However, if z is calculated by one method to be $[+]$ and by another to be $[-]$, then they are incompatible.

To determine the correctness of the results obtained by using the derivatives that were established above, it is necessary to examine how the qualitative values of the derivatives change when the quantities whose value they relate themselves change. According to the theory of differential calculus (Stewart, 1991), when considering the derivative $\partial y/\partial x$ that links y to x, the factor that controls the change in the value of $\partial y/dx$ as x alters is the second derivative of y with respect to x, $\partial^2 y/\partial x^2$. This is simply $\partial y/\partial x$ differentiated with respect to x. If $\partial^2 y/\partial x^2$ has value zero, then the derivative $\partial y/\partial x$ is constant when x changes. Similarly, the change in value of $\partial_s y/\partial_s x$ is determined by the second derivative $\partial_s{}^2 y/\partial_s x^2$. Calculating the second derivatives for probability, possibility and evidence theories gives:

LEMMA 7.2: The values of the partial qualitative derivative $[\partial \mathrm{Val}(c_1)/\partial \mathrm{Val}(a_1)]$ and the separable qualitative derivative $[\partial_s \mathrm{Val}(c_1)/\partial_s \mathrm{Val}(a_1)]$ are constant under changes in the value of $\mathrm{Val}(a_1)$.

Since the value of the qualitative derivatives do not alter in value as $\mathrm{Val}(a_1)$ changes, the predictions made using them are the same as those that take the changes into account, and so the next result immediately follows.

THEOREM 7.9: The qualitative changes predicted by using the qualitative derivatives $[\partial \mathrm{Val}(c_1)/\partial \mathrm{Val}(a_1)]$ and $[\partial_s \mathrm{Val}(c_1)/\partial_s \mathrm{Val}(a_1)]$ when changes in $\mathrm{Val}(a_1)$ are not infinitesimal are compatible with those that would be obtained were the effect of the changes being finite taken into account.

This rather longwinded result makes it clear that there is no problem in using results that are, strictly speaking, only valid in the limit.

A related point is that of the effect on the assumption behind Lemma 7.1—this assumption being that the change in the certainty value with respect to which the derivatives are being determined is no smaller than the change in the certainty value of all the other values of the same variable. Thus when determining $[\partial \mathrm{Val}(c_1)/\partial \mathrm{Val}(a_1)]$, all the results

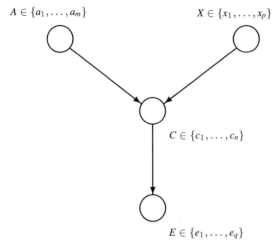

$A \in \{a_1, \ldots, a_m\}$

$X \in \{x_1, \ldots, x_p\}$

$C \in \{c_1, \ldots, c_n\}$

$E \in \{e_1, \ldots, e_q\}$

Figure 7.4
A network relating A to E

so far make the assumption that $\Delta \mathrm{Val}(a_1) \geq \max_{i=2\ldots m} \Delta \mathrm{Val}(a_i)$. This obviously limits the application of the results for probability theory or evidence theory to the case in which the assumption is true, and an important result to determine is what this means for the propagation of qualitative values. Consider the situation depicted in Figure 7.4, in which it is again necessary to propagate a change in the certainty value of one of the values of A to determine its effect on the certainty values of the values of E. To do this the initial information about A must obviously include information about which value of A changes most, the value that will be known as the *driving value* since it drives the propagation, and how this value changes. This requirement seems very reasonable, especially since the initial information will often be of the form "A is observed to have value a_1" in which case information about the relative prior certainty values will be sufficient to establish which is the driving value. Thus this information is sufficient to determine which set of qualitative derivatives are appropriate for determining the changes in the certainty values of the values c_i of C. If $\mathrm{Val}(a_3)$ is the value of A whose certainty value alters most, then the only correct derivatives to use are:

$$\left[\frac{\partial \mathrm{Val}(c_1)}{\partial \mathrm{Val}(a_3)} \right], \ldots, \left[\frac{\partial \mathrm{Val}(c_n)}{\partial \mathrm{Val}(a_3)} \right]$$

These may then be used to establish the changes in $\mathrm{Val}(c_1), \ldots \mathrm{Val}(c_n)$. Now, to use these changes to establish the changes in $\mathrm{Val}(e_1), \ldots \mathrm{Val}(e_q)$, it is necessary to establish which of the $\mathrm{Val}(c_i)$ is the driving value. For this particular example it is necessary to know which value of C changes most given that a_3 is the driving value of the propagation from A to C, and to account for all possible cases it is necessary to which value of C changes most for each value of A being the driving value. At first this seems like a huge burden, and might appear to undermine the advantage of the qualitative approach as a relatively "information light" means of handling uncertainty. However, a few moments reflection suffice to make it clear that if a_3 is the driving value for the propagation from A to C, the driving value for the propagation from C to E will be that value of C, c_j, for which, for all $i \neq j$ and for all x,

$$\Pr(c_j|a_3, x) \geq \Pr(c_i|a_3, x)$$

If such a value cannot be determined, it is not possible to say what the driving value will be, and so no accurate predictions about the certainty values of the possible values of E may be made. However, for the same reason, it will not be possible to say how any possible value of C affects any possible value of E because Theorem 7.3 will only identify the relevant derivatives as having value [?]. Thus to determine the driving value of any hypothesis during propagation, all that is required is knowledge of the relative size of the conditional values—knowledge that is required in order to determine the qualitative behaviour of the links in any case. If this information is not available, or is not true of a c_j for all values of X, then the propagation will founder for lack of a driving value. However, in such a situation it will already have sunk for lack of useful qualitative derivatives since all the relevant derivatives will have value [?]. As a result it is possible to conclude that the assumption in Lemma 7.1 places no practical restrictions on the propagation of values.

Despite the fact that there are no restrictions that it imposes, two final points should be made about the assumption. The first is that, by definition, when the change in the driving value of a variable is zero so are the changes in all other values of that variable. Thus if the change in the driving value of a variable is zero for any reason, propagation effectively terminates at that point with all changes "downstream" from that variable also being zero, thus blocking propagation. The second point is that if the change in the driving value of some variable is has qualitative value [+], then changes in several of the other values of that variable must be [−]. Indeed, overall there must be more values whose change is [−] than there are values whose change is [+]. If this were not the case, then the fact that all the changes sum to zero would means there was a change in value bigger than that of the driving value. A similar argument applies to a driving value of [−].

7.4 Evidential reasoning

The results in the previous section make it possible to analyse the causal propagation of values in networks quantified using probability, possibility and belief values. Since it is often necessary to reason evidentially, this section provides a means of obtaining the qualitative behaviour of evidential propagation from the known qualitative behaviour of causal propagation.

7.4.1 Bayes' rule and its variants

As discussed in Chapter 3, when dealing with quantitative network models, it is usual for the conditional values that quantify such networks to be of the form:

Val(*effect*|*cause*)

which make it possible to carry out causal propagation. Such values are exactly those used in the previous section to determine how qualitative values are propagated. When propagating quantitative values from effects to causes, some variant of Bayes' rule is required to establish (although this is often done implicitly) values of the form:

Val(*cause*|*effect*)

One might therefore expect that to determine the how qualitative values are propagated evidentially it is necessary to use the same variants of Bayes' rule. However this is not always the case since the differential calculus makes some shortcuts possible. The main result that makes such shortcuts possible is (Stewart, 1991):

THEOREM 7.10:   Given that value of the derivative

$$\frac{\partial y}{\partial x}$$

is k, then the value of

$$\frac{\partial x}{\partial y}$$

is $1/k$.

Thus, almost immediately, it is possible to establish:

COROLLARY 7.4:   For two variables A and C such that A is a parent of C, if the certainty value of C taking the value c_1 follows (respectively, varies inversely with) the certainty value of A taking the value a_1, then the certainty value of A taking value a_1 follows (respectively, varies inversely with) the certainty value of C taking value c_1.

This result applies to any formalism for which the differential calculus is applied to establish qualitative changes and so is valid for probability and evidence theories. Possibility theory, as already discussed, requires a different approach, and it turns out that:

THEOREM 7.11:   For two variables A and C such that A is a parent of C:

1. If the possibility of C taking the value c_1 follows the possibility of A taking the value a_1 then the possibility of A taking the value a_1 may follow the possibility of C taking the value c_1.

2. If the possibility of C taking the value c_1 may follow the possibility of A taking the value a_1 up then the possibility of A taking the value a_1 may follow the possibility of C taking the value c_1 down.

3. If the possibility of C taking the value c_1 may follow the possibility of A taking the value a_1 down then the possibility of A taking the value a_1 may follow the possibility of C taking the value c_1 up.

4. If the possibility of a variable C taking the value c_1 is qualitatively independent of the possibility of a variable A taking the value a_1 then the possibility of A taking the value a_1 may follow the possibility of C taking the value c_1.

Thus it is possible to predict the qualitative relationship that controls the propagation of changes in possibility from C to A from that which governs the propagation from A to C. These predictions are, of course, rather weak, all being of the form "may follow."

   These two results might appear to enable evidential propagation in the theory of qualitative change, at least for the formalisms considered in this book. However, this is not so due to an unfortunate corollary of Theorem 7.10:

COROLLARY 7.5:   For two variables A and C such that A is the parent of C, if

$$\frac{\partial \text{Val}(c_1)}{\partial \text{Val}(a_1)} = [0], [0, +] \text{ or } [0, -]$$

then

$$\frac{\partial \text{Val}(a_1)}{\partial \text{Val}(c_1)} = [?]$$

This result makes link-reversal uninformative in many cases involving any formalism for which the differential calculus is applied to establish qualitative changes. Such formalisms include probability and evidence theories, and so the result poses a problem for the theory of qualitative change.

Now, such indeterminate results are typical of all qualitative methods whether applied to reasoning about imperfect information or to modelling physical systems—in some situations they do not generate any useful information. At one level the indeterminacy is perfectly acceptable since it simply reflects the fact that knowing that $\text{Val}(c_1)$ may follow (or may vary inversely with or is independent of) $\text{Val}(a_1)$ does not place enough constraints over the relationship between $\text{Val}(c_1)$ and $\text{Val}(a_1)$ to say how $\text{Val}(a_1)$ will change when $\text{Val}(c_1)$ changes. However, from the point of view of making predictions about changes in value when propagating changes from evidence to hypotheses, it would be useful to be able to say something more precise. It turns out that it is possible to make more precise predictions in evidence theory provided that the disjunctive rule of combination is used since in such a case it is possible to obtain the following result:

THEOREM 7.12:   For two variables A and C such that A is a parent of C, belief in A taking the value a_1 may always follow belief in C taking value c_1 if the relevant beliefs are combined using the disjunctive rule of combination.

This might seem to contradict Corollary 7.5, but a moment's reflection is sufficient to see it does not—it is compatible with the result of the corollary, and may be obtained because particular information about the theory is being used rather than general information about derivatives. The result is that precise predictions can be made when reversing links in evidence theory when the disjunctive rule is used. Obviously it would be helpful if similarly precise predictions could be made in the cases in which probability theory is used and in which evidence theory is used in conjunction with Dempster's rule.

There are two obvious ways in which this may be done. The first is also the easiest from the point of view of developing the theory of qualitative change because it involves stepping outside the theory. It is, simply, to specify the exact qualitative relationship between every $\text{Val}(a_1)$ and $\text{Val}(c_1)$ for which $[\partial \text{Val}(c_1)/\partial \text{Val}(a_1)]$ has one of the troublesome values. Thus whenever $[\partial \text{Val}(c_1)/\partial \text{Val}(a_1)]$ has value $[0]$, $[0, +]$ or $[0, -]$ it necessary to specify either a full set of conditional values such as $\text{Val}(a_i|c_1, y)$ or to specify the relevant qualitative derivative directly. In other words in order to reason evidentially it is necessary to do some more knowledge elicitation, either to obtain the quantitative values or the qualitative influence.

The second way of obtaining more precise results is to make the obvious, though clearly not necessarily correct, assumption that:

$$\left[\frac{\partial \text{Val}(c_1)}{\partial \text{Val}(a_1)}\right] = [0] \Leftrightarrow \left[\frac{\partial \text{Val}(a_1)}{\partial \text{Val}(c_1)}\right] = [0] \tag{7.13}$$

ensuring that the relationships between values are entirely symmetric. This is very appealing. However, if the assumption in 7.13 is made, it is clear that the results obtained will not always be compatible with those that would be obtained were the necessary conditional values known—if $[\partial \text{Val}(c_1)/\partial \text{Val}(a_1)]$ has value $[0]$ then it is quite possible for $[\partial \text{Val}(a_1)/\partial \text{Val}(c_1)]$ to have value $[+]$ and this value will give results that are incompatible with those that would be obtained if $[\partial \text{Val}(a_1)/\partial \text{Val}(c_1)]$ were assumed to be $[0]$. Thus it is sensible to investigate under what conditions the assumption in (7.13) is valid.

It is easy to establish that in probability theory for the assumption to hold it is necessary that:

$$\left[\frac{\partial \Pr(c_i)}{\partial \Pr(a_1)}\right] = [0] \tag{7.14}$$

for all c_i, $i \neq 1$ in addition to the fact that $[\partial \Pr(c_1)/\partial \Pr(a_1)] = [0]$. Thus it is necessary that the probability of all values of C, not just c_1, are independent of the probability of a_1 in order for the influence to reverse in a symmetrical fashion. In other words symmetric reversal in probability theory requires additional constraints on causal propagation between A and C.

In evidence theory, as will be shown below, when using Dempster's rule, symmetric reversal requires:

$$\prod_{y \in \bar{a}_1} \text{Bel}(\mathbf{C} - c_1|y, x)\,(1 - \text{Bel}(\mathbf{C} - c_1|a_1, x)) \tag{7.15}$$

$$= \prod_{y \in \bar{a}_1} \text{Bel}(\mathbf{C} - \mathcal{C}|y, x)\,(1 - \text{Bel}(\mathbf{C} - \mathcal{C}|a_1, x))$$

for all $\mathcal{C} \subseteq \mathbf{C}$ such that $c_1 \in \mathcal{C}$. In fact, this condition is sufficient to ensure qualitative independence in the evidential propagation of beliefs using Dempster's rule without any condition on causal propagation.

Given these results, two directions are possible. The first is to take the theory as described so far and, when reversing an influence between two values, note that only an influence that obeys the above conditions will be symmetric. If this approach is adopted, Corollary 7.5 is replaced with the more specific results:

THEOREM 7.13:   For two variables A and C such that A is a parent of C and

$$\left[\frac{\partial \Pr(c_1)}{\partial \Pr(a_i)}\right] = [0]$$

then if for all values a_i of A, $i \neq 1$:

$$\left[\frac{\partial \Pr(c_1)}{\partial \Pr(a_i)} \right] = [0]$$

then the probability of A taking the value a_1 is qualitatively independent of the probability of C taking the value c_1. Otherwise the probability of A taking the value a_1 has an indeterminate relationship with the probability of C taking the value c_1.

and

THEOREM 7.14:   For two variables A and C such that A is a parent of C, beliefs are combined by Dempster's rule, and:

$$\left[\frac{\partial \mathrm{Bel}(c_1)}{\partial \mathrm{Bel}(a_i)} \right] = [0]$$

then if for all $\mathcal{C} \subseteq \mathbf{C}$ such that $c_1 \in \mathcal{C}$:

$$\prod_{y \in \bar{a}_1} \mathrm{Bel}(\mathbf{C} - c_1 | y, x) \, (1 - \mathrm{Bel}(\mathbf{C} - c_1 | a_1, x))$$

$$= \prod_{y \in \bar{a}_1} \mathrm{Bel}(\mathbf{C} - \mathcal{C} | y, x) \, (1 - \mathrm{Bel}(\mathbf{C} - \mathcal{C} | a_1, x))$$

then belief in A taking the value a_1 is qualitatively independent of belief in C taking the value c_1. Otherwise belief in A taking the value a_1 has an indeterminate relationship with belief in C taking the value c_1.

An alternative approach is to re-write Theorems 7.3 and 7.5 to take conditions (7.14) and (7.15) into account so that two values of two variables are independent of one another only if this condition holds. Taking this approach, we would classify all those influences for which $[\partial \mathrm{Val}(c_i)/\partial \mathrm{Val}(a_j)]$ has value $[0]$ but for which $[\partial \mathrm{Val}(a_j)/\partial \mathrm{Val}(c_i)]$ does not have value $[0]$ as being indeterminate. Here this second course is not adopted since it only has the effect of creating more indeterminate influences—it never makes more precise predictions than the first approach and will often (when propagating in a causal direction) make less precise predictions. However, it should be noted that the results from both approaches are always compatible.

It should be noted that Corollary 7.4 and Theorems 7.13, 7.14 and 7.15 ensure that it is possible to reverse any influence. If the influence between c_1 and a_1 is such that c_1 follows, varies inversely, or is independent of a_1, then the result follows directly. If c_1 may follow (respectively, may vary inversely with) a_1 then either c_1 follows or is independent of (respectively, may vary inversely with or is independent of) a_1 and the result is obtained by composing the results from the two alternatives.

This work, however, is not the whole story of evidential propagation. A little reflection on Theorem 7.14 makes it clear that a more general result is possible. This is the following:

THEOREM 7.15:   For two variables A and C such that A is a parent of C, if for all $\mathcal{C} \subseteq \mathbf{C}$ such that $c_1 \in \mathcal{C}$:

$$\prod_{a_i \neq a_1} \mathrm{Bel}(\mathbf{C} - c_1|a_i)\,(1 - \mathrm{Bel}(\mathbf{C} - c_1|a_1)) > \prod_{a_i \neq a_1} \mathrm{Bel}(\mathbf{C} - \mathcal{C}|a_i)\,(1 - \mathrm{Bel}(\mathbf{C} - \mathcal{C}|a_1))$$

then belief in a_1 follows belief in c_1.

Analogous results for the case in which belief in a_1 follows belief in c_1 may be obtained by replacing $>$ with $<$, and results for the cases in which a_1 may follow and may vary inversely with belief in c_1 may be obtained by the appropriate conjunction with Theorem 7.14.

It is also important to realise that additional information about the nature of the conditionals in order to reverse the direction of propagation is only necessary when the variables joined by the links have three or more values. For binary valued variables, results may be obtained directly by examining the relevant conditional probabilities (those of the form $\mathrm{Val}(a_1|c_1, x)$), having established these by application of the relevant version of Bayes' rule. For probability theory this result is:

THEOREM 7.16:   For two variables A, with possible values $\{a_1, a_2\}$, and C, with possible values $\{c_1, c_2\}$, such that A is the parent of C, if the probability of C taking value c_1 follows (respectively, varies inversely with, is qualitatively independent of) the probability of A taking value a_1, then the probability of A taking value a_1 follows (respectively, varies inversely with, is qualitatively independent of) the probability of C taking value c_1.

As before, these results may be composed to obtain similarly symmetric results for the other possible qualitative relationships between the probabilities of the different values of A and C, and the influence reverses in a completely symmetric fashion. This approach also works very nicely for evidence theory, giving the following result:

THEOREM 7.17:   For two variables A, with possible values $\{a_1, a_2\}$, and C, with possible values $\{c_1, c_2\}$, such that A is the parent of C, belief in A taking value a_1 may always follow belief in C taking value c_1.

Thus reversing binary evidential links with Smets' version of Bayes' rule has the effect of making the relationship between the antecedent of the original link and its consequent such that the belief in the antecedent may follow changes in the belief in the consequent. This seems sensible when the forward propagation is carried out using the disjunctive rule. Using the disjunctive rule means that the consequent always follows the antecedent so it is sensible that the antecedent may follow consequent on reversal. However, when Dempster's rule is used the behaviour of this belief function version of Bayes' theorem seems less satisfactory. Using Dempster's rule, it is possible for $Bel(c_1)$ to vary inversely with $Bel(a_1)$ when reasoning predictively. In such a case it would seem odd that $Bel(a_1)$ may follow $Bel(c_1)$ when the link is reversed. Examination of the proof suggests that this behaviour stems from the assumption that all conditional beliefs of the form $Bel(\emptyset|x,y)$ are zero, and it may therefore be worth considering lifting this restriction in later work.

The results in this section have been sufficiently numerous that it is worth restating them briefly. Considering the reversal of influences formalism by formalism gives the following sets of results for influences relating multiple-valued variables.

1. All possibilistic influences may be reversed using Theorem 7.11.

2. All probabilistic influences may be reversed using a combination of Corollary 7.4 and Theorem 7.13.

3. Influences quantified with evidence theory in which values are combined using the disjunctive rule may be reversed using Theorem 7.12.

4. Influences quantified with evidence theory in which values are combined using Dempster's rule may be reversed either using a combination of Corollary 7.4 and Theorem 7.14 or by using a combination of Theorem 7.14 and Theorem 7.15.

5. When only binary valued variables are considered, Theorems 7.16 and 7.17 may be applied to influences quantified with probabilities and beliefs, respectively.

This section began with the aim of developing the theory of qualitative change so that it was possible to establish the behaviour of evidential propagation across a link from the behaviour of the causal propagation across it. This aim has turned out to be elusive—it seems that for probability and evidence theory it is not possible to establish evidential behaviour from causal behaviour when the variables at either end of the link have more than two possible values. However, in all the cases in which it is not possible to give the evidential behaviour of a link directly from the causal behaviour, it is possible to express the evidential behaviour in terms of the conditional values that determine the causal behaviour. Thus, instead of relating the behaviours at the qualitative level it is possible to relate them at the level of the values which determine them and so it is a reasonable assumption that if one may be determined, so may the other.

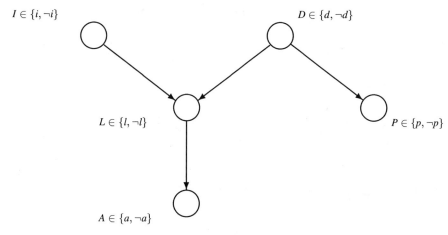

Figure 7.5
The network describing Jack's beliefs about Cody (again)

7.4.2   An example of evidential reasoning

When replying to the letter that led to the example of Section 7.3.3, Jack had reason to be grateful for the results on reversing qualitative influences. For several years he had been encouraging Cody to put down on paper his rambling verses, believing them to be every bit as good as the work of their mutual friend Irwin Garden whose mighty poem "Wail" was making him famous at that time. However, being aware of both the correlation between Cody's writing and drinking and the possibly disastrous effects that Cody's drinking might have upon his family's welfare, Jack was not sure if he should continue his exhortations. Luckily he could answer this question by applying Theorem 7.16 to the model he had already developed and whose underlying network is pictured again in Figure 7.5. Recall that node I represents the variable "ill," L represents the variable "lose job," D represents the variable "drink alcohol," P represents the variable "write poetry" and A represents the variable "adequate income."

When considering the use of probability theory to quantify his beliefs, Jack was able to use Theorem 7.16 to determine that since he was assuming that the probability of the proposition "write poetry" followed the probability of "drinks alcohol", then the probability of the proposition "drinks alcohol" followed the probability of the proposition "write poetry." Thus, were he to encourage Cody to write poetry, and assuming that doing so would might increase the probability that Cody would write poetry (so that

$[\Delta \Pr(p)] = [0, +)$, the change in probability of Cody drinking would be:

$$
\begin{aligned}
[\Delta \Pr(d)] &= \left[\frac{\partial \Pr(d)}{\partial \Pr(p)} \right] \otimes [\Delta \Pr(p)] \\
&= [+] \otimes [+, 0] \\
&= [+, 0]
\end{aligned}
$$

indicating that the probability of Cody drinking might increase. Jack was then able to establish the effect of this possible increase on Cody's income in much the same way as he had done before:

$$
\begin{aligned}
[\Delta \Pr(a)] &= \left[\frac{\partial \Pr(a)}{\partial \Pr(l)} \right] \otimes \left[\frac{\partial \Pr(l)}{\partial \Pr(d)} \right] \otimes [\Delta \Pr(d)] \\
&= [-] \otimes [+] \otimes [+, 0] \\
&= [-, 0]
\end{aligned}
$$

suggesting that Cody's income might fall. This was sufficient to enable Jack to decide that he should not mention poetry in his letter.

Some months later, while talking to Evelyn, Cody's wife, on the telephone, Jack learnt that the family were living in some financial hardship. After the conversation ended, he went back to his model once again in order to see what he could infer from this. Once more he used Theorem 7.16, this time to establish that since the probability of the proposition "adequate income" varies inversely with the probability of the proposition "lose job," the probability of the proposition "lose job" varies inversely with the probability of the proposition "adequate income," and that since probability of the proposition "lose job" may follow the probability of the propositions "ill" and "drink alcohol," then the probability of the both the propositions "drink alcohol" and "ill" may follow the probability of the proposition "lose job." Thus, since he knew that $\Delta \Pr(a) = [-]$, Jack could conclude that both:

$$
\begin{aligned}
[\Delta \Pr(i)] &= \left[\frac{\partial \Pr(i)}{\partial \Pr(l)} \right] \otimes \left[\frac{\partial \Pr(l)}{\partial \Pr(a)} \right] \otimes [\Delta \Pr(a)] \\
&= [+, 0] \otimes [-] \otimes [-] \\
&= [+, 0]
\end{aligned}
$$

and:

$$
\begin{aligned}
[\Delta \Pr(d)] &= \left[\frac{\partial \Pr(d)}{\partial \Pr(l)} \right] \otimes \left[\frac{\partial \Pr(l)}{\partial \Pr(a)} \right] \otimes [\Delta \Pr(a)] \\
&= [+, 0] \otimes [-] \otimes [-]
\end{aligned}
$$

Table 7.3
The probabilities for the gout example

$\Pr(g\|h,s)$	=	0.8			
$\Pr(g\|\neg h,s)$	=	0.6	$\Pr(c\|s,\neg e)$	=	0.7
$\Pr(g\|h,\neg s)$	=	0.6	$\Pr(c\|\neg s,e)$	=	0.3
$\Pr(g\|\neg h,\neg s)$	=	0.2	$\Pr(c\|\neg s,\neg e)$	=	0.3
$\Pr(s\|i)$	=	0.8	$\Pr(l\|c)$	=	0.8
$\Pr(s\|\neg i)$	=	0.1	$\Pr(l\|\neg c)$	=	0.2
$\Pr(a\|g)$	=	0.7			

$$= \quad [+,0]$$

Thus the correct inference from the information that Evelyn gave Jack was that it was now more likely than before that Cody had either been ill or had started drinking.

7.5   Handling incompleteness and integration

As discussed in Chapter 5, the theory of qualitative change provides a means of handling incompleteness. If particular numerical certainty values are missing then, provided that there is enough information to allow the influences that connect them to be established, it is possible to apply the theory as usual. For instance, consider the following example. Half of all measles patients have a fever so $\Pr(fever|measles) = 0.5$. The value of $\Pr(fever|\neg measles)$ is not known, so that it is not possible to propagate values using probability theory. However, because it is known that having measles makes a fever more likely than not having measles, it is possible to deduce that $\Pr(fever|\neg measles) < \Pr(fever|measles)$, and this information is sufficient to apply the theory. In this way, it is possible to handle incompleteness in the example discussed in Section 5.4.2.

7.5.1   An example of handling incompleteness

Recall that the example includes the following medical knowledge. Both alcoholism (S) and hypertension (H) influence the occurrence of gout (G), while alcoholism and hepatitis (E) influence the occurrence of cirrhosis (C). Cirrhosis causes liver failure (L), and gout causes arthritis (A), while alcoholism is caused by a high intake of alcohol (I). Most of the necessary conditional probabilities are available (Table 7.3), so that it is possible to apply Theorem 7.3 to establish that the derivatives relating the various events are as follows.

The probability of gout follows the probability of alcoholism and the probability of

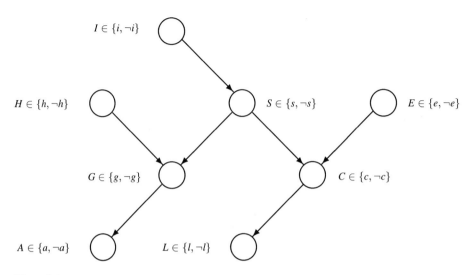

Figure 7.6
The network for the gout example.

hypertension:

$$\frac{\partial \Pr(g)}{\partial \Pr(s)} = [+]$$

$$\frac{\partial \Pr(g)}{\partial \Pr(h)} = [+]$$

the probability of arthritis follows the probability of gout:

$$\frac{\partial \Pr(a)}{\partial \Pr(g)} = [+]$$

the probability of alcoholism follows the probability of high alcohol intake:

$$\frac{\partial \Pr(s)}{\partial \Pr(i)} = [+]$$

and, finally, the probability of liver failure follows the probability of cirrhosis:

$$\frac{\partial \Pr(l)}{\partial \Pr(c)} = [+]$$

In all these cases, the remaining qualitative derivatives relating the variables can be established immediately from Corollary 7.1.

Since the value of $\Pr(c|s,e)$ is unknown, it does not seem initially as though it is possible to determine the qualitative derivatives that relate $\Pr(c)$ to $\Pr(s)$ and $\Pr(e)$. However it is possible to apply the same kind of commonsense argument as for the measles example above to suggest that $\Pr(c|s,e) > \Pr(c|s,\neg e)$ (on the grounds that cirrhosis is more likely to occur if both its causes are present than if just one is present) and then use Theorem 7.3 to obtain:

$$\frac{\partial \Pr(c)}{\partial \Pr(s)} = [+]$$

$$\frac{\partial \Pr(c)}{\partial \Pr(e)} = [+]$$

Again the remaining relevant qualitative derivatives can be determined from Corollary 7.1.

These results may be used to propagate changes in probability stemming from new evidence about the patient's likelihood of having a high intake of alcohol or suffering from hepatitis, to determine the resultant change in their probability of having liver failure. Consider that it is observed that a given patient suffers from hypertension and has a high alcohol intake. Thus $\Delta \Pr(h) = \Delta \Pr(i) = [+]$. This information may be used along with the fact that $\Delta \Pr(e) = [0]$ (since there is no evidence to suggest that the patient is suffering from hepatitis) and the results obtained above, to predict that $\Delta \Pr(s) = [+]$, so that it becomes more likely that the patient is suffering from alcoholism. This, in turn means that $\Delta \Pr(c) = [+]$, $\Delta \Pr(g) = [+]$ so that the patient is more likely to suffer from gout and cirrhosis, and as a result $\Delta \Pr(a) = \Delta \Pr(l) = [+]$. These last changes indicate that the patient should be considered to be more likely to have arthritis and suffer liver failure than before the observations. Clearly it is possible to carry out this kind of reasoning in possibility and evidence theories as well using the results obtained earlier in the chapter.

Because the theory of qualitative change uses so little numerical information, it is possible for it to cope with much more incomplete knowledge than is possible when using numerical formalisms. Indeed, it can cope without having any numerical information at all, so long as there is some knowledge of the relative magnitude of the conditionals. This ability, of course, also means that it can provide a solution to the robustness problem. If the system is moved from the Centre for the Treatment of Gout and Hepatitis to another clinic, the qualitative influences that it employs will be the same despite the different patient population, and so its conclusions will still be valid. This counts as a solution to the robustness problem because the numerical values in Table 7.3 would no longer apply after such a move.

7.5.2   An example of handling integration

It is possible to use the theory of qualitative change to implement integration by change in value, as discussed in Chapter 5. Using the monotonicity assumptions and the principle of degrading together makes it possible to reason in the following way. If the certainty value of hypothesis x, expressed in a given formalism, increases, then the certainty value of x expressed in any other formalism does not decrease. Thus it is possible to translate from one formalism into another. The size of the change in value is unknown, all that is known is the direction of the change. Thus the translation gives quite weak knowledge, and it is knowledge that cannot be used in conventional theories of uncertainty. However, the theory of qualitative change is capable of using this information. In fact knowledge of the direction of changes in value is exactly what the theory manipulates, so that it may be applied equally across any group of formalisms.

Given complete knowledge of the conditional certainty values relating a set of hypotheses, exactly the same values as would be required to propagate the values in probability, possibility, and evidence theories, it is possible to propagate qualitative changes in those formalisms. The conditional values make it possible to establish the qualitative derivatives and these predict how the changes move through the network. Thus it is possible to predict, say, that $\Pr(a)$ increases, $\Pr(b)$ decreases and so does $\Pr(c)$. If belief values relating $\mathrm{Bel}(c)$ to $\mathrm{Bel}(d)$ are known, it is possible to establish the qualitative derivatives that relate the qualitative changes in the two, so that if $\Delta \mathrm{Bel}(c)$ were known it would be possible to establish $\Delta \mathrm{Bel}(d)$. Now, from $\Delta \Pr(c) = [-]$, it is reasonable to assume that $\Delta \mathrm{Bel}(c) = [-]$ or $[0]$, and so $\Delta \mathrm{Bel}(d)$ can be determined. Other translations may be carried out in exactly the same manner.

With this procedure in mind, it is possible to consider how this kind of integration may be performed in practice. Recall the medical example from Section 5.4.2, which concerns trauma and related complaints and is pictured in Figure 7.7. This network encodes the medical information that joint trauma (T) leads to loose knee bodies (K), and that these and arthritis (A) cause pain (P). The incidence of arthritis is influenced by dislocation (D) of the joint in question and by the patient suffering from Sjorgen's syndrome (S). Sjorgen's syndrome affects the incidence of vasculitis (V), and vasculitis leads to vasculitic lesions

Table 7.4
The probabilities for the trauma example

$\Pr(k|t)$	=	0.6	$\Pr(a|d,s)$	=	0.9
$\Pr(k|\neg t)$	=	0.2	$\Pr(a|\neg d,s)$	=	0.6
			$\Pr(a|d,\neg s)$	=	0.6
$\Pr(v|s)$	=	0.1	$\Pr(a|\neg d,\neg s)$	=	0.4
$\Pr(v|\neg s)$	=	0.3			

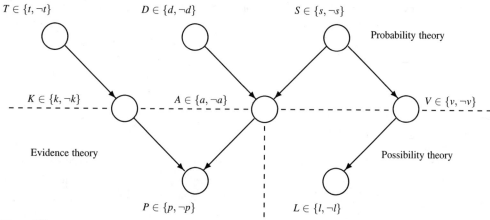

Figure 7.7
The network for the trauma example.

Table 7.5
The possibilities for the trauma example

$\Pi(l\|v)$	=	1	$\Pi(\neg l\|v)$	=	1
$\Pi(l\|\neg v)$	=	0.8	$\Pi(\neg l\|\neg v)$	=	1

Table 7.6
The beliefs for the trauma example

$\mathrm{Bel}(p\|k, a)$	=	0.9	$\mathrm{Bel}(p\|k, a \cup \neg a)$	=	0.7
$\mathrm{Bel}(p \cup \neg p\|k, a)$	=	0.1	$\mathrm{Bel}(p \cup \neg p\|k, a \cup \neg a)$	=	0.3
$\mathrm{Bel}(p\|k, \neg a)$	=	0.7	$\mathrm{Bel}(\neg p\|\neg k, \neg a)$	=	0.5
$\mathrm{Bel}(p \cup \neg p\|k, \neg a)$	=	0.3	$\mathrm{Bel}(p \cup \neg p\|\neg k, \neg a)$	=	0.5
$\mathrm{Bel}(p\|\neg k, a)$	=	0.7	$\mathrm{Bel}(\neg p\|\neg k, a \cup \neg a)$	=	0.4
$\mathrm{Bel}(p \cup \neg p\|\neg k, a)$	=	0.3	$\mathrm{Bel}(p \cup \neg p\|\neg k, a \cup \neg a)$	=	0.6
$\mathrm{Bel}(p\|k \cup \neg k, a)$	=	0.6	$\mathrm{Bel}(\neg p\|k \cup \neg k, \neg a)$	=	0.4
$\mathrm{Bel}(p \cup \neg p\|k \cup \neg k, a)$	=	0.4	$\mathrm{Bel}(p \cup \neg p\|k \cup \neg k, \neg a)$	=	0.6

(L). The strengths of these influences are given as probabilities (Table 7.4), possibilities (Table 7.5), and beliefs (Table 7.6). The effect of these different sets of influences is to partition the network into three parts; a probabilistic part that relates T and K and, separately, D, A, and S; a belief part that relates K, A, and P, and a possibilistic part that relates V and L. Integration by change makes it possible to propagate changes across these different parts of the network to predict how belief in the patient in question being in pain and the possibility that the patient has vasculitic lesions vary when new evidence that she is suffering from Sjorgen's syndrome is obtained. In, particular the change in probability due to the evidence about Sjorgen's syndrome can be propagated through the probabilistic part of the network to find out the change in probability of both arthritis and vasculitis. These changes can then be translated into changes in belief and possibility respectively, and propagated through the relevant parts of the network in order to establish the change in belief in the patient being in pain and the change in possibility of the patient having vasculitic lesions.

From the observation that the patient is suffering from Sjorgen's syndrome, there is an increase in the probability of the disease $\Delta \Pr(s) = [+]$ and, because this is the only observation, the probabilities of the other root nodes of the network do not change so that $\Delta \Pr(t) = [0]$ and $\Delta \Pr(d) = [0]$. Since it is clear from Table 7.1 that there is no qualitative quantity that $[0]$ can be multiplied by in order to give $[+]$ or $[-]$, a change of $[0]$ can never become a change of $[+]$ or $[-]$ and it is possible to ignore changes whose value is $[0]$. Thus the only change that needs to be considered is $\Delta \Pr(s)$. The first step in the propagation is to determine how the change in $\Pr(s)$ affects $\Pr(a)$ and $\Pr(v)$, and this is done by applying Theorem 7.3 to find that:

$$\frac{\partial \Pr(v)}{\partial \Pr(s)} = [-]$$

$$\frac{\partial \Pr(a)}{\partial \Pr(s)} = [+]$$

Once again the remaining derivatives follow from Corollary 7.1.

Combining the derivatives with the information about the known changes in probability gives $\Delta \Pr(a) = [+]$, and $\Delta \Pr(v) = [-]$. From this new information, it is possible to deduce that $\Delta \Pr(\neg a) = [-]$ and $\Delta \Pr(\neg v) = [+]$. To get any further it is necessary to translate from changes in probability to changes in either belief or possibility by using one of the monotonicity assumptions. As a result, because the monotonicity assumptions are all heuristic, any further conclusions are not guaranteed to be correct. However, if at least one of the monotonicity assumptions seems reasonable, then acceptable conclusions may be obtained.

Consider applying the second monotonicity assumption, Assumption 5.3. Using this it is possible to infer that if the probability of a hypothesis increases then both the possibility of that hypothesis and the belief in it do not decrease. Similarly if the probability decreases then the possibility and belief do not increase. Applying that to what is known about $\Pr(a)$ and $\Pr(\neg a)$, it is possible to infer that:

$$\Delta \mathrm{Bel}(a) = [+,0]$$

$$\Delta \mathrm{Bel}(\neg a) = [-,0]$$

$$\Delta \Pi(v) = [-,0]$$

$$\Delta\Pi(\neg v) \quad = \quad [+, 0]$$

Considering the belief part of the network, Theorem 7.5 may be applied to find that:

$$\frac{\partial \text{Bel}(p)}{\partial \text{Bel}(a)} \quad = \quad [+]$$

$$\frac{\partial \text{Bel}(\neg p)}{\partial \text{Bel}(a)} \quad = \quad [-]$$

$$\frac{\partial \text{Bel}(p)}{\partial \text{Bel}(\neg a)} \quad = \quad [0]$$

$$\frac{\partial \text{Bel}(\neg p)}{\partial \text{Bel}(\neg a)} \quad = \quad [+]$$

Combining these derivatives with the result of the translation, it is possible to predict that $\Delta\text{Bel}(p) = [+, 0]$, $\Delta\text{Bel}(\neg p) = [-, 0]$.

Propagating values through the possibilistic part of the network is more complicated. This is because the propagation of possibility values depends upon priors, and there is no information about prior possibility of vasculitis. Now, one solution is to apply the principle of minimum specificity (if, of course, that is acceptable) to do so. In this case, this amounts to assuming that $\Pi(v) = \Pi(\neg v) = 1$, so that both vasculitis and no vasculitis are equally possible. This assumption is embedded in Corollary 7.2 and applying it gives:

$$\frac{\partial \Pi(l)}{\partial \Pi(v)} \quad = \quad [0]$$

$$\frac{\partial \Pi(\neg l)}{\partial \Pi(v)} \quad = \quad [0]$$

$$\frac{\partial \Pi(l)}{\partial \Pi(\neg v)} \quad = \quad [0]$$

$$\frac{\partial \Pi(\neg l)}{\partial \Pi(\neg v)} \quad = \quad [0]$$

and $\Delta\Pi(v) = \Delta\Pi(\neg v) = [0]$. The result of the new evidence is that belief in the patient's pain may increase, while the possibility of the patient having vasculitic lesions is unaffected.

Another approach to ignorance about the prior values is to admit that the prior values are unknown and establish what the qualitative derivatives could be given any prior value using Corollary 7.3. This gives:

$$\frac{\partial \Pi(l)}{\partial \Pi(v)} \quad = \quad [\uparrow]$$

$$\frac{\partial \Pi(\neg l)}{\partial \Pi(v)} \;=\; [\uparrow]$$

$$\frac{\partial \Pi(l)}{\partial \Pi(\neg v)} \;=\; [\uparrow]$$

$$\frac{\partial \Pi(\neg l)}{\partial \Pi(\neg v)} \;=\; [\uparrow]$$

When this is combined with the change in $\Pi(v)$ and $\Pi(\neg v)$ it is clear that $\Delta\Pi(l) = \Delta\Pi(\neg l) = [+, 0]$. Thus the possibility of the patient both having and not having lesions may increase, just as in Chapter 6.

In this way it is possible to use numerical values and qualitative relationships from different uncertainty handling formalisms to reason about the change in the belief of one event given information about the probability of a second event, and can infer whether the possibility of a third event also varies. Thus the theory of qualitative change allows some integration between formalisms. Of course the exact results obtained are influenced by the various assumptions made during the integration. As demonstrated, different results are obtained depending on whether the principle of minimum specificity is accepted or rejected, and different results would be obtained if different monotonicity assumptions were to be employed.

In particular, it is worth mentioning the use of Assumption 5.5—the weakest of the four monotonicity assumptions, and one that it is difficult to argue against. Applying this to the translation of $\Pr(v)$ into $\Pi(v)$ tells gives $\Pi(v) = \Pi(\neg v) = [?]$. This looks initially like vacuous information, but it does turn out to be useful when it is used to find something about L. If it is used in conjunction with the derivatives obtained from Corollary 7.2 it gives the same conclusions as the stronger monotonicity assumption. If is used in conjunction with Corollary 7.3 it leads the conclusion that $\Pi(l) = [+, 0]$ and $\Pi(\neg l) = [+, 0]$, which, in comparison to learning nothing at all about L is reasonably informative. Both of these cases illustrate the blocking that is a characteristic of possibilistic derivatives.

7.6 Summary

This chapter has proposed a new method for qualitative reasoning under uncertainty known as the theory of qualitative change. This method propagates qualitative estimates of changes in values using methods from qualitative physics, in particular the use of qualitative derivatives. Unlike previous methods, the use of qualitative derivatives is equally applicable to all uncertainty handling techniques. All that need be done to find the qualitative relation between two values is to write down the analytical expression relating them and take the derivative of this expression with respect to one of the values. Whereas in qualitative physics the usual preoccupation is taking derivatives of state variables with respect to time, here we are preoccupied with taking derivatives of state variables with respect those variables that influence them. The easy applicability of the method was illustrated by results from the qualitative analysis of propagation through singly-connected networks in each of probability, possibility, and evidence theories. The differences between the behaviours of these theories were discussed at some length, along with details of the causal propagation of values using the method, before an account of evidential propagation was given. The latter concentrated upon establishing the form of evidential propagation from knowledge of the form of causal propagation and, where this was not possible, from the same information that is used to derive the form of causal propagation. Following the results concerning propagation, the theory of qualitative change was used to establish a form of qualitative integration between formalisms. In this integration, numerical and qualitative data expressed in all three formalisms was used to help derive the change in probability of one node in a directed graph from knowledge of a change in the belief in another, related, node. The method of integration was demonstrated upon the example introduced in Chapter 5, and the way that the qualitative analysis may be used to provide a solution to the incompleteness and robustness problems were also discussed. Having provided the basis of the theory, the next step is to extend it to more complex situations, specifically to handle multiply-connected networks, intercausal reasoning, and synergistic relationships.

8 Further results in the theory of qualitative change

Yet who would have thought the old man to have had so much blood in him?

William Shakespeare, *Macbeth*

The results in the previous chapter make it possible to perform both causal and evidential reasoning about qualitative changes in probability, possibility, and belief values in singly-connected networks. These modes of reasoning are sufficient for many problems, but there are also many situations that they cannot handle. The most obvious of these are situations in which networks are multiply-connected. Not only is it desirable to be able to handle such networks from the point of view of completeness, but it is also desirable from the point of view of being able to represent commonly occurring dependencies since (Cooper, 1990):

it appears that large multiply-connected networks are needed for some complex domains, such as medicine.

As a result this chapter extends the theory of qualitative change to multiply-connected networks. These additional results might seem to make the theory of qualitative change broad enough to capture most quantitative models that might be built using probability, possibility and, evidence theories, and so to mark the end of the development of the theory. However, there is more blood than that in this body of work. In particular, there are two areas in which it is desirable to extend the theory in order make it compatible with other qualitative theories. The first of these is in the area of intercausal reasoning, where two common causes of an event effect each other's certainty value when the event is known to occur. Particularly interesting is the case of "explaining away" when an increase in the certainty of one possible value of one cause makes the certainty of one possible value of another decrease. Similar in some ways is the phenomenon of synergy between common causes. In this case it is possible that a change in the certainty of a possible value of one cause will alter the effect of a change in the certainty of a possible value of the other cause, and it is with a consideration of synergy that this chapter opens.

8.1 Synergy

As discussed in Section 4.4.1, in qualitative probabilistic networks (Wellman, 1990b; Druzdzel, 1993), it turns out that just looking at the qualitative influence of one node on another is not sufficient to describe all the possible interactions that may occur between nodes. For instance, consider a node C that is positively influenced by two nodes A and B, which means that as the probabilities of A and B increase, the probability of C taking higher values also increase. If the probabilities of both *A* and *B* taking higher values increase at the same time, the joint effect on the probability of *C* taking higher values may be affected in three ways. It may increase by exactly the sum of the amounts that it would increase by were the changes in *A* and *B* to occur in isolation, or it may increase more or less than this amount. If it increases more, then the increases in *A* and *B* have a positive effect on each other's effect, and in Wellman and Henrion's (1991) terminology (see Section 4.4.1) they have a positive synergistic effect on *C*. If the joint effect is less than the sum of the two individual effects then *A* and *B* are said to have a negative synergistic effect on *C*, and if the joint effect is exactly the sum of the individual effects *A* and *B* are said to have a zero synergistic effect on *C*. When non-zero synergistic effects occur, it may be necessary to take them into account when calculating joint effects since they could effect the result of propagating certain values through a qualitative probabilistic network (in particular in Wellman's work (Wellman, 1990a) they may have an effect on determining dominating decision outcomes).

Now, it seems quite clear that if synergistic relationships are important in qualitative probabilistic networks, it is quite possible for them to both exist and have a noticeable effect on reasoning in the theory of qualitative change. The question is, how should they be investigated? Well, as defined in qualitative probabilistic networks, synergy is a kind of second-order relation—it is a relation between qualitative influences, which are themselves relations between the probabilities of variables. Given that in the theory of qualitative change qualitative influences are determined using derivatives, it seems natural that relations between influences be determined by the relation between derivatives. Differential calculus provides precisely such a mechanism with second derivatives (Stewart, 1991). Given a variable *y*, which is a function of the variables *x* and *z*, the effect of changes in the value of *z* upon the derivative

$$\frac{\partial y}{\partial x}$$

is determined by the second derivative

$$\frac{\partial^2 y}{\partial x \partial z}$$

where this latter is just

$$\frac{\partial y}{\partial x}$$

differentiated with respect to *z*.

Furthermore, since in the theory of qualitative change qualitative influences are defined between the certainty values of individual values of variables rather than over all values of the variables as is the case in qualitative probabilistic networks, it seems natural that synergies be determined by second derivatives of individual values of variables with respect to values of other variables.[1] Thus to determine the form of the synergy that exists between the certainty value of A taking value a_1 and the certainty value of B taking value b_1 upon the certainty value of C taking value c_1 it is necessary to determine the second derivative

$$\frac{\partial^2 \mathrm{Val}(c_1)}{\partial \mathrm{Val}(a_1)\partial \mathrm{Val}(b_1)}$$

which describes the change in

$$\frac{\partial \mathrm{Val}(c_1)}{\partial \mathrm{Val}(a_1)}$$

as $\mathrm{Val}(b_1)$ varies.[2] This leads directly to the definitions of different varieties of synergy in this setting.

DEFINITION 8.1:   There is *strictly positive synergy* between the certainty value of one of the possible values a_1 of variable A and the certainty value of one of the possible values b_1 of variable B with respect to the certainty of value of one of the possible values c_1 of variable C if the certainty value of A taking value a_1 and the certainty value of B taking value b_1 are related to the certainty value of C taking value c_1 such that:

$$\frac{\partial^2 \mathrm{Val}(c_1)}{\partial \mathrm{Val}(a_1)\partial \mathrm{Val}(b_1)} > 0$$

Strictly negative and zero synergy are defined analogously by replacing $>$ with $<$ and $=$ respectively, and it is possible to also define non-strict positive synergy and negative synergy using $\geq$ and $\leq$ respectively.

     With these definitions, it is possible to take the results for causal propagation established in the previous chapter and, by judicious further differentiation, obtain information about the conditions under which synergistic effects take place in the theory of qualitative change. This work is the subject of the next section.

8.1.1   Establishing synergistic relationships

The basic situation in which synergistic effects take place is given in Figure 8.1. Considering only singly-connected networks at this stage, it is quite straightforward to obtain results for networks that are quantified using probabilities. Indeed, the following theorem follows

---

1 Indeed, "product synergy," introduced in Section 4.4.1 is also defined in terms of the individual values of a variable.

2 Exactly this point was independently made by Michelena in his thesis (Michelena, 1991).

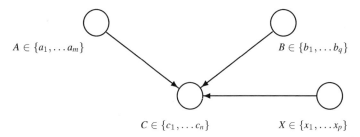

Figure 8.1
A network for synergistic reasoning

almost immediately from previous work:

THEOREM 8.1:   Consider a variable C, with possible values $c_1, \ldots, c_n$, which is part of
a singly connected network. If C has parents A, with possible values $a_1, \ldots, a_m$, B, with
possible values $b_1, \ldots, b_q$, and X, with possible values $x_1, \ldots, x_p$, strictly positive synergy
exists between the probability of a_1 and the probability of b_1 with respect to the probability
of c_1 if, for all other values a_i of A and b_j of B, and all values x of X:

$$\Pr(c_1|a_1, b_1, x) + \Pr(c_1|a_i, b_j, x) > \Pr(c_1|a_1, b_j, x) + \Pr(c_1|a_i, b_1, x)$$

The situations in which there are strictly negative and zero synergies between a_1 and b_1
with respect to c_1 of C are determined analogously, replacing $>$ with $<$ and $=$ respectively,
and the situations in which there are non-strict positive and negative synergies between a_1
and b_1 with respect to c_1 are determined in a similar way, replacing $>$ with $\geq$ and $\leq$
respectively.
    For networks quantified using belief functions there are, as usual, two results. The first
relates to networks in which the propagation of values is carried out using Dempster's rule
of combination:

THEOREM 8.2:   Consider a variable C, with possible values $c_1, \ldots, c_n$, which is part of
a singly connected network. If C has parents A, with possible values $a_1, \ldots, a_m$, B, with
possible values $b_1, \ldots, b_q$, and X, with possible values $x_1, \ldots, x_p$, strictly positive synergy
exists between belief in a_1 and belief in b_1 with respect to belief in c_1 if, for all other values
$\mathbf{a} \subseteq A$, $a_1 \in \mathbf{a}$ and $\mathbf{b} \subseteq B$, $b_1 \in \mathbf{b}$ and all values x:

$$\mathrm{Bel}(c_1|a_1, b_1, x) + \mathrm{Bel}(c_1|\mathbf{a}, \mathbf{b}, x) > \mathrm{Bel}(c_1|a_1, \mathbf{b}, x) + \mathrm{Bel}(c_1|\mathbf{a}, b_1, x)$$

when beliefs are combined using Dempster's rule of combination.

The situations in which there are strictly negative and zero synergies between a_1 and b_1 with respect to c_1 of C are determined analogously, replacing $>$ with $<$ and $=$ respectively, and the situations in which there are non-strict positive and negative synergies between a_1 and b_1 with respect to c_1 are determined in a similar way, replacing $>$ with $\geq$ and $\leq$ respectively.

The second result relates to networks in which propagation is carried out using the disjunctive rule of combination:

THEOREM 8.3: Consider a variable C, with possible values $c_1, \ldots, c_n$, which is part of a singly connected network. If C has parents A, with possible values $a_1, \ldots, a_m$, B, with possible values $b_1, \ldots, b_q$, and X, with possible values $x_1, \ldots, x_p$, strictly positive synergy exists between belief in a_1 and belief in b_1 with respect to belief in c_1 if, for all other values $\mathbf{a} \subseteq A$, $a_1 \in \mathbf{a}$ and $\mathbf{b} \subseteq B$, $b_1 \in \mathbf{b}$ and all values x_i:

$$\prod_{\substack{a \in a_1 \\ b \in b_1 \\ x \in x_i}} \mathrm{Bel}(c_1 | a_i, b_j, x) + \prod_{\substack{a_i \in \mathbf{a} \\ b_j \in \mathbf{b} \\ x \in x_i}} \mathrm{Bel}(c_1 | a_i, b_j, x) >$$

$$\prod_{\substack{a \in a_1 \\ b_j \in \mathbf{b} \\ x \in x_i}} \mathrm{Bel}(c_1 | a, b_j, x) + \prod_{\substack{a_i \in \mathbf{a} \\ b \in b_1 \\ x \in x_i}} \mathrm{Bel}(c_1 | a_i, b_1, x)$$

when beliefs are combined using the disjunctive rule of combination.

The situations in which there are strictly negative and zero synergies between a_1 and b_1 with respect to c_1 of C are determined analogously, replacing $>$ with $<$ and $=$ respectively, and the situations in which there are non-strict positive and negative synergies between a_1 and b_1 with respect to c_1 are determined in a similar way, replacing $>$ with $\geq$ and $\leq$ respectively.

Thus both of the results for evidence theory are, in some sense, a generalisation of the result for probability theory. It is also possible to determine conditions under which synergistic relationships hold in possibility theory. However, as will become apparent, these results will be somewhat easier to obtain if the quest for them is delayed for a while. Instead attention will be turned to how information about synergies may be employed.

Now, a naïve answer to the question of what synergistic relationships might be used for is given by the differential calculus (Stewart, 1991). Calculus dictates that from two first derivatives $\partial y / \partial x$ and $\partial y / \partial z$ and the relevant second derivative $\partial^2 y / \partial x \partial z$, the overall change in y is calculated by:

$$\Delta y = \frac{\partial y}{\partial x} \Delta x + \frac{\partial y}{\partial z} \Delta z + \frac{\partial^2 y}{\partial z \partial x} \Delta z \Delta x + \frac{\partial^2 y}{\partial x \partial z} \Delta x \Delta z$$

the last two terms representing the "corrections" due to the changes in $\partial y/\partial x$ and $\partial y/\partial z$ respectively caused by changes in x and y. Now, it happens to be the case that (Stewart, 1991):

$$\frac{\partial^2 y}{\partial x \partial z} = \frac{\partial^2 y}{\partial z \partial x}$$

Because these two values are the same, the qualitative value of their sum is the same as the qualitative value of either term. In other words:

$$\begin{aligned}
[\Delta y] &= \left[\frac{\partial y}{\partial x}\right] \otimes [\Delta x] \oplus \left[\frac{\partial y}{\partial z}\right] \otimes [\Delta z] \\
&\quad \oplus \left[\frac{\partial^2 y}{\partial z \partial x}\right] \otimes [\Delta z] \otimes [\Delta x] \oplus \left[\frac{\partial^2 y}{\partial x \partial z}\right] \otimes [\Delta x] \otimes [\Delta z] \\
&= \left[\frac{\partial y}{\partial x}\right] \otimes [\Delta x] \oplus \left[\frac{\partial y}{\partial z}\right] \otimes [\Delta z] \oplus \left[\frac{\partial^2 y}{\partial z \partial x}\right] \otimes [\Delta z] \otimes [\Delta x]
\end{aligned}$$

Thus, the qualitative change in the certainty value of the various values of a variable C, which is influenced by variables A and B, is given by:

$$\begin{aligned}
\begin{bmatrix} [\Delta \text{Val}(c_1)] \\ \vdots \\ [\Delta \text{Val}(c_n)] \end{bmatrix} &= \begin{bmatrix} \left[\frac{\partial \text{Val}(c_1)}{\partial \text{Val}(a_i)}\right] \\ \vdots \\ \left[\frac{\partial \text{Val}(c_n)}{\partial \text{Val}(a_i)}\right] \end{bmatrix} \otimes [\Delta \text{Val}(a_i)] \\
&\oplus \begin{bmatrix} \left[\frac{\partial \text{Val}(c_1)}{\partial \text{Val}(b_j)}\right] \\ \vdots \\ \left[\frac{\partial \text{Val}(c_n)}{\partial \text{Val}(b_j)}\right] \end{bmatrix} \otimes [\Delta \text{Val}(b_j)] \\
&\oplus \begin{bmatrix} \left[\frac{d^2 \text{Val}(c_1)}{\partial \text{Val}(a_i)\partial \text{Val}(b_j)}\right] \\ \vdots \\ \left[\frac{d^2 \text{Val}(c_n)}{\partial \text{Val}(a_i)\partial \text{Val}(b_j)}\right] \end{bmatrix} \otimes [\Delta \text{Val}(a_i)] \otimes [\Delta \text{Val}(b_j)]
\end{aligned} \qquad (8.1)$$

This equation is valid when partial derivatives are used. Of course, exactly the same kind of results are possible for separable derivatives and when they are used the change in the certainty values of C is given by:

$$\begin{bmatrix} [\Delta \text{Val}(c_1)] \\ \vdots \\ [\Delta \text{Val}(c_n)] \end{bmatrix} = \begin{bmatrix} \left[\frac{\partial_s \text{Val}(c_1)}{\partial_s \text{Val}(a_1)}\right] & \cdots & \left[\frac{\partial_s \text{Val}(c_1)}{\partial_s \text{Val}(a_m)}\right] \\ \vdots & \ddots & \vdots \\ \left[\frac{\partial_s \text{Val}(c_n)}{\partial_s \text{Val}(a_1)}\right] & \cdots & \left[\frac{\partial_s \text{Val}(c_n)}{\partial_s \text{Val}(a_m)}\right] \end{bmatrix} \otimes \begin{bmatrix} [\Delta \text{Val}(a_1)] \\ \vdots \\ [\Delta \text{Val}(a_n)] \end{bmatrix}$$

$$
\oplus
\begin{bmatrix}
\begin{bmatrix} \dfrac{\partial_s \mathrm{Val}(c_1)}{\partial_s \mathrm{Val}(b_1)} \end{bmatrix} & \cdots & \begin{bmatrix} \dfrac{\partial_s \mathrm{Val}(c_1)}{\partial_s \mathrm{Val}(b_q)} \end{bmatrix} \\
\vdots & \ddots & \vdots \\
\begin{bmatrix} \dfrac{\partial_s \mathrm{Val}(c_n)}{\partial_s \mathrm{Val}(b_1)} \end{bmatrix} & \cdots & \begin{bmatrix} \dfrac{\partial_s \mathrm{Val}(c_n)}{\partial_s \mathrm{Val}(b_q)} \end{bmatrix}
\end{bmatrix}
\otimes
\begin{bmatrix} [\Delta\mathrm{Val}(b_1)] \\ \vdots \\ [\Delta\mathrm{Val}(b_q)] \end{bmatrix}
\tag{8.2}
$$

$$
\oplus
\begin{bmatrix}
\begin{bmatrix} \dfrac{\partial_s{}^2 \mathrm{Val}(c_1)}{\partial_s \mathrm{Val}(a_1)\partial_s \mathrm{Val}(b_1)} \end{bmatrix} & \cdots & \begin{bmatrix} \dfrac{\partial_s{}^2 \mathrm{Val}(c_1)}{\partial_s \mathrm{Val}(a_m)\partial_s \mathrm{Val}(b_q)} \end{bmatrix} \\
\vdots & \ddots & \vdots \\
\begin{bmatrix} \dfrac{\partial_s{}^2 \mathrm{Val}(c_n)}{\partial_s \mathrm{Val}(a_1)\partial_s \mathrm{Val}(b_1)} \end{bmatrix} & \cdots & \begin{bmatrix} \dfrac{\partial_s{}^2 \mathrm{Val}(c_n)}{\partial_s \mathrm{Val}(a_m)\partial_s \mathrm{Val}(b_q)} \end{bmatrix}
\end{bmatrix}
$$

$$
\otimes
\begin{bmatrix} [\Delta\mathrm{Val}(a_1)] \\ \vdots \\ [\Delta\mathrm{Val}(a_m)] \end{bmatrix}
\otimes
\begin{bmatrix} [\Delta\mathrm{Val}(b_1)] \\ \vdots \\ [\Delta\mathrm{Val}(b_q)] \end{bmatrix}
$$

These equations are correct but, as mentioned above, they are also naïve. They are correct because they are just the qualitative versions of the equations given by differential calculus. They are naïve because they are ignoring an important fact about the qualitative first derivatives that requires a little more elaboration.

What the second derivatives do is to provide a correction to the first derivatives. This correction takes account of the fact that, for example, when computing $\partial\mathrm{Val}(c_1)/\partial\mathrm{Val}(a_1)$ it is assumed that changes in $\mathrm{Val}(b_1)$ have no effect. What the correction does is to add in an additional factor that compensates for the effect of the changes in $\mathrm{Val}(b_1)$. In quantitative terms this correction is necessary. In qualitative terms, all this correction does is to point out that if the change in $\mathrm{Val}(b_1)$ tends to make $\partial\mathrm{Val}(c_1)/\partial\mathrm{Val}(a_1)$ smaller, and $\partial\mathrm{Val}(c_1)/\partial\mathrm{Val}(a_1)$ is found to be positive when the change is ignored, then there may come a time when $\partial\mathrm{Val}(c_1)/\partial\mathrm{Val}(a_1)$ is zero or negative. This is quite correct. The reason that it is naïve is that looking at the theorems that determine the value of $\partial\mathrm{Val}(c_1)/\partial\mathrm{Val}(a_1)$ it is clear that if $\partial\mathrm{Val}(c_1)/\partial\mathrm{Val}(a_1)$ is positive, it will be positive whatever the value of $\mathrm{Val}(b_1)$. This is precisely the point of the x in all those theorems—if the synergistic effect could ever make $\partial\mathrm{Val}(c_1)/\partial\mathrm{Val}(a_1)$ negative as well as positive or zero, then the relevant theorem would only give the value of $\partial\mathrm{Val}(c_1)/\partial\mathrm{Val}(a_1)$ as [?]. The fact that the value is given as [+] means that it will always be [+]. This is reason that both the theory of qualitative change and qualitative probabilistic networks (Wellman, 1990b) make no attempt to use synergy to establish how qualitative influences change—instead synergies are propagated in order to find new synergistic relationships (see Section 8.1.2). However, it should be noted that recently Renooij and van der Gaag (1999b) have shown that synergies can be used to resolve ambiguous influences in QPNs.

Having now thought through what synergy is in the theory of qualitative change, it is possible to see what effect synergy will have in possibility theory. It turns out that the effect of synergy in possibility theory is fundamentally different from the effect of synergy in probability and evidence theories. The reason for this is that in possibility theory the way in which changes are propagated from a node A to a node C depends upon the possibility distribution over the values of B where B is any parent of C other than A. For example Theorem 7.4 states that for $\Pi(c_1)$ to follow $\Pi(a_1)$ it is necessary that the following condition holds:

$$\Pi(a_1) < \Pi(c_1|a_1, b), \Pi(b) \tag{8.3}$$

for all values b of B. Thus if the value of $\Pi(b)$ changes, the kind of propagation that takes place between A and C in qualitative terms may also change. In other words, a change in value of $\Pi(b)$ may mean that $\Pi(c_1)$ stops following $\Pi(a_1)$ or even that $\Pi(c_1)$ may start following $\Pi(a_1)$. This is in contrast with probability and evidence theories where, as just discussed, the propagation always stays the same in qualitative terms.

Now that it is established that in possibility theory the effect of synergy is to directly alter the way in which values are propagated, the next thing to consider is how the synergistic effect may be taken into account. This can be done by examining how changes in the value of $\Pi(b)$ may alter the kind of propagation identified by Theorem 7.4. Thus, for example, it is possible to argue that if $\Pi(c_1)$ follows $\Pi(a_1)$ initially so that (8.3) holds and then $\Pi(b)$ increases, there is no synergistic effect because (8.3) will continue to be true no matter how big $\Pi(b)$ becomes. Doing so makes it possible to determine synergistic effects in terms of the changes to the kind of propagation that is possible between A and C. Generalising this argument gives:

THEOREM 8.4:   Consider a variable C, with possible values $c_1, \ldots, c_n$, which is part of a singly connected network. If C has parents A, with possible values $a_1, \ldots, a_m$, B, with possible values $b_1, \ldots, b_q$, and X, with possible values $x_1, \ldots, x_p$, then the following synergistic effects exist between the possibility of a_1 and the possibility of b_1 with respect to the possibility of c_1:

1. If when $\Pi(b_1)$ does not change, $\Pi(c_1)$ follows $\Pi(a_1)$ or may follow $\Pi(a_1)$ up, then when $\Pi(b_1)$ decreases, the relationship between $\Pi(c_1)$ and $\Pi(a_1)$ becomes indeterminate.

2. If when $\Pi(b_1)$ does not change, $\Pi(c_1)$ may follow $\Pi(a_1)$ down, and $\Pi(a_1) \geq \Pi(b_1)$, then when $\Pi(b_1)$ increases, the relationship between $\Pi(c_1)$ and $\Pi(a_1)$ becomes indeterminate.

In all other cases the relationship between $\Pi(c_1)$ and $\Pi(a_1)$ is unchanged by changes in $\Pi(b_1)$.

Thus a lot of the time a change in $\Pi(b_1)$ will have no effect on the relationship between $\Pi(c_1)$ and $\Pi(a_1)$. However, sometimes a change in $\Pi(b_1)$ will make the influence of $\Pi(a_1)$ on $\Pi(c_1)$ indeterminate. It should be noted that these results are pessimistic in that even when $\Pi(b_1)$ changes as described by the theorem, there will not definitely be a change in the relationship between $\Pi(c_1)$ and $\Pi(a_1)$. In other words, the theorem tends towards predicting an indeterminate relationship between A and C if this can possibly be the case. On a more positive note, if anything definite is known about how $\Pi(b_1)$ changes, it is possible to use Theorem 7.4 to determine exactly what the result of the change will be.

However, examination of (8.3) and the other constraints on the propagation of possibility values necessary to arrive at Theorem 8.4 brings another fact to light. If $\Pi(b_1)$ changes in such a way that the relationship between $\Pi(c_1)$ and $\Pi(a_1)$ is altered, then it will be the case that the relationship between $\Pi(c_1)$ and $\Pi(b_1)$ may also be altered. To see why this is the case, consider the following. Assume that initially $\Pi(c_1)$ follows $\Pi(a_1)$ so that (8.3) holds. Now, if $\Pi(b_1)$ decreases so that (8.3) no longer holds it will now be the case that

$$\Pi(b_1) < \Pi(c_1|a_1, b_1), \Pi(a_1)$$

and so it may be the case that the conditions are now set for $\Pi(c_1)$ to follow $\Pi(b_1)$. This matter will be pursued no further here, but a closely related matter will arise later when propagation in multiply-connected networks is considered.

8.1.2   Propagating synergistic relationships

In possibility theory, synergistic relationships between variables have a direct effect on the way in which values are propagated through certainty networks. In probability and evidence theories, however, no such direct effects on propagation occur. Instead, the effects of synergy propagate indirectly. To see what this means, consider Figure 8.2. In the graph, A and B both influence C, which in turn influences D. Consider what happens if value a of A and value b of B have a positive synergistic effect on value c of C and c follows both a and b. If the certainties of both a and b increase then the certainty of c increases, and this increase is greater than if only one of the certainties of a and b had increased. Sometimes it may be useful to know about this synergistic effect (for instance when deciding whether to take actions that increase the certainties of a and b in order to make c more certain) and a natural question is what synergistic effect a and b have on the certainties of various values of D.

As it happens, it is straightforward to determine the synergistic effect of a and b on the values of b given the synergistic effect of a and b on the values of C and the influences between the values of C and the values of D. The way in which this is done is summarised

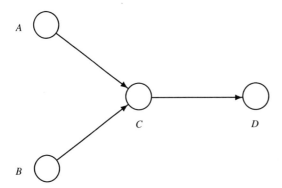

Figure 8.2
Propagating synergistic relationships

by the following result[3]:

THEOREM 8.5:   Consider two variables A and B that are part of a directed graph such that neither is an ancestor of the other. If A and B are both ancestors of a variable C and C has a descendent D then the synergistic effect of $Val(a_1)$ and $Val(b_1)$ on $Val(d_1)$ is the qualitative product of the synergistic effect of $Val(a_1)$ and $Val(b_1)$ on $Val(c_1)$ and the influence of $Val(c_1)$ on $Val(d_1)$.

What this theorem says is very general—from the synergistic effect of any two variables on one of their common descendents it is possible to determine their synergistic effect on any descendent of that descendent. Thus in Figure 8.3 it is possible to take the synergistic effect of $Val(a_1)$ and $Val(b_1)$ on $Val(c_1)$ and use it to compute the synergistic effect of $Val(a_1)$ and $Val(b_1)$ on $Val(d_1)$ as follows:

$$\left[\frac{\partial^2 Val(d_1)}{\partial Val(a_1)\partial Val(b_1)}\right] = \left[\frac{\partial^2 Val(c_1)}{\partial Val(a_1)\partial Val(b_1)}\right] \otimes \left[\frac{\partial Val(d_1)}{\partial Val(c_1)}\right]$$

It is also possible to take the synergistic effect of $Val(a_1)$ and $Val(b_1)$ on $Val(c_1)$ and use it to compute the synergistic effect of $Val(a_1)$ and $Val(b_1)$ on $Val(v_1)$ by taking the synergistic effect of $Val(a_1)$ and $Val(b_1)$ on $Val(c_1)$ and multiplying it by the influence of $Val(c_1)$ on $Val(d_1)$ and the influence of $Val(d_1)$ on $Val(e_1)$ and then the influence of each

---

3 Note that this result and the discussion that follows it depend on the strict use of differential calculus, and so do not apply to networks quantified with possibility values.

$A \in \{a_1, \ldots, a_m\}$

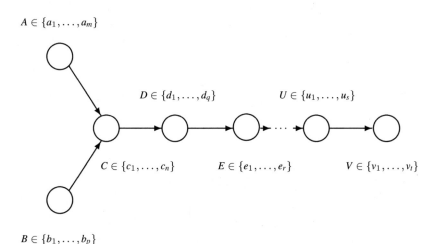

$D \in \{d_1, \ldots, d_q\}$

$U \in \{u_1, \ldots, u_s\}$

$C \in \{c_1, \ldots, c_n\}$

$E \in \{e_1, \ldots, e_r\}$

$V \in \{v_1, \ldots, v_t\}$

$B \in \{b_1, \ldots, b_p\}$

Figure 8.3
More complex synergistic propagation

variable on the next down to V:

$$\left[\frac{\partial^2 \mathrm{Val}(d_1)}{\partial \mathrm{Val}(a_1) \partial \mathrm{Val}(b_1)} \right] = \left[\frac{\partial^2 \mathrm{Val}(c_1)}{\partial \mathrm{Val}(a_1) \partial \mathrm{Val}(b_1)} \right] \otimes \left[\frac{\partial \mathrm{Val}(d_1)}{\partial \mathrm{Val}(c_1)} \right]$$
$$\otimes \left[\frac{\partial \mathrm{Val}(e_1)}{\partial \mathrm{Val}(d_1)} \right] \otimes \ldots \otimes \left[\frac{\partial \mathrm{Val}(v_1)}{\partial \mathrm{Val}(u_1)} \right]$$

In fact it is also possible to use the synergistic effect of any two variables on one of their common descendants to find their synergistic effect on an ancestor of that common descendant. Thus knowing the synergistic effect of $\mathrm{Val}(a_1)$ and $\mathrm{Val}(b_1)$ on $\mathrm{Val}(e_1)$ it is possible to find the synergistic effect of $\mathrm{Val}(a_1)$ and $\mathrm{Val}(b_1)$ on $\mathrm{Val}(d_1)$ by dividing the former by the influence of $\mathrm{Val}(d_1)$ on $\mathrm{Val}(e_1)$. However, such "reverse reasoning" about synergy is only valid in some situations. In Figure 8.3 it is possible to reason backwards from the synergistic effect of $\mathrm{Val}(a_1)$ and $\mathrm{Val}(b_1)$ on $\mathrm{Val}(e_1)$ to find the effect of $\mathrm{Val}(a_1)$ and $\mathrm{Val}(b_1)$ on $\mathrm{Val}(d_1)$ and $\mathrm{Val}(c_1)$, but it is not valid to continue to reason backwards to find the synergistic effect of $\mathrm{Val}(a_1)$ and $\mathrm{Val}(b_1)$ on the values of other parents of C.

8.1.3 An example of the use of synergy

As an example of the use of synergy, consider another couple of scenes from the life and times of our friend Jack Dulouz. This time Jack was staying in his friend Monsanto's cabin down in Big Sur and, feeling rather lonely out in the woods with nobody to talk to, was

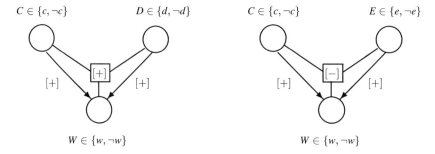

Figure 8.4
Two scenes from the Dulouz legend—planning invitations to Monsanto's cabin

planning to invite some of his friends down for the weekend. Having planned a number of disastrous parties in the past, Jack was paying attention to the possible interactions between his proposed guests, and, as he had done before, was using the theory of qualitative change to build models of what might happen. His first thought was that he should invite his old buddy Cody down, and his second that Dave Wain should come as well. He knew that the more likely it was that Cody came, the more likely it was that he would enjoy the weekend, and the more likely that Dave was to come, the more likely he was to enjoy the weekend. Thus his graphical model of the situation included positive influences between nodes representing Cody's and Dave's presence, and the node representing the quality of the weekend. Then Jack pondered the question of synergy. Using the variable W, with possible values w and $\neg w$, for the proposition "the weekend is good," the variable C, with possible values c and $\neg c$, for the proposition "Cody comes" and the variable D, with possible values d and $\neg d$, for the proposition "Dave comes," Jack assessed that, for all other values x of all other variables that might bear on the quality of the weekend,

$$\Pr(w|c,d,x) + \Pr(w|\neg c, \neg d, x) > \Pr(w|\neg c, d, x) + \Pr(w|c, \neg d, x)$$

so that $\Pr(c)$ and $\Pr(d)$ would have a positive synergistic effect on one another with respect to w. Thus Jack's overall model of that fragment of his beliefs is summarised by the left-hand graph in Figure 8.4. The $[+]$ signs on the influences represent the relationships between $\Pr(c)$ and $\Pr(w)$ and between $\Pr(d)$ and $\Pr(w)$ while the $[+]$ in the box represents the synergistic influence of $\Pr(c)$ and $\Pr(d)$ on each other with respect to $\Pr(w)$ (this notation is borrowed from Wellman (1990b)). Other influences are omitted in the interests of clarity. When used in conjunction with the information that both Dave and Cody could come for the weekend, this told Jack that it was more likely that the party will be good than if he knew that just one of the two could come.

Another person whom Jack was considering inviting is Cody's wife Evelyn. Jack and Evelyn were very close, so her presence on her own would definitely have a positive influence on the party. However, Jack was worried about the effect of inviting both Cody and Evelyn. In his experience, what tended to happen when Cody and Evelyn got together with Jack's other friends is that Cody's usual extrovert behaviour was rather reduced because he was afraid of upsetting Evelyn (because she is rather embarrassed by it), and Evelyn's usual happy demeanour was upset because of her embarrassment (which is unabated by Cody's attempts to calm down) over Cody's loud behaviour. Since Jack enjoyed Cody's outbursts, he felt that the interaction between Cody and Evelyn would have a negatively synergistic effect upon the weekend, and so modelled the situation with the right-hand network of Figure 8.4 where variable E represents the proposition "Evelyn comes." Using this information, Jack made predictions based upon both Cody and Evelyn coming, finding that, together they make the weekend less likely to be good than if either came on their own. However, despite this information, Jack decided to invite both Cody and Evelyn.

Later, while sitting on the beach reflecting about life, Zen, and the theory of qualitative change, Jack realised that this example also highlights a limitation of the representation of synergy in the theory of qualitative change. Because of the symmetry of the probabilistic synergy relation as expressed in the theory of qualitative change, it is not possible for $\Pr(a)$ to have a positive synergistic effect on $\Pr(b)$ with respect to c and for $\Pr(b)$ to have a negative synergistic effect on $\Pr(a)$ with respect to c. Thus, to take a variation on the second of the two scenes above, consider a situation in which Evelyn's presence is likely to have a negative effect on Cody's propensity to contribute to the atmosphere of the weekend as before, but Cody's presence is likely to improve Evelyn's mood (because she is less likely to worry about him running off with other women while she is able to keep an eye on him) and so she is likely to contribute more to the weekend than if she were invited on her own. Such a scenario can only be represented using probabilistic synergy by giving both synergistic relationships a value of [?]. This is not incorrect, since any synergistic relationship could be represented using a value of [?]. It is, however, rather uninformative since it does not allow any definite conclusions to be drawn about the synergistic effect of either Evelyn or Cody coming for the weekend on their own.

Scratching qualitative certainty networks in the sand, Jack also considered extending his model of the forthcoming weekend to include some additional information. In particular he sketched the network of Figure 8.5 where the variable H represents the proposition "Jack is happy" and the variable N represents the proposition "Jack makes good progress on his novel." Now, Jack believed that having a good weekend would have a positive influence on his happiness so that the probability of h follows the probability of w, and also believed that if he is happy he will make good progress on his novel in the days following the weekend,

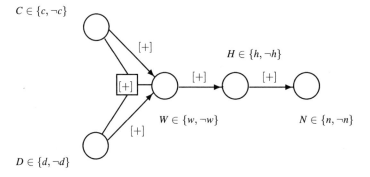

Figure 8.5
How the weekend will affect the next great American novel

so that the probability of n follows the probability of h. He was therefore able to calculate the synergistic effect of $\Pr(d)$ and $\Pr(c)$ on $\Pr(h)$ as follows:

$$\frac{\partial^2 \Pr(n)}{\partial \Pr(c)\partial \Pr(d)} = \frac{\partial^2 \Pr(w)}{\partial \Pr(c)\partial \Pr(d)} \otimes \frac{\partial \Pr(h)}{\partial \Pr(w)} \otimes \frac{\partial \Pr(n)}{\partial \Pr(h)}$$

$$= [+] \otimes [+] \otimes [+]$$

Thus the synergistic effect of $\Pr(d)$ and $\Pr(c)$ on $\Pr(n)$ is positive, and Cody and Dave coming for the weekend makes it more likely that Jack will make good progress on his novel than if either of them came alone.

8.2   Propagation in multiply-connected networks

As presented so far, all of the theory of qualitative change is only applicable to singly-connected networks. Thus the results only relate to the propagation of values through networks in which the certainties of the various values of the parents of a node are conditionally independent (however conditional independence is expressed for that formalism) if the value taken by the node is not known. As mentioned above, this rather restricts the situations in which the theory may be applied and it is therefore interesting to try and extend the theory to multiply-connected networks.

8.2.1   Extending propagation

The theory expounded so far has three main parts—causal propagation, evidential propagation, and synergy—each of which must be re-evaluated in the context of multiply-connected networks. At first sight this appears to be a great deal of work. It turns out, however, that this re-evaluation is relatively easy for probability and possibility theories and impossible for evidence theory, so the amount of work involved is not that large.

The crucial difference in both probability and possibility theories is that the joint certainty value of the parents is no longer a simple function of the certainty values of the parents. This has the following effect. Consider the familiar situation of a node C that has parents A and X. Whereas in a singly-connected network the joint probability of values a of A and x of X is $\Pr(a)\Pr(x)$, in a multiply-connected network it will be $\Pr(x|a)\Pr(a)$. $\Pr(x|a)$ will be equal to $\Pr(x)$ if there is no path connecting X and A except that through C, and otherwise will summarise the conditional probabilities of the links that join X and A. Similarly, the joint possibility of values a of A and x of X is $\min(\Pi(a),\Pi(x))$ in a singly-connected network and $\min(\Pi(x|a),\Pi(a))$ in a multiply-connected network where $\Pi(x|a) = \Pi(x)$ if the only path between X and A is through C. Thus the only new results that must be sought are those for the situation in which there are two or more paths between A and X (including that through C), and the only change in the method of obtaining the results is to substitute $\Pr(x|a)\Pr(a)$ for $\Pr(a)\Pr(x)$ and $\min(\Pi(x|a),\Pi(a))$ for $\min(\Pi(a),\Pi(x))$.

Armed with this information it is possible to obtain results for causal propagation in multiply-connected networks, or, more accurately any kind of network since the results given apply to both singly and multiply-connected nets. Firstly, consider networks in which the influences are expressed using probability values. Such networks yield the following results:

THEOREM 8.6:   For a variable C, with possible values $c_1, \ldots, c_n$, with parents A, with possible values $a_1, \ldots, a_m$, and X, which has possible values $x_1, \ldots, x_p$, the probability of C taking value c_1 follows the probability of A taking value a_1, if, for all other values a_i of A and all values x of X:

$$\Pr(c_1|a_1, x) > \Pr(c_1|a_i, x)$$

The situations in which the probability of C taking value c_1 varies inversely with, and is qualitatively independent of the probability of A taking value a_1 are defined analogously, replacing $>$ with $<$ and $=$ respectively, and the situations in which the probability of C taking value c_1 may follow or may vary inversely with the probability of A taking value a_1 are also defined in a similar way, replacing $>$ with $\geq$ and $\leq$ respectively.

The constraint on the conditional probabilities in this theorem is exactly the same as the constraint for singly-connected networks given in the previous chapter. Thus the qualitative propagation of probability values happens under exactly the same conditions in singly-connected and multiply-connected networks. The reason for this is, broadly speaking, the following. When the probability of a_1 changes, it may influence the probability of c_1 in two ways. The first is directly through the connection between A and C. The other is indirectly through the possible trails from A to X that do not pass through C. What the theory of qualitative change inherits from the differential calculus is the ability to consider these two influences independently, relying on the principle of superposition (Stewart, 1991) embodied in 7.6 to ensure that both are taken into account. This allows the influence of A on C to be calculated as the sum of the direct and indirect influence. Since the indirect influence, if any, will be transmitted to C via X it can be safely ignored. If there is a trail from A to X that does not go through C then when the probability of a_1 changes this change will propagate to X and hence on to C. The effect this has on C will then be taken account of when computing how X affects C and including it in the effect of A on C would be counting it twice. So only the direct effect need be considered, and this is exactly the same as in the singly-connected case. With a little thought the reason why the result should be the same emerges. If $\Pr(c_1|a_1, x) > \Pr(c_1|a_i, x)$ for all x, the condition holds whatever the state of any other parents of C are. Thus it does not matter whether X is affected by A or not, the effect of A on C will be the same, which is that c_1 follows a_1.

There are two important points to make about this result. The first is that since the result hinges on the fact that any indirect influence of A on C will be taken care of when the direct influence of X on C is computed, it is necessary to make sure that all possible influences on C are considered when calculating the change at C. This is in contrast to the case for singly-connected networks, a point that is explored in more detail in Section 9.3.3. The second important point is that, examining the proof in detail, it is clear that the condition given as controlling the influence between a_1 and c_1 is actually stronger than strictly necessary. In both the singly and multiply-connected cases, the precise value that determines how values are propagated is:

$$\left[\Pr(c_1|a_1) - \begin{array}{c}\max\\\min\end{array}_{i=2...n} \Pr(c_1|a_i)\right] \tag{8.4}$$

Using this to determine the derivatives will result in distinct $[+]$ and $[-]$ values in situations in which the stated result gives $[?]$. So why use the stated results rather than (8.4)? The reasons for this are rather subtle, and for a while escaped me completely. Indeed in earlier versions of this work (for example (Parsons and Mamdani, 1993)) the condition in (8.4) was the one used. However, the big disadvantage of using results based upon conditionals like $\Pr(c_1|a_1)$ is that the values of these latter conditionals change—in the situation we have here, $\Pr(c_1|a_1)$ changes in value as the probability distribution over X changes. Such values are thus an artifact of a particular state of the world, and as a result a particular influence might change value as the probability distribution over X changes. In contrast, values such as $\Pr(c_1|a_1, x_1)$, where all the parents of C are to the right of the conditional bar, are constant. The values define the relationship between the variables. As a result it is more realistic to expect to be able to say whether the relationships in the given theorems hold, although it would be possible to use results based on (8.4) with the added proviso that they have to hold "for all probability distributions across the other parents of C."[4] The results as stated also have the advantage of being close to those in qualitative probabilistic networks.

Given the proof of the previous result, it is very easy to establish what separable relationships are possible between two nodes, and again it turns out that for probability theory these are unaffected by the move from singly-connected networks to multiply-connected ones:

THEOREM 8.7:   For a variable C, with possible values $c_1, \ldots, c_n$, with parents A, which possible values $a_1, \ldots, a_m$, and X, which has possible values $x_1, \ldots, x_p$ the probability of C taking value c_1 may always separably follow the probability of A taking value a_1.

Of course, showing that the propagation of qualitative changes is largely unaffected by the move from singly-connected to multiply-connected networks is a very different thing from saying that the way actual changes in value are propagated is unaffected. The actual changes will be affected. As discussed in the section on synergy, the size of the change in probability of a node C that is caused by the change in probability of one of its parents A will be affected by any change in probability of another parent B. In a network in which A and B are only connected through C, the probability of any value a_i of A can change without the probability of any value b_j of B also changing. In a network in which A and B are multiply-connected and one of the connections is causally directed,[5] change in the probability of a_i will always lead to a change in the probability of b_j. Thus it is not possible for the probability of a_i to change without the probability of b_j changing. In such a network the actual change in the probability of any value c_k of C will never be unaffected by the fact that the network is multiply-connected, and it is the need to take this fact into account that makes the exact calculation of probabilities in multiply-connected networks so complex.[6] However, once again the fact that the theory of qualitative change only deals with the direction of changes, not their size, finesses any problem. The fact that the effect of the probability of a_i on that of c_k is defined so that it is not sensitive to the probability of b_j means that whatever happens to B does not make any qualitative difference, and because

---

4 Though one can also imagine systems in which the influences were taken to hold for specific values of C, along the lines of the context specific influences of (Renooij et al., 2001).

5 In other words it is possible to get from A to B following the links in the direction in which they point.

6 Though, as mentioned in Section 3.4.1, methods originally intended for singly-connected networks can give good results on multiply-connected networks.

only qualitative differences are important within the theory, any quantitative differences are ignored.

Turning to networks in which the influences are quantified with possibility values, things become slightly more complicated. The problem stems from the fact that $\Pi(c_1)$ is only influenced by changes in the possibility of a_1 if it is not influenced by changes in possibility of any value of X. Since the possibility of the values of X may themselves be affected by changes in the possibility of a_1, it is not possible to separate out the direct and indirect influences in the same way as in probability theory. The net result is that the effect of changes in $\Pi(a_1)$ on $\Pi(c_1)$ depend upon conditional values such as $\Pi(x_j|a_1)$:

THEOREM 8.8:   For a node C, with possible values $c_1, \ldots, c_n$, which has parents A, with possible values $a_1, \ldots, a_m$, and X, with possible values $x_1, \ldots, x_p$.

1. The possibility of C taking value c_1 follows the possibility of A taking value a_1 if, for some value x_j of X and all other values a_i of A and x_k of X:

$$\Pi(a_1) \quad < \quad \Pi(c_1|a_1,x_j), \Pi(x_j|a_1)$$
$$\Pi(c_1,a_1,x_j) \quad > \quad \Pi(c_1,a_i,x_k)$$

2. The possibility of C taking value c_1 may follow the possibility of A taking value a_1 up if, for some value x_j of X and all other values a_i of A and x_k of X:

$$\Pi(a_1) \quad < \quad \Pi(c_1|a_1,x_j), \Pi(x_j|a_1)$$
$$\Pi(c_1,a_1,x_j) \quad \leq \quad \Pi(c_1,a_i,x_k)$$

3. The possibility of C taking value c_1 may follow the possibility of A taking value a_1 down if, for some value x_j of X and all other values a_i of A and x_k of X:

$$\Pi(a_1) \quad \geq \quad \Pi(c_1|a_1,x_j)$$
$$\Pi(c_1,a_1,x_j) \quad > \quad \Pi(c_1,a_i,x_k)$$

or

$$\Pi(a_1) \quad \geq \quad \Pi(x_j|a_1)$$
$$\Pi(c_1,a_1,x_j) \quad > \quad \Pi(c_1,a_i,x_k)$$

Otherwise the possibility of C taking value c_1 is qualitatively independent of the possibility of A taking value a_1.

The fact that the conditions for propagation depend upon conditional possibilities such as $\Pi(x_j|a_1)$ initially makes it difficult to see how the form of propagation can be determined unless a full set of numerical possibilities are available so that the necessary conditional values can be calculated. However, as in the singly-connected case, the theorem has an important corollary that makes it possible to determine the behaviour of the influence between a_1 and c_1 when there is no information about $\Pi(a_1)$ and $\Pi(x_j|a_1)$ provided that it is thought reasonable to assume that such prior values are 1 as suggested by the principle of minimum specificity. This result is:

COROLLARY 8.1: For a node C, with possible values $c_1, \ldots, c_n$, which has parents A, with possible values $a_1, \ldots, a_m$, and X, which has possible values $x_1, \ldots, x_p$, if nothing is known about the prior distributions over A and X, then applying the principle of minimum specificity means that the possibility of C taking value c_1 may follow the possibility of A taking value a_1 down if, for some value x_j of X and all other values a_i of A and x_k of X:

$$\Pi(c_1|a_1, x) > \Pi(c_1|a_i, x)$$

Otherwise the possibility of C taking value c_1 is qualitatively independent of the possibility of A taking value a_1.

This second result is exactly the same as Corollary 7.2—the corresponding result for the singly-connected case—and it is also possible to obtain a result just like that of Corollary 7.3:

COROLLARY 8.2: Consider a variable C, with possible values $c_1, \ldots, c_n$, which has parents A, with possible values $a_1, \ldots, a_m$, and X, with possible values $x_1, \ldots, x_p$. If nothing is known about the prior distributions over A and X, then the possibility of C taking value c_1 may always follow the possibility of A taking value a_1 up, and may follow the possibility of A taking value a_1 down if, for some value x_j of X and all other values a_i of A and x_k of X:

$$\Pi(c_1|a_1, x_j) > \Pi(c_1|a_i, x_k)$$

These two results will, as discussed in Chapter 7, be of more general use than the theorem that gave rise to them.

At this point it would be appropriate to consider the propagation of belief values in multiply-connected networks. Unfortunately, as noted in Section 3.4.1, it is not possible to extend the theory of qualitative change to multiply-connected networks quantified with belief functions. This is not so much a problem with the theory of qualitative change, as a problem with evidence theory. At the moment establishing the correct method to construct the joint mass assignment over the values of a pair of variables that are not conditionally cognitively independent is an open problem. Once it has been solved then it may be possible to extend the theory of qualitative change to cover multiply-connected networks quantified with belief functions, but until this problem has been solved it is quite impossible to extend the theory. Of course, as Xu and Smets (1991) point out, if the topology of the network can be altered to remove the loops (by merging several variables into one by building the appropriate joint distribution over the cross-product of their possible values) then evidence theory may be applied to the situation and the theory of qualitative change used as before.

Instead, the obvious next step is to look at evidential propagation. Now, thinking about the results in the previous chapter, it becomes obvious that evidential propagation is unaffected by the move from singly-connected to multiply-connected networks. The reason for this is essentially as follows. The main results for evidential propagation given in Chapter 7 are based only upon the results for causal propagation, so they do not depend upon the fact that in singly-connected networks $\Pr(a, c) = \Pr(a) \Pr(x)$ and $\Pi(a, c) = \min(\Pi(a), \Pi(c))$. Since causal propagation occurs under exactly the same conditions in multiply-connected networks as it does in singly-connected networks, it follows that evidential propagation will occur under exactly the same conditions in multiply-connected networks as it does in singly-connected networks. To make this clear it is worth stating the following results. Firstly, consider probability theory. Here there are three results, the first for qualitative derivatives with values $[+]$ and $[-]$:

THEOREM 8.9:   For two variables A and C such that A is a parent of C, if the probability of C taking the value c_1 follows (respectively, varies inversely with) the probability of A taking the value a_1, then the probability of A taking value a_1 follows (respectively, varies inversely with) the probability of C taking value c_1.

The second result takes care of qualitative derivatives with value $[0]$:

THEOREM 8.10:   For two variables A and C such that A is a parent of C and:

$$\left[\frac{\partial \Pr(c_1)}{\partial \Pr(a_i)} \right] = [0]$$

if for all values a_i of A, $i \neq 1$:

$$\left[\frac{\partial \Pr(c_1)}{\partial \Pr(a_i)} \right] = [0]$$

then the probability of A taking the value a_1 is qualitatively independent of the probability of C taking the value c_1. Otherwise the probability of A taking the value a_1 has an indeterminate relationship with the probability of C taking the value c_1.

Together Theorems 8.9 and 8.10 are sufficient to permit evidential reasoning in probabilistic qualitative certainty networks. However, the second result is obtained at the cost of additional conditions over and above those on causal propagation. When only binary variables are concerned, it is possible to handle evidential propagation without the additional conditions even when the derivative relating two values has qualitative value $[0]$.

THEOREM 8.11:   For two variables A, with possible values $\{a_1, a_2\}$, and C, with possible values $\{c_1, c_2\}$, such that A is the parent of C, if the probability of C taking value c_1 follows (respectively, varies inversely with, is qualitatively independent of) the probability of A taking value a_1, then the probability of A taking value a_1 follows (respectively, varies inversely with, is qualitatively independent of) the probability of C taking value c_1.

In contrast with probability theory, possibility theory only requires a single result in order to enable evidential propagation:

THEOREM 8.12:   For two variables A and C such that A is a parent of C:

1. If the possibility of C taking the value c_1 follows the possibility of A taking the value a_1, then the possibility of A taking the value a_1 may follow the possibility of C taking the value c_1.
2. If the possibility of C taking the value c_1 may follow the possibility of A taking the value a_1 up, then the possibility of A taking the value a_1 may follow the possibility of C taking the value c_1 down.
3. If the possibility of C taking the value c_1 may follow the possibility of A taking the value a_1 down, then the possibility of A taking the value a_1 may follow the possibility of C taking the value c_1 up.
4. If the possibility of a variable C taking the value c_1 is qualitatively independent of the possibility of a variable A taking the value a_1, then the possibility of A taking the value a_1 may follow the possibility of C taking the value c_1.

Having extended causal and evidential propagation to the multiply-connected case, it makes sense to consider under what conditions the other form of qualitative interaction, synergy, takes place in multiply-connected networks. However, there is a problem. This is because that idea of synergy was based on calculating the correction necessary because the effect of one parent on the other was ignored when calculating the effect of one parent on the child. In other words, synergy captures the fact that the effects of parents on children differs depending on whether certainty values of parents vary alone or together. If one parent is an ancestor of another, then they cannot vary independently and so there is no synergy between them in the sense introduced in Section 8.1. As a result there are no general results for multiply-connected networks. For two nodes that have only one trail between them, the following result, which is a minor generalisation of Theorem 8.1, holds:

THEOREM 8.13:   Consider a variable C, with possible values $c_1, \ldots, c_n$, which has parents A, with possible values $a_1, \ldots, a_m$, B, with possible values $b_1, \ldots, b_q$, and X, with possible values $x_1, \ldots, x_p$. If the only trail between A and B passes through C, then strictly positive synergy exists between the probability of a_1 and the probability of b_1 with respect to the probability of c_1 if, for all other values a_i of A and b_j of B and all values x:

$$\Pr(c_1|a_1,b_1,x) + \Pr(c_1|a_i,b_j,x) > \Pr(c_1|a_1,b_j,x) + \Pr(c_1|a_i,b_1,x)$$

The situations in which there are strictly negative and zero synergies between a_1 and b_1 with respect to c_1 of C are determined analogously, replacing $>$ with $<$ and $=$ respectively, and the situations in which there are non-strict positive and negative synergies between a_1 and b_1 with respect to c_1 are determined in a similar way, replacing $>$ with $\geq$ and $\leq$ respectively.

Something similar can be shown for possibilistic networks:

THEOREM 8.14:   Consider a variable C, with possible values $c_1, \ldots, c_n$, which has parents A, with possible values $a_1, \ldots, a_m$, B, with possible values $b_1, \ldots, b_q$, and X, with possible values $x_1, \ldots, x_p$. If the only trail between A and B passes through C, then the following synergistic effects exist between the possibility of a_1 and the possibility of b_1 with respect to the possibility of c_1:

1. If when $\Pi(b_1)$ does not change, $\Pi(c_1)$ follows $\Pi(a_1)$ or may follow $\Pi(a_1)$ up, then when $\Pi(b_1)$ decreases, the relationship between $\Pi(c_1)$ and $\Pi(a_1)$ becomes indeterminate.
2. If when $\Pi(b_1)$ does not change, $\Pi(c_1)$ may follow $\Pi(a_1)$ down, and $\Pi(a_1) \geq \Pi(b_1)$ then when $\Pi(b_1)$ increases, the relationship between $\Pi(c_1)$ and $\Pi(a_1)$ becomes indeterminate.

In all other cases the relationship between $\Pi(c_1)$ and $\Pi(a_1)$ is unchanged by changes in $\Pi(b_1)$.

Now, if there is more than one trail between the parents, then there is no synergy between

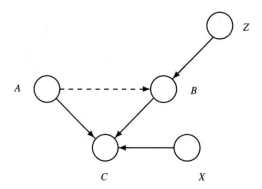

Figure 8.6
A multiply-connected network in which synergistic effects are possible

them in the sense defined in Section 8.1. However, this does not mean that the form of synergy captured by the theory of qualitative change only features in singly-connected sub-graphs of multiply-connected networks. Consider that B has a parent Z such that the only trails between Z and A pass through B. This situation is depicted in Figure 8.6 with the dashed arc indicating the trail between A and B. Here, because Z can vary independently of A, there may be synergistic effects between values of Z and A with respect to values of B and C.

This completes the work necessary to use the theory of qualitative change for probability and possibility theories in multiply-connected networks.

8.2.2   Belief change in sets of propositions

It might not be possible to build multiply-connected networks using evidence theory, making the theory seem less expressive than probability or possibility, but it is possible to build networks that cannot easily be built using probability and possibility theory. Such networks are those in which influences exist between disjunctions of values of variables, as when it is necessary to say express the fact that if it becomes more certain that A has value a_1 or a_2 then it becomes more certain that C has value c_1 or c_2 or c_5. The discussion of the application of the theory of qualitative change to networks quantified with belief functions has not as yet dealt this matter, having instead stressed the fact that it has only been concerned with the influences that hold between individual values of a variable. This was done in order to make the comparison with probability and possibility theories clear, and is rather at odds with the fact that evidence theory is typically used to reason about sets of values of variables. Indeed, it turns out to be perfectly possible to perform a qualitative analysis of the changes in belief of sets of values of variables, and this is the subject of this section.

When considering such changes, there are six obvious situations that must be considered. For a variable C, which has a parent A, these situations are those in which the influences that are investigated are that between a set of values of C and a single value of A, that between a single value of C and a set of values of A, and that between a set of values of C and a set of values of A where in each case, the results need to be specified both for combination by Dempster's rule of combination and for combination using the disjunctive rule. The first of these pairs of results is extremely straightforward to determine. Indeed, they follow quickly from the proofs of Theorems 7.5 and 7.6. The first result concerns the use of Dempster's rule, and is as follows:

THEOREM 8.15:   For a node C, with possible values $\{c_1, \ldots, c_n\}$, and parents A, with possible values $\{a_1, \ldots, a_m\}$, and X, with possible values $\{x_1, \ldots, x_p\}$, belief in C taking a set of values $\mathbf{c} \subseteq \{c_1, \ldots, c_n\}$ follows belief in A taking value a_1 if, for all other values $\mathbf{a} \subseteq A$, $a_1 \in \mathbf{a}$ and all values x of X:

$$\mathrm{Bel}(\mathbf{c}|a_1, x) > \mathrm{Bel}(\mathbf{c}|\mathbf{a}, x)$$

when beliefs are combined using Dempster's rule of combination.

The situations in which belief in C taking a set of values $\mathbf{c} \subseteq \{c_1, \ldots, c_n\}$ varies inversely with and is qualitatively independent of belief in A taking value a_1 are defined analogously, replacing $>$ with $<$ and $=$ respectively, and the situations in which belief in C taking a set of values $\mathbf{c} \subseteq \{c_1, \ldots, c_n\}$ may follow and may vary inversely with belief in A taking value a_1 are also similarly defined by replacing $>$ with $\geq$ and $\leq$ respectively. If none of these relations hold, then the belief in C taking a set of values $\mathbf{c} \subseteq \{c_1, \ldots, c_n\}$ is indeterminate with respect to belief in A taking value a_1.

The second of the pair of results concerns the use of the disjunctive rule of combination, and takes a similar form:

THEOREM 8.16:   For a node C, with possible values $\{c_1, \ldots, c_n\}$, and parents A, with possible values $\{a_1, \ldots, a_m\}$, and X, with possible values $\{x_1, \ldots, x_p\}$, belief in C taking a set of values $\mathbf{c} \subseteq \{c_1, \ldots, c_n\}$ may always follow belief in A taking value a_1 when beliefs are combined using the disjunctive rule of combination.

These results are so easy to obtain, essentially, because the only additional factors that need to be taken into account are the changes in belief in the subsets of $\mathbf{c}$, and these can be simply obtained in exactly the same way as the changes in belief in the individual members of the sets. However, things get slightly more complicated when changes with respect to sets of values of A are considered. The problem is that the the basis on which the previous results about belief functions were determined was that belief in the possible value a of A was simply the mass assigned to it. This is fine for singleton values of A, but is not true for sets of values of A. Instead, it is necessary to first determine how the mass assigned to such sets of values changes and then use this to determine the beliefs. However, despite this complication, reasonably simple results may be obtained to relate changes in sets of values of A to single values of C. The first such result is that obtained when Dempster's rule of combination is used:

THEOREM 8.17: For a node C, with possible values $\{c_1, \ldots, c_n\}$, and parents A, with possible values $\{a_1, \ldots, a_m\}$, and X, with possible values $\{x_1, \ldots, x_p\}$, belief in C taking value c_1 follows belief in A taking a set of values $\mathbf{a} \subseteq A$ if, for all values $\mathbf{A}$ and $\mathcal{A}$ such that $\mathcal{A} \subseteq \mathbf{a} \subseteq \mathbf{A} \subseteq A$, and all values x of X:

$$\text{Bel}(c_1|\mathbf{a}, x) + \text{Bel}(c_1|\mathcal{A}, x) > \text{Bel}(c_1|\mathbf{A}, x)$$

when beliefs are combined using Dempster's rule of combination.

Once again, the situations in which belief in C taking value c_1 varies inversely with and is qualitatively independent of belief in A taking a set of values $\mathbf{a} \subseteq A$ are defined analogously, replacing $>$ with $<$ and $=$ respectively, and the situations in which belief in C taking value c_1 may follow and may vary inversely with belief in A taking a set of values $\mathbf{a} \subseteq A$ are also similarly defined by replacing $>$ with $\geq$ and $\leq$ respectively. If none of these relations hold, then the belief in C taking value c_1 is indeterminate with respect to belief in A taking a set of values $\mathbf{a} \subseteq A$.

When dealing with singleton values of A, c_1 follows a_1 if

$$\text{Bel}(c_1|a_1, x) > \text{Bel}(c_1|\mathbf{y}, x)$$

where $a_1 \in \mathbf{y} \subseteq A$. In other words, c_1 follows a_1 if increase in belief in c_1 due to moving mass from other values of A to a_1 outweighs the loss in support from those values. The same interpretation may be applied to this new result. For belief in $\mathbf{a}$ to increase, mass must move from supersets of $\mathbf{a}$ to $\mathbf{a}$ or its subsets. Provided these latter provide more support for c_1 than it had previously, belief in c_1 will increase.

As usual, there is a complementary result for the use of the disjunctive rule of combination. This result is one that by now is rather familiar:

THEOREM 8.18:   For a node C, with possible values $\{c_1, \ldots, c_n\}$, and parents A, with possible values $\{a_1, \ldots, a_m\}$, and X, with possible values $\{x_1, \ldots, x_p\}$, belief in C taking value c_1 may always follow belief in A taking a set of values $\mathbf{a} \subseteq A$ when beliefs are combined using the disjunctive rule of combination.

These two pairs of results may then be composed to determine the most general results—those for changes in the belief of sets of values of C given changes in sets of values of A. When Dempster's rule is applied, the result is:

COROLLARY 8.3:   For a node C, with possible values $\{c_1, \ldots, c_n\}$, and parents A, with possible values $\{a_1, \ldots, a_m\}$, and X, with possible values $\{x_1, \ldots, x_p\}$, belief in C taking a set of values $\mathbf{c} \subseteq \{c_1, \ldots, c_n\}$ follows belief in A taking a set of values $\mathbf{a} \subseteq A$ if, for all values $\mathbf{A}$ and $\mathcal{A}$ such that $\mathcal{A} \subseteq \mathbf{a} \subseteq \mathbf{A} \subseteq A$, and all values x of X:

$$\mathrm{Bel}(\mathbf{c}|\mathbf{a}, x) + \mathrm{Bel}(\mathbf{c}|\mathcal{A}, x) > \mathrm{Bel}(\mathbf{c}|\mathbf{A}, x)$$

when beliefs are combined using Dempster's rule of combination.

The situations in which belief in C taking a set of values $\mathbf{c} \subseteq \{c_1, \ldots, c_n\}$ varies inversely with and is qualitatively independent of belief in A taking a set of values $\mathbf{a} \subseteq A$ are defined analogously, replacing $>$ with $<$ and $=$ respectively, and the situations in which belief in C taking a set of values $\mathbf{c} \subseteq \{c_1, \ldots, c_n\}$ may follow and may vary inversely with belief in A taking a set of values $\mathbf{a} \subseteq A$ are also similarly defined by replacing $>$ with $\geq$ and $\leq$ respectively. If none of these relations hold, then the belief in C taking a set of values $\mathbf{c} \subseteq \{c_1, \ldots, c_n\}$ is indeterminate with respect to belief in A taking a set of values $\mathbf{a} \subseteq A$.
    When the disjunctive rule is applied, the result is:

COROLLARY 8.4:   For a node C, with possible values $\{c_1, \ldots, c_n\}$, and parents A, with possible values $\{a_1, \ldots, a_m\}$, and X, with possible values $\{x_1, \ldots, x_p\}$, belief in C taking a set of values $\mathbf{c} \subseteq \{c_1, \ldots, c_n\}$ may always follow belief in A taking a set of values $\mathbf{a} \subseteq A$ when beliefs are combined using the disjunctive rule of combination.

For completeness, it is worth stating the result concerning separable derivatives. This is as follows:

THEOREM 8.19:   For a variable C, with possible values $\{c_1, \ldots, c_n\}$, which has parents A, with possible values $\{a_1, \ldots, a_m\}$, and X, with possible values $\{x_1, \ldots, x_p\}$, belief in C taking a set of values $\mathbf{c} \subseteq \{c_1, \ldots, c_n\}$ may always separably follow belief in A taking a set of values $\mathbf{a} \subseteq \{a_1, \ldots, a_m\}$.

Note that this final result holds for both the use of Dempster's rule of combination and the

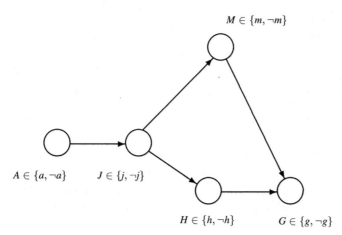

$M \in \{m, \neg m\}$

$A \in \{a, \neg a\}$ $J \in \{j, \neg j\}$

$H \in \{h, \neg h\}$ $G \in \{g, \neg g\}$

Figure 8.7
Jack's model for predicting how his evening would turn out

use of the disjunctive rule.

8.2.3   An example using a multiply-connected network

An example of the use of multiply-connected networks is provided, once again, by an incident from the life of Jack Dulouz. This particular incident took place in Fat City when Jack went there to meet his subterranean friends. One night he was thinking about going out, and was trying to predict what was likely to happen if he went around to see his friend Adam Moorad. As far as he could tell, there were a number things that might happen if he did this. If he went to Adam's house, that would influence whether or not they would go out to a jazz club. The quality of the clubs near Adam's house would influence whether or not they would hear good music, and thus whether or not they would have a good time. In addition, going to the jazz club would influence whether or not they would run into their mutual friend Mardou Fox, and this, again, would affect whether or not the night was enjoyable. Jack realised that this model of events could be captured by the network in Figure 8.7 where A stands for the proposition "go to Adam's house," J for the proposition "go to a jazz club," H for the proposition "hear good music," G for the proposition "have a good time," and M for the proposition "meet Mardou."

Having captured his intuitions about the night's prospects in network form, Jack started thinking about how the model might be used to solve his prediction problem. Consulting his guide to the theory of qualitative change it soon became clear that there was no way he could use evidence theory to solve the problem because evidence theory is unable to deal with multiply-connected networks. This, however, suited Jack who as the astute reader will have already noticed, tends to prefer to use probability theory. This is a decision that really pays off in this scenario—as Jack quickly spotted—because the conditions on probability propagation are exactly the same in singly and multiply-connected networks. This meant he could use the same intuitions to determine the qualitative influences between propositions that he would use were the model singly-connected.

Bearing this in mind he quickly determined that, in his estimation, it was necessary for $\Pr(j)$ to follow $\Pr(a)$, $\Pr(m)$ and $\Pr(h)$ to follow $\Pr(j)$, and $\Pr(g)$ to follow both $\Pr(h)$ and $\Pr(m)$, and consulted Theorem 8.6 to ensure that he was happy with the constraints on the relevant conditional probabilities. Having done this, the procedure for computing predicted changes was no different to that he had used before. He quickly calculated that since he should model going to Adam's house by setting $\Delta \Pr(a) = [+]$ in the usual way, it followed that:

$$
\begin{aligned}
\Delta \Pr(j) &= \left[\frac{\partial \Pr(j)}{\partial \Pr(a)}\right] \otimes \Delta \Pr(a) \\
&= [+] \otimes [+] \\
&= [+]
\end{aligned}
$$

indicating that the probability of going to a jazz club increased. Rolling the propagation on, Jack found that:

$$
\begin{aligned}
\Delta \Pr(m) &= \left[\frac{\partial \Pr(m)}{\partial \Pr(j)}\right] \otimes \Delta \Pr(j) \\
&= [+] \otimes [+] \\
&= [+]
\end{aligned}
\tag{8.5}
$$

and also that:

$$
\begin{aligned}
\Delta \Pr(h) &= \left[\frac{\partial \Pr(h)}{\partial \Pr(j)}\right] \otimes \Delta \Pr(j) \\
&= [+] \otimes [+] \\
&= [+]
\end{aligned}
\tag{8.6}
$$

so that both the probability of running into Mardou, and the probability of hearing good music increased if he decided to go to Adam's house. However, to calculate the joint effect of meeting Mardou and listening to good music on having a good time, Jack had to use (7.6) to combine the two influences, discovering that:

$$
\Delta \Pr(g) = \left[\frac{\partial \Pr(g)}{\partial \Pr(m)}\right] \otimes \Delta \Pr(m) \oplus \left[\frac{\partial \Pr(g)}{\partial \Pr(h)}\right] \otimes \Delta \Pr(h)
\tag{8.7}
$$

$$= \quad [+] \otimes [+] \oplus [+] \otimes [+]$$
$$= \quad [+]$$

Thus Jack could predict from the model that if he went to Adam's house, thus causing $\Pr(a)$ to increase, the probability of having a good time would also increase.

However, being of an inquisitive disposition, Jack did not stop reflecting on the situation described above when he had finished the above calculation. Instead he continued to ponder the deeper mechanisms of the theory. One thing that caught his attention was the fact that the expressions for $\Pr(m)$ and $\Pr(h)$ from (8.5) and (8.6) could be substituted into (8.7) to give:

$$\Delta \Pr(g) \quad = \quad \left[\frac{\partial \Pr(g)}{\partial \Pr(m)} \right] \otimes \Delta \Pr(m) \oplus \left[\frac{\partial \Pr(g)}{\partial \Pr(h)} \right] \otimes \Delta \Pr(h)$$

$$= \quad \left[\frac{\partial \Pr(g)}{\partial \Pr(m)} \right] \otimes \left[\frac{\partial \Pr(m)}{\partial \Pr(j)} \right] \otimes \Delta \Pr(j)$$

$$\oplus \left[\frac{\partial \Pr(g)}{\partial \Pr(h)} \right] \otimes \left[\frac{\partial \Pr(h)}{\partial \Pr(j)} \right] \otimes \Delta \Pr(j)$$

$$= \quad \left(\left[\frac{\partial \Pr(g)}{\partial \Pr(m)} \right] \otimes \left[\frac{\partial \Pr(m)}{\partial \Pr(j)} \right] \oplus \left[\frac{\partial \Pr(g)}{\partial \Pr(h)} \right] \otimes \left[\frac{\partial \Pr(h)}{\partial \Pr(j)} \right] \right) \otimes \Delta \Pr(j)$$

The reason that Jack found this interesting is that he realised that large bracketed term in this last equation was the combined qualitative influence of $\Pr(j)$ on $\Pr(g)$ along both trails. Thus he had demonstrated that computing the influence of a change in $\Delta \Pr(j)$ along two paths and combining the results was equivalent to computing the qualitative influence of a change in $\Pr(j)$ on $\Pr(g)$ along both paths and combining this with the change in $\Pr(j)$.

8.3   Intercausal reasoning

As discussed in Sections 4.4.1 and 5.3.2, intercausal reasoning is another important form of reasoning in network-based models, capturing the interactions between the causes of an event. Recall the discussion in Chapter 5 of the situation captured by the network of Figure 5.1, reproduced in Figure 8.8. Causal and evidential reasoning, respectively, make it possible to capture reasoning of the form "if it rained last night, then it is more likely that the grass is cold and shiny" and "if my shoes are wet, then it is more likely that the sprinkler was on." However, there is no way of relating the events "Rain last night" and "Sprinkler was on" using these forms of reasoning. Intercausal reasoning, on the other hand, only

Rain last night   Sprinkler was on

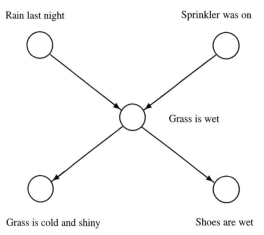

Grass is wet

Grass is cold and shiny   Shoes are wet

Figure 8.8
The graphical representation of the sprinkler example again

relates the events "Rain last night" and "Sprinkler was on." If the grass is known to be wet, it makes it possible to reason that "if the sprinkler was on, then it is less likely that it rained" on the grounds that a single cause is more likely than both.

It might be worth pointing out that this particular example seems to have originated in Southern California where is is indeed unlikely that it would rain at the same time the sprinkler was on. Living in a place where it rains frequently and throughout the year, I found this example most confusing at first, since I could see no reason why using the sprinkler would stop it raining. However, the point of the example is simply that however likely or unlikely it is to rain or for the sprinkler to be on, because no sane person turns the sprinkler on when it is raining, or believes it is likely to rain, the two events tend to occur together less than they occur apart.

The upshot of this discussion is that, whatever form it takes, intercausal reasoning adds an important dimension to any system that reasons under uncertainty. Having dealt with many of the aspects of causal and evidential reasoning within the theory of qualitative change, this section explores what the theory of qualitative change has to say about intercausal reasoning.

8.3.1   Intercausal reasoning and qualitative change

The canonical situation in which intercausal reasoning takes place is depicted in Figure 8.9. The situation involves a variable C, whose value is observed, which is influenced by A, B, and X. A and B are the variables whose intercausal effect on one another is under

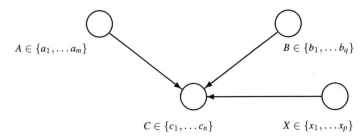

Figure 8.9
A network for intercausal reasoning

investigation, and X summarises all the other influences on C. To analyse the behaviour of the network, the usual procedure for the theory of qualitative change is followed. For a network quantified with probabilities, an expression is written down for a given value of C, $\Pr(c_1)$ say, in terms of the relevant probabilities of A, B and X, and this is used to relate $\Pr(a)$ to $\Pr(b)$ when C has been observed to take the value c_1, so that $\Pr(c_1) = 1$. The derivative of this expression with respect to $\Pr(b)$ is taken, and the landmarks that determine the qualitative values of this derivative established. Of particular interest is the situation in which there is a negative influence between A and B since this is the situation in which explaining away occurs, but it is important to establish the conditions for positive and zero influences as well. For the probabilistic case these are as follows:

THEOREM 8.20:   Consider a node C, with possible values $\{c_1, \ldots, c_n\}$, and parents A, with possible values $\{a_1, \ldots, a_m\}$, B, with possible values $\{b_1, \ldots, b_q\}$, and X, with possible values $\{x_1, \ldots, x_p\}$. When $\Pr(c_1) = 1$:

1. $\Pr(a_1)$ follows $\Pr(b_1)$ if $\Pr(c_1)$ varies inversely with $\Pr(b_1)$;
2. $\Pr(a_1)$ varies inversely with $\Pr(b_1)$ if $\Pr(c_1)$ follows $\Pr(b_1)$;
3. $\Pr(a_1)$ is qualitatively independent of $\Pr(b_1)$ if $\Pr(c_1)$ is qualitatively independent of $\Pr(b_1)$;

In all other cases the relationship between $\Pr(a_1)$ and $\Pr(b_1)$ is indeterminate.

The situations in which $\Pr(a_1)$ may vary inversely with $\Pr(b_1)$ and $\Pr(a_1)$ may follow $\Pr(b_1)$ are similarly defined by suitable composition of the conditions for "varies inversely" and "qualitatively independent" and "follows" and "qualitatively independent" respectively.

Thus the qualitative relation between the probabilities of A and B is determined by the qualitative relation between the probabilities of B and C. If the conditional probabilities connecting B and C are such that $\Pr(c_1)$ normally varies inversely with $\Pr(b_1)$, then, when the value of $\Pr(c_1)$ is fixed at 1, $\Pr(a_1)$ follows $\Pr(b_1)$. Clearly the case in which explaining away occurs is that in which $\Pr(a_1)$ varies inversely with $\Pr(b_1)$, and so explaining away occurs if $\Pr(c_1)$ normally follows $\Pr(b_1)$. The conditions on the intercausal influence between A and B seem entirely reasonable, and may be justified by the following argument. If the probability of c_1 tends to follow that of $\Pr(b_1)$, and $\Pr(b_1)$ increases, then the joint probability of a_1, b_1 and c_1 increases as $\Pr(b_1)$ increases. Since $\Pr(c_1)$ is an increasing function of the joint probability, when $\Pr(c_1)$ is not fixed, the increase in the joint probability will cause it to increase. If, however, the probability of c_1 is fixed, there must be some change in $\Pr(a_1)$ to offset the change in the joint value, and if $\Pr(c_1)$ follows $\Pr(b_1)$ this means that $\Pr(a_1)$ must decrease. Similarly, if $\Pr(c_1)$ varies inversely with $\Pr(b_1)$, $\Pr(a_1)$ must increase as $\Pr(b_1)$ increases in order to offset the change that would otherwise occur in the joint probability. While this explanation seems an adequate justification of the kind of intercausal relationship implied by Theorem 8.20, the fact that the conditions are on the relationship between the probability of C and B, rather than simply on the product of the conditional values of C given its causes, makes it clear that the notion of "explaining away" that is captured here is rather different to that considered by Druzdzel and Henrion (1993c) and Wellman and Henrion (1991). In particular, Wellman and Henrion show that a sufficient and necessary condition for explaining away in the binary case is:

$$\Pr(c_1|a,b,X).\Pr(c_1|\neg a, \neg b, X) \leq \Pr(c_1|\neg a, b, X).\Pr(c_1|a, \neg b, X)$$

whereas in the theory of qualitative change the condition requires that:

$$\begin{aligned}\Pr(c_1|a,b,X) &\geq \Pr(c_1|\neg a, b, X)\\ \Pr(c_1|a, \neg b, X) &\geq \Pr(c_1|\neg a, \neg b, X)\end{aligned}$$

These conditions can coincide (provided, for instance, that $\Pr(c_1|\neg a, \neg b, X)$ is small enough), but they need not.

As an aside, it should be pointed out that my explanation of the way in which the probabilities alter is similar to that used by Tzeng (1992) in his reconstruction of Henrion and Wellman's (1991) result. He examines Pearl's (1988b) method for probability propagation, and considers the flow of probability between the nodes. His result, and its proof, are reconstructed below using the notation and terminology of the theory of qualitative change:

THEOREM 8.21:   For independent binary nodes A, with possible values a_1 and a_2, and B, with possible values b_1 and b_2, which are both parents of a binary node C whose value is known to be c, $\Pr(a_1)$ varies inversely with $\Pr(b_1)$ if

$$\Pr(c|a_1, b_1).\Pr(c|a_2, b_2) < \Pr(c|a_2, b_1).\Pr(c|a_1, b_2)$$

The conditions under which $\Pr(a_1)$ follows $\Pr(b_1)$, may follow $\Pr(b_1)$, may vary inversely with $\Pr(b_1)$ and is qualitatively independent of $\Pr(b_1)$ may be obtained analogously.

When the network is quantified with possibility values, the observation that C takes value c_1 is modelled by setting the value of $\Pi(c_i)$ to 0 for all $i \neq 1$. Since the values are normalised, $\max_i \Pi(c_i) = 1$ and so the effect of the observation on the possibility of c_1 is to ensure that it is 1. This yields the following result:

THEOREM 8.22:   Consider a node C, with possible values $\{c_1, \ldots, c_n\}$, and parents A, with possible values $\{a_1, \ldots, a_m\}$, B, with possible values $\{b_1, \ldots, b_q\}$, and X, with possible values $\{x_1, \ldots, x_p\}$. When $\Pi(c_1) = 1$, $\Pi(a_1)$ varies inversely with $\Pi(b_1)$ if $\Pi(c_1)$ may follow $\Pi(a_1)$ up and may follow $\Pi(b_1)$ down. Otherwise $\Pi(a_1)$ is qualitatively independent of $\Pi(b_1)$.

Thus a form of explaining away is possible in possibility theory, although it is a rather limited one. The inverse relationship between $\Pi(a_1)$ and $\Pi(b_1)$ can only be expressed in such a way that $\Pi(a_1)$ increases as $\Pi(b_1)$ falls. Thus it is the case that evidence for B not taking value b_1 *explains in* A taking value a_1 rather than evidence for B taking value b_1 *explaining away* A taking value a_1. In addition there cannot be a positive relationship between A and B so that $\Pi(a_1)$ can never follow $\Pi(b_1)$. It is also worth noting that for this form of intercausal reasoning between A and B to occur in possibility theory, the conditional possibilities must be such that:

$$\Pi(c_1|a_1, b_i, x_k) = 1$$
$$\Pi(c_1|a_j, b_1, x_l) = 1$$

for $i, j \neq 1$ and some k and l, while all other conditional possibilities are less than one. In other words, c_1 is completely possible if either $A = a_1$ or $B = b_1$ but not both (or A or B take any other value). This suggests that intercausal reasoning relies upon some kind of exclusivity between the causes of C rather as we would expect given the discussion at the start of this section.

Other authors have considered the conditions under which intercausal reasoning and explaining away occur in possibility theory. In particular this topic has been studied by Benferhat and co-authors (Benferhat et al., 1995b, 1996). Just as was the case for probability theory, when examining the work of these authors it becomes clear that the account of intercausal reasoning given by the theory of qualitative change is somewhat different from theirs. Rather then concentrate upon the way in which the $\Pi(b)$ affects $\Pi(a)$, Benferhat et al. (1996) examine what they call Π-based negative influence[7] where $\Pi(a|b,c) < \Pi(a|c)$. The condition for this to be true for the binary case is:

$$\Pi(c|\neg a, b) > \Pi(c|a, b)$$

when all the prior values are 1. In contrast, the theory of qualitative change cannot account for explaining away in the sense of a becoming less possible as evidence for b is known. Indeed it requires $\Pi(a) \neq 1$ and:

$$
\begin{aligned}
1 &= \Pi(c|\neg a, b) > \Pi(c|a, b) \\
1 &= \Pi(c|a, \neg b) > \Pi(c|\neg a, \neg b)
\end{aligned}
$$

as conditions for evidence against b making a more possible. Benferhat et al. (1996) also give conditions for explaining away to occur irrespective of the value of the priors, a situation which is not considered here.

When modelling the situation depicted in Figure 8.9 using evidence theory, there are, as always, two ways of combining the influences of A and B on C. One may either use Dempster's rule of combination that involves the use of conditionals such as $\text{Bel}(c|a, b \cup \neg b)$, or Smets' disjunctive rule which does not need such values, replacing $\text{Bel}(c|a, b \cup \neg b)$ with $\text{Bel}(c|a, b)\text{Bel}(c|a, \neg b)$. Firstly, for Dempster's rule the result is:

THEOREM 8.23: Consider a node C, with possible values $\{c_1, \ldots, c_n\}$, and parents A, with possible values $\{a_1, \ldots, a_m\}$, B, with possible values $\{b_1, \ldots, b_q\}$, and X, with possible values $\{x_1, \ldots, x_p\}$. When $\text{Bel}(c_1) = 1$ and beliefs are combined using Dempster's rule of combination:

1. $\text{Bel}(a_1)$ follows $\text{Bel}(b_1)$ if $\text{Bel}(c_1)$ varies inversely with $\text{Bel}(b_1)$;

2. $\text{Bel}(a_1)$ varies inversely with $\text{Bel}(b_1)$ if $\text{Bel}(c_1)$ follows $\text{Bel}(b_1)$;

3. $\text{Bel}(a_1)$ is qualitatively independent of $\text{Bel}(b_1)$ if $\text{Bel}(c_1)$ is qualitatively independent of $\text{Bel}(b_1)$;

In all other cases, the relationship between $\text{Bel}(a_1)$ and $\text{Bel}(b_1)$ is indeterminate.

The situations in which $\text{Bel}(a_1)$ may vary inversely with $\text{Bel}(b_1)$ and $\text{Bel}(a_1)$ may follow $\text{Bel}(b_1)$ are similarly defined by suitable composition of the conditions for "varies inversely" and "qualitatively independent" and "follows" and "qualitatively independent" respectively.

---

7 Benferhat et al. also deal with what they call N-based negative influence, which is where $\Pi(a, \neg b, c) > \Pi(\neg a, \neg b, c)$.

Thus for explaining away to take place in evidence theory, the conditions that must be met are analogous to those for probability theory, and suggest that the same kind of mechanism is at work. If $\text{Bel}(c_1)$ follows $\text{Bel}(b_1)$ when it is not fixed, then when it is fixed, the inflow of belief into the joint distribution over A, B, C and X from increasing $\text{Bel}(b_1)$ must be matched by a decrease in $\text{Bel}(a_1)$. Similarly, if $\text{Bel}(c_1)$ varies inversely with $\text{Bel}(b_1)$, then when $\text{Bel}(c_1)$ is fixed, the decrease in belief over all three variables in question that results from an increase in $\text{Bel}(b_1)$ must be offset by an increase in $\text{Bel}(a_1)$.

If, on the other hand, the disjunctive rule is used to combine values, the relevant result is:

THEOREM 8.24:   Consider a node C, with possible values $\{c_1, \ldots, c_n\}$, and parents A, with possible values $\{a_1, \ldots, a_m\}$, B, with possible values $\{b_1, \ldots, b_q\}$, and X, with possible values $\{x_1, \ldots, x_p\}$. When $\text{Bel}(c_1) = 1$, and beliefs are combined using the disjunctive rule of combination, $\text{Bel}(a_1)$ may always vary inversely with $\text{Bel}(b_1)$.

Thus if the disjunctive rule is used, then the intercausal propagation of belief always occurs. Furthermore such intercausal propagation always takes the form of explaining away (albeit in a "may" sense). Given the behaviour reported in Theorem 8.23 for combination using Dempster's rule, and the fact that under the disjunctive rule $\text{Bel}(c_1)$ may always follow $\text{Bel}(a_1)$ and $\text{Bel}(b_1)$ (Theorem 7.6), this result is not surprising. It does, however, have some consequences for the expressiveness of the networks that one may build using belief functions and the disjunctive rule. Indeed, the practical result of Theorem 8.24 is that it is not possible to construct a network of the form of Figure 8.9 in which evidence for the values of A causes belief in the values of B to increase when one of the values of C is observed. This is something of a restriction, and may have important consequences for Xu and Smets' evidential networks (Xu and Smets, 1991), which use the disjunctive rule in a similar way to that analysed here.

8.3.2   The uses of intercausal reasoning

At first glance it might seem that the work in this section verges on the irrelevant. After all, the most important forms of reasoning are causal and evidential—causal to make predictions about what observations are to be expected if certain events are known to take place, and evidential to deduce what events must have taken place if certain observations are made. Why is it worth bothering with anything more? There are a number of ways this question can be answered.

One, which was adopted in the introduction to the chapter, is to argue that intercausal reasoning is another mode of reasoning, distinct from causal and evidential, and so deserves to be studied as a way of enriching the theory of qualitative change. However, this is a rather

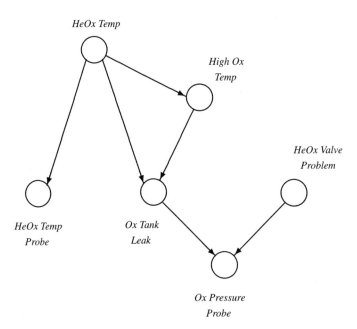

Figure 8.10
Part of a shuttle engine model

unsatisfactory answer since all it really says is "because it is there."

A second answer to the question is to point to the use that Druzdzel (1993) made of intercausal reasoning, a use that demonstrates that intercausal reasoning is not just an interesting phenomenon, but also has practical uses. Druzdzel was interested in using qualitative probabilistic reasoning as a means of explaining probabilistic inference, the idea being that a suitable explanation for the user of a system built on probabilistic causal networks is of the form:

We know that *A* becomes more probable, and we also know that if *A* becomes more probable then *B* becomes more probable. Therefore we can infer that *B* becomes more probable.

Given that this is essentially abstracting probabilistic inference into something approaching a logical syllogism, the usefulness of this kind of explanation might be questioned, but I personally find it helpful. Anyway, in developing this form of explanation, a situation such as that in Figure 8.10 often arises. This network captures some information about the functioning of a space shuttle engine, and originates from (Horvitz et al., 1992) (via (Druzdzel, 1993)). As explained in the latter, this network represents a system that consists of two liquid gas tanks: an oxidizer tank and a helium tank. Helium is used for putting pressure on the oxidizer, necessary for expelling the oxidizer into the combustion subsystem. A potential temperature problem in the neighborhood of the two tanks (*HeOx Temp*) can be discovered by a probe (*HeOx Temp Probe*) built into the valve between the tanks. An increased temperature in the neighborhood of the two tanks can increase the temperature in the oxidizer tank (*High Ox Temp*) and this in turn can cause a leak in the oxidizer tank (*Ox Tank Leak*). A leak in the tank may lead to decreased pressure in the oxidizer tank. A problem with the valve between the two tanks (*HeOx Valve Problem*) can also be a cause of a decreased pressure in the oxidizer tank. The pressure in the oxidizer tank is measured by a pressure gauge (*Ox Pressure Probe*). Of all the variables in this network, only the values of the two probes (*HeOx Temp Probe* and *Ox Pressure Probe*) are directly observable. The others must be inferred.

Now, a typical usage of this network is to determine whether there is a problem with the valve between the helium and oxygen tanks, given probe measurements. Given a measurement of the pressure probe, evidential reasoning alone is sufficient to make the necessary inference. However, if a pressure reading is taken, fixing the value of *Ox Pressure Probe*, and then there is a change in the temperature reading, the only way to infer anything about *HeOx Valve Problem* is to use intercausal reasoning between the parents of *Ox Pressure Probe*.

The third answer to the question at the start of this section is a generalisation of the second. The QCN models with which the theory of qualitative change deals are directed from causes to effects. A great deal of the time they are used to reason from observed effects back to causes, and in the general case more than one effect is observed. There are two ways of modelling the observation of several effects in QCNs. One is to assert all the changes at the same time, in which case evidential reasoning should suffice to establish all the changes at all the nodes in the network. The other way is to assert the changes one at a time, in which case after the first assertion (which fixes the value of one of the effects) it will be necessary to use intercausal reasoning in order to establish all the changes at all the nodes.[8]

Another reasonable question to ask about the use of intercausal reasoning is how it stands in relation to synergy, the sub-text being that since synergy seems to capture the relationship between the parents, why is it necessary to investigate the relationship in terms of intercausal reasoning? The answer to this question is much shorter—synergy and intercausal reasoning are different phenomena. Intercausal reasoning is about inferring changes in certainty values of variables from other changes in certainty values, and in this sense is just like causal reasoning and evidential reasoning. Synergy on the other hand is about inferring how the relationship between variables changes, and so is wholly different

---

8 As mentioned in Section 4.4.1 and discussed in (Renooij et al., 2000b), there is a bit more to handling multiple observations than this, but it does not change the need to handle intercausal reasoning.

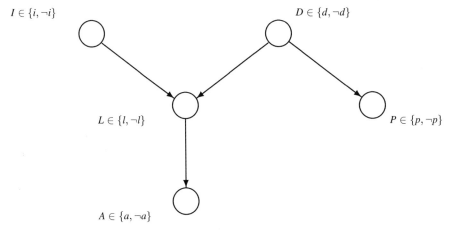

$I \in \{i, \neg i\}$ $D \in \{d, \neg d\}$

$L \in \{l, \neg l\}$ $P \in \{p, \neg p\}$

$A \in \{a, \neg a\}$

Figure 8.11
The network describing Jack's beliefs about Cody (a third time)

to the other kinds of reasoning discussed here.[9]

8.3.3   An example of intercausal reasoning

To illustrate the potential of intercausal reasoning, reconsider the story of Cody Pomeroy and the tyre shack, which was introduced in the previous chapter. Some time after the events described in Chapter 7, Jack spoke to Cody on the telephone. During the conversation, in which Cody talked mainly of his desire to become a brakeman on the railroad, Jack learnt both that Cody had lost his job and that Cody believed that the manager did not find out about his drinking. Armed with this new information, Jack sat down to reason once again about the situation using the same model as before (shown again in Figure 8.11) in which node I represents the variable "ill," L represents the variable "lose job," D represents the variable "drink alcohol," P represents the variable "write poetry," and A represents the variable "adequate income."

Given his initial probabilistic model, in which "lose job" follows both "ill" and "drinks alcohol," Jack found he could apply Theorem 8.20 to determine that, given he knows "lose job" is true, it is the case that evidence against "drinks alcohol" is evidence for "ill" since by Theorem 8.20 the the probability of the latter varies inversely with that of the former. Thus, since on Cody's evidence the probability of "drinks alcohol" may fall, the probability that Cody was ill may increase. Jack got similar results with his evidence theory model. The fact

---

9 Though it should be recalled, as mentioned in Sections 4.4.1 and 8.1.1, that additive synergies can be used to disambiguate influences is qualitative probabilistic networks.

Table 8.1
Possibilities for the example

$\Pi(l\|i,d)$	=	1	$\Pi(i)$	=	0.1
$\Pi(l\|\neg i,d)$	=	1	$\Pi(d)$	=	1
$\Pi(l\|i,\neg d)$	=	0.9			
$\Pi(l\|\neg i,\neg d)$	=	0.05			

that in in his model belief in "lose job" follows belief in both "ill" and "drinks alcohol" meant that whether he combined his beliefs with Dempster's rule or Smets' disjunctive rule, Theorems 8.23 and 8.24 indicate that belief in "ill" may vary inversely with belief in "drinks alcohol" giving the same result as in the probabilistic case.

Things were a little different with Jack's possibilistic model. In this case, it is not possible to avoid using some numerical values since these values themselves are needed to use Theorem 8.22. After some thought, Jack settled on the possibility values in Table 8.1 since they fitted his feelings about Cody's employer as well as the health and drinking status of the tyre shack employees while ensuring that the possibility of "lose job," $\Pi(l)$, follows both those of "ill," $\Pi(i)$, and "drinks alcohol," $\Pi(d)$, in accordance with his initial information. These values are such that $\Pi(l)$ may follow $\Pi(i)$ up and may follow $\Pi(d)$ down, and so obey the conditions imposed by Theorem 8.22 for some form of intercausal relationship to hold between $\Pi(i)$ and $\Pi(d)$.

Thus Jack expected that altering the possibility of d in his model would mean that the possibility of i had to change, and he tested this by carrying out a calculation with two values of $\Pi(d)$. Initially he found that $\Pi(l) = 1$ because $\Pi(d)$ was 1 as was $\Pi(\neg i)$ (since one of $\Pi(i)$ and $\Pi(\neg i)$ must be 1). Reducing the value of $\Pi(d)$, the only way that $\Pi(l)$ could remain at 1 was for $\Pi(i)$ to increase to 1, and so the falling possibility of "drinks alcohol" explained "ill" becoming more possible. This satisfied Jack that intercausal reasoning in possibility theory behaved as he expected.

He also noted that this example clarified another aspect of the theory that he hadn't noticed before. With the initial conditions, Theorem 7.4 indicated that $\Pi(l)$ may follow $\Pi(i)$ up. Since $\Pi(l)$ is already 1, and therefore can't increase, this result seems a little odd. However, as Jack quickly realised, what the result means is that the conditional possibilities are such that at some point $\Pi(i)$ might be the lowest value determining $\Pi(l)$, and if this comes to pass, then increasing $\Pi(i)$ will cause $\Pi(l)$ to increase—the "may" in "may follow" is broad indeed.

8.4   Related work

As is clear from the survey in Chapter 4, the theory of qualitative change introduced in the last couple of chapters is very similar in many respects to work by other authors. This section takes a brief look at those similarities, giving most attention to qualitative probabilistic networks, but giving due attention to other systems. It starts with these other systems.

8.4.1   Relation with other qualitative methods

The first thing to do is to clarify the relationship between the theory of qualitative change and the work on qualitative reasoning that grew out of naïve physics, work typified by (Kuipers, 1994). The relationship is that the theory of qualitative change is the use of the basic principles of qualitative reasoning applied to formalisms for handling uncertainty. All the theory of qualitative change does is to take the idea of looking at changes in value— abstracted away to the point at which the changes are only recognised to be increases, decreases, or no change—and apply it to the propagation of probability, possibility and evidence theories. In fact, as it stands, the theory of qualitative change only makes use of a very small part of the full power of qualitative reasoning. The theory only uses the simplest quantity space of positive and negative values and the single landmark of zero, although the landmarks of 1 and -1 are often implied (since a first derivative that has a qualitative value of $[+]$ can never have a quantitative value which is greater than 1 since the latter is the difference between two conditional probabilities).

The theory of qualitative change also only really uses first derivatives. While it is clear that considering variable values themselves is largely uninteresting because the values are mostly $[+]$, it is not clear whether there is anything to be gained from considering second derivatives in addition to those that determine synergistic interactions. Many second derivatives appear to be zero, but there may be some advantages to be found if they are considered in more detail, a point also made by Michelena (1991). The other main point about the use made of derivatives is, of course, that most work in qualitative reasoning is mainly concerned with derivatives with respect to time. So if one is considering some state variable X, the most interesting derivatives are those like:

$$\frac{dX}{dt}$$

and

$$\frac{d^2X}{dt^2}$$

which describe how the value of X alters with time. The theory of qualitative change is, as the reader is no doubt only too aware by this time, wholly concerned with the derivative of some state variable with respect to some other state variable (where the state variables are the probabilities, possibilities or belief values of particular propositions).

The use of the derivatives also helps to clarify the relationship between the theory of qualitative change and the qualitative algebras introduced in Chapter 6. Once again, this relationship is quite straightforward. The theory of qualitative change is concerned with qualitative abstractions of changes in of probabilities, possibilities, and belief values. The qualitative algebras are concerned with qualitative abstractions of the values themselves. In the case of $Q2$, the qualitative abstractions are almost exactly those used by the theory of qualitative change. In the case of $Q3$, the abstractions are a good deal more precise. However, the relationship between algebras and the theory is the same. In fact, as the perceptive reader will no doubt already have realised, if one was to use the two in conjunction, the result would be a lot like applying some of the more sophisticated techniques suggested by Kuipers (1994) direct to probabilistic, possibilistic or evidential networks.

The final qualitative approach with which the theory of qualitative change has a close connection, other than qualitative probabilistic networks of course, is argumentation, though it must be granted that the connection here is rather more obscure than any of the others. The connection is partly historical in that the theory of qualitative change, in a rather less developed form than it currently has, emerged from the same pool of ideas that produced the strand of argumentation developed by John Fox and colleagues at the Imperial Cancer Research Fund, in particular the logic of argumentation LA (Fox et al., 1992). However, there is some concrete basis to the connection as well. In my, admittedly rather idiosyncratic, view, both theories are attempts to capture the effect of evidence upon certain interesting hypotheses, and both theories attempt to do this without recourse to numbers (because they are intended to be used when numbers are either unavailable or inappropriate). However, their emphasis is rather different. The theory of qualitative change makes it possible to assert pieces of information of the form "the probability of A being true is known to increase," and allows the computation of pieces of information such as "the probability that C is false is known to decrease." LA, on the other hand, makes it possible to assert pieces of knowledge of the form "A is known to be true," and allows the computation of pieces of information such as "since A is known to be true, and A often causes C, there is reason to believe that C is true."

Despite this difference of emphasis, and the fact that the theory of qualitative change is constrained to work using a network representation while LA is essentially logical, it is possible to perform some kind of unification between them. In fact, two slightly different unifications are possible, though both only consider the use of probabilities. One, recorded in (Parsons, 1997a), is achieved by defining a variant of LA in which the main relationship between propositions is a statement about conditional probabilities rather than material implication. Thus $a \to c$ is taken to represent the fact that for all x:

$$\Pr(c|a, x) \geq \Pr(c|\neg a, x)$$

an inequality that is now tiresomely familiar. This means that knowing something about change in probability of a allows something to be established about the change in probability of c, and it is possible to give the idea of an argument for a proposition a meaning in terms of changes in probability. Thus the theory of qualitative change can be annexed to give a semantics to argumentation. The second variant (Parsons, 1998; Parsons and Green, 1999) turns this relationship around, defining a system that looks like LA, but which captures all the relevant relationships between variables needed by the theory of qualitative change. Thus, for instance, it allows the statement of synergistic relationships. Then it is possible to define rules for building arguments that mimic the propagation of qualitative changes, resulting in a system which looks like a logic, but captures the reasoning of a probabilistic qualitative certainty network.

8.4.2 Relation with qualitative probabilistic networks

At a high level, the relationship between qualitative probabilistic networks as introduced by Wellman (1990a) and further developed by Druzdzel (1993) and the theory of qualitative change, is that the latter is a generalisation of the former. While qualitative probabilistic networks capture the shape of the interactions between probabilities, qualitative certainty networks capture the shape of interactions between probabilities, possibilities, and belief values and are capable of dealing with other uncertainty handling formalisms as well. This much is obvious to all but the most casual observer. However, this relationship holds up even under closer inspection.

The first thing that becomes clear when looking in detail at the relationship between qualitative probabilistic networks and the theory of qualitative change is that they are identical for binary probabilistic variables. Given two binary variables A and C, which have possible values $\{a, \neg a\}$ and $\{c, \neg c\}$, a positive qualitative influence between them in a qualitative probabilistic network captures exactly the same behaviour as the qualitative derivative:

$$\left[\frac{\partial \Pr(c)}{\partial \Pr(a)}\right] = [+]$$

Both formalisms here capture the fact that as a becomes more probable, so does c, and a single qualitative value is sufficient to define the behaviour of an influence (as in Corollary 7.1 and the diagrams Jack drew at Big Sur).

When variables have more than two values differences between the formalisms start to emerge. The way that the theory of qualitative change handles such variables is exactly the same way as it handles binary variables. That is it defines relationships between particular values of the variables, identifying monotonic relationships between them. Thus if A and C have possible values $\{a_1, \ldots, a_m\}$ and $\{c_1, \ldots, c_n\}$, then:

$$\left[\frac{\partial \Pr(c_1)}{\partial \Pr(a_1)}\right] = [+]$$

captures exactly the same as in the binary case—that as a_1 becomes more probable, so does c_1. Thus, if you consider plotting the probability of a_1 against that of c_1, what the theory of qualitative change does is to identify the gradient of the resulting curve. Where this curve is monotonically increasing, the derivative has value $[+]$, where it is monotonically decreasing the derivative has value $[-]$, where it is flat the derivatives has value $[0]$, and otherwise the derivative has value $[?]$. It is the fact that such a simple mechanism as the differential calculus is used that makes the theory of qualitative change so general—any formalism expressing something about the relationship between the possible values of A and C will define some set of curves, and the slope of those curves can be explored using the differential calculus.[10]

The way that qualitative probabilistic networks handle variables with more than two values is by using the idea of stochastic dominance. While this is a reasonably complicated idea—to my mind at least, a considerably more complex idea than differential calculus— the idea behind using it is exactly the same, to capture monotonic relationships. Considering A and C once again, what a positive influence between them means is that for particular values c_i of C, and certain values a_j and a_k of A, it is the case that:

$$\Pr(c_i|a_j, x) \geq \Pr(c_i|a_k, x)$$

so certain values of C become more probable if A is known to take certain values. In particular, it means that "higher" values of A make "higher" values of C more probable. For example, if A has values that are temperatures, and C has values that are humidities, then the c_i will be high humidities, the a_j will be high temperatures and the a_k will be low temperatures and the above constraint will capture an association between temperature and humidity such that high values of both go together and low values of both go together. Thinking about this in terms of of the distribution over the possible values of A and C, we can think of a surface delineated by a series of curves, each of which plots the relationship between the probability of some value a_i of A and some value c_j of C. A positive influence identifies a surface that slopes upwards from the corner corresponding to low values of C and A to the corner corresponding to high values of C and A.

One obvious result of this difference is that in qualitative probabilistic networks, the

---

10 Or some discrete approximation to it as in the case of possibility theory.

c_1	a_1	a_2	a_3
b_1	0.3	0.2	0.3
b_2	0.25	0.15	0.25

c_2	a_1	a_2	a_3
b_1	0.2	0.4	0.2
b_2	0.15	0.25	0.15

c_3	a_1	a_2	a_3
b_1	0.35	0.15	0.35
b_2	0.3	0.3	0.3

c_4	a_1	a_2	a_3
b_1	0.15	0.1	0.15
b_2	0.3	0.15	0.3

Figure 8.12
A probability space with interesting contours

relationship between two variables requires a single sign for its representation, whereas in a qualitative certainty network it requires *mn* signs where *m* and *n* are the numbers of possible values of the two variables. This might seem trivial, but it has important consequences for the computational complexity of the propagation of values as will become clear in the next chapter. However, there is a positive side to this from the point of view of the theory of qualitative change, and this is that, because of the additional values, the theory can provide more precise information. That this is the case is quite clear with a little thought. Considering the set of curves described above, there are many influences that qualitative probabilistic networks will only represent as ?. In fact every non-zero influence from A to C for which the surface doesn't slope monotonically upwards (or downwards) from the corner corresponding to low values of C and A to the corner corresponding to high values of C and A will be represented as a ?.[11] However, many of these will be such that the curves joining particular values of A and C are monotonically increasing or decreasing and so have value [+] or [−]. As an example, consider the probability distribution of Figure 8.12 (this should be read so that the intersection of row a_1 and column b_2 in the table labelled c_3 is $\Pr(c_3|a_1, b_2)$). This is the conditional probability table for a variable C with possible values $\{c_1, c_2, c_3, c_4\}$, where the values increase from c_1 to c_4, which has parents A and B. A has possible values $\{a_1, a_2, a_3\}$, which increase in value from a_1 to a_3, and B has possible values $\{b_1, b_2\}$. Now this is admittedly a rather pathological example, since the set of curves relating the probabilities of A, B and C is contoured like an egg box, but nevertheless, every partial derivative

$$\frac{\partial \Pr(c_i)}{\partial \Pr(a_j)}$$

is either [+] or [−] while in a qualitative probabilistic network the influence between A and C would have sign ?. In fact, it is even possible to relax the constraints on the order of the values of C and A without changing this result.

---

11 Such influences are precisely the non-monotonic influences studied by Renooij and van der Gaag (1999b).

There are two other differences between the theory of qualitative change and qualitative probabilistic networks when the formalisms are considered in this kind of detail. The first of these has already been mentioned, but is worth reiterating, and this is that the two approaches deal with intercausal reasoning rather differently. In the theory of qualitative change, the relationship between the parents of the observed node depends upon the respective relationships between the parents and the observed node, while in qualitative probabilistic networks it is independent of them. This is the only place to my knowledge at which the two theories part company in any major way, and this is why the point bears repeating. The other difference has also already been touched on, but again the point is worth developing a little further. This is the difference between the ways in which the two formalisms capture monotonicity, and in particular the use of the differential calculus in the theory of qualitative change. Now, as one might expect, there are both good and bad things about using the differential calculus as opposed to using stochastic dominance. The main advantages of the calculus approach seems to me to be its simplicity and elegance, along with the fact that nice results occasionally drop out almost immediately. Two examples are the fact that results are always "ceteris paribus" in the sense that when the theory gives a relationship between two values that relationship holds whatever else is going on, and the fact that synergistic relationships are exactly identified by the correct second derivative without the need for any additional machinery. On the down side, the calculus approach sometimes leads to a lot of additional work, as in the case of multiply-connected networks.

8.5   Summary

This chapter has continued the work begun in the previous chapter, exploring further aspects of the theory of qualitative change. In particular it has explored three aspects of the theory of qualitative change that are necessary to give the theory enough depth to make it usable. The first of these aspects is synergy. Section 8.1 considered how the theory of qualitative change captures synergistic effects, in other words how the theory captures the fact that the effect of $\Pr(a)$ on $\Pr(c)$ is affected by the value of $\Pr(b)$. It turned out that synergy is one of those things that the theory of qualitative change provides a neat solution to, since the synergistic effect of $\Pr(b)$ on $\Pr(a)$ with respect to $\Pr(c)$ is given directly by:

$$\frac{\partial^2 \Pr(c)}{\partial \Pr(a)\partial \Pr(b)}$$

The second topic covered by this chapter was the question of propagating values in multiply-connected networks. In contrast to synergy, it turned out that propagation in multiply-connected networks is one of the things that the theory of qualitative change does not provide a neat solution to—not because the theory cannot deal with propagation in multiply-connected networks, or because the theory requires some kind of hack to cope with them, but because in order to handle multiply-connected networks it is necessary to step outside differential calculus and think about what applying it entails rather than simply using the machinery it supplies.[12] Doing this gave results that allow propagation for probability and possibility values. Belief values may not be propagated in multiply-connected networks using the theory of qualitative change, but then they can't be propagated in multiply-connected networks using any theory (at the time of writing). When someone provides a mechanism for propagating quantitative belief values in multiply-connected networks, then it may well prove possible to do the same for qualitative values using the theory of qualitative change. As a sop to this gap in the theory, results that make it possible to propagate the effects of *sets* of variables were provided (naturally these only apply to evidence theory). The third thing covered by this chapter was intercausal reasoning, the form of reasoning in which if A is a cause of C and B is a cause of C, then once the value of C is known, information about A may cause a change in what is known about B. The results are sufficient to allow for intercausal reasoning in all of probability, possibility and evidence theories. In addition to these three developments of the theory of qualitative change, this chapter also discussed the relationship between the theory and other qualitative approaches.

Together Chapters 7 and 8 provide an extensive body of work, and the results given make the theory of qualitative change, when concerned with probability values, broadly comparable with qualitative probabilistic networks as developed by Wellman (1990a) and Druzdzel (1993) (clearly the theory goes rather beyond the total of Wellman and Druzdzel's work in its support for theories other than probability). The one area in which the theory presented so far is deficient when compared with qualitative probabilistic networks is in the provision of an algorithm for the propagation of values. This is provided in the next chapter.

---

12 Though in a general way that could be applied to the propagation of any kind of certainty value.

9 Implementing the qualitative approaches

"It's a curious device," said the officer to the traveller, surveying with a look almost of admiration the device with which he was of course so familiar.

Franz Kafka, *In the Penal Colony*

This chapter describes an experimental system, known as Mummu, which implements many of the ideas of discussed in previous chapters. The name is both an acronym for Multiple Uncertainty ManageMent techniqUes and a reference to one of the primordial trinity of Babylonian mythology. According to Sandars (1971), the exact meaning of the name "Mummu" is unknown, and it is often interpreted as "mist" or "cloud." However, in the epic *Myth of Zu* there is a suggestion of another meaning. In the poem,

an arrow speeding from the bow is ordered to return to its mummu, which means that the shaft again becomes part of the living cane from which it was cut, the gut returns to the animal's rump, and the feathers to the bird's wing. In cosmic terms this is a return to the womb of chaos, and in twentieth century language it could stand for the second law of thermodynamics, matter degenerating through loss of energy to its simplest common denominator, so leading to 'a run down universe'; we could therefore understand mummu as entropy. The early Greek philosophers are said by Aristotle to have conceived of a universal first principle, 'that from which a thing first comes-into-being and into which it is finally destroyed', and this is not far removed from the . . . meaning of mummu.

Given the interplay between entropy and uncertainty explored in Chapter 2, the lack of precision in some qualitative values, and the fundamental nature of uncertainty, Mummu seems an apt, if ironic, name for the system.

The main aim of the chapter is to discuss the way in which Mummu implements the use of qualitative algebras and the theory of qualitative change. In particular, the chapter details the propagation methods used for the implementations and proves their correctness, and in doing so digresses a little on the underlying computational mechanisms. The mechanisms in question borrow widely from other people's work. In particular, they make use of valuation systems (Shenoy, 1992c), Pulcinella (Saffiotti and Umkehrer, 1991b), Druzdzel's QPN algorithm (Druzdzel, 1993) and IDEAL (Srinivas and Breese, 1989). As a result it is necessary to understand a little about those other pieces of work to understand the mechanisms—the digressions are rather lengthy and make up the bulk of the chapter. The subsidiary aim of the chapter is to give an account of the structure of the Mummu system and some of its capabilities. However, the chapter stops some way short of being a user manual since providing a definitive guide is a rather futile process for a system that continues to evolve—the current state of the system is documented in (Parsons, 2001).

9.1 Introduction

In a way, to say that Mummu is an implementation of the ideas expounded in this book is rather an exaggeration. In fact, what the system does is to make extensive use of a couple of existing systems for handling uncertainty, adapting and extending them to suit qualitative formalisms. To do this Mummu provides a set of function calls that allow the user to build network-based models and to quantify those networks with either probabilities, possibilities or beliefs whose values may be drawn from the operand sets of $Q2$ or $Q3$, or with the changes and derivatives of the theory of qualitative change. The use of the word "either" is crucial. What Mummu does is to use Pulcinella to propagate values from the qualitative algebras and IDEAL to propagate qualitative changes. It can therefore be thought of as an interface between the user and the other two systems that passes the relevant information to each, makes the relevant queries to each, and invokes the relevant propagations within each. In fact, Mummu does rather more than just provide an interface. Neither Pulcinella nor IDEAL on their own are capable of handling the relevant types of value, so Mummu also comprises a number of extensions to both the other systems—for instance, it provides a number of new "specializations" in the terminology of Pulcinella.

The structure of Mummu dictates the structure of this chapter, with the implementation of the qualitative algebras and the theory of qualitative change considered in different sections. These follow their historical order, with the part that depends on Pulcinella discussed in Section 9.2 and the part that depends on IDEAL discussed in Section 9.3. Each of these sections first introduces the system on which that part of Mummu is built (Sections 9.2.1 and 9.3.1), discusses the mechanism by which the values are propagated and proves that this mechanism is sound (Sections 9.2.2 and 9.3.2), and then discusses the capabilities of the resulting fragment of Mummu (Sections 9.2.3 and 9.3.4). All the code for Mummu is written in Common Lisp. However, because Mummu is implemented as a set of function calls to parts of both Pulcinella and IDEAL, it will not work fully without both Pulcinella and IDEAL and will not work at all without either.

9.2 Implementing qualitative algebras

As noted above, the component of Mummu that propagates interval and qualitative values is built on top of Pulcinella[1] (Saffiotti and Umkehrer, 1991a,b). As already mentioned, this latter makes use of the local computation scheme of Shenoy and Shafer (1990), and so this section deals with the way in which the qualitative algebras of Chapter 6 may be fitted

---

1 I am greatly indebted to all of the developers of Pulcinella for their help and advice in using and modifying the system.

into the local computation scheme. To do this it is first necessary to say a little about both Pulcinella and local computation.

9.2.1   The Pulcinella system

Pulcinella is an implementation of Shenoy's (1992c) idea of valuation-based systems. To understand these it is necessary to give a formal description of the valuation-based language (Shenoy, 1989), which forms the basis of them, the description being based on that in (Saffiotti and Umkehrer, 1991b). The language is made up of two types of component, objects and operators. Objects are used to represent information and operators perform operations on the objects allowing new information to be inferred. There are two kinds of object, variables and valuations, and two kinds of operator, combination and marginalisation.

The first kind of objects to discuss in detail are variables. Consider a finite set of variables. Each variable may range over a finite set of possible values, and this set of values is called the *frame* for that variable. A *configuration* of a finite non-empty set of variables is an element of the Cartesian product of the frames of the variables in this set. The following notation will be used. X denotes the complete set of variables, g, h, and k denote subsets of X. W_g denotes the set of configurations of g, while x and y denote single configurations. In addition, a, b, and c represent sets of configurations. Sometimes it is necessary to project a configuration of one set to another set. A configuration x of g is projected to h, $h \subset g$, by dropping all the elements in x belonging to $g - h$. It is extended to k, $k \supset g$, by building the Cartesian product between the configuration and W_{k-g}. $x^{\downarrow h}$ denotes the projection of x to h, and $x^{\uparrow k}$ denotes the extension of x to k. The second kind of objects to consider are valuations. Given a set of variables h, consider a set V_h. The elements of V_h are called *valuations* on the set h, and these are the objects that represent uncertainty about the members of h. V_g denotes the set of valuations on g, V denotes the set of all valuations on subsets of X, and G and H denote specific valuations. Turning to operators, *combination* is any mapping $\otimes : V \times V \mapsto V$, such that, if G and H are valuations on g and h respectively, then $G \otimes H$ is a valuation on $g \cup h$. For each $h \subseteq X$, there is a mapping $\downarrow h : \bigcup \{V_g : h \subseteq g\} \mapsto V_h$, called *marginalisation* to h such that, if G is a valuation on g and $h \subseteq g$, then $G_{\downarrow h}$ is a valuation on h.

A set of variables and valuations makes up a valuation-based system. When modelling some situation, the important entities in that situation are represented by the variables, and the relationships between them are modelled by the valuations. Thus, in terms of the directed graphs that have been considered widely throughout this book, the variables of a valuation-based system play the same part as nodes and the valuations over variables play the same part as arcs. The generality of the valuation-based system idea means that having decided upon the variables and the relations between them, one is free to choose different formalisms with which to encode these relations, and the kind of valuation is determined by this choice. For example, if one wishes to use probability theory, then the valuations must be probability distributions on the configurations of the variables. Similarly, if possibility theory is chosen, then the valuations must be possibility distributions on the configurations, and if evidence theory is chosen, then the valuations must be mass assignments over sets of configurations. Once a valuation system is defined it is usually useful to evaluate it. One way in which this may be done is to combine all the valuations together to determine the valuation over all the variables in the problem. Given this joint valuation, it is then possible, by marginalisation, to determine the valuation over any set of variables in the problem. Now, computing the valuation over all the variables is, as discussed in Chapter 3, is often computationally infeasible and the whole beauty of the valuation-based approach is that it is dovetails nicely with Shenoy and Shafer's (1990) local computation scheme. Provided that the combination and marginalisation operations appropriate for a particular set of valuations obey three simple axioms, then global computation can be avoided. These axioms are those for the commutativity and associativity of combination:

Axiom 9.1 *Suppose G, H, and K are valuations on g, h, and k respectively. Then:*

$$G \otimes H = H \otimes G$$

and

$$G \otimes (H \otimes K) = (G \otimes H) \otimes K$$

the consonance of marginalisation:

Axiom 9.2 *Suppose G is a valuation on g, and suppose further that $k \subseteq h \subseteq g$, then:*

$$(G^{\downarrow h})^{\downarrow k} = G^{\downarrow k}$$

and the distributivity of marginalisation over combination:

Axiom 9.3 *Suppose G and H are valuations on g and h, respectively. Then:*

$$(G \otimes H)^{\downarrow g} = G \otimes (H^{\downarrow g \cap h})$$

Knowledge of the precise details of the local computation scheme is not necessary in order to understand how Pulcinella works. All that is required is a very rough idea, and roughly speaking, if the relationships between variables can be compiled into a join tree, then passing messages between nodes provides sufficient information to ensure that the valuation over each node is that same as that which would be obtained by computing the global valuation and then marginalising.

9.2.2 Propagating qualitative algebras

Given this brief description of Pulcinella and theory behind it, it is clear what needs to be done in order to use it to implement the qualitative algebras. It is necessary to identify what form valuations take in the algebras and what marginalisation and combination operations are to be used. Ideally it would be possible to do this in such a way that there was one type of valuation and one pair of operators for $Q2$ and one type of valuation and one pair of operators for $Q3$. However, because valuations and operators differ from formalism to formalism, it is necessary to identify six different sets of valuations. These are:

- for probability theory with a mixture of qualitative and point values ($Q2$ probability);
- possibility theory with a mixture of qualitative and point values ($Q2$ possibility);
- evidence theory with a mixture of qualitative and point values ($Q2$ belief);
- probability theory with point and interval values ($Q3$ probability);
- possibility theory with point and interval values ($Q3$ possibility); and finally
- evidence theory with point and interval values ($Q3$ belief).

The different types of valuations are easy to identify since they are based on the valuations for the quantitative formalisms. $Q2$ probability valuations are distributions of point or qualitative probabilities on configurations, $Q2$ possibility valuations are distributions of point or qualitative possibilities on configurations, and $Q2$ belief valuations are assignments of qualitative or point valued masses over sets of configurations. Similarly, $Q3$ probability valuations are distributions of point or interval probabilities on configurations, $Q3$ possibility valuations are distributions of point or interval possibilities on configurations, and $Q3$ belief valuations are assignments of interval or point valued masses over sets of configurations.

Combination and marginalisation operations are also borrowed from the quantitative formalisms. The marginalisation operation for propagating quantitative probability is defined by the following. If $h \subseteq g$ and G is a probability distribution on g then the marginal of G on h is the probability distribution on h defined by:

$$G^{\downarrow h}(x) = \sum \{G(x, y) : y \in W_{g-h}\}$$

for all $x \in W_h$. The combination of G with a probability distribution H on h is defined by:

$$(G \otimes H)(x) = G(x^{\downarrow g})H(x^{\downarrow h})$$

for all $x \in W_{g \cup h}$. The marginalisation and combination operations for $Q2$ probability are similar, but with addition and multiplication replaced by qualitative addition and multiplication respectively. From this it is possible to prove:

THEOREM 9.4:   Axioms 9.1, 9.2, and 9.3 hold for $Q2$ probability.

For $Q3$ probabilities, marginalisation is by interval addition and combination by interval multiplication and:

THEOREM 9.5:   Axioms 9.1, 9.2, and 9.3 hold for $Q3$ probability.

Thus the local computation scheme may be used to propagate both $Q2$ and $Q3$ probability values. Next, the operations for propagating qualitative possibility values must be considered. One set of marginalisation and combination operations for quantitative possibility theory are maximum and minimum (Dubois and Prade, 1991f; Shenoy, 1992b). Using the terminology and notation of valuation systems, if $h \subseteq g$ and G is a possibility distribution on g then the marginal of G on h is the possibility distribution on h defined by:

$$G^{\downarrow h}(x) = \sup\{G(x, y) : y \in W_{g-h}\}$$

for all $x \in W_h$. The combination of G with a possibility distribution H on h is defined by:

$$(G \otimes H)(x) = \min\left(G(x^{\downarrow g}), H(x^{\downarrow h})\right)$$

for all $x \in W_{g \cup h}$. As for probability theory, it is possible to just use the qualitative versions of these operations, which were discussed in Chapter 6. Using these, the following may be proved:

THEOREM 9.6:   Axioms 9.1, 9.2, and 9.3 hold for $Q2$ possibility.

The analogous operations for $Q3$ possibilities are interval max and interval min as discussed in Chapter 6. Using these it is easy to show that:

THEOREM 9.7:   Axioms 9.1, 9.2, and 9.3 hold for $Q3$ possibility.

This is a good point to recall that, as discussed back in Section 3.2.2, propagation in possibility theory may be carried out using product instead of minimum as the combination operation. Such an approach is not considered here (largely because product was not used for combination in the original Pulcinella system), but it is possible. In fact it is easy to show that Axioms 9.1, 9.2, and 9.3 hold for $Q2$ and $Q3$ possibility using max for marginalisation and product for combination.

Finally the operations for propagating belief values are considered. The marginalisation operation for quantitative belief is defined by the following. If $h \subset g$ and G is a mass assignment on g then the marginal of G on h is the mass assignment on h defined by

$$G^{\downarrow h}(a) = \sum \{G(b) : b \subseteq W_g \text{ such that } b^{\downarrow h} = a\}$$

for all $a \subseteq W_h$. The combination of the mass assignments G on g and H on h is the mass assignment on $g \cup h$ defined by

$$(G \otimes H)(c) = \sum \{G(a)H(b) : a^{\uparrow(g \cup h)} \cap b^{\uparrow(g \cup h)} = c\}$$

for all $c \subseteq W_{g \cup h}$, $a \subseteq W_g$, $b \subseteq W_h$. The marginalisation and combination operations for $Q2$ belief values are similar, but with addition and multiplication replaced by qualitative addition and qualitative multiplication. Using these it is possible to prove:

THEOREM 9.8:   Axioms 9.1, 9.2, and 9.3 hold for $Q2$ belief.

For $Q3$ beliefs, marginalisation is by interval addition and combination is as defined above, but with interval addition and interval multiplication replacing addition and multiplication. This gives:

THEOREM 9.9:   Axioms 9.1, 9.2, and 9.3 hold for $Q3$ belief.

Thus Shenoy and Shafer's local computation scheme may be used to propagate $Q2$ and $Q3$ probability, possibility, and belief values.

9.2.3   Mummu/Pulcinella

Thanks to the results obtained in the previous section and the modular way in which Pulcinella is implemented it proved quite straightforward to extend Pulcinella to propagate $Q2$ and $Q3$ versions of probability, possibility and evidence theories. To understand exactly what was done and what the combined Mummu/Pulcinella system provides over and above what is possible with Pulcinella it is first necessary to have a little bit more background on the Pulcinella system.

What Pulcinella provides is a library of Lisp functions that allow the user to create variables and valuations over those variables. The first step in the process of building a model in Pulcinella is to specify which formalism one wishes to use for valuations. The basic system allows the choice of probability theory, possibility theory or evidence theory.[2] Once this choice is made valuations may be entered, values propagated, and the system queried to find the resulting marginal valuation of any variable. Clearly the propagation operations are formalism-dependent, and it turns out that setting valuations also depends upon which formalism is used because the syntax of the valuations varies. This is handled by having a global variable that records which formalism is being used and having the interface functions call different "specializations" (Saffiotti and Umkehrer, 1991b) depending upon the value of this variable. A specialization is a set of functions that together provide the necessary formalism dependent code. The upshot of all this that the same handful of interface functions are used whichever formalism is being used to specify valuations.

From this description it is hopefully clear that what was required in order to implement Mummu/Pulcinella was a series of specializations for setting valuations and carrying out propagation in the $Q2$ and $Q3$ versions of probability, possibility, and evidence theories. This does not sound like much work, and indeed it was even easier than it sounds because the bulk of the propagation mechanism is common to all formalisms—all that it was really necessary to do was to provide was new combination and marginalisation functions along the lines discussed in the previous section, along with some routines for carrying out qualitative and interval arithmetic. Thus the Mummu part of Mummu/Pulcinella consists of six new specializations—$Q2$ and $Q3$ versions of the three theories—plus a module providing the basic arithmetic operations of $Q2$ and $Q3$. From a user's perspective the system looks just like Pulcinella since the same interface functions are used and the same formalisms may be used, the only difference is that it is possible to specify values from the operand sets of $Q2$ and $Q3$ in addition to values from the set of real numbers.

9.3   Implementing the theory of qualitative change

When I first started implementing the theory of qualitative change, my aim was to integrate the implementation closely with the implementation of the qualitative algebras, making it possible to describe problems in terms of both the qualitative influences between variables and the qualitative or interval certainty values of the variables. To do this obviously required the identification of combination and marginalisation operations for qualitative certainty values, interval certainty values, and qualitative changes which all obeyed Axioms 9.1, 9.2, and 9.3. The first operations I looked for were those for interval probability, possibility, and belief values, and, as described in the previous section, these proved easy to adapt from their point valued counterparts. The operations for qualitative probability,

---

2 Pulcinella also allows the use of Boolean values, thus permitting reasoning in propositional logic, but this is not very interesting from the perspective of handling uncertainty.

possibility, and belief values quickly followed. Buoyed up by this success I turned to the operations for qualitative changes convinced that they would be as simple to determine, and at this point the wheels fell off. Despite my best efforts I could find no plausible combination and marginalisation operations for qualitative changes that obeyed Axiom 9.3. Axiom 9.3, of course, is the one that describes the most important property for local computation. I could not even prove that no such operation exists, so the best I can say is that the provision of such operations is an open problem and one that I would like to see solved. However, I strongly suspect that it has no solution.

Anyhow, the upshot of this failure was that I turned to alternative methods of implementing qualitative changes, in particular a modification of Druzdzel's (Druzdzel, 1993; Druzdzel and Henrion, 1993b) message passing algorithm for propagating the effects of evidence through qualitative probabilistic networks, which was mentioned in Section 4.4.1 (and which hadn't been published when I first started implementing the theory of qualitative change). The system that Druzdzel used to implement his algorithm was IDEAL (Srinivas and Breese, 1989) and, taking that as a recommendation, IDEAL was the system I used to implement the qualitative change part of Mummu. As a result, before describing the modification to Druzdzel's algorithm, it is worth spending a little while considering the workings of IDEAL.

9.3.1 The IDEAL system

IDEAL (Srinivas and Breese, 1990, 1989) is a software environment for building and analysing probabilistic causal networks and influence diagrams. It was initially developed as a research tool and takes the form of a set of data structures and a library of functions. The data structures make it possible to represent the nodes in a probabilistic causal network as well as the value and decision nodes of an influence diagram. They also allow the representation of influences between variables, and the probability distributions over these links. The function library includes functions for building causal networks and influence diagrams, editing such networks, and manipulating files that store such networks. The library provides a number of different algorithms for propagating values through models built using causal networks or influence diagrams, including methods based upon message passing, join trees, and influence diagram reduction. This comprehensive collection of algorithms includes all those most widely used at the time the system was built. In addition, and rather more helpfully from the point of view of developing a system for handling QCNs, the system also includes a wide range of lower level network-handling functions that make it possible, for instance, to check that a graph is acyclic and to sort the nodes into graph order.

There is an interesting contrast between Pulcinella and IDEAL from the point of view of using them to develop new systems for propagating certainty values. Pulcinella only provides support for propagation by local computation, and so is only of use when developing methods that obey the local computation axioms. However, Pulcinella provides such an extensive set of relevant functions that the implementation of a new specialization is relatively straightforward. IDEAL, on the other hand is a suitable basis for the development of any system for propagating values through network models. However, it provides little direct support for the development of new methods of propagation beyond basic functions to create nodes and the relations between them.

9.3.2   An algorithm for QPNs

In order to adapt Druzdzel's algorithm for QCNs, it is necessary to do two things. The first is to fully understand the algorithm, and the second is to obtain the necessary results about propagation in QCNs to make it possible to use a similar algorithm. The first of these two tasks is the subject of this section, the other is the subject of Section 9.3.3.

To understand Duzdzel's algorithm it is necessary to first introduce a few formal graph-theoretic concepts in addition to those already stated in Section 5.3.2. Most of these are taken from (Druzdzel, 1993) with three slight alterations. Firstly, where appropriate, they are stated in terms of certainty values so that they are applicable when talking about qualitative certainty networks as well as qualitative probabilistic networks. Secondly they substitute the word "information" for "evidence" since the former term, unlike the latter, does not suggest the preclusion of causal reasoning. Thirdly, the notion of an intercausal link that is given here is less general than that given by Druzdzel since it reflects the less general notion of intercausal reasoning captured by the theory of qualitative change. The basic idea that underpins all the rest is that propagation begins with information about the change in probability at one or more nodes because of some observation:

DEFINITION 9.1:   An *information node* is one about which there is information concerning changes in certainty value that stem from some observation.

For intercausal reasoning it is also important to identify those nodes whose values are known as a result of a previous observation:

DEFINITION 9.2:   A *known node* is one about which there is enough information to completely determine which of its possible values it takes.

The difference between an information node and a known node is as follows. If A is an information node, then as a result of some observation the change in certainty value of all the possible values of A are known. If B is a known node then B is known to take a particular value b. Thus, for instance, if certainty is represented using probability theory, the probability of B taking value b is 1 and the probability of B taking any other value is zero. Thus any known node is also an information node,[3] but information nodes are not, in general, known nodes.

Given the idea of an information node, it is possible to define the notion of an information trail along which the effects of the change in certainty value at the information node is propagated:

DEFINITION 9.3:   An *information trail* between an information node I and a node C is a minimal active trail from I to C.

Such a trail will be made up of links between parent and child nodes, and links between the parents of observed nodes. These two types of link are formalised by the idea of a direct link:

DEFINITION 9.4:   If node A is the parent or the child of node C then there is a *direct link* between A and C.

and the idea of an intercausal link:

DEFINITION 9.5:   If nodes A and B are parents of a head-to-head node C, an *intercausal link* exists between A and B if C is in the set of known nodes.

The sign of an intercausal link in a qualitative probabilistic network is the sign of the product synergy (4.13) between the two nodes involved in the link, and the sign of a direct link is the sign of the qualitative influence between the two nodes involved. This idea can be extended to give the sign of an information trail:

DEFINITION 9.6:   The *sign* of a trail T is the product, determined using $\otimes$, of the signs of all direct and intercausal links on T.

Comparing this with Definition 7.12 and Definition 7.13 highlights the fact that because in a QPN a node and a link have just the one value, the idea of the qualitative influence (in the parlance of the theory of qualitative change) of one value on another and the qualitative influence along a trail coincide, so that both are summarised in the notion of the sign of a trail.

---

3 It is an information node for which the change in certainty value of every possible value is [0]. In other words it is an information node that experiences zero change.

It is also necessary to bring in the idea of the Markov blanket of a node:

DEFINITION 9.7:   The *Markov blanket* of a node *A* is the set that contains all the parents of *A*, all the children of *A*, and the parents of the children of *A*.

The importance of the Markov blanket of a node in most work on probabilistic causal networks is that it *d*-separates that node from the rest of the network. Here it is important because the Markov blanket of a node is the set of all nodes that are directly influenced by a node (the parents and children of the node) plus the set of all nodes which may be intercausally influenced by the node (the other parents of its children).

With these definitions, it is possible to give a local message passing algorithm for propagating the effects of a change in probability through a qualitative probabilistic network (Druzdzel, 1993). What follows is my reconstruction of how and why the algorithm works. The algorithm takes as input a qualitative probabilistic network, the set of known nodes in that network, a particular information node within the network, and the sign of the change in probability at that node. The information node sends a message to each of the relevant nodes in its Markov blanket. Not all nodes in the Markov blanket will receive messages, because not all those that might be intercausally linked to the information node will be. Which will depends on the set of known nodes, and the relevant ones are the nodes to which there are active links. In order that a given node can determine which nodes it has active links to just by interrogating those nodes, each node records whether or not it is one of the known nodes (using the variable *known?*).

Each message passed contains a sign, and the value of that sign is the product (determined using $\otimes$) of the change in probability of the information node and the link that the message traverses. The sign represents the effect of the information upon the node to which it is passed. Each node that receives a message from the information node uses the sign in the message to update its own sign (using $\oplus$), and then passes the message on to all the relevant nodes in its own Markov blanket. In doing so it modifies the sign of the message depending on the influence connecting it to the node it is passing the message to.[4] It is at this point that the possibility of confusion sets in. Does a node pass on the same message that it receives many times, or does it pass on many different messages? For reasons that may become clear later, I have opted to think of the node as passing on many copies of the same message, though any two copies may have different signs. Each node that receives one of these new messages then updates its own sign and passes the message, with suitably modified sign, to each relevant node in its own Markov blanket and the same process

---

4 In Druzdzel's algorithm it is unclear where this information is held, but it is easy to imagine a number of different ways of storing it.

happens again. This recursive process is the basis of Druzdzel's algorithm.

The reason that the algorithm is "local" is that the updating of a particular node only depends on information about that node and its local connections—it is not necessary for a given node to have information about the whole of the network in order to calculate its sign. The reason that the algorithm is sound in the sense that it only calculates signs justified by probability theory is because of Theorem 9.10. This result is proved by Druzdzel (1993)[5]:

THEOREM 9.10:   The qualitative influence of a node I on a node C is equal to the sum of the signs of all the information trails from I to C.

To see why this guarantees soundness, consider the following. In a general network there will be a number of information trails between I and C. The algorithm obviously guarantees that messages will pass along each of these, and so C will receive a number of incoming messages, each of which will contain a sign that represents an influence on the sign of C. These influences will be summed using $\oplus$. Each of these influences is calculated as the product of the sign of I and the signs of all the links traversed as part of the trail. Thus the algorithm guarantees that the sign of C will be the sum of the products of the sign of I and the signs of the information trails between I and C. The theorem then says that given this, the sign of C will be the product of the sign of I and the qualitative influence of I on C, which is exactly as it should be. The completeness of the algorithm follows from the fact that eventually every trail to every node will be traversed.

As described so far, the algorithm is rather inefficient. In fact it will never terminate since every node that receives a message passes it on to at least one node (the node from which the message came since this is obviously in the receiver's Markov blanket). Clearly any realistic algorithm will need to limit the number of messages it generates, and the way to do this is to limit the number of messages passed. An obvious step to take is to modify the algorithm so that messages are only passed to nodes that have not yet been visited by that message. This is easily achieved by having each message carry a list of all the nodes that it has visited. The other trick to reduce the number of messages is a little more devious and comes from observing that not every message that reaches a node need be passed on to other nodes even if the other nodes have not yet received the message. This is because the message may have no effect on the sign of those nodes. Since an incoming sign is combined with the existing sign of the node using $\oplus$, the incoming sign will have no effect on the existing sign if the incoming sign is the same as the existing sign or if the existing sign includes the incoming sign in the sense of Definition 7.14. The sceptical reader is

---

5 The notion of a qualitative influence used in this theorem corresponds to the idea of "overall qualitative influence" defined below rather than to the notions of qualitative influence for qualitative certainty networks that were developed in Chapter 7.

encouraged to check this by considering all possible pairs of incoming and existing sign. If the incoming sign does not change the existing sign, then the incoming message need not be passed on. The `propagate_sign` procedure proposed by Druzdzel and reproduced in Figure 9.1 takes into account these savings in messages. Note that $to : change$ denotes the value of the attribute *change* in the node identified by *to*.

The remainder of the algorithm in Figure 9.1 needs little explanation. The main program starts by setting the change at each node to $'0$ to reflect the fact that the changes calculated are relative to the values before the change at the information node was considered, and the whole process starts by setting the change at the information node i using a call to the procedure `propagate_sign`, which has i as both the node from which the change is being propagated and the node to which it is propagated. It is left to the reader to work out why this is a suitable thing to do. It should be noted that, as discussed in Section 4.4.1 the algorithm as given is only intended to calculate the results of changes at one information node.

If redundant messages are not passed on, then as Druzdzel (Druzdzel, 1993; Druzdzel and Henrion, 1993b) has pointed out, the algorithm becomes quite efficient. The nature of $\oplus$ is such that the sign of a node can change at most twice—first from $'0$ to $'+, '-,$ or $'?$ and second to $'?$ if it is not $'?$ already. This means that the number of messages that will be passed is less than twice the number of nodes in the network, so termination is guaranteed. Furthermore, since each message can only visit each node once, the size of the list of visited nodes in each message is proportional to the number of nodes in the network. Thus the storage required by all various copies of all the messages together is only quadratic in the size of the network.

This should suffice to explain Druzdzel's algorithm, and it is possible to start on the additional work required in order to use an adaptation of it for propagating values in the theory of qualitative change.

9.3.3   Modifying the QPN algorithm

There are a number of results required before a QCN version of Druzdzel's algorithm can be devised. The first of these is is to show that the results given in Chapters 7 and 8 apply to general networks. The need to do this arises from the observation that all the results have been obtained for sub-networks in which a node A influences a node C (or in the case of synergistic and intercausal relationships, a sub-network in which a pair of nodes A and B influence a node C) which has another parent node X. The reader might wonder[6] whether this causes problems when C has parents in addition to X, for instance in the

---

6 Perhaps I am being unkind to the reader. The truth is that at one point I wondered, and only convinced myself by working through the example below (I won't dignify the result by making it a theorem). I hope readers for whom this is obvious will forgive me and skip to the end of the paragraph.

Input: A qualitative probabilistic network *qpn*, a set of known nodes *k*,
   an information node *i* and the change at that node *c*

Output: Updated *qpn* in which every node holds the sign of the influence
   of *i* on that node in its variable *change*

Data structures in each node

   change   (sign of change)
   known?   (is the node in *k*?)

for each node in the network
   do *change* = $'0$;
   propagate_sign($\emptyset$, *i*, *i*, *c*);

propagate_sign(*trail, from, to, sign*)
   trail   (nodes visited)
   from   (sender of the message)
   to   (recipient of the message)
   sign   (sign of the influence between from and to)

begin
   if(*to* : *change* == *sign* $\oplus$ *to* : *change*)
       exit
   to : *change* = *sign* $\oplus$ *to* : *change*;
   trail = *trail* $\cup$ *to*;
   for each *node* in the Markov blanket of *to*
   begin
       influence = sign of link between *node* and *to*;
       if(the link to *n* is active **and** *n* $\notin$ *trail* **and** *node* : *change* $\neq$ *to* : *change* $\otimes$ *influence*)
           propagate_sign(*trail, to, node, to* : *change* $\otimes$ *sign*);
   end
end

Figure 9.1
The local propagation algorithm for qualitative probabilistic networks

situation pictured in Figure 9.2. Happily a simple piece of algebraic manipulation solves the problem. Consider the case in which the network is quantified with probabilities. In this case, according to Theorem 7.3, the propagation between *A* and *C* is controlled by the value of probabilities such as $\Pr(c_1|a_i, X)$ for all values of *X*. If *B* has possible values

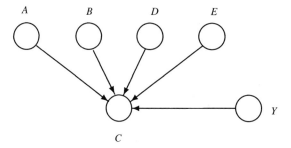

Figure 9.2
A network in which node C has many parents

$\{b_1, \ldots, b_r\}$, D has possible values $\{d_1, \ldots, d_s\}$, E has possible values $\{e_1, \ldots, e_t\}$, and Y has possible values $\{y_1, \ldots, y_u\}$, then the X in the propagation condition is set to be such that:

$$x_1 = b_1 \wedge d_1 \wedge e_1 \wedge y_1$$
$$x_2 = b_2 \wedge d_1 \wedge e_1 \wedge y_1$$
$$\vdots \quad \vdots$$
$$x_p = b_r \wedge d_s \wedge e_t \wedge y_u$$

The conditions are then tested against all these values of X when the necessary theorems are applied.

What this means is that the number of parents does not have any affect on the conditions that determine the direct influence of one node on another. It does not say that additional parents can be ignored when propagating the changes caused by the changes at one parent. In fact, there is a requirement that the change in value of every parent of every node is fed into the calculation. This is necessary because of the subtle change that occurred in moving from singly to multiply-connected networks, and which will require a new paragraph to explain properly.

In singly-connected networks, the effect of any node on the node to which it is directly connected (and hence by Definition 7.12 on any node to which there is a trail from the node in question) is uniquely determined by propagating values along the trail that connects them. This follows from the fact that there is just one trail. In a multiply-connected network there are, in general, multiple trails between any two nodes. Some of these will be mutually reinforcing and some of these will conflict (in the sense that some have a positive influence and some have a negative influence). Since the mechanism by which the influences along these trails will have been established in a QCN is the application of Theorem 8.6 or analogous results,[7] and this gives the direct influence only, it is necessary to take all the trails into account to establish the correct change (which in this general case will be [?]).

One mechanism that could be adopted to ensure that all relevant changes are taken into account is to set the changes in value of all the root and leaf nodes—thus making all such nodes into information nodes—by setting all those for which there is no known change to have a zero change. This approach turns out to be unnecessary because we have the following:

THEOREM 9.11:   Consider a node A, with possible values $\{a_1, \ldots, a_m\}$ that is part of a qualitative certainty network. If the change in certainty value of any value of A is set to $[0]$ this will not result in any possible value of any other node experiencing a non-zero change.

The upshot of Theorem 9.11 is that it is only necessary to feed into the algorithm the changes at nodes whose value is known to be non-zero. However, there is a related problem that also needs solving. This is the problem of what value to assign to nodes by default— the equivalent of the prior value in a numerical network. In a qualitative system, until the system is perturbed by the arrival of new information, all changes are zero, so $[0]$ seems to be the right value to use. From this perspective Theorem 9.11 can be seen as guaranteeing that setting all values which are not known to change to $[0]$ will not result in any spurious inferences. In fact, it is possible to go slightly further, since it is possible to show that:

THEOREM 9.12:   Consider a node A, with possible values $\{a_1, \ldots, a_m\}$ that is part of a qualitative certainty network. If the change in the certainty value of one of the a_i is initially $[0]$, and any value of any node that has a non-zero influence on a_i experiences a subsequent non-zero change, then this will lead to a non-zero change in $\mathrm{Val}(a_i)$.

This guarantees that setting all nodes, other than those whose changes are initially known, to have value $[0]$ will not stop these values being non-zero after all changes have been propagated. This in turn means that setting all values to $[0]$ initially will not invalidate the propagation. Now, in QPNs it is the case that given a non-zero change at a node, there will be a non-zero change at every node along all the trails from that node. However, this is not the case in QCNs, as shown by the following:

THEOREM 9.13:   A set of information nodes $\mathbf{I}$ that have non-zero changes may have zero influences on some nodes on information trails from members of $\mathbf{I}$.

---

7 Remembering that QCNs quantified with belief functions may not be multiply-connected (see Section 8.2).

Thus there is no guarantee that there will be a non-zero change at a node even though it is on a trail from a node whose value is known to change. This in turn means that Theorem 9.12 cannot be strengthened to say that the certainty values of the a_i will change whenever A is on a trail from an information node. This property of the theory of qualitative change has already been encountered in the last example in Chapter 7. There the propagation of possibility values was shown to be blocked in a specific case. Theorem 9.13 shows that the phenomenon can occur whatever values are being propagated.

Before turning to modify the algorithm, there is one further result that is required. This to prove an analogous result to Theorem 9.10 for qualitative changes. This may be proved quite simply, but first requires the following definition:

DEFINITION 9.8:   The *overall qualitative influence between two nodes* is the combined qualitative influence along all trails between them.

Considering how the influences along all the trails interact, gives the necessary theorem.

THEOREM 9.14:   The overall qualitative influence of an information node I on another node C, to which it is connected by a number of different information trails, is the sum of the qualitative influences along all the information trails between them.

In other words, to compute the changes in certainty value at C from those at I one need only compute the effect of the changes in I along all the information trails joining the two nodes and then sum the changes. This result should not come as a surprise. From the earlier discussion of how differential calculus is used to propagate values in the theory of qualitative change, it is clear that the effect of two paths from I to C in a singly-connected network is simply the sum of the changes propagated along those paths. This follows directly from (7.6), which in turn follows from the principle of superposition. In multiply-connected networks, as discussed above, propagation is no different, and so the theorem holds (the proof of Theorem 9.14 is just a slightly more formal version of this argument). A less general result pointing to the same conclusion was also obtained in the course of Jack's adventures with the Subterraneans (see Section 8.2.3).

Now, the importance of Theorem 9.14 is that it makes the necessary algorithm local in exactly the same way as Druzdzel's algorithm is. Thus, in order to determine the change at a given node, it is only necessary to take account of the changes at surrounding nodes. As a result it is possible to use Druzdzel's algorithm almost unchanged. The only difference is that whereas Druzdzel's algorithm only has to compute one change in value at C based upon one change in value at I (because one sign alone describes the change in value at a node in a QPN), the QCN algorithm has to compute the changes in all the possible values

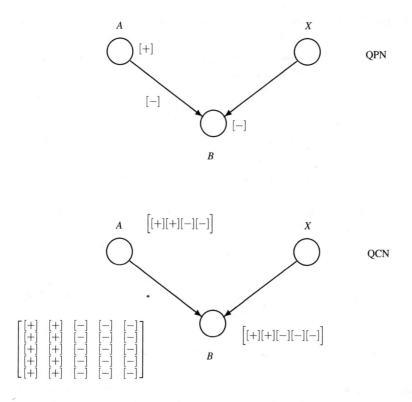

Figure 9.3
Propagating values in QPNs and QCNs

$\{c_1, \ldots, c_n\}$ of C that result from changes in all the possible values $\{i_1, \ldots, i_m\}$ of I.

Consider what this means in practice with reference to Figure 9.3. The calculation of the change at B in the QPN in Figure 9.3 simply involves the qualitative multiplication of the sign of the change at A and the sign of the link joining the two nodes. The calculation of the sign of the change at B in the QCN in Figure 9.3 involves the following matrix calculation:

$$
\begin{bmatrix} [\Delta \text{Val}(b_1)] \\ \vdots \\ [\Delta \text{Val}(b_n)] \end{bmatrix} = \begin{bmatrix} \left[\dfrac{\partial \text{Val}(b_1)}{\partial \text{Val}(a_i)}\right] \\ \vdots \\ \left[\dfrac{\partial \text{Val}(b_n)}{\partial \text{Val}(a_i)}\right] \end{bmatrix} \otimes [\Delta \text{Val}(a_i)]
$$

where a_i is the driving value of A. This calculation is exactly that of (7.4). Now, from the discussion in Section 7.3.4, it should be clear that the driving value for the propagation depends upon the change at A. Given the change at A, it is clear that a_i is the driving value and this value is used to establish the changes at B and the driving value for the nodes that B in turn influences. This, in turn, means that to describe the link joining A and B in Figure 9.3 it will be necessary to store all the derivatives that relate all the possible values of A and B, despite the fact that any particular propagation will only require a subset of these to be used. It will also be necessary to store information about the relationships between possible driving values, so that for a given driving value of A, it is both possible to pick the relevant subset of the derivatives to use for the propagation, and possible to identify the driving value of B. The driving value of B will then be passed to the nodes that B influences.

What all this means in practice for the algorithm is as follows, taking the components in the order they appear in Figure 9.4.

1. Each node needs to store a set of changes in the existing variable *change* rather than a single value.

2. Each link is characterised by a matrix of derivatives rather than a single sign, and also holds a set of relations between driving values in the new variable *drive*.

3. The procedure propagate_sign now holds a list of changes in the variable *sign*, and needs an additional argument *drive*, which is the driving value of the *from* node.

4. Two additional functions are required. The first of these, determine_drive, determines the driving value of the *to* node from that of the *from* node. The second new function, sign_combination, combines the driving value of the *to* node with the link joining the nodes to compute the set of values of the *to* node.

The rest of the algorithm is unchanged. The resulting algorithm is that in Figure 9.4. The new functions are not given because they are quite simple—both are just look-up tables. Note that this algorithm only works for QCNs that are specified using partial derivatives. A very similar algorithm will work for separable derivatives, though such an algorithm does not form part of Mummu/Ideal. Note also that the algorithm given, just like the QPN algorithm on which it is based, has problems handling situations in which there are several information nodes.

As ever, it is useful to consider the complexity of this algorithm, and this is done by imagining a network of n nodes, where each node has m possible values. Thinking of the propagation in the same way as for Druzdzel's network, as a set of messages sent from the information nodes and spreading through the network along the information trails, the following analysis applies. Each of the m values at a node can change at most twice (for exactly the same reason that the sign of a node can change at most twice in

Input: A qualitative certainty network *qcn*, a set of known nodes *k*, an information
node *i*, the change at that node *c*, and its driving value *v*

Output: Updated *qcn* in which every node holds the sign of the influence
of *i* on that node in its variable *change*

Data structures in each node

change	(a list of changes)
known?	(is the node in *k*?)

Data structures in each link

nodes	(nodes joined by link)
derivatives	(matrix of derivatives relating values of nodes)
drive	(relation between driving values)

for each node in the network, **do** *ch* = ′0;
    propagate_sign(∅, *i*, *i*, *c*, *v*);

propagate_sign(*trail, from, to, sign, drive*)

trail	(nodes visited)
from	(sender of the message)
to	(recipient of the message)
sign	(list of changes propagated between from and to)
driving	(the current driving value of from)

begin
    if(*to* : *change* == *sign* ⊕ *to* : *change*), **exit**;
    to : *change* = *sign* ⊕ *to* : *change*;
    trail = *trail* ∪ *to*;
    for each *node* in the Markov blanket of *to*, **do**
    begin
        link is the link between *to* and *node*;
        driving_value = determine_drive(*to*, *link*, *driving*);
        if(the link to *node* is active **and** *node* ∉ *trail*)
            propagate_sign(*trail*, *to*, *node*, sign_combination(*to*, *link*, *driving_value*);
    end
end

Figure 9.4
The local propagation algorithm for qualitative certainty networks

Druzdzel's algorithm). Because the algorithm discards messages that do not change any of the values at a node, this means that each node will receive at most $2m$ messages (this is a worst case figure that assumes each message changes only one of the m values). Thus the maximum number of messages that will be passed around any network is $2mn$. This guarantees termination. Each message holds the vector of the m changes in the last node it passed through along with the list of up to n nodes it has passed through, making a total of $m + n$ pieces of information. Thus the maximum storage requirement for all the messages, assuming that they are all running simultaneously, is:

$$2mn(m + n) = 2m^2n + 2mn^2$$

If the number of nodes in the network is significantly larger than the number of values of each node, this reduces to the result for Druzdzel's algorithm, that the storage requirement is quadratic in the size of the network.

It is also possible to estimate the worst case complexity of the computation. At each node for each message that arrives, there are m multiplications to combine the incoming values and the derivatives and m additions to combine these new values with the existing ones. Given the total number of messages, this gives a total of $2m^2$ additions and multiplications at each node, and thus $2m^2n$ multiplications and $2m^2n$ additions for the network as a whole. Thus, as for Druzdzel's algorithm, the total number of calculations is linear in the size of the network, and the only difference in complexity between the QCN algorithm and Druzdzel's algorithm is the increased number of calculations at each node.

This analysis has, of course, ignored the effect of propagating driving values, while taking in account the advantage of using them. If the driving value is taken into account it turns the m pieces of information in each message into $m + 1$, but otherwise has no effect on the amount of information passed around.[8] Using the driving value does significantly reduce the computation required for each message. Without it, it would be necessary to combine the m incoming values with every one of the m^2 derivatives, resulting in m^3 multiplications.

9.3.4 Mummu/Ideal

Mummu/Ideal provides an implementation of the ideas developed in the previous section. It builds upon the function library and data structures provided by IDEAL in the following way. The existing data structures for representing nodes and the links between them were extended to make it possible to associate qualitative values with them. Each node in Mummu/Ideal has a vector of qualitative values (one value for each of the possible values

---

8 Though the need to store the relationship between the driving values does affect the amount of storage required at each node.

of the nodes) associated with it, and each link has a matrix of qualitative values (one value for each of the relevant qualitative derivatives) associated with it. In addition, there is a data structure to hold the matrix of intercausal influences between the common causes of leaf nodes.

The function library is extended with functions that allow the various data structures to be instantiated with their qualitative values, functions to declare information nodes and the changes at those nodes, and functions to query the values of nodes and links. The final functions, then, are those that implement the propagation algorithm. These functions give Mummu/Ideal a similar programming interface to that of Mummu/Pulcinella—there are a set of functions for declaring the structure of the network, functions for propagating values through the network, and functions for querying the results of the propagation.

9.4 Summary

This chapter has described the Mummu system, an implementation of the ideas introduced in Chapters 6, 7, and 8. The system takes the form of a set of Lisp functions that permit the construction and evaluation of models based on qualitative versions of probability, possibility, and evidence theories. There are two distinct components of the system. The first, Mummu/Pulcinella, is based upon the Pulcinella system (Saffiotti and Umkehrer, 1991b) and allows the construction and evaluation of models that employ qualitative algebras. These models are valuation systems (Shenoy, 1989) and so propagate values using the local computation mechanism proposed by Shenoy and Shafer (Shenoy and Shafer, 1990). The version of the system that exists at the time of writing allows for valuations that use $Q2$ and $Q3$ versions of probability, possibility, and evidence theory— the proof of the soundness of the local computation mechanism for such valuations was the first major contribution of this chapter. The second component of Mummu, Mummu/Ideal, is based upon the IDEAL system (Srinivas and Breese, 1989) and allows the construction and evaluation of qualitative certainty networks. In other words it permits the construction and evaluation of directed graphs in which the focus is the computation of the change in probability, possibility, or belief and in which such computation is mediated by the theory of qualitative change. The propagation of values in Mummu/Ideal takes place by local message passing, and the development of the message passing algorithm from that provided by Druzdzel (Druzdzel, 1993; Druzdzel and Henrion, 1993b) for QPNs was the second major contribution of this chapter.

Having obtained the necessary technical results and described the implementation, it is possible to consider the use of Mummu in dealing with uncertainty in the context of a particular problem—the problem of predicting protein topology.

10 Qualitative protein topology prediction

So... we should seek a whole new idea, something just a little bit strange, perhaps cruel, or even twisted, to get us through this low period.

Hunter S. Thompson, *Generation of Swine*

Up to this point, the qualitative systems developed in Chapters 6, 7 and 8 have only been tested on rather artificial examples. Hopefully these examples have convinced the reader that the systems both behave in a reasonable way and may be used to model intriguing situations, and so have persuaded the reader that the systems are worth studying. However, it is unrealistic to hope that the true value of the systems can be usefully gauged by solving such small problems. After all, the whole reason for developing the qualitative systems is to handle real world problems and so it is not to be expected that much argument can be made for them in the absence of solutions to such problems. In an attempt, therefore, to prove the true worth of the systems developed in Chapters 6, 7 and 8, this chapter looks at how they might be applied to a large and complex problem that requires the modelling of a number of different types of uncertainty. This is the problem of predicting protein topology. In some ways this problem is ideal for the testing of the systems. The problem, at least in the form in which it is tackled here, is reasonably easy to understand, small enough to be manageable, and contains enough imperfect information to intrigue. That is why I started work upon it. However, it does have some drawbacks. The first is that it does involve coming to terms with a little domain knowledge, though I trust that the reader is prepared to persevere enough to make this a minor hitch. The second is more serious. Since the problem is one for which there is no established solution,[1] it is not possible to demonstrate that the methods give a better solution than any other approach. Thus no argument can be made for the methods providing a wonderful new approach from the point of view of molecular biology (though they do offer a natural development of existing approaches to the problem as discussed in Section 10.1). However, merely representing the various imperfections in information in the problem and then generating some solutions is sufficient to demonstrate that the qualitative systems may be usefully applied in real problems, and that is what this chapter aims to do. In doing so, the chapter concentrates mainly upon the use of qualitative algebras, in particular $Q3$. This is because I feel that the case for qualitative probabilistic networks has been made elsewhere—by Wellman (1990a), Druzdzel (1993), Michelena (1991) and most recently by van der Gaag (Druzdzel and van der Gaag, 1995; van der

---

1 The topologies in question are not known and the molecular biology literature merely points to a set of plausible solutions whose likelihood of being correct is a matter of conjecture.

Gaag, 1999)—and that this shows the potential usefullness of the theory of qualitative change.

10.1   Introduction

Proteins are large biological macromolecules that form the main components of living organisms. In addition, in the form of enzymes, hormones, and antibodies, proteins control most of the crucial processes in cells and are thus of vital importance to all living organisms. The reason that the structure of a protein is of such importance is that the function of a particular protein is determined by the chemical interactions at its surface, and these are related to its three dimensional structure. Now, this structure is hard to establish experimentally. In contrast, it is easy to determine the component parts of a protein, and, in theory, it is possible to predict the three dimensional structure from knowledge of these components. This prediction of protein structure is an important problem in molecular biology.

The structure of proteins can be described at various levels of detail, usually identified by the terms "primary," "secondary," and "tertiary." The primary structure of a protein consists of a description of the components of the chains of amino acids that make up the protein. Each amino acid is one of twenty naturally occurring molecules from which all proteins are made. The sequential order of the acids in the protein chain determines the unique structure of the protein, by affecting the way the chain is folded into three dimensions. The secondary structure of a protein is a description of the way that the amino acids are grouped together into substructures within this three dimensional pattern. These substructures can be thought of as energetically stable arrangements and are formed as a result of hydrogen bonding between different amino acids. The two most frequently identified forms of secondary structure are β-sheets, which consist of a number of β-strands, and α-helices. Where a structure is neither an α-helix or a β-strand it is said to be a "coil." The tertiary structure of a protein is the set of three dimensional co-ordinates of every atom in the protein. The term "protein topology" is used to denote an intermediate level, somewhere between secondary and tertiary structure, which specifies how secondary structural units combine together into larger complexes such as α/β-sheets. The prediction of protein topology is particularly interesting because it can be used to guide the choice of experiments to confirm protein structure and to search for similar known structures. It is also much easier to establish the protein topology than the full 3-D structure. For all these reasons it is the prediction of protein topology that will be the focus of this chapter.

Many techniques have been applied to the various computational problems offered by molecular biology, but two are of especial importance from the point of view of this chapter—constraint satisfaction and probabilistic models. Constraint satisfaction techniques have been widely applied (Gaspin et al., 1995), including application to problems such as RNA structure prediction (Gaspin and Regin, 1997; Gaspin and Westhof, 1995), genetic map assembly (Clark et al., 1994), protein tertiary structure prediction (Hayes-Roth et al., 1986), and protein topology prediction (Clark et al., 1992). Probabilistic models have also been widely used, having found application in protein secondary structure prediction (Chen et al., 1999; Delcher et al., 1993a,b; Munson et al., 1993; Sonnhammer et al., 1998), protein tertiary structure prediction (Asai et al., 1993; Schmidt et al., 1998), identification of protein families (Brown et al., 1993; Haussler et al., 1993; Pedersen et al., 1996), RNA structure prediction (Altman, 1993), identification of genes in DNA sequences (Krogh, 1997; Kulp et al., 1996; Salzburg et al., 1996), pedigree analysis (Spiegelhalter, 1990; Szolovits, 1992) and genetic map construction (Schiex and Gaspin, 1997). There have even been a few applications that combine constraint satisfaction and the use of probability and similar measures (Altman and Jardetzky, 1989; Altman, 1994; Clark et al., 1993). The reason for the use of constraint satisfaction and probabilistic methods is that both provide a means of handling one of the two most difficult aspects of molecular biology problems—that they involve huge search spaces, and that they are full of uncertain and noisy information (Allison, 1993). The fact that the search spaces are so large means that it is not feasible to search them exhaustively and so some means of restricting the search is required. The "constrain and generate" methods adopted by systems of constraint satisfaction do precisely this. The fact that data is uncertain and noisy suggests that methods that take this into account by explicitly modelling the imperfections in the data (MacKenzie et al., 1993) will be profitable, and this is borne out by, for instance, the good performance of probabilistic methods for protein structure prediction (Delcher et al., 1993a,b).

This chapter describes some experiments in explicitly representing the uncertainty of a set of constraints used for protein topology prediction, which make use of the models of uncertainty developed in earlier chapters. These experiments thus provide an advance on previous attempts to model the uncertainty in this problem (Clark et al., 1993) and demonstrate the use of these new means of representing and reasoning with uncertainty to complement the existing use of probabilistic networks in this area. As with previous work in this area, the intention is to help a molecular biologist explore the space of possible protein structures, rather than to present her with a structure that is guaranteed to be correct, and the reason for making the connection with the work of Clark and colleagues (Clark et al., 1992) is both to provide a context for the use of the qualitative models and to stress their direct applicability to the real world—with a little work a tool with the potential of being of real use to a molecular biologist could be constructed.

10.2 Protein topology prediction

The major problem with predicting protein topology is that a vast number of possible topologies can be hypothesised for a given secondary structure. For example, a mixed α/β-sheet of n strands, where $n > 1$, can be arranged in

$$\frac{n!(4n-1)}{2}$$

possible ways (Clark et al., 1992). One way to reduce this space is to identify and apply constraints based upon previous analyses of similar proteins. For example, for α/β sheets (Taylor and Green, 1989; Clark et al., 1992) the following constraints might be used[2]:

- C1. For parallel pairs of β-strands, β-α-β and β-coil-β connections are right handed (Richardson, 1976; Sternberg and Thornton, 1977).

- C2. The first β-strand in the sheet is not at the edge of the sheet (Bränden, 1990).

- C3. Only one change in winding direction occurs (Richardson, 1981).

- C4. The β-strands associated with the conserved[3] patterns lie adjacent in the sheet (Walker et al., 1982).

- C5. All strands lie parallel in the β-sheet.

- C6. Unconserved strands are at the edge of the sheet.

- F1. Strands are ordered in the sheet by hydrophobicity (the degree to that they lack an affinity for water), with the most hydrophobic strands central.

- F2. Parallel β-coil-β connections contain at least 10 amino acids.

- F3. Large insertions and deletions[4] are expected to occur on the edge of a domain.

- F4. Most conserved loops lie adjacent in front.

- F5. Long secondary-structure units should lie parallel or anti-parallel to one another, with sequential units being anti-parallel.

These constraints can be applied manually, as described by Taylor and Green (1989), or by generating all possible topologies and removing those that do not conform to the constraints (Cohen and Kuntz, 1987). However manual search is a time-consuming and

---

2 The names of the constraints come from (Taylor and Green, 1989) where $C1$–$C6$ are the constraints applied during the construction of the solutions ($C6$ being implicit as argued in (Clark et al., 1992)), and $F1$–$F5$ are generally applicable "folding rules" used to assess whether predicted structures are valid.

3 When the amino acid sequences of proteins that perform similar functions, but are found in different species, are compared, parts of the sequences are often found to be the same in all proteins. These are said to be conserved.

4 When amino acid sequences are aligned to determine conserved regions, some regions do not match. Thus, to align the conserved regions it is necessary to split up sequences, "inserting" spaces between certain amino acids. Similarly, it may be necessary to "delete" acids in order to match regions.

Table 10.1
The results of checking constraints against eight proteins

Protein ID.	Constraints Violated	Protein ID.	Constraints Violated
p4adh	F1	p1pfk	C5 F1
p5adh	F1	p2pfk	C5 F1
p6adh	F1	p3pfk	C5
p7adh	F1	p4pfk	C5
p1ldx		p1gpd	C3 C5 F1 F2
p3ldh	F1	p1gd1	C3 C5 F1 F2
p4ldh	F1	p2gpd	C3 C5 F1 F2
p3dfr	C3 C5 F1	p3grs	C2 F1
p4dfr	C3 C5 F1 F2		
		p3pgk	F1
p3adk			

error-prone procedure suitable only for small sheets, and exhaustive search is far too inefficient to be applied to large structures. As a result, Clark and colleagues (1992) developed a Prolog program named CBS1 (later re-implemented in ElipSys as CBS1e and CBS2e (Clark et al., 1993)) to apply the constraints. In this constraint-based approach, the search proceeds by incrementally adding components (such as β-strands) to a set of possible structures. After each addition the set of structures is pruned by testing against every constraint. CBS1 was used to reproduce Taylor and Green's results, as well as to identify a new topological hypothesis consistent with the constraints (Clark et al., 1992), indicating that the original search was not exhaustive. As one might imagine, because the constraints are derived from aggregate properties of a collection of proteins, they do not apply to all of them. Clark and colleagues (Clark et al., 1992) assessed the validity of $C1$, $C2$, $C3$, $C5$, $F1$, and $F2$ by checking them against the known structures of eight proteins with similar function. The results are reproduced in Table 10.1, where the structures that are grouped together are those relating to the same protein. For instance $p1gpd$, $p1gd1$, and $p2gpd$ are different experimentally determined structures for D-glyceraldehyde-3-phosphate dehydrogenase. Each of the variations should be considered equally valid, so when a rule holds for one form of a protein and not for another, it is ambiguous whether or not the constraint holds for that protein. Other results support the idea of constraints being uncertain. For instance, King and colleagues (King et al., 1994) found that some of the constraints used by Clark et al. failed to hold for more general classes of proteins. Thus while the folding rules are useful heuristics, they are only true some of the time, suggesting that explicitly modelling the uncertainty in the constraints might be advisable.

10.3   A first approach to modelling the uncertainty

One approach to modelling the uncertainty is to assess the validity of a structure based upon
the constraints to which that structure conforms, and this is one of the methods adopted
here. The same approach was independently proposed in (Clark et al., 1993) though these
authors used a less sophisticated model. The best way of modelling the uncertainty in the
constraints is not clear, and so in the tradition of experimental investigations of the best way
of modelling uncertainty in a given problem (Heckerman, 1990a; Heckerman and Shwe,
1993; Saffiotti et al., 1994) a number of different ways in which the data from Table 10.1
may be represented are discussed. There are, of course, other possibilities that are not
discussed here—only some of the most obvious models are covered.

10.3.1   Using probability theory

Since the data is drawn from a reasonably random population of proteins, the following
simple argument can be made. Table 10.1 holds a list of 8 proteins. Of these, 7 conform
to constraint $C2$, and 1 does not, so a possible protein structure that conforms to $C2$, has a
probability of:

$$\Pr(C2) = \frac{\text{Number of proteins for which } C2 \text{ holds}}{\text{Total number of proteins}}$$
$$= \frac{7}{8}$$

of being a real protein of the relevant class. Since the sample size is very small, the
probabilities will not be very accurate, but they will be the best values that can be obtained
given the data to hand.

However, there is a problem with this approach, which arises because the data is
ambiguous. Of the eight proteins analysed, several have alternative structures and some
constraints hold for some alternative structures and not for others. Thus it is not clear
whether or not some constraints are valid for some proteins. To handle this ambiguity
within probability theory more subtle approaches are required. One is to "disambiguate"
and consider each of the 19 possible structures as a separate entity. Doing this makes it
possible to argue that of these 19 structures, 18 conform to $C2$ and 1 doesn't, so that a
structure that conforms to $C2$ has a probability of:

$$\Pr(C2) = \frac{\text{Number of structures for which } C2 \text{ holds}}{\text{Total number of structures}}$$
$$= \frac{18}{19}$$

of being a real protein. This approach gives the probabilities of Table 10.2. However,

Table 10.2
Probabilities of constraints holding based upon the "disambiguated" interpretation. The total number of structures is 19.

Constraint (x)	Number of cases in which the constraint is violated	Pr(x)
C1	0	1.0
C2	1	0.947
C3	5	0.737
C5	9	0.526
F1	15	0.211
F2	4	0.789

it could be argued that disambiguation distorts the data, and the uncertainty should be modelled in a "purer" way acknowledging the ambiguity. One way of doing this is to use interval probabilities to represent the uncertainty, with the lower bound calculated by counting proteins for which the rule is ambiguous as proteins for which it fails to hold, and the upper bound by counting proteins for which the rule is ambiguous as proteins for which it does hold. So, for a constraint for which there is no ambiguity, for instance $C2$, the probability is as before:

$$\Pr(C2) = \frac{\text{Number of proteins for which } C2 \text{ holds}}{\text{Total number of proteins}}$$

$$= \frac{7}{8}$$

For ambiguous constraints such as $F1$ there are some proteins for which the constraint is known to hold for all structures and some for which it is known to hold for at least one structure, so:

$$\Pr(F1) = \left[\frac{\text{Number of proteins for which } F1 \text{ holds for every structure}}{\text{Total number of proteins}}, \frac{\text{Number of proteins for which } F1 \text{ holds for at least one structure}}{\text{Total number of proteins}} \right]$$

$$= \left[\frac{1}{8}, \frac{3}{8} \right]$$

Using this method the probabilities of Table 10.3 are obtained.

10.3.2   Using possibility theory

It is also possible to model the constraints using possibility theory by adopting the following argument. If a structure conforms to a constraint, it is entirely possible that the structure is that of a naturally occurring protein. However, if a structure fails to conform to a constraint then it becomes less possible that the structure is a naturally occurring protein. Indeed the possibility of the structure being a naturally occurring protein falls to a figure that reflects the proportion of naturally occurring proteins that do not conform to the

Table 10.3
Probabilities of constraints holding based upon the "pure" interpretation. The total number of proteins is 8.

Constraint (x)	Number of cases in which the constraint is violated	Pr(x)
C1	0	1.0
C2	1	0.875
C3	2	0.75
C5	3	0.625
F1	5–7	[0.125, 0.375]
F2	1–2	[0.75, 0.875]

Table 10.4
Possibilities of constraints holding based upon the "disambiguated" interpretation. The total number of structures is 19.

Constraint (x)	Number of cases in which the constraint is violated	$\Pi(x)$	$\Pi(\neg x)$
C1	0	1.0	1.0
C2	1	1.0	0.053
C3	5	1.0	0.263
C5	9	1.0	0.474
F1	15	1.0	0.789
F2	4	1.0	0.211

constraint. This, broadly speaking, is the approach suggested by Farreny and Prade (1985) and discussed in Section 4.5.2. Thus, for each constraint Cx, the possibility that the protein occurs in nature given that Cx holds is 1, $\Pi(Cx) = 1$, while the possibility that the protein occurs in nature given that Cx does not hold, $\Pi(\neg Cx)$, depends upon the data in Table 10.1. Thus, a possible protein structure that does not conform to $C2$ has a possibility of:

$$\Pi(\neg C2) = \frac{\text{Number of proteins for which } C2 \text{ does not hold}}{\text{Total number of proteins}} \qquad (10.1)$$

$$= \frac{1}{8}$$

of being a real protein. Once again there are problems with ambiguity, and again there are a number of possible ways of dealing with it. If the ambiguity is "disambiguated" the following kind of results are obtained:

$$\Pi(\neg C2) = \frac{\text{Number of structures for which } C2 \text{ does not hold}}{\text{Total number of structures}}$$

$$= \frac{1}{19}$$

and Table 10.4 is the outcome. If the ambiguity is acknowledged, then interval possibility values can be used to capture it. While the possibilities of non-ambiguous constraints are

Table 10.5
Possibilities of constraints holding based upon the "pure" interpretation. The total number of proteins is 8.

Constraint (x)	Number of cases in which the constraint is violated	$\Pi(x)$	$\Pi(\neg xA)$
C1	0	1.0	0
C2	1	1.0	0.125
C3	2	1.0	0.25
C5	3	1.0	0.375
F1	5–7	1.0	[0.625, 0.875]
F2	1–2	1.0	[0.125, 0.25]

calculated as in (10.1), for ambiguous constraints such as $F1$ the value is determined by the following method:

$$\Pi(\neg F1) = \left[\frac{\text{Number of proteins for which } F1 \text{ does not hold for every structure}}{\text{Total number of proteins}}, \frac{\text{Number of proteins for which } F1 \text{ does not hold for at least one structure}}{\text{Total number of proteins}} \right]$$

$$= \left[\frac{5}{8}, \frac{7}{8} \right]$$

This approach gives the possibilities of Table 10.5.

10.3.3   Using evidence theory

The information about the applicability of the constraints may also be modelled using evidence theory, and this approach is particularly attractive since evidence theory has a built-in mechanism for handling the ambiguity in the data. Thus, for an ambiguous constraint such as $F1$:

$$m(F1) = \frac{\text{Number of proteins for which } F1 \text{ holds for every structure}}{\text{Total number of proteins}}$$

$$= \frac{1}{8}$$

$$m(\neg F1) = \frac{\text{Number of proteins for which } F1 \text{ does not hold for every structure}}{\text{Total number of proteins}}$$

$$= \frac{5}{8}$$

$$m(\{F1, \neg F1\}) = 1 - \big(m(F1) + m(\neg F1)\big)$$

$$= \frac{1}{4}$$

Table 10.6
Basic mass distribution for the constraints holding. The total number of proteins is 8.

Constraint (x)	Number of cases in which the constraint is violated	$m(x)$	$m(\neg x)$	$m(x \cup \neg x)$
C1	0	1.0	0	0
C2	1	0.875	0.125	0
C3	2	0.75	0.25	0
C5	3	0.625	0.375	0
F1	5–7	0.125	0.625	0.25
F2	1–2	0.75	0.125	0.125

while for one that is not ambiguous, such as $C2$:

$$m(C2) = \frac{\text{Number of proteins for which } C2 \text{ holds for every structure}}{\text{Total number of proteins}}$$

$$= \frac{7}{8}$$

$$m(\neg C2) = \frac{\text{Number of proteins for which } C2 \text{ does not hold for every structure}}{\text{Total number of proteins}}$$

$$= \frac{2}{8}$$

$$m(\{C2, \neg C2\}) = 0$$

Using this method, the basic mass distributions of Table 10.6 are obtained.

10.3.4 The valuation system models

Having considered some of the different ways in which the uncertain nature of the constraints can be modelled, the obvious question is how to employ these models in topology prediction. In particular, how to use the probability, possibility, and evidence values to establish how certain particular structures are to be real proteins. To do this it is necessary to both determine how the various pieces of information interact in determining the certainty, and how to represent the interactions. For the data that is available, the valuation systems used by Mummu are a natural representation since they allow the easy combination of probability, possibility, and belief values in the same model by providing a uniform representation.

The valuation system that was adopted for handling the data in Tables 10.2–10.6 is given in Figure 10.1. This network is based upon that in (Smets and Hsia, 1991), and expresses the fact that the validity of the structure is a combination of the effect of all constraints, and that the constraints hold by default until they are explicitly represented

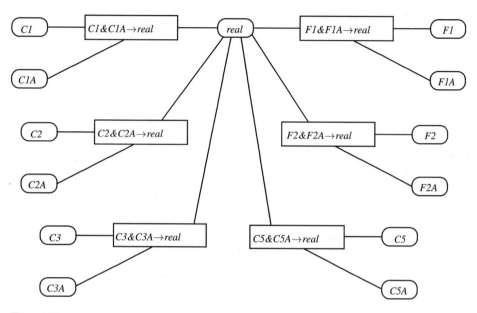

Figure 10.1
A network relating the effects of constraints to the likelihood that a structure is real.

as failing. Thus, for $C1$ there is a node "$C1A$"[5] that is true if $C1$ holds for the structure in question, and false otherwise. The value of this node combined with the value of the nodes "$C1\&C1A \rightarrow real$" and "$C1$." The valuation for the node "$C1\&C1A \rightarrow real$" is intended to capture an implication. Following Smets and Hsia (1991), in a probabilistic model it allocates the same probability of $1/7$ to all combinations of the possible values of $C1$, $C1A$, and *real* except the triple $C1 = true$, $C1A = true$, and $real = false$, this latter being assigned a probability of zero. In a possibilistic mode it allocates a possibility of 1 to all combinations except $C1 = true$, $C1A = true$, and $real = false$, and in a belief model it allocates a belief of 1 to the set that contains all combinations except $C1 = true$, $C1A = true$ and $real = false$. The node $C1$ contains information about the certainty that constraint $C1$ applies, and so holds values from Tables 10.2–10.6. The value obtained from the combination of values from these three nodes is then combined with similar results for other constraints to get an overall measure of the likelihood that the protein is real. This valuation system was then evaluated using Mummu to get the results presented in the next section. It should be noted that this is an extremely simple model since it assumes that the constraints have no effect on each other's applicability. In the absence of any information

5 An arbitrary name, but it can be thought of as capturing information about whether $C1$ *applies* or not.

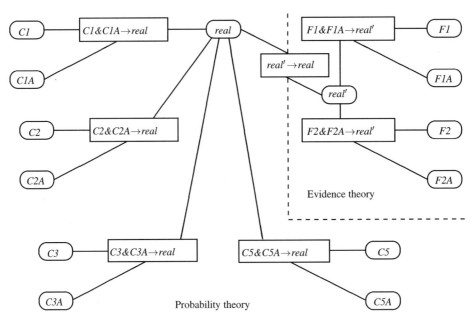

Figure 10.2
A network relating the effects of constraints in which probabilities and beliefs may be combined.

as to how the constraints interact this seems to be a reasonable initial assumption, and if any interactions were established, they could easily be incorporated into the model.

This, of course, is just one possible representation that uses the available data. Another makes use of the work on integrating formalisms presented in Chapter 6. Consider the following argument. There are point probabilities (Table 10.3) that model conformance to $C1$ to $C5$, and there is some ambiguous data best modelled in evidence theory (Table 10.6) that says something about structures that conform to $F1$ and $F2$. This suggests that the network of Figure 10.1 be partitioned into two parts as in Figure 10.2. In this network values are propagated according to evidence theory in the right-hand section until a value for the node *real'* is established. This value is then translated into a probability interval and combined with the results from the rest of the network to establish overall probabilistic measures of validity. To recap, the translation introduced in Chapter 6 uses intervals to model the fact that a belief value may be taken as the lower bound on a probability, thus:

$$\text{Bel}(x) = n \mapsto \text{Pr}(x) = [n, 1] \tag{10.2}$$

and thus:

$$Pr(\neg x) = [0, 1 - n] \tag{10.3}$$

This is only one way of combining formalisms. An alternative is to combine the evidence theory model of the ambiguous data about $F1$ and $F2$ with the possibility model. Such an integration would be carried out in the network of Figure 10.2, but with every probability replaced with a possibility based on values from Table 10.5. The translation here is based upon the fact that a belief is a lower bound on a probability and a possibility is an upper bound, so a belief is a lower bound on a possibility:

$$Bel(x) = n \mapsto \Pi(x) = [n, 1] \tag{10.4}$$

While these translations generate interval probability and possibility values, it should be noted that the belief values are not intervals—they are point belief values just as in the original Dempster-Shafer theory.

10.3.5 Results using the first approach

The results of using the models in Figures 10.1 and 10.2 with the data in Tables 10.2–10.6 is given in tabular form in Tables 10.7–10.9 and in graphical form in Figures 10.3–10.6. In more detail, the results can be related to the initial data as follows.

Table 10.2 has point values for each of the constraint probabilities $Pr(xA)$ that are based on the disambiguated sample of eight proteins. The results of using these in the first valuation system model are given in Figure 10.3(a) and the second column of Tables 10.7, 10.8 and Table 10.9. In the graph each point on the x-axis corresponds to a single set of constraints,[6] with the validity measured up the y-axis. The point numbered 1 on the x-axis corresponds to the first set of constraints in Table 10.7, the point numbered 22 on the x-axis corresponds to the first set of constraints in Table 10.8, and the point numbered 44 on the x-axis corresponds to the first set of constraints in Table 10.9. These results show a range of values from the certainty that a topology will be a real protein when all the constraints hold, to ignorance (a probability of 0.5) when no constraints hold. Note that any structure that conforms to $C1$ is predicted to be certainly real since none of the proteins in the sample had structures that violated $C1$.

Table 10.3 has interval values that represent the ambiguity surrounding $F1$ and $F2$ holding. Results using these values are given in the third column of Tables 10.7, 10.8 and 10.9 and are displayed graphically in Figure 10.3(b). In order to represent intervals as part of the graph they have been transformed into point values by replacing them with their

---

6 It should be noted that the order of the sets of constraints along the x-axis is rather arbitrary, but roughly corresponds to to having large sets of constraints to the left and small sets to the right.

Table 10.7
Results of the first experiment in assessing the validity of sets of constraints

Constraint Set	Pr(real)	Pr(real)	Bel(real)	II(¬real)	II(¬real)	Pr(real)	II(¬real)
{C1, C2, C3, C5, F1, F2}	1.0	[0.467 1.0]	1.0	0	[0 0]	[0.855 1]	[0 0]
{C1, C2, C3, C5, F1}	1.0	[0.467 1.0]	1.0	0	[0 0]	[0.231 1]	[0 0]
{C1, C2, C3, C5, F2}	1.0	[0.467 1.0]	1.0	0	[0 0]	[0.778 1]	[0 0]
{C1, C2, C3, C5}	1.0	[0.467 1.0]	1.0	0	[0 0]	[0 1]	[0 0]
{C1, C3, C5, F1, F2}	1.0	[0.467 1.0]	1.0	0	[0 0]	1.0	[0 0]
{C1, C3, C5, F1}	1.0	[0.467 1.0]	1.0	0	[0 0]	[0.231 1]	[0 0]
{C1, C3, C5, F2}	1.0	[0.467 1.0]	1.0	0	[0 0]	[0.778 1]	[0 0]
{C1, C3, C5}	1.0	[0.467 1.0]	1.0	0	[0 0]	[0 1]	[0 0]
{C1, C2, C5, F1, F2}	1.0	[0.467 1.0]	1.0	0	[0 0]	[0.855 1]	[0 0]
{C1, C2, C5, F1}	1.0	[0.467 1.0]	1.0	0	[0 0]	[0.231 1]	[0 0]
{C1, C2, C5, F2}	1.0	[0.467 1.0]	1.0	0	[0 0]	[0.778 1]	[0 0]
{C1, C2, C5}	1.0	[0.467 1.0]	1.0	0	[0 0]	[0 1]	[0 0]
{C2, C3, C5, F1, F2}	0.999	[0.466 0.998]	0.999	0.053	[0.125 0.125]	[0.854 0.999]	[0 0.125]
{C2, C3, C5, F1}	0.995	[0.463 0.991]	0.992	0.053	[0.125 0.125]	[0.230 0.995]	[0 0.125]
{C2, C3, C5, F1}	0.999	[0.465 0.997]	0.998	0.053	[0.125 0.125]	[0.0.777 0.999]	[0 0.125]
{C2, C3, C5}	0.993	[0.461 0.988]	0.988	0.053	[0.125 0.125]	[0 0.994]	[0 0.125]
{C1, C2, C3, F1, F2}	1.0	[0.467 1.0]	1.0	0	[0 0]	[0.855 1]	[0 0]
{C1, C2, C3, F1}	1.0	[0.467 1.0]	1.0	0	[0 0]	[0.231 1]	[0 0]
{C1, C2, C3, F2}	1.0	[0.467 1.0]	1.0	0	[0 0]	[0.777 1]	[0 0]
{C1, C2, C3, F1, F2}	1.0	[0.467 1.0]	1.0	0	[0 0]	[0 1]	[0 0]
{C1, C2, F1, F2}	1.0	[0.467 1.0]	1.0	0	[0 0]	[0.855 1]	[0 0]

Table 10.8
Results of the first experiment in assessing the validity of sets of constraints

Constraint Set	Pr(real)	Pr(real)	Bel(real)	Π(¬real)	Π(¬real)	Pr(real)	Π(¬real)
{C1, C2, F1}	1.0	[0.467 1.0]	1.0	0	[0 0]	[0.231 1]	[0 0]
{C1, C2, F2}	1.0	[0.467 1.0]	1.0	0	[0 0]	[0.778 1]	[0 0]
{C1, C2}	1.0	[0.467 1.0]	1.0	0	[0 0]	[0 1]	[0 0]
{C1, C3, F1, F2}	1.0	[0.467 1.0]	1.0	0	[0 0]	[0.855 1]	[0 0]
{C1, C3, F1}	1.0	[0.467 1.0]	1.0	0	[0 0]	[0.231 1]	[0 0]
{C1, C3, F2}	1.0	[0.467 1.0]	1.0	0	[0 0]	[0.778 1]	[0 0]
{C1, C3}	1.0	[0.467 1.0]	1.0	0	[0 0]	[0 1]	[0 0]
{C1, C5, F1, F2}	1.0	[0.467 1.0]	1.0	0	[0 0]	[0.855 1]	[0 0]
{C1, C5, F1}	1.0	[0.467 1.0]	1.0	0	[0 0]	[0.231 1]	[0 0]
{C1, C5, F2}	1.0	[0.467 1.0]	1.0	0	[0 0]	[0.778 1]	[0 0]
{C1, C5}	1.0	[0.467 1.0]	1.0	0	[0 0]	[0 1]	[0 0]
{C2, C3, F1, F2}	0.998	[0.464 0.993]	0.997	0.053	[0.125 0.125]	[0.853 0.997]	[0 0.125]
{C2, C3, F1}	0.989	[0.457 0.976]	0.980	0.053	[0.125 0.125]	[0.228 0.988]	[0 0.125]
{C2, C3, F2}	0.997	[0.463 0.993]	0.996	0.053	[0.125 0.125]	[0.775 0.996]	[0 0.125]
{C2, C3}	0.986	[0.453 0.97]	0.969	0.053	[0.125 0.125]	[0 0.985]	[0 0.125]
{C2, C5, F1, F2}	0.996	[0.463 0.992]	0.996	0.053	[0.125 0.125]	[0.852 0.997]	[0 0.125]
{C2, C5, F1}	0.980	[0.452 0.968]	0.970	0.053	[0.125 0.125]	[0.226 0.982]	[0 0.125]
{C2, C5, F2}	0.995	[0.461 0.990]	0.994	0.053	[0.125 0.125]	[0.774 0.995]	[0 0.125]
{C2, C5}	0.975	[0.446 0.955]	0.953	0.053	[0.125 0.125]	[0 0.977]	[0 0.125]
{C3, C5, F1, F2}	0.979	[0.460 0.986]	0.992	0.211	[0.125 0.25]	[0.849 0.993]	[0 0.125]
{C3, C5, F1}	0.910	[0.438 0.938]	0.941	0.263	[0.25 0.25]	[0.223 0.965]	[0 0.25]
{C3, C5, F2}	0.974	[0.457 0.980]	0.988	0.211	[0.125 0.25]	[0.770 0.989]	[0 0.25]

Table 10.9
Results of the first experiment in assessing the validity of sets of constraints

Constraint Set	Pr(real)	Pr(real)	Bel(real)	Π(¬real)	Π(¬real)	Pr(real)	Π(¬real)
{C3, C5}	0.889	[0.427 0.914]	0.906	0.263	[0.25 0.25]	[0 0.955]	[0 0.25]
{C1, F1, F2}	1.0	[0.467 1.0]	1.0	0	[0 0]	[0.855 1]	[0 0]
{C1, F1}	1.0	[0.467 1.0]	1.0	0	[0 0]	[0.231 1]	[0 0]
{C1, F2}	1.0	[0.467 1.0]	1.0	0	[0 0]	[0.778 1]	[0 0]
{C1}	1.0	[0.467 1.0]	1.0	0	[0 0]	[0 1]	[0 0]
{C2, F1, F2}	0.991	[0.458 0.981]	0.990	0.053	[0.125 0.125]	[0.847 0.991]	[0 0.125]
{C2, F1}	0.960	[0.429 0.920]	0.921	0.053	[0.125 0.125]	[0.220 0.954]	[0 0.125]
{C2, F2}	0.989	[0.454 0.973]	0.984	0.053	[0.125 0.125]	[0.767 0.986]	[0 0.125]
{C2}	0.950	[0.415 0.889]	0.875	0.053	[0.125 0.125]	[0 0.941]	[0 0.125]
{C3, F1, F2}	0.958	[0.449 0.963]	0.980	0.211	[0.125 0.25]	[0.840 0.982]	[0 0.125]
{C3, F1}	0.828	[0.397 0.851]	0.843	0.263	[0.25 0.25]	[0.211 0.912]	[0 0.25]
{C3, F2}	0.947	[0.442 0.947]	0.969	0.211	[0.125 0.25]	[0.757 0.973]	[0 0.25]
{C3}	0.792	[0.373 0.8]	0.75	0.263	[0.25 0.25]	[0 0.889]	[0 0.25]
{C5, F1, F2}	0.927	[0.44 0.945]	0.970	0.211	[0.125 0.25]	[0.832 0.974]	[0 0.375]
{C5, F1}	0.728	[0.367 0.792]	0.766	0.474	[0.375 0.375]	[0.201 0.874]	[0 0.375]
{C5, F2}	0.909	[0.431 0.923]	0.953	0.211	[0.125 0.25]	[0.747 0.96]	[0 0.375]
{C5}	0.678	[0.339 0.727]	0.625	0.474	[0.375 0.375]	[0 0.842]	[0 0.375]
{F1, F2}	0.857	[0.404 0.865]	0.922	0.211	[0.125 0.25]	[0.797 0.932]	[0 1]
{F1}	0.559	[0.275 0.588]	0.373	0.789	[0.625 0.875]	[0.167 0.722]	[0 1]
{F2}	0.826	[0.382 0.818]	0.875	0.211	[0.125 0.25]	[0.7 0.9]	[0 1]
{}	0.5	[0.233 0.5]		1	[1 1]	[0 0.667]	[0 1]

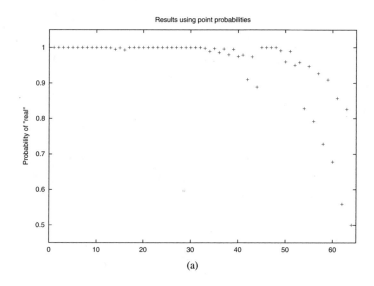

(a)

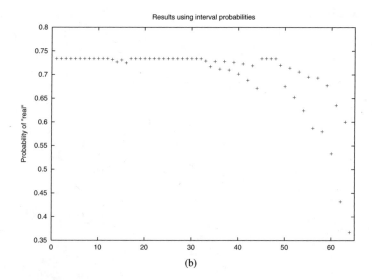

(b)

Figure 10.3
Results based on (a) the point probabilities from Table 10.2, and (b) the interval probabilities from Table 10.3.

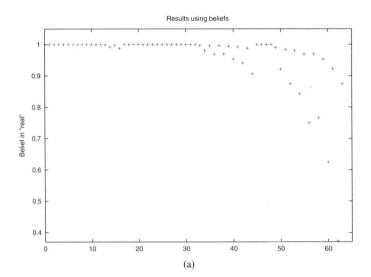

(a)

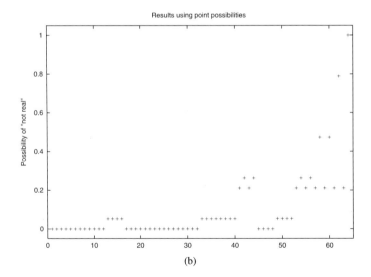

(b)

Figure 10.4
Results based on (a) the point possibilities from Table 10.4, and (b) the interval possibilities from Table 10.5.

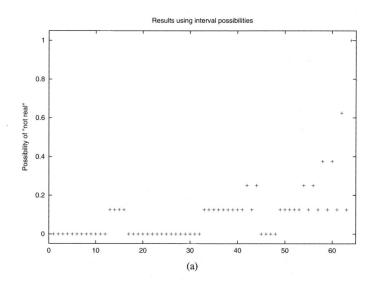

(a)

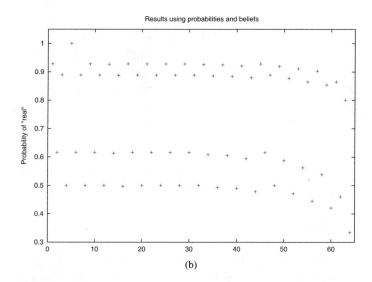

(b)

Figure 10.5
Results based on (a) the mass distribution from Table 10.6, and (b) probabilities from Table 10.3 and beliefs from Table 10.6.

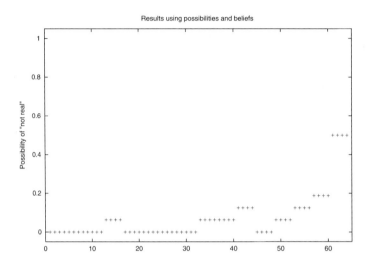

Figure 10.6
Results based on possibilities from Table 10.5 and beliefs from Table 10.6.

mid-points. This transformation is, of course, justified by Theorem 6.3, and is adopted throughout this chapter. The remaining graphs and columns of Tables 10.7, 10.8 and 10.9 give similar results for the remaining sets of data. In particular, they show the results of using the mass distribution of Table 10.6; the point and interval possibility data from Tables 10.4 and 10.5; the combination of the mass distribution of Table 10.6 and the point probabilities from Table 10.3; and the combination of the mass distribution of Table 10.6 and the point possibilities from Table 10.5.

All of the sets of results are dominated by the value attached to $C1$, but some general trends are nevertheless visible. For instance, considering the results of using probability data or the mass distribution data (on its own or in conjunction with the probability data), it is clear that in general as the set of constraints to which a protein conforms is reduced (which is what proceeding along the x-axis broadly represents), the measure of validity of the protein (which is measured up the y-axis) decreases. In other words, the results show that the larger the set of constraints, the higher the validity. However, when a very unreliable constraint is relaxed there is a sharp increase in validity indicating that there is some value in considering the weights of the constraints rather than just the number of constraints that apply. In other words, the "better" the constraints, the higher the validity. The results of using the possibility data, either alone or in combination with the mass distributions, gives results with broadly reversed trends. This is not surprising since the possibilities calculated are those of ¬*real*. The steps in the possibility results are, of course, the result of combination using max and min which mean that the possibility relating to a single constraint dominates the overall result. When using probabilities, the combination has a more averaging effect on the different constraints.

To some extent, of course, the results depend upon the model that is used to obtain them. As mentioned above, the models adopted here, in particular the calculation of the overall validity from the effects of the violation or otherwise of the individual constraints, could be replaced by other models. Obvious alternatives include the Noisy-Or model or one of its generalisations (Henrion, 1989; Srinivas, 1993), some of which allow the use of possibility theory (Parsons and Bigham, 1996). It is also worth noting that the use of interval probabilities and possibilities, while arguably giving a more natural representation of the strength to which the constraints hold, does not greatly affect the results. Thus the results for interval probability, when reduced to their mid-point value, have the same form as those for point probability (Figure 10.3)—the main effect of the intervals is to move the results down the y-axis. This effect is most obvious in the results for the model which combines probabilities and beliefs. Since the beliefs relating to $F1$ and $F2$ translate into interval probabilities with relatively wide intervals, the effects of these intervals dominate the mid-point values in Figure 10.5(b) which otherwise follow the same pattern as for the other probability models.

10.4   A second approach to modeling the uncertainty

The available data can also be interpreted in a slightly different way. Instead of taking the proportion of proteins for which a constraint applies as a measure of how likely it is that the constraint applies to any structure, it can be taken as a measure of how often constraints hold for real proteins, since every structure in the table occurs in nature. Thus the proportion of the proteins for which a given constraint holds is related to the conditional measure of the constraint holding given that the protein is real, thus capturing the fact that the data says nothing about structures that are not real proteins.

10.4.1   Using probability theory

An obvious choice for establishing the necessary probability information is natural sampling (Kleiter, 1993; Gigerenzer, 1994). In order to find out the conditional probability of a constraint holding given the protein is real it is necessary to know both how many proteins obey the constraint and are real, let this be a, and how many proteins do not obey the constraint and are real, let this be b. The conditional probability that constraint holds given

Table 10.10
Conditional probabilities of the constraints holding based upon the "disambiguated" interpretation. The total number of structures is 19.

Constraint (x)	Number of cases in which the constraint is violated	$\Pr(x\|real)$	$\Pr(x\|\neg real)$
C1	0	1.0	0.5
C2	1	0.947	0.5
C3	5	0.737	0.5
C5	9	0.526	0.5
F1	15	0.211	0.5
F2	4	0.789	0.5

Table 10.11
Conditional probabilities of the constraints holding based upon the "pure" interpretation. The total number of proteins is 8.

Constraint (x)	Number of cases in which the constraint is violated	$\Pr(x\|real)$	$\Pr(x\|\neg real)$
C1	0	1.0	[0, 1]
C2	1	0.875	[0, 1]
C3	2	0.75	[0, 1]
C5	3	0.625	[0, 1]
F1	5–7	[0.125, 0.375]	[0, 1]
F2	1–2	[0.750, 0.875]	[0, 1]

the protein is real is then:

$$\frac{a}{a+b}$$

In other words, the probability that the constraint holds given the protein is real is the number of real proteins for which the constraint holds over the total number of proteins (all of which are real) for which data is available. For unambiguous constraints such as $C2$ the calculation is as follows:

$$\Pr(C2|real) = \frac{\text{Number of proteins for which } C2 \text{ holds}}{\text{Total number of proteins}}$$

$$= \frac{7}{8}$$

When there is ambiguity in the data it is possible either to disambiguate to get point conditional values, or to calculate bounds on the conditional value as in Section 10.3.1. The two approaches give the results of Tables 10.10 and 10.11. Now, there is no information about the proportion of proteins for which $C2$ holds yet which are not real, so it is not possible to establish $\Pr(C2|\neg real)$ in the same way. Instead, it is possible to employ the principle of maximum entropy to conclude that $\Pr(C2|\neg real) = 0.5$, or to use $[0, 1]$ as discussed in Chapter 6. Table 10.10 uses maximum entropy, while Table 10.11 uses $[0, 1]$—

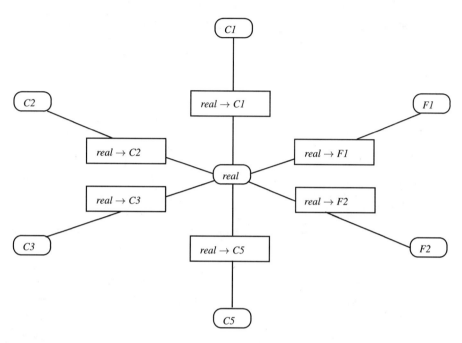

Figure 10.7
A valuation network for relating the effects of constraints using conditional values.

the choice being made arbitrarily to keep point and interval estimates together. Similarly it is possible to take either $\Pr(real) = \Pr(\neg real) = 0.5$ or $\Pr(real) = \Pr(\neg real) = [0, 1]$, and again the former is used with the disambiguated values and the latter with the pure values in order to keep point and interval values together.

One way of predicting the quality of possible topologies using these values would be to build a valuation system like that in Figure 10.7 and then use the values obtained above in much the same way that probability values were used in the previous section. This approach could also be extended to use possibility and evidence theories, and even combinations of theories. However, this would largely be a matter of repeating the work in the previous section and so would do little to add to the argument about the usefullness of the qualitative approaches. Instead this section will examine the use of the theory of qualitative change, which, of course, fits in much better with the use of conditional values of the sort that have just been derived than the kind of values handled in the previous section.

The use of the theory of qualitative change also fits in well with the constraint-satisfaction approach to protein topology prediction reported by Clark et al. (1992; 1993),

and implemented in the system CBS1, which was one of the original motivating examples
for the development of the qualitative approaches. Clark et al.'s approach works as follows.
The search for a topology is initiated with an empty sheet template that contains N slots,
one for each strand, each with three arguments for orientation, sequence number and
connection handedness. The principal operation of the algorithm is to take a set of partly
instantiated templates and add a strand to each. A strand is added at every available strand
position in both orientations (up and down) and directions of handedness (left and right),
provided that the result is not a rotational variant of another template. Then the set of new
templates is tested against every relevant constraint. The procedure is then called again
on the templates and the process is repeated until all the templates are fully instantiated.
At each test against constraints, templates can be pruned according to the constraints they
violate.

Thus, following each step a structure can either conform to the same set of constraints
as before, or to some superset or subset of that set. So, after each step new evidence may
be available about whether or not a constraint holds. If it is possible to relate the fact
that a particular structure conforms to a particular constraint to it being correct, then the
effect of the new knowledge may be propagated to find out how it affects the certainty
that the structure is correct. Thus it is possible to tell whether the protein structure that
is being assembled has become more or less likely to be correct, and whether it should
be rejected or continued with accordingly. This kind of information, about changes in the
certainty of protein being correct with evidence about which constraints it conforms to,
is exactly the kind of information that would be useful in an interactive system in which
a molecular biologist is considering the structural impact of particular constraints as part
of the process of determining the most plausible structure. It is also exactly the kind of
information handled by the theory of qualitative change, and so it seems that using the
theory to provide information on the changing certainty of structures is something that will
be helpful in solving the protein topology prediction problem.

Applying the theory of qualitative change to this situation starts with the conditional
probability values of Table 10.10 and 10.11, all of which are of the form $\Pr(C2|real)$. From
Theorem 7.3 it is clear that these values are sufficient to establish the relationship between
$\Pr(C2)$ and $\Pr(real)$ in terms of the derivative

$$\left[\frac{\partial \Pr(C2)}{\partial \Pr(real)} \right]$$

that relates them. This information, in turn (Corollary 7.4), is sufficient to give:

$$\left[\frac{\partial \Pr(real)}{\partial \Pr(C2)} \right]$$

Table 10.12
The probabilistic qualitative derivatives based upon both "disambiguated" and "pure" interpretations

Constraint (x)	$\left[\dfrac{\partial \Pr(real)}{\partial \Pr(x)} \right]$
$C1$	$[+]$
$C2$	$[+]$
$C3$	$[+]$
$C5$	$[+]$
$F1$	$[-]$
$F2$	$[+]$

which is enough to establish how $\Pr(real)$ changes when there is information about $C2$ holding. From the data available, irrespective of whether the "disambiguated" or "pure" interpretations are adopted, the derivatives are those of Table 10.12. Note that:

$$\left[\frac{\partial \Pr(real)}{\partial \Pr(C1)} \right] = [+]$$

indicates that as $\Pr(C1)$ increases, so does $\Pr(real)$, and

$$\left[\frac{\partial \Pr(real)}{\partial \Pr(F1)} \right] = [-]$$

indicates that as $\Pr(F1)$ increases, $\Pr(real)$ decreases.

This information about changes in probability fits closely with CBS1. In CBS1, at every step, a new component of the protein is added. This new knowledge may be propagated to find out how it affects the likelihood that the structure is correct. Thus it is possible to tell whether the protein structure that is being assembled has become more or less likely to be correct, and whether it should be rejected or continued with accordingly.

10.4.2 Using possibility theory

It is also possible to adopt something akin to the natural sampling approach when using possibility theory. Since it is quite possible for any constraint to hold in a real protein, the conditional possibility of that constraint holding given that a protein is real is 1 for any constraint. However, the possibility of a constraint failing to hold in a real protein is determined by the proportion of real proteins for which the constraint is known not to hold. So, for an unambiguous constraint such as $C2$:

$$\Pi(C2|real) = 1$$

$$\Pi(\neg C2|real) = \frac{\text{Number of proteins for which } C2 \text{ does not hold}}{\text{Total number of proteins}}$$

Table 10.13
Conditional possibilities of constraints holding based upon the "disambiguated" interpretation. The total number of structures is 19.

Constraint (x)	Number of cases in which the constraint is violated	$\Pi(x\vert real)$	$\Pi(\neg x\vert real)$
C1	0	1.0	1.0
C2	1	1.0	0.053
C3	5	1.0	0.263
C5	9	1.0	0.474
F1	15	1.0	0.789
F2	4	1.0	0.211

Table 10.14
Conditional possibilities of the constraints holding based upon the "pure" interpretation. The total number of proteins is 8.

Constraint (x)	Number of cases in which the constraint is violated	$\Pi(x\vert real)$	$\Pi(\neg x\vert real)$
C1	0	1.0	0
C2	1	1.0	0.125
C3	2	1.0	0.25
C5	3	1.0	0.375
F1	5–7	1.0	[0.625, 0.875]
F2	1–2	1.0	[0.125, 0.25]

$$= \frac{1}{8}$$

Again it is possible either to disambiguate or use interval values, and the respective results are contained in Tables 10.13 and 10.14. In both cases, since there is no information about proteins that are not real, nothing is known about $\Pi(C2\vert\neg real)$ and $\Pi(\neg C2\vert\neg real)$ for any of the constraints. Similarly nothing is known about $\Pi(real)$ and $\Pi(\neg real)$. As with probability values there are two ways of resolving this, one of which uses the principle of minimum specificity, and one of which uses interval values. In the former case we get:

$$\Pi(C2\vert\neg real) = 1$$
$$\Pi(\neg C2\vert\neg real) = 1$$

and similarly for all other constraints, along with:

$$\Pi(real) = 1$$
$$\Pi(\neg real) = 1$$

and in the latter case we get:

$$\Pi(C2\vert\neg real) = [0, 1]$$

Table 10.15
The possibilistic qualitative derivatives

Constraint (x)	$\left[\dfrac{\partial\Pi(real)}{\partial\Pi(x)}\right]$	$\left[\dfrac{\partial\Pi(real)}{\partial\Pi(\neg x)}\right]$	$\left[\dfrac{\partial\Pi(\neg real)}{\partial\Pi(x)}\right]$	$\left[\dfrac{\partial\Pi(\neg real)}{\partial\Pi(\neg x)}\right]$
C1	[0, +]	[0, +]	[0, +]	[0, +]
C2	[0, +]	[0, +]	[0, +]	[0, ↑]
C3	[0, +]	[0, +]	[0, +]	[0, ↑]
C5	[0, +]	[0, +]	[0, ⊦]	[0, ↑]
F1	[0, +]	[0, +]	[0, +]	[0, ↑]
F2	[0, +]	[0, +]	[0, +]	[0, ↑]

$$\Pi(\neg C2|\neg real) \;=\; [0,1]$$

and similarly for all other constraints, along with:

$$\Pi(real) \;=\; [0,1]$$
$$\Pi(\neg real) \;=\; [0,1]$$

As in the probability case the first set of values are used with disambiguated values and the latter set with pure values.

Once these values are established it is possible to apply the theory of qualitative change. In particular, it is possible to establish derivatives that define the relationship between $\Pi(real)$ and $\Pi(C2)$. Theorem 7.4 gives:

$$\left[\frac{\partial\Pi(C2)}{\partial\Pi(real)}\right] \;=\; [0]$$

$$\left[\frac{\partial\Pi(\neg C2)}{\partial\Pi(real)}\right] \;=\; [0]$$

$$\left[\frac{\partial\Pi(C2)}{\partial\Pi(\neg real)}\right] \;=\; [0]$$

$$\left[\frac{\partial\Pi(\neg C2)}{\partial\Pi(\neg real)}\right] \;=\; [0,\downarrow]$$

meaning that $\Pi(\neg C2)$ may decrease when $\Pi(real)$ decreases, while it is independent of $\Pi(\neg real)$, and $\Pi(C2)$ is independent of $\Pi(real)$ and $\Pi(\neg real)$. From these values it is possible (Theorem 7.11) to determine that

$$\left[\frac{\partial\Pi(\neg real)}{\partial\Pi(\neg C2)}\right] = [0,\uparrow]$$

while the other derivatives concerning $C1$ are all $[0,+]$. This is an example of the weakness of Theorem 7.11 remarked on in Chapter 7. Similar reasoning about the other constraints

Table 10.16
Conditional beliefs of the constraints holding. Θ_x stands for $\{x, \neg x\}$ and Θ_{real} for $\{real, \neg real\}$. The total number of proteins is 8.

Constraint (x)	Number of cases in which the constraint is violated	$\text{Bel}(x\|real)$	$\text{Bel}(x\|\neg real)$	$\text{Bel}(x\|\Theta_{real})$
C1	0	1	0	0
C2	1	0.875	0	0
C3	2	0.750	0	0
C5	3	0.625	0	0
F1	5–7	0.125	0	0
F2	1–2	0.750	0	0

Constraint (x)	Number of cases in which the constraint is violated	$\text{Bel}(\neg x\|real)$	$\text{Bel}(\neg x\|\neg real)$	$\text{Bel}(\neg x\|\Theta_{real})$
C1	0	0	0	0
C2	1	0.125	0	0
C3	2	0.250	0	0
C5	3	0.375	0	0
F1	5–7	0.625	0	0
F2	1–2	0.125	0	0

Constraint (x)	Number of cases in which the constraint is violated	$\text{Bel}(\Theta_x\|real)$	$\text{Bel}(\Theta_x\|\neg real)$	$\text{Bel}(\Theta_x\|\Theta_{real})$
C1	0	0	1	1
C2	1	0	1	1
C3	2	0	1	1
C5	3	0	1	1
F1	5–7	0.250	1	1
F2	1–2	0.125	1	1

gives Table 10.15—those concerning C1 differ from the rest since all the relevant conditional possibilities are 1.

10.4.3   Using evidence theory

Again it is possible to use evidence theory to model the data in such a way that the ambiguity is neatly incorporated. This time the mass assignments are interpreted as conditional beliefs, and are calculated in a similar way to that in which the probabilistic and possibilistic conditionals were. For example:

$$\text{Bel}(\{F1\}|\{real\}) \quad = \quad m(\{F1\}|\{real\})$$

Table 10.17
The evidential qualitative derivatives

Constraint (x)	$\left[\dfrac{\partial \mathrm{Bel}(\{x\})}{\partial \mathrm{Bel}(\{real\})}\right]$	$\left[\dfrac{\partial \mathrm{Bel}(\{x\})}{\partial \mathrm{Bel}(\{\neg real\})}\right]$	$\left[\dfrac{\partial \mathrm{Bel}(\{x\})}{\partial \mathrm{Bel}(\{real, \neg real\})}\right]$
C1	[+]	[−]	[−]
C2	[+]	[−]	[−]
C3	[+]	[−]	[−]
C5	[+]	[−]	[−]
F1	[+]	[−]	[−]
F2	[+]	[−]	[−]

Constraint (x)	$\left[\dfrac{\partial \mathrm{Bel}(\{\neg x\})}{\partial \mathrm{Bel}(\{real\})}\right]$	$\left[\dfrac{\partial \mathrm{Bel}(\{\neg x\})}{\partial \mathrm{Bel}(\{\neg real\})}\right]$	$\left[\dfrac{\partial \mathrm{Bel}(\{\neg x\})}{\partial \mathrm{Bel}(\{real, \neg real\})}\right]$
C1	[0]	[0]	[0]
C2	[+]	[+]	[−]
C3	[+]	[+]	[−]
C5	[+]	[+]	[−]
F1	[+]	[+]	[−]
F2	[+]	[+]	[−]

Constraint (x)	$\left[\dfrac{\partial \mathrm{Bel}(\{x, \neg x\})}{\partial \mathrm{Bel}(\{real\})}\right]$	$\left[\dfrac{\partial \mathrm{Bel}(\{x, \neg x\})}{\partial \mathrm{Bel}(\{\neg real\})}\right]$	$\left[\dfrac{\partial \mathrm{Bel}(\{x \neg x\})}{\partial \mathrm{Bel}(\{real, \neg real\})}\right]$
C1	[−]	[+]	[+]
C2	[−]	[+]	[+]
C3	[−]	[+]	[+]
C5	[−]	[+]	[+]
F1	[−]	[+]	[+]
F2	[−]	[+]	[+]

$$= \frac{\text{Number of proteins for which } F1 \text{ holds for every structure}}{\text{Total number of proteins}}$$

$$= \frac{1}{8}$$

$$\mathrm{Bel}(\{\neg F1\})|\{real\}) = m(\{\neg F1\})|\{real\})$$

$$= \frac{\text{Number of proteins for which } F1 \text{ does not hold for at least one structure}}{\text{Total number of proteins}}$$

$$= \frac{5}{8}$$

$$\mathrm{Bel}(\{F1, \neg F1\}|\{real\}) = m(\{F1, \neg F1\}|\{real\})$$

$$= 1 - \sum_{f \subset \{F1, \neg F1\}} m(f|\{real\})$$

$$= 1 - \big(\mathrm{Bel}(\{F1\}|\{real\}) + \mathrm{Bel}(\{\neg F1\}|\{real\})\big)$$

Table 10.18
The evidential qualitative derivatives

Constraint (x)	$\left[\dfrac{\partial\mathrm{Bel}(\{real\})}{\partial\mathrm{Bel}(\{x\})}\right]$	$\left[\dfrac{\partial\mathrm{Bel}(\{real\})}{\partial\mathrm{Bel}(\{\neg x\})}\right]$	$\left[\dfrac{\partial\mathrm{Bel}(\{real\})}{\partial\mathrm{Bel}(\{x,\neg x\})}\right]$
C1	$[+]$	$[0]$	$[-]$
C2	$[+]$	$[+]$	$[-]$
C3	$[+]$	$[+]$	$[-]$
C5	$[+]$	$[+]$	$[-]$
F1	$[+]$	$[+]$	$[-]$
F2	$[+]$	$[+]$	$[-]$

Constraint (x)	$\left[\dfrac{\partial\mathrm{Bel}(\{\neg real\})}{\partial\mathrm{Bel}(\{x\})}\right]$	$\left[\dfrac{\partial\mathrm{Bel}(\{\neg real\})}{\partial\mathrm{Bel}(\{\neg x\})}\right]$	$\left[\dfrac{\partial\mathrm{Bel}(\{\neg real\})}{\partial\mathrm{Bel}(\{x,\neg x\})}\right]$
C1	$[-]$	$[0]$	$[+]$
C2	$[-]$	$[-]$	$[+]$
C3	$[-]$	$[-]$	$[+]$
C5	$[-]$	$[-]$	$[+]$
F1	$[-]$	$[-]$	$[+]$
F2	$[-]$	$[-]$	$[+]$

Constraint (x)	$\left[\dfrac{\partial\mathrm{Bel}(\{real,\neg real\})}{\partial\mathrm{Bel}(\{x\})}\right]$	$\left[\dfrac{\partial\mathrm{Bel}(\{real,\neg real\})}{\partial\mathrm{Bel}(\{\neg x\})}\right]$	$\left[\dfrac{\partial\mathrm{Bel}(\{real,\neg real\})}{\partial\mathrm{Bel}(\{x,\neg x\})}\right]$
C1	$[-]$	$[0]$	$[+]$
C2	$[-]$	$[-]$	$[+]$
C3	$[-]$	$[-]$	$[+]$
C5	$[-]$	$[-]$	$[+]$
F1	$[-]$	$[-]$	$[+]$
F2	$[-]$	$[-]$	$[+]$

$$= \frac{2}{8}$$

Since there is no data about proteins that are not real, the Dempster-Shafer model of ignorance is employed to get the following conditional beliefs:

$$\mathrm{Bel}(\{F1\}|\{\neg real\}) = 0$$
$$\mathrm{Bel}(\{\neg F1\}|\{\neg real\}) = 0$$
$$\mathrm{Bel}(\{F1,\neg F1\}|\{\neg real\}) = 1$$
$$\mathrm{Bel}(\{F1\}|\{real,\neg real\}) = 0$$
$$\mathrm{Bel}(\{\neg F1\}|\{real,\neg real\}) = 0$$
$$\mathrm{Bel}(\{F1,\neg F1\}|\{real,\neg real\}) = 1$$

Overall the values of Tables 10.16 are obtained. Of course, ignorance about the conditional beliefs could also be modelled by setting them to $[0,1]$.

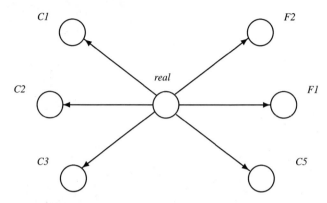

Figure 10.8
A network for computing changes in information about the applicability of constraints.

Once more these conditional values are sufficient to apply the theory of qualitative change. Along with Theorem 7.5 they may be used to ascertain, for instance, that:

$$\left[\frac{\partial \mathrm{Bel}(\{F1\})}{\partial \mathrm{Bel}(\{real\})} \right] \;=\; [+]$$

$$\left[\frac{\partial \mathrm{Bel}(\{\neg F1\})}{\partial \mathrm{Bel}(\{real\})} \right] \;=\; [+]$$

$$\left[\frac{\partial \mathrm{Bel}(\{F1, \neg F1\})}{\partial \mathrm{Bel}(\{real\})} \right] \;=\; [-]$$

Applying the same theorem for all the possible combinations of value of constraint x and *real* gives the derivatives of Table 10.17. These derivatives may be then be transformed, using Corollary 7.4, to give:

$$\left[\frac{\partial \mathrm{Bel}(\{real\})}{\partial \mathrm{Bel}(\{F1\})} \right] \;=\; [+]$$

$$\left[\frac{\partial \mathrm{Bel}(\{real\})}{\partial \mathrm{Bel}(\{\neg F1\})} \right] \;=\; [+]$$

$$\left[\frac{\partial \mathrm{Bel}(\{real\})}{\partial \mathrm{Bel}(\{F1, \neg F1\})} \right] \;=\; [-]$$

Repeating this procedure for the remaining constraints gives the derivatives of Table 10.18.

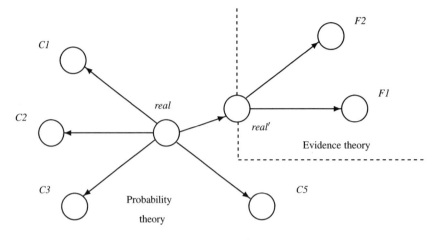

Figure 10.9
A network for computing changes in information about the applicability of constraints which uses probability and evidence theories.

10.4.4   QCN Models

To use the derivatives derived above to make predictions about how the certainty of possible structures changes as constraints are enforced or relaxed, it is necessary to build a qualitative certainty network that captures interactions between the constraints and the proposition *real*. As when using valuation systems and qualitative algebras, there are a number of possible models that can be adopted. Since the aim of this chapter is to show how the theory of qualitative change may be used, it seems sufficient to use a simple model, and that chosen is probably the simplest possible. The model is given in Figure 10.8. This network is simply a qualitative certainty network that corresponds to the valuation system in Figure 10.7, and makes the assumption that there are no interactions between constraints. Such interactions can easily be taken into account in qualitative certainty networks if required. In other words the simplicity of the model is a result of deciding not to model interactions between constraints (again because none have, to my knowledge, been suggested) rather than a limitation enforced by the qualitative certainty network representation.

   This model, of course, is intended for use with a single formalism for handling uncertainty. It can be instantiated with the derivatives established above for probability or possibility theories, and then evaluated using Mummu. This approach to modelling is not restricted to using just a single formalism, however. As discussed in Chapter 7, the various monotonicity assumptions may be applied to translate changes in one formalism

Table 10.19
The results of using the probabilistic qualitative derivatives from Table 10.12

Constraint Added	Change in $\Pr(real)$
C1	[+]
C2	[+]
C3	[+]
C5	[+]
F1	[−]
F2	[+]

Table 10.20
The results of using the possibilistic qualitative derivatives from Table 10.15

Constraint Retracted	Change in $\Pi(\neg real)$
C1	[0, +]
C2	[0, +]
C3	[0, +]
C5	[0, +]
F1	[0, +]
F2	[0, +]

into changes in another formalism, thus making it possible to build models that make use of several different formalisms. As an illustration of this, consider using evidence theory to capture the effect of constraints $F1$ and $F2$, rather as in the last experiments using qualitative algebras. A qualitative certainty network that fits this kind of model is given in Figure 10.9. Information about $F1$ and $F2$ is propagated in the top right-hand corner, establishing the change in $\mathrm{Bel}(real')$ where $real'$ is a dummy variable that separates the two sections of the network. Once this change in belief has been established, it can be translated into a change in probability, and this can be combined with other changes to establish the overall change in $real$. The same network can also be used to combine changes in evidence theory and changes in possibility theory.

10.4.5 Results using the second approach

The particular experiments carried out using the models described above involved changing the applicability of a single constraint, and then using Mummu to propagate the effect of this using the network of Figure 10.8. For the probability model, the change in applicability was modelled by increasing the probability that a constraint held, thus capturing the addition of a constraint. The results of doing this for each constraint in turn is given in Table 10.19 where [+] indicates a rise in $\Pr(real)$, and [−] indicates a fall. These results show that the addition of all constraints except $F1$ causes $\Pr(real)$ to rise, the latter causing it to fall. This outcome is to be expected from the data of Tables 10.2 and 10.3, since $F1$ fails to hold in less than half of all proteins for which there is data.

Table 10.21
The results of using the evidential qualitative derivatives from Table 10.17

Constraint Added	Change in Bel(*real*)
C1	[+]
C2	[+]
C3	[+]
C5	[+]
F1	[+]
F2	[+]

Table 10.22
The results of using the evidential qualitative derivatives from Table 10.17 and probabilistic qualitative derivatives from Table 10.12

Constraint Added	Change in Pr(*real*)
C1	[+]
C2	[+]
C3	[+]
C5	[+]
F1	$[0, +]$
F2	$[0, +]$

The possibility model is slightly different with the changing applicability of the constraints being modelled by increasing the possibility that constraints do not hold. In other words the changing applicability of $C1$ was modelled by increasing $\Pi(\neg C1)$. The results of this procedure are given in Table 10.20, and show that for every constraint this results in a possible increase in $\Pi(\neg real)$. This broadly mirrors the result for the probability model in that it indicates that more constraints means more belief in the structure being a real protein. However, note the difference concerning $F1$. Whereas the probability model takes the low applicability of the constraint to suggest that conforming to it is evidence against a structure being a real protein, the possibility model takes conformance to it to be evidence, albeit weaker evidence than that provided by conformance to other constraints, in favour.

The results of the analysis using evidence theory, given in Table 10.21, can be considered a mixture of the results for the probability model and possibility model in the following sense. Because the approach is to look at the change in Bel(*real*), the results are broadly the same as for the probability model—as constraints are added, Bel(*real*) increases. However, just as for the possibility model, the result of applying $F1$ is exactly the same as for the other constraints and for exactly the same reason. That is the constraint is taken as weak evidence in favour of the conformant structure being a real protein. It should be noted that these results were obtained under the assumption that, *a priori* the applicability of each constraint was modelled by setting, for example, Bel($\{C1, \neg C\}$) to 1, and then the effect of applying the constraint modelled by setting Bel($\{C1, \neg C\}$) to 0 and

Table 10.23
The results of using the evidential qualitative derivatives from Table 10.17 and possibilistic qualitative
derivatives from Table 10.15

Constraint Removed	Change in $\Pi(\neg real)$
$C1$	$[0, +]$
$C2$	$[0, +]$
$C3$	$[0, +]$
$C5$	$[0, +]$
$F1$	$[0, +]$
$F2$	$[0, +]$

$Bel(\{C1\})$ to 1. This focussing of belief is a typical use of evidence theory.

Finally, Tables 10.22 and 10.23 give the results of models that combine evidence theory with, respectively, probability and possibility theories. This is done in the context of the QCN model in Figure 10.9, using Assumption 5.3 to translate between formalisms. The second of these sets of results does not differ from that for the pure possibility model because the evidence theory model relating $\neg F1$ and $\neg F2$ to $\neg real$ does not differ from the possibility theory model. However, the results from the combined evidence/probability theory model are a little different from those for the pure probability model. In particular, the belief in *real* given $F1$ increases, and this translates into a change in probability of $[0, +]$ as opposed to $[-]$ in the probability model. The change due to $F2$ being applied is similarly $[0, +]$, this time as opposed to $[+]$. It is, of course, possible to use any of the monotonicity assumptions discussed in Chapter 5. Some of these, for instance Assumption 5.2, will give different results (and in the case of Assumption 5.2 they are arguably too strong), but others will not. Using Assumption 5.4 to translate to the probability theory model will give exactly the same results as using Assumption 5.3 since the upper and lower measure are the same, while using Assumption 5.5 to translate to possibility theory will give the same results because the qualitative possibilistic derivatives will block the resulting decreasing values.

10.5   Discussion

Since the protein structures considered here have not, so far as I know, been established, there is no gold standard against which to compare the results to determine which is best. Thus, the most that can be hoped for is a more subjective view of what "best" means.[7] A

---

7 Of course, if I was arguing that the approaches introduced here are hugely important from the perspective of molecular biology, then it would be necessary to go out and verify the approaches against a set of known structures. But I am not. I am merely trying to argue that the approaches introduced in this book appear to be of some use when modelling problems like protein structure prediction. This is a much weaker statement, and one that I feel can be justified by the range of types of information that can be represented. Despite this it seems worth considering which of the many results is most attractive and to discuss criteria against which they may be judged.

possible silver standard is to consider the structure picked out by Taylor and Green in their analysis (Taylor and Green, 1989) as the "best" and look favourably on those approaches that give it the highest belief. Doing this for the results from the qualitative algebras shows that the structure Taylor and Green picked out is the one that has all constraints applying. Similarly the results from the qualitative change approach suggest that structures with more constraints will be "better" (exactly which is "best" will depend, of course, on how $F1$ is modelled). However, using this standard is problematic since the idea of using the constraints originated with Taylor and Green's work so it is not surprising that applying the same constraints gives the same results. All it shows is that if we attach values to the constraints we get the same "best" result as if we had taken the constraints to be hard, which is not that informative.

In the absence of a sensible silver standard, it is possible to suggest a number of purely pragmatic criteria for both choosing between results and deciding whether any of them are useful. In doing this, it is worth bearing in mind that the intention of this work is to provide a means of focusing attention on a group of likely structures rather than determining the absolute best structure. For instance the decision about which results are most acceptable will partly depend on which method of dealing with ambiguity is preferred. Thus if one feels that the "pure" values give the best representation, then results based on those values, such as those in the and third and sixth columns of Tables 10.7–10.9, will be preferred over other results using qualitative algebras. Similarly, advocates of pure probability theory might well prefer the values in the second column of the tables, so long as they also agree with the way the initial probability assignment was carried out. Of course, when using the approach based on the theory of qualitative change, it does not matter which interpretation is used.

Thought might also be given to what the results are to be used for, and the decision about which is best made on the basis of which are most useful. In this case, when using qualitative algebras, it may be of little use having a set of values that contain many identical entries, an argument which suggests that the results might be more useful if they were more disparate since, as they stand, they have a value of 1 for any constraint set containing $C1$. On the other hand this could be acceptable as a clear indication of the necessity of having structures conformant with $C1$. Another point is that the prediction of protein topology is only a part of the process of establishing structure. Clearly, if a large number of experiments are required in order to reject each possible structure, it would be advantageous to start with the smallest possible set of structures. This suggests considering the number of possible structures associated with various sets of constraints when considering the usefulness of the results. It is possible to determine the number of structures associated with sets of constraints, and the order of the seven sets for which this has been done (Rawlings, 1995), based upon the number of possible structures, agrees broadly with the order obtained from our results. This suggests that our results are helpful in this regard, though again more disparate values might make things easier.

Finally, the way in which the topology prediction system is to be used can be considered. If it is intended that the system be used in batch mode to predict a group of structures and their respective validities, then the absolute values given using the first two approaches seem to be the most useful. However, this changes if the system is used interactively, with constraints being added and deleted one by one so that their effect on the structure and the validity can be observed. In this case the use of the approach based on the theory of qualitative change seems to be helpful[8] since it gives immediate feedback on the change in validity as the constraint set is altered.

10.6 Summary

This chapter has provided an example of the kinds of problem that may be solved using qualitative algebras and the theory of qualitative change. In particular it shows how these methods may be used to represent and reason with imprecise and ambiguous information, and how they may be used to combine different representations of this information. The chapter therefore illustrates that the qualitative approaches developed in this book can be applied to give a new and interesting perspective to the problem of protein topology prediction. It does not, of course, provide a conclusive argument that the use of these approaches is fundamentally better than previous attempts to build models for protein topology prediction—at best the results are an illustration of what it is possible to do. However, I believe that the results show that methods were worth developing, since they can be used to provide a new approach to a difficult problem.

This latter statement can be made with confidence since the work described in this chapter makes use of much more sophisticated models of handling uncertainty in protein topology prediction than have previously been used. Clark and colleagues (Clark et al., 1993) propose the most sophisticated model of which I am aware in the molecular biology literature. They use a simple weighting that records the penalty associated with constraints holding and failing. The weights are obtained in the same way as "pure" probabilities, and combined additively and with the assumption that they are completely independent. While the methods presented here that are based on probability theory also assume independence, the values used are assessed like probabilities and are combined as one would combine probabilities. Furthermore, the use of the valuation systems and qualitative certainty networks means that it is easy to adapt the method to take account of information about dependencies between constraints as well as to use possibility and evidence theories,

---

8 Perhaps coupled with an optional incremental calculation of the absolute value.

and these go somewhat beyond what Clark et al. propose. Indeed, it is not easy to see how their proposal could be easily extended to incorporate more sophisticated models.

Despite these advantages, it should be acknowledged that the work presented here is, from the molecular biology point of view, rather preliminary. It only represents a fraction of the possible work that could be carried out in this area, and it raises many more questions than it answers—there are many ways in which it could be improved. For instance, as previously noted, the models that were adopted are very simple, and could be greatly refined by considering the dependencies between the constraints, by obtaining more data on the applicability of the constraints, by using different methods for handling the rather imperfect data that is available, or by using any of the many methods for flexible constraint satisfaction (Miguel and Shen, 1999), in particular those that make use of probability (Fargier et al., 1995) and possibility (Schiex, 1992) measures to model soft constraints.

11 Summary and conclusions

As elaborate a waste of human intelligence as you could find anywhere outside an advertising agency.

Raymond Chandler, *The Long Goodbye*

When setting out to write this book there were three things that I wanted to achieve. The first was to promote the use of qualitative methods for reasoning under uncertainty because I believe that they provide an important counterpoint to the usual tendency towards extreme precision in the specification and calculation of measures of uncertainty—a tendency that I believe is often unjustifiable. The second thing that I wanted to achieve was to promote the eclectic position as regards reasoning under uncertainty because I believe that any one uncertainty handling formalism can only deal convincingly with some of the many types of uncertainty. The third thing I wanted to do was to exploit the synergy that I believe exists between qualitative methods and the eclectic position by using qualitative methods to solve some problems with numerical uncertainty handling formalisms, and to use these solutions to argue for the usefulness of the qualitative methods. In particular, I wanted to discuss the solutions to the problem of how to integrate different uncertainty handling formalisms, the problem of how to cope with insufficient information to build models using a specific uncertainty handling formalism, and the problem of how to make models built using uncertainty handling formalisms sufficiently robust that they can be used in different, but similar, environments. Having spent a good deal of time and space trying to achieve these three things, the idea behind this chapter is to discusses the extent to which the attempt has been successful, always bearing in mind the limitations imposed upon this work by the chosen setting of the use of probability, possibility, and evidence theories to propagate values in directed graphs. The chapter also attempts a degree of honesty in identifying some problems with the various qualitative methods that have been presented, and also tries to suggest some future avenues of research that might alleviate these problems. Before doing so, however, it first recaps upon the main arguments made in this book.

11.1 Summary

The foundations that support the qualitative approach, whether using qualitative algebras or considering qualitative changes, are provided by the principle of degrading or, equivalently, the monotonicity assumptions. Everything else follows naturally from these. Starting from the principle of degrading, the argument goes as follows. If the principle of degrading is accepted, then all formalisms, once all the subtleties of their semantics are abstracted away, are essentially saying the same thing. Thus having a possibility for A, $\Pi(A) = 0.4$ say, implies that there is some probability for A, $\Pr(A) = (0, 1]$ (or $\Pr(A) = [+]$) and there is also a belief in A, $\text{Bel}(A) = [0, 1]$. Then all that it is necessary to do is to extend the set of values over which the operations of the various formalisms operate, as is done in the qualitative algebras of Chapter 6, so that the qualitative and interval values generated by the principle of degrading may be combined with more usual point values. When this is done, it is possible translate between different formalisms. If it is necessary to take a probability and translate it into a possibility and then combine it with other possibility values, the probability can be translated into an equivalent qualitative or interval possibility value using the principle of degrading and then combined with other possibility values using a qualitative algebra. It is also possible to handle incomplete models. If a probability model is incomplete in that it is missing critical probability values, then it is possible to complete the model with vacuous interval or qualitative values and use a qualitative algebra to combine the new vacuous values with the previously available ones.

The principle of degrading also leads to the monotonicity assumptions. If all formalisms, once all the subtleties of their semantics are abstracted away, essentially say the same thing then, when the value assigned to a proposition in one formalism changes, it seems reasonable to assume that there will be some restrictions on the changes of the value assigned to the proposition in other formalisms. In other words, at least one of the monotonicity assumptions is reasonable. Depending upon which monotonicity assumption is adopted, one of several alternative solutions may be provided to the problems of how to translate between formalisms and how to complete models, along with a solution to the problem of how to make models robust. Translation between formalisms takes the form of propagating changes in the certainty value of a propositions as expressed in one formalism into changes in the certainty value of that proposition as expressed in another. Thus given that it is known that the probability of A increases, then it is possible to translate information about A into evidence theory by applying a monotonicity assumption to say something about the change in belief in A. This can then be combined with other belief function information to learn something about the beliefs in propositions other than A. Using the theory of qualitative change also provides two solutions to the problem of incomplete models. Firstly, it is possible to use the theory to abstract away from detailed numerical models to allow reasoning at a level at which the missing values are not significant. Alternatively it is possible to use the theory to identify the landmark values of the missing quantities, a move that may make it possible to complete the model at the qualitative level by identifying the assumptions that it must make and allowing them to be recognised as being reasonable. As an example of the first consider the model of the interaction between two variables A and

B, where A is the parent of B, which is only specified as

$$\Pr(b|a, x) > \Pr(b|\neg a, x)$$

for all values x. This is of no use when dealing with numerical probabilities. However, it is sufficient to specify that the qualitative relationship between $\Pr(a)$ and $\Pr(b)$ is that $\Pr(b)$ follows $\Pr(a)$, and so is a fully specified model of qualitative change.[1] As an example of the second, consider that the model of interaction between A and B is only specified by $\Pr(b|a) = 0.6$. Again this is insufficient information to identify the probabilistic interactions between the variables. However, the theory of qualitative change makes it clear that the important information is whether or not $\Pr(b|\neg a)$ is greater than, less than, or equal to 0.6. Furthermore, it identifies what will follow if the value is taken to be greater than, less than, or equal to 0.6, so allowing the impact of any assumption to be estimated. The use of qualitative changes also provides a means of making models robust since the abstract level at which the theory operates makes it reasonable to assume that models built in one environment will continue to be accurate when used in similar environments—an assumption that is not always reasonable when made about numerical models.

It is also possible to start by accepting that at least one of the monotonicity assumptions is reasonable. Then, since it is the case that the different formalisms are related to the degree that a change in the certainty value of a proposition as expressed in one formalism is reflected by some change in the the certainty value of the proposition as expressed in others, it is the case that the formalisms are related at some fundamental level—under all the layers of mathematical differences between them, they are effectively measuring the same thing. This then implies that the principle of degrading holds. Thus whether the principle of degrading or the monotonicity assumptions are taken as a starting point, there are the same reasons for developing qualitative methods, and the same problems may be solved by the qualitative methods.

In fact, it is possible to start the argument from an even earlier point since I think that both (or either, since they are equivalent) the principle of degrading and the monotonicity assumptions follow from the acceptance of the eclectic position. As soon it is acknowledged that there is some merit in different models of handling uncertainty, it follows that the different models are looking at the same information in different ways and that they only disagree on some of the subtleties of different situations and broadly agree on everything else (otherwise they could not have any merit at all because, in general, they would disagree with whatever the correct answer was). The only way to escape this conclusion is to assert that only one formalism is at all correct and so the others are wrong—as soon as

1 The relationships between $\Pr(b)$ and $\Pr(\neg a)$ and $\Pr(\neg b)$ and both $\Pr(a)$ and $\Pr(\neg a)$ are also identified by this information.

it is acknowledged that two formalisms have something useful to say then the eclectic position applies to these two as does the argument that follows from it. Once it is established
that the formalisms broadly agree, then the principle of degrading and the monotonicity
assumptions follow since they capture exactly this notion of broad agreement. An even
more extreme position is that the very fact that there are so many different types of uncertainty, along with the fact that no one formalism is able to represent all of the different
types without somehow adding in constraints that are not warranted by the available data,
means that the eclectic position is inevitable. However, I will resist the temptation to argue
this point again, having already done so at some length, and turn instead to the issue of
assessing whether the work summarised here has lived up to my aspirations for it.

11.2   Conclusions

The question, then, is

Has this book achieved all that I wanted it to?

Unsurprisingly, since it would be a pretty sad admission that after all this time I could not
have produced something that did what I wanted it to, I believe that the answer is

To a large degree, yes.

I think that this book provides a cogent argument for the adoption of the eclectic position
that builds naturally from the diversity of different types of uncertainty and different
models for handling uncertainty to the position that all the different models have something
to offer. I also think that the book provides good evidence of the maturity of qualitative
approaches both by showing that there are a number of well-developed qualitative theories
around, and by developing several new ones. That these may be used, in addition to
their role as additional mechanisms for modelling interesting real-world problems, to
solve some of the difficulties that arise in adopting the eclectic position, not only proves
my third assertion, that qualitative methods may be used to solve some problems with
existing uncertainty handling formalisms including the problem of translating between
such formalisms (which is a particular problem created by the eclectic position), but also
adds weight to the proof of the other two.

It should be noted, however, that the fact that the eclectic position and the use of qualitative methods fit so well together does not mean that they rely on each other for support.
The foundations of the eclectic position are in the diversity of varieties of uncertainty, and
were an alternative method of translating values between formalisms to be found the eclectic position would not rely on the use of qualitative methods. Similarly, even if not used
to translate values, qualitative methods have a useful role in modelling imprecisely known

systems and systems for which robustness is an important issue.

In this regard it should be remembered that, when dealing with these issues, the theory of qualitative change achieves most of the important things that the work of Wellman (1990b; 1990a) and Druzdzel and Henrion (1993b) on qualitative probabilistic networks does. Indeed it goes further since the work described here is applicable to probability, possibility and evidence theories while that of Druzdzel, Henrion and Wellman only relates to probability (though it should also be recalled that in the analysis of qualitative forms of inference the theory of qualitative change does not go quite so far as the work on qualitative probabilistic networks does). It should be also be noted that the approach described here stays completely within the theories of probability, possibility and evidence upon which it is based. As a result, while it is possible to criticise the theories themselves, reasoning based on the qualitative behaviour is to some degree "fireproof" since it is merely a qualitative interpretation of what would have happened if the precise numerical values had been used. Thus when changes in probability are predicted, these are exactly those that would be observed if the quantitative change was established by Pearl's (1988b) method, while the predicted changes for belief and possibility values are qualitatively equal to those generated, respectively, by the methods of Smets (1991a) and Fonck and Straszecka (1991).

Another consequence of the fact that the theory of qualitative change is soundly based upon the underlying uncertainty formalisms is the ease with which it may be extended. All that is necessary in order to extend the theory to cover a new formalism or a new combination rule is to write down the relationship that relates one value to another and differentiate it. Consider the following simple example in which variable A is related to variable C by the following rule, which is quantified by certainty factors (Buchanan and Shortliffe, 1984):

IF A is true THEN C is true (MB, MD)

where MB and MD are the measures of belief attached to the rule. This rule is roughly the equivalent of a causal network joining A and C with MB and MD playing an equivalent role to the conditional values in other formalisms, though the values MB and MD represent changes in subjective belief about the applicability of the conclusion rather than the more usual degrees of subjective belief in its applicability. This difference does not affect the qualitative analysis, since it is still possible to analyse how changes in the certainty factor of A, $CF(A)$, affects the certainty factor of C. The quantitative relationship is:

$$CF(C) = (MB - MD) . \max(0, CF(A))$$

and this may be analysed in much the same way as the possibilistic relationships considered earlier. Doing this gives:

$$\left[\frac{\delta CF(C)}{\delta CF(A)}\right] = \begin{cases} 0 & \text{if } CF(A) \leq 0 \\ [\text{MB} - \text{MD}] & \text{otherwise} \end{cases}$$

This is a result that looks a lot like a hybrid of the results for probability and possibility theories.

Qualitative algebras may also be extended to cope with any formalism. For instance, to extend $Q3$ to handle certainty factors in the situation described above, it is necessary to write down the interval arithmetic version of the equation relating $CF(A)$ and $CF(A)$:

$$CF(C) = ([(MB_L - MD_U), (MB_U - MD_L)]) ([\max(0, CF(A)_L), \max(0, CF(A)_U)])$$

where all the values are of the form

$$CF(A) = ([CF(A)_L, CF(A)_U])$$

and $CF(A)_L \leq CF(A)_U$. Note that when dealing with certainty factors the principle of degrading would have to take into account the fact that certainty factors can be negative.

By the same token, and the same method, it is simple to extend both qualitative algebras and the theory of qualitative change to cope with new combination rules that are necessary to fit different data or new interpretations of the underlying values. Thus, if desired, both the theory of qualitative change and the qualitative algebras could be extended to use the possibilistic combination rule suggested by Martin-Clouaire and Prade (1985):

$$\Pi(a, c) = \frac{\min\left(\Pi(a), \Pi(c)\right)}{\max[\min(\Pi(a), \Pi(c)), \min(1 - N(a), 1 - N(c))]}$$

Thus the methods introduced in this book provide a powerful yet easily extended method for handling incomplete numerical information.

Another point worth bearing in mind is that the means of integration provided by the qualitative methods is a way of integrating any number of uncertainty handling formalisms on a purely syntactic basis. Of course, as mentioned in Chapter 6, it is not possible to ignore semantics altogether. Some semantics must be chosen for the formalisms that are to be integrated. Once the semantics are determined, and whoever is integrating is happy that integration makes sense, then the qualitative methods may be applied whatever semantics have been decided upon since the methods place no constraints on the semantics. It is this concentration on syntax that gives the systems their power. Because the issue of semantics is handled by dealing only with the "degraded" value of every uncertainty value, integration using qualitative approaches is not as open to criticism on semantic grounds as other methods. This contrasts with, for instance, the method proposed by Zhang (1992).

In Zhang's integration, the use of direct translations between values expressed in different formalisms ignores the fact that values expressed in different formalisms mean different things. A different semantic attack could be made upon the work of Agustí-Cullell et al. (1991). Here the translation is between sets of values that are different sets of divisions of the same quantity. Thus the translation is between descriptions at different granularities. As a result it could be said that the translation fails to perform any integration.

Of course, there is a price to be paid for the advantages of the qualitative approaches. Chief among these is that only qualitative information may be derived. Thus, when using the theory of qualitative change, it is only possible to determine information such as "the probability of the patient being in pain increases." It is not possible to say by how much, or what the final probability is. The change could be almost nothing, or almost one. In addition since the initial probability may not be known, it may be even less clear whether the change is important. This leads to problems in determining trade-offs between different hypotheses—if the relative size of the probabilities of two events are not known, how is it possible to determine which is more likely to occur? Similarly, when using qualitative algebras, it is possible that the only available information that may be deduced is in the form of very wide intervals, a scenario that leads to the same problems as may be experienced with the qualitative changes.

There are a number of responses to this criticism. Firstly, the results may well be strong enough to be useful in many situations. When considering possible treatments for a disease, knowing that a certain plan of action will cause pain to increase will be sufficient to rule it out when another, painless, plan that does not decrease the chance of a cure is found. Wellman (1990b) uses a similar argument to justify his use of qualitative values. Qualitative results are also sufficient for explaining the impact of evidence to a human user of a probabilistic decision support system (Druzdzel, 1993) and for reasoning about the relationships between the variables in a design problem (Michelena, 1991). Possibly more importantly, they may be used as a basis for building more detailed numerical models, making it possible to elicit information at a level of detail the domain expert is happy with (Druzdzel and van der Gaag, 1995), and then focus on what additional information is required to answer the queries the users want to ask (van der Gaag, 1999). In addition it seems that qualitative models may be used for validating quantitative models (Parsons and Saffiotti, 1996), making it possible to ensure that the effect of evidence in a quantitative model is as desired without the need for exhaustive testing. Thus, in the worst case, there are definitely some niches in which qualitative methods can flourish. Secondly, if weak results are obtained in situations in which it would otherwise be impossible to derive any results—irrespective of whether this was because it was necessary to complete models, integrate values, or build robust models—even those weak results will be much better than what would otherwise be available. Thirdly, it may be possible to improve the results obtained, strengthening them so that more useful results can be obtained more often.

One might consider that the improvement of the results is one of the more important lines of research to investigate, and in the years since I began work on this book, a number of such pieces of work have appeared. As mentioned in Chapter 4, the weakness of results in terms of qualitative values has long been realised in the qualitative reasoning community, and there has been a considerable amount of work on ways to strengthen the results. Any of these could, in theory, be usefully used in combination with QPNs or QCNs, and some have been in practice. For instance, it is possible (Parsons, 1995) to apply the order of magnitude reasoning system ROM[K] (Dague, 1993b) to augment reasoning with probabilistic changes so that it is possible to determine which hypothesis is best supported by a given piece of evidence. The same style of reasoning has also been applied to the problem of determining the qualitative values of influences that the theory discussed in this book would dismiss as being of unknown value and thus written as [?]. Clearly such influences are either positive or negative in the sense that they will have either a positive or a negative effect in particular situations, it is just that the theory views them at too high a level of abstraction to determine which. Using order of magnitude reasoning to "zoom in" and resolve the matter has been discussed both informally (Parsons and Saffiotti, 1996) and formally (Parsons, 1997b). Another approach to strengthening results is to distinguish between the strengths of different qualitative influences, thus making it possible to identify which of two contradictory influences on a variable has the greater effect. A rather crude mechanism for doing this was provided in (Parsons, 1995), and a much neater solution was given by Renooij and van der Gaag (1999a). As discussed in (Renooij et al., 2000a,b) it is also possible to improve solutions by adapting the QPN propagation algorithm. All three of these latter approaches are qualitative in nature, the first using interval probabilities, the second defining strengths with respect to a landmark, and the third exploiting additional properties of qualitative influences. It is also possible to use detailed quantitative information to deal with this problem, and a way of doing this is discussed by Liu and Wellman (Liu and Wellman, 1998).

Another direction that such work could take is to emulate the work in qualitative reasoning on joint qualitative and quantitative approaches such as that of Berleant and Kuipers (1992). One way in which this might be done is to combine the use of qualitative algebras and the theory of qualitative change. If prior values are known for those uncertainty values known to change it is possible to use $Q3$ to handle the results. If for instance, $\Pr(a) = 0.4$ is known to increase it is possible to say that its posterior value is $\Pr(a)^* = (0.4, 1]$. This can then be compared using the rules of $Q3$ with the posterior probability $\Pr(b)^*$ of the competing hypothesis B that, for instance, is known to fall in the interval $[0, 0.8)$.

Improving the precision of the results of inference is not the only way in which the systems described here might be extended, for there are several other interesting avenues of further research. Firstly the approaches might be extended to cover the propagation of other uncertainty handling formalisms in networks. Particularly interesting would be the generalisation of the methods to cover all non-additive probability values (Dubois and Prade, 1988d) to provide the propagation of a whole a family of uncertainty representations that includes possibility measures and belief functions. Such work would need to consider the wide range of different ways of combining information in such formalisms, for instance the use of product rather than min in possibility theory, and Smets' α-junction operators for belief functions (Smets, 1997a). Secondly it would be interesting to investigate the relationship between the results of the qualitative analysis and work on conditioning (Goodman and Nguyen, 1991), independence (Shenoy, 1992a; Chrisman, 1996; Dawid and Studený, 1999), and causality (Geffner, 1996; Pearl, 2000). Establishing the qualitative effect of one variable on another is deeply concerned with the value of the conditionals, and the independence of the value of one variable from changes in value of another might be one way of determining conditional independence in non-probabilistic formalisms where such matters are not entirely settled, as well as having a bearing on what it means for one variable to be a cause of another.

All of these extensions seek to deepen the theory of qualitative change. However, the theory is already considerable, and what is perhaps more interesting is to look at applying it to new domains where it has advantages over quantitative methods. Such domains are those that are either massively complex (so that full quantitative data would be hard to obtain) and those where there is still little knowledge (where full quantitative data is just not available), and where there are good reasons to want to build predictive models despite the problems in both building models and interpreting the results that qualitative approaches can offer. Two obvious such domains are climate change, for instance to inform the debate on global warming, and macroeconomics, for example to analyse the effect of changes in economic policy in Southeast Asia. A less grandiose domain would be that of marketing, where the techniques devised in this book could be used to analyse the way potential markets will change with the release of new products. The proliferation of such domains suggests that qualitative approaches generally, and those related to the theory of qualitative change in particular, have a bright future.

A   Appendix: Proofs of theorems

Whatever they could prove (which is usually anything you like), they proved there, in an army constantly strengthened by the arrival of new recruits.

Charles Dickens, *Hard Times*

Proof of Theorem 5.6 (page 181): The probability/possibility consistency principle introduced in Section 3.2.2 and (3.44) states that there is a degree of consistency γ between $\Pr(x_i)$ and $\Pi(x_i)$:

$$\gamma = \Pi(x_1) \cdot \Pr(x_1) + \ldots + \Pi(x_n) \cdot \Pr(x_n)$$

which remains constant as the distributions are updated as a result of new information. Consider that $\Pr(x_1)$ increases in value as the result of some evidence, is it possible for γ to remain constant? The only definite result of the increase in $\Pr(x_1)$ is that there must be at least one probability $\Pr(x_i)$, $i \neq 1$, that decreases. None of the monotonicity assumptions put such strong constraints upon $\Pi(x_1)$ that the change in value of $\Pr(x_1).\Pi(x_1)$ cannot be offset by changes in value of some $\Pr(x_j)$ and $\Pi(x_k)$ so that γ does not change. The case in which $\Pr(x_1)$ decreases is similar. Consider instead that $\Pi(x_1)$ increases or decreases. In this case, there is no requirement that $\Pi(x_i)$, $i \neq 1$, changes, and again under any monotonicity assumption, the subsequent change in $\Pr(x_1)$ can be balanced by changes in $\Pr(x_j)$ and $\Pi(x_k)$.

As a result of this, it is quite possible for γ to remain constant, and the monotonicity assumptions do not violate the probability/possibility consistency principle. Now, consider the probability/belief and possibility/belief consistency principles introduced in Section 5.2.3. Since probability is the most restrictive formalism in that an increase in $\Pr(x_1)$ means a definite decrease in some $\Pr(x_i)$, the restrictions entailed by other consistency principles will be no more stringent than those entailed by the probability/possibility consistency principle, and the monotonicity assumptions will not cause them to be violated. □

Proof of Theorem 6.2 (page 213): From (6.24) and (6.25) it is clear that $\min([a,b], [m,n]) = [\min(a,m), \min(b,n)]$. If the inequality $\leq_{Q3}$ is defined in terms of min then $[a,b] \leq_{Q3} [n,m]$ if $\min([a,b], [m,n]) = [a,b]$. This will clearly only be true if $\min(a,m) = a$ and $\min(b,n) = b$ which in turn will only be true if $a \leq m$ and $b \leq n$. □

Proof of Theorem 6.3 (page 214): From the definition of $\leq'_{Q3}$ it follows that a point value is equivalent to an interval if the value represented by the interval is just as likely to be less than the point value as it is to be greater. Clearly then, the point value equivalent to the interval $[m, n]$ is its centre of gravity $(n + m)/2$. Now, one interval is greater than another if its equivalent value is greater than that of the other, so $[a, b] \leq'_{Q_3} [m, n]$ if and only if:

$$\frac{(a + b)}{2} \leq \frac{(m + n)}{2}$$

and the theorem holds. $\square$

Proof of Theorem 7.1 (page 243): The result follows immediately from Definitions 7.1–7.3 and (7.2). $\square$

Proof of Theorem 7.2 (page 244): The result follows immediately from Definitions 7.6–7.9, Definition 7.11 and (7.2). $\square$

Proof of Lemma 7.1 (page 248): Consider differentiating $u_1 = k_1 v_1 + \ldots + k_n v_n$ with respect to v_1. This clearly gives:

$$\frac{du_1}{dv_1} = k_1 + k_2 \frac{dv_2}{dv_1} + \ldots k_n \frac{dv_n}{dv_1}$$

In order to establish the qualitative value of du_1/dv_1 it is necessary to establish the values of the derivatives $dv_2/dv_1 \ldots dv_n/dv_1$. Now, since $\Delta v_1 \geq \Delta v_2, \ldots, \Delta v_n$, the biggest change possible in any of the v_i, $i \neq 1$ is a change of the same magnitude as that in v_1 though since:

$$v_1 = 1 - (v_2 + \ldots + v_n)$$

it will be in the opposite direction. In other words, the largest value of any of the dv_2/dv_1 is -1 and the smallest value is 0. Thus the smallest possible value of du_1/dv_1 will be $k_1 - k_i$ where k_i is the largest of the constant values, and the largest possible value of du_1/dv_1 will be $k_1 - k_j$ where k_j is the smallest of the constant values. From this the result quickly follows. $\square$

Proof of Theorem 7.3 (page 249): From (3.13) it is clear that:

$$Pr(c_1) = \sum_{\substack{A=a_1,\ldots,a_m \\ X=x_1,\ldots,x_p}} Pr(c_1|A,X) Pr(A,X)$$

Since A and X are conditionally independent of one another when C is not known,

$$Pr(A,X) = Pr(A) Pr(X)$$

for all values of A and X. Thus:

$$\Pr(c_1) = \sum_{\substack{A=a_1,\dots,a_m \\ X=x_1,\dots,x_p}} \Pr(c_1|A,X)\Pr(A)\Pr(X)$$

Differentiating with respect to $\Pr(a_1)$ and applying Lemma 7.1 gives:

$$\left[\frac{\partial \Pr(c_1)}{\partial \Pr(a_1)}\right] = \left[\sum_{X=x_1,\dots,x_p} \Pr(c_1|a_1,X)\Pr(X)\right.$$

$$\left. - \frac{\max}{\min}_{i=2\dots m} \sum_{X=x_1,\dots,x_p} \Pr(c_1|a_i,X)\Pr(X)\right]$$

From this the result immediately follows. $\square$

Proof of Corollary 7.1 (page 250): Start by assuming that:

$$\left[\frac{\partial \Pr(c_1)}{\partial \Pr(a_1)}\right] = [+]$$

and so:

$$\Pr(c_1|a_1,x) > \Pr(c_1|a_2,x)$$

Now, obviously:

$$\Pr(c_1|a_2,x) < \Pr(c_1|a_1,x)$$

and so:

$$\left[\frac{\partial \Pr(c_1)}{\partial \Pr(a_2)}\right] = [-]$$

Then, since:

$$\Pr(c_1|a_1,x) = 1 - \Pr(c_2|a_1,x)$$

it follows that:

$$\Pr(c_2|a_1,x) < \Pr(c_2|a_2,x)$$

and so:

$$\left[\frac{\partial \Pr(c_2)}{\partial \Pr(a_1)}\right] = [-]$$

and:

$$\left[\frac{\partial \Pr(c_2)}{\partial \Pr(a_2)}\right] = [+]$$

Similar arguments about the cases in which:

$$\left[\frac{\partial \Pr(c_1)}{\partial \Pr(a_1)}\right]$$

has the other possible qualitative values gives the result. □

Proof of Theorem 7.4 (page 251): From (3.38) it is clear that:

$$\Pi(c_1) = \sup_{\substack{A=a_1,\dots,a_m \\ X=x_1,\dots,x_p}} \min\left(\Pi(c_1|A,X), \Pi(A,X)\right)$$

Since A and X are conditionally independent of one another when C is not known,

$$\Pi(A,X) = \min\left(\Pi(A), \Pi(X)\right)$$

for all values of A and X. Thus:

$$\Pi(c_1) = \sup_{\substack{A=a_1,\dots,a_m \\ X=x_1,\dots,x_p}} \min\left(\Pi(c_1|A,X), \Pi(A), \Pi(X)\right)$$

The only time that $\Pi(c_1)$ will definitely change in value as $\Pi(a_1)$ does is when $\Pi(c_1) = \Pi(a_1)$ initially, in which case

$$\Pi(a_1) < \Pi(c_1|a_1,X)$$
$$\Pi(a_1) < \Pi(X)$$
$$\Pi(c_1,a_1,X) > \Pi(c_1,A,X)$$

for all values x of X and all values of A other than a_1 (the strict inequality is necessary to ensure that $\Pi(c_1)$ changes even if $\Pi(a_1)$ decreases). In this case

$$\left[\frac{\partial \Pi(c_1)}{\partial \Pi(a_1)}\right] = [+]$$

If the first two of the conditions hold and the last doesn't then $\Pi(c_1)$ may increase if $\Pi(a_1)$ does, since the last condition may hold after the increase. Similarly, if the last condition holds and the first two don't, then $\Pi(c_1)$ may decrease if $\Pi(a_1)$ does, since the first two conditions may hold after the decrease. If neither the last condition holds nor both of the first two conditions hold, then $\Pi(c_1)$ will not change as $\Pi(a_1)$ does. From this the result immediately follows. □

Proof of Corollary 7.2 (page 252): Consider applying Theorem 7.4 when $\Pi(a_1) = 1$. Since $\Pi(a_1)$ can never be less than all the $\Pi(c_1|a_1, x_j)$ (or indeed any of them) nor less than any of the $\Pi(x_j)$, the only possible values of the derivative are $[\downarrow, 0]$ or $[0]$, and which applies depends on the value of $\Pi(c_1|a_1, x_j)$. $\square$

Proof of Corollary 7.3 (page 252): Consider applying Theorem 7.4 when $\Pi(a_1) = 0$. Since $\Pi(a_1)$ can never be greater than all the $\Pi(c_1|a_1, x_j)$ (for any non-vacuous link), the only applicable cases from Theorem 7.4 are the first two. However, if $\Pi(a_1) = 0$, then $\Pi(c_1, a_1, x_j) = 0$ so the first cannot apply, and the only applicable case is the second. Looking at the second condition in this case, it is clear that:

$$\Pi(c_1, a_1, x_j) \leq \Pi(c_1, a_i, x_k)$$

whatever the distribution over X, so $\Pi(c_1)$ may follow $\Pi(a_1)$ up. Now, consider applying Theorem 7.4 when $\Pi(a_1) = 1$. No new possibilities arise from considering cases in which $\Pi(x_j) = 0$, but if all have value 1, the situation is that of Corollary 7.2, and the result follows. $\square$

Proof of Theorem 7.5 (page 253): From (3.64) it is clear that:

$$\mathrm{Bel}(c_1) = \sum_{\substack{A \subseteq \{a_1,\ldots,a_m\} \\ X \subseteq \{x_1,\ldots,x_p\}}} \mathrm{Bel}(c_1|A, X)m(A, X)$$

Since A and X are conditionally independent of one another when C is not known,

$$m(A, X) = m(A)m(X)$$

for all values of A and X. Thus:

$$\mathrm{Bel}(c_1) = \sum_{\substack{A \subseteq \{a_1,\ldots,a_m\} \\ X \subseteq \{x_1,\ldots,x_p\}}} \mathrm{Bel}(c_1|A, X)m(A)m(X)$$

Now, by (3.53), the mass of a singleton is same as the belief in that singleton, so that $m(a_1) = \mathrm{Bel}(a_1)$. Thus, differentiating with respect to $\mathrm{Bel}(a_1)$ and applying Lemma 7.1 gives:

$$\left[\frac{\partial \mathrm{Bel}(c_1)}{\partial \mathrm{Bel}(a_1)}\right] = \left[\sum_{X \subseteq \{x_1,\ldots,x_p\}} \mathrm{Bel}(c_1|a_1, X)m(X) \right.$$
$$\left. - \begin{array}{c}\max \\ \min\end{array} \begin{array}{c}y \subseteq A \\ a_1 \in y\end{array} \sum_{X \subseteq \{x_1,\ldots,x_p\}} \mathrm{Bel}(c_1|y, X)m(X)\right]$$

since basic belief mass may only move from sets of hypotheses to subsets of the same set of hypotheses—this means that any change in the belief mass of a_1 will only affect the belief mass of sets of hypotheses that include a_1. From the last equation the result immediately follows. $\square$

Proof of Theorem 7.6 (page 254): From (3.65) it is clear that:

$$\text{Bel}(c_1) = \sum_{\substack{A \subseteq \{a_1,\ldots,a_m\} \\ X \subseteq \{x_1,\ldots,x_p\}}} m(A,X) \prod_{\substack{a \in A \\ x \in X}} \text{Bel}(c_1|a,x)$$

Since A and X are conditionally independent of one another when C is not known,

$$m(A,X) = m(A)m(X)$$

for all values of A and X. Thus:

$$\text{Bel}(c_1) = \sum_{\substack{A \subseteq \{a_1,\ldots,a_m\} \\ X \subseteq \{x_1,\ldots,x_p\}}} m(A)m(X) \prod_{\substack{a \in A \\ x \in X}} \text{Bel}(c_1|a,x)$$

By the same argument as was used in the proof of Theorem 7.5, the requisite derivative is:

$$\left[\frac{\partial \text{Bel}(c_1)}{\partial \text{Bel}(a_1)} \right] = \left[\sum_{X \subseteq \{x_1,\ldots,x_p\}} m(X) \prod_{\substack{a_i \in a_1 \\ x_j \in X}} \text{Bel}(c_1|a_i,x_j) \right.$$

$$\left. - \frac{\max}{\min} \substack{y \subseteq A \\ a_1 \in y} \sum_{X \subseteq \{x_1,\ldots,x_p\}} m(X) \prod_{\substack{y_i \in y \\ x_j \in X}} \text{Bel}(c_1|y,x_j) \right]$$

Now, since each term in the product on the left of the subtraction will also appear in the product on the right of the subtraction (since $a_1 \in y$) and there will be multiplied by other conditional beliefs (which are no greater than 1), the derivative is always positive. $\square$

Proof of Theorem 7.7 (page 254): From (3.13) it is clear that:

$$\text{Pr}(c_1) = \sum_{\substack{A = a_1,\ldots,a_m \\ X = x_1,\ldots,x_p}} \text{Pr}(c_1|A,X) \text{Pr}(A,X)$$

Since A and X are conditionally independent of one another when C is not known,

$$\text{Pr}(A,X) = \text{Pr}(A) \text{Pr}(X)$$

for all values of A and X. Thus

$$\Pr(c_1) = \sum_{\substack{A=a_1,\ldots,a_m \\ X=x_1,\ldots,x_p}} \Pr(c_1|A,X)\Pr(A)\Pr(X)$$

Taking the separable derivative with respect to $\Pr(a_1)$ gives:

$$\left[\frac{\partial_s \Pr(c_1)}{\partial_s \Pr(a_1)}\right] = \left[\sum_{X=x_1,\ldots,x_p} \Pr(c_1|a_1,X)\Pr(X)\right]$$

From which it is clear that the separable derivative will always be non-negative and so $\Pr(c_1)$ may separably follow $\Pr(a_1)$ in all cases. $\square$

Proof of Theorem 7.8 (page 255): From (3.64) it is clear that when Dempster's rule is used:

$$\mathrm{Bel}(c_1) = \sum_{\substack{A\subseteq\{a_1,\ldots,a_m\} \\ X\subseteq\{x_1,\ldots,x_p\}}} \mathrm{Bel}(c_1|A,X)m(A,X)$$

Since A and X are conditionally independent of one another when C is not known,

$$m(A,X) = m(A)m(X)$$

for all values of A and X. Thus:

$$\mathrm{Bel}(c_1) = \sum_{\substack{A\subseteq\{a_1,\ldots,a_m\} \\ X\subseteq\{x_1,\ldots,x_p\}}} \mathrm{Bel}(c_1|A,X)m(A)m(X)$$

Now, by (3.53), the mass of a singleton is same as the belief in that singleton, so that $m(a_1) = \mathrm{Bel}(a_1)$, so, taking the separable derivative with respect to $\mathrm{Bel}(a_1)$ gives:

$$\left[\frac{\partial_s \mathrm{Bel}(c_1)}{\partial_s \mathrm{Bel}(a_1)}\right] = \left[\sum_{X\subseteq\{x_1,\ldots,x_p\}} \mathrm{Bel}(c_1|a_1,X)m(X)\right]$$

From which it is clear that the separable derivative will always be non-negative. When the disjunctive rule is used, (3.65) gives:

$$\mathrm{Bel}(c_1) = \sum_{\substack{A\subseteq\{a_1,\ldots,a_m\} \\ X\subseteq\{x_1,\ldots,x_p\}}} m(A,X) \prod_{\substack{a\in A \\ x\in X}} \mathrm{Bel}(c_1|a,x)$$

Since A and X are conditionally independent of one another when C is not known,

$$m(A,X) = m(A)m(X)$$

for all values of A and X. Thus:

$$\text{Bel}(c_1) = \sum_{\substack{A \subseteq \{a_1,\dots,a_m\} \\ X \subseteq \{x_1,\dots,x_p\}}} m(A)m(X) \prod_{\substack{a \in A \\ x \in X}} \text{Bel}(c_1|a,x)$$

Again $m(a_1) = \text{Bel}(a_1)$, and so the separable derivative is:

$$\left[\frac{\partial_s \text{Bel}(c_1)}{\partial_s \text{Bel}(a_1)} \right] = \left[\sum_{X \subseteq \{x_1,\dots,x_p\}} m(X) \prod_{\substack{a_i \in a_1 \\ x_j \in X}} \text{Bel}(c_1|a_i, x_j) \right]$$

exactly as before. Thus the separable derivative is non-negative, and from these two results, the theorem follows. $\square$

Proof of Lemma 7.2 (page 261): Consider the derivative:

$$\left[\frac{\partial \text{Pr}(c_1)}{\partial \text{Pr}(a_1)} \right] = \left[\sum_{X=x_1,\dots,x_p} \text{Pr}(c_1|a_1, X)\,\text{Pr}(X) \right.$$

$$\left. - \begin{array}{c} \max \\ \min \end{array}_{i=2\dots m} \sum_{X=x_1,\dots,x_p} \text{Pr}(c_1|a_i, X)\,\text{Pr}(X) \right]$$

determined by Theorem 7.3. Because there are no more instances of $\text{Pr}(a_1)$ in this expression, differentiating it again with respect to $\text{Pr}(a_1)$ will give:

$$\left[\frac{\partial^2 \text{Pr}(c_1)}{\partial \text{Pr}(a_1)^2} \right] = 0$$

from which it is clear that

$$\left[\frac{\partial \text{Pr}(c_1)}{\partial \text{Pr}(a_1)} \right]$$

is constant. Applying a similar procedure to the results of Theorems 7.5 and 7.6 it is easy to see that all the requisite second derivatives when dealing with evidence theory are zero. Possibility theory, of course, is slightly different, but considering the proof of Theorem 7.4 makes it clear that the only dependency of the derivative on the value of $\Pi(a_1)$ is already taken into account in the proof. Thus all the crucial qualitative derivatives are constant. $\square$

Proof of Theorem 7.9 (page 261): From Lemma 7.2 the value of both the partial and separable qualitative derivatives relating $\text{Val}(c_1)$ and $\text{Val}(a_1)$ are constant, so there is no difference between the results generated by them and those that would be generated by taking changes in the derivatives into account. Thus the changes calculated by the two methods have the same qualitative value, and so, by Definition 7.15, they are compatible. □

Proof of Corollary 7.4 (page 264): Differential calculus gives:

$$\frac{dy}{dx} = \frac{1}{\frac{dx}{dy}}$$

and if $\text{Val}(c_1)$ follows $\text{Val}(a_1)$ then:

$$\left[\frac{\partial \text{Val}(c_1)}{\partial \text{Val}(a_1)}\right] = [+]$$

so, if $\text{Val}(c_1)$ follows $\text{Val}(a_1)$, then it follows that:

$$\left[\frac{\partial \text{Val}(a_1)}{\partial \text{Val}(c_1)}\right] = \frac{1}{[+]} = [+]$$

Similarly, if $\text{Val}(c_1)$ varies inversely with $\text{Val}(a_1)$ then:

$$\left[\frac{\partial \text{Val}(c_1)}{\partial \text{Val}(a_1)}\right] = [-]$$

and so:

$$\left[\frac{\partial \text{Val}(a_1)}{\partial \text{Val}(c_1)}\right] = \frac{1}{[-]} = [-]$$

from which the result follows. □

Proof of Theorem 7.11 (page 265): If $\Pi(c_1)$ follows $\Pi(a_1)$ then $\Pi(c_1) = \Pi(a_1)$ which is a sufficient condition for $\Pi(a_1)$ to follow $\Pi(c_1)$. However, the conditional possibility values of the form $\Pi(a_1|c_i, x)$ and the possibilities of the values of C other than c_1 may be sufficient to prevent $\Pi(a_1)$ changing when $\Pi(c_1)$ does. Thus $\Pi(a_1)$ may follow $\Pi(c_1)$. If $\Pi(c_1)$ may follow $\Pi(a_1)$ up then $\Pi(c_1) > \Pi(a_1)$. Thus either the other relevant possibility values are such that $\Pi(a_1)$ may follow $\Pi(c_1)$ down, or they are such that $\Pi(a_1)$ is independent of $\Pi(c_1)$. Either way, $\Pi(a_1)$ may follow $\Pi(c_1)$ down. If $\Pi(c_1)$ may follow $\Pi(a_1)$ down then $\Pi(c_1) < \Pi(a_1)$. Thus either the other relevant possibility values are such that $\Pi(a_1)$ may follow $\Pi(c_1)$ up, or they are such that $\Pi(a_1)$ is independent of $\Pi(c_1)$. Either way, $\Pi(a_1)$ may follow $\Pi(c_1)$ up. If $\Pi(c_1)$ is independent of $\Pi(a_1)$ then the relationship between $\Pi(c_1)$ and $\Pi(a_1)$ is unknown. Thus all that may be said is that $\Pi(a_1)$ may follow $\Pi(c_1)$. Thus the theorem holds. □

Proof of Corollary 7.5 (page 265): Differential calculus gives:

$$\frac{dy}{dx} = \frac{1}{\frac{dx}{dy}}$$

and if $\text{Val}(c_1)$ may follow $\text{Val}(a_1)$ then:

$$\left[\frac{\partial \text{Val}(c_1)}{\partial \text{Val}(a_1)}\right] = [0, +]$$

so, if $\text{Val}(c_1)$ may follow $\text{Val}(a_1)$, then it follows that:

$$\left[\frac{\partial \text{Val}(a_1)}{\partial \text{Val}(c_1)}\right] = \frac{1}{[0, +]} = [?]$$

Similarly, if $\text{Val}(c_1)$ may vary inversely with $\text{Val}(a_1)$ then:

$$\left[\frac{\partial \text{Val}(c_1)}{\partial \text{Val}(a_1)}\right] = [0, -]$$

and so:

$$\left[\frac{\partial \text{Val}(a_1)}{\partial \text{Val}(c_1)}\right] = \frac{1}{[0, -]} = [?]$$

From this the result follows. $\square$

Proof of Theorem 7.12 (page 266): By Theorem 7.6 $\text{Bel}(a_1)$ follows $\text{Bel}(c_1)$ whatever the conditionals. Thus the result follows. $\square$

Proof of Theorem 7.13 (page 267): If

$$\left[\frac{\partial \Pr(c_1)}{\partial \text{Val}(a_1)}\right] = [0]$$

then, by definition:

$$\Pr(c_1|a_1, x) = \ldots = \Pr(c_1|a_m, x)$$

for all values $a_1, \ldots a_m$ of A and all values x of X. Now, by Bayes' rule (3.15):

$$\Pr(a_1|c_1, x) = \frac{\Pr(c_1|a_1, x)\Pr(a_1)}{\Pr(c_1)}$$

$$\Pr(a_1|c_2, x) = \frac{\Pr(c_2|a_1, x)\Pr(a_1)}{\Pr(c_2)}$$

For $\Pr(a_1)$ to be independent of $\Pr(c_1)$, it is necessary for these two conditionals to be equal. Thus it is necessary that:

$$\frac{\Pr(c_1|a_1,x)}{\Pr(c_1)} = \frac{\Pr(c_2|a_1,x)}{\Pr(c_2)} \tag{A.1}$$

From (3.13),

$$\Pr(c_1) = \sum_{\substack{A=a_1,\ldots,a_m \\ X=x_1,\ldots,x_p}} \Pr(c_1|A,X)\Pr(A,X)$$

$$= \Pr(c_1|a,x) \sum_{\substack{A=a_1,\ldots,a_m \\ X=x_1,\ldots,x_p}} \Pr(A,X)$$

$$= \Pr(c_1|a,x)$$

where $\Pr(c_1|a,x)$ is any $\Pr(c_1|a_i,x)$ (they are all equal). This means that (A.1) reduces to:

$$\Pr(c_2|a_1,x) = \Pr(c_2)$$

which is true provided that

$$\left[\frac{\partial\Pr(c_2)}{\partial\Pr(a_1)}\right] = [0]$$

Now, to ensure that $\Pr(a_1)$ is independent of $\Pr(c_1)$ it is clearly necessary that this condition is true for all the possible values c_i of C, which leads to the conclusion that:

$$\left[\frac{\partial\Pr(c_i)}{\partial\Pr(a_1)}\right] = [0]$$

for all values c_i of C. From this the result follows. $\square$

Proof of Theorem 7.14 (page 268): By Theorem 7.5,

$$\left[\frac{\partial\mathrm{Bel}(a_1)}{\partial\mathrm{Bel}(c_1)}\right] = \left[\mathrm{Bel}(a_1|c_1,x) - \frac{\max}{\min}\,{}_{\substack{y\subseteq c \\ c_1\in y}}\,\mathrm{Bel}(a_1|y,x)\right]$$

and from the generalisation of Bayes' theorem (3.66) it is possible to establish the conditionals in this expression from those that are available, thus for all x:

$$\mathrm{Bel}(a_1|c_1,x) = \prod_{y\in\bar{a}_1}\mathrm{Bel}(\mathbf{C}-c_1|y,x) - \prod_{z\in A}\mathrm{Bel}(\mathbf{C}-c_1|z,x)$$

$$\mathrm{Bel}(a_1|C,x) = \prod_{y\in\bar{a}_1}\mathrm{Bel}(\mathbf{C}-C|y,x) - \prod_{z\in A}\mathrm{Bel}(\mathbf{C}-C|z,x)$$

for any $\mathcal{C} \subseteq \mathbf{C}$. This reduces to:

$$\mathrm{Bel}(a_1|c_1, x) = \prod_{y \in \bar{a}_1} \mathrm{Bel}(\mathbf{C} - c_1|y, x)\,(1 - \mathrm{Bel}(\mathbf{C} - c_1|a_1, x))$$

$$\mathrm{Bel}(a_1|\mathcal{C}, x) = \prod_{y \in \bar{a}_1} \mathrm{Bel}(\mathbf{C} - \mathcal{C}|y, x)\,(1 - \mathrm{Bel}(\mathbf{C} - \mathcal{C}|a_1, x))$$

Now, the relevant conditional beliefs are those for which $c_1 \in \mathcal{C}$, and since none of these expressions depend upon the conditionals that determine

$$\left[\frac{\partial \mathrm{Bel}(c_1)}{\partial \mathrm{Bel}(a_1)} \right]$$

it is clear that nothing can be deduced about

$$\left[\frac{\partial \mathrm{Bel}(a_1)}{\partial \mathrm{Bel}(c_1)} \right]$$

from information about

$$\left[\frac{\partial \mathrm{Bel}(c_1)}{\partial \mathrm{Bel}(a_1)} \right]$$

Furthermore, since for two sets A and B such that $A \subseteq B$, $\mathrm{Bel}(A) \leq \mathrm{Bel}(B)$ (from (3.51), it follows that:

$$\mathrm{Bel}(\mathbf{C} - c_1|y, x) \geq \mathrm{Bel}(\mathbf{C} - \mathcal{C}|y, x)$$

and:

$$\mathrm{Bel}(\mathbf{C} - c_1|a_1, x) \geq \mathrm{Bel}(\mathbf{C} - \mathcal{C}|a_1, x)$$

which prevents anything conclusive about

$$\left[\frac{\partial \mathrm{Bel}(a_1)}{\partial \mathrm{Bel}(c_1)} \right]$$

to be deduced without adding additional conditions. The only condition under which the relevant conditionals are equal, and thus

$$\left[\frac{\partial \mathrm{Bel}(a_1)}{\partial \mathrm{Bel}(c_1)} \right] = [0]$$

is:

$$\mathrm{Bel}(a_1|c_1, x) = \mathrm{Bel}(a_1|\mathcal{C}, x)$$

for all $C \subseteq \mathbf{C}$ such that $c_1 \in C$, and this condition is just:

$$\prod_{y \in \bar{a}_1} \mathrm{Bel}(\mathbf{C} - c_1|y,x)\,(1 - \mathrm{Bel}(\mathbf{C} - c_1|a_1,x))$$

$$= \prod_{y \in \bar{a}_1} \mathrm{Bel}(\mathbf{C} - C|y,x)\,(1 - \mathrm{Bel}(\mathbf{C} - C|a_1,x))$$

for all C. From these, the result follows. $\square$

Proof of Theorem 7.15 (page 269): By Theorem 7.5:

$$\left[\frac{\partial \mathrm{Bel}(a_1)}{\partial \mathrm{Bel}(c_1)}\right] = \left[\mathrm{Bel}(a_1|c_1,x) - \frac{\max}{\min} {}_{\substack{y \subseteq C \\ c_1 \in y}} \mathrm{Bel}(a_1|y,x)\right]$$

and from the generalisation of Bayes' theorem (3.66) it is possible to establish the conditionals in this expression from those that are available, thus for all x:

$$\mathrm{Bel}(a_1|c_1,x) = \prod_{y \in \bar{a}_1} \mathrm{Bel}(\mathbf{C} - c_1|y,x) - \prod_{z \in A} \mathrm{Bel}(\mathbf{C} - c_1|z,x)$$

$$\mathrm{Bel}(a_1|C,x) = \prod_{y \in \bar{a}_1} \mathrm{Bel}(\mathbf{C} - C|y,x) - \prod_{z \in A} \mathrm{Bel}(\mathbf{C} - C|z,x)$$

for any $C \subseteq \mathbf{C}$. This reduces to:

$$\mathrm{Bel}(a_1|c_1,x) = \prod_{y \in \bar{a}_1} \mathrm{Bel}(\mathbf{C} - c_1|y,x)\,(1 - \mathrm{Bel}(\mathbf{C} - c_1|a_1,x))$$

$$\mathrm{Bel}(a_1|C,x) = \prod_{y \in \bar{a}_1} \mathrm{Bel}(\mathbf{C} - C|y,x)\,(1 - \mathrm{Bel}(\mathbf{C} - C|a_1,x))$$

As in the proof of Theorem 7.14, the relevant conditional beliefs are those for which $c_1 \in C$, and since none of these expressions depend upon the conditionals which determine $[\partial \mathrm{Bel}(c_1)/\partial \mathrm{Bel}(a_1)]$, it is clear that nothing can be deduced about $[\partial \mathrm{Bel}(a_1)/\partial \mathrm{Bel}(c_1)]$ from information about $[\partial \mathrm{Bel}(c_1)/\partial \mathrm{Bel}(a_1)]$. However, substituting back into the expression for $[\partial \mathrm{Bel}(a_1)/\partial \mathrm{Bel}(c_1)]$, it becomes apparent that $[\partial \mathrm{Bel}(a_1)/\partial \mathrm{Bel}(c_1)]$ is:

$$\left[\prod_{y \in \bar{a}_1} \mathrm{Bel}(\mathbf{C} - c_1|y,x)\,(1 - \mathrm{Bel}(\mathbf{C} - c_1|a_1,x))\right.$$

$$\left. - \frac{\max}{\min} {}_{\substack{c_1 \in y \\ y \subseteq C}} \prod_{y \in \bar{a}_1} \mathrm{Bel}(\mathbf{C} - C|y,x)\,(1 - \mathrm{Bel}(\mathbf{C} - C|a_1,x))\right]$$

and from this, the result follows. $\square$

Proof of Theorem 7.16 (page 269): The basis of this proof comes from (Spiegelhalter, 1991). One way to interpret Theorem 7.3 is that the qualitative value of the derivative is given by:

$$\left[\frac{\partial \Pr(c_1)}{\partial \Pr(a_1)}\right] = \bigoplus_x [\Pr(c_1|a_1,x) - \Pr(c_1|a_2,x)]$$

and so

$$\left[\frac{\partial \Pr(a_1)}{\partial \Pr(c_1)}\right] = \bigoplus_x [\Pr(a_1|c_1,x) - \Pr(a_1|c_2,x)]$$

Applying Bayes' rule to $\Pr(a_1|c_1,x)$ and $\Pr(a_1|c_2,x)$ for some x gives:

$$\Pr(a_1|c_1,x) = \frac{\Pr(c_1|a_1,x)\Pr(a_1)}{\Pr(c_1)} \tag{A.2}$$

$$\Pr(a_1|c_2,x) = \frac{\Pr(c_2|a_1,x)\Pr(a_1)}{\Pr(c_2)} \tag{A.3}$$

Writing

$$\Pr(c_1) = \Pr(c_1|a_1,x)\Pr(a_1,x) + \Pr(c_1|a_2,x)\Pr(a_2,x) \tag{A.4}$$
$$\Pr(c_2) = \Pr(c_2|a_1,x)\Pr(a_1,x) + \Pr(c_2|a_2,x)\Pr(a_2,x) \tag{A.5}$$

and dividing (A.2) by (A.3), and simplifying, gives:

$$\frac{\Pr(a_1|c_1,x)}{\Pr(a_1|c_2,x)} = \frac{\Pr(a_1,x) + \Pr(a_2,x)\left(\frac{\Pr(c_2|a_2,x)}{\Pr(c_2|a_1,x)}\right)}{\Pr(a_1,x) + \Pr(a_2,x)\left(\frac{\Pr(c_1|a_2,x)}{\Pr(c_1|a_1,x)}\right)}$$

Now, consider that $\Pr(c_1)$ follows $\Pr(a_1)$, and so:

$$\Pr(c_1|a_1,x) \geq \Pr(c_1|a_2,x)$$

for all x. Since:

$$\Pr(c_1|a_1,x) = 1 - \Pr(c_2|a_1,x)$$

it follows that:

$$\Pr(c_2|a_2,x) \geq \Pr(c_2|a_1,x)$$

for the x we are dealing with. Thus:

$$\frac{\Pr(c_2|a_2,x)}{\Pr(c_2|a_1,x)} \geq 1$$

$$\frac{\Pr(c_1|a_2,x)}{\Pr(c_1|a_1,x)} \leq 1$$

so that:

$$\frac{\Pr(a_1|c_1,x)}{\Pr(a_1|c_2,x)} \geq 1$$

and thus:

$$\Pr(a_1|c_1,x) \geq \Pr(a_1|c_2,x)$$

We can do that same for every x, and $\Pr(a_1)$ follows $\Pr(c_1)$. Similar arguments can be made for the case in which $\Pr(a_1)$ varies inversely with $\Pr(c_1)$ and is independent of it, allowing the conclusion that the influence is symmetric.□

Proof of Theorem 7.17 (page 269): By Theorem 7.5

$$\left[\frac{\partial \mathrm{Bel}(a_1)}{\partial \mathrm{Bel}(c_1)}\right] = [\mathrm{Bel}(a_1|c_1,X) - \mathrm{Bel}(a_1|c_1 \cup c_2,X)]$$

and from the generalisation of Bayes' theorem (3.66) it is possible to establish the conditionals in this expression from those that are available, thus for all x:

$$\mathrm{Bel}(a_1|c_1,x) = \prod_{y\in\tilde{a}_1} \mathrm{Bel}(\mathbf{C}-c_1|y,x) - \prod_{z\in A} \mathrm{Bel}(\mathbf{C}-c_1|z,x)$$

$$\mathrm{Bel}(a|c_1 \cup c_2,x) = \prod_{y\in\tilde{a}_1} \mathrm{Bel}(\emptyset \cup c_2|y,x) - \prod_{z\in A} \mathrm{Bel}(\emptyset|z,x)$$

Since all beliefs of the form $\mathrm{Bel}(\emptyset|x,y)$ are taken to be zero it is clear that $\mathrm{Bel}(a|c_1 \cup c_2,x)$ will always be zero and thus no larger than $\mathrm{Bel}(a_1|c_1,x)$. Thus:

$$\left[\frac{\partial \mathrm{Bel}(a_1)}{\partial \mathrm{Bel}(c_1)}\right] = \left[\prod_{y\in\tilde{a}_1} \mathrm{Bel}(c_2|y,x) - \prod_{z\in\mathbf{A}} \mathrm{Bel}(c_2|z,x)\right]$$

which may be written as:

$$\left[\frac{\partial \mathrm{Bel}(a_1)}{\partial \mathrm{Bel}(c_1)}\right] = \left[\prod_{y\in\tilde{a}_1} \mathrm{Bel}(\mathbf{C}-c_1|y,x)(1 - \mathrm{Bel}(c_2|a_1,x))\right]$$

Since all beliefs are between 1 and zero, this value is not negative, and the result follows.
□

Proof of Theorem 8.1 (page 286): From (3.13) it is clear that:

$$\Pr(c_1) = \sum_{\substack{A=a_1,\ldots,a_m \\ B=b_1,\ldots,b_q \\ X=x_1,\ldots,x_p}} \Pr(c_1|A,B,X)\Pr(A,B,X)$$

Since A, B and X are conditionally independent of one another when C is not known,

$$\Pr(A,B,X) = \Pr(A)\Pr(B)\Pr(X)$$

for all values of A, B, and X. Thus:

$$\Pr(c_1) = \sum_{\substack{A=a_1,\ldots,a_m \\ B=b_1,\ldots,b_q \\ X=x_1,\ldots,x_p}} \Pr(c_1|A,B,X)\Pr(A)\Pr(B)\Pr(X)$$

Differentiating with respect to $\Pr(a_1)$ and applying Lemma 7.1 gives:

$$\left[\frac{\partial\Pr(c_1)}{\partial\Pr(a_1)}\right] = \left[\sum_{\substack{B=b_1,\ldots,b_q \\ X=x_1,\ldots,x_p}} \Pr(c_1|a_1,B,X)\Pr(B)\Pr(X)\right.$$

$$\left. -\,\begin{array}{c}\max\\\min\end{array}_{i=2\ldots m}\sum_{\substack{B=b_1,\ldots,b_q \\ X=x_1,\ldots,x_p}} \Pr(c_1|a_i,B,X)\Pr(B)\Pr(X)\right]$$

Differentiating with respect to $\Pr(b_1)$ and applying Lemma 7.1 gives:

$$\left[\frac{\partial^2\Pr(c_1)}{\partial\Pr(a_1)\partial\Pr(b_1)}\right] =$$

$$\left[\sum_{X=x_1,\ldots,x_p} \Pr(X)\left[\Pr(c_1|a_1,b_1,X) - \begin{array}{c}\max\\\min\end{array}_{i=2\ldots m}\Pr(c_1|a_i,b,X)\right]\right.$$

$$\left. -\sum_{X=x_1,\ldots,x_p} \Pr(X)\left[\begin{array}{c}\max\\\min\end{array}_{j=2\ldots q}\Pr(c_1|a,b_j,X) - \begin{array}{c}\max\\\min\end{array}_{\substack{i=2\ldots m\\j=2\ldots q}}\Pr(c_1|a_i,b_j,X)\right]\right]$$

From this expression and Definition 8.1 the result immediately follows. $\square$

Proof of Theorem 8.2 (page 286): From (3.64) it is clear that:

$$\mathrm{Bel}(c_1) = \sum_{\substack{A\subseteq\{a_1,\ldots,a_m\} \\ B\subseteq\{b_1,\ldots,b_q\} \\ X\subseteq\{x_1,\ldots,x_p\}}} \mathrm{Bel}(c_1|A,B,X)m(A,B,X)$$

Since A, B, and X are conditionally independent of one another when C is not known,

$$m(A, B, X) = m(A)m(B)m(X)$$

for all values of A, B, and X. Thus:

$$\text{Bel}(c_1) = \sum_{\substack{A \subseteq \{a_1,\ldots,a_m\} \\ B \subseteq \{b_1,\ldots,b_q\} \\ X \subseteq \{x_1,\ldots,x_p\}}} \text{Bel}(c_1|A, B, X)m(A)m(B)m(X)$$

Now, by (3.53), the mass of a singleton is same as the belief in that singleton, so that $m(a_1) = \text{Bel}(a_1)$. Thus, differentiating with respect to $\text{Bel}(a_1)$ and applying Lemma 7.1 gives:

$$\left[\frac{\partial \text{Bel}(c_1)}{\partial \text{Bel}(a_1)}\right] = \left[\sum_{\substack{B \subseteq \{b_1,\ldots,b_q\} \\ X \subseteq \{x_1,\ldots,x_p\}}} \text{Bel}(c_1|a_1, B, X)m(B)m(X) \right.$$

$$\left. - \frac{\max}{\min} {\substack{y \subseteq A \\ a_1 \in y}} \sum_{\substack{B \subseteq \{b_1,\ldots,b_q\} \\ X \subseteq \{x_1,\ldots,x_p\}}} \text{Bel}(c_1|y, B, X)m(B)m(X) \right]$$

as in the proof of Theorem 7.5. Differentiating this with respect to $\text{Bel}(b_1)$ and applying Lemma 7.1 gives:

$$\left[\frac{\partial^2 \text{Bel}(c_1)}{\partial \text{Bel}(a_1)\partial \text{Bel}(a_2)}\right] =$$

$$\left[\sum_{X \subseteq \{x_1,\ldots,x_p\}} m(X)\left[\text{Bel}(c_1|a_1, b, X) - \frac{\max}{\min}{\substack{z \subseteq B \\ b_1 \in z}}\text{Bel}(c_1|a_1, z, X)\right]\right.$$

$$\left. - \sum_{X \subseteq \{x_1,\ldots,x_p\}} m(X)\left[\frac{\max}{\min}{\substack{y \subseteq A \\ a_1 \in y}}\text{Bel}(c_1|y, b, X) - \frac{\max}{\min}{\substack{y \subseteq A \ z \subseteq B \\ a_1 \in y, b_1 \in z}}\text{Bel}(c_1|y, z, X)\right]\right]$$

And from this expression and Definition 8.1 the result immediately follows. □

Proof of Theorem 8.3 (page 287): From (3.65) it is clear that:

$$\text{Bel}(c_1) = \sum_{\substack{A \subseteq \{a_1,\ldots,a_m\} \\ B \subseteq \{b_1,\ldots,b_q\} \\ X \subseteq \{x_1,\ldots,x_p\}}} m(A, B, X) \prod_{\substack{a \in A \\ b \in B \\ x \in X}} \text{Bel}(c_1|a, b, x)$$

Since A, B, and X are conditionally independent of one another when C is not known,

$$m(A, B, X) = m(A)m(B)m(X)$$

for all values of A, B, and X. Thus:

$$\text{Bel}(c_1) = \sum_{\substack{A \subseteq \{a_1, \ldots, a_m\} \\ B \subseteq \{b_1, \ldots, b_q\} \\ X \subseteq \{x_1, \ldots, x_p\}}} m(A)m(B)m(X) \prod_{\substack{a_i \in A \\ b_j \in B \\ x_k \in X}} \text{Bel}(c_1 | a_i, b_j, x_k)$$

By the same argument as was used in the proof of Theorem 8.2, the necessary first derivative is:

$$\left[\frac{\partial \text{Bel}(c_1)}{\partial \text{Bel}(a_1)} \right] = \left[\sum_{\substack{B \subseteq \{b_1, \ldots, b_q\} \\ X \subseteq \{x_1, \ldots, x_p\}}} m(B)m(X) \prod_{\substack{b_j \in B \\ x_k \in X}} \text{Bel}(c_1 | a_1, b_j, x_k) \right.$$

$$\left. - \frac{\max}{\min} {}_{\substack{y \subseteq A \\ a_1 \in y}} \sum_{\substack{B \subseteq \{b_1, \ldots, b_q\} \\ X \subseteq \{x_1, \ldots, x_p\}}} m(B)m(X) \prod_{\substack{b_j \in B \\ x_k \in X}} \text{Bel}(c_1 | y, b_j, x_k) \right]$$

Differentiating this with respect to $\text{Bel}(b_1)$ and applying Lemma 7.1 gives:

$$\left[\frac{\partial^2 \text{Bel}(c_1)}{\partial \text{Bel}(a_1) \partial \text{Bel}(a_2)} \right] =$$

$$\left[\sum_{X \subseteq \{x_1, \ldots, x_p\}} m(X) \left[\prod_{\substack{b_j \in b_1 \\ x_k \in X}} \text{Bel}(c_1 | a_1, b_1, x_k) - \frac{\max}{\min} {}_{\substack{z \subseteq B \\ b_1 \in z}} \prod_{\substack{b_j \in z \\ x_k \in X}} \text{Bel}(c_1 | a_1, z, x_k) \right] \right.$$

$$- \sum_{X \subseteq \{x_1, \ldots, x_p\}} m(X) \left[\frac{\max}{\min} {}_{\substack{y \subseteq A \\ a_1 \in y}} \prod_{\substack{b_j \in b_1 \\ x_k \in X}} \text{Bel}(c_1 | y, b_j, x_k) \right.$$

$$\left. \left. - \frac{\max}{\min} {}_{\substack{y \subseteq A \\ a_1 \in y}} {}_{\substack{z \subseteq B \\ b_1 \in z}} \prod_{\substack{b_j \in z \\ x_k \in X}} \text{Bel}(c_1 | y, z, x_k) \right] \right]$$

And from this expression and Definition 8.1 the result immediately follows. $\square$

Proof of Theorem 8.4 (page 290): Consider Theorem 7.4 writing b_1 for x. For $\Pi(c_1)$ to follow $\Pi(a_1)$ or to follow $\Pi(a_1)$ up it is necessary for $\Pi(a_1)$ be less than $\Pi(b_1)$. If $\Pi(b_1)$ decreases then it may be the case that it is no longer less than $\Pi(a_1)$. Thus it may be the case that $\Pi(c_1)$ no longer follows $\Pi(a_1)$ or no longer follows $\Pi(a_1)$ down. Thus the relationship between $\Pi(a_1)$ and $\Pi(c_1)$ becomes indeterminate and (1) is proved. If $\Pi(c_1)$ follows $\Pi(a_1)$ down then either $\Pi(a_1)$ is greater than or equal to $\Pi(c_1|a_1, b_1)$ or $\Pi(a_1)$ is greater than or equal to $\Pi(b_1)$. In the former case changes in $\Pi(b_1)$ will have no effect on the relationship between $\Pi(a_1)$ and $\Pi(c_1)$. In the latter case, if $\Pi(b_1)$ increases it may no longer be less than or equal to $\Pi(a_1)$ so that the relationship between $\Pi(a_1)$ and $\Pi(c_1)$ becomes indeterminate and (2) is proved. (3) follows from the fact that there are no other ways in which the conditions specified in Theorem 7.4 can be affected by changes in value of $\Pi(b_1)$. Thus the theorem is proved. □

Proof of Theorem 8.5 (page 292): Given Definition 8.1, this theorem concerns the way in which

$$\frac{\partial^2 \mathrm{Val}(d_1)}{\partial \mathrm{Val}(a_1)\partial \mathrm{Val}(b_1)}$$

is computed from

$$\frac{\partial^2 \mathrm{Val}(c_1)}{\partial \mathrm{Val}(a_1)\partial \mathrm{Val}(b_1)}$$

and

$$\frac{\partial \mathrm{Val}(d_1)}{\partial \mathrm{Val}(c_1)}$$

Now, by the chain rule of the differential calculus (Stewart, 1991) it is the case that:

$$\frac{\partial \mathrm{Val}(d_1)}{\partial \mathrm{Val}(a_1)} = \frac{\partial \mathrm{Val}(c_1)}{\partial \mathrm{Val}(a_1)} \cdot \frac{\partial \mathrm{Val}(d_1)}{\partial \mathrm{Val}(c_1)}$$

Differentiating both sides with respect to $\mathrm{Val}(b_1)$ gives:

$$\frac{\partial^2 \mathrm{Val}(d_1)}{\partial \mathrm{Val}(a_1)\partial \mathrm{Val}(b_1)} = \frac{\partial}{\partial \mathrm{Val}(b_1)} \left(\frac{\partial \mathrm{Val}(c_1)}{\partial \mathrm{Val}(a_1)} \cdot \frac{\partial \mathrm{Val}(d_1)}{\partial \mathrm{Val}(c_1)} \right)$$

and applying the product rule of the differential calculus (Stewart, 1991) gives:

$$\frac{\partial^2 \mathrm{Val}(d_1)}{\partial \mathrm{Val}(a_1)\partial \mathrm{Val}(b_1)} = \frac{\partial^2 \mathrm{Val}(c_1)}{\partial \mathrm{Val}(a_1)\partial \mathrm{Val}(b_1)} \cdot \frac{\partial \mathrm{Val}(d_1)}{\partial \mathrm{Val}(c_1)}$$
$$+ \frac{\partial}{\partial \mathrm{Val}(b_1)} \left(\frac{\partial \mathrm{Val}(d_1)}{\partial \mathrm{Val}(c_1)} \right) \frac{\partial \mathrm{Val}(c_1)}{\partial \mathrm{Val}(a_1)}$$

From previous results it is clear that $\partial\mathrm{Val}(d_1)/\partial\mathrm{Val}(c_1)$ will not contain any terms that are functions of $\mathrm{Val}(b_1)$ (it will only contain conditional probabilities or beliefs) so that:

$$\frac{\partial}{\partial\mathrm{Val}(b_1)}\left(\frac{\partial\mathrm{Val}(d_1)}{\partial\mathrm{Val}(c_1)}\right) = 0$$

Thus:

$$\frac{\partial^2\mathrm{Val}(d_1)}{\partial\mathrm{Val}(a_1)\partial\mathrm{Val}(b_1)} = \frac{\partial^2\mathrm{Val}(c_1)}{\partial\mathrm{Val}(a_1)\partial\mathrm{Val}(b_1)}\cdot\frac{\partial\mathrm{Val}(d_1)}{\partial\mathrm{Val}(c_1)}$$

so that:

$$\left[\frac{\partial^2\mathrm{Val}(d_1)}{\partial\mathrm{Val}(a_1)\partial\mathrm{Val}(b_1)}\right] = \left[\frac{\partial^2\mathrm{Val}(c_1)}{\partial\mathrm{Val}(a_1)\partial\mathrm{Val}(b_1)}\right] \otimes \left[\frac{\partial\mathrm{Val}(d_1)}{\partial\mathrm{Val}(c_1)}\right]$$

and the result follows. $\square$

Proof of Theorem 8.6 (page 297): From (3.13) it is clear that:

$$\Pr(c_1) = \sum_{\substack{A=a_1,\ldots,a_m \\ X=x_1,\ldots,x_p}} \Pr(c_1|A,X)\Pr(A,X)$$

Since the network is multiply-connected,

$$\Pr(A,X) = \Pr(X|A)\Pr(A)$$

for all values of A and X. Thus:

$$\Pr(c_1) = \sum_{\substack{A=a_1,\ldots,a_m \\ X=x_1,\ldots,x_p}} \Pr(c_1|A,X)\Pr(X|A)\Pr(A)$$

Differentiating with respect to $\Pr(a_1)$ gives:

$$\frac{\partial\Pr(c_1)}{\partial\Pr(a_1)} = \sum_{\substack{A=a_1,\ldots,a_m \\ X=x_1,\ldots,x_p}} \Pr(c_1|A,X)\left(\Pr(X|A)\frac{\partial\Pr(A)}{\partial\Pr(a_1)} + \Pr(A)\frac{\partial\Pr(X|A)}{\partial\Pr(a_1)}\right)$$

Now, the first of the two derivatives on the right hand side of this expression is similar to that which gives the result for the singly-connected case. The second summarises the effect of X on C due to the change in A. What the overall expression is therefore saying is that the way in which $\Pr(c_1)$ changes as $\Pr(a_1)$ changes is the sum of (1) the way in which $\Pr(c_1)$ changes as $\Pr(a_1)$ in the singly-connected case and (2) the way in which $\Pr(c_1)$ changes as the various $\Pr(x)$ change due to the change in $\Pr(a_1)$. Thus what the differential calculus gives is not just the way in which $\Pr(c_1)$ changes due to the direct influence of A but also its indirect influence through X.

This calculation is entirely correct. If A is a parent of X, then the second derivative on the right hand side in the above equation will summarise the effect of $Pr(a_1)$ on the various values of X and so the derivative will calculate the double effect of A on C without having to propagate changes variable by variable along the chain of influences from A to C. If A is not a parent of C, so that there is no trail from A to X that does not go through C, then the second derivative will be zero, $Pr(X|A)$ will become $Pr(X)$ and the expression will reduce to that for the singly-connected case.

However, as is the case elsewhere, the differential calculus goes rather further than is required by the theory of qualitative change. If A is connected to X the indirect influence of A on C will be calculated directly when the influence of X on C is considered. The second derivative can therefore be ignored when determining the qualitative influence of A on C. The important thing that the differential calculus gives is an assurance that there are no additional influences that affect the value of $Pr(c_1)$ besides the same direct influence as in the singly-connected case and the indirect influence through X.

Thus considering the "direct influence" part of the expression for the derivative and applying Lemma 7.1 gives:

$$
\begin{aligned}
\left[\frac{\partial Pr(c_1)}{\partial Pr(a_1)} \right] &= \left[\sum_{X=x_1,\ldots,x_p} Pr(c_1|a_1,X)\,Pr(X|a_1) \right. \\
&\qquad\qquad \left. - \frac{\max}{\min}_{i=2\ldots m} \sum_{X=x_1,\ldots,x_p} Pr(c_1|a_i,X)\,Pr(X|a_i) \right] \\
&= \left[\sum_{X=x_1,\ldots,x_p} Pr(c_1,X|a_1) - \frac{\max}{\min}_{i=2\ldots m} \sum_{X=x_1,\ldots,x_p} Pr(c_1,X|a_i) \right] \\
&= \left[Pr(c_1|a_1) - \frac{\max}{\min}_{i=2\ldots m} Pr(c_1|a_i) \right]
\end{aligned}
\qquad\text{(A.6)}
$$

Which gives a simple condition determining the qualitative value of the derivative. Now, from Theorem 7.3 in the singly-connected case:

$$
\begin{aligned}
\left[\frac{\partial Pr(c_1)}{\partial Pr(a_1)} \right] &= \left[\sum_{X=x_1,\ldots,x_p} Pr(c_1|a_1,X)\,Pr(X) \right. \\
&\qquad\qquad \left. - \frac{\max}{\min}_{i=2\ldots m} \sum_{X=x_1,\ldots,x_p} Pr(c_1|a_i,X)\,Pr(X) \right]
\end{aligned}
$$

$$= \left[\sum_{X=x_1,\dots,x_p} \Pr(c_1, X|a_1) - \frac{\max}{\min}_{i=2\dots m} \sum_{X=x_1,\dots,x_p} \Pr(c_1, X|a_i) \right]$$

$$= \left[\Pr(c_1|a_1) - \frac{\max}{\min}_{i=2\dots m} \Pr(c_1|a_i) \right] \tag{A.7}$$

Thus, if:

$$\sum_{X=x_1,\dots,x_p} \Pr(c_1|a_1, X) \Pr(X) > \frac{\max}{\min}_{i=2\dots m} \sum_{X=x_1,\dots,x_p} \Pr(c_1|a_i, X) \Pr(X)$$

then as above (A.7) and so (A.6) and will be satisfied. Thus if the condition for the singly-connected case is satisfied, then the condition for the multiply-connected case will also be satisfied and the derivatives will have value $[+]$ in both cases. Similar reasoning for other values of the derivative gives the result. □

Proof of Theorem 8.7 (page 299): From (3.13) it is clear that:

$$\Pr(c_1) = \sum_{\substack{A=a_1,\dots,a_m \\ X=x_1,\dots,x_p}} \Pr(c_1|A, X) \Pr(A, X)$$

As in the previous proof, in a multiply-connected network

$$\Pr(A, X) = \Pr(X|A) \Pr(A)$$

for all values of A and X. Thus:

$$\Pr(c_1) = \sum_{\substack{A=a_1,\dots,a_m \\ X=x_1,\dots,x_p}} \Pr(c_1|A, X) \Pr(X|A) \Pr(A)$$

Taking the separable derivative with respect to $\Pr(a_1)$ gives:

$$\left[\frac{\partial_s \Pr(c_1)}{\partial_s \Pr(a_1)} \right] = \left[\sum_{X=x_1,\dots,x_p} \Pr(c_1|a_1, X) \Pr(X|a_1) \right]$$

From which it is clear that the separable derivative will always be non-negative and so $\Pr(c_1)$ may separably follow $\Pr(a_1)$ in all cases. □

Proof of Theorem 8.8 (page 300): From (3.38) it is clear that:

$$\Pi(c_1) = \sup_{\substack{A=a_1,\dots,a_m \\ X=x_1,\dots,x_p}} \min \left(\Pi(c_1|A, X), \Pi(A, X) \right)$$

Since A and X are not conditionally independent of one another:

$$\Pi(A, X) = \min\left(\Pi(X|A), \Pi(X)\right)$$

for all values of A and X. Thus:

$$\Pi(c_1) = \sup_{\substack{A=a_1,\dots,a_m \\ X=x_1,\dots,x_p}} \min\left(\Pi(c_1|A, X), \Pi(X|A), \Pi(A)\right)$$

Just as in the proof of Theorem 7.4 it is possible to argue that the only time that $\Pi(c_1)$ will definitely change in value as $\Pi(a_1)$ does is when $\Pi(c_1) = \Pi(a_1)$ initially, in which case:

$$\begin{aligned}
\Pi(a_1) &< \Pi(c_1|a_1, X) \\
\Pi(a_1) &< \Pi(X|a_1) \\
\Pi(c_1, a_1, X) &> \Pi(c_1, A, X)
\end{aligned}$$

for all values x of X (the strict inequality is necessary to ensure that $\Pi(c_1)$ changes even if $\Pi(a_1)$ decreases). In this case:

$$\left[\frac{\partial\Pi(c_1)}{\partial\Pi(a_1)}\right] = [+]$$

If the first two of the conditions holds and the last doesn't then $\Pi(c_1)$ may increase if $\Pi(a_1)$ does, since the last condition may hold after the increase. Similarly, if the last condition holds and the first two don't then $\Pi(c_1)$ may decrease if $\Pi(a_1)$ does, since the first condition may hold after the decrease. If neither condition holds then $\Pi(c_1)$ will not change as $\Pi(a_1)$ does. This argument suffices to show the result. □

Proof of Corollary 8.1 (page 301): The proof is the same as for Corollary 7.2. □

Proof of Corollary 8.2 (page 301): The proof is the same as for Corollary 7.3, but with $\Pi(x_j|a_i)$ in place of $\Pi(x_j)$. □

Proof of Theorem 8.9 (page 302): The result follows directly from Corollary 7.4 and the fact that the proof of the corollary does not depend upon the variables being in a singly-connected network. □

Proof of Theorem 8.10 (page 302): The result follows directly from Theorem 7.13 and the fact that the proof of this corollary does not depend upon the variables being in a singly-connected network. □

Proof of Theorem 8.11 (page 303): The result follows directly from Theorem 7.16 and the fact that the proof of this theorem does not depend upon the variables being in a singly-connected network. ☐

Proof of Theorem 8.12 (page 303): The result follows directly from Theorem 7.11 and the fact that the proof of this theorem does not depend upon the variables being in a singly-connected network. ☐

Proof of Theorem 8.13 (page 304): If there is only one trail between A and B then as far as the interactions between A, B and C are concerned the network is singly-connected, and so the theorem follows directly from Theorem 8.1. ☐

Proof of Theorem 8.14 (page 304): If there is only one trail between A and B then as far as the interactions between A, B and C are concerned the network is singly-connected, and so the theorem follows directly from Theorem 8.4. ☐

Proof of Theorem 8.15 (page 306): To prove this result, it is necessary to start from a slightly more elementary position than (3.64). If, rather than dealing with belief, basic belief masses are considered, it is the case (Smets, 1991a) that for any set of values $\mathbf{c} \subseteq \{c_1, \ldots, c_n\}$:

$$m(\mathbf{c}) = \sum_{\substack{A \subseteq \{a_1, \ldots, a_m\} \\ X \subseteq \{x_1, \ldots, x_p\}}} m(c_i|A, X)m(A, X)$$

and so from (3.51):

$$\mathrm{Bel}(\mathbf{c}) = \sum_{c \subseteq \mathbf{c}} \sum_{\substack{A \subseteq \{a_1, \ldots, a_m\} \\ X \subseteq \{x_1, \ldots, x_p\}}} m(c|A, X)m(A, X)$$

Thus:

$$\frac{\partial \mathrm{Bel}(\mathbf{c})}{\partial \mathrm{Bel}(a_1)} = \sum_{c \subseteq \mathbf{c}} \sum_{\substack{A \subseteq \{a_1, \ldots, a_m\} \\ X \subseteq \{x_1, \ldots, x_p\}}} \frac{\partial}{\partial \mathrm{Bel}(a_1)} (m(c|A, X)m(A, X))$$

$$= \sum_{c \subseteq \mathbf{c}} \sum_{\substack{A \subseteq \{a_1, \ldots, a_m\} \\ X \subseteq \{x_1, \ldots, x_p\}}} \frac{\partial m(c|A, X)}{\partial \mathrm{Bel}(a)} m(A, X) + \frac{\partial m(A, X)}{\partial \mathrm{Bel}(a)}$$

Since conditional masses are constant,

$$\frac{\partial m(c|A, X)}{\partial \mathrm{Bel}(a)} = 0$$

for all values of A and X, and, as always,

$$0 \le \frac{\partial m(A,X)}{\partial \mathrm{Bel}(a)} \le -1$$

for every $\mathbf{a} \subseteq A$ such that $a \in \mathbf{a}$. Thus:

$$\left[\frac{\partial \mathrm{Bel}(\mathbf{c})}{\partial \mathrm{Bel}(a_1)}\right] = \left[\sum_{c \subseteq \mathbf{c}} \sum_{X \subseteq \{x_1,\dots,x_p\}} m(c|a_1,X)m(X)\right.$$

$$\left. - \frac{\max}{\min} {}_{\substack{\mathbf{a} \subseteq A \\ a_1 \in \mathbf{a}}} \sum_{c \subseteq \mathbf{c}} \sum_{X \subseteq \{x_1,\dots,x_p\}} m(c|\mathbf{a},X)m(X)\right]$$

$$\left[\frac{\partial \mathrm{Bel}(\mathbf{c})}{\partial \mathrm{Bel}(a_1)}\right] = \left[\sum_{c \subseteq \mathbf{c}} m(c|a_1,X) - \frac{\max}{\min} {}_{\substack{\mathbf{a} \subseteq A \\ a_1 \in \mathbf{a}}} \sum_{c \subseteq \mathbf{c}} m(c|\mathbf{a},X)\right]$$

$$\left[\frac{\partial \mathrm{Bel}(\mathbf{c})}{\partial \mathrm{Bel}(a_1)}\right] = \left[\mathrm{Bel}(\mathbf{c}|a_1,X) - \frac{\max}{\min} {}_{\substack{\mathbf{a} \subseteq A \\ a_1 \in \mathbf{a}}} \mathrm{Bel}(\mathbf{c}|\mathbf{a},X)\right]$$

and from this expression, the result follows. □

Proof of Theorem 8.16 (page 306): As with the other proofs of results using the disjunctive rule, the proof of this result follows almost immediately from the proof of the corresponding result using Dempster's rule. Taking the various equations in the proof of Theorem 8.15 and writing the conditionals involving sets of values of A, such as $\mathrm{Bel}(\mathbf{c}|\{a_1,a_2\})$, as products, such as $\mathrm{Bel}(\mathbf{c}|\{a_1\})\mathrm{Bel}(\mathbf{c}|\{a_2\})$, ensures that the crucial derivative is never negative. □

Proof of Theorem 8.17 (page 307): As in previous proofs, (3.64) is applied to obtain:

$$\mathrm{Bel}(c_1) = \sum_{\substack{A \subseteq \{a_1,\dots,a_m\} \\ X \subseteq \{x_1,\dots,x_p\}}} \mathrm{Bel}(c_1|A,X)m(A,X)$$

which, since A and X are conditionally independent of one another when C is not known, becomes:

$$\mathrm{Bel}(c_1) = \sum_{\substack{A \subseteq \{a_1,\dots,a_m\} \\ X \subseteq \{x_1,\dots,x_p\}}} \mathrm{Bel}(c_1|A,X)m(A)m(X)$$

Now, considering a change in belief in $\mathbf{a} \subseteq A$:

$$\frac{\partial \mathrm{Bel}(c_1)}{\partial \mathrm{Bel}(\mathbf{a})} = \frac{\partial}{\partial \mathrm{Bel}(\mathbf{a})} \left(\sum_{\substack{A \subseteq \{a_1,\ldots,a_m\} \\ X \subseteq \{x_1,\ldots,x_p\}}} \mathrm{Bel}(c_1|A,X) m(A) m(X) \right)$$

$$= \sum_{\substack{A \subseteq \{a_1,\ldots,a_m\} \\ X \subseteq \{x_1,\ldots,x_p\}}} \mathrm{Bel}(c_1|A,X) m(X) \frac{\partial m(A)}{\partial \mathrm{Bel}(\mathbf{a})}$$

In previous cases where $\mathbf{a}$ has been a singleton, $\mathrm{Bel}(\mathbf{a})$ has been equivalent to $m(\mathbf{a})$ so that the derivative was easy to establish. The problem is that now the relationship between $m(\mathbf{a})$ and $\mathrm{Bel}(\mathbf{a})$ is specified by (3.51) and (3.53), which in this case give:

$$\mathrm{Bel}(\mathbf{a}) = \sum_{a \subseteq \mathbf{a}} m(a)$$

$$m(\mathbf{a}) = \sum_{a \subseteq \mathbf{a}} (-1)^{|\mathbf{a}-a|} \mathrm{Bel}(a)$$

Thus the derivative is not so easy to resolve. The key is to consider how the mass distribution over the power set of all the possible values of A changes. Consider what happens when $\mathrm{Bel}(\mathbf{a})$ increases. In this case the sum of the mass on $\mathbf{a}$ and its subsets increases and the mass focuses in from large sets of values of A to smaller sets. Thus the mass of some superset of $\mathbf{a}$ decreases just as it is in the case in which $\mathbf{a}$ is a singleton. However, unlike the singleton case, it is also possible that the mass of one or more subsets of $\mathbf{a}$ also increase. As a result the contribution to $\mathrm{Bel}(c_1)$ from the supersets of $\mathbf{a}$ decreases and that from $\mathbf{a}$ and its subsets increases, and whether overall this equates to a positive or negative change in $\mathrm{Bel}(c_1)$ will depend on the relative magnitude of the relevant conditional beliefs.

With this in mind it is clear that applying the reasoning behind Lemma 7.1 will give:

$$\left[\frac{\mathrm{Bel}(c_1)}{\mathrm{Bel}(\mathbf{a})} \right] = \left[\mathrm{Bel}(c_1|\mathbf{a}) + \frac{\max}{\min} {}_{A \subseteq \mathbf{a}} \mathrm{Bel}(c_1|A) - \frac{\max}{\min} {}_{\mathbf{a} \subseteq A \subseteq A} \mathrm{Bel}(c_1|\mathbf{A}) \right]$$

and from this the result follows immediately $\square$

Proof of Theorem 8.18 (page 308): As with the other proofs of results using the disjunctive rule, the proof of this result follows almost immediately from the proof of the corresponding result using Dempster's rule. Taking the various equations in the proof of Theorem 8.17 and writing the conditionals involving sets of values of A, such as $\mathrm{Bel}(c_1|\{a_1, a_2\})$, as products, such as $\mathrm{Bel}(c_1|\{a_1\})\mathrm{Bel}(c_1|\{a_2\})$, ensures that the crucial derivative is never negative. $\square$

Proof of Corollary 8.3 (page 308): The proof follows almost immediately from the proofs of Theorems 8.15 and 8.17. Taking the final equation in Theorem 8.17 and generalising it to the case in which a set of values of C is considered gives:

$$\left[\frac{\mathrm{Bel}(\mathbf{c})}{\mathrm{Bel}(\mathbf{a})}\right] = \left[\mathrm{Bel}(\mathbf{c}|\mathbf{a}) + \frac{\max}{\min} {}_{A \subseteq \mathbf{a}} \, \mathrm{Bel}(\mathbf{c}|A) - \frac{\max}{\min} {}_{\mathbf{a} \subseteq A \subseteq A} \, \mathrm{Bel}(\mathbf{c}|A)\right]$$

from which the result quickly follows. $\square$

Proof of Corollary 8.4 (page 308): As for the previous result, this proof may be obtained by combining the results of two previous theorems, in this case Theorems 8.16 and 8.18. $\square$

Proof of Theorem 8.19(page 308): This proof is remarkably similar to previous proofs about separable derivatives, and is left as an exercise for the interested reader. $\square$

Proof of Theorem 8.20 (page 313): As ever:

$$\Pr(c_1) = \sum_{\substack{A=a_1,\ldots,a_m \\ B=b_1,\ldots,b_q \\ X=x_1,\ldots,x_p}} \Pr(c_1|A,B,X)\Pr(A,B,X)$$

Since $\Pr(c_1) = 1$,

$$1 = \sum_{\substack{A=a_1,\ldots,a_m \\ B=b_1,\ldots,b_q \\ X=x_1,\ldots,x_p}} \Pr(c_1|A,B,X)\Pr(B,X)\Pr(A)$$

and since A is independent of B and X,

$$1 = \sum_{\substack{B=b_1,\ldots,b_q \\ X=x_1,\ldots,x_p}} \Pr(c_1|a_1,B,X)\Pr(B,X)\Pr(a_1)$$

$$+ \sum_{\substack{A=a_2,\ldots,a_m \\ B=b_1,\ldots,b_q \\ X=x_1,\ldots,x_p}} \Pr(c_1|A,B,X)\Pr(B,X)\Pr(A)$$

Thus it is possible to write an expression for $\Pr(a_1)$ in terms of $\Pr(b_1)$:

$$\Pr(a_1) = \frac{1 - \sum_{\substack{A=a_2,\ldots,a_m \\ B=b_1,\ldots,b_q \\ X=x_1,\ldots,x_p}} \Pr(c_1|A,B,X)\Pr(B,X)\Pr(A)}{\sum_{\substack{B=b_1,\ldots,b_q \\ X=x_1,\ldots,x_p}} \Pr(c_1|a_1,B,X)\Pr(B,X)}$$

This can be differentiated using the product and quotient rules of the differential calculus (Stewart, 1991) to get:

$$
\frac{\partial \Pr(a_1)}{\partial \Pr(b_1)} = \frac{1}{V^2} \left(V . \frac{\partial}{\partial \Pr(b_1)} \left(1 - \sum_{\substack{A=a_2,\ldots,a_m \\ B=b_1,\ldots,b_q \\ X=x_1,\ldots,x_p}} \Pr(c_1|A,B,X)\Pr(B,X)\Pr(A) \right) \right.
$$

$$
\left. - \frac{\partial V}{\partial \Pr(b_1)} \left(1 - \sum_{\substack{A=a_2,\ldots,a_m \\ B=b_1,\ldots,b_q \\ X=x_1,\ldots,x_p}} \Pr(c_1|A,B,X)\Pr(B,X)\Pr(A) \right) \right)
$$

where

$$
V = \sum_{\substack{B=b_1,\ldots,b_q \\ X=x_1,\ldots,x_p}} \Pr(c_1|a_1,B,X)\Pr(B,X)
$$

Now, for singly-connected networks we know that:

$$
\Pr(B,X) = \Pr(B).\Pr(X)
$$

so that:

$$
\frac{\partial \Pr(a_1)}{\partial \Pr(b_1)} V^2 =
$$

$$
-V \left(\left(\sum_{\substack{A=a_2,\ldots a_M \\ X=x_1,\ldots,x_p}} \Pr(c_1|A,b_1,X)\Pr(A)\Pr(X) \right. \right.
$$

$$
- \frac{\max}{\min} {}_{B=b_2,\ldots,b_q} \sum_{\substack{A=a_2,\ldots,a_M \\ X=x_1,\ldots,x_p}} \Pr(c_1|A,B,X)\Pr(A)\Pr(X) \Bigg)
$$

$$
- \sum_{\substack{A=a_2,\ldots,a_m \\ B=b_1,\ldots,b_q \\ X=x_1,\ldots,x_p}} \Pr(c_1|A,B,X) \frac{\partial \Pr(A)}{\partial \Pr(b_1)} \Pr(X)\Pr(B) \Bigg)
$$

$$
-\left(1 - \sum_{\substack{A=a_2,\dots,a_m \\ B=b_1,\dots,b_q \\ X=x_1,\dots,x_p}} \Pr(c_1|A,B,X)\Pr(A)\Pr(B)\Pr(X)\right)
$$

$$
\left(\sum_{X=x_1,\dots,x_p} \Pr(c_1|a_1,b_1,X)\Pr(X)\right.
$$

$$
\left.-\,\frac{\max}{\min}{}_{B=b_2,\dots,b_q}\sum_{X=x_1,\dots,x_p}\Pr(c_1|a_1,B,X)\Pr(X)\right)
$$

which we can re-write as:

$$
\frac{\partial \Pr(a_1)}{\partial \Pr(b_1)}V^2 - VW =
$$

$$
-V\left(\sum_{\substack{A=a_2,\dots a_M \\ X=x_1,\dots,x_p}}\Pr(c_1|A,b_1,X)\Pr(A)\Pr(X)\right.
$$

$$
\left.-\,\frac{\max}{\min}{}_{B=b_2,\dots,b_q}\sum_{\substack{A=a_2,\dots a_M \\ X=x_1,\dots,x_p}}\Pr(c_1|A,B,X)\Pr(A)\Pr(X)\right)
$$

$$
-\left(1 - \sum_{\substack{A=a_2,\dots,a_m \\ B=b_1,\dots,b_q \\ X=x_1,\dots,x_p}} \Pr(c_1|A,B,X)\Pr(A)\Pr(B)\Pr(X)\right)
$$

$$
\left(\sum_{X=x_1,\dots,x_p} \Pr(c_1|a_1,b_1,X)\Pr(X)\right.
$$

$$
\left.-\,\frac{\max}{\min}{}_{B=b_2,\dots,b_q}\sum_{X=x_1,\dots,x_p}\Pr(c_1|a_1,B,X)\Pr(X)\right)
$$

where

$$
W = \sum_{\substack{A=a_2,\dots,a_m \\ B=b_1,\dots,b_q \\ X=x_1,\dots,x_p}} \Pr(c_1|A,B,X)\frac{\partial \Pr(A)}{\partial \Pr(b_1)}\Pr(X)\Pr(B)
$$

Now, applying the same argument as in Lemma 7.1, the derivative in W is

$$\frac{\partial \Pr(a_1)}{\partial \Pr(b_1)}$$

multiplied by a value between 0 and -1. This means that the above reduces to:

$$\frac{\partial \Pr(a_1)}{\partial \Pr(b_1)} K =$$

$$-V\left(\sum_{\substack{A=a_2,\ldots,a_m \\ X=x_1,\ldots,x_p}} \Pr(c_1|A, b_1, X) \Pr(A) \Pr(X) \right.$$

$$\left. - \max_{\min B=b_2,\ldots,b_q} \sum_{\substack{A=a_2,\ldots,a_m \\ X=x_1,\ldots,x_p}} \Pr(c_1|A, B, X) \Pr(A) \Pr(X) \right)$$

$$-\left(1 - \sum_{\substack{A=a_2,\ldots,a_m \\ B=b_1,\ldots,b_q \\ X=x_1,\ldots,x_p}} \Pr(c_1|A, B, X) \Pr(A) \Pr(B) \Pr(X) \right)$$

$$\left(\sum_{X=x_1,\ldots,x_p} \Pr(c_1|a_1, b_1, X) \Pr(X) \right.$$

$$\left. - \max_{\min B=b_2,\ldots,b_q} \sum_{X=x_1,\ldots,x_p} \Pr(c_1|a_1, B, X) \Pr(X) \right)$$

where K is a positive constant. The qualitative value of the derivative clearly depends upon the value of the three bracketed terms. Writing:

$$E_1 \quad = \quad \sum_{\substack{A=a_2,\ldots,a_m \\ X=x_1,\ldots,x_p}} \Pr(c_1|A, b_1, X) \Pr(A) \Pr(X)$$

$$- \max_{\min B=b_2,\ldots,b_q} \sum_{\substack{A=a_2,\ldots,a_m \\ X=x_1,\ldots,x_p}} \Pr(c_1|A, B, X) \Pr(A) \Pr(X)$$

$$E_2 \quad = \quad 1 - \sum_{\substack{A=a_2,\ldots,a_m \\ B=b_1,\ldots,b_q \\ X=x_1,\ldots,x_p}} \Pr(c_1|A, B, X) \Pr(A) \Pr(B) \Pr(X)$$

$$E_3 \quad = \quad \sum_{X=x_1,\ldots,x_p} \Pr(c_1|a_1, b_1, X) \Pr(X)$$

$$- \frac{\max}{\min}_{B=b_2,\ldots,b_q} \sum_{X=x_1,\ldots,x_p} \Pr(c_1|a_1,B,X)\Pr(X)$$

the expression simplifies to:

$$\frac{\partial \Pr(a_1)}{\partial \Pr(b_1)} K = -V.E_1 - E_2.E_3$$

Now, since V is positive, and:

$$\Pr(c_1) = \sum_{\substack{A=a_1,\ldots,a_m \\ B=b_1,\ldots,b_q \\ X=x_1,\ldots,x_p}} \Pr(c_1|A,B,X)\Pr(A)\Pr(B)\Pr(X)$$

it follows that:

$$E_2 = 1 - \left(\Pr(c_1) - \sum_{\substack{A=a_1,\ldots,a_m \\ B=b_1,\ldots,b_q \\ X=x_1,\ldots,x_p}} \Pr(c_1|a_1,B,X)\Pr(a_1)\Pr(B)\Pr(X) \right)$$

$$E_2 > 0$$

Thus the qualitative value of the derivative is determined by:

$$\left[\frac{\partial \Pr(a_1)}{\partial \Pr(b_1)} \right] = [-] \otimes ([E_1] \oplus [E_3])$$

Thus the derivative is positive if both E_1 and E_3 are negative, is negative if both E_1 and E_3 are positive, and is zero if both are zero. Otherwise the derivative has qualitative value $[?]$. E_1 is positive if:

$$\sum_{\substack{A=a_2,\ldots,a_m \\ X=x_1,\ldots,x_p}} \Pr(c_1|A,b_1,X)\Pr(A)\Pr(X) >$$

$$\frac{\max}{\min}_{B=b_2\ldots,b_q} \sum_{\substack{A=a_2,\ldots,a_m \\ X=x_1,\ldots,x_p}} \Pr(c_1|A,B,X)\Pr(A)\Pr(X)$$

and E_3 is positive if:

$$\sum_{X=x_1,\ldots,x_p} \Pr(c_1|a_1,b_1,X)\Pr(X) >$$

$$\frac{\max}{\min}_{B=b_2\ldots,b_q} \sum_{X=x_1,\ldots,x_p} \Pr(c_1|a_1,B,X)\Pr(X)$$

The first of these is the condition under which $\Pr(c_1)$ follows $\Pr(b_1)$ when A has any value except a_1 and the second is the condition under which $\Pr(c_1)$ follows $\Pr(b_1)$ when A is known to take the value a_1. Both will be true if $\Pr(c_1)$ follows $\Pr(b_1)$, so:

$$\left[\frac{\Pr(a_1)}{\Pr(b_1)} \right] = [-]$$

if $\Pr(c_1)$ follows $\Pr(b_1)$,

$$\left[\frac{\Pr(a_1)}{\Pr(b_1)} \right] = [+]$$

if $\Pr(c_1)$ varies inversely with $\Pr(b_1)$ and

$$\left[\frac{\Pr(a_1)}{\Pr(b_1)} \right] = [0]$$

if $\Pr(c_1)$ is qualitatively independent of $\Pr(b_1)$. Otherwise

$$\left[\frac{\Pr(a_1)}{\Pr(b_1)} \right] = [?]$$

From this the result follows. □

Proof of Theorem 8.21 (page 314): Considering Pearl's (1988b) algorithm when c is known to be the value that C takes, the evidential flow of probability into node A is such that the ratio of the change in $\Pr(a_1)$ to that in $\Pr(a_2)$ is given by the ratio of $\Pr(c|a_1)$ to $\Pr(c|a_2)$. Now, since A and B are independent:

$$\Pr(c) = \sum_{\substack{A=a_1,a_2 \\ B=b_1,b_2}} \Pr(c|A,B) \Pr(A) \Pr(B)$$

In addition:

$$
\begin{aligned}
\Pr(c|a_1) &= \Pr(c|a_1,b_1) \Pr(b_1) + \Pr(c|a_1,b_2) \Pr(b_2) \\
&= \Pr(c) \left(\Pr(c|a_1,b_1) - \Pr(c|a_1,b_2) \right) + \Pr(c|a_1,b_2)
\end{aligned}
$$

and a similar expression may be written for $\Pr(c|a_2)$. Now, it is necessary to determine the way in which this ratio alters as $\Pr(b_1)$ changes. If the ratio increases, $\Pr(a_1)$ increases as $\Pr(b_1)$ increases, and if the ratio decreases, $\Pr(b_1)$ explains $\Pr(a_1)$ away. To do this it is necessary to determine the qualitative value of the derivative:

$$\frac{\partial}{\partial \Pr(b_1)} \left(\frac{\Pr(c|a_1)}{\Pr(c|a_2)} \right)$$

which is given by:

$$\frac{\partial}{\partial \Pr(b_1)} \left(\frac{\Pr(c|a_1)}{\Pr(c|a_2)} \right)$$

$$= \frac{\partial}{\partial \Pr(b_1)} \left(\frac{\Pr(b_1)\,(\Pr(c|a_1,b_1) - \Pr(c|a_1,b_2)) + \Pr(c|a_1,b_2)}{\Pr(b_1)\,(\Pr(c|a_2,b_1) - \Pr(c|a_2,b_2)) + \Pr(c|a_2,b_2)} \right)$$

Now, the quotient rule of the differential calculus (Stewart, 1991) gives:

$$\frac{\partial}{\partial \Pr(b_1)} \left(\frac{\Pr(c|a_1)}{\Pr(c|a_2)} \right) = \frac{1}{K} \Big(\Pr(b_1)\big(\Pr(c|a_2,b_1) - \Pr(c|a_2,b_2)\big) + \Pr(c|a_2,b_2) \Big)$$

$$\Big(\Pr(c|a_1,b_1) - \Pr(c|a_1,b_2) \Big)$$

$$- \Big(\Pr(b_1)\big(\Pr(c|a_1,b_1) - \Pr(c|a_1,b_2)\big) - \Pr(c|a_1,b_2) \Big)$$

$$\Big(\Pr(c|a_2,b_1) - \Pr(c|a_2,b_2) \Big)$$

where $K = \Pr(c|a_2)^2$. All the terms that are multiplied by $\Pr(b_1)$ cancel out, along with some others, leaving:

$$\frac{\partial}{\partial \Pr(b_1)} \left(\frac{\Pr(c|a_1)}{\Pr(c|a_2)} \right) = \frac{1}{K} \Big(\Pr(c|a_1,b_1)\Pr(c|a_2,b_2) - \Pr(c|a_2,b_1)\Pr(c|a_1,b_2) \Big)$$

K can be ignored since it is always positive and so does not affect the qualitative value of the derivative. Thus:

$$\left[\frac{\partial}{\partial \Pr(b_1)} \left(\frac{\Pr(c|a_1)}{\Pr(c|a_2)} \right) \right] = \Big[\Pr(c|a_1,b_1)\Pr(c|a_2,b_2) - \Pr(c|a_2,b_1)\Pr(c|a_1,b_2) \Big]$$

and the result follows. □

Proof of Theorem 8.22 (page 315): The starting point is that $\Pi(c_1) = 1$ and:

$$\Pi(c_1) = \sup_{\substack{A=a_1,\dots,a_m \\ B=b_1,\dots,b_q \\ X=x_1,\dots,x_p}} \min\left(\Pi(c_1|A, B, X), \Pi(A), \Pi(B), \Pi(X) \right)$$

The question is whether there are circumstances in which if $\Pi(b_1)$ changes it is the case that in order for $\Pi(c_1)$ to remain at 1, $\Pi(a_1)$ must alter. Since $\Pi(c_1) = 1$ initially, it must be the case that for some A, B and X:

$$\Pi(c_1|A, B, X) = 1$$
$$\Pi(A) = 1$$
$$\Pi(B) = 1$$

$$\Pi(X) \quad = \quad 1$$

Now, if $B \neq b_1$ then altering the value of $\Pi(b_1)$ can have no effect on the value of $\Pi(c_1)$ and so can have no effect on $\Pi(a_1)$, so $B = b_1$ in the interesting cases. Similarly, if $A = a_1$, then there is no possible change in $\Pi(a_1)$ (thanks to the min) which will keep $\Pi(c_1)$ at 1. Thus $A \neq a_1$. It is also necessary that initially $\Pi(a_1) < 1$, otherwise it need not change in value to keep $\Pi(c_1)$ at 1.

These conditions ensure that altering $\Pi(b_1)$ is significant and that $\Pi(a_1)$ can be affected by the change. To ensure that $\Pi(a_1)$ is affected, all $\Pi(c_1|A, B, X)$ where $A \neq a_1, B \neq b_1$ must be less than 1 (otherwise the corresponding values of A and B could keep $\Pi(c_1)$ at 1), and it must be possible for $\Pi(c_1)$ to be 1, so that:

$$\Pi(c_1|a_1, B, X) \quad = \quad 1$$
$$\Pi(A) \quad = \quad 1$$
$$\Pi(B) \quad = \quad 1$$
$$\Pi(X) \quad = \quad 1$$

for some $B \neq b_1$ and X. These conditions are exactly those under which $\Pi(c_1)$ may follow $\Pi(a_1)$ up and may follow $\Pi(b_1)$ down when $\Pi(c) = 1$. $\square$

Proof of Theorem 8.23 (page 316): This proof starts with:

$$\mathrm{Bel}(c_1) = \sum_{\substack{A \subseteq \{a_1,\dots,a_m\} \\ B \subseteq \{b_1,\dots,b_q\} \\ X \subseteq \{x_1,\dots,x_p\}}} \mathrm{Bel}(c_1|A, B, X) m(A, B, X)$$

Since $\mathrm{Bel}(c_1) = 1$, and A, B, and X are conditionally independent:

$$1 = \sum_{\substack{A \subseteq \{a_1,\dots,a_m\} \\ X \subseteq \{x_1,\dots,x_p\}}} \mathrm{Bel}(c_1|A, b_1, X) m(A) m(b_1) m(X)$$

$$+ \sum_{\substack{A \subseteq \{a_1,\dots,a_m\} \\ B \subseteq \{b_1,\dots,b_q\}, B \neq \{b_1\} \\ X \subseteq \{x_1,\dots,x_p\}}} \mathrm{Bel}(c_1|A, B, X) m(A) m(B) m(X)$$

The reason for writing the sum like this is that it makes it possible to isolate the term that includes $m(b_1)$, which, since b_1 is a singleton set, is the same as $\text{Bel}(b_1)$. Thus:

$$\text{Bel}(b_1) = \frac{1 - \displaystyle\sum_{\substack{A \subseteq \{a_1,\ldots,a_m\} \\ B \subseteq \{b_1,\ldots,b_q\}, B \neq \{b_1\} \\ X \subseteq \{x_1,\ldots,x_p\}}} \text{Bel}(c_1|A, B, X)m(A)m(B)m(X)}{\displaystyle\sum_{\substack{A \subseteq \{a_1,\ldots,a_m\} \\ X \subseteq \{x_1,\ldots,x_p\}}} \text{Bel}(c_1|A, b_1, X)m(A)m(X)}$$

Now, writing:

$$U \;=\; 1 - \sum_{\substack{A \subseteq \{a_1,\ldots,a_m\} \\ B \subseteq \{b_1,\ldots,b_q\}, B \neq \{b_1\} \\ X \subseteq \{x_1,\ldots,x_p\}}} \text{Bel}(c_1|A, B, X)m(A)m(B)m(X)$$

$$V \;=\; \sum_{\substack{A \subseteq \{a_1,\ldots,a_m\} \\ X \subseteq \{x_1,\ldots,x_p\}}} \text{Bel}(c_1|A, b_1, X)m(A)m(X)$$

It follows from quotient rule of the differential calculus (Stewart, 1991) that:

$$\frac{\partial \text{Bel}(b_1)}{\partial \text{Bel}(a_1)} = \frac{1}{V^2}\left(V\frac{\partial U}{\partial \text{Bel}(a_1)} - U\frac{\partial V}{\partial \text{Bel}(a_1)}\right) \tag{A.8}$$

The second of these partial derivatives is easy to derive:

$$\frac{\partial}{\partial \text{Bel}(a_1)}\left(\sum_{\substack{A \subseteq \{a_1,\ldots,a_m\} \\ X \subseteq \{x_1,\ldots,x_p\}}} \text{Bel}(c_1|A, b_1, X)m(A)m(X)\right)$$

$$= \sum_{X \subseteq \{x_1,\ldots,x_p\}} \text{Bel}(c_1|a_1, b_1, X)$$

$$- \max_{\min A \subseteq \{a_1,\ldots,a_m\}, A \neq \{a_1\}} \sum_{X \subseteq \{x_1,\ldots,x_p\}} \text{Bel}(c_1|A, b_1, X)$$

and, as above, the term:

$$\frac{\partial m(b_1)}{\partial \text{Bel}(a_1)}$$

can be replaced by:

$$\frac{\partial \text{Bel}(b_1)}{\partial \text{Bel}(a_1)}$$

The first partial derivative is more complex:

$$\frac{\partial}{\partial \mathrm{Bel}(a_1)} \left(1 - \sum_{\substack{A \subseteq \{a_1,\ldots,a_m\} \\ B \subseteq \{b_1,\ldots,b_q\}, B \neq \{b_1\} \\ X \subseteq \{x_1,\ldots,x_p\}}} \mathrm{Bel}(c_1 | A, B, X) m(A) m(B) m(X) \right)$$

$$= - \sum_{\substack{B \subseteq \{b_1,\ldots,b_q\}, B \neq \{b_1\} \\ X \subseteq \{x_1,\ldots,x_p\}}} \mathrm{Bel}(c_1 | a_1, B, X) m(B) m(X)$$

$$+ \frac{\max}{\min} {}_{A \subseteq \{a_1,\ldots,a_m\}, A \neq \{a_1\}} \sum_{\substack{B \subseteq \{b_1,\ldots,b_q\}, B \neq \{b_1\} \\ X \subseteq \{x_1,\ldots,x_p\}}} \mathrm{Bel}(c_1 | a_1, B, X) m(B) m(X)$$

$$- \sum_{\substack{A \subseteq \{a_1,\ldots,a_m\} \\ B \subseteq \{b_1,\ldots,b_q\}, B \neq \{b_1\} \\ X \subseteq \{x_1,\ldots,x_p\}}} \mathrm{Bel}(c_1 | A, B, X) m(A) \frac{\partial m(B)}{\partial \mathrm{Bel}(a_1)} m(X)$$

It is not easy to calculate the value of the last term because it is hard to calculate the value of the:

$$\frac{\partial m(b_j)}{\partial \mathrm{Bel}(a_1)}$$

However, applying similar reasoning to that in Lemma 7.1, each of these will be some fraction of the value of

$$\frac{\partial \mathrm{Bel}(b_1)}{\partial \mathrm{Bel}(a_1)}$$

and the final term above can be replaced by:

$$K \left(\frac{\partial \mathrm{Bel}(b_1)}{\partial \mathrm{Bel}(a_1)} \right)$$

Where K is the sum of those fractions, a positive number whose value is less than 1. Substituting everything back into (A.8) and re-arranging gives:

$$\frac{\partial \mathrm{Bel}(b_1)}{\partial \mathrm{Bel}(a_1)} (V^2 + V.K)$$

$$= - \sum_{\substack{A \subseteq \{a_1,\ldots,a_m\} \\ X \subseteq \{x_1,\ldots,x_p\}}} \mathrm{Bel}(c_1 | A, b_1, X) m(A) m(b_1) m(X)$$

$$\left(\sum_{\substack{B \subseteq \{b_1,\ldots,b_q\}, B \neq \{b_1\} \\ X \subseteq \{x_1,\ldots,x_p\}}} \mathrm{Bel}(c_1 | a_1, B, X) m(B) m(X) \right.$$

$$\left. - \max_{\min} {}_{A \subseteq \{a_1,\ldots,a_m\}, A \neq \{a_1\}} \sum_{\substack{B \subseteq \{b_1,\ldots,b_q\}, B \neq \{b_1\} \\ X \subseteq \{x_1,\ldots,x_p\}}} \mathrm{Bel}(c_1 | A, B, X) m(B) m(X) \right)$$

$$- \left(1 - \sum_{\substack{A \subseteq \{a_1,\ldots,a_m\} \\ B \subseteq \{b_1,\ldots,b_q\}, B \neq \{b_1\} \\ X \subseteq \{x_1,\ldots,x_p\}}} \mathrm{Bel}(c_1 | A, B, X) m(A) m(B) m(X) \right)$$

$$\left(\sum_{X \subseteq \{x_1,\ldots,x_p\}} \mathrm{Bel}(c_1 | a_1, b_1, X) m(b_1) m(X) \right.$$

$$\left. - \max_{\min} {}_{A \subseteq \{a_1,\ldots,a_m\}, A \neq \{a_1\}} \sum_{X \subseteq \{x_1,\ldots,x_p\}} \mathrm{Bel}(c_1 | a_1, b_1, X) m(b_1) m(X) \right)$$

where:

$$K = \sum_{\substack{A \subseteq \{a_1,\ldots,a_m\} \\ X \subseteq \{x_1,\ldots,x_p\}}} \mathrm{Bel}(c_1 | A, b_1, X) m(A) m(X)$$

Now, the qualitative value of this expression hinges on the qualitative values of:

$$E_1 = \left(\sum_{\substack{B \subseteq \{b_1,\ldots,b_q\}, B \neq \{b_1\} \\ X \subseteq \{x_1,\ldots,x_p\}}} \mathrm{Bel}(c_1 | a_1, B, X) m(B) m(X) \right.$$

$$\left. - \max_{\min} {}_{A \subseteq \{a_1,\ldots,a_m\}, A \neq \{a_1\}} \sum_{\substack{B \subseteq \{b_1,\ldots,b_q\}, B \neq \{b_1\} \\ X \subseteq \{x_1,\ldots,x_p\}}} \mathrm{Bel}(c_1 | A, B, X) m(B) m(X) \right)$$

$$E_2 = \left(\sum_{X \subseteq \{x_1,\ldots,x_p\}} \mathrm{Bel}(c_1 | a_1, b_1, X) m(b_1) m(X) \right.$$

$$-\begin{array}{c} \max \\ \min \end{array}\underset{\substack{A\subseteq\{a_1,\ldots,a_m\},A\neq\{a_1\} \\ X\subseteq\{x_1,\ldots,x_p\}}}{\sum}\text{Bel}(c_1|a_1,b_1,X)m(b_1)m(X)\Bigg)$$

E_1 and E_2, taken together are closely related to the relationship between $\text{Bel}(c_1)$ and $\text{Bel}(a_1)$. As a result, the value of the derivative

$$\frac{\partial\text{Bel}(b_1)}{\partial\text{Bel}(a_1)}$$

is closely related to the relationship between $\text{Bel}(c_1)$ and $\text{Bel}(a_1)$. In particular, if both E_1 and E_2 are positive, in which case $\text{Bel}(c_1)$ follows $\text{Bel}(a_1)$, then $\text{Bel}(b_1)$ varies inversely with $\text{Bel}(a_1)$. If both E_1 and E_2 are negative, in which case $\text{Bel}(c_1)$ varies inversely with $\text{Bel}(a_1)$, then $\text{Bel}(b_1)$ follows $\text{Bel}(a_1)$. If both both E_1 and E_2 are zero, in which case $\text{Bel}(c_1)$ is qualitatively independent of $\text{Bel}(a_1)$, then $\text{Bel}(b_1)$ is qualitatively independent of $\text{Bel}(a_1)$. Finally, if E_1 and E_2 don't have the same qualitative value, in which case the relationship between $\text{Bel}(c_1)$ and $\text{Bel}(a_1)$ is indeterminate, then the relationship between $\text{Bel}(b_1)$ and $\text{Bel}(a_1)$ is indeterminate. From this the result follows by symmetry. $\square$

Proof of Theorem 8.24 (page 317): From (3.65) it is clear that:

$$\text{Bel}(c_1)=\underset{\substack{A\subseteq\{a_1,\ldots,a_m\} \\ B\subseteq\{b_1,\ldots,b_q\} \\ X\subseteq\{x_1,\ldots,x_p\}}}{\sum}m(A,B,X)\prod_{\substack{a\in A \\ b\in B \\ x\in X}}\text{Bel}(c_1|a,b,x)$$

Since $\text{Bel}(c_1)=1$, and A, B, and X are conditionally independent:

$$1=\underset{\substack{A\subseteq\{a_1,\ldots,a_m\} \\ X\subseteq\{x_1,\ldots,x_p\}}}{\sum}m(A)m(b_1)m(X)\prod_{\substack{a\in A \\ x\in X}}\text{Bel}(c_1|a,b_1,x)$$

$$+\underset{\substack{A\subseteq\{a_1,\ldots,a_m\} \\ B\subseteq\{b_1,\ldots,b_q\},B\neq\{b_1\} \\ X\subseteq\{x_1,\ldots,x_p\}}}{\sum}m(A)m(B)m(X)\prod_{\substack{a\in A \\ b\in B \\ x\in X}}\text{Bel}(c_1|a,b,x)$$

As in the previous proof, this makes it possible to turn the equation into one for $\text{Bel}(b_1)$:

$$\text{Bel}(b_1)=\frac{1-\underset{\substack{A\subseteq\{a_1,\ldots,a_m\} \\ B\subseteq\{b_1,\ldots,b_q\},B\neq\{b_1\} \\ X\subseteq\{x_1,\ldots,x_p\}}}{\sum}m(A)m(B)m(X)\prod_{\substack{a\in A \\ b\in B \\ x\in X}}\text{Bel}(c_1|a,b,x)}{\underset{\substack{A\subseteq\{a_1,\ldots,a_m\} \\ X\subseteq\{x_1,\ldots,x_p\}}}{\sum}m(A)m(X)\prod_{\substack{a\in A \\ x\in X}}\text{Bel}(c_1|a,b_1,x)}$$

The right hand side of this equation, of course, is very similar to the expression that determined the value of $\mathrm{Bel}(b_1)$ in the previous proof. In fact, the only difference is that conditional beliefs of the form:

$$\mathrm{Bel}(c_1 | \{a_1, a_2\}, \{b_1, b_2\}, X)$$

are replaced by products like:

$$\mathrm{Bel}(c_1 | a_1, b_1, X) \mathrm{Bel}(c_1 | a_2, b_1, X) \mathrm{Bel}(c_1 | a_1, b_2, X) \mathrm{Bel}(c_1 | a_2, b_2, X)$$

By now, it should be clear what the effect of this is—crucial values like E_1 in the previous proof can never be negative since every term on the left of the minus sign turns up on the right of it multiplied by another conditional belief (which has a minimum value of 0 and a maximum value of 1). Thus it is always the case that $\mathrm{Bel}(b_1)$ may vary inversely with $\mathrm{Bel}(a_1)$ and the result follows by symmetry. $\square$

Proof of Theorem 9.4 (page 334): Axiom A1 may easily be verified from the combinator tables for qualitative multiplication. For Axiom A2 it is necessary that

$$\sum \{G^{\downarrow h}(x, y) : y \in W_{h-k}\} = \sum \{G(x, y) : y \in W_{g-k}\}$$

Now,

$$G^{\downarrow h} = \sum \{G(x, y) : y \in W_{g-h}\}$$

so that

$$\sum \{G^{\downarrow h}(x, y) : y \in W_{h-k}\} = \sum \{G(x, y) : y \in W_{g-k}\}$$

and the axiom holds. The fact that Axiom A3 holds follows since multiplication distributes over addition. Thus the axioms hold. $\square$

Proof of Theorem 9.5 (page 334): Axiom A1 holds if interval multiplication is commutative and associative. This is proved in (Parsons and Dohnal, 1992) for closed intervals and extending this to open intervals and mixed open and closed intervals is trivial. Axiom A2 holds as in the proof of Theorem 9.4. For A3 to hold, interval multiplication must distribute over addition. Thus it is necessary that

$$[a, b]([c, d] + [e, f]) = [a, b][c, d] + [a, b][e, f]$$

Now, from (6.24), for closed intervals

$$\begin{aligned}
[a, b]([c, d] + [e, f]) &= [a, b][(\min(c, d) + \min(e, f)), (\max(c, d) + \max(e, f))] \\
&= [(\min(a, b).\min(c, d) + \min(a, b).\min(e, f)),
\end{aligned}$$

$$\max(a,b).\max(c,d) + \max(a,b).\max(e,\!f))]$$

and

$$
\begin{aligned}
[a,b][c,d] + [a,b][e,\!f] \ &= \ [\min(a,b).\min(c,d), \max(a,b).\max(c,d)] \\
&\quad + [\min(a,b).\min(e,\!f), \max(a,b).\max(e,\!f)] \\
&= \ [\min(a,b).\min(c,d) + \min(a,b).\min(e,\!f)), \\
&\qquad \max(a,b).\max(c,d) + \max(a,b).\max(e,\!f)]
\end{aligned}
$$

A similar proof is possible for open intervals, and mixed open and closed intervals, so multiplication distributes over addition, and A3 holds. □

Proof of Theorem 9.6 (page 334): The fact that Axiom A1 holds follows directly from the associativity and commutativity of the qualitative minimum operation (Table 6.2). The fact that Axiom A2 holds also follows directly from the definition of qualitative maximum (Table 6.2), and Axiom A3 holds since the minimum operation distributes over the maximum operation. □

Proof of Theorem 9.7 (page 334): The proof follows directly from the definitions of the interval version of the maximum and minimum operations (6.24). □

Proof of Theorem 9.8 (page 335): The proof of this theorem follows simply from the analogous proof for the propagation of real-valued belief functions (Shenoy, 1994a). Extending these proofs for qualitative values, Axiom A1 holds due to the associativity and commutivity of qualitative multiplication (which is clear from the combinator table, Table 6.1), and Axioms A2 and A3 hold because qualitative addition is commutative (again clear from the combinator table, Table 6.1). □

Proof of Theorem 9.9 (page 335): The proof of this theorem again follows from (Shenoy, 1994a). Extending Shenoy's proofs for qualitative values, Axiom A1 holds due to the associativity and commutivity of interval multiplication as discussed in the proof of Theorem 9.5, and Axioms A2 and A3 hold because interval addition is commutative. This is proved in (Parsons and Dohnal, 1992) for closed intervals and by trivial extension is proved for open and mixed open and closed intervals. □

Proof of Theorem 9.11 (page 345): The influence of a given value a_i of A on the value x_j of another node is given by (7.12) to be:

$$[\Delta\text{Val}(x_j)] = \left[\frac{\partial\text{Val}(x_j)}{\partial\text{Val}(a_i)}\right] \otimes [\Delta\text{Val}(a_i)]$$

Since Table 7.1 shows that combining any qualitative value with $[0]$ gives $[0]$, it is not possible for $[\Delta\text{Val}(x_j)]$ to be non-zero and so the result follows. $\square$

Proof of Theorem 9.12 (page 345): By the principle of superposition (Stewart, 1991), as expressed in (7.6), the overall change in $\text{Val}(a_i)$ is the qualitative sum of all the changes in $\text{Val}(a_i)$. The fact that $\oplus$ is commutative and associative ensures that the order in which the values are summed is irrelevant. Following a similar line of reasoning to that in the previous proof, a non-zero change in a value of a node with a non-zero influence on a_i will result in a non-zero change in $\text{Val}(a_i)$ which will then be summed with $[0]$. From Table 7.2, adding any non-zero value to $[0]$ gives the non-zero value, so the change in $\text{Val}(a_i)$ will be non-zero. $\square$

Proof of Theorem 9.13 (page 345): Consider a node I, which has a set of possible values $\{I_1, \dots, I_n\}$, and which is a member of $\mathbf{I}$. The effect of a non-zero change in the value of a $\text{Val}(i_j)$ upon a node X is given by (7.12) to be :

$$\begin{bmatrix} [\Delta\text{Val}(x_1)] \\ \vdots \\ [\Delta\text{Val}(x_m)] \end{bmatrix} = \begin{bmatrix} \left[\frac{\partial\text{Val}(x_1)}{\partial\text{Val}(i_j)}\right] \\ \vdots \\ \left[\frac{\partial\text{Val}(x_m)}{\partial\text{Val}(i_j)}\right] \end{bmatrix} \otimes [\Delta\text{Val}(i_j)]$$

If X is on a trail from I, then by Definition 7.13

$$\left[\frac{\partial\text{Val}(x_i)}{\partial\text{Val}(i_j)}\right]$$

is the product of the derivatives relating to the links that make up the trail. By convention, none of these derivatives will be zero for all pairs of possible values of the variables at the two ends of the link, but it is possible for the overall influence to become zero. Consider the trail:

$$A \to B \to C$$

where A has values $\{a_1, a_2, a_3, a_4\}$, B has values $\{b_1, b_2, b_3, b_4\}$, and C has values $\{c_1, c_2, c_3, c_4\}$. If the derivatives are such that:

$$\left[\frac{\partial \text{Val}(b_1)}{\partial \text{Val}(a_1)}\right] = [+]$$

$$\left[\frac{\partial \text{Val}(b_2)}{\partial \text{Val}(a_2)}\right] = [+]$$

$$\left[\frac{\partial \text{Val}(c_1)}{\partial \text{Val}(b_3)}\right] = [+]$$

$$\left[\frac{\partial \text{Val}(c_2)}{\partial \text{Val}(b_4)}\right] = [+]$$

and all other derivatives have value $[0]$ then A has zero influence on C. This is illustrated by considering what happens if $\text{Val}(a_1)$ goes up and $\text{Val}(a_2)$ goes down. This will cause $\text{Val}(b_1)$ to go up and $\text{Val}(b_2)$ to go down, which will not affect the values of C at all, even though they would be affected were $\text{Val}(b_3)$ and $\text{Val}(b_4)$ to change. $\square$

Proof of Theorem 9.14 (page 346): Let N_j denote the parent node of C on the jth trail from I to C and let that node have m_j values. The principle of superposition means that the qualitative change at C due to changes in all its parents along all the trails is:

$$
\begin{bmatrix} [\Delta \text{Val}(c_1)] \\ \vdots \\ [\Delta \text{Val}(c_n)] \end{bmatrix} = \bigoplus_j \begin{bmatrix} \left[\frac{\partial_s \text{Val}(c_1)}{\partial_s \text{Val}(n_{j_1})}\right] & \cdots & \left[\frac{\partial_s \text{Val}(c_1)}{\partial_s \text{Val}(n_{j_{m_j}})}\right] \\ \vdots & \ddots & \vdots \\ \left[\frac{\partial_s \text{Val}(c_n)}{\partial_s \text{Val}(n_{j_1})}\right] & \cdots & \left[\frac{\partial_s \text{Val}(c_n)}{\partial_s \text{Val}(n_{j_{m_j}})}\right] \end{bmatrix} \otimes \begin{bmatrix} [\Delta \text{Val}(n_{j_1})] \\ \vdots \\ [\Delta \text{Val}(n_{j_{m_j}})] \end{bmatrix} \tag{A.9}
$$

Now, the term:

$$
\begin{bmatrix} [\Delta \text{Val}(n_{j_1})] \\ \vdots \\ [\Delta \text{Val}(n_{j_{m_j}})] \end{bmatrix}
$$

is the change in the various values of a single N_j that result from the changes in value of I. By definition, therefore, the above is just the product of the qualitative influence of I on N_j with the changes at I. If I has possible values $\{i_1, \ldots, i_m\}$, then:

$$
\begin{bmatrix} [\Delta \text{Val}(n_{j_1})] \\ \vdots \\ [\Delta \text{Val}(n_{j_{m_j}})] \end{bmatrix} = \begin{bmatrix} \left[\frac{\partial \text{Val}(n_{j_1})}{\partial \text{Val}(i_1)}\right] \\ \vdots \\ \left[\frac{\partial \text{Val}(n_{j_{m_j}})}{\partial \text{Val}(i_m)}\right] \end{bmatrix} \otimes \begin{bmatrix} [\Delta \text{Val}(i_1)] \\ \vdots \\ [\Delta \text{Val}(i_m)] \end{bmatrix}
$$

Substituting back into (A.9) gives:

$$
\begin{bmatrix} \Delta \mathrm{Val}(c_1) \\ \vdots \\ \Delta \mathrm{Val}(c_n) \end{bmatrix} = \bigoplus_j \begin{bmatrix} \left[\frac{\partial_s \mathrm{Val}(c_1)}{\partial_s \mathrm{Val}(n_{j_1})}\right] & \cdots & \left[\frac{\partial_s \mathrm{Val}(c_1)}{\partial_s \mathrm{Val}(n_{jm_j})}\right] \\ \vdots & \ddots & \vdots \\ \left[\frac{\partial_s \mathrm{Val}(c_n)}{\partial_s \mathrm{Val}(n_{j_1})}\right] & \cdots & \left[\frac{\partial_s \mathrm{Val}(c_n)}{\partial_s \mathrm{Val}(n_{jm_j})}\right] \end{bmatrix}
$$

$$
\otimes \begin{bmatrix} \left[\frac{\partial \mathrm{Val}(n_{j_1})}{\partial \mathrm{Val}(i_1)}\right] \\ \vdots \\ \left[\frac{\partial \mathrm{Val}(n_{jm_j})}{\partial \mathrm{Val}(i_m)}\right] \end{bmatrix} \otimes \begin{bmatrix} [\Delta \mathrm{Val}(i_1)] \\ \vdots \\ [\Delta \mathrm{Val}(i_m)] \end{bmatrix}
$$

The combination of the two matrices of derivatives is just the qualitative influence of I on C along the jth trail, and the result follows. $\square$

B Appendix: Conditional belief calculations

...but formulas are as holy as prayers, decree-laws, and dead languages, and not an iota of them can be changed.

Primo Levi, *The Periodic Table*

Applying (3.66) it is possible to calculate conditional beliefs such as $\mathrm{Bel}(a|p,k)$ from conditional beliefs such as $\mathrm{Bel}(p|k,a)$. The given values are reproduced in Table B.1 and all other values are zero. The calculation of the relevant values proceeds as follows. For $\mathrm{Bel}(a|p,k)$:

$$
\begin{aligned}
\mathrm{Bel}(a|p,k) &= \prod_{y \in \bar{a}} \mathrm{Bel}(\neg p|y,k) - \prod_{z \in A} \mathrm{Bel}(\neg p|z,k) \\
&= \mathrm{Bel}(\neg p|\neg a,k) - \mathrm{Bel}(\neg p|a,k).\mathrm{Bel}(\neg p|\neg a,k).\mathrm{Bel}(\neg p|a \cup \neg a,k) \\
&= 0 - 0 \times 0 \times 0 \\
&= 0
\end{aligned}
$$

For $\mathrm{Bel}(a|p,\neg k)$:

$$
\begin{aligned}
\mathrm{Bel}(a|p,\neg k) &= \prod_{y \in \bar{a}} \mathrm{Bel}(\neg p|y,\neg k) - \prod_{z \in A} \mathrm{Bel}(\neg p|z,\neg k) \\
&= \mathrm{Bel}(\neg p|\neg a,\neg k) \\
&\quad - \mathrm{Bel}(\neg p|a,\neg k).\mathrm{Bel}(\neg p|\neg a,\neg k).\mathrm{Bel}(\neg p|a \cup \neg a,\neg k) \\
&= 0.5 - 0 \times 0.5 \times 0.4 \\
&= 0.5
\end{aligned}
$$

Table B.1
The beliefs for the trauma example

$\mathrm{Bel}(p|k,a)$	=	0.9	$\mathrm{Bel}(p|k,a \cup \neg a)$	=	0.7
$\mathrm{Bel}(p \cup \neg p|k,a)$	=	0.1	$\mathrm{Bel}(p \cup \neg p|k,a \cup \neg a)$	=	0.3
$\mathrm{Bel}(p|k,\neg a)$	=	0.7	$\mathrm{Bel}(\neg p|\neg k,\neg a)$	=	0.5
$\mathrm{Bel}(p \cup \neg p|k,\neg a)$	=	0.3	$\mathrm{Bel}(p \cup \neg p|\neg k,\neg a)$	=	0.5
$\mathrm{Bel}(p|\neg k,a)$	=	0.7	$\mathrm{Bel}(\neg p|\neg k,a \cup \neg a)$	=	0.4
$\mathrm{Bel}(p \cup \neg p|\neg k,a)$	=	0.3	$\mathrm{Bel}(p \cup \neg p|\neg k,a \cup \neg a)$	=	0.6
$\mathrm{Bel}(p|k \cup \neg k,a)$	=	0.6	$\mathrm{Bel}(\neg p|k \cup \neg k,\neg a)$	=	0.4
$\mathrm{Bel}(p \cup \neg p|k \cup \neg k,a)$	=	0.4	$\mathrm{Bel}(p \cup \neg p|k \cup \neg k,\neg a)$	=	0.6

For $\text{Bel}(a|p, k \cup \neg k)$:

$$
\begin{aligned}
\text{Bel}(a|p, k \cup \neg k) &= \prod_{y \in \bar{a}} \text{Bel}(\neg p|y, k \cup \neg k) - \prod_{z \in A} \text{Bel}(\neg p|z, k \cup \neg k) \\
&= \text{Bel}(\neg p|\neg a, k \cup \neg k) \\
&\quad - \text{Bel}(\neg p|a, k \cup \neg k) \\
&\qquad . \text{Bel}(\neg p|\neg a, k \cup \neg k).\text{Bel}(\neg p|a \cup \neg a, k \cup \neg k) \\
&= 0.4 - 0 \times 0.4 \times 0 \\
&= 0.4
\end{aligned}
$$

Now, from these values it is possible to compute what $\text{Bel}(a|p)$ will be for a particular set of values $m(k)$, $m(\neg k)$, $m(k \cup \neg k)$. Since without integration there is no information about this mass distribution, the only way in which progress may be made is by making an assumption. The usual assumption to apply in this kind of situation is that of minimum commitment which in this case comes down to making the assumption that all the belief mass relating to K is placed on the whole frame. With $m(k \cup \neg k) = 1$ and $m(k) = m(\neg k) = 0$, it is possible to calculate $\text{Bel}(a|p)$ as follows:

$$
\begin{aligned}
\text{Bel}(a|p) &= \sum_{w \in K} \text{Bel}(a|p, w)m(w) \\
&= 0.4
\end{aligned}
$$

A similar calculation can be performed to establish $\text{Bel}(\neg a|p)$. It is first necessary to calculate the values of $\text{Bel}(\neg a|p, k)$, $\text{Bel}(\neg a|p, \neg k)$, and $\text{Bel}(\neg a|p, k \cup \neg k)$. For $\text{Bel}(\neg a|p, k)$:

$$
\begin{aligned}
\text{Bel}(\neg a|p, k) &= \prod_{y \in \bar{\neg} a} \text{Bel}(\neg p|y, k) - \prod_{z \in A} \text{Bel}(\neg p|z, k) \\
&= \text{Bel}(\neg p|a, k) - \text{Bel}(\neg p|a, k).\text{Bel}(\neg p|\neg a, k).\text{Bel}(\neg p|a \cup \neg a, k) \\
&= 0 - 0 \times 0 \times 0 \\
&= 0
\end{aligned}
$$

For $\text{Bel}(\neg a|p, \neg k)$:

$$
\begin{aligned}
\text{Bel}(\neg a|p, \neg k) &= \prod_{y \in \bar{\neg} a} \text{Bel}(\neg p|y, \neg k) - \prod_{z \in A} \text{Bel}(\neg p|z, \neg k) \\
&= \text{Bel}(\neg p|a, \neg k) \\
&\quad - \text{Bel}(\neg p|a, \neg k).\text{Bel}(\neg p|\neg a, \neg k).\text{Bel}(\neg p|a \cup \neg a, \neg k) \\
&= 0 - 0 \times 0.5 \times 0.4 \\
&= 0
\end{aligned}
$$

For $\text{Bel}(\neg a|p, k \cup \neg k)$:

$$
\begin{aligned}
\text{Bel}(\neg a|p, k \cup \neg k) &= \prod_{y \in \neg a} \text{Bel}(\neg p|y, k \cup \neg k) - \prod_{z \in A} \text{Bel}(\neg p|z, k \cup \neg k) \\
&= \text{Bel}(\neg p|a, k \cup \neg k) \\
&\quad - \text{Bel}(\neg p|a, k \cup \neg k) \\
&\qquad .\text{Bel}(\neg p|\neg a, k \cup \neg k).\text{Bel}(\neg p|a \cup \neg a, k \cup \neg k) \\
&= 0 - 0 \times 0.4 \times 0 \\
&= 0
\end{aligned}
$$

It is then possible to calculate $\text{Bel}(\neg a|p)$ by making the same assumption as before about $m(k)$, $m(\neg k)$, and $m(k \cup \neg k)$. This gives:

$$
\begin{aligned}
\text{Bel}(\neg a|p) &= \sum_{w \in K} \text{Bel}(\neg a|p, w)m(w) \\
&= 0
\end{aligned}
$$

This indicates that observing pain says nothing about belief in the absence of arthritis.

Glossary

What a jumble! What a jumble! I must tidy up my mind . . . something has been talking, or someone,
that suddenly falls silent and then it all begins again.

Albert Camus, *The Renegade*

The purpose of this glossary is to make this book as self-contained as possible by explaining some mathematical concepts that are sufficiently obscure that some readers might have forgotten what they mean while being common enough that many readers might find a formal definition in the body of the book an annoying waste of space. Most of the terms are simple enough that it is possible to define them precisely in a few lines. Those few that need more space are defined rather loosely along with a pointer to a more precise definition.

Anytime algorithm: an algorithm that is guaranteed to always produce a solution, and also has the property that a later solution will never be worse than an earlier solution.

Arc: that which joins two nodes in a graph.

Boolean algebra: a Boolean algebra of a set is the set of subsets that can be obtained from the original set by means of a finite number of union, intersection, and complementation operations.

Cartesian product: given two sets A and B, the Cartesian product of A and B, written $A \times B$ is the set of all pairs $\langle a, b \rangle$ where a is a member of A and b is a member of B.

Closed interval: to say that a value x is drawn from a closed interval $[n, m]$ is to say that $n \leq x \leq m$.

Conjunction: the conjunction of two sentences a and b, often written as $a \wedge b$, is the sentence that is only true if both a and b are true. The term is sometimes used loosely as a synonym for intersection.

Conditional probability: the conditional probability of some event a given some other event b is the probability that a will occur given that b definitely occurs.

Consequence relation: a consequence relation holds between a set of formulae Δ expressed in some formal system $\mathcal{L}$ and some formula α of that system, if it is possible to obtain α by applying the rules of inference of $\mathcal{L}$ to the formulae in Δ. A consequence relation is thus a means of talking about what can be derived in a formal language.

Convex hull: the convex hull of a set of points S is the intersection of all convex sets containing S.

Convex set: a set S is convex if the line segment joining any pair of points in S lies entirely within S.

Cross product: the same as a Cartesian product.

Decidable: a formal system $\mathcal{L}$ is decidable if it is possible to decide whether any formula α is a consequence of some set of formulae Δ simply by applying the rules of inference of L.

Decision tree: a graphical method for calculating the expected utility of a set of decisions, used as a means of choosing the best decisions to take. Decision trees are discussed in depth by Raiffa (1970).

Directed acyclic graph: a graph in which edges have a direction, and it is not possible to travel in a circle from one node back to the same node while following the direction of the edges.

Directed graph: a graph in which edges have a direction.

Disjunction: the disjunction of two sentences a and b, often written as $a \vee b$, is the sentence that is true if either a or b are true. The term is sometimes used loosely as a synonym for union.

Edge: that which joins two nodes in a graph.

Extension: the logical closure of the union of a set of facts expressed in a non-monotonic logic and the assumptions that may be drawn from those facts.

Expected utility: given a probability distribution P and a utility distribution U over a set of states $S = \{s_1, \ldots, s_n\}$, the expected utility $E(U, P)$ is:

$$E(U, P) = \sum_{i=1,\ldots,n} P(s_i) U(s_i)$$

the sum of the pairwise products of probability and utility of each possible state.

Graph: a pair (N, E), where N is a finite set and E is a collection of two element subsets of N. The elements of N are called nodes, and the elements of E are called edges or arcs.

Greatest lower bound: for three elements x, y, and z of a partially ordered set, z is the greatest lower bound of x and y if $z \leq x$, $z \leq y$, and $w \leq z$ for all w such that $w \leq x$ and $w \leq y$.

Hyperedge: an edge in a hypergraph. It is thus an edge that joins sets of nodes (Berge, 1973).

Hypergraph: a generalisation of a graph in which an arc joins sets of nodes (Berge, 1973).

Hypertree: a generalisation of a tree in which an arc joins sets of nodes.

Infimum: the greatest lower bound of a set.

Interpretation: an assignment of truth values to every proposition in a logical formula or set of formulae. Thus an interpretation for the formula $a \wedge b$ will specify the truth value of a and b.

Intersection: the intersection of two sets A and B is the set of objects that are members of both A and B.

Join tree: a tree whose nodes are sets of variables so arranged that if a variable is in two distinct nodes, it is in every node on the path between the two nodes.

Joint probability: the joint probability of events a and b is the probability of the conjunction $a \wedge b$, the probability that both a and b occur.

Junction tree: a tree whose nodes are sets of variables so arranged that if a variable is in two distinct nodes, it is in every node on the path between the two nodes.

Lattice: a partially-ordered set for which each pair of elements has a least upper bound and a greatest lower bound.

Least upper bound: for three elements x, y, and z of a partially ordered set, z is the least upper bound of x and y if $x \leq z$, $y \leq z$, and $z \leq w$ for all w such that $x \leq w$ and $y \leq w$.

Linear equation: a polynomial equation where each variable is raised to the power 1, for example $y = x + 1$.

Linear function: a function that can be expressed as a linear equation.

Linear program: a method for finding the maximum or minimum of a linear function of a set of variables subject to a set of constraints that are themselves expressed as linear equations or inequalities.

Logical closure: the set of all conclusions that may be deduced from an initial set of facts by applying a set of rules of inference to both the facts and the growing set of conclusions as often as they may be applied.

Marginal probability: the marginal probability of the event a is just the probability of a, so it is the probability of a given all that is known about the current state of the world. The term "the marginal probability of a" is usually used to distinguish this probability from the conditional probability of a given some other event, or the joint probability of a and some other event.

Mean: a property of a probability distribution obtained by taking the product of each value of a variable and its probability and then summing over the values.

Median: the median of a probability distribution is the middle value of the associated set of values such that the values above and below it have equal total probabilities.

Markov tree: another term for a join tree.

Meta-logical rule: a rule relating to a formal system that is not expressed in the language of the system but which specifies something about the system.

Möbius transform: if a and z are complex numbers, and $|a| < 1$, then:

$$\phi_a(z) = \frac{z - a}{1 - a^*z}$$

is a Möbius transformation of a. a^* is the complex conjugate of a, so if $a = x + yi$ then $a^* = x - yi$.

Mode: the mode of a probability distribution is the member of the associated set of values to which the highest probability is assigned.

Model: a model for a set of logical formulae is an interpretation that makes all of the formulae in the set true. Thus the set of formulae $\{a \wedge b, a \vee \neg c\}$ has two models. In one a, b, and c are all true, in the second a and b are true and c is false.

Monte-Carlo method: a method for estimating the results of intractable processes by simulating their outcome probabilistically, and sampling from the results of this simulation.

Node: a member of the set from which a graph is composed.

Normal distribution: a continuous probability distribution with the functional form:

$$\Pr(x) = \frac{1}{\sqrt{\pi 2 \sigma}} e^{\frac{1}{2}\left(\frac{x-\mu}{\sigma}\right)^2}$$

The mean, median and mode of a normal distribution are all equal.

NP-complete: an NP-problem that is NP-hard is said to be NP-complete.

NP-hard: a problem is NP-hard if an algorithm for solving it can be translated into one for solving any other NP-problem. Thus if a problem is NP-hard, it is at least as hard to solve as any NP-problem.

NP-problem: an NP-problem is a problem that is solvable in polynomial time by a non-deterministic Turing machine, that is a computer which can take many computational paths simultaneously without communication between the paths.

#P-problem: In studying NP-problems, the problem is solved if a single solution is found. A similar notion to that of an NP-problem can be developed for problems where the interesting property is the number of solutions. This notion is that of a #P-problem. Thus a #P-problem is one for which the number of solutions can be established in polynomial time by a non-deterministic Turing machine.

Open interval: to say that a value x is drawn from an open interval (n, m) is to say that $n < x < m$.

Partial order: the relation between two members of a partially ordered set.

Partially ordered set: a pair $(S, \leq)$ where S is a non-empty set, and $\leq$ is a binary relation on S such that for $x, y \in S$, $x \leq x$, if $x \leq y$ and $y \leq x$ then $x = y$, and if $x \leq y$ and $y \leq z$ then $x \leq z$.

Polynomial equation: an equation where variables are raised to arbitrary powers, for example $y^2 = x^5 - x^2 + 1$.

Polynomial function: a function that can be expressed as a polynomial equation.

Polynomial time: a problem is said to be solvable in polynomial time if there is an algorithm for solving it that executes in a time which is a polynomial function of the size of the problem. Thus sorting a list is a polynomial time problem because there are algorithms for sorting lists that execute in a time which is a polynomial function of the length of the list.

Polytope: a convex set with a finite number of vertices.

Possibility distribution: a possibility distribution over a set of events can be thought of as a function that gives the possibility of each member of the set.

Probability distribution: a probability distribution over a set of events can be thought of as a function that gives the probability of each member of the set.

Random variable: a variable that may take any of a range of values, and for which the value it takes cannot be predicted with certainty.

Rule of inference: a rule that indicates how conclusions may be drawn from one or more facts in a formal system. Rules of inference are meta-logical rules.

Stochastic dominance: Very informally, one probability distribution F has stochastic dominance over another distribution G iff the expected utility $E(U,F)$ for any utility distribution U is greater than $E(U,G)$. A precise definition may be found in (Whitmore and Findlay, 1978).

Supremum: the least upper bound of a set.

Tree: a graph in which it is not possible to find a path from a node that leads back to the same node without traversing the same arc more than once.

Union: the union of two sets A and B is the set of objects that are members of either A or B.

Utility: a means of representing the value that a particular state of the world has for a decision maker. Utility is used rather than monetary value (or any other objective measure) to make it possible to model the subjective views of the decision maker (Raiffa, 1970).

Utility distribution: a utility distribution over a set of states can be thought of as a function that gives the utility of each member of that set.

Vacuous value: a value that is uninformative. Thus a vacuous mass distribution in evidence theory is one that gives all the mass to the whole frame of discernment.

Valuation network: a graphical representation of a valuation-based system.

References

Abramson, B. (1991). ARCO1: An application of belief networks to the oil market. In *Proceedings of the 7th Conference on Uncertainty in Artificial Intelligence*, pages 1–8, San Mateo, CA. Morgan Kaufmann.

Acid, S. and de Campos, L. M. (1996). BENEDICT: an algorithm for learning probabilistic belief networks. In *Proceedings of the 6th International Conference on Information Processing and the Management of Uncertainty*, pages 979–984.

Adams, E. (1975). *The Logic of Conditionals*. Reidel, Dordrecht, Netherlands.

Adams, J. B. (1976). A probability model of medical reasoning and the MYCIN model. *Mathematical Biosciences*, **32**, 177–186.

Agogino, A. M. and Michelena, N. F. (1993). Qualitative decision analysis. In N. Piera Carreté and M. G. Singh, editors, *Qualitative Reasoning and Decision Technologies*, pages 285–293. CIMNE, Barcelona, Spain.

Agosta, J. M. (1990). The structure of Bayes networks for visual recognition. In R. D. Shachter, T. S. Levitt, L. N. Kanal, and J. F. Lemmer, editors, *Uncertainty in Artificial Intelligence 4*, pages 397–405. Elsevier Science Publishers, Amsterdam, The Netherlands.

Agosta, J. M. (1991). "Conditional inter-causally independent" node distributions, a property of "noisy-or" models. In *Proceedings of the 7th Conference on Uncertainty in Artificial Intelligence*, pages 9–16, San Mateo, CA. Morgan Kaufmann.

Agustí-Cullell, J., Esteva, F., García, P., Godó, L., and Sierra, C. (1991). Combining multiple-valued logics in modular expert systems. In *Proceedings of the 7th Conference on Uncertainty in Artificial Intelligence*, pages 17–25, San Mateo, CA. Morgan Kaufmann.

Agustí-Cullell, J., Esteva, F., García, P., Godó, L., Lòpez de Mántaras, R., Puyol, J., and Sierra, C. (1992). Structured local fuzzy logics in MILORD. In L. A. Zadeh and J. Kacprzyk, editors, *Fuzzy Logic for the Management of Uncertainty*, pages 523–551. John Wiley & Sons, New York, NY.

Aleliunas, R. (1990). A summary of a new normative theory of probabilistic logic. In R. D. Shachter, T. S. Levitt, L. N. Kanal, and J. F. Lemmer, editors, *Uncertainty in Artificial Intelligence 4*, pages 199–206. Elsevier Science Publishers, Amsterdam, The Netherlands.

Allison, L. (1993). Methods for dealing with error and uncertainty in molecular biology computations and databases. In *Proceedings of the 22nd Hawaiian International Conference on System Sciences*, page 704, Los Alamitos, CA. IEEE Computer Society Press.

Altman, R. B. (1993). Probabilistic structure calculations: a three dimensional tRNA structure from sequence correlation data. In *Proceedings of the First International Conference on Intelligent Systems for Molecular Biology*, pages 12–20, Menlo Park, CA. AAAI Press.

Altman, R. B. (1994). Constraint satisfaction techniques for modelling large complexes: application to the central domain of 16S ribosomal RNA. In *Proceedings of the Second International Conference on Intelligent Systems for Molecular Biology*, pages 10–18, Menlo Park, CA. AAAI Press.

Altman, R. B. and Jardetzky, O. (1989). Heuristic refinement method for determination of solution structure of proteins from nuclear magnetic resonance. *Methods in Enzymology*, **177**, 218–246.

Amarger, S., Dubois, D., and Prade, H. (1991). Constraint propagation with imprecise conditional probabilities. In *Proceedings of the 7th Conference on Uncertainty in Artificial Intelligence*, pages 26–34, San Mateo, CA. Morgan Kaufmann.

Amgoud, L. (1999). *Contribution a l'integration des préferences dans le raisonnement argumentatif*. Ph.D. thesis, Université Paul Sabatier, Toulouse.

Andersen, S. K., Jensen, F. V., Olesen, K. G., and Jensen, F. (1989). HUGIN—a shell for building Bayesian belief universes for expert systems. In *Proceedings of the 11th International Joint Conference on Artificial Intelligence*, pages 783–791, San Mateo, CA. Morgan Kaufmann.

Andreassen, S., Woldbye, M., Falck, B., and Andersen, S. K. (1987). MUNIN—a causal probabilistic network for interpretation of electromyographic findings. In *Proceedings of the 10th International Joint Conference on Artificial Intelligence*, pages 366–372, Los Altos, CA. Morgan Kaufmann.

Anrig, B., Haenni, R., Kohlas, J., and Lehmann, N. (1997). Assumption-based modelling using ABEL. In D. M. Gabbay, R. Kruse, A. Nonnengart, and H. J. Ohlbach, editors, *Qualitative and Quantitative Practical Reasoning*, pages 171–182. Springer Verlag, Berlin, Germany.

Antoniou, G. (1996). A comparative survey of default logic variants. In D. M. Gabbay and H. J. Ohlbach, editors, *Practical Reasoning*, pages 15–28. Springer Verlag, Berlin, Germany.

Antoniou, G. (1997). *Nonmonotonic Reasoning*. MIT Press, Cambridge, MA. With contributions by Mary-Anne Williams.

Antoniou, G. (1998). A tutorial on default reasoning. *Knowledge Engineering Review*, **13**, 225–246.

Ardizzone, E., Bonadonna, F., Gaglio, S., Nicolini, C., Ruggiero, C., and Sorbello, F. (1988). Qualitative modelling of cell growth processes. *Applied Artificial Intelligence*, **2**, 251–263.

Arkes, H. R. and Hammond, K. R. (1986). *Judgement and Decision Making: An Interdisciplinary Reader*. Cambridge University Press, Cambridge, UK.

Asai, K., Hayamizu, S., and Onizuka, K. (1993). HMM with protein structure grammar. In *Proceedings of the 22nd Hawaiian International Conference on System Sciences*, pages 783–791, Los Alamitos, CA. IEEE Computer Society Press.

Ayton, P. and Pascoe, E. (1995). Bias in human judgement under uncertainty. *The Knowledge Engineering Review*, **10**, 21–41.

Bacchus, F. (1990a). On probability distributions over possible worlds. In R. D. Shachter, T. S. Levitt, L. N. Kanal, and J. F. Lemmer, editors, *Uncertainty in Artificial Intelligence 4*, pages 217–226. Elsevier Science Publishers, Amsterdam, The Netherlands.

Bacchus, F. (1990b). *Representing and Reasoning with Probabilistic Knowledge*. MIT Press, Cambridge, MA.

Bacchus, F. (1991). Default reasoning from statistics. In *Proceedings of the 10th National Conference on Artificial Intelligence*, pages 392–398, Menlo Park, CA. AAAI Press/MIT Press.

Bacchus, F. (1993). Using first order probability logic for the construction of Bayesian networks. In *Proceedings of the 9th Conference on Uncertainty in Artificial Intelligence*, pages 219–226, San Mateo, CA. Morgan Kaufmann.

Bacchus, F., Grove, A. J., Halpern, J. Y., and Koller, D. (1992). From statistics to beliefs. In *Proceedings of the 10th National Conference on Artificial Intelligence*, pages 602–608, San Mateo, CA. AAAI Press/MIT Press.

Bacchus, F., Grove, A. J., Halpern, J. Y., and Koller, D. (1993). Statistical foundations for default reasoning. In *Proceedings of the 13th International Joint Conference on Artificial Intelligence*, pages 563–569, San Mateo, CA. Morgan Kaufmann.

Bacchus, F., Grove, A. J., Halpern, J. Y., and Koller, D. (1996). From statistical knowledge bases to degrees of belief. *Artificial Intelligence*, **87**, 75–143.

Baldwin, J. F. (1986). Automated fuzzy and probabilistic inference. *Fuzzy Sets and Systems*, **18**, 219–235.

Baldwin, J. F. (1987). Evidential support logic programming. *Fuzzy Sets and Systems*, **24**, 1–26.

Baldwin, J. F. (1990). Towards a general theory of evidential reasoning. In B. Bouchon-Meunier, R. R. Yager, and L. A. Zadeh, editors, *Uncertainty in Knowledge Bases*, pages 360–369. Springer Verlag, Berlin, Germany.

Baldwin, J. F. (1992). Fuzzy and probabilistic uncertainties. In S. Shapiro, editor, *Encyclopaedia of Artificial Intelligence, Volume 1, 2nd Edition*, pages 528–537. John Wiley & Sons, London, UK.

Baldwin, J. F. and Martin, T. P. (1996). Fril as an implementation language for fuzzy information systems. In *Proceedings of the 6th International Conference on Information Processing and the Management of Uncertainty*, pages 289–294.

Baldwin, J. F. and Zhou, S. Q. (1984). A fuzzy relational inference language. *Fuzzy Sets and Systems*, **14**, 155–174.

Banks, I. M. (1993). *The State of the Art*. Orbit, London, UK.

Bar-Hillel, M. (1980). The base-rate fallacy in probability judgements. *Acta Psychologica*, **44**, 211–233.

Barnett, J. A. (1981). Computational methods for a mathematical theory of evidence. In *Proceedings of the 7th International Joint Conference on Artificial Intelligence*, pages 868–875, Los Altos, CA. William Kaufmann.

Baron, J. and Frisch, D. (1994). Ambiguous probabilities and the paradoxes of expected utility. In G. Wright and P. Ayton, editors, *Subjective Probability*, pages 273–294. John Wiley & Sons, Chichester, UK.

Barrow, H. G. (1984). VERIFY: a program for proving correctness of digital hardware. *Artificial Intelligence*, **24**, 437–491.

Beach, L. R. (1966). Accuracy and consistency in the revision of subjective probabilities. *IEEE Transactions on Human Factors in Electronics*, **7**, 29–37.

Beach, L. R. and Braun, G. P. (1994). Laboratory studies of subjective probability: a status report. In G. Wright and P. Ayton, editors, *Subjective Probability*, pages 107–127. John Wiley & Sons, Chichester, UK.

Becker, A. and Geiger, D. (1996). Optimization of Pearl's method of conditioning and greedy-like approximation algorithms for the vertex feedback set problem. *Artificial Intelligence*, **83**, 167–188.

Ben Yaghlane, B. and Mellouli, K. (1999). Updating directed belief networks. In A. Hunter and S. Parsons, editors, *Symbolic and Quantitative Approaches to Reasoning and Uncertainty*, pages 43–54. Springer Verlag, Berlin, Germany.

Benferhat, S. (1994). Handling hard rules and default rules in possibilistic logic. In *Proceedings of the 5th International Conference on Information Processing and the Management of Uncertainty*, pages 1153–1158.

Benferhat, S., Dubois, D., and Prade, H. (1992). Representing default rules in possibilistic logic. In *Proceedings of the 3rd International Conference on Knowledge Representation and Reasoning*, pages 673–684, San Mateo, CA. Morgan Kaufmann.

Benferhat, S., Dubois, D., and Prade, H. (1993). Argumentative inference in uncertain and inconsistent knowledge bases. In *Proceedings of the 9th Conference on Uncertainty in Artificial Intelligence*, pages 411–419, San Mateo, CA. Morgan Kaufmann.

Benferhat, S., Dubois, D., and Prade, H. (1994a). Expressing independence in a possibilistic framework and its application to default reasoning. In *Proceedings of the 11th European Conference on Artificial Intelligence*, pages 150–154, Chichester, UK. John Wiley & Sons.

Benferhat, S., Dubois, D., and Prade, H. (1994b). Some syntactic approaches to the handling of inconsistent knowledge bases: a comparative study. Part 1: The flat case. Rapport IRIT/94-55-R, IRIT.

Benferhat, S., Dubois, D., and Prade, H. (1994c). Some syntactic approaches to the handling of inconsistent knowledge bases: a comparative study. Part 2: The prioritized case. Rapport IRIT/94-55-R, IRIT.

Benferhat, S., Saffiotti, A., and Smets, P. (1995a). Belief functions and default reasoning. In *Proceedings of the 11th Conference on Uncertainty in Artificial Intelligence*, pages 19–26, San Francisco, CA. Morgan Kaufmann.

Benferhat, S., Dubois, D., and Prade, H. (1995b). A conditional approach to possibilistic abduction. In *Proceedings of the 3rd Congress on Intelligent Techniques and Soft Computing*, pages 64–68.

Benferhat, S., Cayrac, D., Dubois, D., and Prade, H. (1996). Explaining away in a possibilistic setting. In *Proceedings of the 6th International Conference on Information Processing and the Management of Uncertainty*, pages 929–934.

Benferhat, S., Dubois, D., and Prade, H. (1997). Syntactic combination of uncertain information: a possibilistic approach. In D. M. Gabbay, R. Kruse, A. Nonnengart, and H. J. Ohlbach, editors, *Qualitative and Quantitative Practical Reasoning*, pages 30–42. Springer Verlag, Berlin, Germany.

Benferhat, S., Dubois, D., and Prade, H. (1999). Possibilistic and standard semantics of conditional knowledge bases. *Journal of Logic and Computation*, **9**, 873–895.

Benferhat, S., Saffiotti, A., and Smets, P. (2000). Belief functions and default reasoning. *Artificial Intelligence*, **122**, 1–69.

Berge, C. (1973). *Graphs and Hypergraphs*. North-Holland, Amsterdam, Netherlands.

Berleant, D. and Kuipers, B. (1992). Qualitative-numeric simulation with Q3. In B. Faltings and P. Struss, editors, *Recent Advances in Qualitative Physics*, pages 3–16. MIT Press, Cambridge, MA.

Besnard, P. (1989). *Introduction to Default Logic*. Springer-Verlag, Berlin, Germany.

Besnard, P. and Kohlas, J. (1995). Evidence theory based on general consequence relations. *International Journal of Foundations of Computer Science*, **6**, 119–135.

Besnard, P. and Siegel, P. (1988). Supposition-based logic for automated nonmonotonic reasoning. In *9th International Conference on Automated Deduction*, pages 592–601. Springer Verlag, Berlin, Germany.

Besnard, P., Quinou, R., and Quinton, P. (1983). A theorem prover for a decidable subset of default logic. In *Proceedings of the 3rd National Conference on Artificial Intelligence*, pages 27–30, Los Altos, CA. William Kaufmann.

Bigham, J. (1990). Computing beliefs according to the Dempster-Shafer and possibilistic logic theories, using the results of propositional inference as a basis. In *Proceedings of the 3rd International Conference on Information Processing and the Management of Uncertainty*, pages 59–61.

Birnbaum, L. (1982). Argument molecules: a functional representation of argument structure. In *Proceedings of the 2nd National Conference on Artificial Intelligence*, pages 63–65, Los Altos, CA. William Kaufmann.

Birnbaum, L. (1991). Rigor mortis: a response to Nilsson's "Logic and artificial intelligence". *Artificial Intelligence*, **47**, 57–77.

Birnbaum, L., Flowers, M., and McGuire, R. (1980). Towards an AI model of argumentation. In *Proceedings of the 1st National Conference on Artificial Intelligence*, pages 313–315, Los Altos, CA. William Kaufmann.

Bobrow, D. G. (1984). *Qualitative Reasoning about Physical Systems*. Elsevier Science Publishers, Amsterdam, The Netherlands.

Bochman, A. (1995). On bimodal nonmonotonic logics and their unimodal and nonmodal equivalents. In *Proceedings of the 14th International Joint Conference on Artificial Intelligence*, pages 1518–1524, San Mateo, CA. Morgan Kaufmann.

Bogler, P. L. (1987). Shafer-Dempster reasoning with applications to multisensor target identification systems. *IEEE Transactions on Systems, Man and Cybernetics*, **17**, 968–977.

Bondarenko, A., Dung, P. M., Kowalski, R. A., and Toni, F. (1997). An abstract argumentation-theoretic approach to default reasoning. *Artificial Intelligence*, **93**, 63–101.

Bonissone, P. P. (1987a). Reasoning, Plausible. In S. Shapiro, editor, *Encyclopaedia of Artificial Intelligence*, pages 854–863. John Wiley & Sons, London, UK.

Bonissone, P. P. (1987b). Summarizing and propagating uncertain information with triangular norms. *International Journal of Approximate Reasoning*, **1**, 71–101.

Bonissone, P. P. and Decker, K. S. (1986). Selecting uncertainty calculi and granularity: an experiment in trading-off precision and granularity. In L. N. Kanal and J. F. Lemmer, editors, *Uncertainty in Artificial Intelligence*, pages 217–247. Elsevier Science Publishers, Amsterdam, The Netherlands.

Bonissone, P. P. and Tong, R. M. (1985). Editorial: reasoning with uncertainty in expert systems. *International Journal of Man-Machine Studies*, **22**, 241–250.

Bonissone, P. P. and Wood, N. C. (1989). T-norm based reasoning in situation assessment applications. In L. N. Kanal, T. S. Levitt, and J. F. Lemmer, editors, *Uncertainty in Artificial Intelligence 3*, pages 241–256. Elsevier Science Publishers, Amsterdam, The Netherlands.

Bonissone, P. P., Gans, S. S., and Decker, K. S. (1987). RUM: a layered architecture for reasoning with uncertainty. In *Proceedings of the 10th International Joint Conference on Artificial Intelligence*, pages 891–898, Los Altos, CA. Morgan Kaufmann.

Boolos, G. (1993). *The Logic of Provability*. Cambridge University Press, Cambridge, UK.

Borgelt, C. and Kruse, R. (1997). Some experimental results on learning probabilistic and possibilistic networks with different evaluation measures. In D. M. Gabbay, R. Kruse, A. Nonnengart, and H. J. Ohlbach, editors, *Qualitative and Quantitative Practical Reasoning*, pages 71–85. Springer Verlag, Berlin, Germany.

Bosc, P. and Prade, H. (1997). An introduction to the fuzzy set and possibility theory-based treatment of flexible queries and uncertain or imprecise databases. In A. Motro and P. Smets, editors, *Uncertainty in Information Systems: From Needs to Solutions*, pages 285–324. Kluwer, Boston, MA.

Bossu, G. and Siegel, P. (1985). Saturation, nonmonotonic reasoning, and the closed world assumption. *Artificial Intelligence*, **25**, 13–64.

Bourne, R. A. (1999). *Default reasoning using maximum entropy and variable strength defaults*. Ph.D. thesis, Department of Electronic Engineering, Queen Mary and Westfield College, London.

Bourne, R. A. and Parsons, S. (1999a). Connecting lexicographic with maximum entropy entailment. In A. Hunter and S. Parsons, editors, *Symbolic and Quantitative Approaches to Reasoning and Uncertainty*, pages 80–91. Springer Verlag, Berlin, Germany.

Bourne, R. A. and Parsons, S. (1999b). Maximum entropy and variable strength defaults. In *Proceedings of the 16th International Joint Conference on Artificial Intelligence*, pages 50–55, San Francisco, CA. Morgan Kaufmann.

Bousson, K. and Travé-Massuyès, L. (1993). Fuzzy causal simulation in process engineering. In *Proceedings of the 13th International Joint Conference on Artificial Intelligence*, pages 1509–1514, San Mateo, CA. Morgan Kaufmann.

Boutilier, C. (1993). The probability of a possibility: addng uncertainty to default rules. In *Proceedings of the 9th Conference on Uncertainty in Artificial Intelligence*, pages 461–468, San Mateo, CA. Morgan Kaufmann.

Boutilier, C., Friedman, N., Goldszmidt, M., and Koller, D. (1996). Context-specific independence in Bayesian networks. In E. Horvitz and F. Jensen, editors, *Proceedings of the 12th Conference on Uncertainty in Artificial Intelligence*, pages 115–123, San Francisco, CA. Morgan Kaufmann.

Brachman, R., Fikes, R., and Levesque, H. (1983). KRYPTON: a functional approach to knowledge representation. *IEEE Computer*, **16**, 67–73.

Brajnik, G. and Lines, M. (1998). Qualitative modeling and simulation of socio-economic phenomena. *Journal of Artificial Societies and Social Simulation*, **1**.

Bränden, C. (1990). Relation between structure and function of α/β proteins. *Quarterly Review of Biophysical Chemistry*, **13**, 317–338.

Breese, J. and Fertig, K. W. (1991). Decision making with interval influence diagrams. In P. P. Bonissone, M. Henrion, L. N. Kanal, and J. F. Lemmer, editors, *Uncertainty in Artificial Intelligence 6*, pages 467–478. Elsevier Science Publishers, Amsterdam, The Netherlands.

Breese, J. S. (1992). Construction of belief and decision networks. *Computational Intelligence*, **8**, 624–647.

Brewka, G. (1986). Tweety—still flying, some remarks on abnormal birds, applicable rules and a default prover. In *Proceedings of the 5th National Conference on Artificial Intelligence*, pages 8–12, Los Altos, CA. Morgan Kaufmann.

Brewka, G. (1991). *Nonmonotonic Reasoning: Logical Foundations of Commonsense*. Cambridge University Press, Cambridge, UK.

Brillouin, L. (1964). *Scientific Uncertainty and Information*. Academic Press, London, UK.

Brown, M., Hughey, R., Krogh, A., Mian, I. S., Sjölander, K., and Haussler, D. (1993). Using Dirchlet mixture priors to derive hidden Markov models for protein families. In *Proceedings of the First International Conference on Intelligent Systems for Molecular Biology*, pages 47–55, Menlo Park, CA. AAAI Press.

Buchanan, B. G. and Shortliffe, E. H., editors (1984). *Rule-based Expert Systems: The MYCIN Experiments of the Stanford Heuristic Programming Project*. Addison-Wesley, Reading, Mass.

Bundy, A. (1985). Incidence calculus: a mechanism for probabilistic reasoning. *Journal of Automated Reasoning*, **1**, 263–284.

Bundy, A. (1990). Incidence calculus. Research Paper 457, Department of Artificial Intelligence, Edinburgh.

Bundy, A. (1991). Clear thinking on artificial intelligence. *The Guardian, December 5th*, page 33.

Cano, A., Cano, J., and Moral, S. (1994). Convex sets of probabilities propagation by simulated annealing. In *Proceedings of the 5th International Conference on Information Processing and the Management of Uncertainty*, pages 978–983.

Cano, J., Moral, S., and Verdegay López, J. F. (1991). Combination of lower and upper probabilities. In *Proceedings of the 7th Conference on Uncertainty in Artificial Intelligence*, pages 61–68, San Mateo, CA. Morgan Kaufmann.

Cano, J., Moral, S., and Verdegay López, J. F. (1992). Propagation of convex sets of probabilities in directed acyclic networks. In *Proceedings of the 4th International Conference on Information Processing and the Management of Uncertainty*, pages 289–292, Palma, Mallorca. Universitat de les Illes Balears.

Cano, J., Delgardo, M., and Moral, S. (1993). An axiomatic framework for propagating uncertainty in directed acyclic networks. *International Journal of Approximate Reasoning*, **8**, 253–280.

Carbogim, D. V., Robertson, D., and Lee, J. (2000). Argument-based applications to knowledge engineering. *The Knowledge Engineering Review*, **15**(2).

Carnap, R., editor (1962). *The Logical Foundations of Probability*. Chicago University Press, Chicago, IL, 2nd edition.

Castillo, E., Gutiérrez, J. M., and Hadi, A. S. (1997). *Expert Systems and Probabilistic Network Models*. Springer

Verlag, Berlin, Germany.

Castro, J. L. and Trillas, E. (1993). The management of the inconsistency in expert systems. *Fuzzy Sets and Systems*, **58**, 51–57.

Catino, C. (1993). *Automated modeling of chemical plants with application to hazard and operability studies.* Ph.D. thesis, Department of Chemical Engineering, University of Pennsylvania.

Cayrol, C. (1995). On the relation between argumentation and non-monotonic coeherence-based entailment. In *Proceedings of the 14th International Joint Conference on Artificial Intelligence*, pages 1443–1448, San Mateo, CA. Morgan Kaufmann.

Chard, T. (1991). Qualitative probability versus quantitative probability in clinical diagnosis: a study using a computer simulation. *Medical Decision Making*, **11**, 38–41.

Charniak, E. (1991). Bayesian networks without tears. *AI Magazine*, **12**, 50–63.

Cheeseman, P. (1983). A method of computing generalised Bayesian probability values for expert systems. In *Proceedings of the 8th International Joint Conference on Artificial Intelligence*, pages 198–202, Los Altos, CA. William Kaufmann.

Cheeseman, P. (1985). In defence of probability. In *Proceedings of the 9th International Joint Conference on Artificial Intelligence*, pages 1002–1009, Los Altos, CA. Morgan Kaufmann.

Cheeseman, P. (1986). Probabilistic vs. fuzzy reasoning. In L. N. Kanal and J. F. Lemmer, editors, *Uncertainty in Artificial Intelligence*, pages 85–102. Elsevier Science Publishers, Amsterdam, The Netherlands.

Cheeseman, P. (1988a). Discussion of the paper by Lauritzen and Spiegelhalter. *Journal of the Royal Statistical Society, B*, **50**, 203.

Cheeseman, P. (1988b). An inquiry into computer understanding. *Computational Intelligence*, **4**, 58–142.

Chen, C. C., Singh, J. P., and Altman, R. B. (1999). Using imperfect secondary structure predictions to improve molecular structure computations. *Bioinformatics*, **15**, 53–65.

Cheng, J. and Druzdzel, M. J. (2000). AIS-BN: an adaptive importance sampling algorithm for evidential reasoning in large Bayesian networks. *Journal of Artificial Intelligence Research*, **13**, 155–188.

Cholewiński, P., Marek, V. W., Mikitiuk, A., and Truszczyński, M. (1999). Computing with default logic. *Artificial Intelligence*, **112**, 105–146.

Chomsky, N. (1992). *Deterring Democracy*. Vintage, London, UK.

Choquet, G. (1953). Theory of capacities. *Annals of the Institute Fourier*, **5**, 131–295.

Chrisman, L. (1996). Independence with lower and upper probabilities. In *Proceedings of the 12th Conference on Uncertainty in Artificial Intelligence*, pages 169–177, San Francisco, CA. Morgan Kaufmann.

Clark, D. A. (1990). Numerical and symbolic approaches to uncertainty management in AI. *Artificial Intelligence Review*, **4**, 109–146.

Clark, D. A., Shirazi, J., and Rawlings, C. J. (1992). Protein topology prediction through constraint-based search and the evaluation of topological folding rules. *Protein Engineering*, **4**, 751–760.

Clark, D. A., Rawlings, C. J., Shirazi, J., Veron, A., and Reeve, M. (1993). Protein topology prediction through parallel constraint logic programming. In *Proceedings of the First International Conference on Intelligent Systems for Molecular Biology*, pages 83–91, Menlo Park, CA. AAAI Press.

Clark, D. A., Rawlings, C. J., and Doursenot, S. (1994). Genetic map construction with constraints. In *Proceedings of the Second International Conference on Intelligent Systems for Molecular Biology*, pages 78–86, Menlo Park, CA. AAAI Press.

Clark, K. L. (1978). Negation as failure. In H. Gallaire and J. Minker, editors, *Logic and Databases*, pages 293–322. Plenum Press, New York, NY.

Clarke, M. (1988). Comments on "Belief functions" by P. Smets. In P. Smets, E. H. Mamdani, D. Dubois, and H. Prade, editors, *Non-Standard Logics for Automated Reasoning*, pages 277–279. Academic Press, London, UK.

Cohen, F. E. and Kuntz, I. D. (1987). Prediction of the three dimensional structure of human growth hormone. *Proteins: Structure, Function and Genetics*, **2**, 162–167.

Cohen, P. R. (1985). *Heuristic Reasoning about Uncertainty: An Artificial Intelligence Approach.* Pitman, London, UK.

Cohen, P. R. and Grinberg, M. R. (1983a). A framework for heuristic reasoning about uncertainty. In *Proceedings of the 8th International Joint Conference on Artificial Intelligence*, pages 355–357, Los Altos, CA. William Kaufmann.

Cohen, P. R. and Grinberg, M. R. (1983b). A theory of heuristic reasoning about uncertainty. *AI Magazine*, **4**, 17–24.

Cohen, P. R. and Lieberman, M. D. (1983). A report on Folio: an expert assistant for portfolio managers. In *Proceedings of the 8th International Joint Conference on Artificial Intelligence*, pages 212–214, Los Altos, CA. William Kaufmann.

Cohen, R. (1987). Analyzing the structure of argumentative discourse. *Computational Linguistics*, **13**, 11–24.

Cohn, A. G. (1989). Approaches to qualitative reasoning. *Artificial Intelligence Review*, **3**, 177–232.

Coiera, E. (1992). The qualitative representation of physical systems. *The Knowledge Engineering Review*, **7**, 55–77.

Cooper, G. F. (1990). The computational complexity of probabilistic inference using belief networks. *Artificial Intelligence*, **42**, 393–405.

Cooper, G. F. and Herskovits, E. (1991a). A Bayesian method for constructing Bayesian belief networks from databases. In *Proceedings of the 7th Conference on Uncertainty in Artificial Intelligence*, pages 86–94, San Mateo, CA. Morgan Kaufmann.

Cooper, G. F. and Herskovits, E. (1991b). A Bayesian method for the induction of probabilistic networks from data. Report SMI-1-93, Section of Medical Informatics, University of Pittsburgh.

Corrêa da Silva, F. S. and Bundy, A. (1990). On some equivalence relations between Incidence Calculus and Dempster-Shafer theory of evidence. Research Paper 470, Department of Artificial Intelligence, University of Edinburgh.

Cowell, R. G., Dawid, A. P., Hutchinson, T. A., and Spiegelhalter, D. J. (1991). A Bayesian expert system for the analysis of an adverse drug reaction. *Artificial Intelligence in Medicine*, **3**, 257–270.

Cowell, R. G., Dawid, A. P., Lauritzen, S. L., and Spiegelhalter, D. J. (1999). *Probabilistic Networks and Expert Systems*. Springer Verlag, Berlin, Germany.

Cox, R. (1946). Probability, frequency and reasonable expectation. *American Journal of Physics*, **14**, 1–13.

Cozman, F. (1997). Robustness analysis of Bayesian networks with local convex sets. In D. Geiger and P. P. Shenoy, editors, *Proceedings of the 13th Conference on Uncertainty in Artificial Intelligence*, pages 108–115, San Francisco, CA. Morgan Kaufmann.

Cozman, F. G. (1999). Irrelevance and independence axioms in quasi-Bayesian theory. In A. Hunter and S. Parsons, editors, *Symbolic and Quantitative Approaches to Reasoning and Uncertainty*, pages 128–136. Springer Verlag, Berlin, Germany.

Cozman, F. G. (2000). Credal networks. *Artificial Intelligence*, **120**, 199–233.

Curley, S. P. and Benson, P. G. (1994). Applying a cognitive perspective to probability construction. In G. Wright and P. Ayton, editors, *Subjective Probability*, pages 185–209. John Wiley & Sons, Chichester, UK.

Dague, P. (1993a). Numeric reasoning with relative orders of magnitude. In *Proceedings of the 11th National Conference on Artificial Intelligence*, pages 541–547, Menlo Park, CA. AAAI Press/MIT Press.

Dague, P. (1993b). Symbolic reasoning with relative orders of magnitude. In *Proceedings of the 13th International Joint Conference on Artificial Intelligence*, pages 1509–1514, San Mateo, CA. Morgan Kaufmann.

Dague, P., Raiman, O., and Devès, P. (1987). Troubleshooting: when modelling is the trouble. In *Proceedings of the 6th National Conference on Artificial Intelligence*, pages 600–605, Los Altos, CA. Morgan Kaufmann.

Dagum, P. and Luby, M. (1993). Approximating probabilistic inference in Bayesian belief networks is NP-hard. *Artificial Intelligence*, **60**, 141–153.

Dagum, P. and Luby, M. (1997). An optimal approximation algorithm for Bayesian inference. *Artificial Intelligence*, **93**, 1–27.

Dagum, P., Galper, A., and Horvitz, E. (1992). Dynamic network models for forecasting. In *Proceedings of the 8th Conference on Uncertainty in Artificial Intelligence*, pages 41–48, San Mateo, CA. Morgan Kaufmann.

D'Ambrosio, B. (1989). A hybrid approach to reasoning under uncertainty. In L. N. Kanal, T. S. Levitt, and

J. F. Lemmer, editors, *Uncertainty in Artificial Intelligence 3*, pages 267–283. Elsevier Science Publishers, Amsterdam, The Netherlands.

Darwiche, A. (1994a). CNETS: a computational environment for causal networks. Technical memorandum, Rockwell International, Palo Alto Laboratories.

Darwiche, A. (1994b). The CNETS user's manual. Technical memorandum, Rockwell International, Palo Alto Laboratories.

Darwiche, A. and Goldszmidt, M. (1994). On the relation between kappa calculus and probabilistic reasoning. In *Proceedings of the 10th Conference on Uncertainty in Artificial Intelligence*, pages 145–153, San Mateo, CA. Morgan Kaufmann.

Darwiche, A. and Pearl, J. (1994). Symbolic causal networks. In *Proceedings of the 12th National Conference on Artificial Intelligence*, pages 238–244, Menlo Park, CA. AAAI Press/MIT Press.

Darwiche, A. and Provan, G. (1997). Query DAGs: A practical paradigm for implementing belief network inference. *Journal of Artificial Intelligence Research*, **6**, 147–176.

Darwiche, A. Y. (1992). Objection-based causal networks. In *Proceedings of the 8th Conference on Uncertainty in Artificial Intelligence*, pages 67–73, San Mateo, CA. Morgan Kaufmann.

Darwiche, A. Y. (1993a). Argument calculus and networks. In *Proceedings of the 9th Conference on Uncertainty in Artificial Intelligence*, pages 420–427, San Mateo, CA. Morgan Kaufmann.

Darwiche, A. Y. (1993b). *A symbolic generalization of probability theory*. Ph.D. thesis, Stanford University.

Darwiche, A. Y. and Ginsberg, M. L. (1992). A symbolic generalization of probability theory. In *Proceedings of the 10th National Conference on Artificial Intelligence*, pages 622–627, San Mateo, CA. AAAI Press/MIT Press.

Davis, R. (1984). Diagnostic reasoning based on structure and behaviour. *Artificial Intelligence*, **24**, 347–410.

Dawes, R. M. (1979). The robust beauty of improper linear models in decision making. *American Psychologist*, **34**, 571–582.

Dawid, A. P. and Studený, M. (1999). Conditional products: an alternative approach to conditional independence. In *Proceedings of the 7th International Workshop on Artificial Intelligence and Statistics*, pages 32–40, San Francisco, CA. Morgan Kaufmann.

Dawkins, R. (1988). *The Blind Watchmaker*. Penguin, Harmondsworth, UK.

de Campos, L. M. and Moral, S. (1995). Independence concepts for convex sets of probabilities. In *Proceedings of the 11th Conference on Uncertainty in Artificial Intelligence*, pages 108–115, San Francisco, CA. Morgan Kaufmann.

de Campos, L. M., Huete, J. F., and Moral, S. (1994). Uncertainty management using probability intervals. In *Proceedings of the 5th International Conference on Information Processing and the Management of Uncertainty*, pages 431–436.

de Campos, L. M., Gebhardt, J., and Kruse, R. (1995). Axiomatic treatment of possibilistic independence. In C. Froidevaux and J. Kohlas, editors, *Symbolic and Quantitative Approaches to Reasoning and Uncertainty*, pages 77–88. Springer Verlag, Berlin, Germany.

de Finetti, B. (1975). *Theory of Probability: A Critical Introductory Treatment*. John Wiley & Sons, Chichester, UK.

de Kleer, J. (1984). How circuits work. *Artificial Intelligence*, **24**, 205–280.

de Kleer, J. (1986). An assumption-based TMS. *Artificial Intelligence*, **28**, 127–162.

de Kleer, J. and Brown, J. S. (1984). A qualitative physics based on confluences. *Artificial Intelligence*, **24**, 7–83.

de Kleer, J. and Williams, B. C. (1987). Diagnosing multiple faults. *Artificial Intelligence*, **32**, 97–130.

Deakin, M. A. B. (1992). The car and the goats. *Function*, **16**, 125–126.

Dean, T. and Boddy, M. (1988). An analysis of time-dependent planning. In *Proceedings of the 7th National Conference on Artificial Intelligence*, pages 49–54, San Mateo, CA. Morgan Kaufmann.

Delcher, A. L., Kasif, S., Goldberg, H. R., and Hsu, W. H. (1993a). Probabilistic prediction of protein secondary structure using causal networks. In *Proceedings of the 11th National Conference on Artificial Intelligence*, pages 316–321, Menlo Park, CA. AAAI Press.

Delcher, A. L., Kasif, S., Goldberg, H. R., and Hsu, W. H. (1993b). Protein structure modelling using probabilistic networks. In *Proceedings of the First International Conference on Intelligent Systems for Molecular Biology*, pages 109–117, Menlo Park, CA. AAAI Press.

Delgardo, M. and Moral, S. (1987). On the concept of possibility-probability consistency. *Fuzzy Sets and Systems*, **21**, 311–318.

Delgrande, J. P. and Schaub, T. (2000). Expressing preferences in default logic. *Artificial Intelligence*, **123**, 41–87.

Dempster, A. P. (1967). Upper and lower probabilities induced by a multi-valued mapping. *Annals of Mathematical Statistics*, **38**, 325–339.

Dempster, A. P. (1968). A generalisation of Bayesian inference (with discussion). *Journal of the Royal Statistical Society B*, **30**, 205–232.

Dempster, A. P. (1988). Comments on 'An inquiry into computer understanding' by Peter Cheeseman. *Computational Intelligence*, **4**, 72–73.

Deutsch-McLeish, M. (1991). A model for non-monotonic reasoning using Dempster's rule. In P. P. Bonissone, M. Henrion, L. N. Kanal, and J. F. Lemmer, editors, *Uncertainty in Artificial Intelligence 6*, pages 481–493. Elsevier Science Publishers, Amsterdam, The Netherlands.

Doherty, P., Łukaszewicz, W., and Szałas, A. (1995). Computing circumscription revisited: preliminary report. In *Proceedings of the 14th International Joint Conference on Artificial Intelligence*, pages 1502–1508, San Mateo, CA. Morgan Kaufmann.

Doherty, P., Łukaszewicz, W., and Szałas, A. (1996). General domain circumscription and its first-order reduction. In D. M. Gabbay and H. J. Ohlbach, editors, *Practical Reasoning*, pages 93–109. Springer Verlag, Berlin, Germany.

Dormoy, J.-L. and Raiman, O. (1988). Assembling a device. *Artificial Intelligence in Engineering*, **3**, 216–226.

Dostoevsky, F. (1966). *The Gambler*. Penguin, Harmondsworth, UK.

Doyle, J. (1979). A truth maintenance system. *Artificial Intelligence*, **12**, 231–272.

Draper, D. L. and Hanks, S. (1994). Localized partial evaluation of belief networks. In *Proceedings of the 10th Conference on Uncertainty in Artificial Intelligence*, pages 170–177, San Francisco, CA. Morgan Kaufmann.

Driankov, D. (1986). A calculus for belief-intervals representation of uncertainty. In B. Bouchon-Meunier and R. R. Yager, editors, *Uncertainty in Knowledge-Based Systems*, pages 205–216. Springer-Verlag, Berlin, Germany.

Druzdzel, M. J. (1993). *Probabilistic reasoning in decision support systems: from computation to common sense*. Ph.D. thesis, Department of Engineering and Public Policy, Carnegie Mellon University.

Druzdzel, M. J. and Henrion, M. (1993a). Belief propagation in qualitative probabilistic networks. In N. Piera Carreté and M. G. Singh, editors, *Qualitative Reasoning and Decision Technologies*, pages 452–460. CIMNE, Barcelona, Spain.

Druzdzel, M. J. and Henrion, M. (1993b). Efficient reasoning in qualitative probabilistic networks. In *Proceedings of the 11th National Conference on Artificial Intelligence*, pages 548–553, Menlo Park, CA. AAAI Press/MIT Press.

Druzdzel, M. J. and Henrion, M. (1993c). Intercausal reasoning with uninstantiated ancestor nodes. In *Proceedings of the 9th Conference on Uncertainty in Artificial Intelligence*, pages 317–325, San Mateo, CA. Morgan Kaufmann.

Druzdzel, M. J. and van der Gaag, L. (1995). Elicitation of probabilities for belief networks: combining qualitative and quantitative information. In P. Besnard and S. Hanks, editors, *Proceedings of the 11th Conference on Uncertainty in Artificial Intelligence*, pages 141–148, San Francisco, CA. Morgan Kaufmann.

Dubois, D. (1996). Personal communication.

Dubois, D. and Prade, H. (1979). Fuzzy real algebra: some results. *Fuzzy Sets and Systems*, **2**, 327–348.

Dubois, D. and Prade, H. (1980). *Fuzzy Sets and Systems: Theory and Applications*. Academic Press, New York, NY.

Dubois, D. and Prade, H. (1983). Upper and lower possibilities induced by a multivalued mapping. In *Fuzzy Information, Knowledge Representation and Decision Analysis*, pages 147–151, Oxford, UK. Pergamon Press.

Dubois, D. and Prade, H. (1986). The principle of minimum specificity as a basis for evidential reasoning. In B. Bouchon-Meunier and R. R. Yager, editors, *Uncertainty in Knowledge-Based Systems*, pages 75–84. Springer-Verlag, Berlin, Germany.

Dubois, D. and Prade, H. (1987a). The mean value of a fuzzy number. *Fuzzy Sets and Systems*, **24**, 279–300.

Dubois, D. and Prade, H. (1987b). Necessity measures and the resolution principle. *IEEE Transactions on Systems, Man and Cybernetics*, **17**, 474–478.

Dubois, D. and Prade, H. (1987c). A tentative comparison of numerical approximate reasoning methodologies. *International Journal of Man-Machine Studies*, **27**, 717–728.

Dubois, D. and Prade, H. (1988a). Comments on *an inquiry into computer understanding*. *Computational Intelligence*, **4**, 73–76.

Dubois, D. and Prade, H. (1988b). Default reasoning and possibility theory. *Artificial Intelligence*, **35**, 243–257.

Dubois, D. and Prade, H. (1988c). An introduction to possibilistic and fuzzy logics. In P. Smets, E. H. Mamdani, D. Dubois, and H. Prade, editors, *Non-Standard Logics for Automated Reasoning*, pages 287–313. Academic Press, London, UK.

Dubois, D. and Prade, H. (1988d). Modelling uncertainty and inductive inference: a survey of recent non-additive probability systems. *Acta Psychologica*, **68**, 53–78.

Dubois, D. and Prade, H. (1988e). On fuzzy syllogisms. *Computational Intelligence*, **4**, 171–179.

Dubois, D. and Prade, H. (1988f). *Possibility Theory: An Approach to Computerized Processing of Uncertainty*. Plenum Press, New York, NY.

Dubois, D. and Prade, H. (1988g). Representation and combination of uncertainty with belief functions and possibility measures. *Computational Intelligence*, **4**, 244–264.

Dubois, D. and Prade, H. (1989a). Fuzzy arithmetic in qualitative reasoning. In A. Blaquière, editor, *Modelling and Control of Systems in Engineering, Quantum Mechanics, Economics and Biosciences*, pages 458–467. Springer-Verlag, Berlin, Germany.

Dubois, D. and Prade, H. (1989b). Order of magnitude reasoning with fuzzy relations. *Revue D'Intelligence Artificielle*, **3**, 69–94.

Dubois, D. and Prade, H. (1990a). Consonant approximations of belief functions. *International Journal of Approximate Reasoning*, **4**, 419–449.

Dubois, D. and Prade, H. (1990b). The logical view of conditioning and its application to possibility and evidence theories. *International Journal of Approximate Reasoning*, **4**, 23–46.

Dubois, D. and Prade, H. (1990c). Modeling uncertain and vague knowledge in possibility and evidence theories. In R. D. Shachter, T. S. Levitt, L. N. Kanal, and J. F. Lemmer, editors, *Uncertainty in Artificial Intelligence 4*, pages 303–318. Elsevier Science Publishers, Amsterdam, The Netherlands.

Dubois, D. and Prade, H. (1990d). Resolution principles in possibilistic logic. *International Journal of Approximate Reasoning*, **4**, 1–21.

Dubois, D. and Prade, H. (1990e). Rough fuzzy sets and fuzzy rough sets. *International Journal of General Systems*, **17**, 191–209.

Dubois, D. and Prade, H. (1991a). Certainty and uncertainty of (vague) knowledge and generalised dependencies in fuzzy databases. In *Proceedings of the International Fuzzy Engineering Symposium*, pages 239–249.

Dubois, D. and Prade, H. (1991b). Conditional objects and non-monotonic reasoning. In *Proceedings of the 2nd International Conference on Principles of Knowledge Representation and Reasoning*, pages 175–185, San Mateo, CA. Morgan Kaufmann.

Dubois, D. and Prade, H. (1991c). Epistemic entrenchment and possibilistic logic. *Artificial Intelligence*, **50**, 223–239.

Dubois, D. and Prade, H. (1991d). Fuzzy sets in approximate reasoning, Part 1: Inference with possibility distributions. *Fuzzy Sets and Systems*, **40**, 143–202.

Dubois, D. and Prade, H. (1991e). Possibilistic logic, preferential models, non-monotonicity and related issues. In *Proceedings of the 12th International Joint Conference on Artificial Intelligence*, pages 24–30, San Mateo, CA. Morgan Kaufmann.

Dubois, D. and Prade, H. (1991f). Propagation in possibilistic hypergraphs. In B. Bouchon-Meunier, R. R. Yager, and L. A. Zadeh, editors, *Uncertainty in Knowledge Bases*, pages 250–259. Springer-Verlag, Berlin, Germany.

Dubois, D. and Prade, H. (1991g). Semantical considerations on order of magnitude reasoning. In M. G. Singh and L. Travé-Massuyès, editors, *Decision Support Systems and Qualitative Reasoning*, pages 223–228. North Holland, Amsterdam, The Netherlands.

Dubois, D. and Prade, H. (1991h). Updating with belief functions, ordinal conditional functions and possibility measures. In P. P. Bonissone, M. Henrion, L. N. Kanal, and J. F. Lemmer, editors, *Uncertainty in Artificial Intelligence 6*, pages 311–329. Elsevier Science Publishers, Amsterdam, The Netherlands.

Dubois, D. and Prade, H. (1992a). Evidence, knowledge, and belief functions. *International Journal of Approximate Reasoning*, **6**, 295–319.

Dubois, D. and Prade, H. (1992b). When upper probabilities are possibility measures. *Fuzzy Sets and Systems*, **49**, 65–74.

Dubois, D. and Prade, H. (1993). Possibilistic abduction. In B. Bouchon-Meunier, L. Valverde, and R. R. Yager, editors, *IPMU '92—Advanced Methods in Artificial Intelligence*, pages 3–12. Springer-Verlag, Berlin, Germany.

Dubois, D. and Prade, H. (1994). Can we enforce compositionality in uncertainty calculi? In *Proceedings of the 12th National Conference on Artificial Intelligence*, pages 149–154, Menlo Park, CA. AAAI Press/MIT Press.

Dubois, D., Lang, J., and Prade, H. (1987). Theorem proving under uncertainty—a possibility-theory based approach. In *Proceedings of the 10th International Joint Conference on Artificial Intelligence*, pages 984–986, Los Altos, CA. Morgan Kaufmann.

Dubois, D., Lang, J., and Prade, H. (1989). Automated reasoning using possibilistic logic: semantics, belief revision and variable certainty weights. In *Proceedings of the 5th Workshop on Uncertainty in Artificial Intelligence*, pages 81–87, Mountain View, CA. Association for Uncertainty in AI.

Dubois, D., Lang, J., and Prade, H. (1990a). POSLOG, an inference system based on possibilistic logic. In *Proceedings of the North American Fuzzy Information Processing Society Conference*, pages 177–180.

Dubois, D., Lang, J., and Prade, H. (1990b). A possibilistic assumption-based truth maintenance system with uncertain justifications, and its application to belief revision. In J. P. Martins and M. Reinfrank, editors, *Truth Maintenance Systems*, pages 87–106, Berlin, Germany. Springer Verlag.

Dubois, D., Lang, J., and Prade, H. (1991a). Fuzzy sets in approximate reasoning, Part 2: Logical approaches. *Fuzzy Sets and Systems*, **40**, 203–244.

Dubois, D., Lang, J., and Prade, H. (1991b). Towards possibilistic logic programming. In *Proceedings of the 8th International Conference on Logic Programming*, pages 581–595, Cambridge, MA. MIT Press.

Dubois, D., Prade, H., Godó, L., and Lòpez de Mántaras, R. (1992). A symbolic approach to reasoning with linguistic quantifiers. In *Proceedings of the 8th Conference on Uncertainty in Artificial Intelligence*.

Dubois, D., Lang, J., and Prade, H. (1994a). Automated reasoning using possibilistic logic: semantics, belief revision and variable certainty weights. *IEEE Transactions on Knowledge and Data Engineering*, **6**, 64–71.

Dubois, D., Fariñas del Cerro, L., Herzig, A., and Prade, H. (1994b). An ordinal view of independence with application to plausible reasoning. In *Proceedings of the 10th Conference on Uncertainty in Artificial Intelligence*, pages 195–203, San Mateo, CA. Morgan Kaufmann.

Dubois, D., Prade, H., and Smets, P. (1994c). Partial truth is not uncertainty. *IEEE Expert*, **9**(4), 15–19.

DuCharme, W. M. and Peterson, C. R. (1968). Intuitive inference about normally distributed populations. *Journal of Experimental Psychology*, **78**, 269–275.

Duda, R. O., Hart, P. E., and Nilsson, N. J. (1976). Subjective Bayesian methods for a rule-based inference system. In *Proceedings of the National Computer Conference*, pages 1075–1082.

Dung, P. M. (1993). On the acceptability of arguments and its fundamental role in nonmonotonic reasoning and logic programming. In *Proceedings of the 13th International Joint Conference on Artificial Intelligence*, pages 852–857, San Mateo, CA. Morgan Kaufmann.

Dung, P. M. (1995). On the acceptability of arguments and its fundamental role in nonmonotonic reasoning, logic programming and *n*-person games. *Artificial Intelligence*, **77**, 321–357.

Eco, U. (1998). *Faith in Fakes: Travels in Hyperreality*. Vintage, London.

Eddy, D. M. (1982). Probabilistic reasoning in medicine: problems and opportunities. In D. Kahneman, P. Slovic, and A. Tversky, editors, *Judgement under uncertainty: Heuristics and biases*, pages 249–267. Cambridge University Press, Cambridge.

Edwards, W. (1954). The theory of decision making. *Psychological Bulletin*, **51**, 380–417.

Edwards, W. (1968). Conservatism in human information processing. In B. Kleinmuntz, editor, *Formal Representation of Human Judgment*, pages 17–52. John Wiley & Sons, New York, NY.

Eiter, T. and Lukasiewicz, T. (2000). Default reasoning from conditional knowledge bases: complexity and tractable cases. *Artificial Intelligence*, **124**, 169–241.

Elkan, C. (1993). The paradoxical success of fuzzy logic. In *Proceedings of the 11th National Conference on Artificial Intelligence*, pages 698–703, Cambridge, MA. AAAI Press/MIT Press.

Elkan, C. (1994a). The paradoxical controversy over fuzzy logic. *IEEE Expert*, **9**(4), 47–49.

Elkan, C. (1994b). The paradoxical success of fuzzy logic. *IEEE Expert*, **9**(4), 3–8.

Ellsberg, D. (1961). Risk, ambiguity, and the Savage axioms. *Quarterly Journal of Economics*, **75**, 643–669.

Elvang-Gøransson, M. and Hunter, A. (1995). Argumentative logics: reasoning with classically inconsistent information. *Data and Knowledge Engineering*, **16**, 125–145.

Elvang-Gøransson, M., Krause, P., and Fox, J. (1993). Dialectic reasoning with inconsistent information. In *Proceedings of the 9th Conference on Uncertainty in Artificial Intelligence*, pages 114–121, San Mateo, CA. Morgan Kaufmann.

Epstein, R. (1992). The quest for the thinking computer. *AI Magazine*, **13**(2), 81–95.

Etherington, D. W. (1987). Relating default logic and circumscription. In *Proceedings of the 10th International Joint Conference on Artificial Intelligence*, pages 489–494, Los Altos, CA. Morgan Kaufmann.

Etherington, D. W. (1988). *Reasoning with Incomplete Information*. Pitman, London, UK.

Even, S. (1979). *Graph Algorithms*. Pitman, London, UK.

Fagin, R. and Halpern, J. (1991). A new approach to updating beliefs. In P. P. Bonissone, M. Henrion, L. N. Kanal, and J. F. Lemmer, editors, *Uncertainty in Artificial Intelligence 6*, pages 347–374. Elsevier Science Publishers, Amsterdam, The Netherlands.

Falkenheiner, B. and Forbus, K. D. (1988). Setting up large-scale qualitative models. In *Proceedings of the 7th National Conference on Artificial Intelligence*, pages 301–306, San Mateo, CA. Morgan Kaufmann.

Fargier, H., Lang, J., Martin-Clouaire, R., and Schiex, T. (1995). A constraint satisfaction framework for decision under uncertainty. In *Proceedings of the 11th Conference on Uncertainty in Artificial Intelligence*, pages 167–174, San Francisco, CA. Morgan Kaufman.

Fariñas del Cerro, L. and Herzig, A. (1994). Possibility and independence. In *Proceedings of the 5th International Conference on Information Processing and the Management of Uncertainty*, pages 820–825.

Fariñas del Cerro, L. and Orłowska, E. (1985). DAL—a logic for data analysis. *Theoretical Computer Science*, **36**, 251–264.

Farley, A. M. and Lin, K.-P. (1991). Qualitative reasoning in microeconomics: an example. In M. G. Singh and L. Travé-Massuyès, editors, *Decision Support Systems and Qualitative Reasoning*, pages 303–306. Elsevier Science Publishers B. V., Amsterdam, The Netherlands.

Farreny, H. and Prade, H. (1985). Default and inexact reasoning with possibility degrees. *IEEE Transactions on Systems, Man, and Cybernetics*, **16**(2), 270–276.

Féray Beaumont, S. (1991). Qualitative model-based reasoning: an application to distillation process. In M. G. Singh and L. Travé-Massuyès, editors, *Decision Support Systems and Qualitative Reasoning*, pages 203–208. Elsevier Science Publishers B. V., Amsterdam, The Netherlands.

Fertig, K. W. and Breese, J. S. (1990). Interval influence diagrams. In M. Henrion, R. D. Shachter, L. N. Kanal, and J. F. Lemmer, editors, *Uncertainty in Artificial Intelligence 5*, pages 149–161. Elsevier Science Publishers, Amsterdam, The Netherlands.

Flowers, M., McGuire, R., and Birnbaum, L. (1982). Adversary arguments and the logic of personal attacks. In W. G. Lehnert and M. H. Ringle, editors, *Strategies for natural language processing*, pages 275–294. Lawrence Erblaum Associates, Hillsdale, New Jersey.

Fonck, P. (1992). Propagating uncertainty in a directed acyclic graph. In *Proceedings of the 4th International Conference on Information Processing and the Management of Uncertainty*, pages 17–20, Palma, Mallorca. Universitat de les Illes Balears.

Fonck, P. (1994). Conditional independence in possibility theory. In *Proceedings of the 10th Conference on Uncertainty in Artificial Intelligence*, pages 221–226, San Mateo, CA. Morgan Kaufmann.

Fonck, P. and Straszecka, E. (1991). Building influence networks in the framework of possibility theory. *Annales Univ. Sci. Budapest, Sect. Comp.*, **12**, 101–106.

Forbus, K. D. (1984). Qualitative process theory. *Artificial Intelligence*, **24**, 85–168.

Forbus, K. D. and de Kleer, J. (1993). *Building Problem Solvers*. MIT Press, Cambridge, MA.

Fox, J. (1981). Towards a reconciliation of fuzzy logic and standard logic. *International Journal of Man-Machine Studies*, **15**, 213–220.

Fox, J. (1986). Three arguments for extending the framework of probability. In L. N. Kanal and J. F. Lemmer, editors, *Uncertainty in Artificial Intelligence*, pages 447–458. Elsevier Science Publishers, Amsterdam, The Netherlands.

Fox, J. and Das, S. (1996). A unified framework for hypothetical and practical reasoning (2): lessons from medical applications. In D. M. Gabbay and H. J. Ohlbach, editors, *Formal and Applied Practical Reasoning*, pages 73–92. Springer Verlag, Berlin, Germany.

Fox, J. and Krause, P. J. (1990). Combining symbolic and numerical methods for defeasible reasoning. In *Proceedings of the IEE Colloquium on Reasoning Under Uncertainty*, London, UK. IEE.

Fox, J., Barber, D., and Bardhan, K. D. (1980). Alternatives to Bayes? A quantitative comparison with rule-based diagnostic inference. *Methods of Information in Medicine*, **19**, 210–215.

Fox, J., Myers, C. D., Greaves, M. F., and Pegram, S. (1985). Knowledge acquisition for expert systems: experience in leukaemia diagnosis. *Methods of Information in Medicine*, **24**, 65–72.

Fox, J., Krause, P., and Ambler, S. (1992). Arguments, contradictions and practical reasoning. In *Proceedings of the 10th European Conference on Artificial Intelligence*, pages 623–627, Chichester, UK. John Wiley & Sons.

Frisch, A. M. and Haddaway, P. (1994). Anytime deduction for probabilistic logic. *Artificial Intelligence*, **69**, 93–122.

Froidevaux, C. and Grossetête, C. (1990). Graded default theories for uncertainty. In *Proceedings of the 9th European Conference on Artificial Intelligence*, pages 283–288, London, UK. Pitman.

Froidevaux, C. and Mengin, J. (1990). A theorem prover for free graded default theories. In *Proceedings of the Workshop of Esprit Basic Research Action 3085, DRUMS*, pages 194–205.

Froidevaux, C. and Mengin, J. (1994). Default logics: a unified view. *Computational Intelligence*, **10**, 332–368.

Fung, R. and Del Favero, B. (1995). Applying Bayesian networks to information retrieval. *Communications of the ACM*, **38**, 42–48,57.

Gabbay, D. (1982). Intuitionistic basis for non-monotonic logic. In D. W. Loveland, editor, *6th Conference on Automated Deduction*, pages 260–273. Springer Verlag, Berlin, Germany.

Gabbay, D. (1985). Theoretical foundations for non-monotonic reasoning in expert systems. In *Proceedings NATO Advanced Study Institute on Logics and Models of Concurrent Systems*, pages 439–457, Berlin, Germany. Springer Verlag.

Gaeth, G. J. and Shanteau, J. (1986). Reducing the influence of irrelevant information on experienced decision makers. In H. R. Arkes and K. R. Hammond, editors, *Judgment and Decision Making: An Interdisciplinary Reader*, pages 449–465. Cambridge University Press, Cambridge, UK.

Gallie, W. B. (1957). Uncertainty as a philosophical problem: 1. In C. F. Carter, G. P. Meredith, and G. L. S. Shackle, editors, *Uncertainty and business decisions: The logic, philosophy and psychology of business decision-making under uncertainty*, pages 1–11. Liverpool University Press.

Gao, Y. and Durrant-Whyte, H. F. (1994). Integrating qualitative reasoning for numerical data fusion tasks. In *Proceedings of the 11th European Conference on Artificial Intelligence*, pages 682–686, Chichester, UK. John Wiley & Sons.

Garbolino, P. (1996). Qualitative reasoning in Bayesian networks. *Mathware & Soft Computing*, **3**, 125–135.

Gärdenfors, P. (1988). *Knowledge in Flux: Modelling the Dynamics of Epistemic States*. MIT Press, Cambridge, MA.

Garriba, S., Lucia, A., Servida, A., and Volta, G. (1988). Fuzzy measures of uncertainty for evaluating nondestructive crack inspection. *Structural Safety*, **5**, 187–204.

Gaspin, C. and Regin, J.-C. (1997). Application of maximal constraint satisfaction problems to RNA folding. In *Proceedings of the CP97 Workshop on Constraints and Bioinformatics and Biocomputing*.

Gaspin, C. and Westhof, E. (1995). An interactive framework for RNA secondary structure prediction with a dynamical treatment of constraints. *Journal of Molecular Biology*, **254**, 163–174.

Gaspin, C., Bessière, C., Moisan, A., and Schiex, T. (1995). Saisfaction de contraintes et biologie moléculaire. *Revue d'Intelligence Artificielle*, **9**.

Gebhardt, J. and Kruse, R. (1993a). The context model: an integrating view of vagueness and uncertainty. *International Journal of Approximate Reasoning*, **9**, 283–314.

Gebhardt, J. and Kruse, R. (1993b). A new approach to semantic aspects of possibilistic reasoning. In M. Clarke, R. Kruse, and S. Moral, editors, *Symbolic and Quantitative Approaches to Reasoning and Uncertainty*, pages 151–159. Springer Verlag, Berlin, Germany.

Gebhardt, J. and Kruse, R. (1994). A numerical framework for possibilistic abduction. In *Proceedings of the 5th International Conference on Information Processing and the Management of Uncertainty*, pages 809–814.

Gebhardt, J. and Kruse, R. (1995). Learning possibilistic networks from data. In *Proceedings of the 5th International Workshop on AI and Statistics*.

Geffner, H. (1990). Causal theories for nonmonotonic reasoning. In *Proceedings of the 9th National Conference on Artificial Intelligence*, pages 524–530, San Mateo, CA. AAAI Press/MIT Press.

Geffner, H. (1994). Causal default reasoning: principles and algorithms. In *Proceedings of the 12th National Conference on Artificial Intelligence*, pages 245–250, Menlo Park, CA. AAAI Press/MIT Press.

Geffner, H. (1996). A formal framework for causal modelling and argumentation. In D. M. Gabbay and H. J. Ohlbach, editors, *Practical Reasoning*, pages 208–222. Springer Verlag, Berlin, Germany.

Geffner, H. and Pearl, J. (1992). Conditional entailment: bridging two approaches to default reasoning. *Artificial Intelligence*, **53**, 209–244.

Geiger, D. and Heckerman, D. (1991). Advances in probabilistic reasoning. In *Proceedings of the 7th Conference on Uncertainty in Artificial Intelligence*, pages 118–126, San Mateo, CA. Morgan Kaufmann.

Geiger, D. and Heckerman, D. (1996). Knowledge representation and inference in similarity networks and Bayesian multinets. *Artificial Intelligence*, **82**, 45–74.

Geiger, D., Verma, T., and Pearl, J. (1990). *d*-separation: from theorems to algorithms. In M. Henrion, R. D. Shachter, L. N. Kanal, and J. F. Lemmer, editors, *Uncertainty in Artificial Intelligence 5*, pages 139–148. Elsevier Science Publishers, Amsterdam, The Netherlands.

Genesereth, M. (1984). The use of design desciptions in automated diagnosis. *Artificial Intelligence*, **24**, 411–436.

Giang, P. H. and Shenoy, P. P. (1999). On transformations between probability and Spohnian disbelief functions. In K. B. Laskey and H. Prade, editors, *Proceedings of the 15th Conference on Uncertainty in Artificial Intelligence*, pages 236–244, San Francisco, CA. Morgan Kaufmann.

Gibson, W. (1993). *Neuromancer*. HarperCollins, London, UK.

Gigerenzer, G. (1994). Why the distinction between single-event probabilities and frequencies is important for psychology (and vice versa). In G. Wright and P. Ayton, editors, *Subjective Probability*, pages 130–161. John Wiley & Sons, Chichester, UK.

Gigerenzer, G., Hell, W., and Blank, H. (1988a). Presentation and content: The use of base rates as a continuous variable. *Journal of Experimental Psychology*, **14**, 513–525.

Gigerenzer, G., Hell, W., and Blank, H. (1988b). Probabilistic mental models: a Brunswikian theory of confidence. *Psychology Review*, **98**, 506–528.

Ginsberg, M. (1984). Non-monotonic reasoning using Dempster's rule. In *Proceedings of the 4th National Conference on Artificial Intelligence*, pages 112–119, Los Altos, CA. William Kaufmann.

Ginsberg, M. L. (1985). Does probability have a place in non-monotonic reasoning? In *Proceedings of the 9th International Joint Conference on Artificial Intelligence*, pages 107–110, Los Altos, CA. Morgan Kaufmann.

Ginsberg, M. L., editor (1987). *Readings in Nonmonotonic Reasoning*. Morgan Kaufmann, San Mateo, CA.

Ginsberg, M. L. (1988). Multivalued logics: a uniform approach to reasoing in artificial intelligence. *Computational Intelligence*, **4**, 265–316.

Ginsberg, M. L. (1989). A circumscriptive theorem prover. *Artificial Intelligence*, **39**, 209–230.

Gleick, J. (1992). *Genius: Richard Feynman and modern physics*. Little, Brown, London, UK.

Glesner, S. and Koller, D. (1995). Constructing flexible dynamic belief networks from first-order probabilistic knowledge bases. In C. Froidevaux and J. Kohlas, editors, *Symbolic and Quantitative Approaches to Reasoning and Uncertainty*, pages 217–226. Springer Verlag, Berlin, Germany.

Glowinski, A., O'Neil, M., and Fox, J. (1989). Design of a generic information system and its application to primary care. In *Proceedings of the European Conference on Artificial Intelligence in Medicine*, pages 221–233. Springer-Verlag.

Goldman, R. P. and Breese, J. S. (1992). Integrating model construction and evaluation. In *Proceedings of the 8th Conference on Uncertainty in Artificial Intelligence*, pages 104–111, San Mateo, CA. Morgan Kaufmann.

Goldman, R. P. and Charniak, E. (1990). Dynamic construction of belief networks. In *Proceedings of the 6th Conference on Uncertainty in Artificial Intelligence*, pages 90–97, Mountain View, CA. Association for Uncertainty in AI.

Goldszmidt, M. and Pearl, J. (1991a). On the consistency of defeasible databases. *Artificial Intelligence*, **52**, 121–149.

Goldszmidt, M. and Pearl, J. (1991b). System-Z^+: a formalism for reasoning with variable-strength defaults. In *Proceedings of the 10th National Conference on Artificial Intelligence*, pages 399–404, Menlo Park, CA. AAAI Press/MIT Press.

Goldszmidt, M. and Pearl, J. (1992). Reasoning with qualitative probabilities can be tractable. In *Proceedings of the 8th Conference on Uncertainty in Artificial Intelligence*, pages 112–120, San Mateo, CA. Morgan Kaufmann.

Goldszmidt, M. and Pearl, J. (1996). Qualitative probabilities for default reasoning, belief revision and causal modelling. *Artificial Intelligence*, **84**, 57–112.

Goldszmidt, M., Morris, P., and Pearl, J. (1990). A maximum entropy approach to nonmonotonic reasoning. In *Proceedings of the 9th National Conference on Artificial Intelligence*, pages 646–652, Menlo Park, CA. AAAI Press/MIT Press.

González, J. C. (1989). *Arquitectura para sistemas expertos con razonamiento aproximado*. Ph.D. thesis, Universidad Politécnica de Madrid.

González, J. C. and Fernández, G. (1990a). ENAMORA: A general framework for approximate reasoning methodologies. In *Proceedings of the North American Fuzzy Information Processing Society Conference*.

González, J. C. and Fernández, G. (1990b). A metalevel architecture for expert systems with approximate reasoning. Technical Report UPM/DIT/LIA 2-90, Universidad Politécnica de Madrid.

Good, I. J. (1950). *Probability and the Weighing of Evidence*. Charles Griffin, London, UK.

Goodman, I. R. and Nguyen, H. T. (1991). Foundations for an algebraic theory of conditioning. *Fuzzy Sets and Systems*, **42**, 103–118.

Gordon, J. and Shortliffe, E. H. (1985). A method for managing evidential reasoning in a hierarchical hypothesis space. *Artificial Intelligence*, **26**, 323–357.

Gottlob, G. (1993). The power of beliefs or translating default logic into standard autoepistemic logic. In *Proceedings of the 13th International Joint Conference on Artificial Intelligence*, pages 563–569, San Mateo, CA. Morgan Kaufmann.

Goyal, N. and Shoham, Y. (1993). Reasoning precisely with vague concepts. In *Proceedings of the 11th National Conference on Artificial Intelligence*, pages 426–431, Menlo Park, CA. AAAI Press/MIT Press.

Gribben, J. (1995). *Schrödinger's Kittens: and the search for reality*. Wiedenfield and Nicolson, London.

Grosof, B. N. (1988). Non-monotonicity in probabilistic reasoning. In J. F. Lemmer and L. N. Kanal, editors, *Uncertainty in Artificial Intelligence 2*, pages 237–249. Elsevier Science Publishers, Amsterdam, The Netherlands.

Grove, A. J. and Halpern, J. Y. (1997). Probability update: conditioning versus cross-entropy. In D. Geiger and P. P. Shenoy, editors, *Proceedings of the 13th Conference on Uncertainty in Artificial Intelligence*, pages 208–214, San Francisco, CA. Morgan Kaufmann.

Grzymala-Busse, J. (1987). Rough set and Dempster-Shafer approaches to knowledge acquisition under uncertainty—a comparison. Technical report, Department of Computer Science, University of Kansas.

Guan, J. W. and Bell, D. A. (1993). A generalisation of the Dempster-Shafer theory. In *Proceedings of the 13th International Joint Conference on Artificial Intelligence*, pages 592–597, San Mateo, CA. Morgan Kaufmann.

Güntzer, U., Kießling, W., and Thöne, H. (1991). New directions for uncertainty reasoning in deductive databases. In *Proceedings ACM SIGMOD International Conference on the Management of Data*, pages 178–187.

Gupta, C. P. (1993). A note on the transformation of possibilistic information into probabilistic information for investment decisions. *Fuzzy Sets and Systems*, **56**, 175–182.

Gustafon, D. H., Tianen, B., and Greist, J. H. (1986). A computer-based system for identifying suicide attemptors. In H. R. Arkes and K. R. Hammond, editors, *Judgment and Decision Making: An Interdisciplinary Reader*, pages 432–445. Cambridge University Press, Cambridge, UK.

Haack, S. (1979). Do we need fuzzy logic? *International Journal of Man-Machine Studies*, **11**, 437–445.

Haenni, R. (1996). *Propositional argumentation systems and symbolic evidence theory*. Ph.D. thesis, Institut für Informatik,Universität Freiburg.

Haenni, R. (1998). Modelling uncertainty with propositional assumption-based systems. In A. Hunter and S. Parsons, editors, *Applications of Uncertainty Formalisms*, pages 446–470. Springer Verlag, Berlin, Germany.

Halpern, J. and Fagin, R. (1992). Two views of belief: belief as generalized probability and belief as evidence. *Artificial Intelligence*, **54**, 275–317.

Halpern, J. Y. (1989). An analysis of the first-order logics of probability. In *Proceedings of the 11th International Joint Conference on Artificial Intelligence*, pages 1375–1381, San Mateo, CA. Morgan Kaufmann.

Halpern, J. Y. (1990). An analysis of the first-order logics of probability. *Artificial Intelligence*, **46**, 311–350.

Halpern, J. Y. (1999a). A counterexample to theorems of Cox and Fine. *Journal of Artificial Intelligence Research*, **10**, 67–85.

Halpern, J. Y. (1999b). Cox's theorem revisited. *Journal of Artificial Intelligence Research*, **11**, 429–435.

Hangos, K. M., Csáki, Z., and Bay Jørgensen, S. (1992). Qualitative model-based intelligent control of a distillation column. *Engineering Applications of Artificial Intelligence*, **5**, 431–440.

Haussler, D., Krogh, A., Mian, I. S., and Sjölander, K. (1993). Protein modelling using Hidden Markov Models: Analysis of globins. In *Proceedings of the 22nd Hawaiian International Conference on System Sciences*, pages 792–802, Los Alamitos, CA. IEEE Computer Society Press.

Hayes, P. (1978). The naive physics manifesto. In D. Michie, editor, *Expert Systems in the Microelectronic Age*, pages 242–270. Edinburgh University Press, Edinburgh.

Hayes, P. (1985a). Naive physics I: Ontology for liquids. In J. R. Hobbs and R. C. Moore, editors, *Formal Theories of the Commonsense World*, pages 71–107. Ablex Publishing Corporation, New Jersey.

Hayes, P. (1985b). The second naive physics manifesto. In J. R. Hobbs and R. C. Moore, editors, *Formal Theories of the Commonsense World*, pages 1–36. Ablex Publishing Corporation, New Jersey.

Hayes-Roth, B., Buchanan, B., Lichtarge, O., Hewett, M., Altman, R., Brinkley, J., Cornelius, C., Duncan, B., and Jardetzky, O. (1986). PROTEAN: deriving protein structure from constraints. In *Proceedings of the 5th National Conference on Artificial Intelligence*, pages 904–909, Los Altos, CA. Morgan Kaufmann.

Heckerman, D. (1995). A Bayesian approach to learning causal networks. In *Proceedings of the 11th Conference on Uncertainty in Artificial Intelligence*, pages 285–295, San Francisco, CA. Morgan Kaufmann.

Heckerman, D., Geiger, D., and Chickering, D. (1994). Learning Bayesian networks: the combination of knowledge and statistical data. In *Proceedings of the 10th Conference on Uncertainty in Artificial Intelligence*, pages 293–301, San Francisco, CA. Morgan Kaufmann.

Heckerman, D., Breese, J. S., and Rommelse, K. (1995). Decision-theoretic troubleshooting. *Communications of the ACM*, **38**, 49–57.

Heckerman, D. E. (1986). Probability interpretation for MYCIN's certainty factors. In L. N. Kanal and J. F. Lemmer, editors, *Uncertainty in Artificial Intelligence*, pages 167–196. Elsevier Science Publishers, Amsterdam, The Netherlands.

Heckerman, D. E. (1990a). An empirical comparison of three inference methods. In R. D. Shachter, T. S. Levitt, L. N. Kanal, and J. F. Lemmer, editors, *Uncertainty in Artificial Intelligence 4*, pages 283–302. Elsevier Science Publishers B.V., Amsterdam, The Netherlands.

Heckerman, D. E. (1990b). Probabilistic similarity networks. *Networks*, **20**, 607–636.

Heckerman, D. E. (1991a). *Probabilistic Similarity Networks*. MIT Press, Cambridge, MA.

Heckerman, D. E. (1991b). Similarity networks for the construction of multiple-fault belief networks. In P. P. Bonissone, M. Henrion, L. N. Kanal, and J. F. Lemmer, editors, *Uncertainty in Artificial Intelligence 6*, pages 51–64. Elsevier Science Publishers, Amsterdam, The Netherlands.

Heckerman, D. E. and Horvitz, E. J. (1987). On the expressiveness of rule-based systems for reasoning under uncertainty. In *Proceedings of the 6th National Conference on Artificial Intelligence*, pages 121–126, Los Altos, CA. Morgan Kaufmann.

Heckerman, D. E. and Horvitz, E. J. (1988). The myth of modularity in rule based systems. In J. F. Lemmer and L. N. Kanal, editors, *Uncertainty in Artificial Intelligence 2*, pages 23–34. Elsevier Science Publishers, Amsterdam, The Netherlands.

Heckerman, D. E. and Nathwani, B. N. (1992). Towards normative expert systems: Part II Probability-based representations for efficient knowledge acquisition and interface. *Methods of Information in Medicine*, **31**, 106–116.

Heckerman, D. E. and Shachter, R. (1994a). A decision-based view of causality. In *Proceedings of the Tenth Conference on Uncertainty in Artificial Intelligence*, pages 302–310, San Fransisco, CA. Morgan Kaufmann.

Heckerman, D. E. and Shachter, R. (1994b). A decision-based view of causality. Technical Report MSR-TR-11, Microsoft Research.

Heckerman, D. E. and Shwe, M. (1993). Diagnosis of multiple faults: a sensitivity analysis. In *Proceedings of the Ninth Conference on Uncertainty in Artificial Intelligence*, pages 80–87, San Mateo, CA. Morgan Kaufmann.

Heckerman, D. E., Horvitz, E. J., and Nathwani, B. N. (1992). Towards normative expert systems: Part I The Pathfinder project. *Methods of Information in Medicine*, **31**, 90–105.

Henrion, M. (1988). Propagating uncertainty in Bayesian networks by probabilistic logic sampling. In J. F. Lemmer and L. N. Kanal, editors, *Uncertainty in Artificial Intelligence 2*, pages 149–163. Elsevier Science Publishers, Amsterdam, The Netherlands.

Henrion, M. (1989). Some practical issues in constructing belief networks. In L. N. Kanal, T. S. Levitt, and J. F. Lemmer, editors, *Uncertainty in Artificial Intelligence 3*, pages 161–173. Elsevier Science Publishers, Amsterdam, The Netherlands.

Henrion, M. (1990). An introduction to algorithms for inference in belief nets. In M. Henrion, R. D. Shachter, L. N. Kanal, and J. F. Lemmer, editors, *Uncertainty in Artificial Intelligence 5*, pages 129–138. Elsevier Science Publishers, Amsterdam, The Netherlands.

Henrion, M. (1993). Personal communication.

Henrion, M. and Cooley, D. R. (1987). An experimental comparison of knowledge engineering for expert systems and for decision analysis. In *Proceedings of the 6th National Conference on Artificial Intelligence*, pages 471–476, Los Altos, CA. Morgan Kaufmann.

Henrion, M. and Druzdzel, M. J. (1990). Qualitative propagation and scenario-based approaches to explanation of probabilistic reasoning. In *Proceedings of the 6th Conference on Uncertainty in Artificial Intelligence*, pages 10–20, Mountain View, CA. Association for Uncertainty in AI.

Henrion, M. and Druzdzel, M. J. (1991). Qualitative propagation and scenario-based schemes for explaining probabilistic reasoning. In P. P. Bonissone, M. Henrion, L. N. Kanal, and J. F. Lemmer, editors, *Uncertainty in Artificial Intelligence 6*, pages 17–32. Elsevier Science Publishers, Amsterdam, The Netherlands.

Henrion, M. and Morgan, M. G. (1985). A computer aid for risk and other policy analysis. *Risk Analysis*, **5**, 195–208.

Henrion, M., Breese, J. S., and Horvitz, E. J. (1991). Decision analysis and expert systems. *AI Magazine*, **12**(4),

64–91.

Henrion, M., Provan, G., Favero, B. D., and Sanders, G. (1994). An experimental comparison of numerical and qualitative probabilistic reasoning. In *Proceedings of the 10th Conference on Uncertainty in Artificial Intelligence*, pages 319–326, San Fransisco, CA. Morgan Kaufmann.

Herskovits, E. and Cooper, G. F. (1990). Kutató: an entropy driven system for construction of probabilistic expert systems from databases. In *Proceedings of the 6th Conference on Uncertainty in Artificial Intelligence*, pages 54–62, Mountain View, CA. Association for Uncertainty in AI.

Hisdal, E. (1978). Conditional possibilities, independence and non-interaction distributions. *Fuzzy Sets and Systems*, **1**, 283–299.

Hofstadter, D. (1986). *Metamagical Themas*. Penguin, London, UK.

Horsch, M. C. and Poole, D. (1990). A dynamic approach to probabilistic inference using Bayesian networks. In *Proceedings of the 6th Conference on Uncertainty in Artificial Intelligence*, pages 155–161, Mountain View, CA. Association for Uncertainty in AI.

Horvitz, E., Ruokangas, C., Srinivas, S., and Barry, M. (1992). A decision-theoretic approach to the display of information for time-critical decisions: Project Vista. Technical Memorandum 96, Rockwell International Science Center, Palo Alto Laboratory.

Horvitz, E. J., Heckerman, D. E., and Langlotz, C. P. (1986). A framework for comparing alternative formalisms for plausible reasoning. In *Proceedings of the 5th National Conference on Artificial Intelligence*, pages 210–214, Los Altos, CA. Morgan Kaufmann.

Horvitz, E. J., Breese, J., and Henrion, M. (1988). Decision theory in expert systems and artificial intelligence. *International Journal of Approximate Reasoning*, **2**, 247–302.

Horvitz, E. J., Suermondt, H. J., and Cooper, G. F. (1989). Bounded conditioning: flexible inference for decisions under scarce resources. In *Proceedings of the 5th Workshop on Uncertainty in Artificial Intelligence*, pages 182–193, Mountain View, CA. Association for Uncertainty in AI.

Horvorka, R., Andreassen, S., Benn, J. J., Olesen, K. G., and Carson, E. R. (1992). Causal probabilistic modeling—an illustration of its role in the management of chronic diseases. *IBM Systems Journal*, **31**, 635–648.

Howard, R. A. (1990). From influence to relevance to knowledge. In R. M. Oliver and J. Q. Smith, editors, *Influence Diagrams, Belief Nets and Decision Analysis*, pages 3–23. John Wiley & Sons, Chichester, UK.

Howard, R. A. and Matheson, J. E. (1984). Influence diagrams. In R. A. Howard and J. E. Matheson, editors, *Readings on the Principles and Applications of Decision Analysis*, pages 719–762. Strategic Decisions Group, Menlo Park, CA.

Hrycej, T. (1990). Gibbs sampling in Bayesian networks. *Artificial Intelligence*, **46**, 351–363.

Hsia, Y.-T. (1990). The belief calculus and uncertain reasoning. In *Proceedings of the 8th National Conference on Artificial Intelligence*, pages 120–125, Menlo Park, CA. AAAI Press/MIT Press.

Hsia, Y.-T. (1991a). A belief function semantics for cautious nonmonotonicity. Technical Report IRIDIA/91-3, IRIDIA, Université Libre de Bruxelles.

Hsia, Y.-T. (1991b). Characterizing belief with minimum commitment. In *Proceedings of the 12th International Joint Conference on Artificial Intelligence*, pages 1184–1189, San Mateo, CA. Morgan Kaufmann.

Hsia, Y.-T. (1991c). Uncertainty about belief, belief function and logic of belief. Technical Report IRIDIA/91-21, IRIDIA, Université Libre de Bruxelles.

Hsia, Y.-T. and Shenoy, P. P. (1989a). An evidential language for expert systems. In Z. W. Ras, editor, *Methodologies for Intelligent Systems 4*, pages 9–16. Elsevier Science Publishers B. V., Amsterdam, The Netherlands.

Hsia, Y.-T. and Shenoy, P. P. (1989b). MacEvidence, a visual environment for constructing and evaluating evidential systems. Working Paper 211, School of Business, University of Kansas, Lawrence.

Hughes, G. E. and Cresswell, M. J. (1968). *An Introduction to Modal Logic*. Methuen, London, UK.

Hunt, J. E. and Cooke, D. E. (1994). Qualitatively modeling photosynthesis. *Applied Artificial Intelligence*, **8**, 307–332.

Hunter, A. (1995). Using default logic in information retrieval. In C. Froidevaux and J. Kohlas, editors, *Symbolic and Quantitative Approaches to Reasoning and Uncertainty*, pages 235–242. Springer Verlag, Berlin, Germany.

Hunter, A. (1996). *Uncertainty in Information Systems: An Introduction to Techniques and Applications.* McGraw-Hill, Maidenhead, UK.

Hunter, A. (2000). Reasoning with inconsistency in structured text. *The Knowledge Engineering Review*, **15**(4).

Hurme, M., Dohnal, M., and Järveläinen, M. (1991). A method of qualitative economic optimisation and its application to a practical engineering problem. In M. G. Singh and L. Travé-Massuyès, editors, *Decision Support Systems and Qualitative Reasoning*, pages 281–284. Elsevier Science Publishers B. V., Amsterdam, The Netherlands.

IEEE Expert (1994). A fuzzy logic symposium. *IEEE Expert*, **9**(4), 2–49.

Imielinski, T. (1985). Results on translating defaults to circumscription. In *Proceedings of the 9th International Joint Conference on Artificial Intelligence*, pages 114–120, Los Altos, CA. Morgan Kaufmann.

Imielinski, T. (1987). Results on translating defaults to circumscription. *Artificial Intelligence*, **32**, 131–146. A short list of errata from the paper can be found on page 413 of volume 33 of the journal.

Israel, D. J. (1987). Some remarks on the place of logic in knowledge representation. In N. Cercone and G. McCalla, editors, *The Knowledge Frontier: Essays in the Representation of Knowledge*, pages 80–91. Springer Verlag, New York, NY.

Jaakkola, T. S. and Jordan, M. I. (1996). Computing upper and lower bounds on likelihoods in intractable networks. In E. Horvitz and F. Jensen, editors, *Proceedings of the 12th Conference on Uncertainty in Artificial Intelligence*, pages 340–348, San Francisco, CA. Morgan Kaufmann.

Jaakkola, T. S. and Jordan, M. I. (1999). Variational probabilistic inference and the QMR-DT network. *Journal of Artificial Intelligence Research*, **10**, 291–322.

Jaffray, J.-Y. (1988). Application of linear utility theory to belief functions. In B. Bouchon-Meunier, L. Saitta, and R. R. Yager, editors, *Uncertainty and Intelligent Systems*, pages 1–8. Springer Verlag, Berlin, Germany.

Jain, P. and Agogino, A. (1988). Arithmetic operations on Bayesian fuzzy probabilities. Working Paper 87-0803-3, Berkley Expert Systems Technology Laboratory.

Jain, P. and Agogino, A. (1990). Stochastic sensitivity analysis using fuzzy influence diagrams. In R. D. Shachter, T. S. Levitt, L. N. Kanal, and J. F. Lemmer, editors, *Uncertainty in Artificial Intelligence 4*, pages 79–92. Elsevier Science Publishers B. V., Amsterdam, The Netherlands.

Jakobovits, H. and Vermeir, D. (1996). Contradiction in argumentation frameworks. In *Proceedings of the 6th International Conference on Information Processing and the Management of Uncertainty*, pages 821–826.

JANCL (1991). Special issue on uncertainty, conditionals and nonmonotonicity. *Journal of Applied Non-Classical Logics*, **1**, 105–197.

Jaynes, E. J. (1979). Where do we stand on maximum entropy? In R. D. Levine and M. Tribus, editors, *The Maximum Entropy Formalism*, pages 15–118. MIT Press, Cambridge, MA.

Jeffrey, R. (1965). *The Logic of Decision.* McGraw-Hill, New York, NY.

Jennings, N. R. (1994). *Cooperation in Industrial Multi-Agent Systems.* World Scientific, London, UK.

Jensen, F. V. (1996). *An Introduction to Bayesian Networks.* UCL Press, London.

Jensen, F. V. (1999). Gradient descent training of Bayesian networks. In A. Hunter and S. Parsons, editors, *Symbolic and Quantitative Approaches to Reasoning and Uncertainty*, pages 190–200. Springer Verlag, Berlin, Germany.

Jensen, F. V. and Andersen, S. K. (1990). Approximations in Bayesian belief universes for knowledge-based systems. In *Proceedings of the 6th Conference on Uncertainty in Artificial Intelligence*, pages 162–169, Mountain View, CA. Association for Uncertainty in AI.

Jensen, F. V., Olesen, K. G., and Andersen, S. K. (1990). An algebra of Bayesian belief universes for knowledge-based systems. *Networks*, **20**, 637–659.

Jitnah, N. and Nicholson, A. (1997). treeNets: a framework for anytime evaluation of belief networks. In D. M. Gabbay, R. Kruse, A. Nonnengart, and H. J. Ohlbach, editors, *Qualitative and Quantitative Practical Reasoning*, pages 350–364. Springer Verlag, Berlin, Germany.

Kahneman, D. and Tversky, A. (1973). On the psychology of prediction. *Psychological Review*, **80**, 237–251.

Kahneman, D. and Tversky, A. (1982a). Subjective probability: a judgement of representativeness. In D. Kahneman, P. Slovic, and A. Tversky, editors, *Judgement under uncertainty: Heuristics and biases*, pages 32–47. Cambridge University Press, Cambridge, UK.

Kahneman, D. and Tversky, A. (1982b). Variants of uncertainty. In D. Kahneman, P. Slovic, and A. Tversky, editors, *Judgement under uncertainty: Heuristics and biases*, pages 509–520. Cambridge University Press, Cambridge, UK.

Kahneman, D., Slovic, P., and Tversky, A. (1982). *Judgement under uncertainty: Heuristics and biases*. Cambridge University Press, Cambridge, UK.

Kakas, A. C., Mancarella, P., and Dung, P. M. (1994). The acceptability semantics for logic programs. In *Proceedings of the 11th International Conference on Logic Porgramming*, pages 504–519, Cambridge, MA. MIT Press.

Kämpke, T. (1988). About assessing and evaluating uncertain inferences within the theory of evidence. *Decision Support Systems*, **4**, 433–439.

Kennes, R. (1992). Computational aspects of the Möbius transformation of graphs. *IEEE Transactions on Systems, Man, and Cybernetics*, **22**, 201–223.

Keren, G. (1994). The rationality of gambling: gamblers' perceptions of probability, chance and luck. In G. Wright and P. Ayton, editors, *Subjective Probability*, pages 485–499. John Wiley & Sons, Chichester, UK.

Kim, J. H. and Pearl, J. (1983). A computational model for causal and diagnostic reasoning in inference systems. In *Proceedings of the 8th International Joint Conference on Artificial Intelligence*, pages 190–193, Los Altos, CA. William Kaufman.

Kim, J. H. and Pearl, J. (1987). CONVINCE: a conversational inference consolidation engine. *IEEE Transactions on Systems, Man, and Cybernetics*, **17**, 120–132.

King, R. D., Clark, D. A., Shirazi, J., and Sternberg, M. J. E. (1994). Inductive logic programming used to discover topological constraints in protein structures. In *Proceedings of the Second International Conference on Intelligent Systems for Molecular Biology*, pages 219–226, Menlo Park, CA. AAAI Press.

Klawonn, F. (1991). Personal communication.

Kleinmuntz, B. (1986). The scientific study of judgment in psychology and medicine. In H. R. Arkes and K. R. Hammond, editors, *Judgment and Decision Making: An Interdisciplinary Reader*, pages 551–567. Cambridge University Press, Cambridge, UK.

Kleiter, G. (2000). Propagating imprecise probabilities in Bayesian networks. *Artificial Intelligence*, **88**, 143–161.

Kleiter, G. and Jiroušek, R. (1996). Learning Bayesian networks under the control of mutual information. In *Proceedings of the 6th International Conference on Information Processing and the Management of Uncertainty*, pages 985–990.

Kleiter, G. D. (1993). Natural sampling: rationality without base rates. In G. H. Fischer and D. Lanning, editors, *Contributions of Mathematical Psychology, Psychometrics, and Methodology*, pages 369–382. Springer Verlag, New York.

Klir, G. J. (1987). Where do we stand on measures of uncertainty, ambiguity, fuzziness, and the like? *Fuzzy Sets and Systems*, **24**, 141–160.

Klir, G. J. and Folger, T. A. (1988). *Fuzzy Sets, Uncertainty and Information*. Prentice Hall Inc., Englewood Cliffs, NJ.

Kohlas, J. (1993). Symbolic evidence, arguments, supports and valuation networks. In M. Clarke, R. Kruse, and S. Moral, editors, *Symbolic and Quantitative Approaches to Reasoning and Uncertainty*, pages 186–198. Springer Verlag, Berlin, Germany.

Kohlas, J. and Brachinger, W. (1994). Mathematical foundations of evidence theory. In *Proceedings of the 5th International Conference on Information Processing and the Management of Uncertainty*, pages 53–58.

Kohlas, J. and Monney, P.-A. (1993). Probabilistic assumption-based reasoning. In *Proceedings of the 9th Conference on Uncertainty in Artificial Intelligence*, pages 485–491, San Mateo, CA. Morgan Kaufmann.

Kohlas, J., Monney, P. A., Haenni, R., and Lehmann, N. (1995). Model-based diagnosis using hints. In C. Froidevaux and J. Kohlas, editors, *Symbolic and Quantitative Approaches to Reasoning and Uncertainty*, pages 259–266. Springer Verlag, Berlin, Germany.

Kohlas, J., Haenni, R., and Moral, S. (1999). Propositional information systems. *Journal of Logic and Computation*, **9**, 651–681.

Koivisto, R., Dohnal, M., and Likitalo, A. (1989). Deep and shallow knowledge integration: a case study of an AI diagnosis of a chemical reactor. In *Proceedings of the 2nd Scandinavian Conference on Artificial Intelligence*.

Konolige, K. (1988). On the relation between default and autoepistemic logic. *Artificial Intelligence*, **35**, 343–382. A short list of errata from the paper can be found on page 115 of volume 41 of the journal.

Konolige, K. (1989). On the relation between autoepistemic logic and circumscription. In *Proceedings of the 11th International Joint Conference on Artificial Intelligence*, pages 1213–1218, San Mateo, CA. Morgan Kaufmann.

Konolige, K. and Myers, K. (1989). Representing defaults with epistemic concepts. *Computational Intelligence*, **5**, 32–44.

Kraus, S., Lehmann, D., and Magidor, M. (1990). Nonmonotonic reasoning, preferential models and cumulative logics. *Artificial Intelligence*, **44**, 167–207.

Krause, P., Ambler, S., Elvang-Gøransson, M., and Fox, J. (1995). A logic of argumentation for reasoning under uncertainty. *Computational Intelligence*, **11**, 113–131.

Krause, P. J. (1998). Learning probabilistic networks. *The Knowledge Engineering Review*, **13**, 321–351.

Krause, P. J. and Clark, D. A. (1993). *Representing Uncertain Knowledge: An Artificial Intelligence Approach*. Intellect, Oxford, UK.

Krause, P. J. and Fox, J. (1994). Combining symbolic and numerical methods for reasoning under uncertainty. In D. J. Hand, editor, *AI and Computer Power: The Impact on Statistics*, pages 99–114. Chapman and Hall, London, UK.

Krogh, A. (1997). Two methods for improving performance of an HMM and their application for gene finding. In *Proceedings of the Fifth International Conference on Intelligent Systems for Molecular Biology*, pages 179–186, Menlo Park, CA. AAAI Press.

Kruse, R., Schwecke, E., and Heinshohn, J. (1991). *Uncertainty and Vagueness in Knowledge Based Systems*. Springer-Verlag, Berlin, Germany.

Kruse, R., Gebhardt, J., and Klawonn, F. (1994). *Foundations of Fuzzy Systems*. John Wiley & Sons, Chichester, UK.

Kubat, M. (1991). Conceptual inductive learning: the case of unreliable teacher. *Artificial Intelligence*, **52**, 169–182.

Kuipers, B. (1984). Commonsense reasoning about causality: deriving behaviour from structure. *Artificial Intelligence*, **24**, 169–203.

Kuipers, B. (1986). Qualitative simulation. *Artificial Intelligence*, **29**, 289–338.

Kuipers, B. (1987). New reasoning methods for artificial intelligence in medicine. *International Journal of Man-Machine Studies*, **26**, 707–718.

Kuipers, B. (1988). The qualitative calculus is sound but incomplete: a reply to Peter Struss. *Artificial Intelligence in Engineering*, **3**, 170–172.

Kuipers, B., editor (1994). *Qualitative Reasoning—Modelling and Simulation with Incomplete Knowledge*. MIT Press, Cambridge, MA.

Kuipers, B. and Berleant, D. (1988). Using incomplete quantitative knowledge in qualitative reasoning. In *Proceedings of the 7th National Conference on Artificial Intelligence*, pages 324–329, San Mateo, CA. Morgan Kaufmann.

Kulp, D., Haussler, D., Reese, M. G., and Eeckman, F. H. (1996). A generalised hidden Markov model for the recognition of human genes in DNA. In *Proceedings of the Fourth International Conference on Intelligent Systems for Molecular Biology*, pages 134–142, Menlo Park, CA. AAAI Press.

Kwan, S., Olken, F., and Rotem, D. (1997). Uncertain, incomplete and inconsistent data in scientific and statistical databases. In A. Motro and P. Smets, editors, *Uncertainty in Information Systems: From Needs to Solutions*, pages 127–153. Kluwer, Boston, MA.

Kyburg, Jr., H. E. (1987). Bayesian and non-Bayesian evidential updating. *Artificial Intelligence*, **31**, 271–293.

Kyburg, Jr., H. E. (1989). Higher order probabilities. In L. N. Kanal, T. S. Levitt, and J. F. Lemmer, editors, *Uncertainty in Artificial Intelligence 3*, pages 15–22. Elsevier Science Publishers, Amsterdam, The Netherlands.

Kyburg, Jr., H. E. and Pittarelli, M. (1992). Some problems for convex Bayesians. In *Proceedings of the 8th Conference on Uncertainty in Artificial Intelligence*, pages 149–154, San Mateo, CA. Morgan Kaufmann.

Kyburg, Jr., H. E. and Pittarelli, M. (1996). Set-based Bayesianism. *IEEE Transactions on Systems, Man and Cybernetics*, **26**, 324–339.

Lakshmanan, L. and Shiri, N. (1996). A generic framework for deduction with uncertainty. In *Proceedings of the 6th International Conference on Information Processing and the Management of Uncertainty*, pages 295–300.

Lam, F. C. and Yeap, W. K. (1992). Bayesian updating: on the interpretation of exhaustive and mutually exclusive assumptions. *Artificial Intelligence*, **53**, 245–254.

Lam, W. and Bacchus, F. (1994). Learning Bayesian belief networks: an approach based on the MDL principle. *Computational Intelligence*, **10**, 269–293.

Lamata, M. T. and Moral, S. (1994). Calculus with linguistic probabilities and beliefs. In M. Fedrizzi, J. Kacprzyk, and R. R. Yager, editors, *Advances in the Dempster Shafer Theory of Evidence*, pages 133–152. John Wiley & Sons, New York, NY.

Lang, J. (1990). Semantic evaluation in possibilistic logic: application to min-max discrete optimisation problems. In B. Bouchon-Meunier, R. R. Yager, and L. A. Zadeh, editors, *Uncertainty in Knowledge Bases*, pages 260–268. Springer Verlag, Berlin, Germany.

Lang, J. (2000). Possibilistic logic: complexity and algorithms. In J. Kohlas and S. Moral, editors, *Handbook of Algorithms for Uncertainty and Defeasible Reasoning*. Kluwer Academic Publishers, Boston, MA.

Laskey, K. B. and Lehner, P. E. (1990). Assumptions, beliefs and probabilities. *Artificial Intelligence*, **32**, 65–77.

Lauritzen, S. L. and Jensen, F. (1996). Local computation with valuations from a commutative semigroup. Research Report R-96-2028, Department of Mathematics and Computer Science, Aalborg University.

Lauritzen, S. L. and Shenoy, P. P. (1995). Computing marginals using local computation. Working Paper 267, School of Business, University of Kansas, Lawrence.

Lauritzen, S. L. and Spiegelhalter, D. J. (1988). Local computations on graphical structures, and their application to expert systems. *Journal of the Royal Statistical Society, B*, **50**, 157–224.

Léa Sombé (1990). *Reasoning under Incomplete Information in Artificial Intelligence*. John Wiley & Sons, New York, NY.

Lehmann, D. (1989). What does a conditional knowledge base entail? In *Proceedings of the 1st International Conference on Knowledge Representation and Reasoning*, pages 212–222, San Mateo, CA. Morgan Kaufmann.

Lehmann, D. and Magidor, M. (1992). Nonmonotonic reasoning, preferential models and cumulative logics. *Artificial Intelligence*, **55**, 1–60.

Lehmann, N. and Haenni, R. (1999). An alternative to outward propagation for Dempster-Shafer belief functions. In A. Hunter and S. Parsons, editors, *Symbolic and Quantitative Approaches to Reasoning and Uncertainty*, pages 256–267. Springer Verlag, Berlin, Germany.

Levesque, H. J. (1990). All I know: a study in autoepistemic logic. *Artificial Intelligence*, **42**, 263–309.

Lichtenstein, S., Fishhoff, B., and Phillips, L. D. (1982). Calibration of probabilities: the state of the art to 1980. In D. Kahneman, P. Slovic, and A. Tversky, editors, *Judgement under uncertainty: Heuristics and biases*, pages 306–334. Cambridge University Press, Cambridge, UK.

Lifschitz, V. (1986). Pointwise circumscription: preliminary report. In *Proceedings of the 5th National Conference on Artificial Intelligence*, pages 406–410, Los Altos, CA. Morgan Kaufmann.

Lifschitz, V. (1989). Between circumscription and autoepistemic logic. In *Proceedings of the 1st International Conference on Knowledge Representation and Reasoning*, pages 235–244, San Mateo, CA. Morgan Kaufmann.

Lifschitz, V. (1994). Minimal belief and negation as failure. *Artificial Intelligence*, **70**, 53–72.

Lin, F. (1993). An argument-based approach to non-monotonic reasoning. *Computational Intelligence*, **9**, 254–267.

Lin, F. and Shoham, Y. (1989). Argument systems: a uniform basis for nonmonotonic reasoning. In *Proceedings of the 1st International Conference on Knowledge Representation and Reasoning*, pages 245–255, San Mateo,

CA. Morgan Kaufmann.

Lin, F. and Shoham, Y. (1992). A logic of knowledge and justified assumptions. *Artificial Intelligence*, **57**, 271–289.

Lindley, D. V. (1965). *Introduction to Probability and Statistics from a Bayesian Viewpoint.* Cambridge University Press, Cambridge, UK.

Lindley, D. V. (1975). *Making Decisions.* John Wiley & Sons, Chichester, UK.

Linke, T. and Schaub, T. (1999). On bottom-up pre-processing techniques for automated default reasoning. In A. Hunter and S. Parsons, editors, *Symbolic and Quantitative Approaches to Reasoning and Uncertainty*, pages 190–200. Springer Verlag, Berlin, Germany.

Linke, T. and Schaub, T. (2000). Alternative foundations for Reiter's default logic. *Artificial Intelligence*, **124**, 31–86.

Liu, C.-L. and Wellman, M. P. (1998). Incremental tradeoff resolution in qualitative probabilistic networks. In G. F. Cooper and S. Moral, editors, *Proceedings of the 14th Conference on Uncertainty in Artificial Intelligence*, pages 338–353, San Francisco, CA. Morgan Kaufmann.

Loui, R. (1986). Interval-based decisions for reasoning systems. In L. N. Kanal and J. F. Lemmer, editors, *Uncertainty in Artificial Intelligence*, pages 459–472. Elsevier Science Publishers, Amsterdam, The Netherlands.

Loui, R. (1987). Defeat among arguments: a system of defeasible inference. *Computational Intelligence*, **3**, 100–106.

Lowrance, J. D., Garvey, T. D., and Strat, T. M. (1986). A framework for evidential-reasoning systems. In *Proceedings of the 5th National Conference on Artificial Intelligence*, pages 896–903, Los Altos, CA. Morgan Kaufmann.

Łukaszewicz, W. (1985). Two results on default logic. In *Proceedings of the 9th International Joint Conference on Artificial Intelligence*, pages 459–461, Los Altos, CA. Morgan Kaufmann.

Łukaszewicz, W. (1988). Considerations on default logic: an alternative approach. *Computational Intelligence*, **4**, 1–16.

MacKenzie, T., Platt, D., and Dix, T. (1993). Modelling errors in restriction mapping. In *Proceedings of the 22nd Hawaiian International Conference on System Sciences*, pages 613–619, Los Alamitos, CA. IEEE Computer Society Press.

Madsen, A. and D'Ambrosio, B. (1999). Lazy propagation and independence of causal influence. In A. Hunter and S. Parsons, editors, *Symbolic and Quantitative Approaches to Reasoning and Uncertainty*, pages 293–304. Springer Verlag, Berlin, Germany.

Madsen, A. L. (1999). Lazy propagation: A junction tree inference algorithm based on lazy evaluation. *Artificial Intelligence*, **113**, 203–245.

Mamdani, E. H. and Gaines, B. R., editors (1981). *Fuzzy Reasoning and its Applications.* Academic Press, New York, NY.

Marek, W. and Truszczyński, M. (1989). Relating autoepistemic and default logics. In *Proceedings of the 1st International Conference on Knowledge Representation and Reasoning*, pages 276–288, San Mateo, CA. Morgan Kaufmann.

Martin, T. P., Baldwin, J. F., and Pilsworth, B. W. (1987). The implementation of FProlog—a fuzzy Prolog interpreter. *Fuzzy Sets and Systems*, **23**, 119–129.

Martin-Clouaire, R. and Prade, H. (1985). On the problems of representation and propagation of uncertainty. *International Journal of Man-Machine Studies*, **22**, 251–264.

Mavrouniotis, M. L. and Stephanopoulos, G. (1987). Reasoning with orders of magnitude and approximate relations. In *Proceedings of the 6th National Conference on Artificial Intelligence*, pages 626–630, Los Altos, CA. Morgan Kaufmann.

Mavrouniotis, M. L. and Stephanopoulos, G. (1988). Formal order-of-magnitude reasoning in process engineering. *Computers in Chemical Engineering*, **12**, 867–880.

Mavrouniotis, M. L. and Stephanopoulos, G. (1989). Order-of-magnitude reasoning with O[M]. *Artificial Intelligence in Engineering*, **4**, 106–114.

McAllester, D. A. (1980). An outlook on truth maintenance. AI Memo 551, AI Laboratory, MIT.

McCarthy, J. (1980). Circumscription—a form of non-monotonic reasoning. *Artificial Intelligence*, **13**, 27–39.

McCarthy, J. (1986). Applications of circumscription to formalising commonsense knowledge. *Artificial Intelligence*, **28**, 89–116.

McCorduck, P. (1979). *Machines who Think*. W. H. Freeman, San Francisco, CA.

McDermott, D. (1991). A general framework for reason maintenance. *Artificial Intelligence*, **50**, 289–329.

McDermott, D. V. (1982). Nonmonotonic logic II: nonmonotonic modal theories. *Journal of the ACM*, **29**, 37–57.

McDermott, D. V. and Doyle, J. (1980). Non-monotonic logic I. *Artificial Intelligence*, **13**, 41–72.

McGuire, R., Birnbaum, L., and Flowers, M. (1981). Opportunistic processing in arguments. In *Proceedings of the 7th International Joint Conference on Artificial Intelligence*, pages 58–60, Menlo Park, CA. American Association for Artificial Intelligence.

McLeish, M. (1988). Probabilistic logic: some comments and possible use for nonmonotonic reasoning. In J. F. Lemmer and L. N. Kanal, editors, *Uncertainty in Artificial Intelligence 2*, pages 55–62. Elsevier Science Publishers, Amsterdam, The Netherlands.

McLeish, M. (1989). Nilsson's probabilistic entailment extended to Dempster-Shafer theory. In L. N. Kanal, T. S. Levitt, and J. F. Lemmer, editors, *Uncertainty in Artificial Intelligence 3*, pages 23–35. Elsevier Science Publishers, Amsterdam, The Netherlands.

McNeil, B. J., Pauker, S. G., Sox, Jr., H. C., and Tversky, A. (1986). On the elicitation of preferences for alternative therapies. In H. R. Arkes and K. R. Hammond, editors, *Judgment and Decision Making: An Interdisciplinary Reader*, pages 386–393. Cambridge University Press, Cambridge, UK.

Meehl, P. E. (1966). *Clinical versus Statistical Prediction: A Theoretical Analysis and a Review of the Evidence*. University of Minnesota Press, Minneapolis, MN.

Mellouli, K. (1994). Decision making using belief functions: evaluation of information. In *Proceedings of the 5th International Conference on Information Processing and the Management of Uncertainty*, pages 47–52.

Mellouli, K., Shafer, G., and Shenoy, P. P. (1986). Qualitative Markov networks. In B. Bouchon and R. R. Yager, editors, *Uncertainty in Knowledge-Based Systems*, pages 69–74. Springer-Verlag, Berlin, Germany.

Mengin, J. (1991). Un démonstrateur de théorèmes pour la logique des défauts libres gradués. In *Actes du 8ème Congrès Reconnaissance des Formes et Intelligence Artificielle*, pages 363–368.

Mengin, J. (1995). A theorem prover for default logic based on prioritized conflict resolution and an extended resolution principle. In C. Froidevaux and J. Kohlas, editors, *Symbolic and Quantitative Approaches to Reasoning and Uncertainty*, pages 301–310. Springer Verlag, Berlin, Germany.

Michelena, N. F. (1991). *Monotonic influence diagrams: application to optimal and robust design*. Ph.D. thesis, Berkeley Expert Systems Technology Laboratory, Berkeley.

Michelena, N. F. and Agogino, A. M. (1993a). Monotonic influence diagrams: extension to stochastic programming and application to probabilistic design. *Engineering Optimisation*, **21**, 99–120.

Michelena, N. F. and Agogino, A. M. (1993b). Monotonic influence diagrams: foundations and application to optimal design. *Engineering Optimisation*, **21**, 79–97.

Miguel, I. and Shen, Q. (1999). Hard, flexible and dynamic constraint satisfaction. *The Knowledge Engineering Review*, **14**, 199–220.

Milgrom, P. R. (1981). Good news and bad news: representation theorems and applications. *Bell Journal of Economics*, **12**, 380–391.

Miller, III, A. C., Merkhofer, M. W., Howard, R. A., Matheson, J. E., and Rice, T. R. (1976). Development of automated aids for decision analysis. Technical Report DO #27742, Stanford Research Institute, Menlo Park, CA.

Mohammed, J. and Simmons, R. (1986). Qualitative simulation of semiconductor fabrication. In *Proceedings of the 5th National Conference on Artificial Intelligence*, pages 794–799, Los Altos, CA. Morgan Kaufmann.

Moinard, Y. (1993). Unifying various approaches to default logic. In B. Bouchon-Meunier, L. Valverde, and R. R. Yager, editors, *IPMU '92—Advanced Methods in Artificial Intelligence*, pages 33–42. Springer-Verlag,

Berlin, Germany.

Moore, R. C. (1983). Semantical considerations on nonmonotonic logic. In *Proceedings of the 8th International Joint Conference on Artificial Intelligence*, pages 272–79, Los Altos, CA. William Kaufmann.

Moore, R. C. (1985). Semantical considerations on nonmonotonic logic. *Artificial Intelligence*, **25**, 75–94.

Moore, R. C. (1988). Autoepistemic logic. In P. Smets, E. H. Mamdani, D. Dubois, and H. Prade, editors, *Non-Standard Logics for Automated Reasoning*, pages 106–126. Academic Press, London, UK.

Moore, R. E. (1966). *Interval Analysis*. Prentice-Hall, Inc., Englewood Cliffs, N.J.

Moral, S. (1992). Calculating uncertainty intervals from conditional convex sets of probabilities. In *Proceedings of the 8th Conference on Uncertainty in Artificial Intelligence*, pages 199–206, San Mateo, CA. Morgan Kaufmann.

Moral, S. and de Campos, L. M. (1991). Updating uncertain information. In B. Bouchon-Meunier, R. R. Yager, and L. A. Zadeh, editors, *Uncertainty in Knowledge Bases*, pages 59–67. Springer-Verlag, Berlin, Germany.

Moral, S. and de Campos, L. M. (1993). Partially specified belief functions. In *Proceedings of the 9th Conference on Uncertainty in Artificial Intelligence*, pages 492–499, San Mateo, CA. Morgan Kaufmann.

Moral, S. and Salmerón, A. (1999). A Monte-Carlo algorithm for combining Dempster-Shafer belief based on approximate pre-computation. In A. Hunter and S. Parsons, editors, *Symbolic and Quantitative Approaches to Reasoning and Uncertainty*, pages 305–315. Springer Verlag, Berlin, Germany.

Moral, S. and Wilson, N. (1994). Markov chain Monte-Carlo algorithms for the calculation of Dempster-Shafer belief. In *Proceedings of the 12th National Conference on Artificial Intelligence*, pages 269–274, Menlo Park, CA. AAAI Press/MIT Press.

Moral, S. and Wilson, N. (1996). Importance sampling Monte-Carlo algorithms for the calculation of Dempster-Shafer belief. In *Proceedings of the 6th International Conference on Information Processing and the Management of Uncertainty*, pages 1337–1344.

Morgan, M. G. and Henrion, M. (1990). *Uncertainty: A Guide to Dealing with Uncertainty in Quantitative Risk and Policy Analysis*. Cambridge University Press, Cambridge, UK.

Moses, Y. and Shoham, Y. (1993). Belief as defeasible knowledge. *Artificial Intelligence*, **64**, 299–321.

Motro, A. (1990). Accomodating imprecision in database systems: issues and solutions. *SIGMOD RECORD*, **19**, 69–74.

Motro, A. (1997). Sources of uncertainty, imprecision and inconsistency in information systems. In A. Motro and P. Smets, editors, *Uncertainty in Information Systems: From Needs to Solutions*, pages 9–34. Kluwer, Boston, MA.

Munson, P. J., Di Francesco, V., and Porelli, R. (1993). Secondary structure prediction using penalised likelihood models. In *Proceedings of the 25th Symposium on the Interface of Computer Science and Statistics*.

Murphy, K. P., Weiss, Y., and Jordan, M. I. (1999). Loopy belief propagation for approximate inference: an empirical study. In K. B. Laskey and H. Prade, editors, *Proceedings of the 15th Conference on Uncertainty in Artificial Intelligence*, pages 467–475, San Francisco, CA. Morgan Kaufmann.

Murthy, S. S. (1988). Qualitative reasoning at multiple resolutions. In *Proceedings of the 7th National Conference on Artificial Intelligence*, pages 296–300, San Mateo, CA. Morgan Kaufman.

Musman, S. A. and Chang, L. W. (1993). A study of scaling issues in Bayesian belief networks for ship classification. In *Proceedings of the 9th Conference on Uncertainty in Artificial Intelligence*, pages 32–39, San Mateo, CA. Morgan Kaufmann.

Nanda, S. and Majumdar, S. (1992). Fuzzy rough sets. *Fuzzy Sets and Systems*, **45**, 157–160.

Neapolitan, R. (1993). The interpretation and application of belief functions. *Applied Artificial Intelligence*, **7**, 195–204.

Neapolitan, R. E. (1990). *Probabilistic Reasoning in Expert Systems: Theory and Algorithms*. John Wiley & Sons, New York, NY.

Neapolitan, R. E. (1996). Is higher-order uncertainty needed? *IEEE Transactions on Systems, Man and Cybernetics*, **26**, 294–302.

Neufeld, E. (1989). Defaults and probabilities: extensions and coherence. In *Proceedings of the 1st International*

Conference on Knowledge Representation and Reasoning, pages 312–323, San Mateo, CA. Morgan Kaufman.

Neufeld, E. (1990). A probabilistic commonsense reasoner. *International Journal of Intelligent Systems*, **5**, 565–594.

Neufeld, E. and Poole, D. (1989). Towards solving the mutiple extension problem: combining defaults and probability. In L. N. Kanal, T. S. Levitt, and J. F. Lemmer, editors, *Uncertainty in Artificial Intelligence 3*, pages 35–44. Elsevier Science Publishers, Amsterdam, The Netherlands.

Neufeld, E., Poole, D., and Aleliunas, R. (1990). Probabilistic semantics and defaults. In R. D. Shachter, T. S. Levitt, L. N. Kanal, and J. F. Lemmer, editors, *Uncertainty in Artificial Intelligence 4*, pages 121–131. Elsevier Science Publishers, Amsterdam, The Netherlands.

Ng, R. T. and Subrahmanian, V. S. (1991a). Non-monotonic negation in probabilistic deductive databases. In *Proceedings of the 7th Conference on Uncertainty in Artificial Intelligence*, pages 249–256, San Mateo, CA. Morgan Kaufmann.

Ng, R. T. and Subrahmanian, V. S. (1991b). A semantical framework for supporting subjective and conditional probabilities in deductive databases. In *Proceedings of the 8th International Conference on Logic Programming*, pages 556–580, Cambridge, MA. MIT Press.

Ng, R. T. and Subrahmanian, V. S. (1992a). Empirical probabilities in monadic deductive databases. In *Proceedings of the 8th Conference on Uncertainty in Artificial Intelligence*, pages 215–222, San Mateo, CA. Morgan Kaufmann.

Ng, R. T. and Subrahmanian, V. S. (1992b). Probabilistic logic programming. *Information and Computation*, **101**, 150–201.

Nguyen, H. T. (1978). On conditional possibility distributions. *Fuzzy Sets and Systems*, **1**, 299–311.

Nicolas, P. and Duval, B. (1995). A theorem prover for Łukaszewicz' open default theory. In C. Froidevaux and J. Kohlas, editors, *Symbolic and Quantitative Approaches to Reasoning and Uncertainty*, pages 311–319. Springer Verlag, Berlin, Germany.

Nicolas, P. and Schaub, T. (1998). The XRay system: an implementation platform for local query-answering in default logics. In A. Hunter and S. Parsons, editors, *Applications of Uncertainty Formalisms*, pages 354–378. Springer Verlag, Berlin, Germany.

Niemelä, I. (1988). Decision procedure for autoepistemic logic. In E. Lusk and R. Overbeek, editors, *9th International Conference on Automated Deduction*, pages 675–684. Springer Verlag, Berlin, Germany.

Nilsson, N. J. (1986). Probabilistic logic. *Artificial Intelligence*, **28**, 71–87.

Nilsson, N. J. (1993). Probabilistic logic revisited. *Artificial Intelligence*, **59**, 39–42.

Nordvik, J.-P., Smets, P., and Magrez, P. (1988). Fuzzy qualitative modeling. In B. Bouchon-Meunier, L. Saitta, and R. R. Yager, editors, *Uncertainty and Intelligent Systems*, pages 360–369. Springer Verlag, Berlin, Germany.

Olesen, K. G. and Andersen, S. K. (1988). Discussion of the paper by Lauritzen and Spiegelhalter. *Journal of the Royal Statistical Society, B*, **50**, 199–200.

Olesen, K. G., Kjaerulff, U., Jensen, F., Jensen, F. V., Falck, B., Andreassen, S., and Andersen, S. K. (1989). A MUNIN network for the median nerve—a case study in loops. *Applied Artificial Intelligence*, **3**, 385–404.

Ormsby, A. R. T., Hunt, J. E., and Lee, M. H. (1991). Towards an automated FMEA assistant. In G. Rzevski and R. A. Adey, editors, *Applications of Artificial Intelligence in Engineering VI*, pages 739–752. Computational Mechanics Publications, Southampton, UK.

Orponen, P. (1990). Dempster's rule of combination is #P-complete. *Artificial Intelligence*, **44**, 245–253.

Paaß, G. (1991). Second order probabilities for uncertain and conflicting evidence. In P. P. Bonissone, M. Henrion, L. N. Kanal, and J. F. Lemmer, editors, *Uncertainty in Artificial Intelligence 6*, pages 447–456. Elsevier Science Publishers, Amsterdam, The Netherlands.

Paris, J. B. (1994). *The Uncertain Reasoner's Companion*. Cambridge University Press, Cambridge, UK.

Paris, J. B. and Vencovska, A. (1990). A note on the inevitability of maximum entropy. *International Journal of Approximate Reasoning*, **4**, 183–223.

Parsons, S. (1990). On using qualitative algebras in place of metatheories for reasoning under uncertainty: a preliminary report. Technical report, Department of Electronic Engineering, Queen Mary and Westfield College.

Parsons, S. (1991). Qualitative and semiqualitative methods for integrating uncertainty handling formalisms. Technical report, Department of Electronic Engineering, Queen Mary and Westfield College.

Parsons, S. (1993). Using interval algebras to model order of magnitude reasoning. *Artificial Intelligence in Engineering*, **8**, 87–98.

Parsons, S. (1994). Some qualitative approaches to applying the Dempster-Shafer theory. *Information and Decision Technologies*, **19**, 321–337.

Parsons, S. (1995). Refining reasoning in qualitative probabilistic networks. In *Proceedings of the 11th Conference on Uncertainty in Artificial Intelligence*, pages 427–434, San Francisco, CA. Morgan Kaufman.

Parsons, S. (1996a). Comparing normative argumentation to qualitative systems. In *Proceedings of the 6th International Conference on Information Processing and the Management of Uncertainty*, pages 137–142.

Parsons, S. (1996b). Defining normative systems for qualitative argumentation. In D. M. Gabbay and H. J. Ohlbach, editors, *Practical Reasoning*, pages 449–465. Springer Verlag, Berlin, Germany.

Parsons, S. (1997a). Normative argumentation and qualitative probability. In D. M. Gabbay, R. Kruse, A. Nonnengart, and H. J. Ohlbach, editors, *Qualitative and Quantitative Practical Reasoning*, pages 466–480. Springer Verlag, Berlin, Germany.

Parsons, S. (1997b). On qualitative probability and order of magnitude reasoning. In *Proceedings of the 10th Florida Artificial Intelligence Research Symposium*, pages 198–203, St Petersburg, FL. Florida AI Research Society.

Parsons, S. (1998). A proof theoretic approach to qualitative probabilistic reasoning. *International Journal of Approximate Reasoning*, **19**, 265–297.

Parsons, S. (1999). Order of magnitude reasoning and qualitative probability. Technical report, Department of Electronic Engineering, Queen Mary and Westfield College.

Parsons, S. (2001). The Mummu user manual. Technical report, Department of Computer Science, University of Liverpool.

Parsons, S. and Bigham, J. (1996). Possibility theory and the generalised Noisy OR model. In *Proceedings of the 6th International Conference on Information Processing and the Management of Uncertainty*, pages 853–858.

Parsons, S. and Dohnal, M. (1992). Qualitative, semiqualitative and interval algebras and their application to engineering problems. *Engineering Applications of Artificial Intelligence*, **5**, 553–560.

Parsons, S. and Dohnal, M. (1993). A semiqualitative approach to reasoning in probabilistic networks. *Applied Artificial Intelligence*, **7**, 223–235.

Parsons, S. and Dohnal, M. (1995). The qualitative and semiqualitative analysis of environmental problems. *Environmental Software*, **10**, 75–85.

Parsons, S. and Fox, J. (1991). Qualitative and interval algebras for robust decision making under uncertainty. In M. G. Singh and L. Travé-Massuyès, editors, *Decision Support Systems and Qualitative Reasoning*, pages 163–168. Elsevier Science Publishers B. V., Amsterdam, The Netherlands.

Parsons, S. and Fox, J. (1994). A general approach to handling imperfect information in deductive databases. In L. V. S. Lakshmanan, editor, *Proceedings of the Post-ILPS'94 Workshop on Uncertainty in Databases and Deductive Systems*, pages 37–48. Also available as Technical Report 283 of the Advanced Computation Laboratory, Imperial Cancer Research Fund, London, UK.

Parsons, S. and Green, S. (1999). Argumentation and qualitative decision making. In A. Hunter and S. Parsons, editors, *Symbolic and Quantitative Approaches to Reasoning and Uncertainty*, pages 328–339. Springer Verlag, Berlin, Germany.

Parsons, S. and Mamdani, E. H. (1993). On reasoning in networks with qualitative uncertainty. In *Proceedings of the 9th Conference on Uncertainty in Artificial Intelligence*, pages 435–442, San Mateo, CA. Morgan Kaufmann.

Parsons, S. and Saffiotti, A. (1996). A case study in the qualitative verification and debugging of numerical uncertainty. *International Journal of Approximate Reasoning*, **14**, 187–216.

Parsons, S., Kubat, M., and Dohnal, M. (1992). A rough logic for reasoning under uncertainty. In *Proceedings of the 6th Annual Computer Conference*, pages 119–120, Los Alamitos, CA. IEEE Computer Society Press.

Parsons, S., Kubat, M., and Dohnal, M. (1995). Rough set reasoning under uncertainty. *Journal of Experimental and Theoretical Artificial Intelligence*, **7**, 175–193.

Pawlak, Z. (1982). Rough sets. *International Journal of Information and Computer Sciences*, **11**, 341–356.

Pawlak, Z. (1984). Rough classification. *International Journal of Man-Machine Studies*, **20**, 469–483.

Pawlak, Z. (1985). Rough sets and fuzzy sets. *Fuzzy Sets and Systems*, **17**, 99–102.

Pawlak, Z. (1991). *Rough Sets, Theoretical Aspects of Reasoning About Data*. Kluwer Academic Publishers, Dordrecht, The Netherlands.

Pawlak, Z. (1992). Rough sets—basic concepts. ICS Research Report 13/92, Institute of Computer Science, Warsaw University of Technology.

Pawlak, Z., Słowinski, K., and Słowinski, R. (1986). Rough classification of patients after highly selective vagotomy for duodenal ulcer. *International Journal of Man-Machine Studies*, **24**, 413–433.

Pearl, J. (1982). Reverend Bayes on inference engines: a distributed hierarchical approach. In *Proceedings of the National Conference on Artificial Intelligence*, pages 133–136. American Association for Artificial Intelligence.

Pearl, J. (1985). How to do with probabilities what people say you can't. In *Proceedings of IEEE Conference on Artificial Intelligence Applications*, pages 6–12. IEEE.

Pearl, J. (1986a). A constraint-propagation approach to probabilistic reasoning. In L. N. Kanal and J. F. Lemmer, editors, *Uncertainty in Artificial Intelligence*, pages 357–369. Elsevier Science Publishers, Amsterdam, The Netherlands.

Pearl, J. (1986b). Fusion, propagation, and structuring in belief networks. *Artificial Intelligence*, **28**, 9–15.

Pearl, J. (1986c). On evidential reasoning in a hierarchy of hypotheses. *Artificial Intelligence*, **29**, 241–288.

Pearl, J. (1987). Evidential reasoning using stochastic simulation of causal models. *Artificial Intelligence*, **32**, 245–257.

Pearl, J. (1988a). Embracing causality in default reasoning. *Artificial Intelligence*, **35**, 259–271.

Pearl, J. (1988b). *Probabilistic Reasoning in Intelligent Systems: Networks of Plausible Inference*. Morgan Kaufmann, San Mateo, CA.

Pearl, J. (1989). Probabilistic semantics for nonmonotonic reasoning. In *Proceedings of the 1st International Conference on Knowledge Representation and Reasoning*, pages 505–516, San Mateo, CA. Morgan Kaufmann.

Pearl, J. (1990a). Reasoning with belief functions: an analysis of compatibility. *International Journal of Approximate Reasoning*, **4**, 363–389.

Pearl, J. (1990b). System Z: a natural ordering of defaults with tractable applications to default reasoning. In *Proceedings of the 3rd Conference on Theoretical Aspects of Reasoning about Knowledge*, pages 121–135, San Mateo, CA. Morgan Kaufmann.

Pearl, J. (1991). Epsilon semantics. In S. Shapiro, editor, *Encyclopaedia of Artificial Intelligence, 2nd Edition*, pages 468–475. John Wiley & Sons, London, UK.

Pearl, J. (1993). From conditional oughts to qualitative decision theory. In *Proceedings of the 9th Conference on Uncertainty in Artificial Intelligence*, pages 12–20, San Mateo, CA. Morgan Kaufmann.

Pearl, J. (2000). *Causality: models, reasoning and inference*. Cambridge University Press, Cambridge, UK.

Pedersen, A. G., Baldi, P., Brunak, S., and Chauvan, Y. (1996). Characterization of prokaryotic and eukaryotic promoters using hidden Markov models. In *Proceedings of the Fourth International Conference on Intelligent Systems for Molecular Biology*, pages 182–191, Menlo Park, CA. AAAI Press.

Peot, M. A. and Shachter, R. D. (1991). Fusion and propagation with multiple observations in belief networks. *Artificial Intelligence*, **48**, 299–318.

Peterson, C. R., Ulehla, Z. J., Miller, A. J., Bourne, L. E., and Stilson, D. W. (1965). Internal consistency of subjective probabilities. *Journal of Experimental Psychology*, **70**, 526–533.

Phillips, L. D. and Edwards, W. (1966). Conservatism in a simple probability inference task. *Journal of Experimental Psychology*, **72**, 346–354.

Phillips, L. D., Hays, W. L., and Edwards, W. (1966). Conservatism in complex probabilistic inference. *IEEE Transactions on Human Factors in Electronics*, **7**, 7–18.

Piatetsky-Shapiro, G. (1997). Knowledge discovery and acquisition from imperfect information. In A. Motro and P. Smets, editors, *Uncertainty in Information Systems: From Needs to Solutions*, pages 155–188. Kluwer, Boston, MA.

Piera, N. and Travé-Massuyès, L. (1989). About qualitative equality: axioms and properties. In *Proceedings of the 9th International Conference on Expert Systems and their Applications*.

Pinkas, G. and Loui, R. P. (1992). Reasoning from inconsistency: a taxonomy of principles for resolving conflict. In *Proceedings of the 3rd International Conference on Knowledge Representation and Reasoning*, pages 709–719, San Mateo, CA. Morgan Kaufmann.

Pittarelli, M. (1994). An algebra for probabilistic databases. *IEEE Transactions on Knowledge and Data Engineering*, **6**, 293–303.

Platt, C. (1995). What's it mean to be human anyway? *Wired*, **April**, 80–85.

Pollock, J. (1995). *Cognitive Carpentry*. MIT Press, Cambridge, MA.

Pollock, J. L. (1987). Defeasible reasoning. *Cognitive Science*, **11**, 481–518.

Pollock, J. L. (1991). A theory of defeasible reasoning. *International Journal of Intelligent Reasoning*, **6**, 33–54.

Pollock, J. L. (1992). How to reason defeasibly. *Artificial Intelligence*, **57**, 1–42.

Pollock, J. L. (1994). Justification and defeat. *Artificial Intelligence*, **67**, 377–407.

Pollock, J. L. (1996a). OSCAR—a general-purpose defeasible reasoner. *Journal of Applied Non-Classical Logics*, **6**, 89–113.

Pollock, J. L. (1996b). Reasoning in a changing world. In D. M. Gabbay and H. J. Ohlbach, editors, *Practical Reasoning*, pages 495–509. Springer Verlag, Berlin, Germany.

Poole, D. (1988). A logical framework for default reasoning. *Artificial Intelligence*, **36**, 27–47.

Poole, D. (1989). Explanation and deduction: an architecture for default and abductive reasoning. *Computational Intelligence*, **5**, 97–110.

Poole, D. (1991). Representing Bayesian networks within probabilistic horn clause abduction. In *Proceedings of the 7th Conference on Uncertainty in Artificial Intelligence*, pages 271–278, San Mateo, CA. Morgan Kaufmann.

Poole, D. (1993a). Average-case analysis of a search algorithm for estimating prior and posterior probabilities in Bayesian networks with extreme probabilities. In *Proceedings of the 13th International Joint Conference on Artificial Intelligence*, pages 606–612, San Mateo, CA. Morgan Kaufmann.

Poole, D. (1993b). Probabilistic horn abduction and Bayesian networks. *Artificial Intelligence*, **64**, 81–129.

Poole, D. (1995). Exploiting the rule structure for decision making within the independent choice logic. In P. Besnard and S. Hanks, editors, *Proceedings of the 11th Conference on Uncertainty in Artificial Intelligence*, pages 454–463, San Francisco, CA. Morgan Kaufmann.

Poole, D., Goebel, R. G., and Aleliunas, R. (1988). Theorist: a logical reasoning system for defaults and diagnosis. In N. Cercone and G. McCalla, editors, *The Knowledge Frontier: Essays in the Representation of Knowledge*, pages 331–352. Springer Verlag, New York, NY.

Poznański, V. (1990). Dempster-Shafer ranges for an RMS. In *Proceedings of the IEE Colloquium on Reasoning Under Uncertainty, London, UK*.

Prade, H. (1983). A synthetic view of approximate reasoning techniques. In *Proceedings of the 8th International Joint Conference on Artificial Intelligence*, pages 130–136, Los Altos, CA. William Kaufmann.

Prade, H. (1993). Personal communication.

Prakken, H. and Sator, G. (1996). A system for defeasible argumentation, with defeasible priorities. In D. M. Gabbay and H. J. Ohlbach, editors, *Practical Reasoning*, pages 510–524. Springer Verlag, Berlin, Germany.

Prakken, H. and Vreeswijk, G. (2000). Logics for defeasible argumentation. In D. Gabbay, editor, *Handbook of Philosophical Logic*. Kluwer Academic Publishers, Dordrecht, The Netherlands.

Provan, G. (1991). Dynamic network updating techniques for diagnostic reasoning. In *Proceedings of the 7th Conference on Uncertainty in Artificial Intelligence*, pages 279–286, San Mateo, CA. Morgan Kaufmann.

Provan, G. M. (1988). Solving diagnostic problems using extended assumption-based truth maintenance systems: foundations. Technical Report 88-10, Department of Computer Science, University of British Columbia.

Provan, G. M. (1990). A logic-based analysis of Dempster-Shafer theory. *International Journal of Approximate*

Reasoning, **4**, 451–495.

Quinlan, J. R. (1983a). Consistency and plausible reasoning. In *Proceedings of the 8th International Joint Conference on Artificial Intelligence*, pages 137–144, Los Altos, CA. William Kaufmann.

Quinlan, J. R. (1983b). INFERNO: a cautious approach to uncertain inference. *Computer Journal*, **26**, 255–269.

Raiffa, H. (1970). *Decision Analysis: Introductory Lectures on Choices under Uncertainty*. Addison-Wesley, Reading, MA.

Raiman, O. (1986). Order of magnitude reasoning. In *Proceedings of the 5th National Conference on Artificial Intelligence*, pages 100–104, Los Altos, CA. Morgan Kaufmann.

Raiman, O. (1991). Order of magnitude reasoning. *Artificial Intelligence*, **51**, 11–38.

Rawlings, C. J. (1995). Personal communication.

Reece, S. (1998). *Qualitative model-based multi-sensor data fusion: the qualitative Kalman filter*. Ph.D. thesis, Department of Engineering Science, University of Oxford.

Reed, C. (1998). *Generating arguments in natural language*. Ph.D. thesis, Department of Computer Science, University College, London.

Rege, A. and Agogino, A. M. (1988). Topological framework for representing and solving probabilistic inference problems in expert systems. *IEEE Transactions on Systems, Man, and Cybernetics*, **18**, 402–414.

Reichgelt, H. (1991). *Knowledge Representation: An AI Perspective*. Ablex Publishing Corporation, Norwood, New Jersey.

Reiter, R. (1978). On closed world databases. In H. Gallaire and J. Minker, editors, *Logic and Databases*, pages 55–76. Plenum Press, New York, NY.

Reiter, R. (1980). A logic for default reasoning. *Artificial Intelligence*, **13**, 81–132.

Reiter, R. and Criscuolo, G. (1981). On interacting defaults. In *Proceedings of the 7th International Joint Conference on Artificial Intelligence*, pages 270–276, Menlo Park, CA. American Association for Artificial Intelligence.

Reiter, R. and Criscuolo, G. (1983). Some representational issues in default reasoning. *International Journal of Computation and Mathematics with Applications*, **9**, 15–27.

Renooij, S. (2000). *Qualitative approaches to quantifying probabilistic networks*. Ph.D. thesis, Institute of Information and Computing Sciences, University of Utrecht.

Renooij, S. and van der Gaag, L. (1998). Decision making in qualitative influence diagrams. In *Proceedings of the 11th International FLAIRS Conference*, pages 410–414, San Mateo, CA. AAAI Press.

Renooij, S. and van der Gaag, L. (1999a). Enhancing QPNs for trade-off resolution. In K. B. Laskey and H. Prade, editors, *Proceedings of the 15th Conference on Uncertainty in Artificial Intelligence*, pages 559–566, San Francisco, CA. Morgan Kaufmann.

Renooij, S. and van der Gaag, L. (1999b). Exploiting non-monotonic influences in qualitative belief networks. In *Proceedings of the 11th Belgium-Netherlands Conference on Artificial Intelligence*, pages 131–138.

Renooij, S., van der Gaag, L., Parsons, S., and Green, S. (2000a). Pivotal pruning of trade-offs in QPNs. In C. Boutillier and M. Goldszmidt, editors, *Proceedings of the 16th Conference on Uncertainty in Artificial Intelligence*, San Francisco, CA. Morgan Kaufmann.

Renooij, S., van der Gaag, L., and Parsons, S. (2000b). Propagation of multiple observations in qualitative probabilistic networks. In *Proceedings of the 12th Belgium-Netherlands Conference on Artificial Intelligence*, pages 235–242.

Renooij, S., Parsons, S., and van der Gaag, L. (2001). Context-specific sign-propagation in qualitative probabilistic networks. In *Proceedings of the 17th International Joint Conference on Artificial Intelligence*.

Rescher, N. and Manor, R. (1970). On inference from inconsistent premises. *Theory and Decision*, **1**, 179–217.

Rhodes, P. C. and Garside, G. R. (1995). The use of maximum entropy as a methodology for probabilistic reasoning. *Knowledge-Based Systems*, **8**, 249–258.

Rich, E. (1983). Default reasoning as likelihood reasoning. In *Proceedings of the 3rd National Conference on Artificial Intelligence*, pages 348–351, Los Altos, CA. William Kaufmann.

Richardson, J. S. (1976). Handedness of crossover connections in β-sheets. *Proceedings of the National*

Academy of Science, **73**, 2619–2623.

Richardson, J. S. (1981). The anatomy and taxonomy of protein structure. *Advances in Protein Chemistry*, **34**, 167–339.

Rickel, J. and Porter, B. (1994). Automated modeling for answering prediction questions: selecting the time scale and system boundary. In *Proceedings of the 12th National Conference on Artificial Intelligence*, Menlo Park CA/Cambridge MA. AAAI Press/MIT Press.

Riese, M. (1993). Diagnosis of communicating systems: Dealing with incompleteness and uncertainty. In *Proceedings of the 13th International Joint Conference on Artificial Intelligence*, pages 1480–1485, San Mateo, CA. Morgan Kaufmann.

Roos, N. (1992). A logic for reasoning with inconsistent information. *Artificial Intelligence*, **57**, 69–103.

Russell, S. (1997). Rationality and intelligence. *Artificial Intelligence*, **94**, 57–77.

Russell, S. and Norvig, P. (1995). *Artificial Intelligence: A Modern Approach*. Prentice Hall, Upper Saddle River, NJ.

Saffiotti, A. (1987). An AI view of the treatment of uncertainty. *The Knowledge Engineering Review*, **2**, 75–97.

Saffiotti, A. (1989a). De propagationibus. Technical Note TR/IRIDIA/89-15, IRIDIA, Université Libre de Bruxelles.

Saffiotti, A. (1989b). De rerum shaferis. Technical Note IRIDIA/ARCHON/TN-001, IRIDIA, Université Libre de Bruxelles.

Saffiotti, A. (1990). A hybrid framework for representing uncertain knowledge. In *Proceedings of the 9th National Conference on Artificial Intelligence*, pages 653–658, San Mateo, CA. AAAI Press/MIT Press.

Saffiotti, A. (1991). A belief function logic: preliminary report. Technical Report TR/IRIDIA/91-25, IRIDIA Université Libre de Bruxelles.

Saffiotti, A. (1992). A belief function logic. In *Proceedings of the 10th National Conference on Artificial Intelligence*, pages 642–647, San Mateo, CA. AAAI Press/MIT Press.

Saffiotti, A. (1993). Personal communication.

Saffiotti, A. and Umkehrer, E. (1991a). PULCINELLA: a general tool for propagating uncertainty in valuation networks. In *Proceedings of the 7th Conference on Uncertainty in Artificial Intelligence*, pages 323–331, San Mateo, CA. Morgan Kaufmann.

Saffiotti, A. and Umkehrer, E. (1991b). PULCINELLA user's manual. Technical Report TR/IRIDIA/91-5, IRIDIA Université Libre de Bruxelles.

Saffiotti, A. and Umkehrer, E. (1994). Inference driven construction of valuation systems from first-order clauses. *IEEE Transactions on Systems, Man, and Cybernetics*, **24**, 1611–1624.

Saffiotti, A. and Umkehrer, U. (1991c). Choosing between uncertainty management techniques. Technical Report TR/IRIDIA/91-7, IRIDIA, Université Libre de Bruxelles.

Saffiotti, A., Parsons, S., and Umkehrer, E. (1994). A case study in comparing uncertainty management techniques. *Microcomputers in Civil Engineering: Special Issue on Uncertainty in Expert Systems*, **9**, 367–380.

Salmerón, A., Cano, A., and Moral, S. (2000). Importance sampling in Bayesian networks using probability trees. *Computational Statistics and Data Analysis*, **34**, 387–413.

Salzburg, S., Chen, X., Henderson, J., and Fasman, K. (1996). Finding genes in DNA using decision trees and dynamic programming. In *Proceedings of the Fourth International Conference on Intelligent Systems for Molecular Biology*, pages 201–210, Menlo Park, CA. AAAI Press.

Sandars, N. K. (1971). *Poems of Heaven and Hell from Ancient Mesopotamia*. Penguin, Harmondsworth, UK.

Sandri, S. A. (1991). Structuring bodies of evidence. In *Proceedings of the 7th Conference on Uncertainty in Artificial Intelligence*, pages 332–338, San Mateo, CA. Morgan Kaufmann.

Schiex, T. (1992). Possibilistic constraint satisfaction problems: or how to handle soft constraints. In *Proceedings of the 8th Conference on Uncertainty in Artificial Intelligence*, pages 268–275, San Mateo, CA. Morgan Kaufmann.

Schiex, T. and Gaspin, C. (1997). CARTHAGENE: constructing and joining maximum likelihood genetic maps. In *Proceedings of the Fifth International Conference on Intelligent Systems for Molecular Biology*, pages 258–

267, Menlo Park, CA. AAAI Press.

Schmidt, J. P., Cheng, C. C., Cooper, J. L., and Altman, R. B. (1998). A surface measure for probabilistic structural computations. In *Proceedings of the 6th International Conference on Intelligent Systems for Molecular Biology*, pages 148–156, Menlo Park, CA. AAAI Press.

Schmidt, T. and Shenoy, P. P. (1998). Some improvements to the Shenoy-Shafer and Hugin algorithms for computing marginals. *Artificial Intelligence*, **102**, 323–333.

Schum, D. A., Goldstein, I. L., and Southard, J. R. (1966). Research on simulated Bayesian information-processing system. *IEEE Transactions on Human Factors in Electronics*, **7**, 37–48.

Schwarz, G. (1996). On embedding default logic into Moore's autoepistemic logic. *Artificial Intelligence*, **80**, 349–359.

Schweitzer, B. and Sklar, A. (1963). Associative functions and abstract semigroups. *Publicationes Mathematicae Debrecen*, **10**, 69–81.

Selman, B. and Kautz, H. A. (1990). Model-preference default theories. *Artificial Intelligence*, **45**, 287–322.

Shachter, R. (1986a). Evaluating influence diagrams. *Operations Research*, **34**, 871–882.

Shachter, R. (1986b). Intelligent probabilistic inference. In L. N. Kanal and J. F. Lemmer, editors, *Uncertainty in Artificial Intelligence*, pages 371–382. Elsevier Science Publishers, Amsterdam, The Netherlands.

Shachter, R. and Ndilikilikesha, P. (1994). Using potential influence diagrams for probabilistic inference and decision making. In *Proceedings of the 10th Conference on Uncertainty in Artificial Intelligence*, pages 383–390, San Francisco, CA. Morgan Kaufmann.

Shachter, R. and Peot, M. (1992). Decision making using probabilistic inference methods. In *Proceedings of the 8th Conference on Uncertainty in Artificial Intelligence*, pages 276–283, San Mateo, CA. Morgan Kaufmann.

Shachter, R. D. (1988). DAVID: influence diagram processing system for the Macintosh. In J. F. Lemmer and L. N. Kanal, editors, *Uncertainty in Artificial Intelligence 2*, pages 191–196. North-Holland, Amsterdam, The Netherlands.

Shackle, G. L. S. (1961). *Decision, Order and Time in Human Affairs*. Cambridge University Press, Cambridge, UK.

Shafer, G. (1976). *A Mathematical Theory of Evidence*. Princeton University Press, Princeton, NJ.

Shafer, G. (1981a). Constructive probability. *Synthese*, **48**, 1–60.

Shafer, G. (1981b). Jeffrey's rule of conditioning. *Philosophy of Science*, **48**, 337–362.

Shafer, G. (1986). Probability judgement in artificial intelligence. In L. N. Kanal and J. F. Lemmer, editors, *Uncertainty in Artificial Intelligence*, pages 127–135. Elsevier Science Publishers, Amsterdam, The Netherlands.

Shafer, G. (1988). Comments on 'an inquiry into computer understanding' by Peter Cheeseman. *Computational Intelligence*, **4**, 121–124.

Shafer, G. (1990). Perspectives on the theory and practice of belief functions. *International Journal of Approximate Reasoning*, **4**, 323–362.

Shafer, G. (1991a). An axiomatic study of computation in hypertrees. Working Paper 232, School of Business, The University of Kansas.

Shafer, G. (1991b). The early development of mathematical probability. Working Paper 228, School of Business, The University of Kansas.

Shafer, G. (1991c). What is probability? Working Paper 229, School of Business, The University of Kansas.

Shafer, G. (1992). Can the various meanings of probability be reconciled? In G. Keren and C. Lewis, editors, *A Handbook for Data Analysis in the Behavioural Sciences*. Lawrence Erblaum, Hillsdale, NJ.

Shafer, G. (1994). Foreword. In M. Fedrizzi, J. Kacprzyk, and R. R. Yager, editors, *Advances in the Dempster Shafer Theory of Evidence*. John Wiley & Sons, New York, NY.

Shafer, G. and Logan, R. (1987). Implementing Dempster's rule for hierarchical evidence. *Artificial Intelligence*, **33**, 271–298.

Shafer, G. and Tversky, A. (1985). Languages and designs for probability judgement. *Cognitive Science*, **9**, 309–339.

Shafer, G., Shenoy, P. P., and Mellouli, K. (1987). Propagating belief functions in qualitative Markov trees. *International Journal of Approximate Reasoning*, **1**, 349–400.

Shannon, C. E. (1948). The mathematical theory of communication. *Bell System Technical Journal*, **27**, 379–423, 623–656.

Shen, Q. and Leitch, R. (1993). Fuzzy qualitative simulation. *IEEE Transactions on Systems, Man and Cybernetics*, **23**, 1038–1061.

Shenoy, P. P. (1989). A valuation-based language for expert systems. *International Journal of Approximate Reasoning*, **3**, 383–411.

Shenoy, P. P. (1990a). Valuation-based systems for Bayesian decision analysis. Working Paper 220, School of Business, University of Kansas, Lawrence.

Shenoy, P. P. (1990b). Valuation-based systems for discrete optimisation. Working Paper 221, School of Business, University of Kansas, Lawrence.

Shenoy, P. P. (1990c). Valuation networks, decision trees, and influence diagrams: a comparison. Working Paper 227, School of Business, University of Kansas, Lawrence.

Shenoy, P. P. (1991a). A fusion algorithm for solving Bayesian decision problems. In *Proceedings of the 7th Conference on Uncertainty in Artificial Intelligence*, pages 361–369, San Mateo, CA. Morgan Kaufmann.

Shenoy, P. P. (1991b). On Spohn's rule for revision of beliefs. *International Journal of Approximate Reasoning*, **5**, 149–181.

Shenoy, P. P. (1992a). Conditional independence in uncertainty theories. In *Proceedings of the 8th Conference on Uncertainty in Artificial Intelligence*, pages 284–291, San Mateo, CA. Morgan Kaufmann.

Shenoy, P. P. (1992b). Using possibility theory in expert systems. *Fuzzy Sets and Systems*, **52**, 129–142.

Shenoy, P. P. (1992c). Valuation-based systems: a framework for managing uncertainty in expert systems. In L. A. Zadeh and J. Kacprzyk, editors, *Fuzzy Logic for the Management of Uncertainty*, pages 83–104. John Wiley & Sons, New York, NY.

Shenoy, P. P. (1994a). Using Dempster-Shafer's belief function theory in expert systems. In M. Fedrizzi, J. Kacprzyk, and R. R. Yager, editors, *Advances in the Dempster Shafer Theory of Evidence*. John Wiley & Sons, New York, NY.

Shenoy, P. P. (1994b). Valuation networks and asymmetric decision problems. In *Proceedings of the 5th International Conference on Information Processing and the Management of Uncertainty*, pages 153–158.

Shenoy, P. P. (1997). Binary join trees for computing marginals in the Shenoy-Shafer architecture. *International Journal of Approximate Reasoning*, **17**, 239–263.

Shenoy, P. P. and Shafer, G. (1986). Propagating belief functions with local computations. *IEEE Expert*, **1**, 43–52.

Shenoy, P. P. and Shafer, G. (1990). Axioms for probability and belief function propagation. In R. D. Shachter, T. S. Levitt, L. N. Kanal, and J. F. Lemmer, editors, *Uncertainty in Artificial Intelligence 4*, pages 169–198. North-Holland, Amsterdam, The Netherlands.

Shenoy, P. P., Shafer, G., and Mellouli, K. (1988). Propagation of belief functions: a distributed approach. In J. F. Lemmer and L. N. Kanal, editors, *Uncertainty in Artificial Intelligence 2*, pages 325–335. North-Holland, Amsterdam, The Netherlands.

Shoham, Y. (1987). Nonmonotonic logics: meaning and utility. In *Proceedings of the 10th International Joint Conference on Artificial Intelligence*, pages 388–393, Los Altos, CA. Morgan Kaufmann.

Shoham, Y. (1988). *Reasoning about Change: Time and Causation from the Standpoint of Artificial Intelliegnce.* MIT Press, Cambridge, MA.

Shortliffe, E. H. (1976). *Computer-Based Medical Consultations: MYCIN.* Elsevier, New York, NY.

Shortliffe, E. H. and Buchanan, B. G. (1975). A model of inexact reasoning in medicine. *Mathematical Biosciences*, **23**, 351–379.

Simari, G. R. and Loui, R. P. (1992). A mathematical treatment of defeasible reasoning and its implementation. *Artificial Intelligence*, **53**, 125–157.

Sisson, J. C., Schoomaker, E. B., and Ross, J. C. (1986). Clinical decision analysis: the hazard of using additional data. In H. R. Arkes and K. R. Hammond, editors, *Judgement and Decision Making: An Interdisciplinary Reader*, pages 354–363. Cambridge University Press, Cambridge, UK.

Słowinski, R. (1992). *Intelligent Decision Analysis. Handbook of Applications and Advances of Rough Set Theory*. Kluwer Academic Publishers, Dordrecht, The Netherlands.

Smets, P. (1983). Information content of an evidence. *International Journal of Man-Machine Studies*, **19**, 33–43.

Smets, P. (1986). Bayes' theorem generalised for belief functions. In *7th European Conference on Artificial Intelligence*, pages 169–537.

Smets, P. (1988a). Belief functions. In P. Smets, E. H. Mamdani, D. Dubois, and H. Prade, editors, *Non-Standard Logics for Automated Reasoning*, pages 253–275. Academic Press, London, UK.

Smets, P. (1988b). Transferable belief model versus Bayesian model. In *Proceedings of the 8th European Conference on Artificial Intelligence*, pages 495–500, London, UK. Pitman.

Smets, P. (1989). Constructing the pignistic probability function in a context of uncertainty. In *Proceedings of the Fifth Workshop on Uncertainty in AI*, pages 319–326, Mountain View, CA. Association for Uncertainty in AI.

Smets, P. (1990). The combination of evidence in the transferable belief model. *IEEE Transactions on Pattern Analysis and Machine Intelligence*, **12**, 447–458.

Smets, P. (1991a). Belief functions: the disjunctive rule of combination and the generalized Bayesian theorem. *International Journal of Approximate Reasoning*, **9**, 1–35.

Smets, P. (1991b). Personal communication.

Smets, P. (1991c). Varieties of ignorance and the need for well-founded theories. *Information Sciences*, **57–58**, 135–144.

Smets, P. (1993). Quantifying beliefs by belief functions: an axiomatic justification. In *Proceedings of the 13th International Joint Conference on Artificial Intelligence*, pages 598–603, San Mateo, CA. Morgan Kaufmann.

Smets, P. (1995). The canonical decomposition of a weighted belief. In *Proceedings of the 14th International Joint Conference on Artificial Intelligence*, pages 1896–1901, San Mateo, CA. Morgan Kaufmann.

Smets, P. (1997a). The α-junctions: combination operators applicable to belief functions. In D. M. Gabbay, R. Kruse, A. Nonnengart, and H. J. Ohlbach, editors, *Qualitative and Quantitative Practical Reasoning*, pages 131–153. Springer Verlag, Berlin, Germany.

Smets, P. (1997b). Imperfect information: imprecision and uncertainty. In A. Motro and P. Smets, editors, *Uncertainty in Information Systems: From Needs to Solutions*, pages 225–254. Kluwer, Boston, MA.

Smets, P. and Hsia, Y.-T. (1990). Default reasoning and the transferable belief model. In *Proceedings of the 6th Conference on Uncertainty in Artificial Intelligence*, pages 529–537, Mountain View, CA. Association for Uncertainty in AI.

Smets, P. and Hsia, Y.-T. (1991). Default reasoning and the transferable belief model. In P. P. Bonissone, M. Henrion, L. N. Kanal, and J. F. Lemmer, editors, *Uncertainty in Artificial Intelligence 6*, pages 495–504. Elsevier Science Publishers, Amsterdam, The Netherlands.

Smets, P. and Kennes, R. (1991). Computational aspects of the Möbius transformation. In P. P. Bonissone, M. Henrion, L. N. Kanal, and J. F. Lemmer, editors, *Uncertainty in Artificial Intelligence 6*, pages 401–416. Elsevier Science Publishers, Amsterdam, The Netherlands.

Smets, P. and Kennes, R. (1994). The transferable belief model. *Artificial Intelligence*, **66**, 191–234.

Smets, P. and Magrez, P. (1987). Implication in fuzzy logic. *International Journal of Approximate Reasoning*, **1**, 327–347.

Smets, P., Mamdani, E. H., Dubois, D., and Prade, H., editors (1988). *Non-Standard Logics for Automated Reasoning*. Academic Press, London, UK.

Smith, C. A. B. (1961). Consistency in statistical inference and decision. *Journal of the Royal Statistical Society*, **B23**, 218–258.

Smithson, M. (1989). *Ignorance and Uncertainty: Emerging Paradigms*. Springer Verlag, New York, NY.

Snow, P. (1986). Bayesian inference without point estimates. In *Proceedings of the 5th National Conference on Artificial Intelligence*, pages 233–237, Los Altos, CA. Morgan Kaufmann.

Snow, P. (1991). Improved posterior probability estimates from prior and conditional linear constraint systems.

IEEE Transactions on Systems, Man and Cybernetics, **21**, 464–469.

Snow, P. (1992). Intuitions about ordered beliefs leading to probabilistic models. In *Proceedings of the 8th Conference on Uncertainty in Artificial Intelligence*, pages 298–302, San Mateo, CA. Morgan Kaufmann.

Snow, P. (1994a). The emergence of ordered belief from initial ignorance. In *Proceedings of the 12th National Conference on Artificial Intelligence*, pages 281–286, Menlo Park, CA. AAAI Press/MIT Press.

Snow, P. (1994b). Ignorance and the expressiveness of single- and set-valued probability models of belief. In *Proceedings of the 10th Conference on Uncertainty in Artificial Intelligence*, pages 531–537, San Francisco, CA. Morgan Kaufmann.

Snow, P. (1995). An intuitive motivation of Bayesian belief models. *Computational Intelligence*, **11**, 449–459.

Snow, P. (1996a). Inference using conditional probabilities despite prior ignorance. *IEEE Transactions on Systems, Man and Cybernetics*, **26**, 349–360.

Snow, P. (1996b). Personal communication—Coherent credal orderings described by possibility measures.

Snow, P. (1998a). On the correctness and reasonableness of Cox's theorem for finite domains. *Computational Intelligence*, **11**, 449–459.

Snow, P. (1998b). Personal communication.

Snow, P. (1998c). The vulnerability of the transferable belief model to Dutch books. *Artificial Intelligence*, **105**, 345–354.

Snow, P. (1999). Diverse confidence levels in a probabilistic semantics for conditional logics. *Artificial Intelligence*, **113**, 269–279.

Sonnhammer, E. L. L., von Hijne, G., and Krogh, A. (1998). A hidden Markov model for predicting transmembrane helices in protein sequences. In *Proceedings of the 6th International Conference on Intelligent Systems for Molecular Biology*, pages 175–182, Menlo Park, CA. AAAI Press.

Spiegelhalter, D. (1990). Fast algorithms for probabilistic reasoning in influence diagrams, with applications in genetics and expert systems. In R. M. Oliver and J. Q. Smith, editors, *Influence Diagrams, Belief Nets and Decision Analysis*, pages 361–383. John Wiley & Sons Ltd., New York, NY.

Spiegelhalter, D. J. (1986). Probabilistic reasoning in predictive expert systems. In L. N. Kanal and J. F. Lemmer, editors, *Uncertainty in Artificial Intelligence*, pages 47–67. Elsevier Science Publishers, Amsterdam, The Netherlands.

Spiegelhalter, D. J. (1991). Personal communication.

Spiegelhalter, D. J., Dawid, A. P., Hutchinson, T. A., and Cowell, R. G. (1990). Probabilistic causality assessment after a suspected adverse drug reaction: a case study in Bayesian network modelling. Report 90-11, MRC Biostatistics Unit.

Spohn, W. (1990). A general non-probabilistic theory of inductive reasoning. In R. D. Shachter, T. S. Levitt, L. N. Kanal, and J. F. Lemmer, editors, *Uncertainty in Artificial Intelligence 4*, pages 149–158. Elsevier Science Publishers, Amsterdam, The Netherlands.

Srinivas, S. (1993). A generalisation of the Noisy-Or model. In *Proceedings of the 9th Conference on Uncertainty in Artificial Intelligence*, pages 208–215, San Mateo, CA. Morgan Kaufmann.

Srinivas, S. and Breese, J. (1989). IDEAL: Influence Diagram Evaluation and Analysis in LISP. Documentation and User Guide. Technical Memorandum No. 23, Rockwell International Science Center.

Srinivas, S. and Breese, J. (1990). IDEAL: a software package for analysis of influence diagrams. In *Proceedings of the 6th Conference on Uncertainty in Artificial Intelligence*, pages 212–219, Mountain View, CA. Association for Uncertainty in AI.

Srinivas, S., Russell, S., and Agogino, A. (1989). Automated construction of sparse Bayesian networks from unstructured probabilistic models and domain information. In *Proceedings of the 5th Workshop on Uncertainty in Artificial Intelligence*, pages 343–350, Mountain View, CA. Association for Uncertainty in AI.

Sternberg, M. J. and Thornton, J. M. (1977). On the conformation of proteins: an analysis of β-pleated sheets. *Journal of Molecular Biology*, **110**, 269–283.

Stewart, J. (1991). *Calculus*. Brooks/Cole Publishing Company, Pacific Grove, CA, 2nd edition.

Steyer, J. P., Queinnec, I., and Simoes, D. (1992). BIOTECH: a real time application of artificial intelligence for fermentation processes. In *Proceedings of the IFAC/IFIP/IMACS International Symposium on AI in Real Time Control*, pages 353–358, Delft, Netherlands. IFAC.

Sticklen, J., Kamel, A., and Bond, W. E. (1991). Integrating quantitative and qualitative computations in a functional framework. *Engineering Applications of Artificial Intelligence*, **4**, 1–10.

Strat, T. (1989a). Decision analysis using belief functions. *International Journal of Approximate Reasoning*, **4**, 391–417.

Strat, T. (1989b). Making decisions with belief functions. In *Proceedings of the 5th Workshop on Uncertainty in Artificial Intelligence*, pages 351–360, Mountain View, CA. Association for Uncertainty in AI.

Struss, P. (1988a). Mathematical aspects of qualitative reasoning. *Artificial Intelligence in Engineering*, **3**, 156–169.

Struss, P. (1988b). Some remarks on Ben Kuipers' reply. *Artificial Intelligence in Engineering*, **3**, 172–173.

Studený, M. (1990). Conditional independence relations have no finite complete characterisation. In S. Kubík and J. A. Víšek, editors, *Information Theory, Statistical Decision Functions, Random Processes: Transactions of the 11th Prague Conference*, pages 377–396. Kluwer, Dordrecht.

Studený, M. (1993). Formal properties of conditional independence in different calculi of AI. In M. Clarke, R. Kruse, and S. Moral, editors, *Symbolic and Quantitative Approaches to Reasoning and Uncertainty*, pages 341–348. Springer Verlag, Berlin, Germany.

Sucar, L. E., Gillies, D. F., and Gillies, D. A. (1993). Objective probabilities in expert systems. *Artificial Intelligence*, **61**, 187–208.

Suermondt, H. J. and Cooper, G. F. (1991). Initialization for the method of conditioning in Bayesian belief networks. *Artificial Intelligence*, **50**, 83–94.

Sullivan, M. and Cohen, P. R. (1985). An endorsement-based plan recognition program. In *Proceedings of the 9th International Joint Conference on Artificial Intelligence*, pages 475–479, Los Altos, CA. Morgan Kaufmann.

Suppes, P. (1994). Qualitative theory of subjective probability. In G. Wright and P. Ayton, editors, *Subjective Probability*, pages 17–37. John Wiley & Sons, Chichester, UK.

Szolovits, P. (1992). Compilation for fast calculation over pedigrees. *Cytogenetics and Cell Genetics*, **59**, 136–138.

Tan, S.-W. (1994). Exceptional sub-classes in qualitative probability. In *Proceedings of the 10th Conference on Uncertainty in Artificial Intelligence*, pages 553–559, San Mateo, CA. Morgan Kaufmann.

Tan, S.-W. and Pearl, J. (1994a). Qualitative decision theory. In *Proceedings of the 12th National Conference on Artificial Intelligence*, pages 928–933, Menlo Park, CA. AAAI Press/MIT Press.

Tan, S.-W. and Pearl, J. (1994b). Specification and evaluation of preferences under uncertainty. In *Proceedings of the 4th International Conference on Knowledge Representation and Reasoning*, pages 530–539, San Francisco, CA. Morgan Kaufmann.

Tan, S.-W. and Pearl, J. (1995). Specificity and inheritance in default reasoning. In *Proceedings of the 14th International Joint Conference on Artificial Intelligence*, pages 1480–1486, San Mateo, CA. Morgan Kaufmann.

Taylor, W. R. and Green, N. M. (1989). The predicted secondary structure of the nucleotide binding sites of six cation-transporting ATPases leads to a probable tertiary fold. *European Journal of Biochemistry*, **179**, 241–248.

Teigen, K. H. (1994). Variants of subjective probabilities: concepts, norms and biases. In G. Wright and P. Ayton, editors, *Subjective Probability*, pages 211–238. John Wiley & Sons, Chichester, UK.

Tessem, B. (1993). Approximations for efficient computation in the theory of evidence. *Artificial Intelligence*, **61**, 315–329.

Thöne, H., Güntzer, U., and Kießling, W. (1992). Towards precision of probabilistic bounds propagation. In *Proceedings of the 8th Conference on Uncertainty in Artificial Intelligence*, pages 315–322, San Mateo, CA. Morgan Kaufmann.

Tong, R. M. and Shapiro, D. G. (1985). Experimental investigations of uncertainty in a rule-based system for information retrieval. *International Journal of Man-Machine Studies*, **22**, 265–282.

Travé-Massuyès, L. and Piera, N. (1989). The orders of magnitude models as qualitative algebras. In *Proceedings of the 11th International Joint Conference on Artificial Intelligence*, pages 1261–1266, San Mateo, CA. Morgan

Kaufmann.

Travé-Massuyès, L., Piera, N., and Missier, A. (1989). What can we do with the qualitative calculus today? In *Proceedings of the IFAC/IMACS/IFORS International Symposium on Advanced Information Processing in Automatic Control*, pages 258–263.

Tu, S. W., Kemper, C. A., Lane, N. M., Carlson, R. W., and Musen, M. A. (1993). A methodology for determining patient's eligibility for clinical trials. *Methods of Information in Medicine*, **32**, 317–325.

Turtle, H. R. and Croft, W. B. (1990). Inference networks for document retrieval. In *Proceedings of the 13th International Conference on Research and Development in Information Retrieval*, pages 1–24. Association for Computaing Machinery.

Turtle, H. R. and Croft, W. B. (1997). Uncertainty in information retrieval systems. In A. Motro and P. Smets, editors, *Uncertainty in Information Systems: From Needs to Solutions*, pages 289–224. Kluwer, Boston, MA.

Tversky, A. and Kahneman, D. (1971). Belief in the law of small numbers. *Psychological Bulletin*, **76**, 105–110.

Tversky, A. and Kahneman, D. (1974). Judgement under uncertainty: Heuristics and biases. *Science*, **185**, 1124–1131.

Tversky, A. and Kahneman, D. (1982a). Causal schemas in judgments under uncertainty. In D. Kahneman, A. Tversky, and P. Slovic, editors, *Judgement under uncertainty: Heuristics and biases*, pages 117–128. Cambridge University Press, Cambridge, UK.

Tversky, A. and Kahneman, D. (1982b). Judgements of and by representativeness. In D. Kahneman, P. Slovic, and A. Tversky, editors, *Judgement under uncertainty: Heuristics and biases*, pages 84–98. Cambridge University Press, Cambridge, UK.

Tversky, A. and Kahneman, D. (1983). Extensional versus intuitive reasoning: The conjunction fallacy in probability judgement. *Psychological Review*, **90**, 293–315.

Tzeng, C.-H. (1992). A plausible reasoning in Bayesian networks. In *Proceedings of the 10th European Conference on Artificial Intelligence*, pages 51–52, Chichester, UK. John Wiley & Sons.

Uhrik, C. T. (1982). PLANT/ds revisited: non-homogeneous evaluation schema in expert systems. In *Proceedings of the 2nd National Conference on Artificial Intelligence*, pages 217–220, Los Altos, CA. William Kaufmann.

van Dam, K. (1996). *Intelligent control of radio communication systems*. Ph.D. thesis, Queen Mary and Westfield College.

van Dam, K. (1998). Using uncertainty techniques in radio communication systems. In A. Hunter and S. Parsons, editors, *Applications of Uncertainty Formalisms*, pages 76–87. Springer Verlag, Berlin, Germany.

van der Gaag, L. C. (1990). Different notions of uncertainty in quasi-probabilistic models. *International Journal of Man-Machine Studies*, **33**, 595–606.

van der Gaag, L. C. (1991). Computing probability intervals under independency constraints. In P. P. Bonissone, M. Henrion, L. N. Kanal, and J. F. Lemmer, editors, *Uncertainty in Artificial Intelligence 6*, pages 457–466. Elsevier Science Publishers, Amsterdam, The Netherlands.

van der Gaag, L. C. (1999). Personal communication.

van Eemeren, F. H., Grootendorst, R., Henkemans, F. S., Blair, J. A., Johnson, R. H., Krabbe, E. C. W., Plantin, C., Walton, D. N., Willard, C. A., Woods, J., and Zarefsky, D. (1996). *Fundamentals of Argumentation Theory: A Handbook of Historical Backgrounds and Contemporary Developments*. Lawrence Erlbaum Associates, Mahwah, NJ.

van Emden, M. H. (1986). Quantitative deduction and its fixpoint theory. *Journal of Logic Programming*, **3**, 37–53.

van Melle, W. (1980). *A domain-independent system that aids in constructing knowledge-based consultation programs*. Ph.D. thesis, Department of Computer Science, Stanford.

van Wylen, G. J. and Sonntag, R. E. (1985). *Fundamentals of Classical Thermodynamics*. John Wiley & Sons, New York, NY, 3rd edition.

Verma, T. and Pearl, J. (1990). Causal networks: semantics and expressiveness. In R. D. Shachter, T. S. Levitt, L. N. Kanal, and J. F. Lemmer, editors, *Uncertainty in Artificial Intelligence 4*, pages 69–76. Elsevier Science Publishers, Amsterdam, The Netherlands.

Vogel, C. (1996). Human reasoning with negative defaults. In D. M. Gabbay and H. J. Ohlbach, editors, *Practical Reasoning*, pages 606–621. Springer Verlag, Berlin, Germany.

Voorbraak, F. (1989). A computationally efficient approximation of Dempster-Shafer theory. *International Journal of Man-Machine Studies*, **30**, 525–536.

Voorbraak, F. (1991). On the justification of Dempster's rule of combination. *Artificial Intelligence*, **48**, 171–197.

Voorbraak, F. (1993). Preference based semantics for nonmonotonic logics. In *Proceedings of the 13th International Joint Conference on Artificial Intelligence*, pages 584–589, San Mateo, CA. Morgan Kaufmann.

Vreeswijk, G. (1989). The feasibility of defeat in defeasible reasoning. In *Proceedings of the 1st International Conference on Knowledge Representation and Reasoning*, pages 526–534, San Mateo, CA. Morgan Kaufmann.

Wainer, J. (1992). Combining circumscription and modal logic. In *Proceedings of the 10th National Conference on Artificial Intelligence*, pages 648–653, San Mateo, CA. AAAI Press/MIT Press.

Walker, J. E., Saraste, M., Runswick, W. J., and Gay, N. J. (1982). Distantly related sequences in the α and β-subunits of ATP synthase, myosin, kinases and other ATP-requiring enzymes and a common nucleotide binding fold. *The EMBO Journal*, **1**, 945–951.

Walley, P. (1996). Measures of uncertainty in expert systems. *Artificial Intelligence*, **83**, 1–58.

Wallsten, T. S. and Budescu, D. V. (1995). A review of human linguistic probability processing: general principles and empirical evidence. *The Knowledge Engineering Review*, **10**, 43–62.

Watkins, F. A. (1995). False controversy: fuzzy and non-fuzzy fauz pas. *IEEE Expert*, **10**(2), 4–5.

Weber, S. (1983). A general concept of fuzzy connectives, negations and implications based on t-norms and t-conorms. *Fuzzy sets and systems*, **11**, 115–134.

Weber, S. (1996). On the semantics of the unknown. In D. M. Gabbay and H. J. Ohlbach, editors, *Practical Reasoning*, pages 622–636. Springer Verlag, Berlin, Germany.

Weichselberger, K. and Pöhlmann, S. (1990). *A Methodology for Uncertainty in Knowledge-Based Systems*. Springer Verlag, Berlin, Germany.

Weiss, Y. and Freeman, W. T. (1999). Correctness of belief propagation in Gaussian graphical models of arbitrary topology. Technical Report TR UCB//CSD-99-1046, Department of Computer Science, University of California at Berkeley.

Wellman, M. P. (1988). Qualitative probabilistic networks for planning under uncertainty. In J. F. Lemmer and L. N. Kanal, editors, *Uncertainty in Artificial Intelligence 2*, pages 197–208. Elsevier Science Publishers, Amsterdam, The Netherlands.

Wellman, M. P. (1990a). *Formulation of Tradeoffs in Planning under Uncertainty*. Pitman, London, UK.

Wellman, M. P. (1990b). Fundamental concepts of qualitative probabilistic networks. *Artificial Intelligence*, **44**, 257–303.

Wellman, M. P. (1991). Exploiting functional dependencies in qualitative probabilistic reasoning. In P. P. Bonissone, M. Henrion, L. N. Kanal, and J. F. Lemmer, editors, *Uncertainty in Artificial Intelligence 6*, pages 3–15. Elsevier Science Publishers, Amsterdam, The Netherlands.

Wellman, M. P. (1994). Some varieties of qualitative probability. In *Proceedings of the 5th International Conference on Information Processing and the Management of Uncertainty*, pages 437–442.

Wellman, M. P. and Henrion, M. (1991). Qualitative intercausal relations, or explaining "explaining away". In *Proceedings of the 2nd International Conference on Principles of Knowledge Representation and Reasoning*, pages 535–546, San Mateo, CA. Morgan Kaufmann.

Wellman, M. P., Breese, J. S., and Goldman, R. P. (1992). From knowledge bases to decision models. *The Knowledge Engineering Review*, **7**, 35–53.

Wen, W. X. (1991). From relational databases to belief networks. In *Proceedings of the 7th Conference on Uncertainty in Artificial Intelligence*, pages 406–413, San Mateo, CA. Morgan Kaufmann.

Weydert, E. (1995). Numeric defaults: about an expressive first-order framework for reasoning with infinitesimal probabilities. In C. Froidevaux and J. Kohlas, editors, *Symbolic and Quantitative Approaches to Reasoning and Uncertainty*, pages 420–427. Springer Verlag, Berlin, Germany.

Weydert, E. (1996). System J—revision entailment: default reasoning through ranking measure updates. In D. M.

Gabbay and H. J. Ohlbach, editors, *Practical Reasoning*, pages 637–649. Springer Verlag, Berlin, Germany.

Whitmore, G. A. and Findlay, M. C., editors (1978). *Stochastic Dominance: An Approach to Decision-Making Under Risk*. D. C. Heath, Lexington, MA.

Williams, B. C. (1984). Qualitative analysis of MOS circuits. *Artificial Intelligence*, **24**, 281–346.

Williams, B. C. (1988). A symbolic approach to qualitative algebraic reasoning. In *Proceedings of the 7th National Conference on Artificial Intelligence*, pages 264–269, San Mateo, CA. Morgan Kaufmann.

Williams, B. C. (1991). A theory of interactions, unifying qualitative and quantitative algebraic reasoning. *Artificial Intelligence*, **51**, 39–94.

Wilson, N. (1990). Rules, belief functions, and default logic. In *Proceedings of the 6th Conference on Uncertainty in Artificial Intelligence*, pages 443–449, Mountain View, CA. Association for Uncertainty in AI.

Wilson, N. (1991). A Monte-Carlo algorithm for Dempster-Shafer belief. In *Proceedings of the 7th Conference on Uncertainty in Artificial Intelligence*, pages 414–417, San Mateo, CA. Morgan Kaufmann.

Wilson, N. (1992a). The combination of belief: when and how fast? *International Journal of Approximate Reasoning*, **6**, 377–388.

Wilson, N. (1992b). How much do you believe? *International Journal of Approximate Reasoning*, **6**, 345–365.

Wilson, N. (1992c). *Some theoretical aspects of the Dempster-Shafer theory*. Ph.D. thesis, Oxford Polytechnic.

Wilson, N. (1993a). The assumptions behind Dempster's rule. In *Proceedings of the 9th Conference on Uncertainty in Artificial Intelligence*, pages 527–534, San Mateo, CA. Morgan Kaufmann.

Wilson, N. (1993b). Default logic and Dempster-Shafer theory. In M. Clarke, R. Kruse, and S. Moral, editors, *Symbolic and Quantitative Approaches to Reasoning and Uncertainty*, pages 372–379. Springer Verlag, Berlin, Germany.

Wilson, N. (1995). An order of magnitude calculus. In *Proceedings of the 11th Conference on Uncertainty in Artificial Intelligence*, pages 548–555, San Francisco, CA. Morgan Kaufman.

Wilson, N. (1996). Extended probability. In *Proceedings of the 12th European Conference on Artificial Intelligence*, pages 667–671, Chichester, UK. John Wiley & Sons.

Wilson, N. and Mengin, J. (1999). Logical deduction using the local computation framework. In A. Hunter and S. Parsons, editors, *Symbolic and Quantitative Approaches to Reasoning and Uncertainty*, pages 386–396. Springer Verlag, Berlin, Germany.

Wilson, N. and Moral, S. (1994). A logical view of probability. In *Proceedings of the 11th European Conference on Artificial Intelligence*, pages 386–390, Chichester, UK. John Wiley & Sons.

Wilson, N. and Moral, S. (1996). Fast Markov chain algorithms for calculating Dempster-Shafer belief. In *Proceedings of the 12th European Conference on Artificial Intelligence*, pages 672–676, Chichester, UK. John Wiley & Sons.

Wise, B. P. and Henrion, M. (1986). A framework for comapring uncertain inference systems to probability. In L. N. Kanal and J. F. Lemmer, editors, *Uncertainty in Artificial Intelligence*, pages 69–83. Elsevier Science Publishers, Amsterdam, The Netherlands.

Wittig, F. and Jameson, A. (2000). Exploiting qualitative knowledge in the learning of conditional probabilities of Bayesian networks. In C. Boutillier and M. Goldszmidt, editors, *Proceedings of the 16th Conference on Uncertainty in Artificial Intelligence*, San Francisco, CA. Morgan Kaufmann.

Wong, S. K. M. and Lingras, P. (1994). Representation of qualitative user preference by quantitative belief functions. *IEEE Transactions on Knowledge and Data Engineering*, **6**, 72–78.

Wong, S. K. M. and Wang, Z. W. (1994). On axiomatization of probabilistic conditional independence. In *Proceedings of the 10th Conference on Uncertainty in Artificial Intelligence*, pages 591–597, San Francisco, CA. Morgan Kaufmann.

Wong, S. K. M., Yao, Y. Y., and Lingras, P. (1991). Compatibility of quantitative and qualitative representations of belief. In *Proceedings of the 7th Conference on Uncertainty in Artificial Intelligence*, pages 418–424, San Mateo, CA. Morgan Kaufmann.

Wong, S. K. M., Wang, L. S., and Yao, Y. Y. (1992). Interval structure: a framework for representing uncertain information. In *Proceedings of the 8th Conference on Uncertainty in Artificial Intelligence*, pages 336–343, San

Mateo, CA. Morgan Kaufmann.

Wong, S. K. M., Xiang, Y., and Nie, X. (1994). Representation of Bayesian networks as relational databases. In *Proceedings of the 5th International Conference on Information Processing and the Management of Uncertainty*, pages 159–165.

Wong, S. K. M., Butz, C. J., and Xiang, Y. (1995). A method for implementing a probabilistic model as a relational database. In *Proceedings of the 11th Conference on Uncertainty in Artificial Intelligence*, pages 556–564, San Francisco, CA. Morgan Kaufmann.

Wright, G. and Ayton, P. (1994). *Subjective Probability*. John Wiley & Sons, Chichester, UK.

Wright, S. (1921). Correlation and causation. *Journal of Agricultural Research*, **20**, 557–585.

Xiang, Y., Poole, D., and Beddoes, M. P. (1993). Multiply sectioned Bayesian networks and junction forests for large knowledge-based systems. *Computational Intelligence*, **9**, 171–220.

Xu, H. (1991a). An efficient implementation of belief function propagation. In *Proceedings of the 7th Conference on Uncertainty in Artificial Intelligence*, pages 425–432, San Mateo, CA. Morgan Kaufmann.

Xu, H. (1991b). TRESBEL: User's Manual. Technical Report TR/IRIDIA/91-11, IRIDIA, Université Libre de Bruxelles.

Xu, H. (1992a). A decision calculus for belief functions in valuation-based systems. In *Proceedings of the 8th Conference on Uncertainty in Artificial Intelligence*, pages 352–359, San Mateo, CA. Morgan Kaufmann.

Xu, H. (1992b). An efficient tool for reasoning with belief functions. In *Proceedings of the 4th International Conference on Information Processing and the Management of Uncertainty*, pages 65–68, Palma, Mallorca. Universitat de les Illes Balears.

Xu, H. (1995). Computing marginals for arbitrary subsets from marginal representation in Markov trees. *Artificial Intelligence*, **74**, 177–189.

Xu, H. and Kennes, R. (1994). Steps towards an efficient implementation of Dempster-Shafer theory. In M. Fedrizzi, J. Kacprzyk, and R. R. Yager, editors, *Advances in the Dempster Shafer Theory of Evidence*, pages 153–174. John Wiley & Sons, New York, NY.

Xu, H. and Smets, P. (1991). Evidential reasoning with conditional belief functions. In *Proceedings of the 10th Conference on Uncertainty in Artificial Intelligence*, pages 598–605, San Mateo, CA. Morgan Kaufmann.

Xu, H., Hsia, Y.-T., and Smets, P. (1993). A belief-function based decision support system. In *Proceedings of the 9th Conference on Uncertainty in Artificial Intelligence*, pages 535–542, San Mateo, CA. Morgan Kaufmann.

Yager, R. R. (1983). An introduction to applications of possibility theory. *Human Systems Management*, **3**, 246–269.

Yager, R. R. (1987). Using approximate reasoning to represent default logic. *Artificial Intelligence*, **31**, 99–112.

Yip, K. M. (1993). Model simplification by asymptotic order of magnitude reasoning. In *Proceedings of the 11th National Conference on Artificial Intelligence*, pages 634–640, Menlo Park, CA. AAAI Press/MIT Press.

Yip, K. M. (1996). Model simplification by asymptotic order of magnitude reasoning. *Artificial Intelligence*, **80**, 309–348.

Zadeh, L. A. (1965). Fuzzy sets. *Information and Control*, **8**, 338–353.

Zadeh, L. A. (1977). PRUF—a language for the representation or meaning in natural languages. In *Proceedings of the 5th International Joint Conference on Artificial Intelligence*, page 918, Pittsburg, PA. Department of Computer Science, Carnegie Mellon University.

Zadeh, L. A. (1978). Fuzzy sets as a basis for a theory of possibility. *Fuzzy Sets and Systems*, **1**, 1–28.

Zadeh, L. A. (1979). A theory of approximate reasoning. In J. E. Hayes, D. Michie, and L. I. Mikulich, editors, *Machine Intelligence 9*, pages 149–194. Ellis Horwood, Chichester, UK.

Zadeh, L. A. (1983a). Commonsense knowledge representation based on fuzzy logic. *IEEE Computer*, **October**, 61–65.

Zadeh, L. A. (1983b). The role of fuzzy logic in the management of uncertainty in expert systems. *Fuzzy Sets and Systems*, **11**, 199–227.

Zadeh, L. A. (1984a). Book review of "A Mathematical Theory of Evidence" by Glenn Shafer. *AI Magazine*, **5(3)**, 81–83.

Zadeh, L. A. (1984b). Fuzzy probabilities. *Information Processing & Management*, **3**, 363–372.

Zadeh, L. A. (1985). Syllogistic reasoning in fuzzy logic and its application to usuality and reasoning with dispositions. *IEEE Transactions on Systems, Man and Cybernetics*, **15**, 754–763.

Zadeh, L. A. (1986). Is probability theory sufficient for dealing with uncertainty in AI? a negative view. In L. N. Kanal and J. F. Lemmer, editors, *Uncertainty in Artificial Intelligence*, pages 103–116. Elsevier Science Publishers, Amsterdam, The Netherlands.

Zadeh, L. A. (1994). Why the success of fuzzy logic is not paradoxical. *IEEE Expert*, **9**(4), 43–46.

Zarley, D. (1988). An evidential reasoning system. Working Paper 206, School of Business, University of Kansas, Lawrence.

Zarley, D., Hsia, Y.-T., and Shafer, G. (1988). Evidential reasoning using Delief. In *Proceedings of the 7th National Conference on Artificial Intelligence*, pages 205–209, San Mateo, CA. Morgan Kaufmann.

Zhang, C. (1992). Co-operation under uncertainty in distributed expert systems. *Artificial Intelligence*, **56**, 21–69.

Zhang, C. (1994). Heterogeneous transformation of uncertainties of propositions among inexact reasoning models. *IEEE Transactions on Knowledge and Data Engineering*, **6**, 353–360.

Zhang, N. L. and Poole, D. (1999). On the role of context-specific independence in probabilistic inference. In *Proceedings of the 16th International Joint Conference on Artificial Intelligence*, pages 1288–1293, San Francisco, CA. Morgan Kaufmann.

Ziarko, W. P. (1993). *Rough Sets, Fuzzy Sets and Knowledge Discovery*. Springer Verlag, London, UK.

Zukerman, I., McConarchy, R., and Korb, K. (1999). Exploratory interaction with a Bayesian argumentation system. In *Proceedings of the 16th International Joint Conference on Artificial Intelligence*, pages 1294–1299, San Francisco, CA. Morgan Kaufmann.

Index

Additive synergy
In qualitative probabilistic networks, 125
Additivity
In evidence theory, 39, 56
In possibility theory, 49, 50
In probability theory, 39, 41
Ancestor node, 189
Anytime algorithm
For propagating probabilities, 77
ARCO, 77
Argumentation
And defeasible reasoning, 150–155
And handling uncertainty, 152, 153
And logic programming, 154
And probability, 133
Relationship with qualitative certainty networks, 323, 324
ATMS, 101, 165
Autoepistemic logic, 138, 139, 162, 163

Base rate fallacy, 21, 22, 27
Base rate neglect, 27
Bayes' rule
In evidence theory, 58, 59
In possibility theory, 50
In probability theory, 42
Naïve, 42, 43
Bayesian belief function
In evidence theory, 56
Bayesian multinets, 93, 94
Belief function
Definition of, 54
Biases in human reasoning
Base rate fallacy, 21, 22, 27
Base rate neglect, 27
Conservatism, 20, 21
Extension law, 23, 24
Gambler's fallacy, 23, 25
Overconfidence, 22, 28

Callibration
Of human subjects, 22
Capacities, 118, 119
Causal networks
And logic, 133
Dynamic construction of, 85–89
For evidence theory, 79
For possibility theory, 79, 80
For probability theory, 74–78
Causal reasoning
In certainty networks, 188, 189
In qualitative certainty networks, 247–255
Certainty factors
Birth of, 3
In qualitative certainty networks, 395, 396
Relation to rules, 66

Certainty networks
Causal reasoning, 188, 189
Definition of, 186, 187
Evidential reasoning, 188, 189
Intercausal reasoning, 189
Certainty value
Definition of, 185, 186
Child node, 189
Circumscription, 137, 138, 162, 163
Clique-tree, 76
CNETS, 78
Combination, 331–337
Role in valuation networks, 81
Compatibility
Of qualitative values, 260, 261
Conditional cognitive independence
Definition of, 59
Relation to d-separation, 79
Conditional independence
In evidence theory, 59
In possibility theory, 50–53
In probability theory, 40
Relation to d-separation, 79
Conditional possibility
Definition of, 49
Conditional probability
Definition of, 40
Conservatism bias, 20, 21
Consonant belief function
In evidence theory, 56
Context model
As a solution to the translation problem, 175
To compare quantitative measures, 160
Contradiction
In evidence theory, 54
Convex sets of probabilities, 119
CONVINCE, 77
Cox's axioms
Critique by Shafer, 30
Definition of, 29, 30
To compare quantitative measures, 156, 158

d-separation
Definition of, 191
In evidence theory, 79
In possibility theory, 79
In probability theory, 79
DAVID, 90
Decision making
Coverage in this book, xiv
Influence diagrams, 89
With kappa values, 132
Default logic, 135–137, 162–164
Defeasible reasoning
And qualitative probabilistic networks, 145, 146
Circumscription, 137, 138

Default logic, 135–137
    Definition of, 134, 135
    Modal approaches, 138, 139
    Nonmonotonic consequence relations, 140, 141
    Nonmonotonic logic, 135–143
    Numerical approaches, 143–150
    Preferential models, 139, 140
    Using evidence theory, 148
    Using kappa values, 146–148
    Using possibility theory, 148–150
    Using probability theory, 140–148
Delief, 83
Dempster's rule
    Definition of, 57
Dempster-Shafer theory, See Evidence theory
Descartes
    The ideally rational man, 8
Descendant node, 189
Direct link, 339
Disbelief functions, See Kappa values
Disjunctive rule
    Definition of, 58
Divisible experiments
    And probability theory, 31
Driving value, 262, 263, 348–350
DRUMS, xiii
Dutch book
    Against evidence theory, 61

Eclectic position
    And types of uncertainty, 35
    Emergence of, 4
    In decision making, 65
    Issues arising from, 4, 5
    Leading to the integration problem, 174
    Manifesto for, xiv
    Probability and evidence theories, 59
    Promotion as aim of book, 391
    Relationship to qualitative methods, 394, 395
    Solution to the incompleteness problem, 182
    Statement of, xi, 172–174
Eco
    Umberto, xiii
Empirical evaluation
    Of quantitative measures, 155, 156
    Of qualitative measures, 358
EMYCIN, 176
ENAMORA, 160, 161
Endorsements, 151
Engineering out
    Of imperfect information, 2, 18
Entropy
    In thermodynamics, 18
    Of information, 19, 20

ENVISION, 109
Epistemic belief, See kappa values
Evidence theory
    #P-completeness of Dempster's rule, 94
    And ATMS, 165
    And default logic, 164, 165
    And defeasible reasoning, 148
    And logic, 101, 102
    As a variant of probability theory, 38
    As upper and lower probabilities, 60
    Bayes' rule, 58, 59
    Bayesian belief function, 56
    Belief function, 54
    Birth of, 3
    Causal networks, 79
    Commonality function, 55
    Computational problems with, 74
    Consistency with possibility theory, 181
    Consistency with probability theory, 181
    Consonant belief function, 56
    Contradiction, 54
    Credal level, 61, 64
    d-separation, 79
    Decision making in, 63–65
    Dempster's rule, 57, 58, 62
    Disjunctive rule, 58
    Efficient computation, 95, 96
    Focal elements, 55
    Frame of discernment, 53
    In protein topology prediction, 380–383
    Jeffrey's rule, 58
    Linguistic values, 121
    Mass distribution, 53
    Normalisation, 58, 62
    NP-completeness of Dempster's rule, 94
    Pignistic level, 61, 64
    Pignistic transformation, 65
    Plausibility, 54
    Principle of minimum commitment, 55
    Probability of provability, 60, 61, 133
    Relation to possibility theory, 56
    Relation to probability theory, 56
    Relation to upper and lower probabilities, 47
    Relationship to possibility theory, 158, 159
    Relationship with rough sets, 162
    Simple support function, 55, 56
    Transferable belief model, 61
    Vacuous belief function, 54
    Varieties of belief, 59–63
    Why studied, 38
Evidential reasoning
    In certainty networks, 188, 189
    In qualitative certainty networks, 263–271
Evidenzia, 134

Explaining away
  In qualitative certainty networks, 311–317
  In qualitative probabilistic networks, 125, 314

Focal elements
  Definition of, 55
FOG, 113, 114
FOLIO, 151
Frame of discernment
  In evidence theory, 53
Fuzzy sets
  And logic, 102–104
  Birth of, 3
  Fuzzy probability, 69, 70
  Introduction to, 66
  Linguistic quantifier, 69
  Membership functions, 67–69
  Relation to possibility theory, 47, 68, 69
  Relationship with rough sets, 161, 162
  Triangular norms, 68, 70

Gambler's fallacy, 23, 25

Head-to-head node, 190
Heuristics in human reasoning
  Anchoring and adjustment, 24, 26
  Availability, 24, 25
  Representativeness, 24, 25
Hidden variables
  Relation to uncertainty, 18
Hooptedoodle
  Explanation of, 7
HUGIN, 78

IDEAL, 78, 86, 90, 329, 330, 337, 338, 350, 351
Ignorant induction, 129
Imperfect information
  Engineering it out, 2, 18
  Fundamental nature of, 2, 7–9
  Hidden variable interpretation, 18
  Numerical measures of, 2, 3
  Qualitative measures of, 5
  Quantitative measures of, 2, 3
  Relation to measurement, 15–18
  Taxonomy by Bonissone and Tong, 12, 13
  Taxonomy by Bosc and Prade, 13
  Taxonomy by Smets, 11, 12
  Taxonomy by Smithson, 10, 11
  Taxonomy for this book, 14, 15
Incompleteness problem
  An example, 196–199
  Definition of, 169, 170
  Example solved by $Q2$, 229, 230
  Example solved by $Q3$, 231–233
  Example solved by qualitative certainty networks,
    273–275

Solution by monotonicity assumption, 392, 393
  Solution through degrading, 182–184, 392
  Solution using $Q2$, 208
  Solution using $Q3$, 219
INFERNO, 46
Infinitesimal probabilities, 129–132
Influence diagrams, 89–91
Information
  Relation to uncertainty, 19
Information node, 338
Information theory, 18
Information trail, 339
Integration problem
  An example, 191–196
  Definition of, 171, 172
  Example solved by $Q2$, 221–224
  Example solved by $Q3$, 225–228
  Example solved by qualitative certainty networks,
    276–280
  Solution through degrading, 177–179
  Solved by qualitative certainty networks, 238
  Stemming from the eclectic position, 174
Intelligence
  Definition of, 1
Intercausal link, 339
Intercausal reasoning
  In certainty networks, 189
  In qualitative certainty networks, 311–319
  In qualitative probabilistic networks, 125

Jack Dulouz
  And Cody's poetry, 271–273
  And the letter, 257–260
  And the telephone call, 320, 321
  And the weekend, 293–296
  On the mountain, 214–217
  With the Subterraneans, 309–311
Jeffrey's rule
  In evidence theory, 58
  In possibility theory, 50
  In probability theory, 41, 42
Join tree, 76, 121

Kappa values
  And decision making, 132
  And local computation, 130
  As linguistic probabilities, 131
  As possibility values, 73
  As probability values, 72, 73, 129–132
  Combination of, 73
  Comparison with probability values, 131, 132
Known node, 338

Law of small numbers, 23
Leaf node, 190

Linguistic probabilities
    As kappa values, 131
    Human fondness for, 33
Linguistic quantifier
    In fuzzy sets, 69
Linguistic values
    In evidence theory, 120
    In probability theory, 120, 121
Local computation
    For $Q2$ and $Q3$, 333–335
    In Pulcinella, 83, 84, 331, 332
    In valuation networks, 80–84
    With kappa values, 130
Logic
    And evidence theory, 101, 102, 133, 134
    And fuzzy sets, 102–104
    And possibility theory, 100, 101
    And probability theory, 97–100, 133
    And qualitative probabilistic networks, 133
    And rough sets, 104
Lower previsions, 120
LTMS, 165

MacEvidence, 83
Marginalisation, 331–337
    Role in valuation networks, 81
Markov blanket, 340
Markov-tree, 76
Membership functions
    Of fuzzy sets, 67–69
MILORD, 176
Monotonicity assumption
    Consistency with consistency principles, 181
    Definition of, 179, 180
    Follows from degrading, 392
    Foundation of the qualitative approach, 391
    In protein topology prediction, 387
    In qualitative certainty networks, 278, 280
    Leads to principle of degrading, 393
    Solution to the incompleteness problem, 392, 393
    Solution to the translation problem, 392
Multi-valued mapping
    Inducing upper and lower possibilities, 53
    Inducing upper and lower probabilities, 47
Multiple-observations
    In qualitative certainty networks, 348
    In qualitative probabilistic networks, 127, 128, 319, 342
Multiply-connected
    Definition of, 76
    Qualitative certainty networks, 296–305
Mummu, xii
    And IDEAL, 350, 351
    And Pulcinella, 335, 336
    For handling qualitative algebras, 333–336
    For handling qualitative change, 342–351
    In protein topology prediction, 362, 363
    Origin of the name, 329
    Relation to IDEAL and Pulcinella, 330
MUNIN, 77, 78
MYCIN, 176
Myth of Zu, 329

Natural conditional functions, See kappa values
Naïve Bayes rule, 42, 43
Naïve physics
    Manifesto, 109
    Qualitative reasoning, 109–112
    Relationship with qualitative certainty networks, 322, 323
Negative influence
    In qualitative certainty networks, 240
Non-interactivity
    Definition of, 52, 53
Non-zero change at a node
    In qualitative certainty networks, 246
Non-zero change in value
    In qualitative certainty networks, 242
Non-zero influence
    In qualitative certainty networks, 241
Normalisation
    In evidence theory, 58, 62
    In possibility theory, 48
Normativeness
    Of human reasoning, 24, 26, 29, 34
    Versus irrationality, 24
    Why formality helps, 37
Numerical measures
    For handling imperfect information, 2, 3
    Obtaining numerical values, 107

O[M], 114, 115
Objective probability
    As frequentist, 44
    As opposed to subjective, 26
Ordinal conditional functions, See kappa values
OSCAR, 154
Overall qualitative influence, 346
Overconfidence bias, 22, 28
Oxford System of Medicine, 191

Parent node, 189
Path
    Through a graph, 190
Perfect information
    Impossibility of, 7, 8
Pignistic transformation
    As a solution to the translation problem, 176
    Definition of, 65

Plain belief
  Introduction to, 72
Positive influence
  In qualitative certainty networks, 240
Possibilistic ATMS, 101
Possibilistic logic, 100, 101
Possibility theory
  Alternative combination functions, 52
  And default logic, 164
  And logic, 100, 101
  And upper and lower probabilities, 159
  As a variant of probability theory, 38
  Bayes' rule, 50
  Causal networks, 79, 80
  Computational problems with, 74
  Conditional independence, 50–53
  Conditional possibility, 49
  Consistency with evidence theory, 181
  Consistency with probability theory, 51
  d-separation, 79
  In protein topology prediction, 359–361, 377–380
  Jeffrey's rule, 50
  Necessity measure, 50
  Non-interactivity, 52, 53
  Normalisation, 48
  Possibility distribution, 47
  Possibility measure, 49
  Principle of minimum specificity, 48, 49
  Relation to evidence theory, 56, 158, 159
  Relation to fuzzy sets, 47, 68, 69
  Relation to kappa values, 73, 159, 160
  Relation to probability theory, 159, 160
  Specificity, 48
  Subadditivity in, 49
  Superadditivity in, 50
  Upper and lower possibilities, 53
  Varieties of, 52
  Why studied, 38
POSSINFER, 80
Predecessor node, 189
Premature mathematization, 37
Principle of degrading
  Definition of, 177
  Follows from monotonicity assumption, 393
  Foundation of the qualitative approach, 391
  Leads to monotonicity assumption, 392
  Solution to the incompleteness problem, 182–184
  Solution to the integration problem, 177–179
  Solution to the translation problem, 392
Principle of maximum entropy
  And information theory, 20
  Applied in diagnosis, 198
  In evidence theory, 55
  In possibility theory, 48, 49

  In probability theory, 43, 44
  Used in $Q3$, 213
Principle of minimum commitment
  In evidence theory, 55
Principle of minimum specificity
  And information theory, 20
  Applied in diagnosis, 193, 195
  In possibility theory, 48, 49
  In qualitative certainty networks, 252, 280, 301
Probabilistic logic, 97–99
Probability of provability
  Interpretation of evidence theory, 60, 61
Probability theory
  Addition law, 40
  Additivity in, 41
  And argumentation, 133
  And defeasible reasoning, 140–148
  And divisible experiments, 31
  And logic, 97–100
  And seriable experiments, 31
  And System P, 146
  As a normative theory, 24
  Bayes' rule, 42
  Causal networks, 74–78
  Computational problems with, 73, 74
  Conditional independence, 40
  Conditional probability, 40
  Consistency with evidence theory, 181
  Consistency with possibility theory, 51
  Convex sets of probabilities, 119
  Convexity law, 40
  d-separation, 79
  Fuzzy probability, 69, 70, 122
  In protein topology prediction, 358, 359, 373–377
  Infinitesimal probabilities, 129–132
  Interval values, 117–123
  Jeffrey's rule, 41, 42
  Linguistic values, 120, 121
  Lower previsions, 120
  Multiplication law, 40
  NP-hardness of propagation, 76
  Odds-likelihood formulation, 45
  Principle of maximum entropy, 43, 44
  Probability distribution, 39
  Probability measure, 39
  Problems with, 3
  Qualitative probabilistic networks, 123–129
  Relation to evidence theory, 56
  Relation to kappa values, 73
  Relationship to possibility theory, 159, 160
  Subjective and objective, 26
  Symbolic values, 132
  Total probability, 41
  Upper and lower probabilities, 47, 118, 119

Varieties of, 44, 45
Why studied, 38
Product synergy
    In qualitative probabilistic networks, 125
Protein topology prediction
    Introduction to, 354–357
    Using *Q3*, 358–373
    Using qualitative certainty networks, 376–387
Psychology
    Human reasoning under uncertainty, 20–29
Pulcinella
    And Mummu, 335, 336
    As an implementation of valuation networks, 83,
        84
    Local computation mechanism, 331, 332

Q1, 114, 202
Q2
    Definition of, 202–204
    Example solution to the incompleteness problem,
        229, 230
    Example solution to the integration problem, 221–
        224
    Handling evidence theory, 205, 206
    Handling possibility theory, 205, 206
    Handling probability theory, 205, 206
    Solution to the incompleteness problem, 208
    Solution to the translation problem, 207, 208
    The role of semantics, 396
    Valuation-based systems, 333–335
Q3
    And qualitative certainty networks, 398
    Comparing intervals, 213, 214
    Definition of, 209, 210
    Example solution to the incompleteness problem,
        231–233
    Example solution to the integration problem, 225–
        228
    Handling certainty factors, 396
    Handling evidence theory, 212
    Handling possibility theory, 211, 212
    Handling probability theory, 211, 212
    In protein topology prediction, 358–373
    Solution to the incompleteness problem, 219
    Solution to the translation problem, 217–219
    The role of semantics, 396
    Valuation-based systems, 333–335
QCN, See Qualitative certainty networks
QPN, See Qualitative probabilistic networks
QSIM, 109, 111, 113
Qualitative algebra
    For qualitative influences, 220, 221
Qualitative algebras
    For certainty values, 202
    For qualitative reasoning, 114–117

The role of semantics, 396
Qualitative certainty networks
    And causality, 398
    And *Q3*, 398
    Causal reasoning, 247–255
    Complexity of propagation, 350
    Conditions on certainty factor influences, 395, 396
    Conditions on evidential influences, 253–255, 266,
        268, 269, 287, 288, 306–308, 316, 317
    Conditions on possibilistic influences, 251, 252,
        265, 290, 291, 300, 301, 303, 304, 315, 316
    Conditions on probabilistic influences, 249, 250,
        254, 267–269, 286, 297–299, 302–304, 313–
        315
    Driving value, 262, 263, 348–350
    Evidential reasoning, 263–271
    Example solution to the incompleteness problem,
        273–275
    Example solution to the integration problem, 276–
        280
    Explaining away, 311–317
    In protein topology prediction, 376–387
    Intercausal reasoning, 311–319
    Introduced, 237
    Monotonicity assumptions in, 278, 280
    Multiple observations, 348
    Multiply-connected, 296–305
    Negative influence, 240
    Non-zero change at a node, 246
    Non-zero change in value, 242
    Non-zero influence, 241
    Positive influence, 240
    Possible futures, 399
    Principle of minimum specificity, 252, 279
    Propagation algorithm, 342–350
    Qualitative derivative, 242–244
    Qualitative independence, 240
    Qualitative influence, 239
    Qualitative influence along a trail, 256, 257
    Relationship to argumentation, 323, 324
    Relationship to naïve physics, 322, 323
    Relationship to qualitative physics, 322, 323
    Relationship to qualitative probabilistic networks,
        314, 324–327, 395
    Separable derivative, 245
    Sets of propositions, 305–309
    Solution to the integration problem, 238
    Synergy, 283–293
    Zero change at a node, 246
    Zero change in value, 242
    Zero influence, 240
Qualitative certainty values
    Solution to the robustness problem, 237
Qualitative derivative

And synergy, 284, 285
  In qualitative certainty networks, 242–244
Qualitative differential equations
  In qualitative physics, 110
Qualitative independence
  In qualitative certainty networks, 240
Qualitative influence
  Along a trail, 256, 257
  As a qualitative algebra, 220, 221
  In qualitative certainty networks, 239
  In qualitative probabilistic networks, 123–125
  Overall between two nodes, 346
Qualitative measures
  Compatibility of, 260, 261
  Definition of, 38, 108
  For handling imperfect information, 5
  QPNs, 123–129
  Qualitative probabilistic networks, 123–129
  Types of abstraction, 123
Qualitative physics
  Order of magnitude reasoning, 112–114
  Qualitative differential equations, 110
  Qualitative reasoning, 109–112
  Relationship to qualitative certainty networks, 322, 323
Qualitative probabilistic networks
  Additive synergy, 125
  And defeasible reasoning, 145, 146
  Complexity of propagation, 342
  Explaining away, 125, 314
  For constructing probabilistic networks, 128
  Intercausal reasoning, 126
  Multiple observations, 127, 128, 319, 342
  Product synergy, 125
  Propagation algorithms, 126, 127, 338–343
  Qualitative influence, 123–125
  Qualitative synergy, 125
  Relationship to qualitative certainty networks, 314, 324–327, 395
  Relationship to monotonic influence diagrams, 128
  Relationship to qualitative certainty networks, 314, 324–327
  Relationship to qualitative probability, 129
  Resolving trade-offs, 127
Qualitative probability
  Relationship to qualitative probabilistic networks, 129
Qualitative reasoning
  In qualitative physics, 109–112
  Problems with, 112
  Qualitative differential equations, 110
  Semiqualitative reasoning, 115
  With numerical information, 114
  With qualitative algebras, 114–117

Qualitative synergy
  Additive synergy, 125
  In qualitative certainty networks, 283–293
  In qualitative probabilistic networks, 125
  Product synergy, 125
QUALQUANT, 78
Quantitative measures
  Brief history of, 3, 4
  Definition of, 38
  Experimental comparisons, 155, 156
  For handling imperfect information, 3
  Obtaining numerical values, 107
Quantity space
  In naïve physics, 110

Robustness problem
  An example, 199
  Definition of, 170, 171
  Solved by qualitative certainty networks, 237
ROM[ℜ], 114
ROM[K], 114
Root node, 190
Rose
  By any other name, xiii
Rough sets
  And indiscernability, 71
  And logic, 102
  Introduction to, 70
  Relationship with evidence theory, 162
  Relationship with fuzzy sets, 161, 162
  Upper and lower approximations, 71, 72
RUM, 32, 70

Schrödinger
  And his cats, 18
  Negentropy, 18
Semiqualitative measures, 38
Semiqualitative reasoning, 115
Semiquantitative reasoning, 115
Separable derivative
  In qualitative certainty networks, 245
Seriable experiments
  And probability theory, 31
Sign of a trail, 339
Similarity networks, 91, 92
Simple support function
  Definition of, 55, 56
Singly-connected
  Definition of, 75, 76
SOLOMON, 151
SR1, 115, 203
Strictly positive synergy, 285
Subadditivity
  In evidence theory, 56
  In possibility theory, 49

Subjective probability
    As opposed to objective, 26
    Bayesian view, 45
    Personalist and necessarian, 44, 45
Superadditivity
    In evidence theory, 56
    In possibility theory, 50
Synergy
    Additive, 125
    In qualitative certainty networks, 283–293
    In qualitative probabilistic networks, 125
    Product, 125
System P
    And evidence theory, 102
    And preferential models, 140
    And probability theory, 146
System-Z, 147, 148

Theorist, 153
Track
    Through a graph, 190
Trade-offs
    In qualitative certainty networks, 397, 398
    In qualitative probabilistic networks, 127
Trail
    Active, 190
    Minimal, 190
    Through a graph, 190
Transferable belief model
    Definition of, 61
Translation problem
    Definition of, 175, 176
    In protein topology prediction, 364, 365, 384, 385,
        387
    Solution by monotonicity assumption, 392
    Solution using $Q2$, 207, 208
    Solution using $Q3$, 217–219
    Some solutions suggested, 176
TresBel, 83, 84
Triangular norms
    For combining fuzzy sets, 68, 70

Uncertainty
    Dictionary definition of, 9, 10
    Hidden variable interpretation, 18
    Inevitability of, 7–9, 34
    Irreducible, 8
    Relation to information, 19
    Relation to measurement, 15–18
    Taxonomy by Bonissone and Tong, 12, 13
    Taxonomy by Bosc and Prade, 13
    Taxonomy by Smets, 11, 12
    Taxonomy by Smithson, 10, 11
    Taxonomy for this book, 14, 15
Upper and lower possibilities

From a multi-valued mapping, 53
Upper and lower probabilities
    And possibility theory, 159
    From a multi-valued mapping, 47
    Relation to evidence theory, 47

Vacuous belief function
    Definition of, 54
Valuation networks
    Combination and marginalisation, 81, 331–337
    Dynamic construction of, 87
    For quantitative measures, 80–84
    Valuation-based systems, 81, 82
Valuation-based systems
    For $Q2$, 333–335
    In Mummu, 327
    In Pulcinella, 331
    Valuation networks, 81, 82
VPROP, 77
VSBD, 83, 84

Weather reports, 2

Zero change at a node
    In qualitative certainty networks, 246
Zero change in value
    In qualitative certainty networks, 242
Zero influence
    In qualitative certainty networks, 240